COORDINAT[...] RESEARCH FROM WEST

Social Security Disability Practice
Charles T. Hall

Medical Proof of Social Security Disability
David A. Morton III, M.D.

Social Security Claims and Procedures
Harvey L. McCormick

Elderlaw: Advocacy for the Aging
Joan M. Krauskopf, Robert N. Brown, Karen Tokarz and Allan D. Bogutz

Medicare and Medicaid Claims and Procedures
Harvey L. McCormick

Guidelines for State Court Decision Making in Life-Sustaining Medical Treatment Cases
National Center for State Courts

Federal Social Security Laws Selected Statutes and Regulations
Annual Pamphlet

SOCIAL SECURITY REPORTING SERVICE

Cases
Code
Regulations
Rulings
Topical Index
Digest Index
Bi-weekly Pamphlet Service
West's Social Security Library on CD–ROM

WESTLAW®
Social Security Databases

FGB–CFR   Code of Federal Regulations
FGB–CS   Federal Cases
FGB–FR   Federal Register
FGB–SSR   Social Security Rulings
FGB–HALLEX   Social Security Administration Documents
FHTH–FDA   FDA Enforcement Reports
FPEN–NR   Federal Pension and Retirement
Benefits—News Releases
GB–TP   Law Reviews, Texts and Journals Related to
Government Benefits
MGB–CS   Multistate Government Benefits Cases
SSRS   Social Security Reporting Service

COORDINATED RESEARCH FROM WEST

WLD–GVT   West's Legal Directory—Government Agencies and Programs

———————

WIN®

WEST*fax*®

WEST*Check*® and WESTMATE®

West CD–ROM Libraries™

———————

West Books, CD–ROM Libraries, Disk Products and WESTLAW
The Ultimate Research System

———————

To order any of these Social Security practice tools, call your West Representative or 1–800–328–9352.

THE LAW OF MEDICARE
AND
MEDICAID FRAUD
AND ABUSE

1998 Edition

By
TIMOTHY STOLTZFUS JOST
Newton D. Baker, Baker and Hostetler Chair,
Ohio State University College of Law
and
Professor, Ohio State University College of Medicine
and Public Health

SHARON L. DAVIES
Assistant Professor of Law
Ohio State University College of Law

WEST GROUP

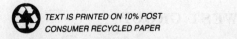 TEXT IS PRINTED ON 10% POST
CONSUMER RECYCLED PAPER

1st Reprint–1998

We dedicate this book to our families:
Ruth, Jacob, Micah, David
Alan, Heather, Tyler

PREFACE

$23,000,000,000. That is the amount that the Office of Inspector General of the Department of Health and Human Services recently estimated the Medicare program paid out "improperly" in 1996, much of it in response to provider fraud and abuse. The Medicaid program also loses billions of dollars a year. Federal and state resources are tight and getting tighter, therefore fraud and abuse is a major concern to government. Year after year new legislation and regulations appear, piling up criminal, civil, and administrative fraud and abuse sanctions.

Health care providers and those attorneys who represent them must understand this bewildering, and constantly growing and changing, body of law. The consequences of not doing so are enormous: civil penalties that have in some cases amounted to hundreds of millions of dollars, exclusion from Medicare and Medicaid participation, even jail sentences for felonies.

This book offers a straightforward and comprehensive guide through this maze. After exploring the nature of fraud and abuse in the health care industry generally and each of its sectors, it analyzes each of the major bodies of substantive fraud and abuse law: false claims, bribes and kickbacks, and self-referrals. It then explores the law peculiar to each type of fraud and abuse sanction: administrative penalties, civil actions (including qui tam), criminal investigations, and criminal sentencing. It orders and explores thoroughly statutory and regulatory authority, judicial and administrative decisions. It makes fraud and abuse law manageable.

The authors wish to thank those who have aided them in this endeavor, Dean Gregory Williams of the Ohio State University College of Law, and their research assistants, Tracy Kozicki, Toby Williams, Stephanie Greene, Tamara Lynd, Marcie Edwards, and Scott Kelly.

TIMOTHY S. JOST
SHARON L. DAVIES

Columbus, Ohio 1997

WESTLAW® ELECTRONIC RESEARCH GUIDE

WESTLAW, Computer–Assisted Legal Research

WESTLAW is part of the research system provided by West Group. With WESTLAW, you find the same quality and integrity that you have come to expect from West books. For the most current and comprehensive legal research, combine the strengths of West books and WESTLAW.

WESTLAW Adds to Your Library

Whether you wish to expand or update your research, WEST-LAW can help. For instance, WESTLAW is the most current source for case law, including slip opinions and unreported decisions. In addition to case law, the online availability of statutes, statutory indexes, legislation, court rules and orders, administrative materials, looseleaf publications, texts, periodicals, news and business information makes WESTLAW an important asset to any library. Check the online WESTLAW Directory or the print WESTLAW Database Directory for a list of available databases and services. Following is a brief description of some of the capabilities that WESTLAW offers.

Natural Language Searching

You can search most WESTLAW databases using WIN®, the revolutionary Natural Language search method. As an alternative to formulating a query using terms and connectors, WIN allows you to simply enter a description of your research issue in plain English:

> What is the government's obligation to warn military
> personnel of the danger of past exposure to radiation?

WESTLAW then retrieves the set of documents that have the highest statistical likelihood of matching your description.

Retrieving a Specific Document

When you know the citation to a case or statute that is not in your library, use the Find service to retrieve the document on WESTLAW. Access Find and type a citation like the following:

> 181 ne2d 520
> in st 27-1-12-1

Updating Your Research

You can use WESTLAW to update your research in many ways:

- Retrieve cases citing a particular statute.

- Update a state or federal statute by accessing the Update service from the displayed statute using the Jump marker.

- Retrieve newly enacted legislation by searching in the appropriate legislative service database.

- Retrieve cases not yet reported by searching in case law databases.

- Read the latest U.S. Supreme Court opinions within an hour of their release.

- Update West digests by searching with topic and key numbers.

Determining Case History and Retrieving Citing Cases

KeyCite$_{SM}$, the new citation research service developed by West Group and made available through the WESTLAW computer-assisted legal research service, integrates all the case law on WESTLAW, giving you the power to

- trace the history of a case;

- retrieve a list of all cases on WESTLAW that cite a case; and

- track legal issues in a case.

Citing references from the extensive library of secondary sources on WESTLAW, such as ALR® annotations and law review articles, are covered by KeyCite as well. You can use these citing references to find case discussions by legal experts.

Now, in this one service on WESTLAW, you receive

- the case-verification functions of Insta-Cite®;

- the case-citing functions of Shepard's® and Shepard's Pre-View®; and

- the currentness of QuickCite®.

In addition, KeyCite is completely integrated with West's Key Number System so that it provides the tools for navigating the case law databases on WESTLAW. Only KeyCite combines the up-to-the-minute case-verification functions of an online citator service with the case-finding tools needed to find relevant case law.

Additional Information

For more detailed information or assistance, contact your WESTLAW account representative or call 1-800-REF-ATTY (1-800-733-2889).

SUMMARY OF CONTENTS

(Including New and Retitled Sections)

TABLE OF CONTENTS

(Including New and Retitled Sections)

TABLE OF CONTENTS

TABLE OF CONTENTS

CHAPTER 4. SELF–REFERRALS: FEDERAL AND STATE PROHIBITIONS

TABLE OF CONTENTS

CHAPTER 5. ADMINISTRATIVE PENALTIES AND EXCLUSIONS

CHAPTER 6. THE CIVIL FALSE CLAIMS ACT AND QUI TAM ACTIONS

TABLE OF CONTENTS

TABLE OF CONTENTS

CHAPTER 8. SENTENCING CONSIDERATIONS FOR HEALTH CARE FRAUD OFFENDERS

TABLE OF CONTENTS

MEDICARE AND MEDICAID FRAUD AND ABUSE

1998 Edition

Chapter 1

AN INTRODUCTION TO MEDICARE AND MEDICAID FRAUD AND ABUSE

Table of Sections

WESTLAW Electronic Research

See WESTLAW Electronic Research Guide preceding the Summary of Contents.

Library References:

West's Key No. Digests, Social Security and Public Welfare ⬯18.

1

§ 1–1. Introduction

The Medicare and Medicaid programs are by any definition enormous programs. In 1995, approximately $184 billion was spent by the Medicare program, $133 billion by Medicaid. Human nature being what it is, it is not surprising that programs spending money in these amounts attract more than a few persons willing to break, or at least to stretch, the law to get some of this money for themselves (or more than their share). In fact, the General Accounting Office and Department of Human Services recently estimated that Medicare pays out about $23 billion a year in improper payments.[1] There are several characteristics of these programs beyond their sheer size, however, that make them particularly vulnerable to fraud and abuse. This chapter will first consider briefly the kinds of providers who commit Medicare and Medicaid fraud. It then will turn to the incentives and opportunities that the Medicare and Medicaid programs present to providers who are willing to defraud the program. Finally, it will explore the types of fraud and abuse likely to occur in particular corners of the health care industry.

§ 1–2. What is Fraud and Abuse?

We begin with definitions. We use the term "fraud and abuse," as it is customarily used, to cover financial misconduct in the delivery and financing of health care. Fraud and abuse occur when one party to a health care transaction intentionally or recklessly (or sometimes negligently) attempts to obtain something of value that the party is not entitled to under the statutory, regulatory, or contractual rules that govern the relationship.

It is possible to distinguish conceptually between fraud and abuse. Fraud denotes practices that are tantamount to theft by deception, defined under the regulations as "an intentional deception or misrepresentation made by a person with the knowledge that the deception could result in some unauthorized benefit to himself or to some other person."[1] Fraud occurs, for example, when a physician claims payment for a service he did not deliver, or for a service that he delivered knowing it to be unnecessary. Abuse, on the other hand, occurs when a party "games the system." The Medicaid regulations define it as "provider practices that are inconsistent with sound fiscal, business, or medical practices, and result in an unnecessary cost to the Medicaid program, or in reimbursement for services that are not medically necessary or that fail to

§ 1–1

1. HCFA's $23 Billion Error Rate Said to Show Need for Random Audits, BNA Health Care Daily, July 18, 1997.

§ 1–2

1. 42 U.S.C.A. § 455.2.

meet professionally recognized standards for health care."[2] A provider, for example, actually delivers a service but "upcodes," claiming reimbursement for a more technical or extensive service than that actually delivered, or "unbundles," claiming reimbursement separately for the component parts of a service that should have been billed as a comprehensive service. Abuse, like fraud, usually involves "willing and knowing" misconduct, but in abusive situations, health care is usually in fact provided, while in fraudulent situations financial misconduct can take place independent of the actual delivery of health care.

The boundary between fraud and abuse is often difficult to discern, however, and the laws that proscribe fraud and abuse rarely attempt to make the distinction. In practice, the primary distinction is that prosecutors, judges, and juries are likely to take fraud more seriously in terms of the allocation of investigative and prosecutorial resources or the imposition of penalties.[3]

§ 1–3. Who Enforces the Fraud and Abuse Laws?

The primary responsibility for enforcing the federal fraud and abuse laws resides with the Department of Justice (DOJ), and with the U.S. Attorneys who work within it. The DOJ prosecutes criminal cases and brings civil false claim actions against fraud and abuse perpetrators. The Federal Bureau of Investigation of the DOJ has made health care fraud a top priority, and has allocated hundreds of agents to investigating fraud. Within the Department of Health and Human Services the primary responsibility for investigating suspected incidents of fraud and abuse, and for bringing administrative sanction cases, rests with the Office of Inspector General (OIG). Under memorandum of understanding between the OIG and DOJ the OIG works together with the DOJ in developing fraud cases, and only brings administrative penalty actions when the DOJ has completed or declined criminal or civil actions.[1] States are generally required by federal law to have Medicaid Fraud Control Units to take primary responsibility for prosecuting Medicaid fraud, and all but three states have such units. Medicaid fraud is also prosecuted by local prosecutors. The role of the DOJ, FBI, OIG , and the states in investigating fraud and abuse are explored in detail in chapter 7.

---

2. See 42 C.F.R. § 455.2; Medicare Carrier's Manual § 14002.4(A).

3. See e.g., United States v. Krizek, 859 F.Supp. 5 (D.D.C.1994), supplemented by, 909 F.Supp. 32, 34 (D.D.C. 1995), aff'd in part & remanded, 111 F.3d 934 (D.C.Cir.1997)(district court's

lenient treatment of physician guilty of abuse).

§ 1–3

1. This memorandum was entered into pursuant to 42 U.S.C.A. § 1320a–7a(c)(1), and is subject to certain exceptions.

§ 1-4. Who Commits Medicare and Medicaid Fraud and Abuse?

Criminal, civil, and administrative actions charging Medicare or Medicaid fraud and abuse have been brought against almost every type of person or entity that provides items or services to the Medicare and Medicaid program: physicians, hospitals, nursing facilities, pharmacies, laboratories, chiropractors, durable medical equipment suppliers, and many others. They have even been brought against the private contractors that process claims and recipients and beneficiaries.

Those who commit fraud and abuse fall into several categories in terms of their relative culpability. First, there are "hard core" criminals, persons who steal from the Medicare and Medicaid programs without any pretense of justification. This group includes, for example, persons who obtain provider numbers and submit Medicare claims based on forged or fraudulent certifications or prescriptions without providing any services.[1] These offenders are often simultaneously pursuing related criminal activity, such as controlled substance violations or tax fraud. In recent years, criminal fraud and abuse schemes have become more complex, while they increasingly involve national or regional entities.[2] Providers who fall into this category are most likely to be criminally prosecuted, but often are poor candidates for civil or administrative penalty actions. They often operate through shell corporations that dissolve leaving few assets behind when attempts are made to recover funds.[3] Providers in this group often end up being excluded from the Medicare and Medicaid programs through administrative exclusions, but sometimes reenter the program under an alias or a new corporate form.

A second category of providers are those who are in fact providing some services, but either out of venality or out of a belief

---

§ 1-4

1. See GAO, Medicare, Antifraud Technology Offers Significant Opportunity to Reduce Health Care Fraud (GAO/AIMD-95-77, Aug. 11, 1995) (describing several instances of this type of behavior, including a case where a Florida company that existed only to bill Medicare without rendering any medical services, was paid about $2 million over a 5 month period. By the time the scheme was detected and a court order was issued to seize the corporation's assets, most of the funds and the company's owner had disappeared. In another instance, an unemployed tow-truck driver filed 717 false electronic claims for more than $300,000 in two weeks on behalf of a nonexistent medical laboratory. An additional $300,000 in claims were being processed when the scam was discovered).

2. William S. Cohen, Gaming the Health Care System, 2 (Investigative Staff Report of Minority Staff of the Senate Special Committee on Aging, July 7, 1994).

3. In 10–20% of the cases investigated annually by the California regional OIG office, for example, the provider declares bankruptcy and leaves no assets behind. GAO, Medicare, Adapting Private Sector Techniques Could Curb Losses to Fraud and Abuse (GAO/T-HEHS-95-211, July 19, 1995).

that they are not being fairly treated by the system, consciously engage in "creative" billing to maximize their own income. Practices engaged in by these providers include:

- upcoding—billing for a service that is similar but more complicated than that they in fact provide;

- fragmentation—billing separately for discrete components of one service that is supposed to be billed comprehensively;

- unbundling—billing for a comprehensive service, but also additionally and duplicatively for its components;

- global service period violations—billing separately for services that occur immediately before or after a procedure covered by a global payment that is supposed also to cover the separately billed service;

- pattern billing—billing all services the same (e.g., coding all patients seen with the same diagnosis);

- assignment or participation agreement violations, or illegal demands for recipient supplementation;

- gang billing—billing for a number of visits to separate nursing home residents based on a single walk through the facility;

- billing for services that are not necessary or are not provided in compliance with program requirements (e.g., without required physician supervision or without proper physician certification of medical necessity); or

- supplying inferior products and charging for higher priced products.[4]

Providers in this second category often realize that what they are doing violates the letter of the law, but rationalize their actions as a justifiable reaction to program complexity or to inadequate payment levels. Minor deviations from billing requirements often go undetected or are ignored. If these providers go too far beyond the boundaries, however, they may find themselves being criminally prosecuted. Once criminally convicted, they are subject to mandatory exclusion from program participation for at least five years. They also are in some instances pursued for civil or administrative penalty recoveries.

Third are those providers who believe themselves to be within the bounds of the law, but steer too close to the boundaries and

---

4. See Alice G. Gosfield, Unintentional Part B False Claims: Pitfalls for the Unwary, in 1993 Health Law Handbook, 205, 212–16 (Alice G. Gosfield ed., 1993) (describing these practices); GAO, Medicare, Miscoded Part B Claims (GAO/AIMD–95–135, May 5, 1995). Unbundling, fragmentation, and global period violations resulted in 93% of the improperly claimed procedures identified through a recent study. Id.

occasionally stray beyond. Providers reimbursed on a cost basis who have executive compensation packages beyond the boundaries of reasonableness; physicians who code too aggressively; or home health agencies that are too ambitious in marketing their services might fall into this category. These providers are often large institutions or wealthy individuals, and occasionally end up settling qui tam or civil false claims actions for considerable sums of money. They are less likely to end up in jail, however.

Finally, there are the genuinely confused and bewildered. Providers who meant to deliver only authorized services, to bill only for services actually rendered, and to code accurately the services provided, but who are overwhelmed by the confusion and complexity of the program. Most providers charged with fraud or abuse claim to be in this category; some undoubtedly are. This is particularly true when major program changes are implemented.

When Medicare implemented its new evaluation and management codes for physicians in 1992, it was estimated that six months into implementation, 40% of submitted claims were improper.[5] On the other hand, a recent GAO study applying up-to-date commercial technology to review miscoded claims found that 92% of the providers in its sample billed correctly and that only 4% of claims it reviewed had to be adjusted.[6] It would appear that most providers are able to bill correctly most of the time once they become accustomed to program requirements.

In most instances where providers are identified who failed to bill correctly simply because of confusion, they are asked to return excess compensation. Occasionally, however, these providers end up being pursued administratively, civilly, or even criminally for their mistakes and misdeeds.

§ 1-5. Incentives and Opportunities for Medicare and Medicaid Fraud and Abuse

a. Incentives

The methods used by both Medicare and Medicaid to pay providers and practitioners create a considerable motivation for fraud. Both programs rely primarily on administered-price payment systems. Medicare, for example, pays hospitals for inpatient hospital care under a diagnosis-related groups prospective payment system. It pays physicians based on a resource-based relative value scale. Medicaid pays hospitals based on rates that are determined (often by the court of last resort) to be "reasonable and adequate to meet the costs which must be incurred by efficiently and economi-

---

5. Gosfield, supra note 4, at 219.

6. GAO, Medicare, Miscoded Part B Claims (GAO/AIMD-95-135, May 5, 1995).

cally operated facilities."[1] Neither program relies on markets to set prices.

One can argue whether it is wise for Medicare and Medicaid to use administered price systems, or whether they should move toward more reliance on market mechanisms for purchasing care.[2] Certainly the market for health care bears little resemblance to a perfect market, such as the market for commodities. It is difficult to conceive of how a market could be created in which Medicare beneficiaries or Medicaid recipients would purchase health care items and services directly and competitively. The existence of any insurance program, but particularly one that is financed through taxes, will inevitably distort consumer decisions. Conceivably Medicare or Medicaid could purchase some services directly through competitive bidding,[3] though experience in the defense industry shows that the use of competitive bidding does not eliminate fraud. Alternatively, Medicare or Medicaid could provide vouchers permitting beneficiaries and recipients to purchase health insurance. This may well, however, simply result in fraud against insurers replacing fraud against Medicare and Medicaid.

Whether or not markets for health care exist or could be created at this point, it is quite clear that when Medicare began in the mid–1960s there was no competitive market for health care in any meaningful sense. Medicare and Medicaid were set up to pay for services just like the private third-party payers then in existence, i.e. on a direct payment or indemnity fee-for-service basis. From these origins, Medicare, and in some states Medicaid, have evolved toward more sophisticated and economical administered price systems, but they have continued to set prices rather than to purchase services in the open market, whatever that could mean. Even when Medicare purchases managed care rather than discrete services, it does so based on an administered formula.

It can certainly be argued that Medicare spends less purchasing services through administered prices than it would using some sort of market mechanism. It has very low administrative costs compared to private insurers, and is often able to pay lower prices than do private insurers. Arguably, Medicare pursues the same strategy used by many large employers who operate self-funded medical benefit plans, paying for services directly at a discounted rate. The use of administered price systems, however, creates significant incentives for fraud. These incentives, and the types of fraud that

§ 1–5

1. 42 U.S.C.A. § 1396a(a)(13)(A); 42 C.F.R. § 430.10.

2. See Symposium, Debating the Future of Medicare, Health Affairs, Winter 1995, at 7 (discussing market-based approaches to restructuring Medicare, their strengths and weaknesses).

3. The Balanced Budget Act of 1997 authorizes competitive bidding demonstration projects. Pub. L. 105–32, § 4319.

they encourage, vary depending on whether the Medicare and Medicaid price is above the market price, below the market price, or includes some combination of above and below market prices for a combination of services.

Though Medicare and Medicaid tend to pay providers and practitioners prices that are quite low when compared to reported charges, Medicare in particular occasionally sets prices for items and services at above-market rates. A recent GAO report, for example, offered as examples glucose monitors for which Medicare paid from $144 to $211 each in 1992 when they were available for under $50 commercially; or one type of gauze pad for which Medicare paid 86 cents when it was available in the market for less than half that cost.[4] Often these high prices occur when Medicare offers initial high prices for new technologies and fails to revise the price downward as the technologies mature and become more widely available and the cost of providing the item or service declines.[5]

If Medicare sets the price it will pay for an item or service too high, this may result in excess provision of services in relationship to "need" as defined in terms of either medical criteria or in terms of the services that would be purchased in a functioning market. From time to time Medicare suddenly experiences dramatic increases in the purchase of certain services, signaling that an opportunity for generous profits has been discovered. Between 1990 and 1992, for example, Medicare claims for orthotic body jackets increased 6400% from 275 to 17,910 while total allowed charges increased 8200% from $217,000 to $18 million. Medicare paid on average $800 per jacket during this time, though they cost only about $100 to produce.[6]

Excessively high prices also create situations where a person or entity providing the overpriced item or service may be willing to share some of the excess profits with those in a position to generate volume through referrals. If Medicare pays above market rates for laboratory services, for example, laboratories might pay physicians to refer patients to them.

Alternatively, those in a position to generate referrals may start providing the overpriced item or service themselves.[7] A physician might herself purchase a laboratory and then refer the pa-

4. GAO, Medicare, Modern Management Strategies Needed to Curb Program Exploitation, 2 (GAO/T–HEHS–95–183, June 15, 1995).

5. One recent study found very high utilization levels for newly covered health care items not yet subject to utilization policies. GAO, Medicare, Excessive Payments for Medical Supplies Continue Despite Improvements (GAO/HEHS–95–171, Aug. 8, 1995).

6. William S. Cohen, Gaming the Health Care System 12–13 (Investigative Staff Report of Minority Staff of the Senate Special Committee on Aging, July 7, 1994).

7. See § 4.1.

tients to it. Indeed, physicians may be willing to conspire with providers of items or services to generate billings independent of the referral of actual patients. Some physicians, for example, have been willing to sell certificates documenting the necessity of durable medical equipment (DME) to DME companies for patients they have never seen.[8] Some providers have engaged in direct telemarketing to convince patients to order services or items they do not medically require, or simply obtained the identification numbers of patients to file claims for services in fact never delivered.

Problems also arise, however, if prices are set too low relative to the market. Medicaid in particular often pays providers only a fraction of their actual costs. First, low prices may only be acceptable to providers who are not otherwise able to compete in the market. Occasionally these are otherwise competent providers or practitioners who are less competitive because of characteristics not necessarily related to quality (such as foreign origin).[9] It is likely, however, that practitioners or providers who end up caring for Medicaid patients are often of lower quality.

Low prices may also encourage fraud and abuse, however. It is sometimes possible for providers to compensate for low prices by providing services in high volume. This may happen, for example, when the provider is paid on a per-service basis but has the capacity for performing more services during the same period of time by cutting the time spent on each service. When this happens, quality may suffer. It is also possible that high volume providers will provide services that are unnecessary, or at least unnecessary in the extent provided. Unnecessary services are wasteful, they may also be harmful. Providers may also attempt to "unbundle," to submit multiple bills for different segments of the same item or service. At worst, they may simply bill for more services than they in fact provide.

When the price for some services is set high relative to the price charged for other, closely related services, the provider may deliver one item or service, but bill for a more costly similar item or service. A common example of this is when pharmacists bill for brand name drugs but provide a generic equivalent. The provider may "upcode," providing a 15 minute consultation, for example, but billing for 30 minutes. Claims may be submitted asserting that services were provided by more highly qualified staff than were actually used to provide the service, or that unsupervised staff were in fact supervised by more highly qualified professionals.

---

8. Cohen, supra note 6, at 14–15.

9. One recent study of high volume Medicaid physicians in New York found that 94% of them were born outside of the United States, Gerry Fairbrother, et al., New York City Physicians Service High Volumes of Medicaid Children: Who Are They and How Do They Practice?, 32 Inquiry 345 (1995).

When prices are based on reported costs, as has historically often been the case with Medicare and Medicaid, a significant temptation is created to inflate costs or to seek reimbursement for costs that are not legally reimbursable. Providers reimbursed on a cost-related basis may also contract with a related organization, essentially selling themselves items or services at prices they themselves set, and then passing these prices on as costs.

Switching from fee-for-service to capitated payment systems solves many of these problems, but causes others.[10] Providers paid on a capitated basis lack an incentive to provide or to bill for excessive services because they get the same payment no matter how many services they provide. They are also unlikely to pay or seek kickbacks for referrals for items or services. On the other hand, capitated providers have an incentive to claim to serve patients who in fact are not receiving services from them or to engage in marketing schemes intended to attract large numbers of patients (preferably low-risk patients), regardless of whether the patients understand what services they should be receiving or from whom the services will be received. More important, perhaps, capitated providers face incentives to underserve their patients—to provide fewer services than their patients need. Capitated providers, moreover, often subcontract for services from specialists or from institutional providers on a fee-for-service basis, thus the fee-for-service problems described above often surface again in capitated systems, but at a lower level where they are less visible.

b. Opportunities

While Medicare and Medicaid payment structures create incentives that encourage fraud and abuse, the administrative structures through which the Medicare and Medicaid programs are managed often provide the opportunities necessary for fraud and abuse to occur. Medicare is administered through an incredibly complex and cumbersome system.[11] The Medicare program consists of two parts: Part A which pays primarily for institutional services and Part B which pays primarily for professional and other non-institutional services. Claims processing and auditing in both programs are handled on a decentralized basis by private contractors, generally insurers and data processors, called intermediaries in the Part A program, carriers in the Part B program. HCFA currently contracts with about 73 private companies to provide these services.[12] While

10. Sharon Davies & Timothy Stoltzfus Jost, Managed Care: Placebo or Wonder Drug for Health Care Fraud and Abuse?, 31 Ga. L. Rev. 373 (1997).

11. See Furrow, et al., Health Law, Chapter 13 (1995).

12. GAO, Control Over Fraud and Abuse Remains Elusive, 6–12 (GAO/T–HEHS–97–165, June 27, 1997); GAO, Medicare, Modern Management Strategies Needed to Curb Program Enforce-

overall payment policy is set by Congress and by the Health Care Financing Administration, many coverage questions and payment policies, as well as the review and payment of individual claims, are left to these intermediaries and carriers.[13] Medicaid programs are administered on a state by state basis, and some states subcontract with private administrators for administration of all or part of the state Medicaid program. Together these programs process more than four billion claims annually.[14]

This complexity and unwieldiness of program organization offers opportunities for sophisticated providers to game the system. Until recently, for example, payment policies for durable medical equipment (DME) varied significantly from carrier to carrier. Fraudulent DME suppliers would obtain post boxes in the areas covered by particularly generous or inattentive carriers simply for the purpose of submitting bills to maximize reimbursement, a practice known as "carrier shopping."[15] Rehabilitation therapy providers have been known to submit multiple bills for the same patients to different carriers in different parts of the country, resulting in payments far in excess of what would have been obtained if only one carrier had been billed.[16] Since there is no effective coordination to assure that each beneficiary is only covered by one carrier, such schemes are possible. Moreover, some items, like surgical dressings, can be billed either to an intermediary as part of a cost covered by Part A (a cost of nursing home care for example) or to a carrier as a charge covered by Part B (by a medical supply company, for example). Sometimes the same item is billed to both.[17]

The payment systems administered by these programs and contractors are themselves extraordinarily complex. Even with the best of intentions, providers often become confused by Medicare and Medicaid coding and coverage policy. Providers who approach the programs with bad intentions can in many cases plausibly claim that they were confused or misled by the complexity of the programs if they get caught. Often, however, the complexity of the program makes it less likely that they will be caught at all.

State Medicaid programs and the contractors that manage Medicare claims often lack the sophisticated technology used by

ment 2 (GAO/T–HEHS–95–183, June 15, 1995).

13. See, e.g., GAO, Medicare Part B, Reliability of Claims Processing Across Four Carriers 3–4 (GAO/PEMD–93–27, Aug. 11, 1993).

14. Cohen, supra note 6, at 9.

15. In 1993, DME claims processing was transferred to four carriers which handle all claims on a regional basis. See GAO, Medicare, Excessive Payments for Medical Supplies Despite Improvements (GAO/HEHS–95–171, Aug. 8, 1995).

16. GAO, Medicare Claims, High–Risk Series (GAO/HR–95–8, Feb. 1995).

17. GAO, Medicare: Medical Supplies (GAO/HEHS–95–171, Aug. 8, 1995).

some private insurance programs to ferret out fraud and abuse.[18] A recent GAO study estimated that Medicare could have saved $640 million in 1994, about 1.8% of total Medicare expenditures, simply by using screening technology already used by commercial insurers to identify code manipulation.[19] Medicare carriers do use computer technology to review claims both before and after payment, and are able to identify some patterns and trends that indicate abusive claims.[20] The fraud-detection screens commonly used by carriers focus on only a small number of variables, however, ignoring obvious problems such as billings for services provided on Sundays or outside of a provider's geographic service area.[21] Medicare and Medicaid have in some instances paid fraudulent claims that could have been identified through screens that are readily available in the commercial market, but not used by Medicare contractors or by Medicaid. Examples include payments made to a psychiatrist who billed for over 24 hours of services a day over a prolonged period of time,[22] or payments made by intermediaries in the late 1980s to hospitals and skilled nursing facilities (SNFs) for beneficiaries who were also at the same time receiving hospice benefits which should have fully covered hospital and SNF services.[23] In particular, Medicare contractors have not adopted artificial intelligence, fuzzy logic, link analysis, or neural network technology that would permit the coordinated and concurrent review of a variety of different factors across claims to identify subtle patterns of fraudulent activity.[24] HCFA is developing a national automatic data processing system that will assure greater uniformity and attentiveness in claims processing once it is operational, but it will not be on line for some time yet and is experiencing tremendous implementation prob-

18. GAO, Medicare, Adapting Private Sector Techniques Could Curb Losses to Fraud and Abuse, 3–4 (GAO/T–HEHS–95–211, July 19, 1995). An excellent recent study of current use of fraud control technology and how it could be improved is Malcolm K. Sparrow, License to Steal: Why Fraud Plagues America's Health Care System (1996).

19. GAO, Medicare, Commercial Technology Could Save Billions Lost to Billing Abuse (GAO/AIMD–95–135, May 5, 1995).

20. See, criticizing claims processing procedure, GAO, Medicare, Inadequate Review of Claims Payments Limits Ability to Control Spending (GAO/HEHS–94–42, Apr. 28, 1994).

21. GAO, Medicare, Antifraud Technology Offers Significant Opportunity to Reduce Health Care Fraud (GAO/AIMD–95–77, Aug 11, 1995).

22. GAO, Medicare, Modern Management Strategies Needed to Curb Program Exploitation, 4 (GAO/T–HEHS–95–183, June 15, 1995).

23. HHS Office of Inspector General, Review of Improper Payments Made to Hospitals and Skilled Nursing Facilities for Beneficiaries Electing Hospice Benefits [1995–2 Transfer Binder] Medicare & Medicaid Guide (CCH) ¶ 43,436 (June 7, 1995).

24. GAO, Medicare, Antifraud Technology Offers Significant Opportunity to Reduce Health Care Fraud (GAO/AIMD–95–77, Aug. 11, 1995). A recent Texas statute requires the state Medicaid agency to use such technology. Tex. Govt. Code § 531.106.

lems.[25]

Constraints on carrier resources are the primary factor limiting their ability to enhance their technological sophistication. Between 1989 and 1995 overall per-claim funding of Medicare contractors declined from $2.74 to $2.05, an inflation-adjusted 37.2% decline, while funding for medical review declined from $.32 to .15 per claim, an inflation-adjusted decline of 61.8%.[26] Between 1989 and 1994, HCFA lowered its targets for percent-of-claims-reviewed-by-its-contractors from 20% to 5% and reduced by a third the number of audits its contractors were required to perform.[27] Between 1987 and 1996 the percentage of home health claims reviewed dropped from 62% to 3%, while the likelihood of an institutional provider's cost report being audited dropped from 1 in 6 to 1 in 13.[28] These cuts are the result of federal budget constraints, and in particular of budgeting processes that mandate that any increase in Medicare fraud and abuse detection expenditures be matched by decreases elsewhere in similar programs.[29]

A particular problem has been assuring the integrity, indeed assuring the actual existence, of providers that submit claims to the Medicare and Medicaid systems. While some professionals and institutions must establish licensure or accreditation status before contracting with Medicare, others, such as DME suppliers or physiological laboratories have historically been subject to few such controls.[30] Numerous examples can be found where providers with dubious credentials, or perhaps even providers who have not actually delivered any services, were able to get provider numbers and bill Medicare. Often these providers have used elaborate, multi-layered corporations and dissolved the billing entity as quickly as Medicare discovers problems associated with its billing.[31] One medical supply company was recently found to have 20 different Medicare provider numbers attached to shell corporations over which it would spread its billings to avoid detection.[32]

Fraud against Medicare and Medicaid is also facilitated by the lack of law enforcement resources dedicated to investigating it and to rooting it out. Within the Medicare program responsibility for

---

25. GAO, Medicare Transaction System: Success Depends Upon Correcting Critical Managerial and Technical Weaknesses (GAO/AIMD–97–789) (May 1997); GAO, Medicare Claims, High–Risk Series (GAO/HR–95–8, Feb. 1995).

26. GAO, Medicare, Adapting Private Sector Techniques Could Curb Losses to Fraud and Abuse (GAO/T–HEHS–95–211, July 19, 1995).

27. GAO, Medicare Claims, High–Risk Series (GAO/HR–95–8, Feb. 1995).

28. GAO, Control Remains Elusive, supra note 12, at 8–9.

29. Id.

30. GAO, Medicare, Modern Management Strategies Needed to Curb Program Exploitation, 6 (GAO/T–HEHS–95–183, June 15, 1995).

31. Id. at 5–6.

32. GAO, Medicare, Adapting Private Sector Techniques Could Curb Losses to Fraud and Abuse (GAO/T–HEHS–95–211, July 19, 1995).

policing fraud falls mainly to the Department of Health and Human Services Office of Inspector General (OIG), supplemented by fraud and abuse identification units in the carriers and intermediaries and by such investigative resources as are made available by the Department of Justice.[33] Both the OIG and the FBI together currently have only about one full time equivalent employee for approximately every 9 million claims, and prosecution is limited to only the most egregious instances of fraud.[34] Moreover, the investigative agencies have not traditionally coordinated their investigative efforts well, further restricting the effectiveness of their efforts.[35] The OIG's office has, in particular, had a difficult time securing appropriate exclusion referrals from the states, and has often acted sluggishly and inconsistently in processing exclusion referrals.[36] Many of these problems are attributable to lack of resources. Ninety percent of the cases handled by the OIG that it considers to have merit are settled through negotiation.[37]

State Medicaid programs also generally lack the resources necessary to identify and prosecute aggressively any but the most egregious instances of fraud. A recent GAO review of Medicaid prescription drug fraud cases, for example, found that few providers went to prison; many convicted individuals or providers reappeared later serving Medicaid patients; over half of the reviewed cases resulted in assessed restitution amounting to less than $5000; and in one case where the provider was assessed $200,000, Medicaid ultimately recovered only $4000.[38]

The patterns of fraud, the incentives to which it responds, and the opportunities that exist for its fulfillment, vary from sector to sector within the health care industry. The next section presents an overview of fraud and abuse in the various sectors of the health care industry.

§ 1–6. Fraud and Abuse in Specific Industry Sectors

a. Physicians

Of all the practitioners and providers who participate in the health care industry, physicians most commonly appear as defen-

---

33. See, describing the roles of the carriers and intermediaries in discovering fraud, Donald Goldman & Timothy Blanchard, Health Care Fraud and Abuse in Medicare Part B—Billing, Claims, Errors and Fraud, in American Bar Association, Health Care Fraud, 1996 at J–1.

34. Cohen, supra note 6, at 9.

35. Id. at 9–11.

36. GAO, Medicare Fraud and Abuse: Stronger Action Needed to Re-

move Excluded Providers from Federal Health Programs (GAO/HEHS–97–63, (1997)).

37. GAO, Medicare, Adapting Private Sector Techniques Could Curb Losses to Fraud and Abuse, 10 (GAO/T–HEHS–95–211, Sept. 19, 1995).

38. GAO, Medicare, Modern Management Strategies Needed to Curb Program Exploitation (GAO/T–HEHS–95–183, June 15, 1995).

dants or respondents in Medicare or Medicaid fraud actions. In the criminal law cases reviewed by Professor Bucy in a study of health care fraud, 47% of the defendants were physicians.[1] Our own review of reported federal court decisions involving criminal and civil Medicare and Medicaid false claim actions found that 38% of defendants were physicians. In both studies, no other category of health care provider was involved in nearly so many cases.[2]

One can speculate as to why physicians are so frequently the subjects of fraud and abuse actions. Though only about 22% of Medicare and 11% of Medicaid dollars go to pay for physician's services,[3] physicians control the access beneficiaries or recipients enjoy to most other Medicare and Medicaid services. Physicians are, therefore, often the originators of or integral participants in fraudulent schemes. Unlike suppliers of home health or durable medical equipment, which can be shell corporations with few assets and ephemeral existence, physicians are real persons, often with substantial assets and ties to a community, and are likely to stay in place until an investigation can be completed and a judgment reached. On the other hand, unlike hospitals and nursing homes, physicians are rarely essential to their communities, and can be excluded from program participation if the seriousness of their offenses warrants this sanction, without disastrous consequences for the program's beneficiaries. Because of the position of trust that physicians occupy and their often sanctimonious rationalizations for illegal behavior, dishonest physicians may be particularly galling to enforcers.[4]

Fraud and abuse cases brought against physicians involve a range of conduct. First, some of these cases address fairly straightforward criminal fraud, such as intentionally billing for fictitious services or patients. In one scheme, for example, an ophthalmologist would sew a stitch too tight when performing cataract surgery, intentionally causing astigmatism. When the patient returned complaining of the problem, the physician would cut the stitch and bill Medicare for the service as a $2000 corneal transplant. During a four year period the physician billed Medicare $1.3 million for over 680 eye operations.[5] Another doctor timed his visits with an egg

§ 1–6

1. Pamela Bucy, Fraud by Fright: White Collar Crime by Health Care Providers?, 67 N.C. L. Rev. 855, 883 (1989).

2. In Professor Bucy's study, the next nearest groups were pharmacists and nursing homes and their employees, each of which accounted for 10% of defendants. Id. In our study, the next closest group was laboratories, which accounted for about 11% of the cases.

3. Katherine R. Levit et al., National Health Expenditures, 1995, 18 Health Care Fin. Rev. 175, 210 (1996).

4. Paul Jesilow et al., Fraud by Physicians Against Medicaid, 266 JAMA 3318, 3321 (1991).

5. Office of Inspector General, Semi-Annual Report, Oct. 1, 1994–March 31, 1995, reprinted in [1995 Transfer Binder] Medicare & Medicaid Guide (CCH) ¶ 42,947.

timer so that he would not spend more than 3 minutes with each patient, rewarded staff during "EKG month" for performing more EKGs than the year before, and scheduled tests for patients before they were even seen to make certain that every patient was tested.[6] Other cases involve doctors who have falsely billed Medicaid for prescribing drugs to substance abusers on request or for surgeries during which they sexually assaulted their patients.[7] Still other cases involve double billing or billing for services never provided or for clearly unnecessary services.[8]

More commonly, however, fraud and abuse actions are used to police the billing practices of physicians or their relationship with other health care providers.[9] Physicians are in most instances compensated for the services they provide Medicare patients on a fee-for-service basis based on Medicare's resource based relative value scale.[10] To obtain compensation physicians must:

- deliver a compensable service;

- certify that the service was "medically indicated and necessary for the health of the patient";

- certify that the service was personally furnished by the physician or furnished incident to his or her professional service by an employee under his or her immediate personal supervision; and

- determine the appropriate diagnosis and procedure code with which to the describe the problem and the service for billing purposes.[11]

Where a single procedure has separately identifiable components, the physician must in some instances bill for the service as a unit, and not bill for its separate component parts.[12] Where physician-ordered ancillary items or services (pharmaceuticals, durable medical equipment, home health care, etc.) are necessary, the

6. United States v. Hale, 106 F.3d 402 (6th Cir.1997), cert. denied __ U.S. __, __ S.Ct. __, __ L.Ed.2d __, 1997 WL 436824 (1997).

7. See Office of Inspector General, Semi–Annual Report, Oct. 1, 1993–March 31, 1994, reprinted in [1994 Transfer Binder] Medicare & Medicaid Guide (CCH) ¶ 42,490. See also Paul Jesilow et al., Prescription for Profit: How Doctors Defraud Medicaid 105, 115–19, 140–46 (1993).

8. William S. Cohen, Gaming the Health Care System, 13–14 (Investigative Staff Report of Minority Staff of Senate Special Committee on Aging, July 7, 1994).

9. See Alice Gosfield, Slouching Toward the Millennium: False Claims in Medicare Physician Billing, in Health Law Handbook, 51 (Alice Gosfield, ed. 1997).

10. 42 U.S.C.A. § 1395w–4.

11. James Sheehan, The False Claims Act, in American Bar Association, Health Care Fraud, 1996, K–47; James Sheehan, The False Claims Act and the HCFA 1500 Form, in Practicing Law Institute, Qui Tam: Beyond Government Contracts (1993).

12. Alice G. Gosfield, Unintentional Part B False Claims: Pitfalls for the Unwary, in 1993 Health Law Handbook, 205, 220 (Alice G. Gosfield ed., 1993).

physician must prescribe them or certify their medical necessity.[13] The physician also must comply with a host of billing limitations, including requirements that the physician fill out designated forms and refrain from balance-billing of patients for amounts in excess of the limits permitted by Medicare.[14] Physicians must also in most cases attempt to collect the 20% beneficiary copayment obligation.[15] Violation of most of these requirements could potentially result in administrative fines or exclusions, or even in civil penalties under the False Claims Act or criminal prosecution for false claims or statements or for mail or wire fraud.[16]

In fact billing slip-ups and oversights rarely result in a sanction. Indeed, administrative sanctions are only available for some types of violations if the offense is repeated, knowing, and willful.[17] Attempts by the Office of Inspector General or Department of Justice to use fraud prosecutions to police billing technicalities have in some cases provoked considerable resistance and skepticism from the courts.[18] In one recent case, for example, the trial court held a doctor whose office had engaged in egregious miscoding liable for fraud only for instances where the doctor billed for more than twenty-four hours of psychiatric sessions in a twenty-four hour period.[19] The court used the case, moreover, as a vehicle for castigating the government for inadequacies of both its payments and coding system.

Where physicians engage in clearly inappropriate billing practices, however, courts will find them guilty of fraud.[20] Psychiatrists

---

13. See, e.g., 42 C.F.R. §§ 424.10–.24 (hospital, SNF, and home health care).

14. See, e.g., 42 U.S.C.A. § 1395w–4(g)(4) (penalties for using improper claims form); 42 U.S.C.A. §§ 1395u(j)(1), 1395w–4(g)(1)(B) (penalties for knowing, willful, and repeated violation of limiting charge requirements).

15. See, St. Louis Doctor Ordered to Pay $4.1 Million in Medicare Fraud Suit, BNA Health Care Daily, Oct. 18, 1996.

16. See chapter 2.

17. See, e.g., 42 U.S.C.A. § 1395u(p) (knowingly, willfully, and on a repeated basis failing to include diagnostic codes on bills after having been notified of the obligation to do so). Recent amendments to the Medicare and Medicaid administrative penalty statute explicitly provide that a "person who engages in a pattern or practice of presenting or causing to be presented a claim for an item or service that is based on a code that the person knows or should know will result in a greater payment to the person than the code the person knows or should know is

applicable to the item or service actually provided" may be sanctioned. 42 U.S.C.A. § 1320a–7a(a)(1)(A). The recent amendments also provide for sanctions where "a pattern or medical or other items or services that a person knows or should know are not medically necessary" is established. 42 U.S.C.A. § 1320a–7a(a)(1)(E).

18. See, e.g., United States v. Siddiqi, 959 F.2d 1167, 1172–73 (2d Cir. 1992), remanded, 98 F.3d 1427 (2d Cir. 1996).

19. United States v. Krizek, 859 F.Supp. 5 (D.D.C.1994), supplemented by, 909 F.Supp. 32, 34 (D.D.C.1995), rev'd 111 F.3d 934 (D.C.Cir.1997)(the Court of Appeals held that the prosecution was not given an opportunity to oppose this standard).

20. See, e.g., United States v. Hooshmand, 931 F.2d 725, 731 (11th Cir. 1991); United States v. Campbell, 845 F.2d 1374, 1381–82 (6th Cir.1988), cert. denied 488 U.S. 908, 109 S.Ct. 259, 102 L.Ed.2d 248 (1988).

seem particularly prone to be sanctioned for billing problems, perhaps because they bill for their time and are thus more visible when they submit inflated bills.[21] A recent fraud alert addressed the problem of psychiatrists billing for time-consuming interactive individual psychotherapy where they should use codes appropriate for pharmacological management of mental problems.[22] From time to time, moreover, physicians are sanctioned for a small number of what appear on their face to be rather petty violations.[23] Though these cases may be instances where the prosecution only brings before the court the tip of the iceberg of improper billing, the cases still create the impression that minor slip-ups may result in major sanctions.

The fraud and abuse laws, particularly the bribe and kickback prohibition and the self-referral laws, are also used to police the relationships between physicians and other health care providers. These laws, for example, severely limit the ability of physicians to own or receive compensation from laboratories or suppliers of many health care items and services, and strictly channel their relationships with hospitals and other health care institutions. The full contours of these prohibitions will be explored in later chapters. Suffice it to say here, however, that physicians must always carefully consider the constraints of the fraud and abuse laws in forming relationships with other providers and practitioners.

b. Other Practitioners

Though physicians are the professionals most likely to be sanctioned for Medicare and Medicaid fraud and abuse, other practitioners, including dentists,[24] podiatrists,[25] chiropractors,[26] optometrists,[27] psychologists,[28] and pharmacists[29] have also been sanc-

21. Jesilow, supra note 4, at 105; William S. Cohen, supra note 8, at 17–19.

22. Office of Inspector General, Fraud Alert—Improper Use of CPT Code, OIG97–03 [1997–1 Transfer Binder] Medicare & Medicaid Guide (CCH) ¶ 45,211 (Jan. 1997).

23. See, e.g., Manocchio v. Kusserow, 961 F.2d 1539, 1540–41 (11th Cir.1992) (doctor excluded from Medicare participation for five years based on guilty plea to misdemeanor of having filed a single fraudulent Medicare claim for $62.40).

24. United States v. Nichols, Nos. 91–6374, 91–6375, 1992 WL 238264 at *1 (6th Cir.1992); United States v. Lorenzo, 768 F.Supp. 1127, 1130 (E.D.Pa. 1991).

25. Kahn v. Inspector General, 848 F.Supp. 432, 434 (S.D.N.Y.1994).

26. Bernstein v. Sullivan, 914 F.2d 1395, 1397 (10th Cir.1990); Mayers v. Department of Health & Human Servs., 806 F.2d 995, 996 (11th Cir.1986); People v. Bovee, 285 N.W.2d 53, 55, 92 Mich.App. 42, 46 (Ct.App.1979).

27. United States v. Gold, Nos. 83–3230, 83–3231, 83–3267, 1984 WL 48339 at *1 (11th Cir.1984); United States ex rel. Fahner v. Alaska, 591 F.Supp. 794, 794–95 (N.D.Ill.1984) (Medicaid fraud).

28. Scott v. Bowen, 845 F.2d 856, 856 (9th Cir.1988); United States v. Cegelka, 853 F.2d 627, 627–28 (8th Cir. 1988), cert. denied 488 U.S. 1011, 109 S.Ct. 798, 102 L.Ed.2d 789 (1989).

29. Pharmacists are probably the profession most likely to be sanctioned for fraud and abuse after physicians. They are discussed separately below.

tioned under the fraud and abuse laws. Practitioners who can bill for their services independently, e.g. dentists or podiatrists, commit many of the same offenses committed by physicians, including improper coding or billing for uncovered or unnecessary services or for services not rendered.[30] Medicare reimbursement for the services of many non-physician professionals is very limited, however. There is, therefore, an incentive for these professionals to falsify their claims to create the appearance that they had delivered a covered service when in fact they had not.[31] Where professionals can only bill for their services upon a referral by a physician, professionals also face a temptation to forge or falsify physician certifications or to pay bribes or kickbacks to physicians to secure certification.[32] Where non-physician professionals can only deliver services under the supervision of a physician, questions arise as to whether services were properly supervised by a physician or otherwise meet program requirements.[33] Finally, non-physician professionals from time to time engage in wholly criminal enterprises.

c. Hospitals

Though hospitals account for 61% of Medicare and 39% of Medicaid expenditures,[34] they are rarely prosecuted for Medicare and Medicaid fraud. Hospitals can only become Medicare providers if they are either accredited by a national accrediting agency or certified by Medicare for participation.[35] It is difficult to conceive of an enterprise formed solely for fraudulent purposes meeting these requirements. Hospitals are usually institutions of considerable stature in their communities, and cannot be lightly charged with fraud nor easily excluded from Medicare or Medicaid participation.

Hospitals have, however, from time to time succumbed to the temptation to cross legal boundaries when they engage in aggres-

---

30. See United States ex rel. Fahner v. Alaska, 591 F. Supp. at 796–97; United States v. Nichols, 977 F.2d 583, 1992 WL 238264 at *1 (6th Cir.1992) (billing for services not rendered, inflating charges, waiving co-payments, and billing for more expensive services when less expensive services were in fact rendered).

31. United States v. Gold, 1984 WL 48339 at *1 (optometrist billing for ordinary glasses or sunglasses, which are not covered by Medicare, as special glasses necessary for patients with cataracts, which are); United States v. Lorenzo, 768 F.Supp. 1127, 1130–31 (E.D.Pa.1991) (routine dental check-ups, not covered by Medicare, billed as oral cancer screening, which may be covered under some circumstances).

32. United States v. Cegelka, 853 F.2d 627, 628 (8th Cir.1988) (psychologist falsifying physician referrals), cert. denied 488 U.S. 1011, 109 S.Ct. 798, 102 L.Ed.2d 789 (1989).

33. Anesthesiologists Affiliated v. Sullivan, 941 F.2d 678, 679–80 (8th Cir. 1991) (nurse anesthetist services); Matter of William J. and Patricia Mayers, [1986 Transfer Binder] Medicare & Medicaid Guide (CCH) ¶ 34,892 (DAB Aug. 11, 1985) (chiropractor's services). See also Office of Inspector General, Semi–Annual Report, April 1, 1994— Sept. 30, 1994 (an OIG audit determined that in 4 out of 5 cases reimbursed as physical therapy in physician's office, true physical therapy was not provided).

34. Levit, supra note 3, at 210.

35. 42 U.S.C.A. §§ 1395aa, 1395bb.

sive Medicare or Medicaid billing or to get involved in prohibited relationships with other practitioners or providers. Most hospitals are now paid by Medicare through a prospective payment system in which payment is based on a patient's discharge diagnosis.[36] By manipulating diagnosis coding, hospitals can secure higher payments. Some hospitals have crossed the line between aggressive coding and fraud, and have been penalized for it. Hospitals that are still paid on a cost basis, such as rehabilitation or psychiatric hospitals, have from time to time been sanctioned for cost-report fraud for claiming costs not in fact incurred or allowable.[37] Hospitals that have failed promptly to refund credit balances based on mistaken overbilling or double-billing have been a concern to the OIG for some time.[38] Hospital-physician relationships have increasingly come under scrutiny for violation of the bribe and kickback or self-referral laws, since physicians are in a position to make referrals to hospitals.[39] Physician recruitment, purchase of physician practices, and space or equipment rental arrangements are particularly problematic areas.[40] Finally, hospitals that bill for services not meeting quality standards may be billing for services not properly rendered and thus be submitting false claims.[41]

In the recent past, hospitals have become increasingly the targets of fraud enforcement.[42] A major area of concern to the OIG has been hospital billing for outpatient testing and services during the 72 hour period prior to inpatient admission. These services are supposed to be covered by global inpatient surgery DRG payments,

36. 42 U.S.C.A. § 1395ww(d).

37. See United States v. Oakwood Downriver Medical Ctr., 687 F.Supp. 302, 303–04 (E.D.Mich.1988).

38. See, e.g., Office of Inspector General, Update on Findings Developed in Our National Review of Medicare Beneficiary Accounts with Credit Balances (Dec. 1992), reported in [1992 Transfer Binder] Medicare & Medicaid Guide (CCH) ¶ 39,608; Office of Inspector General, Outpatient Accounts Receivable with Credit Balances at Selected Hospitals, (Aug. 29, 1991) reported in [1992 Transfer Binder] Medicare & Medicaid Guide (CCH) ¶ 39,608.

39. See, e.g., Office of Inspector General, Fraud Alert, Hospital Incentives to Physicians, reprinted in [1992 Transfer Binder] Medicare & Medicaid (CCH) ¶ 40,200; infra chapters 3 & 4.

40. See Kennestone Hospital settlement, described in Sanford Teplitzky et al., 1993–1994 Developments in Health Care Fraud and Abuse, in 1995 Health Law Handbook 271, 283–85 (Alice G. Gosfield ed., 1995).

41. United States ex rel. Aranda v. Community Psychiatric Ctrs. of Oklahoma, 945 F.Supp. 1485 (W.D.Okla. 1996). This case was subsequently settled for a $750,000 payment, BNA Health Care Daily, Feb. 12, 1997. See also United States ex rel. Sanders v. East Ala. Healthcare Auth., 953 F.Supp. 1404 (M.D.Ala.1996) (claims submitted by hospital that allegedly improperly obtained Certificate of Need could be false claims).

42. See Adam Steiner, The False Claims Act Applied to Health Care Institutions: Gearing up for Corporate Compliance, 2 DePaul J. Health L. 1, 22–35 (1996); Sanford Teplitzky & S. Craig Holden, 1996 Developments in Health Care Fraud and Abuse, in Health Law Handbook, 3, 32–39 (Alice Gosfield ed., 1997); John Steiner, Current Trends in Health Care Fraud and Abuse Enforcement, in American Bar Association, Health Care Fraud, 1996 at I–27.

but have often been billed by hospitals on an unbundled basis.[43] A second area of concern has been improper hospital billing for experimental procedures and devices that are not covered by Medicare.[44] A third issue is billing by staff physicians under Part B for resident services covered under Part A.[45] Finally, the DOJ and OIG have achieved significant settlements in cases alleging that hospitals have submitted claims for unnecessary care or paid kickbacks to secure overutilization of care.[46] The federal government has increasingly been willing to take on large and prestigious hospitals that it suspects of improper billing practices.[47]

More frightening to hospitals, however, has been the rise of qui tam (whistleblower) actions in health care (see chapters 2 and 6). Hospitals are ideal qui tam defendants. They submit large numbers of claims, thus per-claim penalty recoveries can be enormous in size. They are stable institutions with sizable assets, unlikely to become judgment-proof. There are often a number of persons who have inside knowledge regarding their questionable billing practices, and who are thus possible qui tam plaintiffs. Hospitals have become increasingly anxious, therefore, about the potential of qui tam litigation.

d. Nursing Facilities

Most nursing facilities are run for profit. There is a long history in the United States of scandals involving both quality and financial problems in nursing facilities.[48] It is not surprising, therefore, that nursing facilities are also involved fairly often in fraud and abuse proceedings.[49]

Medicare and most state Medicaid programs pay nursing homes on a cost-related basis. One of the most common types of fraud in nursing facilities, therefore, is fraudulent reporting of false or inflated costs.[50] Nursing home operators have been convicted of

---

43. See 42 U.S.C.A. § 1395ww(a)(4); Billing Fraud, Reimbursement Among Top Medicare Legal Issues in 1996, 5 BNA Health L. Rptr. 165 (1996).

44. Secret Witness Tells Senate Panel of Medicare Medical Device Billing Fraud, 5 BNA Health Law Daily 265 (1996).

45. See Pa. Health System to Pay $30 Million in Largest Settlement, DOJ Says, 4 BNA Health Law Reporter 1875 (1994).

46. United States v. National Psychiatric Hospitals Inc. (NME–PHI), No. CR–94–0268 (D.D.C. 1992) ($379 million settlement in case against hospital chain for provision of unnecessary care and for kickbacks) described in Teplitzky, supra

note 40, at 286–87; and in Howard E. O'Leary, Regulating Health Care Costs Through Fraud Enforcement, 62 Def. Couns. J. 211, 213 (1995).

47. Teplizky, supra note 40, at 286–87.

48. See, e.g., Bruce Vladeck, Unloving Care (1979).

49. See Kenneth Bickenstaff, Health Care Fraud: The Nursing Home Setting, in American Bar Association, Health Care Fraud, 1996 (describing typical fraud cases); Office of Inspector General, Fraud Alert, Fraud and Abuse in Provision of Medical Supplies to Nursing Facilities, August 1995.

50. See, e.g., Chapman v. United States Dep't of Health & Human Servs.,

including in Medicaid cost reports items such as swimming pools, jewelry or the owner's nanny.[51] Nursing homes can also be sanctioned for claiming unpermitted costs incurred for tax penalties, late charges, excessive promotional advertising, or excessive costs for recreational trips or luxury items. A variant on this theme is nursing home operators who improperly inflate their reported costs by contracting for services with related organizations.[52]

Nursing facilities also serve as venues where fraud is carried out by other professionals and suppliers. Gang visits to nursing home residents by physicians have already been noted. Speech, physical and occupational therapists, or companies that provide them, have been charged with billing Medicare or Medicaid for services to nursing home residents that were not necessary or not performed.[53] Between 1990 and 1993 the amount Medicare paid for such therapy services tripled from $1 to $3 billion, raising questions about the extent to which fraud and abuse was involved.[54] Some suppliers have also been known to bill Medicare under Part B for services provided in nursing facilities that were also covered as costs reimbursed to the facility under Part A.[55] Because residents of nursing homes are usually very debilitated, it is often difficult to discover or to prove that items or services for which payment is claimed were not in fact provided.

Some of the most spectacular instances of overbilling for unnecessary or unprovided services in recent years have involved supplies allegedly provided to nursing home residents. One such practice was billing adult diapers provided to nursing home patients as "female external urinary collection devices."[56] From 1990 to 1993, the amount Medicare Part B spent on incontinence supplies increased from $88 million to $290 million, though the number of beneficiaries receiving such supplies dropped during the period.[57] In

821 F.2d 523, 525 (10th Cir.1987); Commonwealth v. Minkin, 436 N.E.2d 955, 957, 14 Mass.App.Ct. 911, 911–12 (1982); Frye v. State, 369 So.2d 892, 894–95 (Ala.Crim.App.1979).

51. Ohio Group Home Operator Convicted of Submitting False Medicaid Bills, BNA Health Care Daily, May 12, 1997; Cohen, supra note 21, at 20.

52. United States ex rel. Woodard v. Country View Care Ctr., Inc., 797 F.2d 888, 890–91 (10th Cir.1986).

53. See GAO, Medicare, Tighter Rules Needed to Curtail Overcharges for Therapy in Nursing Homes, 5–6 (GAO/HEHS–95–23, Mar. 30, 1995).

54. Id. at 4.

55. See Office of Inspector General Special Fraud Alert, Fraud and Abuse in the Provision of Medical Supplies to Nursing Facilities, August 1995, reprinted in [1995 Transfer Binder] Medicare & Medicaid Guide (CCH) ¶ 43,517.

56. Florida Man Gets 10–Year Jail Term for Fraudulent Adult Diaper Scheme, BNA Health Care Fraud Report, March 26, 1997 at 201; Office of Inspector General, Fraud Alert, Fraud and Abuse in the Provision of Medical Supplies to Nursing Facilities, August 1995.

57. Office of Inspector General, Questionable Medical Payments for Incontinence Supplies (1994), reprinted in [1995 Transfer Binder] Medicare & Medicaid Guide (CCH) ¶ 42,965. During that time the amount billed to Medicare for lubricants grew from $.5 million to $32 million while the amount spent on

some cases, the supplier provided a bribe or kickback to the nursing facility for permitting it to bill for services the supplier provided or claimed to have provided within the facility, or waived copayments as an inducement to get residents to accept these items.[58] Fraud concerns also arise when institutional pharmacies contract to provide pharmacy services in nursing homes, and pay kickbacks to the nursing home for the privilege, or violate state Medicaid requirements in billing for drugs.

Finally, Medicare and Medicaid nursing facility exclusions are frequently based on neglect and abuse of nursing home residents themselves. One of the four grounds under which exclusion is mandatory under the Medicare and Medicaid fraud and abuse law is conviction of neglect and abuse of a nursing home resident.[59] Exclusions have been imposed for physical abuse of residents, financial abuse of residents, failure to report abuse of residents, and practices that result in neglect of residents.[60] The fraud and abuse statutes also require nursing homes to accept Medicaid as payment in full and impose criminal penalties for requiring patients and their relatives to supplement Medicaid payments.[61]

e. Home Health and Home Infusion Therapy

Because home health care permits beneficiaries and recipients who might otherwise require nursing facility care to remain in their homes, and because it has been perceived by policy-makers as less costly than nursing facility care, the number of beneficiaries and recipients receiving home health care and the amount of money spent on this benefit have increased dramatically in recent years. Between 1983 and 1994 the number of persons receiving home health Medicare benefits grew from 1.3 million to 3.2 million, while expenditures grew from $1.6 billion to $13 billion.[62] Medicaid expenditures for home health grew from .6% of total expenditures in 1975 to 6% in 1993.[63]

---

female pouches grew from $20,000 to 15.3 million. Id.

58. HHS Office of Inspector General, Marketing of Incontinence Supplies (1994), reprinted in [1995 Transfer Binder] Medicare & Medicaid Guide (CCH) ¶ 42,966.

59. 42 U.S.C.A. § 1320a–7(a)(2); 42 C.F.R. § 1001.101(b).

60. See, e.g., Westin v. Shalala, 845 F.Supp. 1446, 1451 (D.Kan.1994) (failure to report neglect and abuse); Barrett v. Dep't of Health & Human Servs., 14 F.3d 26, 27 (8th Cir.1994) (failure to report sex abuse); Edmonson v. Inspector General, [1993 Transfer Binder]

Medicare & Medicaid Guide (CCH) ¶ 40,-993 (DAB May 21, 1992) (assault on resident); Gregory v. Inspector General, [1992 Transfer Binder] Medicare & Medicaid Guide (CCH) ¶ 41,665 (DAB June 25, 1993) (misapplication of patient trust property by nursing home business manager).

61. 42 U.S.C.A. § 1320–7b(d).

62. PPAC, Medicare and the American Health Care System, Report to Congress 69–70 (1995).

63. Anthony De Lew, The First 30 Years of Medicare and Medicaid, 274 JAMA 262, 266 (1995).

It would be difficult to design a program more vulnerable to fraud than the Medicare home health program.[64] Providers are paid on a cost basis. Beneficiaries are not responsible for copayments or deductibles, and historically have not received explanations of benefits. Home health entities are often for-profit organizations. Their services are often received by debilitated patients with only minimal physician oversight. Though home health agencies are licensed by states, they have historically had neither the visibility in the community enjoyed by hospitals nor the notoriety suffered by nursing homes, and thus have often received little regulatory supervision.

The types of fraud and abuses that have been perpetrated by home health agencies fit into a by-now-familiar litany. Agencies have submitted claims for visits not made, for visits made to beneficiaries not eligible for home health services because they are not homebound, for visits to beneficiaries not otherwise requiring covered services, or for visits not properly authorized by a physician.[65] Examples of the perpetrators of such fraud include an agency that billed Medicare for 123 visits to a patient who in fact never received a single visit. Another agency billed for services to a beneficiary so ambulatory that he volunteered several times a week at a local hospital. Another agency forged patient signatures on visit logs and physician signatures on care certificates.[66]

Some home health agencies have also engaged in cost report fraud. The owner of ABC Home Health Care Services Inc., one of the nation's largest home health agencies, was convicted of 70 counts of criminal fraud charges and ABC itself on 72 charges based on allegations that ABC had defrauded Medicare of more than $1 million for personal airplane trips for the family and friends of the owners to Cozumel, Mexico and to college football games, and for political contributions and ghost employees.[67] The successor corporation to ABC eventually entered into a civil settlement with the government for $255 million.[68] Another home health agency was accused of billing the New York state Medicaid agencies for services provided by untrained and unqualified aids, including the services of a 14–year old girl.[69] As with nursing homes, home

64. See Office of Inspector General, Special Fraud Alert, Home Health Fraud, June 1995.

65. Office of Inspector General, Special Fraud Alerts, 60 Fed. Reg. 40,847, 40,848 (1995).

66. Id.

67. ABC Home Health Services, Owner Convicted of Medicare Fraud, 5 BNA Health Law Reporter 202–03 (1995). See also GAO, Medicare, Allega-

tions Against ABC Home Health Care (GAO/OSI–95–17 July 19, 1995); and for another example, Godwin v. Visiting Nurse Assoc. Home Health Servs., 831 F.Supp. 449, 450–53 (E.D.Pa.1993), aff'd 39 F.3d 173 (7th Cir. 1994).

68. Home Health Company to Pay $255 Million to Settle Fraud Charges, BNA Health Care Daily, Oct. 22, 1996.

69. Cohen, supra note 8, at 28.

health agencies have also been known to improperly pass on to Medicare costs improperly billed by related organizations[70]

Home health agencies depend on physicians for certifying the need of beneficiaries and recipients for home health, and upon physicians, hospitals, nursing facilities, and retirement homes and adult congregate living facilities for referrals. Agencies have offered and paid remuneration, sometimes in services or personnel rather than cash, to individuals or entities in a position to make referrals to them.[71] They have also offered illegal incentives to beneficiaries, including services such as housekeeping or grocery-shopping, not covered by Medicare.[72]

Home Infusion therapy—the provision of intravenous drugs and nutritional therapy to patients at home—is one of the fastest growing segments of the home health industry.[73] Home infusion is covered under Medicare Part B.[74] There have been repeated concerns about overcharging, kickbacks, and improper marketing arrangements in the home infusion industry.[75] Until amendments to the self-referral law that went into effect in 1995 banned physician ownership of home infusion providers, physician ownership, with its attendant interest conflicts, was also common.[76] One of the largest settlements of a fraud and abuse case to date involved kickbacks and overbilling by a home infusion agency.[77]

On September 15, 1997, President Clinton, citing the prevalence of fraud and abuse in the home health industry, imposed a six month moratorium on the entry of new home health agencies into the Medicare program. During this time tough new regulations will be drafted to make it more difficult for fraudulent home health agencies to enter the program. It was also announced that audits and claim reviews involving home health agencies would be increased.[78]

---

70. See Executives for Home Health Agency Indicted for Defrauding Medicare, 4 BNA Health Law Reporter 402–03 (1995). This indictment later resulted in conviction, 4 BNA 1254, 1694 (1995).

71. HHS Office of Inspector General, Special Fraud Alerts, 60 Fed. Reg. at 40,848–49.

72. Id.

73. Office of Inspector General, Medicare Home Infusion Therapy (Sept. 1993), reprinted in [1994 Transfer Binder] Medicare & Medicaid Guide (CCH) ¶ 41,926.

74. Id.

75. Id.; Cohen, supra note 8, at 28.

76. Office of Inspector General, Medicare Home Infusion Therapy (Sept. 1993), reprinted in [1994 Transfer Binder] Medicare & Medicaid Guide (CCH) ¶ 41,926.

77. Settlement Reached with Caremark over Medicare Overbilling, Kickbacks, 4 BNA Health Law Reporter 1321 (1995). Ultimately Caremark settled for $161 million in civil and criminal fines.

78. Clinton Calls for Moratorium on Entry of Home Health Agencies into Medicare, BNA Health Care Daily, Sept. 16, 1997.

f. Pharmacies, Pharmacists, and Pharmaceutical Companies

Though Medicare provides minimal coverage for pharmaceuticals (they are only covered when provided by professionals or institutions as part of the delivery of a covered service), most Medicaid programs cover prescription drugs, and Medicaid programs spend proportionately more of their budgets on drugs than on any other form of non-institutional care.[78.5] Pharmacists and pharmacies are second only to physicians in the volume of fraud actions.[79] This is particularly true with respect to state criminal prosecutions.

Drugs present unique opportunities for fraud and abuse. First, drugs are very valuable. This is obviously true with respect to controlled substances, which have a high street value, but is also true with many prescription drugs. The provider willing to engage in fraud, therefore, can profit from the fraud twice—first by billing Medicaid for a drug not actually provided to a Medicaid recipient (or not provided in the number of tablets or strength claimed); and second by reselling the drug for which Medicaid has already paid through illicit channels.[80] Investigations have uncovered complex networks of providers and others involved in drug diversion schemes, which are estimated to have cost the state of New York alone $75 million in 1990, 10% of the state's Medicaid prescription drug expenditures.[81] Medicaid recipients have in some schemes been paid in merchandise, or even lottery tickets, for prescriptions obtained from obliging doctors, which were then used to support bills to Medicaid for diverted drugs.[82] One of the best publicized FBI investigations, Operation Goldpill, involved an extensive drug diversion scheme.[83]

Most reported cases involve, at least in the facts revealed in the court opinions, less sophisticated schemes. By far the most common problem identified in reported cases is billing Medicaid for brand-

---

78.5 De Lew, supra note 63, at 266.

79. Professor Bucy found pharmacists and pharmacies to be tied with nursing homes and their employees in second place behind physicians for number of criminal fraud actions brought between 1908 and 1988. See Bucy, supra note 1, at 883. Our own study found pharmacists and pharmacies also in second place behind physicians if both federal and state actions are considered, though, they drop to third place behind laboratories if only federal actions are considered.

80. In one case, for example, a pharmacist purchased prescribed drugs back from Medicaid recipients and then re-sold them at a higher price. United States v. Carter, No. 96 CR 512, 1996 WL 627722 (N.D.Ill.1996).

81. GAO, Medicaid Drug Fraud, Federal Leadership Needed to Reduce Program Vulnerabilities (GAO/HRD–93–118, Aug. 2, 1993).

82. GAO, Medicaid, A Program Highly Vulnerable to Fraud, 2–3 (GAO/HEHS–94–106, Feb. 25, 1994).

83. U.S. Dept. of Justice, Federal Bureau of Investigation, Operation Goldpill Targets Health Care Crime, Press Release, June 30, 1992.

name drugs when generic drugs were in fact dispensed.[84] As brand-name drugs cost considerably more than generic, this practice allows the pharmacist or pharmacy to pocket a sizable profit. These cases often involve other fraudulent conduct, including billing for larger amounts of drugs or stronger dosages than those actually dispensed.[85]

Other areas of increasing concern include the resale of drug samples or sale of expired or adulterated drugs.[86] These schemes have sometimes involved scraping or rubbing the word "sample" off of the pills before dispensing them.[87] Insofar as these schemes result in patients obtaining drugs that are adulterated or of sub-therapeutic strength, they are particularly troublesome.

Practices such as dispensing brand name drugs rather than generics in the absence of physician authorization required under a state drug substitution law; refilling prescriptions repeatedly without physician authorization or on the basis of forged authorizations; or billing state Medicaid programs higher rates than those charged to other payers when state law requires Medicaid to be given the lowest price, are also being investigated by fraud and abuse prosecutors.

The drug sector, moreover, presents a variety of bribe and kickback issues. There is a long history of drug companies conducting marketing programs offering physicians various benefits.[88] Increasingly the Office of Inspector General and other law enforcers have become concerned with marketing schemes that appear to violate the bribe and kickback prohibition of 42 U.S.C.A. § 1320a–7b(b).[89] Schemes identified in a recent fraud alert as potentially violative of that statute include "fee-for-switch" or "product conversion" programs, where a pharmacist is paid by a drug company each time the pharmacist secures a change to the paying company's product from that of another company; "frequent flier" programs, where a drug company offers a physician, managed care company, mail order pharmacy, or other supplier frequent flier miles or other incentives for prescribing or ordering a particular drug; "research grant" programs where drug companies make substantial payments to physicians or others who prescribe or order their products in

---

84. See, e.g., United States v. Brown, 763 F.2d 984, 985–87 (8th Cir.1985), cert. denied 474 U.S. 905, 106 S.Ct. 273, 88 L.Ed.2d 234 (1985); Greene v. Sullivan, 731 F.Supp. 835, 836 (E.D.Tenn. 1990); State v. Heath, 513 So.2d 493, 495 (La.Ct.App.1987).

85. State v. Vogelsong, 612 N.E.2d 462, 463–64, 82 Ohio App.3d 354, 356 (Ct. App. 1992); State v. Beatty, 308 S.E.2d 65, 67–68, 64 N.C.App. 511, 514–15 (Ct.App.1983).

86. Cohen, supra note 8, at 25–26.

87. Id.

88. Marc A. Rodwin, Medicine, Money and Morals 90–94, 107–10 (1993).

89. Office of Inspector General, Special Fraud Alert, Prescription Drug Marketing Scheme (1994), reprinted in [1994 Transfer Binder] Medicare and Medicaid Guide (CCH) ¶ 42,609.

exchange for minimal recordkeeping characterized as "research"; or other marketing programs where pharmacists are paid by drug companies for performing sale-oriented "educational" or "counselling" tasks.[90] Sizable settlements reached by the OIG with Caremark and Hoffman–LaRouche in the recent past involved allegedly fictitious research programs. Continuing education programs that focus on particular products rather than conditions and are offered by drug companies to physicians in exotic locations for free or at reduced cost are also suspect. Some drug companies have attempted to "carve out" from their marketing programs drugs provided through the Medicaid program, and thus to limit their exposure to bribe and kickback prosecution.[91] These programs may nevertheless find themselves in trouble under state fraud and abuse or consumer protection laws.

Some practices that could be characterized as bribes and kickbacks are less clearly undesirable. In particular, discounts offered to pharmacy benefit management programs or to high volume pharmacies may lower pharmaceutical costs but may not fit neatly within an existing safe harbor, such as the discount or managed care safe harbors.[92] Token gifts such as pens or notepads provided by detail men to physicians are also probably not a major concern, and will probably continue to flow forth from the pharmaceutical companies.

g. Durable Medical Equipment, Prosthetics, Orthotics, and Supplies

In 1993, Medicare spent $2.7 billion on durable medical equipment (DME), prosthetics, orthotics and supplies.[93] DME includes wheelchairs, walkers, canes, and oxygen systems; prosthetics are replacement body parts; orthotics are braces; supplies include disposable items including wound dressings and catheters.[94] DME, prosthetics and orthotics are covered under Part B and paid for on a fee schedule basis.[95] Supplies are covered under Part B on a fee schedule basis,[96] but can be paid for under Part A on a fee schedule or reasonable cost basis if the claims are submitted by hospitals or other institutions.

DME and supplies has been a persistent fraud and abuse problem area. First, historically the program participation requirements for suppliers of DME and medical supplies have been mini-

90. Id.

91. Joseph Wetro, Pharmaceutical and Pharmacy Issues, National Health Lawyers Association, 1995 Fraud and Abuse Conference Binder, 13.

92. Id.

93. GAO, Durable Medical Equipment, Regional Carriers' Coverage Criteria Are Consistent with Medicare Law, 1–2 (GAO/HEHS–95–185, Sept. 19, 1995).

94. Id. at 3.

95. 42 U.S.C.A. § 1395m(a), (h).

96. 42 U.S.C.A. § 1395m(i), (j).

mal, and suppliers that in fact did not exist have been able to bill Medicare.[97] Though a National Supplier Clearinghouse has been created to review supplier applications, as recent as 1995 it still did not perform background checks to verify the information suppliers provide.[98] Second, the possibility of billing under either Part A or Part B for supplies provided in institutions has led to double billing.[99] Double billing of both Medicare and Medicaid for the same equipment has occurred.[100] Third, Medicare pays above-market prices for some supplies, creating significant incentives for fraud and abuse.[101] A particular area of concern has been surgical dressings, where a recent GAO study found that Medicare could have saved $20 million had it paid wholesale prices for 44 types of dressings.[102]

Medicare contractor review of supplier claims has historically had serious deficiencies. A GAO review of 85 high-dollar medical supply claims submitted by Part A intermediaries determined that 89% of the claims and 61% of the dollars billed for claims for which documentation was received should have been totally or partially denied.[103] Prior to 1993, carrier policies as to payment and coverage for DME and supplies varied, and suppliers engaged in "carrier shopping," billing the carrier with the most favorable prices even though the items billed were not provided in the carrier's coverage area.[104] Though consolidation of coverage under four regional durable medical equipment regional carriers (DMERCs) has ended this abuse, claims are still not policed with sufficient vigor. A recent GAO review of surgical dressings found one supplier billing Medicare for surgical tape sufficient to wrap each of the beneficiaries for which claims were made in 60 to 240 yards of tape a day.[105]

The DME and supply area has been plagued with claims for items not actually supplied, items that were substandard or did not meet program definitions, or items that were not medically neces-

97. GAO, Medicare Spending, Modern Management Strategies Needed to Curb Billions in Unnecessary Payments (GAO/HEHS–95–210, Sept. 19, 1995); Cohen, supra note 8, at 13–14.

98. GAO, Medicare Spending, Modern Management Strategies Needed to Curb Billions in Unnecessary Payments (GAO/HEHS–95–210, Sept. 19, 1995).

99. GAO, Medicare: Excessive Payments for Medical Supplies Continue Despite Improvements, 6–7 (GAO/T–HEHS–96–5, Oct. 2, 1995).

100. California Man Sentenced to 11 Years in Prison for Medicare, Medicaid Fraud, BNA Health Care Daily, Nov. 21, 1996.

101. Id. at 2–3.

102. Id.

103. Id. at 4. Amendments in OBRA 1993 require better documentation for some supplier Part A claims, though other supplies are still billed under broad codes that permit abuse. 42 U.S.C.A. § 1395m(i).

104. United States v. Weiss, 930 F.2d 185, 190–91 (2d Cir.1991), cert. denied 502 U.S. 842, 112 S.Ct. 133, 116 L.Ed.2d 100 (1991).

105. GAO, Medicare, Excessive Payments for Medical Supplies Continue Despite Improvements, 6–7 (GAO/T–HEHS–96–5, Oct. 2, 1995).

sary.[106] A particular problem area, mentioned above, has been the provision of supplies and dressings to nursing homes.[107] DME suppliers have been charged with forging physician signatures on or altering certificates of medical necessity (which are required for payment for some products) or with having paid kickbacks to physicians or others to obtain certificates and authorizations.[108] DME suppliers have engaged in telemarketing schemes to encourage beneficiaries to obtain their products, though recent legislation limits telemarketing abuses.[109] Perhaps most disturbing was a scheme involving the sale of tainted pacemakers that were past their expiration date and perhaps contaminated.[110] The scheme, which resulted in several criminal convictions, also involved kickbacks to physicians who used the tainted products, including vacation trips and the services of prostitutes.[111] Other problem areas have been incontinence supplies and nebulizers.[112]

h. Laboratories

Medicare and state Medicaid programs cover a variety of clinical, physiological and imaging laboratory services. Historically, laboratory services has been another major problem area for fraud and abuse.

Laboratories are not licensed in many states, and licensure is only required for Medicare participation for laboratories located in states that offer licensure.[113] Historically, therefore, entities claiming to deliver laboratory services could obtain provider numbers (and sometimes multiple provider numbers) with relative ease.[114] Although clinical laboratories have recently come under closer supervision under the federal Clinical Laboratories Improvement Act,[115] the laboratory area generally is still less tightly supervised by the states than other health care sectors.

106. Cohen, supra note 8, at 11–13; United States v. Freshour, Nos. 94–5448, 94–5759, 94–5758, 1995 WL 496662 at *1 (6th Cir.1995) (items not provided as claimed), cert. denied, ___ U.S. ___, 116 S.Ct. 910, 133 L.Ed.2d 842 (1996) and ___ U.S. ___, 116 S. Ct. 1045, 134 L.Ed.2d 192 (1996); United States v. Fesman, 781 F.Supp. 511, 512 (S.D.Ohio 1991) (used seat lift chairs claimed as new).

107. Office of Inspector General, Special Fraud Alert, Provision of Medical Supplies in Nursing Homes, reprinted in [1995 Transfer Binder] Medicare & Medicaid Guide (CCH) ¶ 43,517 (1995).

108. United States ex rel. Piacentile v. Wolk, No. Civ. A. 93–5773, 1995 WL 20833 at *1 (E.D.Pa.1995) (alteration of

signed certificates by supplier); Cohen, supra note 8, at 14–15.

109. 42 U.S.C.A. § 1395m(a)(17). See Cohen, supra note 8, at 14.

110. Cohen, supra note 8, at 16–17.

111. Id.

112. See HHS Office of Inspector General, Medicare Allowances for Incontinence Supplies (1997) and HHS Office of Inspector General, Questionable Practices Involving Nebulizer Therapy (1997).

113. 42 U.S.C.A. § 1395x(s)(15).

114. See, GAO, Medicare, One Scheme Illustrates Vulnerabilities to Fraud, 8–9 (GAO/HRD–92–76, Aug. 26, 1992).

115. 42 U.S.C.A. § 263a.

The most common abuses in the laboratory sector (as in most other sectors) are billing for services not actually rendered, not necessary, or not provided as claimed. One practice that has resulted recently in sizable settlements involved marketing a single sequential multiple analysis computer (SMAC) blood chemistry test to physicians as a profile test that included HDL cholesterol tests, but then billing Medicare separately for the HDL test, even in circumstances where the HDL test was not necessary. National Health Laboratories settled a case involving this practice in 1992 for around $100 million, while MetPath and MetWest laboratories settled a similar case in 1993 for almost $40 million.[116] Other cases against laboratories have involved tests that were billed but not performed;[117] tests billed as performed manually that were actually performed on automated equipment to obtain higher payment rates;[118] tests billed with false diagnosis codes;[119] tests falsely claimed as ordered by doctors that had not in fact been so ordered;[120] or mileage billed for collecting specimens for trips not made as billed.[121] Laboratory Corporation of America (Labcorp) and Damon Clinical Laboratories entered into settlements of $182 million and $119 million respectively in 1996 for abuses involving unnecessary testing.[122]

Because laboratory tests must be ordered by a physician, laboratories have often in the past either been owned by physicians (who were thereby able to profit by their own referrals) or have offered financial incentives to physicians to secure referrals. Bribes, kickbacks, and self-referrals have thus been a particular concern in this area. Three of the leading cases interpreting the bribe and kickback prohibition, Greber,[123] Kats,[124] and Hanlester,[125] involved financial relationships between physicians and laboratories. The original Stark legislation was concerned solely with physician investment and compensation arrangements with laboratories. A recent fraud alert focused on other problem areas—provision of phlebotomists to physicians; offers of preferential rates to end state renal disease (ESRD) facilities for certain tests the ESRD facility

---

116. See United States ex rel. Dowden v. MetPath, Inc., No. 91–1843, 1993 WL 397770 (C.D.Cal.1993); Teplitzky, supra note 40, at 285–86 (the NHL case also involved serum ferritin tests).

117. United States v. Grewal, No. 93–10284, 1994 WL 587395 at *1 (9th Cir.1994).

118. United States v. Precision Medical Labs., Inc., 593 F.2d 434, 437–39 (2d Cir. 1978).

119. United States ex rel. Wagner v. Allied Clinical Labs., No. C–1–94–092, 1995 WL 254405 at *1 (S.D.Ohio 1995).

120. State v. Ijaz, No. 92AP–942, 1992 WL 385649 at *1 (Ohio. Ct. App. 1992).

121. Clinical Lab Agrees to Fine for Medicare Double Billing, BNA Health Care Daily, July 2, 1997.

122. Medical Lab to pay $187 Million in Civil, Criminal Fraud Penalties, BNA Health Care Daily, Nov. 25, 1996.

123. United States v. Greber, 760 F.2d 68 (3d Cir.1985).

124. United States v. Kats, 871 F.2d 105 (9th Cir.1989).

125. Hanlester Network v. Shalala, 51 F.3d 1390 (9th Cir.1995).

must pay for itself to gain the opportunity to bill Medicare directly for other tests; and reduction of charges for managed care patients to attract non-managed care referrals from physicians.[126]

Labs have also been known to offer "free" tests to recipients, which tests were then billed to Medicare after physicians, who received kickbacks of various types from the laboratories, provided diagnoses justifying the tests.[127] Tests that are poorly performed under these circumstances can generate numerous false positives, resulting in the need for expensive follow-up testing and in considerable anxiety for beneficiaries.[128]

Some clinical laboratories are operated by large national enterprises with considerable assets. These entities have become major qui tam targets. At the other end of the spectrum, however, laboratories have also been operated by corporations that dissolve as rapidly as they attract the attention of investigators, making effective sanctions difficult. One such "rolling labs" scheme operated under more than 500 organizational names.

i. Managed Care

It has often been observed that managed care organizations (MCOs) are not as prone to engage in fraudulent practices as fee-for-service providers.[129] MCOs that are paid on a capitation basis lack the incentives possessed by fee-for-service practitioners to engage in some fraudulent practices, such as providing unnecessary services or upcoding, unbundling, or otherwise misrepresenting the services provided. Providers and practitioners providing care through MCOs are also unlikely to engage in bribes, kickbacks, or self-referrals, since they have nothing to gain by increasing the volume of services they provide.[130]

Nonetheless, moving from fee-for-service to managed care does not eliminate the possibility, or perhaps substantially reduce the danger of fraud.[131] One particular area of concern has been fraudulent marketing practices. Since Medicare and Medicaid pay HMOs on a capitation basis, the more patients an HMO can recruit, and

126. Office of Inspector General, Special Fraud Alert, Clinical Laboratory Services (1994), reprinted in [1994 Transfer Binder] Medicare & Medicaid Guide (CCH) ¶ 42,712.

127. United States v. White, 27 F.3d 1531, 1533 (11th Cir.1994); GAO, Medicare, One Scheme Illustrates Vulnerabilities to Fraud, 16 (GAO/HRD–92–76, Aug. 26, 1992).

128. United States v. White, 27 F.3d at 1533.

129. Sharon Davies & Timothy Stoltzfus Jost, Managed Care: Placebo or Wonder Drug for Health Care Fraud and Abuse?, 31 Ga. L. Rev. 373 (1997).

130. James F. Blumstein, The Fraud and Abuse Statute in an Evolving Health Care Marketplace: Life in the Health Care Speakeasy, 22 Am. J. L. & Med. 205 (1996).

131. See id.; Pamela Bucy, Health Care Reform and Fraud by Health Care Providers, 38 Vill. L. Rev. 1003 (1993) (contrasting incentives for fraud in managed care and in fee for service medicine).

particularly, the more healthy patients it recruits, the more money it makes. During the early days of the Tenncare Medicaid managed care program, HMO recruiters signed up felons in the state's prison, even though they were ineligible for Medicaid, and canvassed housing projects looking for healthy prospects.[132]

Other types of fraud also occur with managed care, however. If MCOs are paid on a cost basis,[133] they may defraud the government by inflating their costs. MCOs can also defraud the government by making false statements to Medicare or Medicaid about their financial condition or about the extent to which they can have providers available to provide care. MCOs can defraud beneficiaries or recipients who receive services from them by misrepresenting the extent to which they have available services or providers.[134] MCOs can defraud providers with whom they contract by misrepresenting their financial or operational arrangements, intentionally delaying payment, withholding money in bad faith, or deselecting providers for impermissible reasons.[135] MCOs can also be defrauded by providers or practitioners, particularly if they pay providers on a fee-for-service basis, as is often the case with specialists. Though defrauding an organization that submits claims to the federal government is illegal, there is a concern that MCOs will be reluctant to report providers who defraud them for fear of defamation litigation, but will rather terminate such providers quietly.[136]

Although the risk of self-referrals and bribes and kickbacks is considerably diminished in managed care, it is not entirely eliminated.[137] MCOs might pay persons in a position to direct subscribers to them. MCOs may offer impermissible "bribes" to potential low cost subscribers to get their business. Managed care contracts frequently contain "carve-outs" under which certain kinds of care are provided on a fee-for-service basis or by a provider outside of the managed care contract (e.g. for nursing home care). MCOs could fraudulently steer patients into the "carve-out" to increase their income or decrease their costs.

The biggest concern regarding managed care, however, is that MCOs will defraud both their subscribers and the government by underproviding services.[138] MCOs that are paid on a capitation

---

132. Martin Gottlieb, A Free-for-All in Swapping Medicaid for Managed Care, New York Times, Oct. 2, 1995 at A1.

133. See 42 C.F.R. § 417.800.

134. Jonathan Lindke, Fraud and Abuse by and Against HMOs and Other MCOs, NHLA Fraud and Abuse Conference Binder, 1995.

135. Id.

136. See Jeannine Mjoseth, Underutilization in Managed Care New Target of Joint Fraud Efforts, 4 BNA Health L. Rptr. 1809 (1995).

137. Timothy Jost & Sharon Davies, The Fraud and Abuse Statute: Rationalizing or Rationalization, 15 Health Aff. 129 (1996).

138. See James Sheehan & Kirsten McAuliffe Raleigh, The Effect of Managed Care on Mental Health Services, in

basis, and providers or practitioners within them who bear risk, face a significant incentive to deny their subscribers services that those subscribers might need. When MCOs fail to provide necessary services, they both deny their subscribers services to which they are entitled and which they have been promised, and deprive the government of services it has paid for.

In theory, at least, MCOs could be held liable for false claims, false statements, and mail or wire fraud when they claim to have provided services and claim payment for services that were not in fact delivered. It may be quite difficult, however, to prove that an MCO has intentionally denied its patients services to which they are entitled.[139]

There are also specific statutes and regulations that provide for civil penalties and suspension of enrollment of or payment for new subscribers in Medicare and Medicaid MCOs that are found to have committed certain abuses. First, MCOs that deny medically necessary items or services to individuals where the denial has an adverse effect or is substantially likely to have an adverse effect can be penalized for up to $25,000 for each determination.[140] "Adverse effect" is defined to cover situations where denial of care "has presented an imminent danger to the health, safety, or well-being of the patient or has placed the patient unnecessarily in a high-risk situation."[141] Second, MCOs that charge their subscribers charges that are not permitted can be fined up to $25,000 for each instance, plus twice the amount of the overcharge.[142] Third, Medicare MCOs that wrongfully expel or refuse to re-enroll eligible individuals can be penalized for up to $25,000 per determination and Medicare and Medicaid MCOs that engage in favorable selection by denying or discouraging enrollment by eligible individuals whose medical condition or history indicates that they will need substantial medical services in the future can be penalized for up to $100,000 per determination plus $15,000 for each person not enrolled.[143] Fourth, MCOs that misrepresent or falsify information provided to the government or to individuals and entities can be penalized for up to $100,000 per determination.[144] Fifth, Medicare MCOs can be penalized up to $25,000 per determination for failing to make prompt

Health Law Handbook, 87 (Alice Gosfield ed., 1997).

139. Id.

140. 42 U.S.C.A. §§ 1395mm(i)(6)(B)(i), 1396b(m)(5)(A)(i); 42 C.F.R. §§ 417.500(a)(1), 434.67(a)(1), 1003.102(b)(3).

141. 42 C.F.R. § 1003.101.

142. 42 U.S.C.A. §§ 1395mm(i)(6)(B)(i), 1396b(m)(5)(A)(ii); 42 C.F.R. §§ 417.500(a)(2), 434.67(a)(2).

143. 42 U.S.C.A. §§ 1395mm(i)(6)(B)(ii), 1396b(m)(5)(A)(iii); 42 C.F.R. §§ 417.500(a)(3), (4), 434.67(3).

144. 42 U.S.C.A. §§ 1395mm(i)(6)(B)(i), 1396b(m)(5)(A)(iv); 42 C.F.R. §§ 417.500(a)(5), 434.67(a)(4), 1003.102(a)(2), (4).

payment of claims to persons or entities that provide services or supplies to their subscribers.[145] Sixth, Medicare MCOs can be penalized for up to $25,000 per determination for contracting with persons or entities excluded from participation in Medicare or with entities that deliver services through excluded individuals or entities.[146] For each of these offenses, Medicare may also suspend enrollment of and payment for new subscribers until the violation is corrected.[147]

The Balanced Budget Act of 1997 adopts a number of additional prohibitions specifically pertaining to Medicaid managed care entities. These provisions prohibit managed care entities from contracting with or having as directors, officers, partners, or more than 5% owners persons debarred by federal agencies;[148] require managed care entities to use only marketing materials that are not false or materially misleading and are approved by the State and that are distributed throughout the entire service area and prohibit linking enrollment in Medicaid managed care to the purchase of other insurance and "cold-call" door-to-door or other telephonic marketing;[149] and require states to have conflict of interest policies with respect to managed care contracting and default enrollment processes.[150]

The Medicare and Medicaid statutes also put limits on physician incentive plans. For MCOs to save medical costs they must persuade physicians to practice conservative medicine and avoid unnecessary care. This is commonly done by putting the physician at risk for the cost of his or her patient's care, or offering the physician financial incentives to limit care. The federal law attempts to strike a compromise, permitting risk sharing or incentive programs, but only if specific payments are not made to physicians or physician groups to reduce or limit medically necessary care with respect to specific individuals; the plan provides stop-loss protection for physicians and physician groups; and the plan surveys enrollees and former enrollees to determine the degree of enrollee access to care and satisfaction.[151] HHS published final rules in 1996 to implement this requirement. These rules specify that physicians are at substantial financial risk if they are at risk for 25% of the

145. 42 U.S.C.A. § 1395mm(i)(6)(B)(i); 42 C.F.R. §§ 417.500(a)(6), 1003.103(f)(1)(v).

146. 42 U.S.C.A. § 1395mm(i)(6)(B)(i); 42 C.F.R. §§ 417.500(a)(8), 1003.103(e)(2).

147. 42 U.S.C.A. § 1395mm(i)(6)(B)(ii), (iii); 42 C.F.R. § 417.500(d).

148. Pub. L. No. 105–32, § 4707(a), to be codified at 42 U.S.C.A. 1396v.

149. Id.

150. Id.

151. 42 U.S.C.A. §§ 1395mm(i)(8). MCOs that violate this provision are subject to civil fines of up to $25,000 per violation. 42 U.S.C.A. § 1395mm(i)(6)(B)(1). The 1997 Balanced Budget Act extends these protections to the new Medicare + Choice managed care plans created by that Act. Pub.L.No. 105–32, § 4001.

maximum potential payments they could receive if referrals were low enough, and require plans in which physicians are at substantial risk to meet certain requirements, including the provision of stop-loss protection for 90% of the costs that exceed the 25% aggregate level or a specified per patient level.[152]

j. Other

The Medicare and Medicaid programs include or touch upon a host of other individuals and entities that from time to time become involved in fraudulent practices. Ambulance and medical transportation companies seem to be particularly problem prone. The primary problems in this area are claims for ambulance transportation that is not medically necessary,[153] overcharging for services rendered,[154] and billing for services not in fact provided.[155] As the manner in which health care is provided continues to evolve, fraud litigation is beginning to move beyond traditional settings to emerging providers, such as ambulatory surgical centers[156] or hospices.[157]

Contractors that help administer Medicare and Medicaid often handle large contracts and sums of money, and, not surprisingly, occasionally find themselves charged with fraud. Fraud cases have involved Part A intermediaries,[158] Part B carriers,[159] and Peer Review organizations.[160] Because these contractors are large organizations with substantial financial resources, they are particularly attractive defendants for qui tam relators.

Finally, there are a host of organizations that do not provide Medicare services directly, but carry on activities related to the Medicare or Medicaid programs. Coding services or billing consultants, which assist Medicare and Medicaid providers and practitioners in maximizing reimbursement, get both themselves and their clients in trouble when they attempt to file improper claims.[161] In

152. HCFA & OIG, Medicare and Medicaid Programs: Requirements for Physician Incentive Plans in Prepaid Health Care Organizations, 61 Fed. Reg. 13,430, 69,034 (1996) (to be codified at 42 C.F.R. §§ 417, 434, 1003).

153. See United States v. Mischler, 787 F.2d 240, 242 (7th Cir.1986).

154. United States v. Lennartz, 948 F.2d 363, 365–66 (7th Cir.1991).

155. People v. Nicholos, 108 A.D.2d 1015, 485 N.Y.S.2d 585, 586 (1985).

156. See Ninth Circuit Upholds Montana Ophthalmologist's Fraud Conviction, 5 BNA Health L. Rptr. 152 (1995) (ambulatory surgical center is co-defendant).

157. Florida Hospice Received Medicare Overpayments of $6.5 Million, IG Says, BNA Health Care Daily, Nov. 18, 1996.

158. United States ex rel. Flynn v. Blue Cross/Blue Shield of Mich., No. C93–1794, 1995 WL 71329 at *2 (D.Md. 1995).

159. United States ex rel. Burr v. Blue Cross & Blue Shield of Fla., 153 F.R.D. 172 (D.Fla.1994); California Blue Shield Agrees to Pay $12 Million for False Medicare Claims, BNA Health Care Daily, May 5, 1997.

160. United States ex rel. McCoy v. California Medical Rev., Inc., 723 F.Supp. 1363 (D.Cal.1989).

161. United States v. DeSalvo, 41 F.3d 505, 506–07 (9th Cir.1994); United States v. Metzinger, No. Civ. A. 94–7520, 1995 WL 398714 at *1 (E.D.Pa.

rare cases, bookkeepers employed by Medicare or Medicaid providers or practitioners have been prosecuted along with their employers.[162] Bookkeepers have also been known to defraud their employers as well as payers. Insurance companies that have allegedly violated statutory requirements that they serve as primary payers for insureds who are insured both by the insurer and by Medicare or Medicaid, have been sued under the false claims statutes.[163] A case has even been brought against a laundry which paid kickbacks to nursing homes.[164] Finally, recipients are occasionally charged with Medicare or Medicaid fraud, though recipient fraud is beyond the scope of this book.[165]

§ 1–7. Fraud Against Other Health Care Payers

This book is concerned with Medicare and Medicaid fraud and abuse. Fraud and abuse is not limited to the Medicare and Medicaid programs, but also affects other government programs such as the Veteran's administration programs, CHAMPUS, or the federal civil service health care system. More broadly, fraud and abuse affects private health care insurers and MCOs. Because more money is spent by the private sector for health care than is spent by Medicare and Medicaid, it is quite possible that fraud in these sectors costs our society more in the end than does fraud against the Medicare and Medicaid programs.

Fraud against private health payers is usually prosecuted under state criminal laws prohibiting theft or fraud.[1] It has also historically been prosecuted under federal mail or wire fraud statutes.[2] Under the recently adopted Health Insurance Portability and Accountability Act, fraud against private health care plans is now specifically a federal crime.[3] The types of fraud most commonly perpetrated against private health payers are much like those perpetrated against Medicare and Medicaid: billing for services not rendered or for unnecessary services, drug scams and misrepresenting services rendered.[4]

1995); Office of Inspector General, Fraud Alert—Billing Consultant Practices, OIG 97–01 [1997–1 Transfer Binder] Medicare & Medicaid Guide (CCH) ¶ 45,208 (Dec. 1996).

162. Sheriff, Clark County v. Spagnola, 706 P.2d 840, 844, 101 Nev. 508, 514 (1985) (evidence insufficient to establish probable cause against bookkeeper in fraud indictment).

163. United States ex rel. Stinson, Lyons, Gerlin & Bustamante, P.A. v. Provident Life & Accident Ins. Co., 721 F.Supp. 1247 (S.D.Fla.1989).

164. N.J. Nursing Homes, Laundry Firm, Charged with Filing False Claims, 5 BNA Health L. Rptr. 862 (1996).

165. See United States v. Carter, No. 96 CR 512, 1996 WL 627722 (N.D.Ill. 1996).

§ 1–7

1. See infra, § 2–6.

2. See infra, § 2–2.

3. 18 U.S.C.A. § 1347.

4. See Pamela Bucy, Fraud by Fright: White Collar Crime by Health Care Providers?, 67 N.C. L. Rev. 855, 883 (1989).

A few types of fraud are more likely to affect private than public payers, most notably auto accident fraud. Auto accident schemes usually involve a combination of doctors, attorneys, and "victims" who stage automobile accidents to take advantage of liability or uninsured motorist insurers.[5]

On the other hand, some conduct that is illegal if perpetrated against the federal or state government is not necessarily illegal if carried out against private payers. Bribes and kickbacks and self-referrals are only prohibited under federal law with respect to Medicare and state health care programs, and thus are not fraudulent with respect to private insurers unless they are independently prohibited under a state's law. Thus some remuneration-for-referral arrangements explicitly "carve out" Medicare or Medicaid transactions and apply only to transactions financed by private insurance. However, most of the conduct discussed in this book is illegal whether it is perpetrated against public or private payers.

5. Id. at 899–905.

Chapter 2

FALSE CLAIMS

Table of Sections

WESTLAW Electronic Research

See WESTLAW Electronic Research Guide preceding the Summary of Contents.

---

§ 2–1. Introduction

Though, as noted in the previous chapter, the rubric "Medicare and Medicaid fraud" covers a wide variety of conduct, the clear majority of criminal prosecutions, civil recoveries, and administrative penalty and sanction cases brought against Medicare and Medicaid providers (including suppliers and professionals) involve false claims.[1] False claims encompass a broad range of conduct, explored more fully below. While false claims include claims for services simply not rendered, essentially theft by deception, they also include an assortment of other attempts to manipulate the Medicare and Medicaid payment systems to receive reimbursement

---

§ 2–1

1. Year after year the semi-annual reports of the Office of Inspector General identify false claims as the most common kind of criminal fraud, as well as the most common ground for recovery under the civil monetary penalty act.

Insofar as false claims result in criminal convictions, they also generally lead to exclusion from program participation. See, e.g., OIG, Semi–Annual Report, Oct. 1, 1995–Mar. 31, 1996, reprinted in [1996–2 Transfer Binder] Medicare & Medicaid Guide (CCH) ¶ 44,468.

to which a provider is not entitled, including cost report fraud, upcoding, unbundling, or billing for unnecessary services.

The primary purpose of the law of false claims is to protect the government from paying for goods or services that have not been provided or that were not provided in accordance with government requirements. But false claims law also polices the boundaries of the Medicare and Medicaid payment systems, assuring that providers code, claim, and report costs in accordance with program regulations and directives. The various payment systems used by Medicare and Medicaid establish various incentives. False claims law polices providers whose responses to these incentives are so aggressive as to imperil other program goals. The false claims prohibitions, moreover, protect the health of patients to the extent that false claims prosecutions deter providers from overprovision of unnecessary or underprovision of necessary medical care. False claims are often, finally, accompanied by other criminal conduct, such as income tax evasion, money laundering, or diversion of controlled substances to unlawful purposes, which are often prosecuted in tandem with the false claims. False claims prosecutions and actions, therefore, serve a variety of ends.

The federal and state governments have available a host of tools for dealing with false claims. First, federal law makes it a felony knowingly and willfully to make or cause to be made a false claim or statement under any health benefit program which receives federal funding (other than the Federal Employees Health Benefit Program) or a state health program, including Medicaid.[2] Recently adopted legislation also makes it a federal crime to knowingly and willfully execute, or attempt to execute, a scheme or artifice to defraud any health care benefit program; to steal or embezzle money from a health care program, make a materially false statement to or conceal material information from a health benefit program, obstruct the criminal investigation of health care offenses, or launder money in connection with federal health care offenses.[3] Knowingly making or presenting false or fraudulent claims to the United States government is also a crime,[4] as is the making of false or fraudulent statements or representations.[5] Use of the mails for the purposes of obtaining money or property by fraud constitutes the federal crime of mail fraud,[6] and use of electronic communications to defraud is wire fraud.[7] Submission of

---

2. 42 U.S.C.A. § 1320a–7b(a). Until 1996, Medicare was the only federal program covered by the statute. See, surveying criminal laws dealing with health care provider crimes, Pamela Bucy, Crimes by Health Care Providers, 1996 U.Ill.L.Rev. 589 (1996).

3. 18 U.S.C.A. §§ 1347, 669, 1035, 1518, 1956(c)(7)(F).

4. 18 U.S.C.A. § 287.

5. 18 U.S.C.A. § 1001.

6. 18 U.S.C.A. § 1341.

7. 18 U.S.C.A. § 1343.

false claims on two or more occasions in association with an "enterprise" engaged in interstate commerce may constitute a violation of RICO, the Racketeer Influenced and Corrupt Organizations statute.[8] Assisting another in creating or presenting a false claim is aiding and abetting,[9] while conspiracy to submit a false claim is also a separate offense.[10]

False claims are not only subject to criminal prosecutions, however, but also to civil and administrative actions. The Federal False Claims Act permits the federal government to recover from a person who "knowingly" submits false claims a civil penalty of $5000 to $10,000 per claim, plus three times the amount of damages sustained by the federal government.[11] Private individuals can also bring qui tam actions to enforce the False Claims Act.[12] Qui tam actions have become a major concern of health care providers in recent years, as disgruntled employees or disaffected and knowledgeable corporate insiders can potentially make a fortune from a successful qui tam action brought against a large provider.

Administrative sanctions are also a real threat to providers who submit false claims. The Office of Inspector General of HHS can proceed administratively under the Medicare and Medicaid Statutes to impose civil penalties of up to $10,000 per false claim plus three times the amount claimed.[13] Alternatively, the Attorney General can proceed under the general federal Administrative Remedies for False Claims and Statements statute to claim $5000 per claim plus twice the amount claimed through administrative procedures.[14] The Medicare and Medicaid statutes are also thick with specific civil penalty and exclusion provisions for specific kinds of conduct.

False claims submitted to state health programs in most instances also violate state criminal statutes that specifically prohibit Medicaid fraud, more generally prohibit presentation of false claims or statements, or most broadly prohibit larceny or theft.[15] Many states also have civil or administrative remedies for health care fraud. States are required under federal law to have state Medicaid Fraud Control Units, and these units commonly focus on pursuit of Medicaid false claims.

8. 18 U.S.C.A. § 1961. See United States v. Hale, No. 95–5915, 1997 WL 34697 (6th Cir. Jan. 28, 1997), cert. denied, 118 S.Ct. 161 (1997); RICO Charges Place Health Fraud in Realm of Organized Crime, BNA's Health Care Fraud Report, Feb. 26, 1997 at 128 (reporting successful use of RICO against five persons who defrauded Medicare of $25 million marketing DME to nursing homes).

9. 18 U.S.C.A. § 2.

10. 18 U.S.C.A. § 286.

11. 31 U.S.C.A. § 3729(a).

12. 31 U.S.C.A. § 3730(b).

13. 42 U.S.C.A. § 1320a–7a.

14. 31 U.S.C.A. §§ 3801–12.

15. See infra, § 2–6.

False claims frequently result in more than one type of sanction, or in both federal and state action. Although the Double Jeopardy Clause ultimately limits the possibility of piling on sanctions,[16] it does not limit the ability of the government to exclude providers convicted of criminal fraud charges from government programs, and only limits the government's ability to pursue civil or administrative money penalties if those penalties are "excessive." The Double Jeopardy Clause also does not preclude both state and federal prosecution. Double jeopardy issues are explored more thoroughly in chapter 8.

False claims actions can involve virtually any kind of health care provider. Reported false claims court decisions most commonly involve physicians, but cases involving laboratories, suppliers of durable medical equipment, pharmacists, and nursing homes are also common. False claims actions are not only brought against providers, moreover, but also against recipients, coding consultants, insurers, carriers, intermediaries, and Peer Review Organizations.

The conduct that is most frequently sanctioned by reported false claims actions is billing for goods or services not provided. A common example would be a physician billing for a particular procedure allegedly rendered to a particular patient that was not in fact provided. Almost as many cases, however, involve goods or services that were in fact provided, but without meeting key program requirements. Examples would be services provided without a physician referral where such a referral is necessary under program requirements, or services rendered by a provider who was excluded from program participation. Even claims for payment for services that do not meet quality standards have been treated as false claims.[17] Other common problems resulting in sanctions include billing for unnecessary services; upcoding (billing for a more expensive service than that actually provided); unbundling (submitting multiple bills for a service that should be billed as a single service); billing Medicaid for name-brand drugs when generics were supplied; double billing; and filing of inflated cost reports or cost reports that include non-allowable costs.

False claims actions sometimes involve conduct that is obviously culpable, where intent to defraud the government seems quite obvious. Examples include providers who bill for a service that was

---

16. See United States v. Halper, 490 U.S. 435, 109 S.Ct. 1892, 104 L.Ed.2d 487 (1989) discussed in chapter 8.

17. See Scienter Is Key in Defending Accusations of FCA Violations, BNA Health Care Fraud Report, May 21, 1997 at 315; Patric Hooper, Defending Against Accusations of Health Care False Claims du Jour, in American Bar Association CLE, Health Care Fraud, C–1, C–4 (1997). See also Michael Mustokoff, Jody Werner & Michael Yecies, The Government's Use of the Civil False Claims Act to Enforce Standards of Quality of Care: Ingenuity or the Heavy Hand of the 800–Pound Gorilla, 6 Ann. Health L. 147 (1997); David Hoffman, The Role of the Federal Government in

simply and clearly not provided (an abortion to a woman who was not pregnant) or for a cost indisputably not covered by the program (the cost of remodeling a nursing home owner's summer home). Often cases involve closer questions, however: was a patient contact properly coded as a "consultation"? Was a patient properly referred by a physician for services received from a chiropractor or psychologist?

In most false claims cases, providers defend their conduct claiming that they did not understand complex program rules or directives, or, alternatively, that their staff may have billed improperly but that they were wholly innocent. One study of interviews of physicians convicted of Medicaid fraud concluded:

> Perhaps most marked in the interviews was the almost ubiquitous unwillingness of members of the sample to indicate greed as the root cause of their difficulties. None of the physicians took full personal blame for his or her violation, in the sense of describing it as a deliberate self-serving act in violation of a legitimate law or rule. . . .
>
> The physicians typically saw themselves as sacrificial lambs hung out to dry because of incompetent or backstabbing employees, stupid laws, bureaucratic nonsense, and a host of similar reasons. . . .[18]

Medicaid providers in particular often seem to believe that "creative" billing is an appropriate response to inadequate Medicaid payment rates, that they are somehow equitably entitled to the amount they claim, whether or not their claims comply with program rules.[19] They express anger and frustration at what they view as intolerable and irrational program complexity, and tend to view Medicaid fraud as victimless crime.[20] Medicare, as well as Medicaid cases, however, also at times involve aggressive and imaginative approaches to coding, intended perhaps to go only to the margins of what is permissible, but straying beyond into the realm of fraud.

Although providers often characterize fraud cases as ordinary billing disputes that have resulted in brutal prosecutorial overreactions, only a tiny proportion of cases that involve questionable billing end up being investigated, and even fewer end up in prosecution. Physicians, supply companies, or diagnostic laboratories have only a 3 in 1000 chance of having their billing practices audited by

Ensuring Quality of Care in Long–Term Care Facilities, 6 Ann.Health L. 147 (1997).

18. Paul Jesilow et al., Fraud by Physicians Against Medicaid, 266 JAMA 3318, 3320 (1991).

19. Id.; United States v. Nazon, 940 F.2d 255, 257–58 (7th Cir.1991).

20. Jesilow, supra note 18, at 3320–21.

Medicare in a given year.[21] Most cases in which problems are identified are settled with the provider agreeing to make restitution.[22] Often penalties are not pursued because the provider declares bankruptcy or otherwise hides its assets after the fraud is detected, making the pursuit of a recovery futile.[23] In sum, though federal and state prosecutors and agencies possess a considerable armamentarium for dealing with false claims, most questionable claims seem to go unpunished.

This chapter examines first the various criminal statutes that are used to prosecute false claims. It then explores the Federal False Claims Act and qui tam actions brought under that act. It then considers federal administrative remedies for false claims. Finally it turns to state law responses to false claims.

§ 2–2. Criminal False Claims Prosecutions

Federal criminal prosecutions for false claims have in the past been most commonly brought under 18 U.S.C.A. § 287, which prohibits "false, fictitious, or fraudulent claims;" 18 U.S.C.A. § 1001, which proscribes "false, fictitious or fraudulent statements or representations;" and 18 U.S.C.A. § 1341, which forbids mail fraud. Federal prosecutors tend to proceed under these general statutes rather than under § 1128A of the Social Security Act (42 U.S.C.A. § 1320a–7b(a)). These statutes are more familiar to both the prosecutors and the courts than the more specific Federal Health Care Program Fraud criminal statutes. Jury instructions and caselaw are readily available under them. Prosecutors proceeding under these statutes are less likely, therefore, to end up in uncharted legal territory. An additional advantage to proceeding under § 287, § 1001, or § 1341 has until recently been that a prosecutor bringing a prosecution under these sections may also move under 18 U.S.C.A. § 1345 for an injunction freezing the bank accounts of a person or entity alleged to have violated these statutes.[1] When (as is often the case) the alleged fraud is being perpetrated by a fly-by-night operation, the ability to immediately freeze the entity's assets is a substantial strategic benefit. Under newly adopted legislation creating federal health care offenses,

---

21. GAO, Medicare, Reducing Fraud and Abuse Can Save Millions, 7 (GAO/T–HEHS–95–157, May 16, 1995).

22. GAO, Medicare, Modern Management Strategies Needed to Curb Program Exploitation, 7–8 (GAO/T–HEHS–95–183, June 15, 1995).

23. GAO, Medicare, Adapting Private Sector Techniques Could Curb Losses to Fraud and Abuse, 9–10 (GAO/T–HEHS–95–211, July 19, 1995).

§ 2–2

1. United States v. Brown, 988 F.2d 658, 660–63 (6th Cir.1993). Only assets related to the alleged fraud may be frozen. Id. at 664. See James Sheehan, The False Claims Act, in American Bar Association, Health Care Fraud, 1996, K–47, K–52—K–53 (describing the use of the mail fraud injunction in health care fraud cases.)

however, the injunctive power is now available for any health care offense litigation.[2] There is no problem with the government proceeding under these statutes in Medicare and Medicaid cases rather than under the more specific Federal Health Care Program Fraud statute.[3]

This chapter will examine the substantive provisions of these criminal statutes. Subsequent chapters will consider procedural issues involved in criminal investigations and prosecutions (chapter 7), as well as criminal sentencing (chapter 8).

a. Federal Health Care Offenses

Library References:

West's Key No. Digests, Social Security and Public Welfare ⚷18.

The Health Care Portability and Accountability Act of 1996 dramatically expands federal criminal jurisdiction over health fraud, creating a series of new federal health care offenses. These offenses carry substantial penalties and are accompanied by important enforcement tools including freezing of assets, investigative demand procedures, and forfeitures for health care offenses. They may replace the more traditional statutes discussed below as the tool of choice for federal criminal prosecutors. All of the statutes apply to "health care benefit programs," defined in the statute as "any public or private plan or contract, affecting commerce, under which any medical benefit, item, or service is provided to any individual," including "any individual or entity who is providing a medical benefit, item, or service for which payment may be made under the plan or contract."[4] This definition creates federal criminal jurisdiction over virtually any fraud committed against a health insurer or health benefit plan. It also seems, albeit awkwardly, to criminalize fraud against subcontractors. An IPA which provided care to the beneficiaries of an HMO under contract would meet the definition of a "health care benefit program" under this statute, and a specialist subcontractor who fraudulently submitted a bill to the IPA would violate the statute.

The first offense created by the new statute is the crime of health care fraud.[5] The statute provides that a person who

"knowingly and willfully executes, or attempts to execute, a scheme or artifice–

(1) to defraud any health care benefit program; or

---

2. 18 U.S.C.A. § 1345(a)(1)(C).

3. United States v. Adler, 623 F.2d 1287, 1290 (8th Cir.1980); United States v. Gordon, 548 F.2d 743, 744–45 (8th Cir.1977); United States v. Radetsky, 535 F.2d 556, 567 (10th Cir.1976).

4. 18 U.S.C.A. § 24(b).

5. 18 U.S.C.A. § 1347.

(2) to obtain, by means of false or fraudulent pretenses, representations, or promises, any of the money or property owned by, or under the custody or control of, any health care benefit program,

in connection with the delivery of or payment for health care benefits, items or services,"

penalty may be fined or imprisoned for up to 10 years, or both.[6] If the fraud results in serious bodily injury, the perpetrator can be imprisoned for up to 20 years, and if it results in death, a term of life imprisonment can be imposed.[7]

The conference report accompanying this provision states that this provision is not intended to be interpreted to prohibit claims for complementary, alternative, innovative, experimental or investigational medical or health care, or coverage of such claims. The Act should not be interpreted to penalize those who make a controversial diagnosis or offer a controversial treatment if it is done in the good faith exercise of professional judgment.[8]

Second, the statute provides that a person who:

"knowingly and wilfully embezzles, steals, or otherwise without authority converts to the use of any person other than the rightful owner, or intentionally misapplies any of the moneys, funds, securities, premiums, credits, or other assets of a health care benefit program,"

penalty may be fined or imprisoned for up to 10 years, (but only for up to one year if the embezzlement or theft did not involve more than $100), or both fined and imprisoned.[9]

Third, the statute provides that a person who:

"in any matter involving a health care benefit program, knowingly and willfully–

(1) falsifies, conceals, or covers up by any trick, scheme, or device a material fact; or

(2) makes any materially false, fictitious, or fraudulent statements or representations, or makes or uses any materially false writing or document knowing the same to contain any materially false, fictitious, or fraudulent statement or entry,

in connection with the delivery of or payment for health care benefits, items, or services,

6. Id.

7. Id. An example of a case in which fraud and abuse results in death might be a case where an unnecessary surgery was done to obtain payment, and the surgery resulted in death.

8. 142 Cong. Rec. H9473, H9538.

9. 18 U.S.C.A. § 669.

may be imprisoned for up to 5 years, or fined, or both.[10] Note that this provision clearly includes a requirement that the false statement must be material, unlike the more general federal false statements prohibition, which is equivocal on this matter.

Fourth, the statute provides that a person who:

"willfully prevents, obstructs, misleads, delays or attempts to prevent, obstruct, mislead, or delay the communication of information or records relating to a violation of a Federal health care offense to a criminal investigator,"

(defined as a person authorized by an agency of the U.S. to investigate or prosecute health care offenses), may be fined or imprisoned for up to five years, or both.[11]

Finally, the statute extends the coverage of the federal money laundering statute to federal health care offenses.[12] The statute also provides for asset freezing injunctions, investigative demands, and forfeitures in cases involving health care offenses.[13] These provisions are discussed further in chapter 7. For purposes of these additional remedies, and for the obstruction of investigation and money laundering provisions, federal health care offense is defined not just to mean offenses under the new provisions created by the statute, but also offenses under other statutes, such as the federal false claims, false statements, or mail or wire fraud statutes, if the offenses affect health care benefit programs.[14]

b. 18 U.S.C.A. § 287, False Claims

Library References:

C.J.S. United States § 173.
West's Key No. Digests, United States ☞123.

18 U.S.C.A. § 287 states:

Whoever makes or presents to any person or officer in the civil, military, or naval service of the United States, or to any department or agency thereof, any claim upon or against the United States, or any department or agency thereof, knowing such claim to be false, fictitious, or fraudulent, shall be imprisoned not more than five years and shall be subject of a fine in the amount provided in this title.

---

10. 18 U.S.C.A. § 1035.

11. 18 U.S.C.A. § 1518.

12. 18 U.S.C.A. § 1956(c)(7)(F).

13. 18 U.S.C.A. §§ 981, 982(a)(6), 1345(a)(1), 1963, 3486. See Robert W. Biddle et al., Asset Forfeitures and Freezes in Health Care Fraud Litigation, in American Bar Association, Health Care Fraud 1997, P–1; Sanford Teplitzky & S. Craig Holden, 1996 Develop-

ments in Health Care Fraud and Abuse, in Health Law Handbook 3, 44–48 (Alice Gosfield ed., 1997). See, as examples of health care fraud cases in which assets were frozen under 18 U.S.C.A. § 1345, United States v. G–4 Medical Ctrs., No. 95–7171 (S.D. Fla. 1995); United States v. Fang, 937 F.Supp. 1186 (D.Md.1996).

14. 18 U.S.C.A. § 24(a).

18 U.S.C.A. § 286 further proscribes agreements, combinations and conspiracies to present such claims.[15]

To violate § 287, a defendant must 1) present a claim to the United States; 2) the claim must be "false, fictitious, or fraudulent" and 3) the defendant must know that the claim was false, fictitious or fraudulent.[16] The term claim is not defined in § 287, but is defined in the companion civil false claims act, discussed below.[17] Although disputes arise in other contexts as to whether a "claim" has actually been submitted to the government (e.g. in cases involving loan applications or bids[18]), this is generally not an issue in Medicare and Medicaid cases.

A more serious problem is whether a claim has been "presented" to the government. Medicare Part A is administered by intermediaries and Part B by carriers. These entities are insurers, Blue Cross and Blue Shield plans, or data processors. Medicaid is administered by the states, which sometimes contract with subcontractors to administer parts of their programs. Defendants, charged with false claims, therefore, occasionally claim that they have not presented their claim to the United States, but rather to a carrier, intermediary, or state Medicaid agency. The courts routinely reject this defense, either recognizing that these entities are effectively acting as agents of the United States in receiving claims, or that presentment of a false claim to these entities "causes" them to consequently present a false claim to the United States.[19] For the same reasons, an indictment that alleges that the defendant presented a claim to Blue Cross is sufficient to state a claim under § 287 where Blue Cross is acting an agent for the United States.[20] A defendant can also not defeat prosecution under the act by claiming that an employee or agent presented the claim rather than the defendant, if the agent's actions were authorized by the defendant.[21]

Whether or not a claim is false, fictitious or fraudulent is a question of fact. Often, as noted earlier, the truth or falsity of a claim depends on whether it complies with program requirements. Submission of a claim for unnecessary and inappropriate care, for

---

15. 18 U.S.C.A. § 371, which more generally prohibits conspiracies to commit an offense against the United States, can also be charged in criminal false claims cases.

16. See Tedd J. Kochman & Garen Meguerian, False Claims, 31 Am. Crim. L. Rev. 525, 528 (1994).

17. See 31 U.S.C.A. § 3729(c).

18. See Kochman & Meguerian, supra note 16, at 528–29.

19. United States v. Precision Medical Labs., Inc., 593 F.2d 434, 442 (2d Cir.1978) (claims submitted to Blue Cross and state Department of Social Services); United States v. Catena, 500 F.2d 1319, 1322–23 (3d Cir.1974), cert. denied, 419 U.S. 1047, 95 S.Ct. 621, 42 L.Ed.2d 641 (1974) (claims submitted to Blue Shield and Travelers Insurance Co.).

20. United States v. Hooshmand, 931 F.2d 725, 735 (11th Cir.1991).

21. United States v. Precision Medical Labs., Inc., 593 F.2d at 441.

example, is a false claim when the physician certifies on the claim form that the care was "medically indicated and necessary for the health of the patient."[22]

Section 287 does not on its face require that the false claim be material, though most circuits consider materiality to be an element of the charge.[23] To the extent materiality is required, it is probably an issue that must be submitted to the jury in a jury trial.[24] Thus United States v. White held that even if Medicare does not require a blank on a form to be filled in, the claim is false if the blank is filled in falsely and the statement "has a natural tendency to influence, or was capable of influencing" the decision of Medicare to pay the claim.[25]

To violate § 287, the claim must not only be false, but the defendant must submit the claim "knowing" it to be false. Knowledge of the falsity of a claim can be inferred from the facts and circumstances surrounding the claim.[26] Some courts have held that the scienter requirement of § 287 is simply "knowledge" of the falsity of the claim.[27] Other courts consider "fraudulent intent" or "intent to deceive" to be elements of the charge.[28] "Conscious avoidance" of knowledge of the truth or reckless disregard for the truth can form the basis of a finding of "knowledge" of falsity, though mere negligence is not sufficient.[29] Where the government has through ambiguous program instructions rendered reimbursement policy unclear, however, it cannot establish intent to submit a false claim.[30] The government is also not permitted to shift the theory of its case as the trial proceeds in an attempt to find a billing violation that fits the conduct that is proved.[31]

Section 287 mandates imprisonment and a fine for all convictions. The maximum fine is $250,000 per claim.[32]

---

22. United States v. Campbell, 845 F.2d 1374, 1381–82 (6th Cir.1988), cert. denied 488 U.S. 908, 109 S.Ct. 259, 102 L.Ed.2d 248 (1988).

23. See discussion in United States v. White, 27 F.3d 1531, 1534–35 (11th Cir.1994).

24. See United States v. Gaudin, 515 U.S. 506, 115 S.Ct. 2310, 132 L.Ed.2d 444 (1995).

25. United States v. White, 27 F.3d at 1535.

26. United States v. Adler, 623 F.2d 1287, 1289 (8th Cir.1980).

27. United States v. Precision Medical Labs., Inc., 593 F.2d 434, 443 (2d Cir.1978). See Kochman & Meguerian, supra note 16, at 531–33; United States v. Nazon, 940 F.2d 255, 260–61 (7th

Cir.1991) (omission of "intent to defraud" charge not plain error).

28. See United States v. Campbell, 845 F.2d 1374, 1382 (6th Cir.1988), cert. denied 488 U.S. 908, 109 S.Ct. 259, 102 L.Ed.2d 248 (1988); Kochman & Meguerian, supra note 16, at 530–31.

29. United States v. Nazon, 940 F.2d at 258–60; United States v. Precision Medical Labs., Inc., 593 F.2d at 442–446.

30. United States v. Levin, 973 F.2d 463, 469 (6th Cir.1992).

31. Siddiqi v. United States, 98 F.3d 1427 (2d Cir.1996).

32. 18 U.S.C.A. §§ 3559, 3571. False claims submitted to the defense department may result in fines up to $1,000,-000 per claim. Department of Defense Authorization Act of 1986, Pub. L. No.

c.   18 U.S.C.A. § 1001, False Statements

Library References:

C.J.S. Fraud § 154.
West's Key No. Digests, Fraud ☞68.10.

Prosecutions brought under § 287 are also often brought under § 1001, which prohibits false statements. Section 1001(a) provides:

> [W]hoever, in any matter within the jurisdiction of the executive, legislative, or judicial branch of the Government of the United States, knowingly and willfully (1) falsifies, conceals, or covers up by any trick, scheme, or device a material fact; (2) makes any materially false, fictitious, or fraudulent statement or representation; or (3) makes or uses any false writing or document knowing the same to contain any materially false, fictitious, or fraudulent statement or entry; shall be fined under this title or imprisoned not more than five years, or both.

The elements that must be proven to establish a charge of false statements include 1) the defendant made a statement; 2) regarding a matter within the jurisdiction of a United States department or agency; 3) the statement was made "knowingly and willfully"; and 4) the statement was false.[33] Most circuits also impose an additional requirement that the statement be material.[34]

In other contexts § 1001 raises perplexing issues of interpretation and application, as when it is used to punish negative exculpatory responses to government agents pursuing investigations.[35] In the context of Medicare and Medicaid fraud and abuse, however, the statute is normally applied to claims or reports submitted by defendants to the Medicare or Medicaid programs, and its application is quite straightforward. Violation of § 1001 is usually charged in tandem with charges of violation of § 287, though § 1001 arguably covers conduct not covered by § 287, such as submission of a false cost report that is not in itself a claim for payment.[36]

Under § 1001, as under § 287, a statement made to a carrier, fiscal intermediary, or state Medicaid agency is considered a statement made "within the jurisdiction of a department or agency of the United States."[37] Whether or not a statement is within the jurisdiction of a department or agency is a question of fact rather than law.[38] A false entry in a medical record made to support a false Medicare claim (asserting that a procedure was medically neces-

99–145, tit. IX, § 931, 1985 U.S.C.C.A.N. (99 Stat.) 699.

33. Jennifer L. Kraft & David A. Sadoff, False Statements, 31 Am. Crim. L. Rev. 539, 541 (1994).

34. Id.; United States v. Abadi, 706 F.2d 178, 180 (6th Cir.1983).

35. Kraft & Sadoff, supra note 33, at 544–45.

36. See United States v. Smith, 523 F.2d 771, 777–78 (5th Cir.1975).

37. United States v. Goldstein, 695 F.2d 1228, 1236 (10th Cir.1981).

38. Id.

sary, for example, when it in fact was not), can form the basis of § 1001 conviction, even though the falsified record was not in fact submitted to the government, since the entry was made to conceal material facts from the government.[39]

The scienter requirement of § 1001 is "knowingly and willfully." "Knowingly" requires that the defendant acted with knowledge; "willfully" implies that the defendant acted "deliberately and with knowledge."[40] Reckless disregard for the truth of a statement or conscious avoidance of learning its untruthfulness constitutes "knowledge" of its falsity, for purposes of § 1001.[41] Knowledge and willfulness may, of course, be inferred from the circumstances, as where a doctor billed for office visits on days when he had not seen patients.[42] A defendant may be convicted for willfully authorizing another to make a claim on his behalf, if he has knowledge of its falsity.[43] A defendant may also be convicted for filing cost reports that inaccurately describe costs or conceal important facts regarding costs intending to obtain a greater payment than that to which he was legally entitled.[44]

Up until recently, the most often contested issue in § 1001 prosecutions involving Medicare and Medicaid fraud was whether or not a false statement had to be "material," and, if so, how materiality was to be judged.[45] In United States v. Gaudin, however, the Supreme Court assumed, based on a concession by the government, that materiality was an essential element of the § 1001 offense.[46] This position was questioned by the concurring opinion of Justice Rehnquist, in which Justices O'Connor and Breyer joined,[47] but will be difficult to challenge after *Gaudin*. Though § 1001 on its face does not include a materiality requirement, courts generally had read a materiality requirement into the statute even prior to *Gaudin* to exclude prosecution for trivial falsehoods, and many refer to materiality as an essential element of the statute. Materiality is defined in terms of having "a natural tendency to influence, or [being] capable of influencing, the decision of the decisionmaking body to which it was addressed."[48] The

[margin note: Materiality def.]

---

39. United States v. Rutgard, 116 F.3d 1270 (9th Cir. 1997).

40. United States v. Smith, 523 F.2d at 774. If the indictment only alleges knowing, and not willful conduct, it is not sufficient to state a charge under § 1001. United States v. Mekjian, 505 F.2d 1320, 1323 (5th Cir.1975).

41. United States v. Evans, 559 F.2d 244, 245–46 (5th Cir.1977).

42. United States v. Adler, 623 F.2d 1287, 1289 (8th Cir.1980).

43. United States v. Blazewicz, 459 F.2d 442, 443 (6th Cir.1972).

44. United States v. Calhoon, 97 F.3d 518 (11th Cir.1996).

45. United States v. Abadi, 706 F.2d 178, 180 (6th Cir.1983); United States v. Adler, 623 F.2d at 1291; Kraft & Sodoff, supra note 33, at 541.

46. 515 U.S. 506, 115 S.Ct. 2310, 132 L.Ed.2d 444 (1995).

47. 515 U.S. at 506.

48. Id. (quoting Kungys v. United States, 485 U.S. 759, 770, 108 S.Ct. 1537, 1546, 99 L.Ed.2d 839 (1988)). See also United States v. Adler, 623 F.2d at 1290 (quoting United States v. East, 416

application of this standard is not always clear. Thus one circuit has held that false statements in a claim for a service that is not covered by Medicare do not violate § 1001,[49] whereas another has held that such statements are illegal if they in fact put the claimant in a position to obtain payment, whether payment is otherwise proper or not.[50] The Supreme Court has held that the question of materiality must be decided by the jury in a jury case,[51] though the failure to submit the question to the jury in a case antedating *Gaudin* may be harmless error.[52]

The penalties under § 1001 are fines of up to $250,000 and/or imprisonment for up to five years for individuals.

d. 18 U.S.C.A. § 1341, Mail Fraud

Library References:

C.J.S. Postal Service and Offenses Against Postal Laws § 23.
West's Key No. Digests, Postal Service ⏅35.

The most common statutory basis for Medicare and Medicaid fraud prosecutions is 18 U.S.C.A. § 1341, the federal mail fraud statute. It may seem initially surprising that prosecutions would be brought under the general mail fraud statute when there are more specific federal statutes dealing with false claims and statements made to the federal government, and an even more specific federal statute proscribing false federal health care claims. Section 1341 is one of the statutes most commonly used by federal prosecutors,[53] and the general familiarity of prosecutors with the statute undoubtedly explains much of its appeal in this context. Though the reach of the mail fraud statute is potentially disturbingly broad,[54] the conduct generally prosecuted in Medicare and Medicaid fraud cases is clearly within the scope of that covered by the statute. The federal mail fraud statute can be used not only to prosecute schemes to defraud federal health care programs, but also state programs,[55] or even private insurers.[56]

F.2d 351, 353 (9th Cir.1969)), defining materiality in terms of "whether the falsification is calculated to induce action or reliance by an agency of the United States; is it one that could affect or influence the exercise of government functions, does it have a natural tendency to influence or is it capable of influencing agency decisions."

49. United States v. Radetsky, 535 F.2d 556, 571–74 (10th Cir.1976).

50. United States v. Adler, 623 F.2d at 1291.

51. United States v. Gaudin, 515 U.S. 506, 115 S.Ct. 2310, 132 L.Ed.2d 444 (1995).

52. United States v. McGhee, No. 95–6323, 1997 WL 392714 (6th Cir. 1997); United States v. Calhoon, 97 F.3d 518 (11th Cir.1996).

53. Gregory H. Williams, Good Government by Prosecutorial Decree: The Use and Abuse of Mail Fraud, 32 Ariz. L. Rev. 137, 143 (1990).

54. See id. at 137–38.

55. United States v. Goldstein, 695 F.2d 1228, 1233 (10th Cir.1981).

56. United States v. Duncan, 919 F.2d 981, 990–92 (5th Cir.1990), cert. denied 500 U.S. 926, 111 S.Ct. 2036, 114 L.Ed.2d 121 (1991).

Section 1341 provides, in relevant part:

Whoever, having devised or intending to devise any scheme or artifice to defraud, or for obtaining money or property by means of false or fraudulent pretenses, representations, or promises ..., for the purpose of executing such scheme or artifice or attempting so to do, [uses or causes to be used the federal mails or the services of a private or commercial interstate carrier] shall be fined under this title or imprisoned not more than five years, or both....

The elements of mail fraud are 1) a scheme to defraud, and 2) the use of the mails for executing the scheme.[57] It is not necessary that the scheme succeed, resulting in actual loss to the government, only that success be intended.[58] Further, it is not required that the use of the mails be an essential part of the scheme.[59] It is not even necessary that the false representations themselves be mailed, as long as the mails are used at some stage in the scheme.[60] Moreover, a defendant may be convicted of aiding and abetting mail fraud or of conspiracy to commit mail fraud even if the defendant did not personally prepare or mail a false claim, if the defendant participated in some stage of the scheme.[61]

It is not necessary that a mail fraud prosecution involving Medicare or Medicaid fraud entail conduct that is otherwise violative of a specific Medicare or Medicaid law, as long as the conduct is intended to defraud the program.[62] "Fraudulent representations ... may be effected by deceitful statements of half-truths or the concealment of material facts...." The Medicaid or Medicare program regulations are therefore relevant to a mail fraud charge to the extent that they establish the material facts that the defendant should have known needed to be disclosed in a Medicare or Medicaid claim.[63]

Mail fraud involves intentional conduct.[64] But the intent to defraud, again, is usually inferred from the circumstances.[65] Defen-

---

57. United States v. Lennartz, 948 F.2d 363, 370 (7th Cir.1991); United States v. Campbell, 845 F.2d 1374, 1382 (6th Cir.1988), cert. denied 488 U.S. 908, 109 S.Ct. 259, 102 L.Ed.2d 248 (1988); United States v. Goldstein, 695 F.2d at 1233.

58. United States v. Nichols, Nos. 91–6374, 91–6375, 1992 WL 238264 at *2 (6th Cir.1992).

59. United States v. Lennartz, 948 F.2d at 369.

60. United States v. Campbell, 845 F.2d at 1382.

61. United States v. Turner, Nos. 88–5617, 88–5622, 1990 WL 29182 at

*3–4 (4th Cir.1990), cert. denied 498 U.S. 860, 111 S.Ct. 164, 112 L.Ed.2d 129 (1990).

62. United States v. Goldstein, 695 F.2d 1228, 1233 (10th Cir.1981).

63. Id.

64. United States v. Campbell, 845 F.2d at 1382.

65. United States v. Freshour, Nos. 94–5448, 94–5759, 94–5758, 1995 WL 496662 at *3–4 (6th Cir.1995), cert. denied, ___ U.S. ___, 116 S.Ct. 910, 133 L.Ed.2d 842 (1996), and cert. denied, ___ U.S. ___, 116 S.Ct. 1045, 134 L.Ed.2d 192 (1996) ("the intent to defraud was

dants commonly assert in these cases that they did not intend to defraud the government, but were simply confused or mistaken regarding government policies regarding claims and reimbursement. Though this defense sometimes succeeds when reimbursement policy or communications are particularly obscure or misleading,[66] it fails when the evidence shows that the defendant was intentionally attempting to obtain payment that was not authorized.[67] Conscious avoidance of knowledge or deliberate ignorance here again is treated as the equivalence of knowledge.

The elements of wire fraud are identical to those of mail fraud except that wire fraud involves use of interstate television, radio, or wire communications.[68] As electronic submission of Medicare and Medicaid claims becomes more common, prosecutions will more commonly involve wire fraud rather than mail fraud.

The penalties for mail fraud are, again, up to five years in prison and/or fines of up to $250,000 for individuals.

e. Miscellaneous Crimes

Library References:

West's Key No. Digests, Social Security and Public Welfare ⏀18.

Federal Medicare and Medicaid fraud cases frequently involve schemes in which a number of persons or organizations have taken part. Thus prosecutions often involve secondary charges of aiding and abetting[69] or conspiracy,[70] theft of government property,[71] or charges of a pattern of criminal activity under the Racketeer Influenced and Corrupt Organizations Act (RICO).[72] They also from time to time involve related criminal activity, such as money laundering,[73] forgery or counterfeiting of contracts or documents,[74]

---

evidenced by the shear volume and variety of fraudulent claims submitted, undercutting the Tino defendant's contention that the false claims were the result of mistake or accident").

66. United States v. Levin, 973 F.2d 463, 466–67 (6th Cir.1992).

67. United States v. Lennartz, 948 F.2d 363, 368 (7th Cir.1991); United States v. Weiss, 930 F.2d 185, 192–94 (2d Cir.1991); United States v. Collins, 596 F.2d 166, 168 (6th Cir.1979).

68. 18 U.S.C.A. § 1343.

69. 18 U.S.C.A. § 2.

70. 18 U.S.C.A. § 371. See United States v. Gold, Nos. 83–3230, 83–3231, 83–3267, 1984 WL 48339 (11th Cir. 1984).

71. 18 U.S.C.A. § 641.

72. 18 U.S.C.A. §§ 1961–68; United States v. Huber, 603 F.2d 387, 393–94 (2d Cir.1979).

73. 18 U.S.C.A. §§ 1956, 1957. See Pamela Bucy, Crimes by Health Care Providers, 1996 U. Ill. L. Rev. 589, 620–22 (1996), discussing the application of this statute in healthcare fraud settings. See United States v. Freshour, Nos. 94–5448, 94–5759, 1995 WL 496662 at *5–7 (6th Cir.1995), cert. denied, ___ U.S. ___, 116 S.Ct. 910, 133 L.Ed.2d 842 (1996), and cert. denied, ___ U.S. ___, 116 S.Ct. 1045, 134 L.Ed.2d 192 (1996). The Ninth Circuit has recently held that a doctor who transferred practice revenues to an offshore bank could not be convicted of money laundering under 18 U.S.C.A. § 1957 unless the government could prove that his entire practice was "permeated with fraud," a high stan-

obstruction of justice,[75] or tax evasion. In addition to other sanctions, a defendant convicted of defrauding health care programs can be ordered to pay restitution under the Victim and Witness Protection Act of 1988.[76] For cases arising after 1990 amendments to the Act, restitution may be ordered to persons directly harmed by the defendant's schemes, even though they were not identified in the counts of conviction.[77]

f. Federal Health Care Program Fraud

Library References:

West's Key No. Digests, Social Security and Public Welfare ⊕18.

In addition to the general federal prohibitions against mail fraud and false claims and statements, there is a specific prohibition against false claims in federal and state health care programs, including the Medicare and Medicaid programs. For the purposes of this prohibition, a "claim" is defined as "an application for payments for items and services."[78] It is a felony, punishable by up to five years imprisonment and a fine of up to $25,000, knowingly and willfully to make or cause to be made a false statement or representation of a material fact in a claim for a benefit or payment or for use in determining rights to such benefits or payment under programs that provide health benefits, funded directly in whole or in part by the federal government, or for state health care programs.[79] It is also a felony to conceal or to fail to disclose knowledge of the occurrence of an event affecting an individual's right to a benefit or payment with the intent to secure fraudulently the benefit or payment; to convert a benefit or payment intended for the use of another; or to bill for a physician's service knowing that the individual that provided the service was not a physician.[80] It is a misdemeanor, punishable by a fine of up to $10,000 and up to one year's imprisonment, for a person other than one who furnishes medical items or services (e.g. a secretary or billing clerk) to commit one of these offenses.[81]

The prosecution must prove that the defendant in a federal health care program false claims case knew the claim to be false at

---

dard, or unless fraudulently obtained funds could be traced. United States v. Rutgard, 116 F.3d 1270 (9th Cir. 1997).

74. 18 U.S.C.A. §§ 494–95.

75. 18 U.S.C.A. § 1505.

76. 18 U.S.C.A. §§ 3363–64. United States v. Davis, 117 F.3d 459 (11th Cir. 1997).

77. See United States v. Rutgard, 116 F.3d 1270 (9th Cir. 1997).

78. 42 U.S.C.A. § 1320a–7a(i)(2). See also 42 C.F.R. § 1003.101.

79. 42 U.S.C.A. § 1320a–7b(a). Prior to 1996, the statute applied only to Medicare, Medicaid, or a state health care program funded through a federal block grant under Titles V or XX.

80. Id.

81. Id.

the time it was submitted.[82] It is not sufficient that the defendant knew that a claim was submitted that was in fact false, if there is no proof that the defendant knew of its falsity.[83] It is not necessary, however, for the government to prove additionally that the defendant specifically intended to defraud or deceive the government.[84] The false statement at issue must be "material", i.e. it must have a "natural tendency to influence, or be capable of influencing" a function performed by a government agency, but it need not in fact result in government action.[85] The materiality issue is a question of law to be determined by the court.[86] Intent is usually proved by circumstantial evidence.[87] Once it is shown that the agent of a corporation possessed the requisite intent, however, this intent will be attributed to the corporation.[88]

While physicians, providers, or suppliers most commonly violate these provisions by billing for services that they did not render, the provisions also prohibit upcoding a service to receive a higher reimbursement rate than is appropriate or certifying a service as medically necessary when it in fact was not. In *United States v. Larm*,[89] the Court of Appeals upheld the conviction of an allergist on seventeen counts of Medicaid Fraud for using CPT Code 90040, "brief examination, evaluation and/or treatment same or new illness," rather than CPT Code 90030, "minimal service: injections, minimal dressings, etc. not necessarily requiring the presence of a physician," for nurse administered allergy shots.[90]

In addition to the general prohibition against false claims, the Medicare and Medicaid statutes contain a number of specific prohibitions that carry criminal penalties. The statute provides criminal penalties for knowing and willful violation of a physician or supplier participation agreement or Medicare assignment of benefits agreement.[91] Knowing and willful charging for services to a Medicaid patient at rates in excess of those allowed by the state Medicaid plan or charging, soliciting, or receiving consideration as a precondition of admitting or retaining a Medicaid patient in a hospital, nursing facility or intermediate care facility for the mentally retard-

82. United States v. Laughlin, 26 F.3d 1523, 1525–26 (10th Cir.1994), cert. denied 513 U.S. 965, 115 S.Ct. 428, 130 L.Ed.2d 342 (1994).

83. Id.

84. United States v. Cegelka, 853 F.2d 627, 629 (8th Cir.1988), cert. denied 488 U.S. 1011, 109 S.Ct. 798, 102 L.Ed.2d 789 (1989) (interpreting similar provisions of former 42 U.S.C.A. § 1395nn(a)(1)).

85. United States v. Nichols, Nos. 91–6374, 91–6375, 1992 WL 238264 at *3 (6th Cir.1992).

86. Id.; United States v. Brown, 763 F.2d 984, 993 (8th Cir.1985), cert. denied 474 U.S. 905, 106 S.Ct. 273, 88 L.Ed.2d 234 (1985).

87. See, e.g., United States v. Brown, 763 F.2d at 989.

88. Id.

89. United States v. Larm, 824 F.2d 780 (9th Cir.1987), cert. denied 484 U.S. 1078, 108 S.Ct. 1057, 98 L.Ed.2d 1019 (1988).

90. Id. at 782–83.

91. 42 U.S.C.A. § 1320a–7b(e).

ed is also a crime.[92] Finally, criminal penalties exist for other false statements and representations, including false representations concerning requirements of the Social Security Act;[93] false representations to elicit information regarding the date of birth, employment, wages, or benefits of an individual from HHS;[94] and false statements or representations made to qualify for certification or recertification for Medicare provider status.[95]

§ 2–3. Civil False Claims

The general federal Civil False Claims Act, 31 U.S.C.A. § 3729, was, like its companion criminal law provision, 18 U.S.C.A. § 287, adopted during the civil war to address the problem of rampant war contract fraud.[1] It has become one of the most frequently used tools in the war against health care fraud. It is attractive to the government because its remedial provisions permit recoveries of three times the amount of damages sustained by the government, plus penalties of $5000 to $10,000 per claim. The Civil False Claims Act offers the government prosecutor advantages not available under alternative criminal statutes. First, the government need only meet the civil, preponderance of the evidence, standard of proof.[2] Second, as amended in 1986, the statute permits recoveries without proof of specific intent to defraud. The statute is also popular with private litigants, who can recover a portion of the damages to which the government is entitled under the statute's qui tam provisions.[3]

Section 3729 provides:

(a) Any person who—

(1) knowingly presents, or causes to be presented, to an officer or employee of the United States Government ... a false or fraudulent claim for payment or approval;

(2) knowingly makes, uses, or causes to be made or used, a false record or statement to get a false or fraudulent claim paid by the government;

(3) conspires to defraud the Government by getting a false claim allowed or paid; ...

---

92. 42 U.S.C.A. § 1320a–7b(d).

93. 42 U.S.C.A. § 1307. An example would be making false statements about Medicare deductibles or coinsurance for the purpose of marketing a Medigap policy.

94. 42 U.S.C.A. § 1307(b)(1).

95. 42 U.S.C.A. § 1320a–7b(c).

§ 2–3

1. Adam G. Snyder, The False Claims Act Applied to Health Care Insti-

tutions: Gearing Up for Corporate Compliance, 1 DePaul J. of Health Care L. 1, 6 (1996).

2. 31 U.S.C.A. § 3731(c).

3. See chapter 6. The Civil False Claims Act and its qui tam provisions are treated exhaustively in an excellent treatise by John Boese, Civil False Claims and Qui Tam Actions (1995).

is liable to the United States Government for a civil penalty of not less than $5,000 and not more than $10,000, plus 3 times the amount of damages which the Government sustains because of the act of that person, [except in cases of prompt and voluntary self-disclosure, double damages may be assessed]. A person violating this subsection shall also be liable to the United States Government for the costs of a civil action brought to recover any such penalty or damages.

(b) For purposes of this section, the terms "knowing" and "knowingly" mean that a person, with respect to information—

(1) has actual knowledge of the information;

(2) acts in deliberate ignorance of the truth or falsity of the information;

(3) acts in reckless disregard of the truth or falsity of the information,

and no proof of specific intent to defraud is required.

(c) For purposes of this section, "claim" includes any request or demand, whether under a contract or otherwise, for money or property which is made to a contractor, grantee, or other recipient, if the United States Government provides any portion of the money or property which is requested or demanded, or if the Government will reimburse such contractor, grantee, or other recipient for any portion of the money or property which is requested or demanded.

Section 3729 also contains several other prohibitions dealing with purchase from or provision of property to the government and with obligations to the government, which are not generally applicable to Medicare and Medicaid fraud.

To establish liability under § 3729(a)(1), the government must show that the defendant "1) presented or caused to be presented, for payment or approval, to the Government of the United States a claim upon or against the United States; (2) the claim was false, fictitious or fraudulent; and (3) [the defendant] knew that the claim was false, fictitious, or fraudulent."[4] Where the government sues under § 3729(a)(2), the elements are identical, except that the claim involves the making or causing to be made of a false record or statement.[5]

A claim is a "request or demand" for payment.[6] Thus, a claim is defined (for purposes of counting the number of claims subject to

---

4. United States ex rel. Fahner v. Alaska, 591 F.Supp. 794, 798 (N.D.Ill. 1984).

5. United States v. Warning, No. Civ. A. 93–4541, 1994 WL 396432 at *3 (E.D.Pa.1994).

6. 31 U.S.C.A. § 3729(c).

penalties) in terms of a form submitted by a provider for payment, not each individual service identified on the form.[7] The statutory definition of "claim," added by the 1986 amendments, makes it perfectly clear that claims submitted to state Medicaid agencies or to Medicare carriers or intermediaries are considered to be claims presented against the federal government, thus obviating the question of presentment that arises under other false claims and statements statutes. This understanding of the statute, however, had already been accepted by cases antedating the 1986 amendments.[8] The definition of "claim" would also seem to cover claims submitted to managed care organizations (e.g. by specialists who contract with the managed care organization independently to provide services) which in turn contract with Medicare or Medicaid, though there are no reported cases on this issue as of this date. To be held liable under the Act, a defendant must actually participate in the presentation of a claim. Mere knowledge that others are submitting false claims and failure to take action to stop the submission is not enough to establish liability.[9]

False claims are defined broadly to encompass more than simple common law fraud. Reported cases often involved claims submitted for services that were in fact provided, but where the defendant failed to comply with program requirements. In *United States ex rel. Piacentile v. Wolk*, for example, the defendant was held liable for submitting bills for medical equipment, having altered certificates of medical necessity that were required to support these claims by either deleting information supplied by the physician and substituting false information or by adding information without the authorization of the physician.[10] In *United States v. Nazon* the court permitted a false claim case to proceed against a doctor who had allegedly billed for services provided at a time he was excluded from Medicare participation.[11] In *United States v. Lorenzo*, the court entered a false claims judgment against a dentist who billed the Medicare program for oral cancer examinations that were in fact performed, but that were not properly ordered by a physician as required by Medicare.[12] False statements on cost reports that form the basis for subsequent payments may also be considered false claims,[13] as may claims for services that were in

---

7. United States v. Krizek, 111 F.3d 934, 939–40 (D.C.Cir.1997).

8. United States ex rel. Fahner v. Alaska, 591 F. Supp. at 798; United States v. Jacobson, 467 F.Supp. 507, 507 (S.D.N.Y.1979); United States ex rel. Davis v. Long's Drugs, Inc., 411 F.Supp. 1144, 1146–49 (S.D.Cal.1976).

9. United States ex rel. Piacentile v. Wolk, No. Civ. A. 93–5773, 1995 WL 20833 at *4 (E.D.Pa.1995).

10. Id. at *2.

11. United States v. Nazon, No. 93 C 5456, 1993 WL 410150 at *1 (N.D.Ill. 1993).

12. United States v. Lorenzo, 768 F.Supp. 1127, 1130–31 (E.D.Pa.1991).

13. United States ex rel. Thompson v. Columbia/HCA Healthcare Corp., 1997 WL 619314 (5th Cir. Oct. 23, 1997); United States v. Oakwood Down-

fact provided, but that were not medically necessary.[14] While some courts have stated that it is not necessary for the government to show that the false claim resulted in actual loss to the government,[15] there is substantial authority for the proposition that the representation must be likely to cause eventual reliance by the government.[16]

Whether or not a claim is "false" often involves an interpretation of underlying program regulations and requirements. A claim is not "false" if it is based on a reasonable interpretation of a program requirement.[17]

One potential means of confronting false claims actions (including qui tam actions) might be to request declaratory and injunctive relief challenging the enforceability of Medicare or Medicaid policy on which false claims allegations are based. Twenty-four hospitals, who are being sued in a qui tam action for submitting claims in violation of HCFA's policy for payment of investigative medical devices, are currently suing HHS, claiming that its policy was promulgated in violation of the Administrative Procedures Act and is thus unenforceable.[18] A recent opinion of the Ninth Circuit in this case, however, observed in a jurisdictional ruling that if a provider knowingly files a false claim or statement in order to receive payment for goods or services not covered under a rule or manual provision, the fact that the rule or provision is subsequently declared invalid will not excuse the provider from false claims liability.[19] Should this ruling be followed in the companion false claims case, the strategy would be of little value.

The outer reach of the false claims statute is not clear, however. Courts have permitted suits to go forward based on allegations that a psychiatric hospital submitted false claims when it requested payment for services without having taken appropriate precautions

river Medical Ctr., 687 F.Supp. 302, 303–04, 309 (E.D.Mich.1988).

14. United States v. Crescent City EMS, Inc., No. Civ. A. 91–4150, 1994 WL 518171 at *3 (E.D.La.1994), aff'd, 72 F.3d 447 (5th Cir.1995) (use of ambulances for transporting dialysis patients); United States ex rel. Mikes v. Straus, 853 F.Supp. 115, 118 (S.D.N.Y. 1994) (spirometry tests).

15. United States v. Kensington Hosp., 760 F.Supp. 1120, 1127–28 (E.D.Pa.1991).

16. Boese, supra note 3, at 2–13 to 2–19.

17. United States v. Krizek, 859 F.Supp. 5, 10–11 (D.D.C.1994), modified

909 F.Supp. 32 (D.D.C.1995), aff'd in part and rev'd in part, 111 F.3d 934 (1997); Boese, supra note 3, at 2–45 to 2–47.

18. See Russell Hayman, The Use of Affirmative Civil Litigation to Defend Against a Qui Tam Suit: The Investigational Cardiac Devices Controversy, in American Bar Association, Health Care Fraud, 1996, I–13.

19. Cedars–Sinai Medical Center v. Shalala, Medicare and Medicaid Guide (CCH) ¶ 45,621 (9th Cir. 1997), citing United States v. Weiss, 914 F.2d 1514, 1522–23 (2d Cir. 1990).

to provide a reasonably safe environment for patients, as required by Medicaid regulations,[20] or that a hospital had submitted claims while it was operating under a fraudulently obtained Certificate of Need.[21] Arguably any claim submitted to Medicare or Medicaid that involves conduct otherwise proscribed under the Medicare or Medicaid law, such as bribes and kickbacks or self-referrals, is a false claim.[22] Two district court cases have refused to dismiss cases alleging that claims were for services provided on the basis of referrals that were tainted by illegal kickbacks.[23] The only court of appeals decision to consider the question held that a hospital could be found liable for submitting both a false claim and a false statement if it had certified compliance with Medicare statutes and regulations (including the Stark laws) and payment of claims was conditional on such certification.[24] Some commentators have argued, however, that in the bribes and kickbacks and self-referral statutes themselves Congress established the sanctions that it considered appropriate for those offenses, and that the false claims statute, with its attendant penalties, should not be applied in addition to those offenses.[24.5]

Liability under the Civil False Claims Act is based currently on "knowingly" submitting a false claim or statement. Prior to 1986, the courts were split between those that held that the government had to prove intent to defraud, those that held that the defendant could be convicted for having submitted a claim with knowledge that it was false, and those that were willing to premise liability on negligent misrepresentations.[25] The 1986 amendments make clear that "knowing" conduct includes not only actual knowledge, but also deliberate ignorance or "reckless disregard" for the truth. While the statute does not cover merely negligent conduct, "reck-

20. United States ex rel. Aranda v. Community Psychiatric Ctrs. of Okla., 945 F.Supp. 1485 (W.D.Okla.1996).

21. United States ex rel. Sanders v. East Ala. Healthcare Auth., 953 F.Supp. 1404 (M.D.Ala.1996).

22. See, debating this point, Priscilla Budeiri, Kickbacks, Self–Referrals Make Claims "False under FCA" and Sanford Teplitzky and Harry Silver, False Claims Act Does Not Encompass Kickbacks or Violations of Stark, 1 BNA Health Care Fraud Report 302–304 (1997).

23. United States ex rel. Roy v. Anthony, 914 F.Supp. 1504, 1505–07 (S.D.Ohio 1994); United States ex rel. Pogue v. American Healthcorp., Inc., 914 F.Supp. 1507 (M.D.Tenn.1996). In United States v. Kensington Hosp., 760 F.Supp. 1120 (E.D.Pa.1991) and United States v. Northwestern Institute of Psychiatry, Inc., No. Civ. A. 93–CV–0132 (E.D. Pa. 1993), the government's assertions in false claims cases that claims based on kickbacks were false claims also survived motions to dismiss, though both cases were settled before they went to trial.

24. United States ex rel. Thompson v. Columbia/HCA Healthcare Corp., 1997 WL 619314 (5th Cir. 1997).

24.5 Robert Salcido, Mixing Oil and Water: The Government's Mistaken Use of the Medicare Anti–Kickback Statute in False Claims Act Prosecutions, 6 Ann. Health L. 105 (1997).

25. Boese, supra note 3, at 2–66 to 2–67; United States ex rel. Fahner v. Alaska, 591 F.Supp. at 799.

less disregard" has been defined as "gross negligence-plus."[26] Deliberate ignorance is sufficient to meet the standard.[27] Under this definition, a defendant who submitted claims in the face of rejection of the claims by a carrier and warnings from others that the claims were not covered, was found to have acted recklessly, even though he claimed to have relied on advice from a consultant that his billing was proper.[28] So was a psychiatrist who permitted improper bills to be submitted on his behalf without adequate supervision.[29] On the other hand, a home health service was granted summary judgment in a case in which the government failed to produce evidence that the defendant knew it was not entitled to payments it received or that it acted with reckless disregard of its nonentitlement.[30]

Corporations will normally be held liable for false claims submitted by their employees if the employee was acting within the scope of his or her official duty and the act was taken to benefit the corporation.[31] Individuals, however, cannot be held strictly liable for false claims filed by their employees unless it can be shown that they were at least reckless in permitting the claim to be filed.[32] Individuals also cannot be held liable as corporate officers or shareholders for the false claims of corporations unless they participated in the corporation's illegal conduct.[33] The conspiracy provisions of § 3729(a)(3) cannot be used to reach joint conduct involving corporations and their officers or employees, but individuals who are also employed by the same corporation can be sanctioned under the statute for conspiracies that extend beyond their corporation to involve others.[34]

Under § 3731(d) a final judgment in favor of the United States in a criminal proceeding involving fraud and false statements collaterally estops the defendant from denying the essential ele-

---

26. United States v. Krizek, 111 F.3d 934, 941–42 (D.C.Cir.1997).

27. Krizek, 111 F.3d at 942.

28. United States v. Lorenzo, 768 F.Supp. 1127, 1130 (E.D.Pa.1991).

29. United States v. Krizek, 111 F.3d 934 (D.C.Cir.1997).

30. United States v. American Health Enters., Inc., 1996 WL 331106 (D.C.N. Ga.1996).

31. Boese, supra note 3, at 2–92. See United States v. Lorenzo, 768 F. Supp. at 1133. There is some authority outside of the health care area for extending this liability to situations involving "collective knowledge" where no single employee possesses knowledge that a claim is false, but the fraud would become clear if the knowledge of several employ-

ees were combined. See Boese, supra note 3, at 2–93 to 2–97. Under this theory a corporate health care entity could be held liable if one employee submits a bill based on erroneous transmission of information from another employee who failed to perform a service as billed.

32. Compare United States v. Nazon, No. 93 C 5456, 1993 WL 459966 at *2 (N.D.Ill.1993) (no strict liability for acts of employees) with United States v. Krizek, 111 F.3d 934 (D.D.C. 1997) (liability for reckless failure to supervise filing of claims).

33. United States ex rel. Piacentile v. Wolk, No. Civ. A. 93–5773, 1995 WL 20833 at *4 (E.D.Pa.1995).

34. United States v. Warning, No. Civ. A. 93–4541, 1994 WL 396432 at *4–5 (E.D.Pa.1994).

ments of the false claim offense in a civil false claims action involving the same transaction. A plea of guilty or nolo contendere has the same effect for these purposes as a guilty verdict after trial.[35] The preclusive effect of a guilty plea, however, does not extend beyond the counts to which the defendant pleaded guilty, regardless of the broader scope of findings of fact entered for sentencing purposes.[36] The government may also be bound in pursuing civil remedies by agreements it accepts as part of a plea agreement.[37] Finally, double jeopardy considerations limit the ability of the government to impose civil penalties in addition to criminal sanctions.[38]

Procedural and remedial issues relating to civil money penalty and qui tam actions are discussed below in chapter 6.

Library References:

C.J.S. United States § 174.
West's Key No. Digests, United States ⟜122.

§ 2–4. Beneficiary Incentive Program

The Health Insurance Portability and Accountability Act of 1996 creates a new program to provide Medicare beneficiaries an incentive to identify false claims and other program abuses. Under Section 203 of the Act, HHS is required to provide an explanation of benefits (EOB) form to a Medicare beneficiary every time a Medicare item or service is provided.[1] HHS is required to establish a program to encourage beneficiaries to report false claims and other abuses to HHS.[2] If the report results in the collection of $100 or more, HHS "may pay a portion of the amount collected to the individual" who reports, following procedures similar to those applicable under § 7623 of the Internal Revenue Code.[3] Bounties may also be paid to individuals who make suggestions to HHS for improving the efficiency of the Medicare program, if the suggestion in fact results in savings.[4]

The Balanced Budget Act of 1997 further provides that beneficiaries may file a written request with a physician, supplier or provider for an itemized list of items and services provided, and

---

35. 31 U.S.C.A. § 3731(d).

36. United States v. Mickman, No. Civ. A. 89–7826, 1993 WL 541683 at *3 (E.D.Pa.1993).

37. Stern v. Shalala, 14 F.3d 148, 149–50 (2d Cir.1994).

38. United States v. Halper, 490 U.S. 435, 446–48, 109 S.Ct. 1892, 1900–01, 104 L.Ed.2d 487 (1989). See infra, chapter 8.

§ 2–4

1. 42 U.S.C.A. § 1395b–5(a).

2. 42 U.S.C.A. § 1395b–5(b). The program is supposed also to discourage the provision of frivolous and irrelevant complaints, and to not consider such complaints.

3. 42 U.S.C.A. § 1395b–5(b)(2).

4. 42 U.S.C.A. § 1395b–5(c).

such a list must be provided within 30 days.[5] If the list is not provided, the physician, supplier, or provider may be fined $100 for each failure.[6] An individual who believes that the list reflects items and services not provided as claimed or other billing irregularities may request HHS to review the list.[7] HHS shall make a finding as to whether unnecessary payments were made, and recover such payments.[8]

§ 2–5. Federal Administrative False Claims Remedies

Criminal false claims prosecutions and civil false claims lawsuits are initiated by the Department of Justice. Within the Department of Health and Human Services, which administers the Medicare and Medicaid programs, the Office of Inspector General (OIG) has responsibility for identifying and investigating program fraud and abuse.[1] The Social Security Act authorizes the Department of Health and Human Services to assess administrative civil penalties of up to $10,000 per claim plus three times the amount claimed against persons who file false claims in federal health care programs.[2] The Department may also exclude from program participation persons convicted of program fraud, or persons who submit excessive charges or charges for unnecessary care.[3] Providers can also be fined or excluded from federal health care programs for a violation of specific program requirements under a host of specific provisions scattered throughout the Social Security Act. Finally, the general federal Administrative Remedies for False Claims and Statements statute permits the Attorney General to impose administrative civil penalties of up to $5000 and twice the amount claimed for false claims or statements.[4]

When the OIG identifies a potential fraud and abuse case, it must refer the case to the relevant United States Attorney (or in larger cases to the Department of Justice, Civil Division) for consideration of criminal or civil prosecution.[5] Only if the United States Attorney (or, where relevant, the Department of Justice) declines prosecution (or after the United States Attorney has concluded a

---

5. Pub. L. No. 105–32, § 4311(b).

6. Id.

7. Id.

8. Id.

§ 2–5

1. See Statement of Organizations, Functions and Delegations of Authority, Office of Inspector General, 50 Fed. Reg. 45,488 (1985).

2. 42 U.S.C.A. § 1320a–7a. Until the 1996 amendments to the program, the amount was $2000 per claim plus double the amount wrongfully claimed.

3. 42 U.S.C.A. § 1320a–7(a)(1), (b)(1), (6).

4. 31 U.S.C.A. §§ 3801–12.

5. Memorandum of Understanding Between the Department of Health and Human Services and the Department of Justice Regarding Implementation of Section 1128A of the Social Security Act, 1983. This memorandum implements the requirements of 42 U.S.C.A. § 1320a–7a(c)(1).

criminal prosecution), may the OIG proceed with its own administrative sanction proceeding.

Substantive provisions relevant to administrative false claims remedies will be considered here. Procedural and remedial issues relevant to administrative civil penalty and exclusion proceedings are considered in chapter 5, while investigative issues are examined in chapter 7.

a. Administrative Penalties under the Federal Health Care Program False Claims Statute

Library References:

C.J.S. United States § 174.
West's Key No. Digests, United States ⟛122.

Section 1128A (42 U.S.C.A. § 1320a–7a) of the Social Security Act provides:

> Any person (including an organization, agency, or other entity, but excluding a beneficiary) ... that—
>
>> (1) knowingly presents or causes to be presented to an officer, employee, or agent of the United States, or of any department or agency thereof, or of any State agency ... a claim ... that the Secretary determines—
>>
>>> (A) is for a medical or other item or service that the person knows or should know was not provided as claimed, [or]
>>>
>>> (B) is for a medical or other item or service and the person knows or should know the claim is false or fraudulent, ...
>
> shall be subject, in addition to any other penalties that may be prescribed by law, to a civil money penalty of not more than $10,000 for each item or service.... In addition, such a person shall be subject to an assessment of not more than 3 times the amount claimed for each such item or service in lieu of damages sustained by the United States or a State agency because of such claim. In addition the Secretary may make a determination in the same proceeding to exclude the person from participation in [Medicare] and to direct the appropriate State agency to exclude the person from participation in any State health care program.[6]

---

6. 42 U.S.C.A. § 1320a–7a(a)(1)(A), (B). The terms "claim", "item or service" and "request for payment" are defined in the statute and regulations. See 42 U.S.C.A. § 1320a–7a(i)(2), (3); 42 C.F.R. § 1003.101.

The standard of scienter under 1128A has, until recently, been less demanding than that under the criminal or civil statutes discussed above, though after 1996 amendments to the statute the standard is probably now the same. Under 1128A, a person is liable for civil penalties if that person "knows or should know" that the claim is false or that the service was "not provided as claimed."

The original statute, which imposed liability under a "knows or has reason to know standard," created difficulties for the prosecution when a physician asserted, as is common, that the false claim was the fault of a billing clerk. Congress thus amended the statute to impose the "knows or should know" standard. The meaning of the "should know" standard, as it existed until 1996, is discussed in the preface to the rules implementing the Medicare and Medicaid Patient and Program Protection Act.[7] The standard subsumed reckless disregard for the consequences of one's actions, as well as negligence in the preparing and submitting, or in supervising the preparing and submitting, of claims.[8]

---

7. 57 Fed. Reg. 3298, 3324 (1992).

8. See Mayers v. United States Dep't of Health & Human Servs., 806 F.2d 995, 999–1000 (11th Cir.1986); Anesthesiologists Affiliated v. Sullivan, 941 F.2d 678, 680–81 (8th Cir.1991). The OIG's comments also referenced the Restatement of Torts (2d) at Section 12 (1965), which states that

The words "should know" are used throughout the Restatement * * * to denote the fact that a person of reasonable prudence and intelligence or of the superior intelligence of the actor would ascertain the fact in question in the performance of this duty to another, or would govern his conduct upon the assumption that such fact exists. See Inspector General v. Hobbs [1990 Transfer Binder] Medicare & Medicaid Guide (CCH) ¶ 38,294 at 21,-641 (DAB Dec. 5, 1989).

An Administrative Law Judge, interpreting the "should know" standard, stated:

The "should know" standard is quite similar to the "reason to know" standard, except that the duty to inquire (the duty to ascertain the truth and accuracy of a claim) exists at all times and does not require any special circumstances to bring attention to the duty.

* * *

The "should know" standard includes reckless disregard for the consequences of a person's acts and simple negligence in preparing, presenting, or in supervising the preparation and presentation of claims ... Respondent was obliged to pay attention to her billing, read the Manual and bulletins, and resolve any ambiguities before submitting claims which she should have known were not proper. Id. See similarly, Inspector General v. Hume, [1989 Transfer Binder] Medicare & Medicaid (CCH) ¶ 38,029 (DAB Aug. 22, 1989).

The standard, did not impose strict liability, however, and the OIG had to prove at least negligence by the preponderance of the evidence. The proceeding is civil in nature rather than criminal, thus the preponderance of evidence standard applies rather than a beyond a reasonable doubt standard. Scott v. Bowen, 845 F.2d 856, 856 (9th Cir. 1988). In Inspector General v. Wesley Hal Livingston and Shoals Medical Equipment Supply Co., Inc., for example, the Departmental Appeals Board, Appellate Division, held that the OIG had failed to show that a Medicare contractor failed to act reasonably in not uncovering the fraud of its subcontractor. Inspector General v. Livingston, [1993 Transfer Binder] Medicare & Medicaid Guide (CCH) ¶ 41,629 (DAB Apr. 19, 1993), aff'd on reconsideration, [1993 Transfer Binder] Medicare & Medicaid Guide (CCH) ¶ 41,630 (DAB July 15, 1993).

In 1996 Congress amended the statute to define "should know" to mean:

> "that a person, with respect to information–
>
> (1) acts in deliberate ignorance of the truth or falsity of the information; or
>
> (2) acts in reckless disregard of the truth or falsity of the information, and no proof of specific intent to defraud is required."[9]

The intent of Congress seems clearly to require more than mere negligence in the imposition of claims.

The statute also states, however, that "[A] principal is liable . . . under this section for the actions of the principal's agent acting within the scope of the agency,"[10] and presumably permits the imposition of vicarious liability on physicians, providers and suppliers.[11] Liability can be found under this provision even though the principal is completely without fault.[12]

Here, as elsewhere in false claims law, penalties can be imposed for miscoding as well as for fictitious claims. In Anesthesiologists Affiliated v. Sullivan,[13] for example the court upheld a $258,-000 penalty assessment despite arguments that the physicians had merely described services rendered "unartfully." The court stated, "The standard of care imposed by this requirement is an exacting one, and an "unartful" description of medical services in a Medicare claim *is* a description of services that were not provided as claimed."[14] Recent amendments to the statute explicitly provide that a "person who engages in a pattern of practice of presenting or causing to be presented a claim for an item or service that is based on a code that the person knows or should know will result in a greater payment to the person than the code the person knows or should know is applicable to the item or service actually provided" may be sanctioned.[15] The recent amendments also provide for sanctions where "a pattern of medical or other items or services that a person knows or should know are not medically necessary" is established.[16] The legislative history of this provision specifies that Congress did not intend by this provision to deter the practice of

9. 42 U.S.C.A. § 1320a–7a(i)(7).

10. 42 U.S.C.A. § 1320a–7a(*l*).

11. See, Sanford V. Teplitzky et al., Medicare and Medicaid Fraud and Abuse, in 1989 Health Law Handbook 507, 513–14 (Alice G. Gosfield ed., 1989) (discussing history of provision). See also, discussing application of the "knows or should know" standard, Sanford V. Teplitzky & S. Craig Holden, 1989 Developments in Medicare and Medicaid Fraud and Abuse, in 1990 Health Law Handbook 433, 435–36 (Alice G. Gosfield ed., 1990).

12. See Inspector General v. Livingston, Medicare & Medicaid Guide (CCH) ¶ 41,630.

13. Anesthesiologists Affiliated v. Sullivan, 941 F.2d 678 (8th Cir.1991).

14. Id. at 681.

15. 42 U.S.C.A. § 1320a–7a(a)(1)(A).

16. 42 U.S.C.A. § 1320a–7a(a)(1)(E).

complementary or alternative medicine, to penalize the good faith exercise of medical judgment where treatment choices are supported by significant evidence or would be chosen by a significant minority of providers, to penalize providers who submit claims to Medicare for noncovered service so that their patients can document noncoverage prior to submitting the claim to secondary payers, or to sanction doctors who inform their patients that services are not covered by Medicare.[17] A person who is concerned that activities or proposed activities violate the Medicare and Medicaid fraud laws can request an advisory opinion.[18]

Issues of procedure and of determination of penalties under the administrative False Claims Act are considered below at chapter 5.

b. Administrative Penalties in Other Statutes

As an alternative to the civil penalties that can be imposed under 42 U.S.C.A. § 1320a–7(a), civil penalties of $5000 per claim plus assessments of double the amount of the false claim can also be imposed administratively for false claims under the general federal Program Fraud and Civil Remedies Act.[19] This statute permits greater penalties than those available under the more specific Medicare and Medicaid false claims statute and permits penalties for statements that omit material facts as well as false statements.[20] It also, however, requires proof that the claimant "knows or has reason to know" that a statement is false.[21] Perhaps most importantly, an assistant attorney general must approve any penalty actions before they are filed.[22] Because of these limitations, the Program Fraud Act is not used in practice for prosecuting Medicare and Medicaid false claims.

The administrative sanction of exclusion from program participation, on the other hand, is used quite frequently. In 1994, 1265 providers were excluded from the Medicare program, though many of these were excluded for non-payment of student loans rather than for program-related offenses.[23] Conviction of a criminal offense relating to the delivery of an item or service reimbursed under Medicare, Medicaid, or a state health care program funded under Title V or XX, results in a mandatory exclusion from participation in those programs for at least five years.[24] Commission of an

---

17. 142 Cong.Rec. H9473, H9537.

18. 42 U.S.C.A. § 1320a–7d(b); 42 C.F.R. § 1008.5(a)(5).

19. 31 U.S.C.A. §§ 3801–12.

20. 31 U.S.C.A. § 3802(a)(1).

21. Id.

22. 31 U.S.C.A. § 3803(b)(1)(A).

23. GAO, Medicare, Adapting Private Sector Techniques Could Curb Losses to Fraud and Abuse (GAO/T–HEHS–95–211, July 19, 1995).

24. 42 U.S.C.A. § 1320a–7(a)(1). Conviction is defined broadly to include nolo contendere pleas or entrance into diversion programs. 42 U.S.C.A. § 1320a–7(i). It even includes Alford pleas, in which the defendant pleads not guilty but accepts the conviction to avoid a trial. Hein v. Inspector General, [1993

offense in violation of the civil money penalties or criminal provisions of the statute can also result in an exclusion.[25] An exclusion may be imposed on a physician based on a criminal plea even though the plea purported to settle all civil and criminal claims, as a Medicare exclusion is not a civil or criminal claim.[26] Exclusions are considered further in chapter 5.

The Medicare and Medicaid statutes also contain a variety of other provisions authorizing civil sanctions or exclusions for improper billing practices. The list of such provisions grows with every budget reconciliation act. It currently includes:

    1) civil money penalties of up to $2000 for each claim presented for physician's services (or for items or services incident to a physician's services) by persons who knew or should have known that the person providing the services was not a licensed physician or was a physician who had procured a license through fraud, or by persons who had represented to the patient that the physician was specialty board certified when this was not in fact true;[27]

    2) civil money penalties of up to $2000 for each claim for an item or service provided by a person excluded from the program under which the claim was made;[28]

    3) civil money penalties of up to $2000 per claim for each claim presented in violation of a) a Medicare assignment of claims agreement (an agreement to accept payment directly from Medicare and to accept the Medicare payment as payment in full—exclusive of beneficiary cost-sharing obligations—in lieu of billing the beneficiary who then collects from Medicare); b) an agreement with a State agency under Medicaid not to charge a person for an item or service in excess of the amount permitted under the program; c) a Medicare participating physician or supplier agreement; or d) an agreement not to charge for inpatient hospital services for which payment was denied by a Medicare Peer Review Organization as inappropriate or unnecessary;[29]

Transfer Binder] Medicare & Medicaid Guide (CCH) ¶ 41,366 (DAB Feb. 26, 1993).

25. 42 U.S.C.A. § 1320a–7(b)(7).

26. United States v Potrocky, 2 BNA Health Law Reporter 436 (1993). See, discussing settlement issues generally, James M. Becker et al., Avoiding Multiple Sanctions and Collateral Consequences When Settling Fraud and Abuse Cases, in 1993 Health Law Handbook 187 (Alice G. Gosfield ed., 1993).

27. 42 U.S.C.A. § 1320a–7a(a)(1)(C).

28. 42 U.S.C.A. § 1320a–7a(a)(1)(D).

29. 42 U.S.C.A. § 1320a–7a(a)(2). The Peer Review Organizations are entities responsible for assuring that Medicare beneficiaries are not provided care that is unnecessary, inappropriate, or of substandard quality. See Barry Furrow, et al., Health Law Treatise, §§ 3–26—3–35 (1995).

4) civil penalties of up to $2000 or exclusion for knowingly, willfully, or on a repeated basis billing for clinical diagnostic laboratory tests on other than an assignment basis (excluding tests performed in a rural health clinic);[30]

5) civil money penalties of up to $2000 for knowingly and willfully billing for intraocular lens insertion related to cataract surgery by an ambulatory surgical center in violation of an agreement to accept by assignment an all-inclusive fee as payment in full;[31]

6) civil money penalties of up to $2000 for knowingly and willfully billing a recipient directly for the services of a certified registered nurse anesthetist (CRNA), which must be billed on an assignment basis;[32]

7) civil money penalties of up to $2000 and exclusion for knowingly and willfully failing to furnish durable medical equipment (DME) without charge when the equipment is furnished on a rental basis and rental payments may no longer be made by Medicare;[33]

8) civil money penalties of up to $2000 and exclusion against nonparticipating physicians who knowingly and willfully bill for radiologist services in excess of the "limiting charge" of 115% of the allowable fee schedule;[34]

9) civil money penalties of up to $2000 and exclusion against nonparticipating physicians who knowingly, willfully, and on a repeated basis violate the limiting charge requirements of the Medicare program;[35]

10) civil money penalties of up to $2000 and exclusion for knowingly and willfully billing for the services of an assistant for a cataract operation unless the services are approved by a Medicare Peer Review Organization;[36]

11) civil money penalties of up to $2000 and exclusion against non-participating physicians who knowingly and willfully fail to refund on a timely basis charges paid by a beneficiary for services determined by a Medicare Peer Review Orga-

---

30. 42 U.S.C.A. § 1395l(h)(5)(D).

31. 42 U.S.C.A. § 1395l(i)(6).

32. 42 U.S.C.A. § 1395l(l)(5)(B).

33. 42 U.S.C.A. § 1395m(a)(11).

34. 42 U.S.C.A. § 1395m(b)(5)(C). See United States v. Corson, No. 93–CV–3637, 1993 WL 332268 at *2 (E.D. Pa.1993) (settlement based on limiting charge violations).

35. 42 U.S.C.A. §§ 1395u(j)(1), 1395w–4(g)(1). HHS may not exclude under this authority a "sole community physician or the source of essential specialized services" and must take into account access of beneficiaries to physician's services before imposing an exclusion under this statute. 42 U.S.C.A. § 1395u(j)(3). The provision also permits HHS to make restitution to beneficiaries from excessive charges from civil penalties and assessments. 42 U.S.C.A. § 1395u(j)(4).

36. 42 U.S.C.A. § 1395u(k)(1).

nization to have not been reasonable or necessary,[37] or who fail to either disclose to a beneficiary in writing prior to an elective surgical procedure the estimated charge for the procedure, the approved charge under Part B, the excess of the charge over the approved charge, and the applicable coinsurance amount; or to refund an excess charge on a timely basis;[38]

12) civil money penalties of up to $2000 and exclusion against physicians who charge a mark-up or otherwise improperly charge for purchased diagnostic tests;[39]

13) civil money penalties of up to $2000 against physicians who do not take assignment and do not provide diagnostic codes upon request, and exclusions for physicians who knowingly, willfully, and on a repeated basis fail to include diagnostic codes on bills after having been notified of their obligation to do so;[40]

14) civil money penalties of up to $2000 and exclusion against physicians, suppliers and others who do not accept assignment and fail to submit unassigned Medicare claim forms within one year of the date of service or who charge for providing this service;[41]

15) civil money penalties of up to $2000 and exclusion against physicians who knowingly and willfully fail to bill on an assignment basis for services to persons enrolled under Medicare Part B and eligible for Medicaid;[42]

16) civil penalties of up to $2000, exclusion, and 10% reduction in payment for claims submitted by physicians, suppliers, and others (including employers or facilities that properly bill for physician's services) that are not submitted on the proper specified claim form;[43]

17) reduction of Medicaid payments by up to three times the amount improperly sought for billing persons eligible for Medicaid or their responsible relatives or representatives for medical expenses which third parties (such as insurers) are liable to pay;[44]

18) civil money penalties of up to $2000 for knowingly and willfully presenting a bill inconsistent with an arrangement required under the Medicare law to preclude liability for payment by the patient for services provided in a hospital by a

37. 42 U.S.C.A. § 1395u(1).

38. 42 U.S.C.A. § 1395u(m).

39. 42 U.S.C.A. § 1395u(n).

40. 42 U.S.C.A. § 1395u(p).

41. Omnibus Budget Reconciliation Act of 1989, Pub. L. No. 101–239, § 6102(g)(4), 1989 U.S.C.C.A.N. (103 Stat.) 2106, 2182.

42. 42 U.S.C.A. § 1395w–4(g)(3).

43. 42 U.S.C.A. § 1395w–4(g)(4).

44. 42 U.S.C.A. §§ 1396a(g), 1396a(a)(25)(C).

person other than a physician, CRNA, physician's assistant, certified nurse midwife or qualified psychologist;[45]

19) civil money penalties of up to $2000 for violation of the unbundling prohibition for hospital outpatient services;[46] and

20) civil money penalties of up to $2000 and exclusion for knowingly and willfully billing for interpretation of an electrocardiogram performed or ordered as part of a physician visit.[47]

The Balanced Budget Act of 1997 requires DME suppliers, Home Health Agencies, CORFs, and Rehabilitation Agencies and other suppliers or providers (other than physicians) where appropriate, to file $50,000 bonds as a condition of participation in Medicare unless HHS determines that the entity is required to file a comparable bond under state law.[48] These bonds would presumably be available to cover penalties where necessary.

§ 2–6. State False Claims Law

Though the federal fraud and abuse laws have garnered more attention in recent years, the states have also been active in prosecuting Medicaid fraud and abuse. Federal law authorizes 90% federal funding for getting state Medicaid fraud control units (MFCUs) underway.[1] States were required to establish such units as of 1995 unless they could demonstrate that the unit would not be cost-effective because minimal Medicaid fraud exists in the state and beneficiaries are adequately protected from neglect and abuse without a MFCU.[2] All but three states have now established MFCUs.[3] MFCUs are responsible for facilitating and coordinating state efforts to identify and prosecute Medicaid fraud. MFCUs are defined as entities that are either located in the State Attorney General's office or otherwise are capable of statewide coordination of criminal prosecution efforts; are separate from the entity that administers Medicaid in the state; conduct a statewide program for investigation or prosecution of fraud and abuse; have procedures for reviewing patient abuse and neglect complaints; provide for

---

45. 42 U.S.C.A. § 1395cc(g).

46. 42 U.S.C.A. § 1395cc(g).

47. 42 U.S.C.A. § 1395w–4(b)(3).

48. Pub. L. No. 105–32, § 4312, to be codified at 42 U.S.C.A. §§ 1395m(a), 1395x(o), 1395x(v)(1)(H), 1395m(a)(16), 1395cc(2) and 1395x(p).

2. 42 U.S.C.A. § 1396a(a)(61).

3. See, e.g., Haw. Rev. Stat. § 28–91; Ind. Code § 4–6–10–1; Nev. Rev. Stat. § 228.410; N.H. Rev. Stat. Ann. § 21–M:8–a; W.Va. Code § 9–7–1.

§ 2–6

1. 42 U.S.C.A. § 1396b(a)(6). After the initial 12 calendar quarters of operation the funding decreases to 75%.

collection or referral for collection of overpayments they discover; employ necessary personnel to promote the effective and efficient conduct of their activities; and submit annual reports to HHS.[4] Because of the increasing presence of MFCUs, as well as the increasing urgency of Medicaid fraud as a state fiscal issue, it is likely that state Medicaid fraud actions will become more and more common.

Most states have statutes specifically prohibiting Medicaid fraud.[5] These laws commonly prohibit false claims or obtaining payments through misrepresentation.[6] They often closely track the current federal Medicare and Medicaid false claims law, or some earlier version of it.[7] Several states, however, have additional prohibitions supplementing the federal law.[8] For example, some states have prohibitions against the provision of unnecessary care[9] or care of inadequate quality.[10] Several prohibit providers and practitioners from charging Medicaid a fee higher than they charge

---

4. 42 U.S.C.A. § 1396b(q); 42 C.F.R. §§ 1007.1–.21.

5. See, e.g., Me. Rev. Stat. Ann. tit. 17–A, § 354; N.Y. Penal Law § 175.35. See also, listing state Medicaid fraud statutes, Gregory P. Miller, Recent Developments in the Enforcement and Interpretation of Medicare/Medicaid Anti-Fraud and Abuse Statutes, in Medicare Fraud and Abuse: Understanding the Law 32, 36–39 (Jeanie M. Johnson & Janet Seifert eds., 1986); Mary J. Cavins, Annotation, Criminal Prosecution or Disciplinary Action Against Medical Practitioner for Fraud in Connection with Claims under Medicaid, Medicare, or Similar Welfare Program for Providing Medical Services, 50 A.L.R.3d 549 (1973). The North Carolina Medicaid Investigations Unit has compiled a comprehensive digest of published federal and state appellate court decisions involving Medicare and Medicaid cases.

6. See Conn. Gen. Stat. § 17b–99; Fla. Stat. ch. 409.920; Haw. Rev. Stat. § 346–43.5; Kan. Stat. Ann. § 21–38460; La. Rev. Stat. Ann. § 14:70.1; Mich. Comp. Laws § 400.607; Miss. Code Ann. §§ 43–13–13, 43–13–129, 43–13–205, 43–13–213, 43–13–217; N.H. Rev. Stat. Ann. §§ 167:17–b, 61–a; N.M. Stat. Ann. § 30–44–4; Ohio Rev. Code Ann. § 2913.40.

7. E.g., Ill. Rev. Stat. ch. 23, ¶ 8A–3; Md. Ann. Code art. 27, § 230B; N.J. Rev. Stat. § 30:4D–17. Recent amendments to the Maryland fraud law track recent amendments to the federal law by

providing for life imprisonment for persons convicted of Medicaid fraud where the fraud resulted in the death of an individual, Md. Health Gen. § 15–123.1(d)(2).

8. See, e.g., N.M. Stat. Ann. § 30–44–5 (crime to fail to retain records documenting Medicaid claims for 5 years); R.I. Gen. Laws § 40–8.2–3(A)(3) (submitting claim for which provider has already received or claimed reimbursement from another source).

9. Conn. Gen. Stat. Ann. § 17b–103 (performing services not needed or without prior authorization, where required); Fla. Stat. ch. 409.913 (furnishing inappropriate, unnecessary or harmful goods and services, administrative sanctions only); Mich. Comp. Laws § 400.607 (falsely representing services medically necessary in accordance with professionally accepted standards); 62 Pa. Cons. Stat. § 1407(a)(6) (services not documented in record and of little or no benefit, below accepted standards or unneeded). See also, applying the Michigan statute, In re Wayne County Prosecutor, 329 N.W.2d 510, 510–11, 121 Mich.App. 798, 799 (Ct.App.1982) (claim that medical tests were necessary when in fact they were not is a false claim).

10. Fla. Stat. ch. 409.913 (inferior quality, administrative sanctions only); Ill. Rev. Stat. ch. 23, ¶ 12–4.25(A)(e) (termination for care that is harmful or of "grossly inferior quality").

members of the general public.[11] One state makes it a criminal offense not to collect a copayment from a patient.[12] Recently adopted statutes prohibit fraud against Medicaid managed care plans[13] or by managed care plans.[14] Most states also have laws prohibiting bribes and kickbacks and self-referrals. These laws are discussed in chapters 3 and 4. Though state Medicaid fraud statutes are broadly worded, they are routinely upheld against constitutional challenges based on vagueness.[15]

State statutes authorizing or requiring courts to impose penalties for Medicaid fraud are increasingly common.[16] Many of these statutes require restitution of the money wrongfully claimed with interest.[17] Most also authorize penalties based on double or triple the amount fraudulently obtained plus fines or penalties of specified amounts.[18] Also common are provisions for assessment of the cost of the investigation and prosecution in addition to any other penalties.[19] A few states provide for forfeiture of profits or property

11. E.g. 62 Pa. Cons. Stat. § 1407(a)(8).

12. Fla. Stat. ch. 409.920(2)(f).

13. Md. Health Gen. § 15-123.1(a)(6), (b).

14. Tex. Hum. Res. § 36.002(10).

15. People v. Bynum, 197 Ill.App.3d 959, 963–64, 145 Ill.Dec. 468, 470–71, 557 N.E.2d 238, 240–41 (1990); State v. Dorn, 496 A.2d 451, 455, 145 Vt. 606, 613 (1985).

16. See Francis M. Dougherty, Annotation, Imposition of Civil Penalties, Under State Statute, Upon Medical Practitioner for Fraud in Connection with Claims Under Medicaid, Medicare, or Similar Welfare Programs for Providing Medical Services, 32 A.L.R.4th 671 (1984).

17. See Ark. Code Ann. § 5–55–107; Ann. Code Md. Art. 27 § 230D; Nev. Rev. Stat. § 422.410; N.H. Rev. Stat. Ann. § 167:61; N.Y. Soc. Serv. Law § 145–b; 62 Pa. Cons. Stat. § 1407; Tex. Hum. Res. Code Ann. § 36.004(a)(1), (2); Utah Code Ann. § 26–20–9.5. Criminal restitution awards are not dischargeable in bankruptcy, but litigation in the bankruptcy court may be necessary to determine the amount of damages for which restitution can be properly awarded if the defendant was not given an adequate opportunity to litigate the question in the criminal proceedings. In re Sokol, 113 F.3d 303 (2d Cir.1997).

18. See, e.g., Ark. Code Ann. §§ 5–55–107(b) ($3000 per claim), 5–55–108 (double amount fraudulently received plus up to $2000 for each claim judicially found to be fraudulently claimed), 20–77–903 ($5000 to $10,000 per claim); Ill. Rev. Stat. ch. 23, ¶ 8A–7(b) (triple damages plus $2000 per violation); United States ex rel. Fahner v. Alaska, 591 F.Supp. 794 (N.D.Ill.1984) (assessing $2000 plus treble damages for each of 551 claims); La. Rev. Stat. Ann. § 46:442; Miss. Code Ann. § 43–13–225 (triple the amount received); N.H. Rev. Stat. Ann. § 167:61 (the greater of three times amount or $2000); N.M. Stat. Ann. § 30–44–8 (two times the amount plus $5000 per claim); N.Y. Soc. Serv. Law § 145–b; (three times the amount paid or $5000, whichever is greater for fraud, a penalty of up to $2000 per claim for abuse); Ohio Rev. Code Ann. § 5111.03 ($5000 to $10,000 per claim plus three times amount of excess payments); Okla. Stat. tit. 56, § 1007 (twice the amount or $2000 per violation); 62 Pa. Stat. § 1407 (treble damages); R.I. Gen. Laws §§ 40–8.2–5 (treble damages), 40–8.2–12(d)($1000 per violation); Tex. Hum. Res. Code Ann. § 36.004 (twice the amount paid plus $1000 to $10,000 per violation); Utah Code § 26–20–9.5 (three times the amount claimed or up to $2000 per violation); W.Va. Code § 9–7–6 (treble damages); Wis. Stat. § 49.49(1)(c) (three times actual damages).

19. See, e.g., Ark. Code Ann. § 20–77–903(b); N.M. Stat. Ann. § 30–44–8(C); Ohio. Rev. Code Ann. §§ 2913.40(F), 5111.03(B)(4); Okla. Stat. tit. 56, § 1007(A)(3); Utah Code Ann. § 26–20–9.5; W. Va. Code § 9–7–6.

attributable to the offense,[20] or for injunctive relief.[21] A couple of states have provisions for return of improperly obtained payments with interest, but without additional penalties, where no intention to defraud is shown.[22] Finally, the Arkansas and Texas statutes authorize lower penalties for providers who voluntarily disclose information regarding violations they have committed within 30 days of their becoming aware of the violation and before any proceedings with respect to the violation have begun.[23]

In some states these penalties are imposed pursuant to a criminal conviction by the criminal court.[24] Also common are statutes resembling the federal False Claims Act, authorizing recoveries through civil litigation without the need for a criminal conviction.[25] As with the federal law, such civil penalties are generally held to be civil in nature and thus not to create double jeopardy problems where there is also a criminal conviction.[26] A recent New York case held that a criminal conviction collaterally estops the defendant from contesting liability in a subsequent civil penalty case, and that civil penalties were cumulative to restitution awarded in the criminal case.[27] A few states have adopted qui tam statutes permitting private litigants to recover bounties in civil actions brought against persons who submit false claims.[28] These are discussed further in chapter 6.

---

20. See, e.g., Ill. Rev. Stat. ch. 23, ¶ 8A–3(d); Ohio Rev. Code Ann. § 2933.73. See also Kuriansky v. Bed–Stuy Health Care Corp., 135 A.D.2d 160, 525 N.Y.S.2d 225 (1988) (upholding forfeiture proceeding).

21. R.I. Gen. Laws § 40–8.2–12; Tex. Hum. Res. Code Ann. § 36.004(e)(1).

22. See, e.g., N.J. Rev. Stat. § 30:4D–17(f); Ohio Rev. Code Ann. § 5111.03(D).

23. Ark. Code Ann. § 20–77–903(a); Tex. Hum. Res. Code § 36.004(c). Under the Texas law the disclosure must be made before an investigation is initiated, under the Arkansas law it must be made before the provider becomes aware of an investigation.

24. Ark. Code Ann. § 5–55–107; Nev. Rev. Stat. § 422.410; 62 Pa. Cons. Stat. § 1407(b)(2). Under the Wisconsin law a separate civil action must be brought, but proof of a criminal conviction is conclusive evidence of liability in such a proceeding. Wis. Stat. § 49.49.

25. Ark. Code Ann. § 20–77–903; La. Rev. Stat. Ann. § 442; Miss. Code Ann. § 43–13–225; Okla. Stat. tit. 15, § 1007; 62 Pa. Cons. Stat. § 1407(c)(1); R.I. Gen. Laws §§ 40–8.2–5, 40–8.2–12(d);

Utah Code Ann. § 26–20–9.5; W. Va. Code § 9–7–6.

26. People ex rel. Dep't Pub. Aid v. Bell, 121 Ill.App.3d 1017, 77 Ill.Dec. 422, 460 N.E.2d 478 (Ill.Ct.App.1984); State Dep't of Public Aid v. Greenlee, 61 Ill. App.3d 649, 19 Ill.Dec. 78, 378 N.E.2d 579 (Ill.Ct.App.1978); Matter of Garay, 89 N.J. 104, 444 A.2d 1107 (N.J. 1982); Kuriansky v. Professional Care, Inc. 147 Misc.2d 782, 555 N.Y.S.2d 1 (1990); Harvey–Cook v. Miroff, 130 A.D.2d 621, 515 N.Y.S.2d 551 (N.Y.App.Div.1987), app. denied, 70 N.Y.2d 616, 526 N.Y.S.2d 436, 521 N.E.2d 443 (N.Y. 1988). See also, Matter of Kaplan, 178 N.J.Super. 487, 429 A.2d 590 (N.J.Super.Ct.App.Div.1981) (stating that the purpose of civil penalties is to recover state's cost of investigation and prosecution).

27. State v. Stokols, 652 N.Y.S.2d 7 (App. Div. 1996). See also, Kuriansky v. Orvieto, 653 N.Y.S.2d 953 (App. Div. 1997), upholding a default judgment entered in a civil penalty case brought on the basis of a criminal judgment.

28. Cal. Gov't Code § 12650–55 (relator may retain 15–33% of recovery where state intervenes, 25–50% where it

Specific statutes outlawing Medicaid fraud are only one of the paths open to the states for addressing Medicaid false claims. As is true on the federal side, state criminal prosecutors tend to bring prosecutions under laws prohibiting theft or larceny;[29] theft or larceny by deception;[30] obtaining money under false pretenses;[31] or general state laws prohibiting false claims.[32]

As in federal false claims cases, the most frequently litigated substantive issues in state false claim cases are whether the claim was in fact false and fraudulent and whether the claim was presented with the requisite intent. Obviously the treatment of these issues varies somewhat from state to state depending on the statutes at issue.

With respect to the first issue, a claim can be found false and fraudulent if the services claimed were in fact not rendered, or were not rendered in the required fashion.[33] A claim can also be found false or fraudulent if the code submitted does not describe the service in fact rendered.[34] Cost reports that claim costs improperly are also characteristic of false claims.[35] In several cases a fraud conviction has been upheld where the defendant claimed payment for services he had not performed, even though the defendant argued that services he did in fact perform were of equivalent value.[36] A defendant can also be convicted for billing for "unnecessary" services under a general prohibition against false, fictitious and fraudulent claims.[37] As under the federal law, if coding requirements are unclear and the defendant adopts a "not unreasonable"

declines to do so); Fla. Stat. ch. 68,081–92 (Supp. 1995) (relator may retain 15–25% of recovery if state intervenes, 25–30% if it fails to do so); Tenn. Code Ann. §§ 56–26–401 ("The Tennessee Health Care False Claims Act"), 71–5–182 ("The Tennessee Medicaid False Claims Act"); Ill. Rev. Stat. ch. 740, ¶ 174. See, examining state false claims acts, John Boese, Civil False Claims and Qui Tam Actions chapter 6 (1995).

29. People v. Evans, 199 A.D.2d 191, 605 N.Y.S.2d 287 (N.Y.App.Div.1993); People v. Weinberg, 183 A.D.2d 931, 586 N.Y.S.2d 224 (N.Y.App.Div.), app. denied, 80 N.Y.2d 977, 591 N.Y.S.2d 147, 605 N.E.2d 883 (N.Y. 1992); State v. Alizadeh, 87 A.D.2d 418, 452 N.Y.S.2d 425 (N.Y.App.Div.1982).

30. State v. Brown, 99 Ohio App.3d 604, 651 N.E.2d 470 (1994); State v. Quinn, 43 Wash.App. 696, 719 P.2d 936 (Wash.Ct.App.1986); State v. Kennedy, 105 Wis.2d 625, 314 N.W.2d 884 (Wis. Ct.App.1981) (theft by fraud).

31. Sheriff, Clark County v. Spagnola, 101 Nev. 508, 706 P.2d 840 (Nev. 1985); People v. Bovee, 92 Mich.App. 42, 285 N.W.2d 53 (Mich.Ct.App.1979).

32. People v. Weinberg, 183 A.D.2d 931, 586 N.Y.S.2d 224 (N.Y.App.Div. 1992); People v. Tarikere, 173 A.D.2d 660, 570 N.Y.S.2d 235 (N.Y.App.Div. 1991).

33. State v. Heath, 513 So.2d 493 (La.Ct.App.1987) (generic drugs billed as name brand by pharmacist).

34. See State v. Romero, 533 So.2d 1264 (La.Ct.App.1988), aff'd in part and dismissed in part, 574 So.2d 330 (La. 1990); State v. Cargille, 507 So.2d 1254 (La.Ct.App. 1987).

35. Commonwealth v. Minkin, 14 Mass.App.Ct. 911, 436 N.E.2d 955 (1982).

36. People v. Freda, 817 P.2d 588 (Colo.Ct.App.1991).

37. In re Wayne County Prosecutor, 121 Mich.App. 798, 329 N.W.2d 510 (1982).

interpretation of those requirements, the defendant is not guilty even though the state urges a different interpretation.[38]

A defendant can be convicted of filing false claims even though the claim was actually prepared by an intermediary at the defendant's instruction.[39] Conversely, a provider can be convicted of submitting fraudulent claims, even though the claims deceived Blue Cross, which made payments for the state, and the state was only defrauded through Blue Cross.[40] Indeed, courts in several states have held that a provider can be convicted for presented a fraudulent claim even though the fraud does not actually succeed in the sense of causing the state to lose money.[41]

With respect to the state of mind that must be shown to establish liability, most statutes require a showing that the defendant knowingly committed an offense.[42] A physician can be found guilty of knowingly filing a false claim if he was on notice of proper billing guidelines and deviated from these guidelines.[43] Though appellate courts occasionally reject trial court findings of intent to defraud where it is not sufficiently clear,[44] they generally affirm trial court verdicts based on circumstantial evidence.[45] A defen-

---

38. Commonwealth v. Stein, 519 Pa. 137, 546 A.2d 36 (1988); Clark County v. Spagnola, 101 Nev. 508, 706 P.2d 840, 844 (1985).

39. State v. Freda, 817 P.2d 588 (Colo.Ct.App.1991).

40. Id.

41. State v. Griffon, 448 So.2d 1287 (La.1984); State v. Hunte, 436 So.2d 806 (Ala.1983).

42. One statute defines knowingly in terms of a person being "aware that his conduct will probably cause a certain result or will probably be of a certain nature." Ohio Rev. Code Ann. § 2901.22(B), cited in State v. Brown, 99 Ohio App.3d 604, 651 N.E.2d 470 (1994).

43. People v. Orzame, Nos. 194559, 95–003154–AR, 194566, 95–003153–AR, 1997 WL 405354 (Mich.Ct.App. July 15, 1997)

44. People v. Lee, 134 Mich.App. 278, 351 N.W.2d 294, 300 (1984) (statistical evidence of improbability of treatment not enough); Commonwealth v. Lurie, 524 Pa. 56, 569 A.2d 329 (1990) (Medicaid fraud requires proof of knowing or intentional conduct, mere recklessness or negligence do not suffice); People v. Alizadeh, 87 A.D.2d 418, 452 N.Y.S.2d 425 (1982) (court interpreted evidence to show ineptitude and inexperience in billing by physician rather than intentional fraud).

45. See, e.g., State v. Romero, 574 So.2d 330 (La.1990) (instructions to bill for comprehensive visits regardless of services rendered constitute fraud); State v. McDermitt, 406 So.2d 195 (La. 1981); State v. Romero, 533 So.2d 1264 (La.Ct.App.1988) (billing practices constitute Medicaid fraud); State v. Heath, 513 So.2d 493 (La.Ct.App.1987) (billing for brand-name drugs while supplying generic sufficient evidence of intent to defraud); State v. Cargille, 507 So.2d 1254 (La.Ct.App.1987) (pattern of billing in violation of state regulations despite repeated warnings); People v. American Medical Ctrs. of Mich., 118 Mich.App. 135, 324 N.W.2d 782 (Ct.App.1982) (constructive knowledge sufficient to convict clinic and physician of Medicaid fraud); In re Wayne County Prosecutor, 121 Mich.App. 798, 329 N.W.2d 510 (Ct.App. 1982) (physician's possession and use of Medicaid Manual and authorization for noncompensable services provided factual support for inference that defendant knew claims were false); State v. Brown, 99 Ohio App.3d 604, 651 N.E.2d 470, 472 (Ct.App.1994) (evidence that doctor billed repeatedly incorrectly despite possession of the provider handbook explaining coding and earlier warning from an auditor); State v. Venman, 564 A.2d 574, 580 (Vt.1989) (doctor's conduct showed that he understood defini-

dant's assertion that he believed himself morally entitled to improper payments because of the inadequacy of Medicaid rates is not a defense to a claim of intent to defraud.[46] Though professionals cannot be found vicariously liable for false claims filed by their employees and agents, circumstantial evidence can be relied upon to demonstrate knowledge of, and legal accountability for, fraudulent billing by professionals even though the bill was submitted by others.[47] This is particularly true where the defendant in fact signed the false claim. The Florida statute goes the farthest in imposing liability by creating an inference that one who signs a false claim knows it to be false.[48]

The state cases, like their federal counterparts, also raise a host of procedural and evidentiary issues. For the most part, these questions arise under the general criminal and civil law of the state, though at least one state has a statute authorizing investigative demands for Medicaid fraud cases.[49] Issues of privileges tend to be particularly contentious. These issues are discussed in chapter 7.

§ 2–7. Proof of False Claims Cases

False claims cases generally involve complex facts that can only be proved through expert testimony. In cases involving billing or cost report issues, testimony from experts on billing, coding, or cost reporting will often be necessary.[1] Evidence comparing the defendant's billing practices to those of peers may also be instructive.[2] In cases in which the medical necessity of services is at issue, testimony by medical experts may be required. Cases alleging that the defendant did not in fact provide services for which payment was claimed may require testimony from patient witnesses as well.[3]

tion of "consultation" under Medicaid program, despite assertions to the contrary).

46. People v. Freda, 817 P.2d 588 (Colo.Ct.App.1991); State v. Cargille 507 So.2d 1254, 1260 (La.Ct.App.1987).

47. State v. Quinn, 43 Wash.App. 696, 719 P.2d 936 (1986); State v. Heath, 513 So.2d 493 (La.Ct.App.1987).

48. Fla. Stat. ch. 409.920(6). The Florida statute also provides that repayment of Medicaid payments wrongfully obtained is not a defense to criminal charges for Medicaid fraud. Fla. Stat. ch. 409.920(3). See also, Nev. Stat. § 422.530(2), providing that a person shall be deemed to have made a false claim if he had responsibility for making, authorizing, or supervising the person who made the claim and exercised or failed to exercise that responsibility,

resulting, directly or indirectly, in the false claim.

49. R.I. Gen. Laws § 40–8.2–14.

§ 2–7

1. See United States v. Gold, 743 F.2d 800 (11th Cir.1984); State v. Ruud, 259 N.W.2d 567 (Minn.1977); Sheriff v. Spagnola, 101 Nev. 508, 706 P.2d 840 (1985).

2. Peer group comparisons can be used by the government to show that the defendant's billing practices were unique, Spagnola, 706 P.2d at 843, or by the defendant to show that the defendant's billing practices were like those of other physicians, and thus not based on an intent to defraud, United States v. Hooshmand, 931 F.2d 725, 732 (11th Cir.1991).

3. United States v. Hooshmand, 931 F.2d at 733; People v. American Medical

Where intent is at issue, as it often is in false claims cases, proof of extrinsic criminal acts may be admissible.[4] Cases involving large numbers of claims will often involve computer generated summaries.[5] They may also involve statistical extrapolations from a relatively small but statistically significant sample of claims to the entire universe of a defendant's claims.[6]

The evidentiary issues encountered in proving false claims cases are not in general unique, or even particular, to these cases. They are discussed at length in other sources,[7] and not treated in this Treatise in detail.

Ctrs. of Mich., 118 Mich.App. 135, 324 N.W.2d 782, 791 (Ct.App.1982).

4. United States v. Hooshmand, 931 F.2d at 736.

5. See Pamela Bucy, The Poor Fit of Traditional Evidentiary Doctrine and Sophisticated Crimes, An Empirical Analysis of Health Care Prosecutions, 63 Fordham L. Rev. 383, 438–49 (1994).

6. Sherryl Michaelson, Use of Statistical Evidence in Criminal Health Care Fraud Prosecutions, in American Bar Assoc., Health Care Fraud, 1996, at J–21.

7. Mark Biros, Complex Trial Issues in Health Care Fraud Cases, American Bar Assoc. Health Care Fraud, 1995 at E–1; Pamela Bucy, Health Care Fraud: Criminal, Civil and Administrative Law, § 7.01 et seq.; Bucy, supra note 5.

Chapter 3

THE ANTI–KICKBACK LAWS

Table of Sections

WESTLAW Electronic Research

See WESTLAW Electronic Research Guide preceding the Summary of Contents.

Library References:

West's Key No. Digests, Social Security and Public Welfare ⋘18.

§ 3–1.　Introduction

Federal and state anti-kickback statutes provide health care providers with another major basis for concern about civil, administrative and criminal liability. Anti-kickback laws prohibit the exchange of remuneration for referrals of patients, or for goods or services for which compensation may later be sought under publicly funded health care programs. The federal government and three-quarters of the states have enacted anti-kickback laws. The premise of these laws is that when a medical professional is motivated to make a referral by how much of a profit the referral will bring him rather than the quality of treatment his patients will receive, his patients will suffer, program funds will be unnecessarily depleted, and taxpayer dollars will be wasted. Anti-kickback provisions are thus designed to stop the drain on program funds that would result from health care providers overutilizing medical services for their own profit.

As explored more fully below, Congress passed the first federal anti-kickback statute in 1972,[1] making it a misdemeanor for any individual or entity to solicit, offer or receive a kickback or bribe in connection with any item or service reimbursable under the Medicare or Medicaid programs. In the ensuing decades, the Social Security Act of 1972 was repeatedly amended, both to strengthen the provisions[2] and to exclude from the reach of the provisions (or carve out "safe harbors" for) certain business arrangements deemed innocent and beneficial that otherwise would have been prohibited under the Act.[3]

Although the anti-kickback law's objective—deterring providers from referring Medicare or Medicaid business in order to increase their own profits—might seem uncontroversial, in practice the provisions have generated enormous controversy. Indeed, controversy surrounding the federal anti-kickback statute has greatly exceeded that surrounding the much more frequently used False Claims Act. Why? At least part of the answer has to do with the complexity of the anti-kickback rules themselves and the width of the net that the rules cast. While False Claims Act prosecutions have historically targeted the unquestionably corrupt billing practices of a small sector of the health care community, providers fear

---

§ 3–1

1. The Social Security Amendments of 1972, Pub.L.No. 92–603, 86 Stat. 1329 (1972).

2. See The Medicare and Medicaid Anti–Fraud and Abuse Amendments of 1977, Pub.L.No. 95–142, 91 Stat. 1175 (1977), which enhanced anti-kickback violations from misdemeanor to felony status, increased the criminal fine and term of imprisonment that could be imposed for a violation of the anti-kickback provisions, and broadened the language of the statute to allow for the prosecution of more members of the health care industry. See discussion infra at § 3–6. See also The Medicare and Medicaid Patient and Program Protection Act of 1987, Pub.L.No. 100–93, 101 Stat. 680, (1987) (codified as amended at 42 U.S.C.A. § 1320a–7(b)(7)), which added an administrative sanction against health care providers who engaged in unlawful kickback activity by authoriz-

ing the Department of Health and Human Services' (HHS's) Office of Inspector General (OIG) to exclude a provider from participation in the federally funded programs. See § 3.9; see also Chapter 5.

3. See Medicare and Medicaid Patient and Program Protection Act of 1987, Pub.L.No. 100–93, 101 Stat. 680 (1987)(codified as amended at 42 U.S.C.A. § 1320a–7(b)(7)) (excluding from the reach of the statute properly disclosed discount agreements and payments to bona fide employees); Omnibus Reconciliation Act of 1980, Pub.L.No. 96–499, 94 Stat. 2599 (1980) (adding an intent element to the statute); See The Medicare and Medicaid Patient and Program Protection Act of 1987, Pub.L.No. 100–93, § 14, 101 Stat. 680, 697 (1987) (directing the Secretary of HHS to promulgate "safe harbors" to protect legitimate or innocuous business arrangements).

that the anti-kickback provisions will outlaw "innocent" referral arrangements used throughout the industry.

In truth, prosecutors have relied on the anti-kickback provisions far less frequently than other health care fraud statutes as the basis for prosecution, and the intensifying battle over the mental state required for a kickback violation will likely cause prosecutors to shy away from the statute even more.[4] Nevertheless, the anti-kickback laws arm federal and state investigators with powerful weapons to defend publicly-funded health care programs against abusive referral behavior. Defenders of the provisions contend that anti-kickback laws are a requisite part of the arsenal needed to deter or punish providers who would contribute to the nation's spiraling health care costs by placing profit over the best interests of their patients.

This chapter first examines the federal anti-kickback statute and traces the statute's evolution through legislative amendment, agency and judicial interpretation and the promulgation of "safe harbor" regulations. The chapter reviews the guidance that the Department of Health and Human Services (HHS) has provided to the industry over time regarding the meaning and effect of the federal anti-kickback provisions through advisory opinions, intermediary letters and special fraud alerts. Also considered is the judiciary's varied response to the provisions, and in particular, the raging debate over the statute's *mens rea* requirement. The chapter also examines the newly mandated advisory opinion process. Finally it considers the response of the states to the problem of corrupt referral practices.

§ 3–2. The Current Federal Anti–Kickback Law

The federal anti-kickback statute[1] makes it a felony for individuals or entities knowingly and willfully to offer or pay[2] or to solicit or receive,[3] remuneration in order to induce business reimbursed under any federal health care program.[4] Subsection 1128B(b)(1) of the Social Security Act, amended as recently as August 1996,[5] provides as follows:

4. See discussion infra § 3–13.

§ 3–2

1. 42 U.S.C.A. § 1320a–7b(b)(1) and (2).

2. See 42 U.S.C.A. § 1320a–7b(b)(2).

3. See 42 U.S.C.A. § 1320a–7b(b)(1).

4. The term "Federal health care program" is defined as "any plan or program that provides health benefits, whether directly, through insurance, or otherwise, which is funded directly, in

whole or in part, by the United States Government," or "any State health care program, as defined in section 1128(h)." HIPAA, Pub.L.No. 104–91, § 204(a)(7), 110 Stat. 1936, 2000 (1996).

5. See Health Insurance Portability and Accountability Act of 1996 (hereinafter HIPAA), Pub.L.No. 104–191, Title II § 204, 110 Stat. 1936 (1996), 42 U.S.C.A. 1320a–7b (West Supp.1997).

(1) Whoever knowingly and willfully solicits or receives any remuneration (including any kickback, bribe, or rebate) directly or indirectly, overtly or covertly, in cash or in kind—

(A) in return for referring an individual to a person for the furnishing or arranging for the furnishing of any item or service for which payment may be made in whole or in part under a Federal health care program, or

(B) in return for purchasing, leasing, ordering, or arranging for or recommending purchasing, leasing, or ordering any good, facility, service, or item for which payment may be made in whole or in part under a Federal health care program, shall be guilty of a felony....[6]

Section 1128B(b)(2) of the Social Security Act provides:

(2) whoever knowingly and willfully offers or pays any remuneration (including any kickback, bribe, or rebate) directly or indirectly, overtly or covertly, in cash or in kind to any person to induce such person—

(A) to refer an individual to a person for the furnishing or arranging for the furnishing of any item or service for which payment may be made in whole or in part under a Federal health care program, or

(B) to purchase, lease, order, or arrange for or recommend purchasing, leasing, or ordering any good, facility, service, or item for which payment may be made in whole or in part under a Federal health care program, shall be guilty of a felony....[7]

Each violation of the statute is punishable by a fine of up to $25,000,[8] a term of imprisonment of up to five years, or both,[9] in addition to mandatory exclusion of at least five years from federal health care programs following a criminal conviction.[10] The statute provides a narrow discretionary exception to mandatory exclusion upon conviction:

---

6. 42 U.S.C.A. § 1320a–7b(b)(1)(A) and (B) (West Supp.1997).

7. 42 U.S.C.A. § 1320a–7b(b)(2)(A) and (B) (West Supp.1997).

8. 42 U.S.C.A. § 1320a–7b(b)(1) and (2) (1994).

9. 42 U.S.C.A. § 1320a–7b(b)(1) and (2) (1994). Upon conviction, the exact length of the term of imprisonment will be determined at sentencing with reference to the United States Sentencing Guidelines. The Guidelines are discussed more fully in Chapter 8.

10. An order of exclusion of at least five years must be imposed upon any person or entity convicted of a "criminal offense related to the delivery of an item or service" under the Medicare, Medicaid or other state health care program, 42 U.S.C.A. § 1320a–7(a)(1), or a "criminal offense relating to neglect or abuse of patients in connection with the delivery of a health care item or service." 42 U.S.C.A. § 1320a–7(a)(2). For a more complete discussion of the Secretary's exclusion authority see Chapter 5.

(B) In the case of an exclusion under subsection (a) of this section, the minimum period of exclusion shall be not less than five years, except that, upon the request of a State, the Secretary may waive the exclusion under subsection (a)(1) of this section in the case of an individual or entity that is the sole community physician or sole source of essential specialized services in a community. The Secretary's decision whether to waive the exclusion shall not be reviewable.[11]

Exclusion is mandatory even if the conviction results from a voluntary plea of guilt rather than a verdict of guilt by jury after trial.[12] In addition, the Secretary of Health and Human Services is permitted to bring an exclusion action against any individual or entity convicted of a host of other offenses (including fraud, theft, embezzlement, breach of fiduciary responsibility and financial misconduct) in connection with the delivery of an item or service financed by one of the federally funded health care programs. Obstructing an official investigation of any such offense also provides the basis for an order of exclusion.[13] The Balanced Budget Act of 1997[14] added new penalties to the Secretary's arsenal. The Act included an enhanced civil monetary penalty provision for violators of the anti-kickback statute[15] as well as a "three-strikes-you're-out" provision mandating the permanent exclusion from any federal health care program of any provider convicted of three health care-related offenses.[16] Providers convicted of a second health care-related of-

11. 42 U.S.C.A. § 1320a–7(c)(3)(B) (1994).

12. See Travers v. Sullivan, 791 F.Supp. 1471 (E.D.Wash.1992), aff'd sub nom. Travers v. Shalala, 20 F.3d 993 (9th Cir. 1994) (physician who pled no contest to charge of knowingly filing false medical claim involving Medicaid reimbursement was "convicted" of "program-related crime" and thus five-year exclusion was mandatory). At least one court has held further that federal district courts lack the power to stay a congressionally mandated suspension of a physician following criminal conviction during pendency of a habeas corpus proceeding. See Einaugler v. Dowling, 862 F.Supp. 793 (E.D.N.Y.1994)(memorandum order).

13. See 42 U.S.C.A. § 1320a–7(b)(2) (1994).

14. Pub.L.No. 105–33, Title V, § 4304; 111 Stat. 251 (1997), amending the Social Security Act, § 1128(c)(3), (to be codified at 42 U.S.C.A. 1396v).

15. See Social Security Act, § 1128A(a), 42 U.S.C.A. 1320a–7a(a), as amended by Pub.L.No. 105–33, § 4304(b) (1997), which permits the Secretary to impose civil monetary penalties on any person who "commits an act described in paragraph (1) or (2) of section 1128B(b)." The new authority is applicable to any kickback violation occurring after the enactment of the Balanced Budget Act. See Pub.L.No. 105–33, § 4304(c). The amount of the civil monetary penalties that may be imposed has been set at $50,000 for each kickback violation, or "damages of not more than 3 times the total amount of remuneration offered, paid, solicited, or received, without regard to whether a portion of such remuneration was offered, paid, solicited, or received for a lawful purpose." Social Security Act § 1128A(a), 42 U.S.C.A. § 1320a–7a(a), as amended by Pub.L.No. 105–33, § 4304.

16. Pub.L.No. 105–33, Title V, § 4301, 111 Stat. 251 (1997), amending the Social Security Act, § 1128(c)(3)(G)(i).

fense will face a mandatory 10–year exclusion term under the proposed provisions.[17]

§ 3-3. The Varied Face of Unlawful Kickback Arrangements

Health care fraud investigators will look behind the formal labels of a business arrangement and scrutinize a transaction's underlying intent. A provider's self-serving description of a remuneration arrangement (by, for example, referring to the exchange as a "consulting fee," "interpretive fee," "loan," etc.), will not save the arrangement if a prosecutor is able to establish that the provider was actually motivated to make the payments by the prospect of receiving patient referrals for whom goods or services financed in whole or part by one of the programs. Indeed, a wide array of incentives offered within the industry have been considered unlawful kickbacks under the federal statute, including "consulting fees" paid by a laboratory to osteopathic physicians to induce them to send their patients' specimens to the laboratory for testing;[1] payments from a laboratory to a mobile medical group president substantially in excess of the value of the services provided by the group to the laboratory;[2] "interpretation fees" paid to referring physicians by a medical diagnostic company that provided reimbursable Halter monitor services to referred patients;[3] compensation for "consulting services" paid by an ambulance service company to a hospital employee who was responsible for considering ambulance service bids on the hospital's behalf;[4] grant offers made by a prescription drug company to physicians in a position to prescribe the company's products nominally in exchange for performing inconsequential studies of the company's drugs;[5] loan

---

17. See id. Providers may face additional difficulties if private individuals are permitted to bring actions under the False Claims Act (see Chapter 2) based on an alleged violation of the anti-kickback provisions. See, e.g., United States ex rel. Pogue v. American Healthcorp, Inc., 914 F.Supp. 1507 (M.D.Tenn.1996). But see United States ex rel. Thompson v. Columbia/HCA Healthcare Corp., 938 F.Supp. 399 (S.D.Tex.1996). See also Chapter 4, § 4–3.

§ 3-3

1. See United States v. Tapert, 625 F.2d 111 (6th Cir.1980).

2. See United States v. Lipkis, 770 F.2d 1447 (9th Cir.1985).

3. See United States v. Greber, 760 F.2d 68 (3d Cir. 1985), cert. denied, 474 U.S. 988, 106 S.Ct. 396, 88 L.Ed.2d 348 (1985), overruled in part on other

grounds by United States v. Friedberg, 1997 WL 36997 (E.D.Pa.1997).

4. See United States v. Bay State Ambulance and Hospital Rental Serv., Inc., 874 F.2d 20 (1st Cir.1989).

5. See settlement reached between the Office of Inspector General of the Department of Health and Human Services and Hoffman–LaRoche. Hoffman–LaRoche agreed to pay $450,000 and to establish a corporate integrity program to settle civil and administrative charges that it had violated the anti-kickback provisions by selecting for its grant program physicians who were able to prescribe Hoffman–LaRoche's product, and had paid some of these physicians despite the fact that they had not completed research for the studies. See 3 BNA's Health Law Reporter 36 (Sept. 15, 1994).

guarantees, lucrative lease agreements and "practice enhancement payments" made by a health home care organization to physicians in exchange for referrals;[6] payments solicited and received by the president of a medical center from medical laboratories in exchange for referring blood specimens from Medicare beneficiaries to the labs for analysis and testing;[7] "consulting" payments made by an oxygen supply company to a group of physicians to induce referrals,[8] alcoholic beverages provided by pharmaceutical supplier to administrator of nursing homes,[9] salaries of a physician's receptionist paid by a laboratory to which the physician referred business,[10] and more.

§ 3–4. The Evolution of the Federal Anti–Kickback Provisions

Since its creation almost a quarter of a century ago, the federal anti-kickback law has been the subject of criticism and praise, expansion and retrenchment. Significant refinements of the statute took effect on January 1, 1997.[1] Additional amendments were enacted as a part of the 1997 budget negotiations.[2]

Disputes over the federal anti-kickback provisions have centered on the breadth of the statute and the proper construction of its terms. Critics of the statute maintain that the provisions paint conduct as unlawful with too broad a stroke, and that if the provisions are not construed narrowly, desirable competitive conduct within the health care marketplace will be stifled.[3] Providers complain further that the provisions are impossible to fathom and that calls for guidance from the Department of Health and Human Services (HHS) on how the provisions impact particular business arrangements occurring within the industry have gone unheeded. In light of these difficulties, it is urged, the statute should be construed narrowly so as to avoid ensnaring innocent providers understandably perplexed by the statute's imprecise terms. Sup-

6. See Plea Agreement of United States v. Horizon Group Enterprises Inc., 97 Cr. 0022 (N.D. Ind.) (filed April 28, 1997) discussed in 1 BNA's Health Care Fraud Reports 330 (May 21, 1997).

7. See United States v. Lima, No. 96–390–CR–G (S.D.F.L. 1996), discussed in Health Care Fraud Litigation Reporter 14–15 (January 1997).

8. See Settlement Agreement, United States v. Apria Healthcare Group, Inc., No. 1:95–CV–2142–FMH (N.D. Ga. February 4, 1997) as discussed in DME Supplier, Three Providers Settle Medicare Fraud Charges for $2 Million, BNA Health Care Daily (Feb. 5, 1997).

9. See United States v. Perlstein, 632 F.2d 661 (6th Cir.1980)(per curiam), cert. denied, 449 U.S. 1084, 101 S.Ct. 871, 66 L.Ed.2d 809 (1981).

10. See Illinois v. Bynum, 197 Ill. App.3d 959, 557 N.E.2d 238, 145 Ill.Dec. 468 (1990).

§ 3–4

1. See HIPAA, Pub.L.No. 104–91, Title II, 110 Stat. 1936 (1996).

2. See The Balanced Budget Act of 1997, Pub.L.No. 105–33, 111 Stat. 251 (1997).

3. See James Blumstein, Rationalizing the Fraud and Abuse Statute, 15 Health Affairs 118 (Winter 1996).

porters of the provisions answer that kickback arrangements are common to the industry and that the arrangements have depleted program funds and contributed to rapidly escalating health care costs. Such unscrupulous behavior, it is argued, ultimately threatens the integrity of the federal programs. In this view, only a broad construction of the statute, and severe punishment of offenders will deter costly overutilization of program goods and supplies.

The truth of the matter likely falls somewhere in between these conflicting views. The language of the statute itself is indeed broad, providing the government with the authority to challenge a wide assortment of referral arrangements taking place in the industry. In practice, however, the government has relied on the anti-kickback statute far less often than the other health care fraud provisions as a means for addressing programmatic abuses. When it has been relied upon, the unlawful nature of the referral arrangement has typically been readily apparent.[4] No matter which side of the battlefield one finds oneself on, one of the biggest challenges in this dynamic area of the law is understanding the genesis of the federal anti-kickback law, the major quarrels that the law has engendered over time, and the evolving judicial and legislative responses to criticism of the anti-kickback provisions. We begin by tracing the statute from its early origins.

§ 3–5. The Social Security Act of 1972

Congress passed the first anti-kickback provisions as a part of the Social Security Amendments of 1972 to bolster public confidence in the integrity of the Medicare and Medicaid programs.[1] The ground-breaking provisions were intended to augment laws already available to prosecutors to combat fraud within the industry,[2] and

---

4. See e.g., United States v. Greber, 760 F.2d 68 (3d Cir. 1985), cert. denied, 474 U.S. 988, 106 S.Ct. 396, 88 L.Ed.2d 348 (1985), overruled in part on other grounds by United States v. Friedberg, 1997 WL 36997 (E.D.Pa.1997). But see Hanlester Network v. Shalala, 51 F.3d 1390 (9th Cir.1995).

§ 3–5

1. Section 242(b) of the Social Security Amendments of 1972, Pub.L.No. 92–603, 86 Stat. 1329 (1972), added Sections 1877 and 1909 to the Act, which applied respectively to the Medicare and Medicaid programs. Initially, separate anti-kickback provisions were adopted for the Medicare and Medicaid programs. For the Medicare provision see The Social Security Act Amendments of 1972, Pub.L.No. 92–603, § 242(b), 86

Stat. 1329, 1419 (1972)(codified as amended at 42 U.S.C.A. § 1320a–7b(b)), which added § 1877(b) to the Act. For the Medicaid provision see The Social Security Act Amendments of 1972, Pub. L.No. 92–603, § 242(c), 86 Stat. 1329, 1419–20 (1972)(codified as amended at 42 U.S.C.A. § 1320a–7b(b)), which added § 1909(b) to the Act. In 1987, Congress combined the separate provisions into one. See Medicare and Medicaid Patient and Program Protection Act of 1987, Pub.L.No. 100–93, § 4(c)-(e), 101 Stat. 680, 689 (1987) (codified at 42 U.S.C.A. § 1320a–7b(b) (1994)).

2. Prior to the adoption of the anti-kickback provision, only fraudulent misrepresentations by providers were unlawful under the Act, (see § 208 of the Social Security Act), and the bulk of claims against providers were prosecut-

to spur the prosecution of any provider who "attempt[ed] by unlawful means to obtain payments not due him under the plan."[3] As originally drafted, the anti-kickback law made it a misdemeanor for any individual to furnish, solicit, offer or receive any kickback, bribe or rebate in connection with any item or service for which payment could be made under the Medicare or Medicaid programs. Sections 1877(b) and 1909(b) provided:

> (b) Whoever furnishes items or services to an individual for which payment is or may be made under this title and who solicits, offers, or receives any—

> (1) kickback or bribe in connection with the furnishing of such items or services or the making or receipt of such payment, or

> (2) rebate of any fee or charge for referring any such individual to another person for the furnishing of such items or services, shall be guilty of a misdemeanor.

Conviction under the provisions could lead to the imposition of a fine of up to $10,000, a maximum term of imprisonment of one year, or both.[4]

Several vexing issues under the statute quickly arose. What, if any, *mens rea* was required to violate the statute? What types of business arrangements did the statute preclude? Did joint venture arrangements that were beginning to mushroom in the health care market fall on the right or the wrong side of the law? The statute's express terms provided little help with these questions. The provisions themselves neither defined the terms "kickback, bribe or rebate," nor required prosecutors to prove that a health care provider intended to engage in conduct prohibited by the statute in order to obtain a conviction. Differences over the proper interpretation of the statute's pivotal terms soon spilled into the courts.

a. Early Conflicting Judicial Views of the Anti–Kickback Statute

The first courts to construe the anti-kickback statute did so narrowly, to the benefit of those charged with violations. These courts required prosecutors to prove the intentional exchange of a "corrupt payment" as a predicate for a kickback conviction. If the

---

ed under the federal false claims or general conspiracy provisions. For a thoughtful review of the early history of the anti-kickback statute, see Theodore N. McDowell, Comment, The Medicare–Medicaid Anti–Fraud and Abuse Amendments: Their Impact on The Present Health Care System, 36 Emory Law Journal 691, 715 (1987).

3. H.R. Rep. No. 92–231, pt. III(B)(2) (1972), reprinted in 1972 U.S.C.C.A.N. 4989, 5176.

4. Social Security Amendments of 1972, Pub.L.No. 92–603, § 242(b), 86 Stat. 1329, 1419 (1972)(codified as amended at 42 U.S.C.A. § 1320a–7b (1994)).

government failed to make such a showing, the courts dismissed anti-kickback charges or vacated jury verdicts of guilty. Later decisions, however, gave a more expansive reading to the statute's terms, permitting prosecutions to go forward even where the government was unable to show an actual loss emanating from the alleged kickback activity or actual interference with the proper functioning of a government-run program. The development of these conflicting judicial constructions is traced below.

b. The *Zacher* and *Porter* Decisions

Illustrative of the courts' early view of the statute is the interpretation first given to the term "bribe" by the United States Court of Appeals for the Second Circuit in *United States v. Zacher*.[5] William Zacher, joint-owner of a nursing home in Buffalo, New York, was convicted of soliciting "bribes" from the families of several Medicaid patients admitted to Zacher's nursing home. The government's proof established that Zacher would admit to the nursing home only those Medicaid patients whose families agreed to pay him an annual fee for the privilege of staying there. The government argued at trial that by demanding such a fee, Zacher had solicited bribes in violation of the anti-kickback provisions. Zacher defended the payments on the ground that they simply squared the fees that the home received from its Medicaid patients with those received from its private patients. (Zacher charged his private patients $29 per day, but the Medicaid program reimbursed him at a rate of only $25 per day. To make up the difference, Zacher required the families of all admitted Medicaid patients to pay an additional $4 per day to supplement the Medicaid reimbursements.) The government's view of the statute prevailed, and Zacher was convicted by a jury of violating the anti-kickback law. On appeal, however, the Second Circuit set aside the verdict and ordered that Zacher's indictment be dismissed. In a decision critical of the "sparse" and "inconclusive" legislative history underlying the statute, the court looked to common sense and the common law to construe the term "bribe," and concluded that the statute required a showing that Zacher had been given or offered a "corrupt payment" that was intended "to induce him to act dishonestly while acting in a position of trust."[6] According to the court, a payment (such as that made to Zacher) that did not either increase the government's costs, decrease the quality of care purchased by the government, or involve some misapplication of government funds, could not be characterized as corrupt.[7]

---

5. 586 F.2d 912 (2d Cir.1978). Although decided after the anti-kickback provision was amended, the court assessed the propriety of Zacher's conduct under the terms of original statute. See id. at 913.

6. Id. at 916.

7. See id.

A similar result was reached in *United States v. Porter*,[8] in which the United States Court of Appeals for the Fifth Circuit reversed a conviction secured under the original anti-kickback provisions based on a narrow interpretation of the term "kickback." In *Porter*, a group of Florida physicians sent their Medicare patients' blood samples to a laboratory in exchange for a "handling fee" for each specimen. The laboratory sought payment from the Medicaid program for the tests performed on the specimens.[9] After trial, the defendants were found guilty of having received kickbacks under the 1972 statute. The Fifth Circuit reversed. As in *Zacher*, the court concluded that the physicians had accepted no "bribes" within the meaning of the statute. Extending *Zacher* even further, the court held that the term "kickback" also required proof of " 'a corrupt payment or receipt of payment in violation of the duty imposed on providers of services to use federal funds only for intended purposes and only in the approved manner.' "[10] Unconvinced that such a corrupt payment had been made to the physicians, the court vacated the jury verdict.

The *Zacher* and *Porter* opinions spawned considerable debate about the proper interpretation of the 1972 statute. Although heralded by members of the industry, critics of the decisions argued that the court's constricted interpretations of the statute threatened to hamstring the government's efforts to ferret out fraud within the industry.

c. The *Hancock* and *Tapert* Decisions and Beyond

Other federal courts confronted with the question of how to construe the terms of the anti-kickback statute rejected the narrow interpretations of the *Zacher* and *Porter* courts and adopted a view more generous to the government.[11] In *United States v. Hancock*,[12] for example, the Seventh Circuit affirmed the convictions of a group of chiropractors who had accepted "handling fees" in exchange for referring to a laboratory the blood and tissue specimens of their Medicare and Medicaid patients. The court held that even if corrupt payments were required by the statute, the defendants' agreement to receive payments for referrals sufficiently exhibited that corruption.[13] In a later case, the same court rejected the suggestion that the government's costs had to have been increased in order for

8. 591 F.2d 1048 (5th Cir.1979).

9. See id. at 1051.

10. Id. at 1054 (quoting Zacher, 586 F.2d at 916).

11. See United States v. Hancock, 604 F.2d 999 (7th Cir.1979)(per curiam)

and United States v. Tapert, 625 F.2d 111 (6th Cir.1980). See also United States v. Lipkis, 770 F.2d 1447 (9th Cir. 1985).

12. 604 F.2d 999 (7th Cir.1979)(per curiam).

13. See id. at 1001.

payments to be considered unlawful.[14] It was enough, the court ruled, that the business arrangement had the potential to increase costs by encouraging the overutilization of goods and services which could be paid for by the programs,[15] or that the arrangement interfered with the public's right to an honestly run program.[16]

The United States Court of Appeals for the Sixth Circuit reached a similar result in *United States v. Tapert.*[17] There, the court affirmed the conviction of a group of physicians who had sent their patients' urine and blood samples to certain laboratories in return for payments referred to by the parties as "consulting fees." Relying on *Hancock*, the court upheld the denial of the defendants' motion to dismiss the charges holding that no actual interference with a governmental function was necessary to support a conviction under the statute.[18]

The courts' conflicting interpretations of the 1972 anti-kickback provisions added to the uncertainty generated by the indefinite wording of the statute itself. Prosecutors could not be sure that a challenged exchange of money or other property would be construed to be a kickback when the conduct was scrutinized by a reviewing court. At the same time providers had little assurance that their commercial arrangements would not be the subject of investigation and prosecution, or provide the basis for a criminal conviction or exclusion from a federally funded program.

14. See United States v. Ruttenberg, 625 F.2d 173 (7th Cir.1980) (nursing home owners who solicited and received monthly fees from a druggist for the opportunity to provide drugs and pharmaceutical services to its residents violated the 1972 fraud and abuse provisions even though the government had fixed the price of the drugs and services).

15. The Ruttenberg court placed special emphasis on the point that an arrangement need only have the potential to add to the costs of the program to be unlawful. It wrote:

Whether the costs were directly and immediately increased by those particular payments ... is irrelevant. The potential for increased costs if such 'fee' agreements become an established and accepted method of business is clearly an evil with which the court was concerned and one Congress sought to avoid in enacting § 1396(b)(1) ... [T]he law does not make increased cost to the govern-

ment the sole criterion of corruption. In prohibiting "kickbacks," Congress need not have spelled out the obvious truisms that, while unnecessary expenditure of money earned and contributed by taxpaying fellow citizens may exacerbate the result of the crime, kickback schemes can freeze competing suppliers from the system, can mask the possibility of government price reductions, can misdirect program funds, and, when proportional, can erect strong temptations to order more drugs and supplies than needed.

Id. at 176–77.

16. See id. at 177 n.9 ("A compassionate people have established and paid for a program of care for the aged among them. Nothing in that program gave to its empowered and privileged conductors carte blanche to manipulate within its fixed costs.... ").

17. See United States v. Tapert, 625 F.2d 111, 113 (6th Cir.1980).

18. See id. at 121.

§ 3–6. The Medicare and Medicaid Anti–Fraud and Abuse Amendments of 1977

Responding to calls for clarification of the original anti-kickback provisions, Congress held hearings in 1977 to consider the allegations of some that fraud continued to plague the health care system, and the complaints of others that the provisions went too far by branding innocent commercial arrangement as criminal kickbacks.[1] Following the hearings, Congress enacted the Medicare and Medicaid Anti–Fraud and Abuse Amendments of 1977 (MMAAA).[2] The amendments were at once an exercise in expansion and retrenchment. They exhibited both a concern that fraudulent and abusive practices continued to thrive within the publicly financed programs and a recognition that not all payment practices falling under the anti-kickback provisions improperly drained the programs.

To address the perceived abuses of the programs,[3] Congress extended the reach and strengthened the punch of the anti-kickback provisions in two important ways: it substituted the phrase "any remuneration" for the controversial phrase "bribes and kickbacks,"[4] and it stiffened penalties that could be imposed on any person or entity convicted of violating the statute.[5] Under the

§ 3–6

1. Several United States Attorneys complained during their testimony at those hearings that the courts' conflicting interpretations of the statute made it impossible for prosecutors to secure convictions of those engaged in wrongful kickback practices. See 123 Cong. Rec. S31772 (daily ed. Sept. 30, 1977) (statement of Sen. Church) ("U.S. attorneys ... testified that language of the Medicare/Medicaid fraud statute needs clarification.... New language will help better define what constitutes an illegal 'kickback' or 'rebate.' ").

2. Pub.L.No. 95–142, 91 Stat. 1175 (1977).

3. "Medicaid mills" (entities that derived the bulk of their profits from the "treatment" of anyone sporting a Medicaid number) were considered to be the most flagrant abusers of the Medicaid program. See H.R. Rep. No. 95–393, at 45 (1977), reprinted in 1977 U.S.C.C.A.N. 3039, 3047; see also Staff of Subcommittee on Health of House Committee on Ways and Means and of House Committee on Interstate and Foreign Commerce, 95th Cong., 1st Sess., Fraud and Abuse in the Medicare and Medicaid Programs 2 (Comm. Print 1977). Also of concern were the kickback practices of independent clinical laboratories, pharmaceutical companies, nursing homes, and independent physician practices. See, e.g., H.R. Rep. No. 95–393, pt. II, at 46–48 (1977), reprinted in 1977 U.S.C.C.A.N. 3039, 3048–49; Staff of Subcomm. on Oversight and Investigation of the House Comm. on Interstate and Foreign Commerce, 95th Cong., 1st Sess., Fraud and Abuse in Nursing Homes: Pharmaceutical Kickback Arrangements (Comm. Print 1977).

4. 42 U.S.C.A. §§ 1320a–7b(b)(1)(A) and (B)(West Supp. 1997), Social Security Act §§ 1128B (b)(1) and (2).

5. See 123 Cong. Rec. S31770 (daily ed. Sept. 30, 1977) (statement of Sen. Dole) ("In the past, our attempts to control these problems [of fraud and abuse in these programs] have met with limited success. This bill provides us with an opportunity to wage a stronger battle, with stronger weapons at our disposal."); 123 Cong. Rec. S31767 (daily ed. Sept. 30, 1977) (statement of Sen. Talmadge) (These amendments provide "an opportunity for the Congress to give a clear, loud signal to the thieves and the crooks and the abusers that we mean to call a halt to their exploitation of the public and the public purse.").

amended provisions, violations of the statute were upgraded from misdemeanor to felony status, with a maximum fine of up to $25,000 per violation, and a term of imprisonment of up to five years, or both.[6] The legislative history of the MMAAA amendments indicated the provisions were intended to be read broadly in favor of the government.[7] Congress apparently expected the phrase "any remuneration" to receive a more generous interpretation than had its predecessor phrase "bribes and kickbacks."

Although the MMAAA provision strengthened the hand of prosecutors in some respects, the provisions also reflected agreement with the concern that the provisions could be construed unfairly to treat genuinely innocent business transactions as criminal kickback arrangements. To acknowledge and nurture the beneficial effects of certain payment practices in the industry, Congress cabined the reach of the provisions by adding two new exceptions to the statute. The first exception protected transactions involving discounts or reductions in price, provided those discounts or reductions were "properly disclosed and appropriately reflected in the costs claimed or charges made by the provider or entity."[8] The second exception exempted payments made to employees under a bona fide employment relationship from the reach of the anti-kickback law.[9] The scope of these and other later-enacted statutory exceptions[10] is discussed below.[11]

Rather than quelling the controversy over the anti-kickback law, the 1977 amendments caused considerable alarm within the industry due to their breadth. A particular source of worry was the substitution of the undefined phrase "any remuneration" for the discarded phrase "bribes and kickbacks." As reworded, the statute's express terms broadly prohibited the receipt, solicitation, offer or payment of "any remuneration (including any kickback, bribe, or

---

6. 42 U.S.C.A. §§ 1320a–7b(b)(1) and (2) (West Supp. 1997), Social Security Act §§ 1128B(b)(1) and (2).

7. "The substance rather than simply the form of a transaction should be controlling." 123 Cong. Rec. H30280 (daily ed. Sept. 22, 1977) (statement of the Chairperson of the House Committee on Ways and Means and principal author of H.R. 3, Representative Daniel Rostenkowski). See also H.R. Rep. No. 95–393, pt. II, at 53 (1977), reprinted in 1977 U.S.C.C.A.N. 3039, 3056; S.Rep. No. 95–453, at 12 (1977).

8. See 42 U.S.C.A. § 1320a–7b(b)(3)(A) (1994); H.R. Rep. No. 95–393, pt. II, at 53 (1977), reprinted in 1977 U.S.C.C.A.N. 3039, 3056. The legislative history of the statute indicates that Congress sought to encourage the

use of discounts as a good business practice that would reduce program costs. Id.

9. 42 U.S.C.A. § 1320a–7b(b)(3)(B) (1994).

10. A third exception was carved out in 1986 when Congress exempted payments to group purchasing organizations (GPOs). See Social Security Act § 1128B(b); 42 U.S.C.A. § 1320a–7b(b)(3)(C) (1994). A fourth was later adopted to cover certain waivers of Medicare Part B coinsurance obligations by federally qualified health care centers. See 42 U.S.C.A. § 1320a–7b(b)(3) (1994). A final exemption covering managed care organizations was added by the HIPAA. See 42 U.S.C.A. § 1320a–7b(b)(3) (1994).

11. See § 3–10 and § 3–11a.

rebate) directly or indirectly, overtly or covertly, in cash or in kind."[12] A literal interpretation of this language appeared to preclude the transfer of *anything* of value in exchange for an item or service reimbursable under the Medicare or Medicaid programs, including transactions involving no direct cash payment for referrals. The offer of discount to a purchaser to induce the purchaser to buy larger quantities, for example, could be viewed as a violation of the statute, if the discount fell outside the scope of the discount statutory exemption.[13] The revised statute could also be read to outlaw incentives offered to recruit physicians to join a hospital's staff, a practice widely engaged in by many hospitals at the time. Some commentators warned that a broad construction of the provisions would punish not only unscrupulous providers who traded money for referrals, but innocuous and socially beneficial arrangements as well.[14]

§ 3-7.   The Omnibus Reconciliation Act of 1980—The Requirement of Specific Intent

In 1980 Congress acted to assuage some of the industry's misgivings about the 1977 revisions by amending the anti-kickback statute further to include for the first time an express scienter requirement.[1] The added culpability requirement was designed to preclude the possibility that an individual or entity who acted improperly but inadvertently could be convicted of engaging in kickback activity.[2] With this addition, only those offenders who "knowingly and willfully" engaged in conduct proscribed by the anti-kickback statute would face prosecution and/or exclusion under the provisions. Although added to quiet fears of unwarranted prosecutions under the provisions, the new scienter requirement has itself been the source of heated dispute, as explored more fully below.[3]

---

12. 42 U.S.C.A. §§ 1320a–7b(b)(1) and (2) (1994).

13. H.R. Rep. No. 95–393, pt. II, at 53 (1977), reprinted in 1977 U.S.C.C.A.N. 3039, 3056.

The bill would specifically exclude the practice of discounting or other reductions in price from the range of financial transactions to be considered illegal under Medicare and Medicaid, but only if such discounts are properly disclosed and reflected in the cost for which reimbursement could be claimed. The committee included this provision to ensure that the practice of discounting the normal course of business transactions would not be deemed illegal. In fact, the committee would encourage providers to seek dis-

counts as a good business practice which results in savings to Medicare and Medicaid program costs.

14. See, e.g., David M. Frankford, Creating and Dividing the Fruits of Collective Economic Activity: Referrals Among Health Care Providers, 89 Colum. L. Rev. 1861, 1875–76 (December 1989). See also 56 Fed. Reg. 35,952, 35,-952 (1991).

§ 3–7

1. The Omnibus Reconciliation Act of 1980, Pub.L.No. 96–499, 94 Stat. 2599 (1980).

2. H.R. Rep. No. 96–1167, at 59 (1980), reprinted in 1980 U.S.C.C.A.N. 5526, 5572.

3. See § 3–13.

§ 3–8. Agency Interpretations of the Amended Anti-Kickback Provisions

The willingness of the HHS and HCFA to provide the industry guidance about its view of the anti-kickback law has wavered over time. Between 1977 and 1981, through a series of early advisory opinions, intermediary letters and special fraud alerts, HHS and HCFA publicized its view of the anti-kickback statute's effect on certain business arrangements popular within the industry. In 1981, however, under pressure from the Department of Justice, HCFA reported that it would no longer issue advisory statements concerning the scope of the anti-kickback provisions. The advisory opinion process was discontinued on the grounds that interpretation of a criminal statute was best left to the judiciary, and that ultimate prosecutorial and decision-making authority vis-a-vis the statute fell within the province of the DOJ.[1] The agencies maintained this position for more than a decade until the enactment of the Health Insurance Portability and Accountability Act of 1996 (HIPAA)[2] which directed the OIG to once again begin to issue advisory opinions upon the receipt of an inquiry about the anti-kickback safe harbor provisions.[3] At least for the near future, this mandatory advisory opinion process entitles members of the industry to some administrative guidance. A more detailed discussion of the new advisory opinion procedures is included later in this chapter.[4]

The agency's early advisory statements remain instructive of the government's construction of the provisions and are summarized below.

a. HCFA's Advisory Letters and Opinions

Between 1977 and 1981, the Office of Program Integrity of the Health Care Financing Administration (HCFA) issued a series of advisory letters and opinions in response to calls from the industry for advice about the propriety of certain business transactions. Even today these official statements can assist providers who are attempting to navigate the maze of anti-kickback provisions and safe harbor regulations. At bottom, the advisory statements confirm that, despite the broad wording of the anti-kickback statute, not all financially beneficial referral arrangements between a provider or other professional and a health care facility will be considered to

---

§ 3–8
1. See 56 Fed. Reg. at 35,960.
2. Pub.L.No. 104–191, Title II, 110 Stat. 1936 (1996).

3. See id. at § 205, 110 Stat. at 2000.
4. See § 3–17.

violate the law. As reflected in one advisory letter, for example, a physician may lawfully benefit from a system of referrals to a health care facility in which the physician has a financial interest, provided the physician does not condition her acquisition, or ownership of, or ownership interest in the facility on a promise of referrals.[5]

b. The Intermediary Letters

In addition to HCFA's early advisory opinions, glimpses of the government's construction of the anti-kickback provisions can be obtained from letters issued by HCFA to the intermediaries and carriers[6] that help to police the programs' expenditures. Commonly known as the "intermediary letters," these carrier and intermediary alerts address a variety of referral arrangements that HCFA believes may violate the anti-kickback provisions.[7]

Although somewhat instructive, the intermediary letters may be of limited use to the health care provider struggling to assess the legality of a proposed or existing business transaction. With one notable exception discussed below, the letters tend to highlight conduct that few would regard as lawful. Thus the letters may offer little useful counsel to providers appraising the legality of complex features of a joint venture in today's health care marketplace.[8]

Not all of the intermediary letters were well received by the industry. One intermediary letter in particular was the source of serious disagreement. Issued in 1984, the intermediary letter constructed a hypothetical fee-for-service arrangement between a durable medical equipment (DME) supplier and a respiratory therapist.[9] Under the fictitious arrangement, the DME supplier agreed to pay the therapist a finder's fee for referring patients who needed home

---

5. See Eugene Tillman, Gregory P. Miller and Edwin M. Bladen, Overview of Fraud and Abuse Statutes and Regulations, in MEDICARE FRAUD AND ABUSE, UNDERSTANDING THE LAW 10 (Jeanie M. Johnson, ed. 1986).

6. For a discussion of the role played by carriers and intermediaries in fraud and abuse investigations, see Chapter 7, § 7-2.

7. See, e.g., Rebates to Dialysis Facilities, HCFA Intermediary Letter No. 83-13/83-7 (Sept. 1983), reprinted in Medicare and Medicaid Guide (CCH) ¶ 33,083 (Sept. 1983); Rebates, Kickbacks and/or "Free Goods" in Return For the Purchase of Pacemakers and Intraocular Lenses, HCFA Intermediary Letter No. 83-19/83-11 (Dec. 1983), reprinted in Medicare and Medicaid Guide (CCH) ¶ 33,083 (Dec. 1983); Suppliers of Dura-

ble Medical Equipment Offering "Finders" and "Referral" Fees, HCFA Intermediary Letter No. 84-9, (Sept. 1984), reprinted in Medicare and Medicaid Guide (CCH) ¶ 34,127 (Sept. 1984) and HCFA's follow-up Program Memo (Carriers) No. B85-2 (April 1985), reprinted in Medicare and Medicaid Guide (CCH) ¶ 34,544 (April 1985).

8. Eugene Tillman, Gregory P. Miller and Edwin M. Bladen, Overview of Fraud and Abuse Statutes and Regulations, in MEDICARE FRAUD & ABUSE: UNDERSTANDING THE LAW 11 (Jeanie M. Johnson, ed. 1986).

9. Suppliers of Durable Medical Equipment Offering "Finders" and "Referral" Fees, HCFA Intermediary Letter No. 84-9 (Sept. 1984), reprinted in Medicare and Medicaid Guide (CCH) ¶ 34,127 (Sept. 1984).

oxygen therapy equipment to the supplier. The DME supplier also agreed to pay the therapist a fee to set up any equipment determined to be necessary for the patients' care, to instruct the patients in the use of the equipment, or to perform monthly maintenance on the equipment provided by the DME supplier.[10] Assuming *arguendo* that the fees paid for services under the agreement were reasonable and intended to compensate necessary services, HCFA questioned the legality of the entire business arrangement, including not only the finder's fee but also the fee for services, reasoning that the provision of any opportunity to generate a fee, even a customary fee obtained for services rendered, could constitute an improper form of remuneration.[11]

HCFA's decision not to draw a distinction between the agreement to pay a fee specifically to induce referrals and the agreement for fees for services actually rendered was roundly criticized. Critics argued that the agency interpretation would jeopardize joint venture arrangements pervasive throughout the industry. Others challenged the agency's conclusion on its merits, arguing that the challenged fee arrangement should properly be considered either a lawful agreement between a bona fide employer and employee (and fall therefore within one of the statutory exceptions)[12] or a fee-for-service arrangement not motivated by an unlawful desire for referrals.[13] In response to the controversy created by its letter, HCFA retracted its statement about the illegality of such fee-generating opportunities and has since taken the position that the lawfulness of such arrangements cannot be prejudged without considering the particular facts and circumstances involved in each case.[14] Although, as of January 1, 1997, the OIG is required to respond to the industry's questions about the legality of particular business arrangements pursuant to the advisory opinion provisions of HI-

10. See id.

11. The intermediary letter read:

The opportunity to generate a fee is itself a form of remuneration. The offer or receipt of such fee opportunities is illegal if intended to induce a patient referral. Thus, a supplier who induces patient referrals by offering therapists fee-generating opportunities is offering illegal remuneration, even if the therapist is paid no more than his or her usual fee.

Id.

12. See § 3–10.

13. See, e.g., Adams, Fraud and Abuse Implications of Joint Ventures, in JOINT VENTURES BETWEEN HOSPITALS AND PHYSICIANS: A COMPETITIVE STRATEGY FOR THE HEALTHCARE MARKETPLACE 129, 135 (L. Burns & D. Mancino, eds. 1987).

14. Suppliers of Durable Medical Equipment Offering "Finders" and "Referral" Fees, HCFA Program Memo (Carriers) No. B85–2 (April 1985), reprinted in Medicare and Medicaid Guide (CCH) ¶ 34,544 (April 1985) (setting forth a list of relevant factors and practice patterns that have to be considered before a particular arrangement is determined to be unlawful). Although HCFA's position created a furor, its view that purchasing a fee-generating opportunity violates the statute was essentially upheld five years later in United States v. Bay State Ambulance and Hospital Rental Services, Inc., 874 F.2d 20 (1st Cir.1989).

PAA,[15] the government continues to require particularized information about a transaction before it will issue any advice about its legality.

c. The OIG Special Fraud Alerts

A particularly rich source of administrative guidance regarding the meaning of the federal anti-kickback provisions has been the special fraud alerts issued by the Office of the Inspector General. The OIG has issued eight special fraud alerts since March 1984 which provide assistance to individuals and entities attempting to comply with the federal health care statutes, and to Medicare carriers trying to identify health care fraud schemes.[16] The fraud alerts highlight referral-seeking practices that have been observed on a national scale and are considered by HHS to violate the anti-kickback provisions.[17] The alerts address myriad potentially unlawful business arrangements or payment practices within the industry, including the legality of joint venture arrangements;[18] the routine waiver of Medicare Part B copayments and deductibles;[19] the provision of hospital incentives to referring physicians;[20] prescription drug marketing practices;[21] arrangements for the provision of clinical laboratory services;[22] fraud in the home health care field;[23] the provision of medical supplies to nursing facilities;[24] and fraud and abuse in the provision of services to patients of nursing facilities.[25] Health care providers who pay careful attention to the special fraud alerts may uncover important clues that can help them avoid entering into unlawful arrangements or enable them to correct questionable referral practices before those practices attract

---

15. See HIPAA, Pub.L.No. 104–191, § 205(b), 110 Stat. 1936, 2001 (1996), 42 U.S.C.A. 1320a-7d(b) (West Supp.1997). See also discussion infra at § 3–17 regarding the advisory opinion process.

16. See 62 Fed. Reg. 7350 I(B) (1997). The first five Special Fraud Alerts were originally printed and distributed directly to all Medicare program providers. On December 19, 1994, the OIG republished those five alerts in the Federal Register, see 59 Fed. Reg. 65,372 (1994), and announced that all future alerts would be made available to all affected program providers and the public at large through the Federal Register. See id.

17. See 56 Fed. Reg. at 35,959 (1991) and 59 Fed. Reg. at 65,372 (1994).

18. See Joint Venture Arrangements (1989), reprinted in 59 Fed. Reg. 65,372 (1994).

19. See Routine Waiver of Copayments or Deductibles under Medicare

Part B (1991), reprinted in 59 Fed. Reg. 65,372 (1994).

20. See Hospital Incentives to Physicians (1992), reprinted in 59 Fed. Reg. 65, 372 (1994).

21. See Prescription Drug Marketing Schemes (1994), reprinted in 59 Fed. Reg. 65,372 (1994).

22. See Arrangements for the Provision of Clinical Lab Services (1994), reprinted in 59 Fed. Reg. 65,372 (1994).

23. See Home Health Fraud, OIG 95–08 (June 1995), reprinted in 60 Fed. Reg. 40,847 (1995).

24. See Fraud and Abuse in the Provision of Medical Supplies to Nursing Facilities, OIG 95–09 (August 1995), reprinted in 60 Fed. Reg. 40,847 (1995).

25. See Fraud and Abuse in the Provision of Services in Nursing Facilities (May 1996), reprinted in 61 Fed. Reg. 30,623 (1996).

the attention of federal or state investigators. The substance of each of the special fraud alerts concerning possible kickback violations is summarized later in this chapter.[26]

§ 3–9. The Medicare–Medicaid Patient and Program Protection Act of 1987

In the 1980s as dissatisfaction with the anti-kickback provisions intensified, industry groups redoubled their efforts to curb what they perceived to be a statute run amuck. Critics argued that the judiciary's expansive reading of the statute[1] threatened to bridle the industry's ability to cultivate market-driven business arrangements that had no harmful purpose or effects, and stepped up demands to Congress that it require the government to issue advisory opinions about the legality of particular arrangements.[2] The industry's concerns that innovative and beneficial arrangements were either outlawed or chilled by the anti-kickback statute swelled with the 1982 adoption of the Prospective Payment System (PPS). By placing a ceiling on the fees that would be paid for in-hospital services, PPS forced hospitals and providers to pool their capital and create more integrated health care delivery systems to remain competitive.[3] As the variety of alliances among providers exploded to meet the demands of the dramatically changing marketplace, concerns about the legality of those alliances intensified.

Congress signaled its agreement that the broadly worded anti-kickback statute could indeed be read to impede the beneficial development of innocent and efficient business practices when it enacted the Medicare–Medicaid Patient and Program Protection Act of 1987 (MMPPPA).[4] The MMPPPA directed the Secretary of HHS to promulgate regulations, known as safe harbors, describing conduct which would not be subject to criminal prosecution or exclusion. The safe harbors would serve to narrow the statute's reach and protect legitimate or innocuous business arrangements which might otherwise fall under the statute's broad terms. The 1987 amendments also provided new authority to the OIG to exclude an individual or entity from participation in the Medicare

---

26. See § 3–16.

§ 3–9

1. See discussion regarding the courts' interpretation of the *mens rea* requirement of the statute at § 3–13a.

2. See § 3–17.

3. See David M. Frankford, Creating and Dividing the Fruits of Collective Economic Activity: Referrals Among Health Providers, 89 Colum. L. Rev. 1861, 1865 (1989).

4. Pub.L.No. 100–93, § 14. Congress declined, until August 1996, to include a requirement that the HHS issue advisory opinions to assist the industry. A provision requiring the issuance of such advisory statements was finally adopted with the enactment of the Health Insurance Portability and Accountability Act of 1996, Pub.L.No. 104–191, § 205(b), 110 Stat. 1936, 2001 (1996), 42 U.S.C.A. § 1320a–7d(b) (West Supp.1997). See infra at § 3–17.

and State health care programs if it determined that the party had engaged in an unlawful referral scheme.[5]

Pressure to supplement the safe harbor regulations has continued unabated. The Health Insurance Portability and Accountability Act of 1996 (HIPAA)[6] requires the Secretary to solicit each year proposals to modify the existing safe harbor regulations and to create new safe harbors.[7] The OIG has already received and is reviewing a number of suggestions proposing the addition of new safe harbors and the modification of existing safe harbor provisions.[8] In addition, HIPAA directs the OIG to issue special fraud alerts in response to a request for guidance when the Secretary of HHS deems it to be appropriate.[9] Providers and health care associations have begun to ask for special fraud alerts addressing the legality of several other types of transactions that continue to perplex the industry, including the propriety of financial arrangements between hospitals and hospital-based physicians, the legality of financial arrangements between hospice providers and nursing homes, and the validity of discount agreements between providers and Medicare supplemental carriers.[10]

To date, five statutory exceptions to the federal anti-kickback statute have been enacted, thirteen final safe harbors (including HHS's clarifications of the statutory exceptions) have been promulgated, and eight safe harbor regulations have been proposed but not finalized. Each of the statutory exceptions, safe harbors and proposed safe harbor regulations are considered below.

§ 3–10. The Statutory Exceptions

The 1977 amendments to the anti-kickback statute protected two billing practices otherwise violative of the statute's literal terms—discounts and payments made within a bona fide employment relationship. Since 1977, Congress has added three more statutory exceptions to protect: (i) group purchasing organizations (GPOs), (ii) routine waivers of Medicare Part B coinsurance obligations, and (iii) certain risk-sharing arrangements of managed care organizations.[1]

5. See MMPPPA, Pub.L.No. 100–93, § 2, 101 Stat. 680, 682 (codified at 42 U.S.C.A. § 1320a–7(b)(7) (1994)).

6. Pub.L.No. 104–191, 110 Stat. 1936 (1996).

7. See id. at § 205, 110 Stat. at 2000.

8. See Administration Readies Legislation to Repeal Fraud and Abuse Provisions, 6 BNA Health Law Reporter 393, 394 (March 13, 1997).

9. HIPAA, Pub.L.No. 104–191, Title II, § 205(1)(A)(iv). Special fraud alerts are to be published in the Federal Register. See id.

10. See BNA's Health Law Reporter, Vol. 6 at 394 (March 13, 1994).

§ 3–10

1. See 42 U.S.C.A. § 1320a–7b(b)(3) (1994).

For a business arrangement to qualify for protection under one of the finalized safe harbors, *every* standard of all applicable safe harbor provisions must be met. For example, if a particular business arrangement contemplates making payments for different purposes, each purpose of each payment will have to be analyzed separately to determine if the standards of all the applicable safe harbor provisions are fulfilled. Individuals and entities who enter into arrangements that comply with one of the safe harbors, but not with others, may face civil or criminal enforcement action.[2] The Office of Inspector General has rejected arguments that providers who "substantially comply" with the provisions commit only "technical violations" of the statute, or that making or accepting "de minimis payments" is protected.[3]

Health care providers attempting to structure financial relationships must proceed with caution. Although the federal safe harbor regulations do not purport to comprise the universe of acceptable billing practices under the anti-kickback law, neither do they assure that a provider will be free from investigation, prosecution or exclusion under concurrent state anti-kickback provisions. They simply enumerate particular types of business arrangements that may escape federal criminal or administrative sanction if the provider fully complies with each of the terms of each applicable safe harbor provision.

a. Discounts

The first statutory exemption relates to discounts or other reductions in price obtained by a provider of services or other entity.[4] Such a discount is permissible provided it has been properly disclosed and appropriately reflected in the costs claimed or charges made by the provider or entity.[5] The discount exception is designed to encourage price competition in the Medicare and Medicaid pro-

---

2. See 56 Fed. Reg. 35,952, 35,957 (1991) ("A person engaged in a 'multipurpose' payment practice who seeks protection will need to document separately his or her compliance with the safe harbor applicable to each purpose being served by the payment practice. Compliance with one provision (for one of the purposes of the payment practice) would not insulate the entire payment practice from criminal prosecution or program exclusion, where another purpose of the payment practice is implemented in a manner which violates the statute.").

3. See id.

4. See 42 U.S.C.A. § 1320a–7b(b)(3) (1994) provides:

(3) Paragraphs (1) and (2) shall not apply to—

* * *

(A) a discount or other reduction in price obtained by a provider of services or other entity under subchapter XVIII of this chapter or a State health care program if the reduction in price is properly disclosed and appropriately reflected in the costs claimed or charges made by the provider or entity under subchapter XVIII of this chapter or a State health care program . . .

5. 42 U.S.C.A. § 1320a–7b(b)(3)(A) (1994).

grams, and covers the use of rebate checks, redeemable coupons, credits and, for cost-report buyers, end-of-the-year discounts.[6] A safe harbor regulation promulgated in 1989 clarified the scope and prerequisites of the discount statutory exemption.[7] That safe harbor regulation is discussed further below.[8]

b.   Employer/Employee

Payments by an employer to an employee in the context of a bona fide employment relationship are similarly exempt from the reach of the anti-kickback prohibitions.[9] Like the discount exemption, the bona fide employment statutory exemption is also the subject of a safe harbor regulation[10] that clarifies the scope of the exemption. That clarification is discussed below.[11]

c.   Group Purchasing Organizations (GPOs)

Amounts paid by a vendor of goods or services to a purchasing agent who acts on behalf of a group purchasing organization (GPO) are exempted, provided the vendor has a written contract with each member of the GPO stipulating the fixed amount or fixed percentage of the value of the purchases to be paid the agent, and, where purchases are made for a Medicare provider, the vendor discloses to the provider (and to HHS on request) the amount the vendor paid for each purchase.[12] A safe harbor regulation promulgated in 1981 clarified the GPO statutory exemption,[13] and is discussed below in the section dealing with safe harbors.[14]

---

6. See id.

7. See 42 C.F.R. § 1001.952(h).

8. See § 3–11a(1).

9. See 42 U.S.C.A. § 1320a–7b(b)(3) (1994), which provides in pertinent part:

(3) Paragraphs (1) and (2) shall not apply to—

* * *

(B) any amount paid by an employer to an employee (who has a bona fide employment relationship with such employer) for employment in the provision of covered items or services

. . .

10. See § 3–11a(2).

11. See § 3–11a(3).

12. See 42 U.S.C.A. § 1320a–7b(b)(3) (1994), which provides:

(3) Paragraphs (1) and (2) shall not apply to—

* * *

(C) any amount paid by a vendor of goods or services to a person authorized to act as a purchasing agent for a group of individuals or entities who are furnishing services reimbursed under subchapter XVIII of this chapter or a State health care program if—

(i) the person has a written contract, with each such individual or entity, which specifies the amount to be paid the person, which amount may be a fixed amount or a fixed percentage of the value of the purchases made by each such individual or entity under the contract, and

(ii) in the case of an entity that is a provider of services (as defined in section 1395x(u) of this title), the person discloses (in such form and manner as the Secretary requires) to the entity and, upon request, to the Secretary the amount received from each such vendor with respect to purchases made by or on behalf of the entity . . .

13. See 42 C.F.R. § 1001.952(j).

14. See § 3–11.

d. Waivers of Coinsurance Obligations

Federally qualified health care centers may waive without fear of sanction the Medicare Part B coinsurance obligations of individuals who qualify for subsidized services under the Public Health Service Act.[15]

e. Managed Care Organizations (MCOs)

In August 1996, Congress added a new statutory exception to the anti-kickback statute for certain risk-sharing organizations.[16] The exception permits remuneration between an organization and an individual or entity providing items or services under a written agreement if the organization is an eligible organization under Section 1876 (*i.e.*, any organization with a contract with HCFA), or if, through a risk-sharing arrangement, the agreement places the individual or entity at "substantial financial risk" for the cost or utilization of the items or services which the individual or entity is obligated to provide. Section 216 of HIPAA required the Secretary to promulgate standards by which risk-sharing arrangements will be assessed under the managed care exception, and negotiated rule-making is currently underway. Although the statutorily-prescribed target date for these proposed standards was January 1, 1997, the OIG has been unable to meet that deadline due to delays associated with the negotiated rule-making process. Nevertheless, the risk-sharing statutory exception took effect on that date even in the absence of regulations to implement the exception.[17]

The Balanced Budget Act of 1997[18] recognizes a number of new MCOs under the Medicare and Medicaid programs.[19] The finalized budget agreement did not, however, simultaneously extend the list

---

15. See 42 U.S.C.A. § 1320a–7b(b)(3) (1994) provides:

(3) Paragraphs (1) and (2) shall not apply to—

* * *

(D) a waiver of any coinsurance under part B of subchapter XVIII of this chapter by a Federally qualified health care center with respect to an individual who qualifies for subsidized services under a provision of the Public Health Service Act [42 U.S.C.A. § 201 et seq.] . . .

16. See 42 U.S.C.A. § 1320a–7b(b)(3) (1994), which provides:

(3) Paragraphs (1) and (2) shall not apply to—

* * *

(F) any remuneration between an organization and an individual or enti-ty providing items or services, or a combination thereof, pursuant to a written agreement between the organization and the individual or entity, if the organization is an eligible organization under section 1395mm of this title or it the written agreement, through a risk-sharing arrangement, places the individual or entity at substantial risk for the cost or utilization of the items or services, or a combination thereof, which the individual or entity is obligated to provide . . .

17. See HIPAA, Pub.L.No. 109–141, Title II, § 216, 110 Stat. 1936, 2007 (1996), 42 U.S.C.A. § 1320a–7b(b)(3), Social Security Act § 1128B(b)(3).

18. Pub.L.No. 105–33, 111 Stat. 251, to be codified at 42 U.S.C.A. § 1396v.

19. See Pub.L.No. 105–32, § 4001 (Medicare) and §§ 4701–4710 (Medicaid).

of recognized MCOs described in the anti-kickback statutory exemption provision,[20] the safe harbor provision[21] or the self-referral provision.[22] While this may have simply been an oversight (easily remedied by a future technical amendment), the law as it currently stands expressly addresses only the MCOs described below. It is possible, however, that the newly recognized MCOs would be recognized as federally qualified HMOs and thus be entitled to shelter under the safe harbor that applies to such HMOs.

f. Other Practices

Also excluded from the coverage of the anti-kickback prohibitions are any other practices for which the Secretary of HHS creates a safe harbor regulation. As discussed below, the Secretary has exercised this significant power on several occasions.

§ 3–11. The Safe Harbor Regulations

The OIG published its first set of proposed safe harbor regulations in the Federal Register on January 23, 1989.[1] The regulations described eight safe harbors under which certain payment practices would not be treated as criminal offenses or serve as a basis for program exclusion. The proposed regulations underwent a process of public comment and significant revision before they were finalized. On July 29, 1991, HHS published the first safe harbor regulations in final form.[2] The regulations clarified aspects of the statutory exceptions to the anti-kickback provisions and added several new safe harbors that would provide shelter to certain business arrangements. Payment practices falling outside the safe harbors regulations or the statutory exceptions would violate the anti-kickback law.[3]

---

20. See § 3–10.

21. See § 3–11(h).

22. See Chapter 4, § 4–5d.

§ 3–11

1. See 54 Fed. Reg. 3,088 (1989). Approximately one month earlier, HHS had published in the Federal Register a different set of proposed regulations which, among other things, contemplated the creation of a process by which HHS could advise members of the health care community (by issuing informal advisory letters, for example) on issues not specifically addressed by the regulations. See 53 Fed. Reg. 51,856 (1988). Resistance from the Department of Justice, however, caused HHS to rescind the proposed regulations five days after their publication. See 53 Fed. Reg. 52,448 (1988).

2. Although the Medicare and Medicaid Patient and Program Protection Act of 1987, Pub.L.No. 100–93, 110 Stat. 680 (1987), required the HHS to issue final regulations by August 18, 1989, the final rules were substantially delayed by the combination of voluminous public comments received after publication of the proposed regulations, and differences that developed between the OIG, HHS, the Office of Management and Budget and the Justice Department in the process of finalizing the rules.

3. HHS has indicated that the safe harbor regulations supersede any prior communications from the Department regarding business practices considered not subject to prosecution (such as the HCFA advisory letters). See 56 Fed. Reg. 35,952, 35,960 (1991).

a. Safe Harbors That Clarify The Statutory Exceptions—42 C.F.R. §§ 1001.952(h)–(j)

Three of the safe harbors promulgated in 1989 clarified the (then) existing statutory exceptions to the anti-kickback rules for discounts, employees, and group purchasing organizations. While these provisions reassure members of the industry of the legality of some practices, they also identify as unlawful practices that might have previously been thought to fall within the statutory exceptions.

(1) Discount Safe Harbor—42 C.F.R. § 1001.952(h)

The discount safe harbor regulation clarifies that a "discount" (a reduction in the price of a good or service reimbursable under one of the federal health care programs) must be offered and accepted as a part of an "arms length" transaction to be protected under the discount statutory exception.[4] General price reductions offered equally to all buyers across the board are not considered to be discounts at all, and thus are not prohibited by the statute, since such diffuse price reductions are not likely to induce any particular buyer to purchase or order program-reimbursable goods or services.[5]

Although the discount safe harbor provides expanded protection for rebates, redeemable coupons and credits, several restrictions apply. First, coupons can be redeemed only by the seller, they may not be negotiated by the recipient to third parties. Second, rebate checks, redeemable coupons and credits can only be applied to the good or service that was purchased or provided, they cannot be used toward the purchase of anything else. Third, the discounts must be fully and accurately reported. Finally, except as noted below, such discounts must be given at the time the good or service was purchased or provided.[6]

---

4. 42 C.F.R. § 1001.952(h). The Secretary offered the following example to illustrate a discount that would fail the "arms length transaction" requirement:

For example, in some cases a reference laboratory performs testing for another laboratory at a discount price in accordance with a management contract. In other cases, the services the reference laboratory provides are paid on the basis of a percentage of revenues that the joint venture receives from Medicare. These arrangements are not arms length transactions where the joint venture entity shops around for the best price on a good or service. Rather, it has entered into a collusive arrangement with a particular provider or supplier of items or services that seeks to share its profits with referring physician partners. To clarify that we do not intend to protect these types of transactions which are sometimes made to appear as "discounts," we are clarifying the definition of "discounts" in paragraph (h)(3) of this section to permit only transactions made on an arms length basis.

56 Fed. Reg. at 35,977–78.

5. See 56 Fed. Reg. at 35,977.

6. See 42 C.F.R. § 1001.952(h); see also 56 Fed. Reg. at 35,979. Buyers must report credits on the applicable cost report or claim form covering the goods or

106

End-of-year discounts for cost report buyers are also protected by the discount safe harbor regulation when all of the following conditions are met: 1) the end-of-year discounts are calculated based on purchases of the same good or service in a single fiscal year; 2) the entity claims the benefit of the discount from the seller in the fiscal year in which the discount is earned or the following year; 3) the buyer fully and accurately reports the discount in the cost report for the fiscal year in which the discount is received, and 4) the buyer provides the appropriate invoices from the seller upon the request of the Secretary or a state Medicaid agency.[7]

Also sheltered by the discount safe harbor are discounts provided to health management organizations (HMOs) and competitive medical plans (CMPs) that have risk contracts with HCFA or a state health care program.[8] Such health plans need only report discounts they receive as required under their risk contracts.

Discounts to buyers paid on a charge basis will be protected under the safe harbor only under the following three conditions. First, the discount must be made at the time of the original sale of the good or service. Second, when an item or service is separately claimed for payment with HHS or a state agency, the buyer must fully and accurately report the discount. Third, upon the request of the HHS or a state health care program, the buyer must provide certain information it has received from the seller.[9]

The discount safe harbor provides some protection to sellers as well. Sellers that offer discounts to an HMO or CMP, for example, need not report the discount.[10] A seller providing a discount to any other health care provider, however, must inform the buyer of the buyer's reporting obligations, and either fully and accurately report the discount on its invoice or statement, or, in the event the value of the discount is not known at the time of the purchase, report the existence of its discount program and report the discount when its value is determined.[11]

Although some are protected by other provisions, a number of discounting practices common to the industry fall outside of the statutory discount exception and its safe harbor. These practices include contracts for personal or management services,[12] warranties,[13] arrangements for "bundled goods" (where a seller gives away or reduces the price of one good in connection with the purchase of

services for which the credit is being used.

7. 42 C.F.R. § 1001.952(h)(1)(i).

8. 42 C.F.R. § 1001.952(h)(1)(ii).

9. 42 C.F.R. § 1001.952(h)(1)(iii).

10. 42 C.F.R. § 1001.952(h)(2)(i).

11. 42 C.F.R. § 1001.952(h)(2)(ii).

12. To be protected, these arrangements must fit within the safe harbor provision for personal services and management contracts. See § 3–11c(3).

13. See 56 Fed. Reg. at 35,976–77. To be protected such a practice must fit within the safe harbor promulgated expressly for warranties. See § 3–11f.

another),[14] routine waivers for coinsurance and deductible amounts,[15] discounts to beneficiaries, and end-of-the-year discounts to charge-reimbursed purchasers.[16]

(2) Employee Safe Harbor—42 C.F.R. § 1001.952(i)

According to the HHS clarification, the employee safe harbor allows an employer to hire and pay a person to solicit program-related business provided the person is acting within a bona fide employer-employee relationship. The term "employee" is defined in accordance with provisions of the Internal Revenue Code.[17] Other personal service relationships, such as independent contractor agreements, fall outside the scope of the provision.[18]

(3) GPO Safe Harbor—42 C.F.R. § 1001.952(j)

The group purchasing organization (GPO) statutory exception protects payments made by vendors to certain entities that are authorized to act on behalf of a group of individuals or entities furnishing Medicare or Medicaid services. The final safe harbor adopted in 1991, excludes from the definition of a GPO all entities that are part of the same corporate family as the entities for which the GPO makes purchases.[19] Like the GPO statutory exception,[20] the GPO safe harbor mandates that the GPO and the individuals or entities it represents execute a written agreement that specifies the amount the vendor will pay the GPO.[21] This mandate is satisfied if the GPO discloses the fees it will receive from the vendors that provide goods or services to that provider. The safe harbor also permits the agreement to specify that the vendor will pay the GPO a fee of 3% or less of the purchase price of the vendor's goods, but if the fee is more than 3%, the agreement must specify that the amount of the GPO payment by each vendor (or if that amount is unknown, the maximum amount).[22] The GPO need not disclose to any individual or entity fees from vendors that do not provide goods or services to that particular individual or entity.[23]

---

14. See id. at 35,978.

15. But see the statutory exception for such waivers, discussed below at § 3–10d. See also discussion of the safe harbor for waivers connected to certain inpatient hospital care at § 3–11g.

16. 42 C.F.R. § 1001.952(h)(1) and (2); 56 Fed. Reg. at 35,979.

17. See 42 C.F.R. § 1001.952(i); see also 56 Fed. Reg. at 35,981.

18. See id. However, health care providers may obtain protection for payments to independent contractors by drafting their contracts to satisfy the safe harbor provision for personal services and management contracts.

19. 42 C.F.R. § 1001.952(j).

20. See § 3–10c.

21. 42 C.F.R. § 1001.952(j)(1)(ii).

22. See id. In the event that the fee cannot be ascertained at the time of the contract or the fee is not fixed at 3 percent or less, the contract must state the maximum amount that could be paid to the GPO by the vendor. See 56 Fed. Reg. at 35,982.

23. See 42 C.F.R. § 1001.952(j).

b. The Investment Interests Safe Harbor—42 C.F.R. § 1001.952(a)

Perhaps the most complex safe harbor adopted to date is the investment interest safe harbor regulation. The investment interest safe harbor is most easily understood when it is read in tandem with the OIG's widely disseminated Special Fraud Alert on Joint Ventures (discussed more fully later in this chapter)[24] which describes particular characteristics of proposed or existing joint ventures considered to be inherently suspect.[25]

In contrast to the special fraud alert on joint ventures, the investment interest safe harbor identifies joint ventures and other investment interests that are not suspect, *i.e.*, that are lawful under the anti-kickback statute. The safe harbor carves out a shelter for certain investments made by providers in large publicly traded corporations and in smaller entities (such as a partnership or other joint venture) provided the parties comply with certain stringent restrictions. Thus, the safe harbor provides protection for the physician who invests in a health care entity to which she refers patients or prescribes medication manufactured by a company from which she receives dividend payments, provided the profit distributions from the physician's investment do not serve as an inducement for referrals.

It should be noted, of course, that the investment interest safe harbor only protects such a provider from prosecution or exclusion under the anti-kickback rules. It does not shield the provider from action under the Stark self-referral provisions. For this reason, the investment interest safe harbor may largely be of historical interest to the health care provider who is attempting to structure an investment in a more modern vertically integrated health care delivery system. Even if the provider's investment finds shelter from the anti-kickback provisions under the investment interest safe harbor, it might not fare as well under the self-referral provisions[26] if the entity in which the investment is made is

---

24. See § 3–16a.

25. See "Special Fraud Alert: Joint Venture Arrangements" OIG–89–04 (1989), reprinted in 59 Fed. Reg. 65,372 (1994), which included on its list of suspect joint ventures arrangements under which: selected investors are a potential source of referrals; investment shares are offered to physician investors in proportion to the volume of their referrals; physician investors are encouraged either to make referrals to the entity or to divest their investment interests if their referrals fall below an "acceptable level" or if the physicians become otherwise

unable to make referrals to the entity; investment interests are nontransferable; the joint entity is essentially a "shell" existing primarily to channel business to another entity or to channel profits to its investors; a disproportionately high return on a physician's investment is offered to the physician investor or the physician is permitted to obtain an investment interest in the entity for a disproportionately small amount (or an amount borrowed from the entity itself).

26. See Chapter 4, §§ 4–1, 4–3, 4–6.

included within the Stark prohibitions. The legality of the investment must be analyzed separately under the self-referral provisions and the anti-kickback provisions.

Although the protection afforded by the investment interest self-referral safe harbor was greatly diminished with the enactment of the self-referral law, the safe harbor is not obsolete. The Stark self-referral laws do not apply to all health care services,[27] and some entities not encompassed within the self-referral laws are encompassed within the anti-kickback law. Investment interests in those entities must comply with the investment interest safe harbor to be lawful.

(1) Publicly Traded Corporations

The investment interest safe harbor[28] permits a physician to directly or indirectly[29] obtain an investment interest in a large[30] publicly traded corporation, provided that the investment interest is obtained at fair market value through trading on a publicly regulated exchange.[31] If the foregoing requirements are met, profit distributions made to a referring investor are protected.

The investment interest safe harbor protects debt as well as equity instruments. However, to be protected, investors may have

---

27. See Chapter 4.

28. 42 C.F.R. § 1001.952(a).

29. An investment interest may be indirectly held where a family member of a referring physician holds an investment interest in the joint venture entity, or a referring physician has a legal or beneficial interest in an entity (such as a group practice, a trust or a holding company) which holds an investment interest in the joint venture entity. In either case, the physician will be considered to have an ownership interest in the joint venture entity. See 56 Fed. Reg. at 35,-964. An indirect ownership interest in an entity held by a family member is treated in the same manner as a direct ownership interest to assure that investors who make referrals to that entity do not circumvent the anti-kickback provisions by having investments held in the name of family members instead of their own names. See id.

30. The assets of the entity exceed $50 million. See 56 Fed. Reg. at 35,964–35,965.

31. This provision was loosely based on the SEC registration rules from 15 U.S.C.A. § 781(g) and 17 C.F.R.

§ 240.12g–1, which generally require entities with more than $5 million in assets and more than 500 investors to register with the SEC.

The assets of the entity are to be measured any time within the previous fiscal year or the previous 12 month period, see 56 Fed. Reg. at 35,964, and the entity must possess $50 million in the form of undepreciated net tangible assets. Intangible assets, such as the company's valuation of its name recognition and stock and other forms of goodwill, are excluded, and the company's assets must be reduced by any outstanding liabilities. The reporting of net tangible assets must be based on the net acquisition costs of purchasing the assets from an unrelated entity, rather than on a company's current market valuations of the assets. Further, the acquisition costs must be based on a bona fide purchase through an arm's length transaction. See Medicare related-party rule, 42 C.F.R. § 413.17. Finally, assets unrelated to a company's health care line of business may not be used in the calculation of its assets. See 56 Fed. Reg. at 35,965.

to satisfy additional standards depending on the nature of the investment interest.[32] For example, an investment interest in an equity security must be registered with the SEC under 15 U.S.C.A. §§ 781(b) or (g),[33] and, if the investor is in a position to influence referrals, the investment must be obtained on terms equally available to the public through a registered national securities exchange, such as the New York Stock Exchange or the American Stock Exchange or the National Association of Securities Dealers Automated Quotation (NASDAQ) system.[34] Strict compliance with this standard is required. Hence, no protection will be afforded to an investor who exchanges a limited partnership interest for shares in a newly formed entity that is publicly traded, or to a physician who is given an opportunity to purchase the available shares of an entity before it becomes publicly traded.[35] For the shelter of the safe harbor to apply, the public must be afforded a genuine opportunity to invest in these publicly traded entities.

(2) Investments in Small Entities

The investment interest safe harbor also protects payments from investments in small entities, such as joint venture limited partnership and general partnership interests.[36] Significant safeguards were adopted with the safe harbor to minimize the potentially corrupting influence that such an investment could have on a physician-investor's decision about when and where to refer a patient. The safe harbor regulation includes a number of conditions designed to exclude from the regulation's shelter the abusive practices highlighted in the OIG's special fraud alert on joint ventures[37] while protecting payments made to investors (whether limited or general partners, shareholders, or holders of debt securities) who meet the regulation's stringent conditions. The conditions differ

---

32. See 42 C.F.R. §§ 1001.952(a)(1)(i)–(ii).

33. See 42 C.F.R. § 1001.952(a)(1)(i). This registration requirement does not apply to investment interests that involve debt securities. See 56 Fed. Reg. at 35,965.

34. See 42 C.F.R. § 1001.952(a)(1)(ii). No safe harbor protection exists for securities traded through the so-called "pink sheets" or "non-NASDAQ" securities that are traded through the OTC Bulletin Board Service. See 56 Fed. Reg. at 35,965.

35. See id.

36. See 42 C.F.R. § 1001.952(a)(2).

37. See Special Fraud Alert: Joint Venture Arrangements, OIG–89–04 (1989), reprinted in 59 Fed. Reg. 65,372 (1994) and discussed infra § 3–16a; see also OIG, Financial Arrangements Between Physicians and Health Care Businesses (Office of Analysis and Inspections, May 1989) which disclosed both the extensive ownership of joint ventures by physicians, and the additional services received by patients of these

depending on whether the party is an "active"[38] or "passive"[39] investor. Some of the standards must be met by both passive and active investors, others need only be met by passive investors.

The prerequisites set forth in the investment interest safe harbor provision address three of the OIG's concerns about investment interests joint ventures: the manner in which small entity investors are selected and retained, the nature of the business structure of such entities, and the financing and profit distributions of such joint ventures.[40]

Three of the investment interest safe harbor's standards were adopted to address OIG's concerns about the manner in which investors are *selected*. First, under the so-called "60–40 investor rule," investors who make referrals, or who are in a position to make referrals, or who furnish items or services, may not own more than 40 percent of the value of investment interests within each class of investments in the entity. Persons who are not in a position to make referrals must have a bona fide opportunity to invest in the entity and collectively must hold at least 60 percent of the value of the investment interests in each class of investments.[41] If, for example, a hospital seeks to structure a joint venture with a group of physicians on its staff, the hospital will have to secure 60% of the capital for the joint venture from outside investors who are not in a position to refer business to the joint venture.

Second, safe harbor protection is not available for investment opportunities that are conditioned upon a passive investor's ability to influence referrals, furnish items or services, or otherwise generate business for the entity. An entity may offer investments to such investors only on the same terms as those offered to passive investors not in a position to influence the flow of business to the entity.[42]

physicians as compared to all Medicare patients in general.

38. An active investor is either a general partner (under the Uniform Partnership Act) who is responsible for the day-to-day management of the entity, or an individual or entity who agrees in writing to undertake liability for the partnership, including the acts of its agents. See 42 C.F.R. § 1001.952(a)(2)(viii).

39. Passive investors are those who are not active investors, such as limited partners in a partnership or shareholders in a corporation. See id.

40. See discussion at § 3–16a; see also 56 Fed. Reg. at 35,967.

41. See 42 C.F.R. § 1001.952(a)(2)(i). A joint venture may use any consistent internal accounting principles it chooses to monitor its compliance with the 60–40 investment rule within one of two alternative time periods. The measurement period can either be a joint venture's prior fiscal year or the previous 12 month period.

42. See 42 C.F.R. § 1001.952(a)(2)(ii). This limitation does not apply to active investors, since it is precisely a physician's familiarity with the health care field that may cause her to be chosen as a general partner and offered different investment terms from those offered to passive investors. See 56 Fed. Reg. at 35,968.

Third, when an investment interest is offered to a person in a position to make referrals (whether an active or passive investor), an entity is prohibited from offering favorable terms based on the person's past or expected referrals or amount of business otherwise generated for the entity (e.g., an offer of more shares to a prospective general partner who is expected to generate more business for the entity).

Similar restrictions apply to the manner in which an entity may *retain* investors.[43] Entities are barred from requiring passive investors to make referrals or remain in a position to make referrals as a condition for retaining their investment. Entities and investors are also barred from marketing or furnishing items or services to passive investors on terms more favorable than those offered to non-investors and from promoting the services of other entities as part of a cross-referral agreement.[44] To prevent small entities from operating primarily on referrals from investing physicians, under the so-called 60–40 revenue rule, no more than 40 percent of an entity's gross revenue may come from referrals from investors, or items or services furnished by investors.[45] To assure that investments are bona fide, i.e., that investors' funds are genuinely at risk, an entity may not loan an investor the funds to make the investment, nor guarantee a loan that is used by an investor to make the investment. This prohibition is designed to ensure that physicians and other investors provide new capital and that the joint venture is not simply a sham to facilitate the distribution of payments for referrals. In addition, profit distributions to each investor must be directly proportional to the investor's capital investment.[46] To be protected, dividend payments must parallel the number of shares owned by the investor, and not the investor's referrals. However, the dividend payments of investors who contribute capital in the form of pre-operational services or sweat equity may reflect the fair market value of those services rendered.[47]

(3) Relation to the Stark Self–Referral Prohibitions

As noted above, the impact of the investment interest self-referral safe harbor has been severely limited by the Stark self-

43. See 42 C.F.R. §§ 1001.952(a)(2)(iv)-(v).

44. In a cross-referral agreement, investors in entity "A" are explicitly or implicitly encouraged to refer services to entity "B," which in turn encourages its investors to refer services to entity "A."

45. See 42 C.F.R. § 1001.952(a)(2)(vi). Again, joint ventures may employ any consistent internal accounting principle it chooses to monitor its compliance with this requirement over one of two alternative time periods, either the joint venture's prior fiscal year, or the previous 12 month period. See 56 Fed. Reg. at 35,969.

46. See 42 C.F.R. §§ 1001.952(a)(1)(iv)-(v) and (a)(2)(vii)-(viii).

47. See 56 Fed. Reg. at 35,970.

referral provisions. Under the Stark self-referral prohibitions, a physician is banned from referring a Medicare or Medicaid patient to an entity in which the physician holds an ownership interest.[48] Thus, notwithstanding the investment interest safe harbor, no reimbursements may be made under the federal health care programs to a physician with an investment interest in, or financial relationship with, the entity to whom a referral is made.

c. Space and Equipment Rentals, Personal Services and Management Contracts—42 C.F.R. §§ 1001.952(b)-(d)

Three safe harbors have been adopted to shelter from the reach of the anti-kickback provisions certain space and equipment rentals and personal and management contracts. To avoid pitfalls experienced in the past, when some of these arrangements were nothing more than thinly veiled kickback schemes, strict standards must be met to qualify for the protection of the safe harbors.

(1) Space Rentals—§ 1001.952(b)

If interpreted literally, the terms of the anti-kickback statute could be construed to prohibit a rental agreement between two parties where one of the parties is in a position to make referrals to the other, even if the parties have no understanding regarding referrals. To recognize the legitimacy of certain rental arrangements, while protecting against the possibility that "rent" payments may disguise payments actually intended to induce referrals, this safe harbor provision exempts rental arrangements provided: (a) access to the space is for periodic intervals, which intervals are prospectively established in the lease agreement and are not conditioned on the number of referred patients; (b) the lease is for at least one year, a requirement designed to prevent the possibility of frequent readjustments which might constitute disguised compensation for prior referrals; and (c) the charges for the space reflect the fair market value for the property.[49] Strict compliance is required, and the OIG has indicated that it will look beyond the facially neutral terms of a lease agreement to determine whether the agreement is in fact a vehicle for making payments for referrals.[50]

---

48. See Chapter 4.

49. See 42 C.F.R. § 1001.952(b). For example, a violation of the anti-kickback provisions might be inferred where a group of doctors owning a medical building leases space in that building to a diagnostic laboratory at a rent substantially above that which the laboratory would pay for the same amount of space at a nearby location. OIG has indicated that fair market value "contemplates a rental fee falling within a reasonable commercial range, but not taking into account any value attached by either party based upon the property's proximity or convenience to referral sources." See 56 Fed. Reg. at 35,971.

50. For example, a physician who purports to rent office space to a clinical laboratory to furnish laboratory services by leasing insufficient space or space

(2) Equipment Rentals—§ 1001.952(c)

Because there is always the chance that rental payments purporting to compensate the use of diagnostic and other medical equipment may in truth be a vehicle for the reimbursement of referrals, a safe harbor has been adopted to cover certain equipment rentals. The safe harbor includes safeguards similar to those that apply to space rentals described above.

(3) Personal   Services   and   Management   Contracts—§ 1001.952(d)

This safe harbor permits health care providers to arrange to perform services for each other on a mutually beneficial basis, but prohibits them from arranging to vary the payment for "services" with the volume of referrals. The safe harbor also makes joint ventures and other arrangements involving payments for personal services or management contracts lawful, so long as the joint venturers or other contracting parties satisfy certain standards designed to limit the possibility that financial incentives are being exchanged for referrals. The safe harbor requires that the services to be paid at fair market value, and incorporates requirements similar to those set forth in the safe harbors for space and equipment rentals.

d.   Sale of Practice—42 C.F.R. § 1001.952(e)

This safe harbor exempts from criminal or civil liability the traditional sale of a practice by a retiring physician. The safe harbor provision provides protection for the sale of a physician practice that occurs as the result of retirement or some other event that removes the physician from the practice of medicine or from the service area in which he or she was practicing. It does not cover, however, the sale of a practice made for the purpose of obtaining or conferring an ongoing source of patient referrals, or the situation in which a non-retiring physician sells or appears to sell a practice to a hospital while continuing to practice on its staff. Further, sale or option agreements that extend beyond one year are not protected. Thus, the practitioner must no longer be in a position to refer program-related business to the purchaser after a year has passed from the date of the sale agreement.[51]

that is not actually occupied by laboratory personnel at any time, will not be sheltered by the safe harbor if the physician refers most or all laboratory work to this lessee. See 56 Fed. Reg. at 35,-972.

51. 42 C.F.R. § 1001.952(e). See also § 3–12b for a proposed safe harbor to cover the purchase of a practice by a hospital for recruitment purposes, and § 3–12a(3), for a discussion of the proposed safe harbor for the purchase of group practices.

e.   Referral Services—42 C.F.R. § 1001.952(f)

This safe harbor exempts from criminal or civil liability the practice, common among both professional societies and consumer groups, of operating referral services for a fee. Because such a service fee could be construed to constitute a payment for referrals under the plain terms of the anti-kickback statute, the HHS established a specific safe harbor to shelter this practice. The safe harbor protects payments by practitioners and other health care providers "qualified"[52] to participate in the referral services. In order to safeguard against abuse, however, the referral services safe harbor is only available when several standards are met. The referral service must disclose to all persons seeking a referral the criteria it uses to determine who is qualified as a participant, how a particular provider is selected for the referral, the relationship between the participant and the referral service (e.g., that the provider selected is on the hospital's active medical staff), and what criteria the service uses to exclude an individual or entity from continuing as a participant (e.g., if a malpractice allegation is raised against the provider, or the provider refuses to treat a certain level of uncompensated care cases).[53]

The referral service safe harbor protects only those fee payments related to the cost of operating the service. The provision does not protect fees that are based on the volume or value of Medicare or Medicaid referrals made by the service.[54]

f.   Warranties—42 C.F.R. § 1001.952(g)

The warranty safe harbor permits a health care provider to offer a consumer a warranty to induce the consumer to purchase a product. The safe harbor provision is premised on the belief that warranties generally benefit consumers as well as the Medicare and Medicaid program, although they technically violate the statute.

g.   Waiver of Coinsurance and Deductible Amounts for In-patient Hospital Care—§ 1001.952(k)

With the advent of the prospective payment system (PPS) for paying hospitals for inpatient care, some hospitals began to advertise the routine waiver of Medicare coinsurance and deductible amounts as a means of attracting patients to their facilities. HHS

---

52. The determination of whether a health care provider is "qualified" to participate in a referral service may be decided by the referral service according to its own criteria, so long as the criteria are applied equally to all participants. See 56 Fed. Reg. at 35,975–76. For example, hospital referral services may require participants to be employees, while professional organizations may require only that participants pay dues.

53. See 42 C.F.R. § 1001.952(f)(4). The referral service must also maintain a written certification that such disclosures have been made, signed either by the person seeking a referral or the individual making the disclosure. See id.

54. See 42 C.F.R. § 1001.952(f)(2).

proposed a safe harbor for such waivers.[55] The safe harbor was initially limited to waivers connected to inpatient hospital care, and required that the waivers be made available to all Medicare beneficiaries without regard to diagnosis or length of stay and that the costs to the hospital of waiving the coinsurance and deductible amounts not be passed on to any Federal program as a bad debt or in any other way.[56] The safe harbor for waivers of beneficiary coinsurance and deductibles was amended in November 1992 to include the waiver or reduction of inpatient hospital coinsurance or deductible amounts made pursuant to a contract between the hospital and a Medicare SELECT insurer for the furnishing of items or services to Medicare SELECT beneficiaries.

h. Safe Harbor for Managed Care Organizations—42 C.F.R. § 1001.952(*l*)

In the original set of safe harbor regulations, HHS noted the increasing variety of arrangements among health care entities grouped under such generic headings as "preferred provider organizations" (PPOs) and "managed care" or "health management organizations" (HMOs), but declined to delineate a safe harbor provision to cover these arrangements. Instead, HHS took the view that one or more of the safe harbors described above would protect legitimate relationships in preferred provider and managed care networks. HHS invited public comment, however, regarding a safe harbor that would provide additional protection for HMOs, PPOs, and other managed care plans.

Late the next year, in response to voluminous comments about the vulnerability of HMOs, PPOs and other managed care plans to civil and criminal exposure under the anti-kickback provisions,[57] HHS proposed two new safe harbors and amended an existing one "to protect the essential activities of prepaid health plans."[58] The safe harbors were published in final rule form on January 25, 1996.[59] If the various standards and guidelines set forth in the safe harbors are met, a "health plan"[60] is sheltered from criminal

---

55. 42 C.F.R. § 1001.952(k)(1). See generally on the waiver of cost-sharing obligations, Mark S. Lachs, et al., "The Forgiveness of Coinsurance, Charity or Cheating? " 322 New Eng. J. Med. 1599 (1990).

56. See 42 C.F.R. § 1001.952(k)(2); see also 57 Fed. Reg. 52,723, 52,727–28 (1992). The amendment is discussed more fully below at § 3–11h(4).

57. See 57 Fed. Reg. at 52,724.

58. See 42 C.F.R. § 1001.952(1)(2).

59. See 61 Fed. Reg. 2,122 (1996).

60. To constitute a "health plan", an entity must either (1) furnish, or arrange under agreement with contract health care providers for the furnishing of, items or services to enrollees, or (2) as with some PPOs, furnish health insurance coverage for the provision of such items or services. See 42 C.F.R. § 1001.952(1)(2). In either case, the entity must charge a premium (with certain exceptions below) for such covered benefits. Such premiums may be paid by a variety of sources, including HCFA, a State agency, an employer, or the enrollee. In addition, the health plan must

prosecution or civil sanction.[61]

(1) Price reductions offered to enrollees by health plans

The first safe harbor designed to provide shelter to MCOs covers certain marketing incentives that health care plans use to attract "enrollees,"[62] including increased benefits coverage, reduced premiums and reduced cost-sharing amounts (such as coinsurance, deductibles or copayments).

While incentives offered to enrollees are not *per se* violations of the anti-kickback statute,[63] the statute may be implicated when discounts on premiums or other incentives are offered. Health plans offer a host of incentives to attract enrollees, including increasing covered benefits, reducing or eliminating the beneficiary's obligation to pay cost-sharing amounts (such as coinsurance, deductibles, and copayments), or reducing or eliminating the beneficiary's obligation to pay the premium amounts attributable to the cost of furnishing the covered benefits.

either operate under a contract or agreement with HCFA or a State health care program, or be subject to State regulation of its premium structure.

The requirement that health plans operate in accordance with a contract or agreement with HCFA or State health care program, grew out of a concern that providers might create bogus insurance plans where for a "premium" of $1 all Medicare coinsurance and deductibles would be covered. The premium structure of such a plan plainly would not be based on a bona fide assessment of the risk of providing health benefits to enrollees. Therefore, such a health plan would not be considered a legitimate form of health insurance or prepaid health care, but rather would constitute an unlawful copayment waiver program. See 57 Fed. Reg. at 52,724–25.

A health plan that is covered by the safe harbor may also be subject to oversight under state insurance laws or state enabling statutes governing HMOs or PPOs, may be a federally qualified HMOs under 42 U.S.C.A. § 300e, or may operate under the Employee Retirement Income Security Act of 1974 (ERISA). Health plans may exist in a variety of forms, including provider-based plans, union-sponsored plans or company plans. Health plans may also be Medicare supplemental (Medigap) policies, such as a Medicare SELECT plan issued under the terms of Section 1881(t)(1) of the Act. Id. at 52,725.

61. 42 C.F.R. § 1001.952(*l*). For a cogent discussion of this safe harbor, see Gabriel L. Imperato, 1992–1993 Developments in Health Care Fraud and Abuse, in 1993 Health Law Handbook 147, 168–79 (Alice G. Gosfield, ed., 1993).

62. An "enrollee" is an individual who has entered into a contractual relationship with a health plan (or on whose behalf an employer, or other private or governmental entity has entered into such a relationship) under which the individual is entitled to receive specified health care items and services, or insurance coverage for such items and services, in return for payment of a premium. See 57 Fed. Reg. at 52,725.

63. Indeed, incentives to enrollees may be mandated under the Social Security Act or are offered with HCFA's express approval. For example, under certain conditions HMOs and CMPs are required to offer additional benefits or reduce beneficiary cost-sharing amounts. See § 1876 of the Act and implementing regulations. Further, beneficiaries who enroll in HMOs and CMPs are required to pay the Medicare coinsurance and deductible amounts, but HCFA regularly permits health plans to waive the monthly premiums the plans would otherwise charge the beneficiaries to cover the cost of such coinsurance and deductible amounts. See § 1876 of the Act and implementing regulations.

The safe harbor provision is divided into two parts and covers any health plan that operates pursuant to a contract or agreement with HCFA or a state health care program. The first part of the provision protects incentives offered by risk-based contract health plans, such as an HMO, PHP, or CMP,[64] provided that the plan does not discriminate in the offering of these incentives.[65] The provision evidences HHS's view that there is a difference between a prepaid health plan's routine waiver of a beneficiary's obligation to pay coinsurance and deductible amounts, and such a routine waiver granted by other health care providers, such as hospital outpatient departments, physicians, or durable medical equipment suppliers. This is so because a health plan's routine waiver program is inextricably intertwined with the offering of a comprehensive package of covered benefits, rather than being offered for the purchase of an individual program-related item or service. Typically, a routine waiver of cost-sharing amounts by a pre-paid plan will be made in the form of a waiver of the beneficiary's premium or combined with an offer of increased covered benefits. As a result, a pre-paid plan's routine waiver of cost-sharing amounts will not normally lead a plan to use a particular item or service at the time it is furnished. Further, although cost-sharing requirements can serve to control utilization, HMOs and other health plans under contract with HCFA or a state health care program have built-in incentives to control unnecessary utilization, or have their utilization and costs monitored by HCFA or the state programs. Thus, the issue of potential overutilization (with increased costs to the Medicare and Medicaid programs) is adequately addressed without imposing an obligation on beneficiaries to pay coinsurance and deductible amounts.

The second part of the safe harbor protects incentives offered to enrollees by HMOs, CMPs, PHPs, HCPPs and other health plans that are paid on a reasonable cost or similar basis.[66] Again, to be entitled to protection under this provision, the health plan must offer the same incentives to all enrollees for all covered services. In addition, the health plan may not claim the cost of these incentives as bad debts, or otherwise shift the burden of these incentives onto Medicare, Medicaid, other payors, or individuals. Such incentives must be offered because they make economic sense for the health plan, not because of a desire to shift costs.

64. See 42 C.F.R. § 1001.952(*l*)(1)(i).

65. The health plan must offer the same incentives to all enrollees unless otherwise specifically approved by HCFA or a state health care program. This condition minimizes the chance that a health plan might improperly favor certain healthy beneficiaries or offer incentives to improperly encourage utilization at the time an item or particular service is furnished. See 57 Fed. Reg. at 52,725.

66. See 42 C.F.R. § 1001.952(*l*)(1)(i); 57 Fed. Reg. at 52,-725–26.

The health plans must operate in accordance with section 1876(g) or 1903(m) of the Act, under a Federal statutory demonstration authority, or under other Federal statutory or regulatory authority, and the safe harbor does not protect incentives to enrollees offered by health plans that do not have a contractual relationship with HCFA or a State health care program.

An example of an incentive that would not be protected under the safe harbor provision is an agreement between a PPO and a contract health care provider under which the provider agrees not to charge the PPO or enrollee all or part of the coinsurance and deductible amounts. Under such an agreement (which typically would require the contract provider to "accept Medicare payment as payment in full"), the provider agrees to waive all coinsurance and deductibles and agrees to bill the program directly. Although such a waiver agreement could constitute a legitimate means by which to provide a package of health care benefits (similar to the waiver programs protected by the safe harbor provision), HHS's concern that such an agreement might lead to overutilization led it to place such agreements outside the scope of protection. As discussed above, the utilization and costs of health plans that waive cost-sharing amounts are controlled or monitored by HCFA or a state health care program. By contrast, HMOs, PPOs or their providers may bill the Medicare and Medicaid programs on a fee-for-service basis.

(2) Increased coverage, reduced cost-sharing amounts, or reduced premium amounts offered by health plans

The second managed care safe harbor, effective November 5, 1992, protects certain negotiated price reduction agreements between health care plans and "contract health care providers."[67] Under such agreements contract health care providers agree to furnish the health plans, or arrange for the furnishing of, covered items and services at reduced prices. For example, a health care provider might agree to furnish items and services to a health plan's enrollees at a discount from the provider's usual fee in return for obtaining a large volume of patients.

As with the safe harbor provision discussed above, this safe harbor provision is divided into two parts related to risk-based and cost-reimbursed health plans that operate in accordance with a

---

67. A "contract health care provider" is defined as an individual or entity under contract with a health plan to furnish to the health plan's enrollees items or services that are covered by the health plan, Medicare, or a State health care program. Although health care providers may contract with health plans to perform a variety of other functions, such as marketing or peer review, the term "contract health care provider" under these two safe harbor provisions is limited to contracts to furnish covered items and services. See 57 Fed. Reg. at 52,726.

120

contract or agreement with HCFA or a state health care program. In addition, the price reduction safe harbor provision provides protection for other health plans that do not have contracts or agreements with HCFA or a state health care program provided additional standards are met.

The first part of the price reduction safe harbor provision (§ 1001.952(m)(1)(i)) protects risk-based HMOs, PHPs and CMPs under contract with HCFA or a state health care program.[68] As with the preceding safe harbor, except as specifically authorized by HCFA or a state health care program, contract health care providers may not separately bill Medicare, Medicaid or another State health care program for items or services furnished under the agreement with the health plan.[69] Nor may the contract health care provider otherwise shift the burden of the agreement onto Medicare, Medicaid, other payors, or individuals. Risk-based contract health plans must also meet the three prerequisites discussed below.[70]

The second part of the price reduction safe harbor (§ 1001.952(m)(1)(ii)) protects those health plans that have contracted with HCFA or a state health care program to have payment made on a reasonable cost or similar basis.[71] Price reduction agreements negotiated between such health plans and contract health care providers will be protected, provided four standards are satisfied:

    1) The term of the agreement may not be for less than one year;

    2) the agreement must specify in advance the covered items and services that the contract health care provider will furnish to enrollees and the methodology for computing the payment to the contract health care provider;

    3) the health plan must fully and accurately report to HCFA or the state health care program the amount it has paid the contract health care provider pursuant to the agreement; and

    4) the contract health care provider may not claim payment in any form unless specifically authorized by HCFA or the State health care program, or otherwise shift the burden of such an agreement onto Medicare, Medicaid, other payors, or individuals for the costs of furnishing the items and services.

68. See 57 Fed. Reg. at 52,726. As with the preceding safe harbor, such risk-based health care plans must be operating in accordance with section 1876(g) or 1903(m) of the Act, under a federal statutory demonstration authori-ty, or under other federal statutory or regulatory authority.

69. See 57 Fed. Reg. at 52,727.

70. See id.

71. See id.

Any claim for reimbursement made directly by the contract health care provider to Medicare, Medicaid or other state health care program for items or services for which payment was made by the health plan would constitute an unlawful false claim.

The third part of the price reduction safe harbor (§ 1001.952(m)(1)(iii)) protects price reductions offered by contract health care providers to all other health plans, provided six standards are satisfied:

1) The term of the price reduction agreement may not be for less than one year;

2) the agreement must specify in advance the covered items and services, which party (whether the health plan or the contract health care provider) is to file claims or requests for payment with Medicare, Medicaid and the other state health care programs, and the schedule of fees that the contract provider will be paid (*i.e.*, the parties must agree to a set fee schedule);

3) the fee schedule must remain in effect throughout the term of the agreement unless a fee update is specifically authorized by Medicare or a state health care program;

4) the party submitting claims for items or services furnished under the agreement may not claim or request payment for amounts in excess of the fee schedule;[72]

5) the health plan or the contract health care provider must fully and accurately report costs; and

6) the entity (whether the health plan or the contract health care provider) that is not responsible under the agreement for seeking reimbursement from Medicare, Medicaid and any other state health care program is prohibited from claiming payment or otherwise shifting the burden of the price reduction onto Medicare, Medicaid, other payors, or individuals.

(3) Additional Requirements for Safe Harbor Protection

In addition to the foregoing restrictions, the price reduction safe harbor provision contains three additional prerequisites that apply regardless of the nature of the health plan.[73] First, the negotiated price reduction must equal the provider's reduction of its usual charges for the services. The safe harbor does not cover

---

72. This fourth standard does not restrict the contract provider from claiming or requesting payment in amounts in excess of this fee schedule when it negotiates a different fee schedule with another health plan or when it is furnishing items or services directly to enrollees on a fee-for-service basis. See 57 Fed. Reg. at 52,727.

73. See 42 C.F.R. § 1001.952(m)(1).

reductions that are applicable only to a specific part or portion of the health care provider's charge (such as coinsurance and deductibles). It applies only to reductions in the provider's total customary fee. Any other form of remuneration offered or paid by a contract health care provider to a health plan is not protected, and HHS has announced its intention to "closely review any forms of other such remuneration to ensure that improper payments are not employed to induce the health plan to issue a contract or otherwise steer patients to the person paying the remuneration."[74]

Second, the terms of the agreement between the parties must be in writing. This requirement is intended to assist the HHS in understanding the parties' intent. HHS has warned that it will look behind a written contract to determine whether the true intent of the parties is fully disclosed.

Third, the agreement must be entered into for the sole purpose of having the contract health care provider furnish to enrollees items or services that are covered by the health plan, Medicare, or Medicaid. The provision does not protect agreements under which the contract health care provider contracts to furnish services not covered by the programs, such as agreements to furnish peer review, marketing services, or pre-enrollment screening.[75]

(4) Amendment of waiver of copayment safe harbor

Finally, the safe harbor relating to the waiver of coinsurance and deductible amounts for inpatient hospital care was expanded to cover certain agreements between hospitals and Medicare SELECT insurers.[76]

HHS recognized that in return for becoming a preferred provider under the Medicare SELECT plan, a health care provider might be willing to be paid less to treat Medicare SELECT benefi-

---

74. See 57 Fed. Reg. at 52,726.

75. Remuneration attributable to the furnishing of other services will only be protected if it complies with the personal service/management contracts safe harbor (42 C.F.R. § 1001.952(d)) as set forth in the safe harbor regulations published in the Federal Register on July 29, 1991. See 56 Fed. Reg. 35,952 (1991); see also supra at § 3–11c(3).

76. HHS designated 15 states in which state insurance regulators were authorized to approve the issuance of Medicare supplemental (Medigap) insurance policies that restrict Medigap benefits to services provided through a network of providers if the standards in section 1882(t)(1) of the Act are met. See Pub.L.No. 101–508, § 4358, 104

Stat. 1388–135 (codified at 42 U.S.C.A. § 1395ss (1994)). Under this authority, known as Medicare SELECT, approved insurers are authorized to contract with health care providers to furnish items or services to policyholders. Subject to the approval of the respective state insurance commissioners, a Medicare SELECT insurer may pay less than full Medigap benefits for services obtained outside this provider network. Medicare SELECT only applies to Medicare supplemental (Medigap) insurers who meet specific statutory criteria in one of 15 States designated by the Secretary. Initially, Medicare SELECT was approved to operate only for a three year period, commencing on January 1, 1992 and lasting through the end of 1994.

ciaries. The Medicare SELECT insurer, in turn, might be willing to provide health care to its beneficiaries at a lower price. Because such arrangements between Medicare SELECT insurers and provider entities would violate the terms of the anti-kickback statute (either because the provider would offer or pay remuneration in the form of a reduction of its charges to induce the referral of Medicare patients by the insurer to the provider, or the insurer would solicit or receive remuneration from the provider in return for the insurer's referral of Medicare beneficiaries), HHS decided to grant certain arrangements between Medicare SELECT insurers and providers safe harbor protection. Two types of arrangements between Medicare SELECT insurers and providers that would otherwise implicate the statute are entitled to safe harbor protection: 1) payments between Medicare SELECT insurers and health care providers are protected under the safe harbor for price reductions offered to health plans;[77] and 2) waivers or the reduction of inpatient hospital coinsurance and deductible payments by a hospital pursuant to an agreement with a Medicare SELECT insurer are protected under the safe harbor effective on July 29, 1991 for the reduction or waiver of coinsurance or deductible amounts for inpatient hospital services paid for under the prospective payment system.[78]

To receive safe harbor protection under this second type of arrangement, the parties must satisfy certain additional standards:

1) The hospital may not claim the waived amount as bad debt or otherwise shift the cost of the waiver;

2) the hospital may not discriminate in offering reductions or waivers based on the reason for the patient's admission; and

3) the reduction or waiver may not result from an agreement between the hospital and a third-party payor.

Furthermore, to be protected by this safe harbor, the waiver of coinsurance or deductible amounts provided for under the agreement must be limited to beneficiaries covered by the insurer's Medicare SELECT policy.

By contrast, no safe harbor protection is provided for other types of arrangements between Medicare SELECT insurers and providers. For example, HHS continues to consider routine waivers of coinsurance and deductibles under Part B of Medicare unlawful under both the anti-kickback and the federal false claims provi-

---

77. See 42 C.F.R. § 1001.952(m)(1).

78. See 42 C.F.R. § 1001.952(k)(1); see also 57 Fed. Reg. at 52,727. To qualify for protection under this safe harbor, an insurer must have issued a Medicare SELECT insurance policy that meets all of the requirements of section 1882(t)(1), that is, the policy must have been approved by a state insurance commissioner for use in one of the 15 States designated by the Secretary of HHS.

sions.[79] As demonstrated by an advisory opinion issued by the OIG in September 1997,[80] a provider who fails to make reasonable efforts to collect the copayment and deductible obligations of a Medicare beneficiary, violates Section 231(h) of HIPAA and the anti-kickback statute and may be subject to criminal and civil monetary penalties.[81]

§ 3–12. Proposed Safe Harbors

On September 21, 1993, the Secretary of HHS proposed additional safe harbors yet to become effective.[1] These proposals would expand by seven the list of safe harbors currently published in final form.

a. Proposed Supplementary Investment Interests Safe Harbors

Three safe harbors have been proposed to supplement the existing investment interest safe harbor. If made final, these provisions will provide further protection for remuneration received by investors who do business with an entity in which they have invested.

(1) Proposed Safe Harbor for Investment Interests in Rural Areas

Rural areas have had difficulty complying with the twin 60–40 investor and revenue rules that apply to the small entity investment interest safe harbor.[2] The "60–40 investor rule" mandates that no more than 40 percent of the investment interests of an entity be held by investors who are in a position to make or influence referrals to, furnish items or services to, or otherwise generate business for the entity. The "60–40 revenue rule" directs that no more than 40 percent of the gross revenue of an entity be derived from referrals or business generated from investors. The effect of these restrictions may be particularly harsh in areas in which medical investment resources are scarce. In rural areas, for example, physicians may be the only available source of investment capital, and entities in which they invest may be the only available

---

79. See discussion regarding the OIG's Special Fraud Alert on Routine Waiver of Copayments or Deductibles Under Medicare Part B, § 3–15b.

80. See Advisory Opinion No. 97–4 (September 25, 1997), reprinted in full in 1 BNA's Health Care Fraud Rptr. 675 (October 8, 1997). For a discussion of the advisory opinion process see infra § 3–17.

81. See id.

§ 3–12

1. See 58 Fed. Reg. 49,008 (1993). Compliance with the proposed safe harbors does not ensure protection at the present time. Rather, only behavior in compliance with a safe harbor provision published in final form is guaranteed protection.

2. See 42 C.F.R. §§ 1001.952(a)(2)(i) and (vi).

facility to which they can refer program-related patients or business. As a result, HHS has proposed a third investment interest safe harbor which would eliminate the 60–40 investment and revenue rules for entities serving rural areas (as defined by the Office of Management and Budget—a definition also used by the Bureau of the Census).[3]

The proposed safe harbor would prohibit an entity from conditioning an offer of an investment interest on a prospective investor's ability to make or influence referrals to the entity, or to furnish items or services to, or otherwise generate business for the entity. The entity would be required to make a bona fide offer of an investment interest in a good faith nondiscriminatory manner to any potential source of capital. In addition, in lieu of the 60–40 revenue rule, HHS proposes to require that at least 85 percent of the dollar volume of the entity's business in the previous fiscal year, or previous 12 month period, be derived from the service of persons who reside in a rural area. If an entity has not been in business for 12 months, compliance will be determined by examining the source of the entity's business over the entire period of its existence.

(2) Proposed Safe Harbor for Investment Interests in Ambulatory Surgical Centers

HHS has proposed a fourth investment interest safe harbor that would protect certain payments made to surgeons who invest in an ambulatory surgical center (ASC), refer patients directly to the ASC, and personally perform surgery on referred patients. Normally, a physician-investor in such a situation would receive both a professional fee for furnishing the service, and a profit distribution from the entity (which is based in part on the facility fee the entity receives from the program as a result of the surgeon's referral). While the former payment may not implicate the statute, the latter easily could, since the physician's investment interest in the entity could potentially motivate her to refer to Medicare or Medicaid patients to it. To guard against such overutilization, the safe harbor is designed to protect only payments made to a referring-physician whose professional fee greatly exceeds the facility fee that is generated by the referral (*i.e.*, cases in which the physician's profit distribution payment is so outstripped by her professional fee that it is not likely to constitute a significant inducement for referrals). ASC profit distributions generally fit this description. Accordingly, the safe harbor proposes to protect the payment of profit distributions from an ASC to investors where all investors in

_____

3. HHS has solicited comments on the usefulness of this definition of a rural area. See 58 Fed. Reg. at 49,009.

the ASC are surgeons in a position to refer to the ASC and perform services. The proposed safe harbor applies only to ASCs certified under 42 C.F.R. part 416, and will not protect an ASC located on a hospital's premises that shares operating or recovery room space with the hospital for treatment of the hospital's inpatients or outpatients.[4]

Further, to be eligible, the ACS may not offer an investor better investment terms based on past or expected referrals or the amount of services furnished to the entity,[5] passive investors must not be required to make referrals to the entity in order to continue as investors,[6] the entity or any investor may not loan funds to the investor to obtain the investment interest,[7] the payments to the investor must not be based on referrals,[8] and the practitioner must agree to treat Medicare and Medicaid patients.[9] The proposed safe harbor would not extend protection to investment interests held by physicians who are not in a position to refer patients directly to an ASC and perform surgery.

(3) Proposed Safe Harbor for Investment Interests in Group Practices Composed Exclusively of Active Investors

A final investment interest safe harbor has been proposed to protect payments to investors in entities composed only of "active investors" in a "group practice."[10] Three standards (derived from the second investment interest safe harbor)[11] must be met to be eligible for protection under this proposed safe harbor: (i) the terms of the investment interest given to physicians in the group practice cannot be based on expected referrals; (ii) the entity or another investor cannot loan or guarantee a loan to the investor to obtain the investment interest; and (iii) the rate of return must be directly proportional to the capital invested.

b. Proposed Safe Harbor for Practitioner Recruitment

OIG has proposed safe harbor protection for certain payments or benefits offered by rural hospitals and entities in their efforts to recruit physicians and other practitioners to join their staffs. Hospitals located in rural areas often have trouble attracting physicians

---

4. See 58 Fed. Reg. at 49,009.

5. See id.

6. See id.

7. See id.

8. See id.

9. See id.

10. OIG has solicited comments on the appropriate definition of "group practice." It appears, however, that it is inclined to adopt the definition in section 1877(h)(4) of the Act (as amended by section 6204(a) of the Omnibus Budget Reconciliation Act of 1989, Public Law 101–239). See 58 Fed. Reg. at 49,-010. Alternatively the definition of "group practice" that appears in the regulations implementing section 1877(h)(4) of the Act when that regulation is published in final form; see 57 Fed. Reg. 8,588 (1992), or the definition of the term in 42 CFR 417.100, might be employed. See 58 Fed. Reg. at 49,010.

11. See discussion supra, at § 3–11b.

needed to serve the medical needs of the community. The proposed safe harbor would attempt to provide those facilities greater flexibility without shielding payment practices designed simply to channel Medicare and Medicaid related business to recruiting hospitals. The safe harbor is restricted to hospitals and other entities located in "rural areas" (as that term is defined in the proposed investment interest safe harbor for entities located in rural areas) and protects only the recruitment of either a relocating practitioner (a physician who will have to relocate to a new geographic area and start a new practice) or a new practitioner (a physician who is starting a practice or specialty after completing an internship or residency program). Payments made by a hospital to obtain the referrals of an established physician, or a physician who works elsewhere in the same area, would not be covered. In addition, to secure protection for recruitment activity: (i) the terms of the arrangement must be written; (ii) an established practitioner must establish her new primary place of practice not less than 100 miles from the location of her established primary place of practice, and at least 85 percent of the revenue of the new practice must be generated from patients not previously seen by the practitioner at her former practice; (iii) the duration of the payments or benefits to the relocating practitioner may not exceed 3 years unless the new primary place of practice is designated a health professional shortage area (HPSA) for the practitioner's HPSA specialty category during the entire duration of the payments or benefits; (iv) benefits may not be conditioned on the practitioner's referral of business to the entity; (v) the practitioner may not be barred from establishing staff privileges at, or referring business to, another entity; (vi) the entity may not vary, adjust or renegotiate the amount or value of benefits based on the volume of business the physician generates for the entity; and (vii) the practitioner must treat Medicare and Medicaid patients.

c. **Proposed Safe Harbor for Obstetrical Malpractice Insurance Subsidies**

Another proposed safe harbor provision would protect an entity's full or partial payments of the malpractice insurance premiums of a practitioner whose primary practice is obstetrical medicine in a HPSA[12] provided: (i) the agreement is in writing; (ii) at least 85 percent of the practitioner's obstetrical patients covered by the malpractice insurance reside within the HPSA or are a part of a designated shortage area population; (iii) the practitioner is not required to refer any number of patients to the entity; (iv) the practitioner is not barred from establishing staff privileges at,

---

12. "Practitioner" would include a "certified nurse-midwife" as defined in   section 1861(gg) of the Act. See 58 Fed. Reg. at 49,011.

referring patients to, or otherwise generating business for, other entities; (v) payment does not vary based on the number of referrals made by the practitioner to the entity; (vi) the practitioner agrees to treat Medicaid patients; and (vii) a bona fide insurance policy exists.

d. Proposed Safe Harbor for Referral Agreements for Specialty Services

The OIG has further proposed to protect referral agreements for specialty services in which one individual or entity agrees to refer a patient to another individual or entity for specialty services in return for an agreement that the specialist will refer the patient back at a certain time or under certain circumstances.[13] An example of such an agreement would be where a primary care physician conditions a referral of a patient to a specialist on the understanding that the primary care physician will resume the patient's treatment when the patient reaches a particular stage of recovery. It is believed that referral agreements for special services benefit patients by assuring both continuity of care and ready access to competent specialists, and thereby warrant safe harbor protection.

Safe harbor protection would be afforded exclusively to referral agreements for specialty services—that is, services outside the medical expertise of the referring individual or entity, and within the special expertise of the party receiving the referral. To be protected, neither party may pay the other for the referral. The only permissible exchange of value between the parties would be the opportunity to receive remuneration directly from a third-party payor or the patient for professional services (with the sole exception that referring parties who belong to the same group practice may share revenues of the group practice) that accompanies the referral.

e. Proposed Safe Harbor for Cooperative Hospital Service Organizations

A final proposed safe harbor would protect most cooperative hospital service organizations (CHSOs) that qualify under Section 501(c)(3) of the Internal Revenue Code. A CHSO is a cooperative of two or more tax exempt hospitals referred to as "patron-hospitals."[14] The CHSO provides solely for its patron hospitals certain enumerated services (such as purchasing, billing, and clinical services) and is required to distribute to its patrons "all net earnings ... on the basis of services performed."[15] The OIG has proposed

---

13. See 58 Fed. Reg. at 49,011–12.

14. Patron hospitals are tax exempt under the IRC. See 58 Fed. Reg. at 49,-012.

15. 26 U.S.C.A. § 501(e)(2).

safe harbor protection for the payments CHSOs are obligated by IRS regulations to make to their patron-hospitals, and payments patron-hospitals make to CHSOs to support the CHSOs' operational costs. To be eligible for protection, the CHSO must be wholly owned by its patron-hospital. In addition, if the CHSO acts as a group purchasing organization (GPO) or receives discounts for its patrons, the CHSO and its patron-hospitals must comply with the safe harbor provisions that apply to GPOs and discounts discussed above.

Despite the promulgation of the safe harbor provisions, questions about the scope of the anti-kickback statute continue to trouble the industry. Providers worry that they will be exposed to severe criminal and civil sanctions if they conclude in error that their business arrangements fall within a safe harbor or statutory exception. This fear may or may not be justified, depending on each provider's purpose when entering into a particular arrangement, and the way in which the mental element of the statute is interpreted. Increasingly the industry has looked to the scienter requirements of the anti-kickback law as a means for avoiding liability.

§ 3–13. The Scienter Requirements of the Anti–Kickback Statute

Although frequently lumped together by the courts and commentators, the anti-kickback cases present two separate *mens rea* issues. The first concerns the criminal purpose the government must show a health care provider had when soliciting, receiving, offering or paying remuneration. In other words, what proof of *mens rea* is needed to show that the remuneration was given or accepted "in return" for a reimbursable item or service? The second issue concerns whether an individual or entity must know that a particular exchange of remuneration is unlawful to fit within the statute's prohibition of "willful" conduct. At present the courts disagree whether, in order to establish liability, the government must prove that the defendant knew that a payment violated the kickback statute.

a. Purpose to Induce Future Referrals

The anti-kickback statute prohibits the knowing and willful solicitation, offer, payment or receipt of remuneration "in return" for an item or service reimbursable under the programs.[1] Thus, under the plain terms of the provisions, in addition to proving the existence of some payment, and the referral of program-related

§ 3–13

1. 42 U.S.C.A. § 1320a–7b(b)(1) and (2).

goods or services, the government must also show that the payment was made *for the purpose of inducing* the referral. If remuneration is exchanged for some other purpose, the anti-kickback provisions will not come into play. Health care providers sometimes defend against kickback allegations by asserting an innocent purpose for their payments. For example, providers have argued that alleged unlawful kickbacks were actually "interpretive fees,"[2] "consulting fees,"[3] "handling fees,"[4] "marketing fees"[5] and "management fees."[6] The crux of such a defense is that the payment was not made for the purpose of acquiring referrals of program-financed goods or services, but was made for some other, innocent, purpose.

Although the government must prove the unlawful purpose of a payment challenged under the statute, to date the courts have uniformly held that the transfer of referrals need not be the *sole* purpose of the payment. The presence of some innocent purpose by itself will not shield a party from criminal liability. If a party acts with a purpose to exchange remuneration for goods or services reimbursable under the programs, the statute is violated, although a separate innocent purpose for the payment exists simultaneously. As put by one court, "[E]ven if the physician performs some service for the money received, the potential for unnecessary drain on the Medicare system remains."[7]

In such "mixed purpose" cases, the courts have described the wrongful purpose the government must show in a variety of ways. In increasing order of difficulty for the government: one court has held that a conviction under the statute will stand so long as the government establishes that "one purpose" of the challenged payment practice was to acquire future referrals;[8] another has held that proof of a "material purpose" to obtain money for the referral of services is needed to support a conviction under the statute;[9] still another has held that proof that a "primary purpose" of the payment was to induce future referrals is required.[10]

Whatever the level of purpose required, if the payment exceeds the reasonable or fair market value for the proffered innocent justification, unlawful remuneration is likely to be found. In *United*

2. See United States v. Greber, 760 F.2d 68 (3d Cir.1985).

3. See id.; United States v. Bay State Ambulance & Hospital Rental Service, 874 F.2d 20 (1st Cir.1989).

4. See United States v. Hancock, 604 F.2d 999 (7th Cir.1979).

5. See United States v. Jain, 93 F.3d 436 (8th Cir.1996).

6. See United States v. Lipkis, 770 F.2d 1447 (9th Cir.1985).

7. United States v. Kats, 871 F.2d 105, 108 (9th Cir.1989)(quoting Greber, 760 F.2d at 71).

8. Greber, 760 F.2d at 69.

9. See United States v. Kats, 871 F.2d at 108.

10. See United States v. Bay State Ambulance and Hospital Rental Service, 874 F.2d 20, 22 (1st Cir.1989).

States v. Greber,[11] for example, the birthplace of the "one purpose" test, the court upheld a kickback conviction where the trial evidence belied a defendant's claim that payments were made for services rendered, and not, at least in part, for referrals.

The case involved the investigation and prosecution of Dr. Alvin Greber, which began when a number of physicians informed the Federal Bureau of Investigation (FBI) that CardioMed, a company controlled and partially owned by Greber, had paid the physicians each time they referred a patient who ordered a Halter monitor. At trial, and later on appeal, Greber defended the payments on the ground that they were lawful "interpretive fees"[12] that compensated the physicians for evaluative services the physicians had actually rendered. Greber challenged the instruction of the trial court which allowed the jury to convict upon proof that CardioMed paid the fees to the physicians with the intent to induce them to order services from CardioMed. Greber argued that without a demonstration that the only purpose behind the fee was to induce program-funded business, the fees could not be considered unlawful kickbacks.

The Third Circuit rejected this view, concluding that the anti-kickback provisions are violated whenever fees are paid for the purpose of inducing referrals, regardless of whether the fees are also intended to compensate for actual services rendered. Thus, even if the physicians had performed nominal interpretive services for CardioMed, Greber's payments would still constitute unlawful kickbacks if the evidence established that at least *one purpose* for the payments was to acquire their referrals. This was easily found, since the proof at trial established that CardioMed had paid the physicians even when Greber himself had performed the evaluations, and that the fees paid by CardioMed exceeded the amount that Medicare authorized for such services. In other words, the fees exceeded the market value of the interpretive services provided. Indeed, the court concluded that the modest services provided by the referring physicians not only failed to erase the wrongful nature of the payments, they revealed a calculated attempt by Greber to disguise the true character of the fees being paid.[13] Even without proof that a payment exceeded the fair market value of a

---

11. 760 F.2d 68 (3d Cir.), cert. denied, 474 U.S. 988, 106 S.Ct. 396, 88 L.Ed.2d 348 (1985), overruled in part on other grounds, United States v. Friedberg, 1997 WL 36997 (E.D.Pa.1997).

12. Greber also characterized the fees paid to the physicians as "consulting" and "referral" fees. See id. at 70.

13. See also United States v. Lipkis, 770 F.2d 1447 (9th Cir.1985) (evidence sufficient to support conviction of laboratory charged with paying unlawful kickbacks to the management company, despite defense that the payments compensated services provided by the management company, where the government established that the fair market value of those services was considerably less than the payments made to the management company).

service provided, a court may send to the jury the question whether the payment was made for an improper purpose. Such was the case in *United States v. Bay State Ambulance & Hospital Rental Service, Inc.*[14] In *Bay State*, the trial court allowed the jury to decide whether an ambulance company had paid co-defendant John Felci, a hospital official, with the "primary purpose" of inducing Felci to recommend Bay State for a lucrative contract with the hospital. At trial, Felci denied that Bay State had paid him to influence the hospital to award it the ambulance services contract and claimed that the money he had received from Bay State was for bona fide "consulting" services. Felci asked the trial court to instruct the jury that it could not convict him under the statute unless the government proved that the payments were not compensation for his consulting services or that he had been "substantially overpaid" for those services. Instead, the trial court instructed the jury to determine the legality of the payments by examining the intent that underlay the payments, and that if there was more than one purpose for the payments, it could convict if the government had proved that the primary purpose of the payments was to induce Felci to secure an ambulance services contract for Bay State.[15] The First Circuit upheld this instruction on appeal.[16]

In cases in which the payment does not clearly exceed the market value of legitimate services provided, the description of the requisite criminal purpose becomes more important. Differences between whether a court has adopted the "one purpose"[17] "material purpose"[18] or "primary purpose"[19] test could affect the outcome.

b. Knowledge of the Law

Notwithstanding the advent of safe harbor regulations, critics of the federal anti-kickback statute have continued to argue that members of the health care community cannot reasonably be expected to know when the industry's increasingly complex business relationships will violate the anti-kickback rules. This concern underlies one of the most hotly contested issues under the statute:

---

14. 874 F.2d 20 (1st Cir.1989).

15. The pertinent portion of the trial court's instruction read as follows:

The Government has to prove that the payments were made with a corrupt intent, that they were made for an improper purpose. If you find that payments were made for two or more purposes, then the Government has to prove that the improper purpose is the primary purpose or was the primary purpose in making and receiving the payments. It need not be the only purpose, but it must be the primary purpose for making the payments and for receiving them. You cannot convict if you find that the improper purpose was an incidental or minor one in making the payments.

Bay State, 874 F.2d at 29.

16. See id. at 30.

17. See Greber, 760 F.2d at 69.

18. Kats, 871 F.2d at 108.

19. Bay State, 874 F.2d at 29.

whether the scienter requirement includes knowledge of a payment's illegality. The industry achieved a significant victory on this score in the *Hanlester Network v. Shalala.*[20]

In *Hanlester,* the United States Court of Appeals for the Ninth Circuit held that the statute's "knowing and willful" language requires the government to prove not only that the defendant intentionally engaged in conduct prohibited by the statute, but that the defendant did so with the knowledge that his conduct violated the law.[21] Under this view, the government must show not only that the defendant intentionally entered into a referral arrangement later determined to violate the statute, but also that when the defendant entered into the arrangement, or while the defendant benefited from it, he or she knew the arrangement violated the dictates of the anti-kickback law.

Hanlester was the first case to challenge the propriety of a physician self-referral joint venture agreement under the anti-kickback provisions. In a fairly complex financial arrangement, Hanlester Network, a California general partnership, served as the general partner for three limited partnerships (PPCL, Placer and Omni), each of which operated a licensed laboratory. Limited partnership interests in each of the three laboratories were offered to and held by physicians who practiced in the geographical area of the laboratories and who, as a result, were able to refer business to the labs. SmithKline Beecham Clinical Laboratories, Inc. (SKBL) entered into management agreements with each of the laboratories to operate the laboratories, pursuant to which SKBL was paid either 80% of the laboratories' collections, or a fixed monthly fee, whichever was greater. SKBL also entered into a "Master Agreement" with Hanlester under which SKBL received a discount on its services. With these various agreements in place, approximately 85 to 90 percent of all of the tests ordered by physicians from the Network's laboratories were actually performed at SKBL facilities.[22]

In December 1989, the Inspector General of HHS notified the Network and several individuals that they had violated § 1128B(b)(2) of the Social Security Act by offering and paying remuneration to the Network's physician-investors to induce them to refer their patients' tests to the three Hanlester labs. HHS alleged further that the Network had violated § 1128B(b)(1) of the Act by soliciting and receiving remuneration from SKBL in return for referring lab tests to SKBL. HHS sought to exclude the Network defendants (the limited partnerships, the Hanlester general

20. 51 F.3d 1390 (9th Cir.1995).   **22.** See id. at 1395.
21. See id. at 1400.

partners and SKBL)[23] from participation in the Medicare and state health care programs, under the Secretary's civil exclusion authority.[24]

After protracted administrative proceedings, a federal district court upheld an administrative law judge's (ALJ's) finding that all of the named defendants had violated § 1128(B)(b)(2) by knowingly and willfully offering or paying remuneration to the physician-investors to induce them to refer program-related business, and that seven of the nine defendants had violated § 1128(B)(b)(1) by knowingly and willfully soliciting or receiving remuneration in return for referrals.[25] The Ninth Circuit reversed, however, holding that the Secretary had failed to show that the Hanlester defendants (with the exception of the marketing agent) had acted "willfully"[26] as that term had been defined by the United States Supreme Court in *Ratzlaf v. United States*[27] and *Cheek v. United States*.[28] To satisfy the statute's requirement of willful conduct, held the Ninth Circuit, the government had to prove not only that the Network knew that it was offering or paying remuneration to induce referrals, but that it "engage[d] in [such] prohibited conduct with the specific intent to disobey the law."[29] The government's petition asking the Ninth Circuit to rehear the case en banc was denied, and HHS fared no better when it attempted to persuade the Solicitor General to file a petition for certiorari. The Solicitor General decided not to seek Supreme Court review in the case for the proffered reason that *Hanlester* was the first federal appellate decision on the issue.[30]

Under the *Hanlester* scienter standard, ignorance of the law becomes a defense. If a health care provider is unaware that the anti-kickback statute prohibits its remunerative business dealings, it is safe from prosecution. Only defendants who are shown to have known they were breaking the law by entering into an unlawful referral agreement will be subject to a kickback conviction. The government would appear to have no recourse, for example, against a defendant provider who is able to convince the court or fact-finder that he believed, albeit incorrectly, that the challenged financial arrangement fit within one of the many safe harbors. Nor could a

23. SKBL avoided prosecution without an admission of guilt by paying a multi-million dollar fine.

24. See Chapter 5, § 5.2.

25. See 51 F.3d. at 1395.

26. See id. at 1399–1401. The court based its decision on Ratzlaf v. United States, 510 U.S. 135, 138, 114 S.Ct. 655, 657–58, 126 L.Ed.2d 615, 620 (1994), a anti-structuring case that construed the term "willfulness" in 31 U.S.C.A. § 5324 to require both knowledge of the reporting requirement and a specific in-

tent to violate that reporting requirement.

27. 510 U.S. 135, 138, 114 S.Ct. 655, 657, 126 L.Ed.2d 615, 620 (1994).

28. See 498 U.S. 192, 111 S.Ct. 604, 112 L.Ed.2d 617 (1991).

29. See id. at 1400.

30. See D.O.J. Refuses to Ask Supreme Court Review of Hanlester Anti–Kickback Case, 5 BNA's Health Law Reporter 6 (February 8, 1996).

provider who knowingly accepted money in exchange for referring his patient's blood specimens to a particular laboratory be convicted if the defendant successfully persuades the finder of fact that he was somehow unaware that Congress had passed a statute that outlawed such an arrangement.

c. The Aftermath of *Hanlester*—Acquittal of *Caremark* Defendants

Not surprisingly, health care providers facing prosecution under the federal anti-kickback statute have pointed to *Hanlester* in defense of their own challenged referral arrangements. Relying on *Hanlester*, a federal district court in Minnesota granted motions for acquittal filed by three home care executives in a much publicized prosecution, *United States v. Caremark.* In *Caremark*, the court held that the government had failed to show that executives had the specific intent to violate the anti-kickback statute when they paid a physician to prescribe their company's growth hormone.

A California state court has also applied the *Hanlester* intent standard to a prosecution brought under the state's anti-kickback statute[31] and found that the state Attorney General had failed to prove that local clinical laboratory's payments to doctors for sending business had been made with the specific intent to violate the statute.[32] The court concluded that the government had to prove the same intent found by the *Hanlester* court to be required under the federal anti-kickback provisions, even though the California state statute does not contain an express scienter requirement.

d. An Alternative View: *United States v. Jain* and *United States v. Neufeld*

Not all courts have been persuaded that the anti-kickback statute requires knowledge of the law.[33] In *United States v. Jain*,[34] for instance, the Eighth Circuit took a different approach to the anti-kickback conviction of a Missouri psychologist and the company through which he practiced. The government's proof at trial established that the psychologist had entered into an agreement with a psychiatric hospital under which the hospital was to make monthly payments to Jain for purported "marketing services." At trial, the government argued that the agreement was actually a promise to pay Jain for patient referrals and that Jain had in fact

31. See California Wel. and Inst. Code § 14107.2 (1996).

32. See California v. Duz–Mor Diagnostic Laboratory, Inc., No. BC 123965 (Calif. Super. Ct. April 15, 1997).

33. See United States v. Jain, 93 F.3d 436, 440–41 (8th Cir.1996); United States v. Neufeld, 908 F.Supp. 491, 495 (S.D.Ohio 1995); Med. Development Network, Inc. v. Professional Respiratory Care/Home Medical Equip. Services, Inc., 673 So.2d 565, 567 (Fla.Dist.Ct. App.1996).

34. 93 F.3d 436 (8th Cir.1996).

referred almost fifty patients (one of whom was a Medicare patient, and thirty of whom were insured under CHAMPUS) to the hospital in return for payments totaling $40,500. The jury returned a verdict of guilt on all charges.

On appeal, the defendants argued that the court had incorrectly instructed the jury on the term "willfully." The trial court had charged the jury that the term means "unjustifiably and wrongfully, known to be such by" Jain. Relying on *Ratzlaf* and *Cheek*, defendants urged that the charge should have required a showing that they voluntarily and intentionally violated "a known legal duty."[35] The government urged in opposition that the term "willfully" "refers to consciousness of the act but not to consciousness that the act is unlawful."[36] Referring to the traditional principle in the criminal law that ignorance of the law is no excuse, the Eighth Circuit held that the trial court properly adopted a middle position by instructing the jury that the government had to prove that Jain knew his conduct was wrongful, but not that he knew it violated a known legal duty.[37] The court distinguished the willfulness term in the anti-kickback statute from the willfulness term in the *Ratzlaf* currency statute by finding that the former modified a list of enumerated and prohibited acts, whereas the latter modified a clause that prohibited the violation of another statutory provision.[38] Thus, a prosecutor need only show that a defendant "unjustifiably and wrongfully" committed one of the acts prohibited by the anti-kickback statute to support a conviction under its terms.

Jain filed a petition for certiorari with the United States Supreme Court in early 1997 asking the Court to review the disputed intent requirement. As specifically framed in the petition, Jain's attorney's asked the Court to decide: "What is the scienter requirement for 'knowingly and willfully' paying or receiving remu-

---

35. Id. at 440.

36. Id.

37. See id.

38. See id. at 441 (citing Ratzlaf, 510 U.S. at 140–41). Ratzlaf concerned the proper construction of 31 U.S.C § 5324(a)(3), the statute that prohibits structuring transactions "for the purpose" of evading the financial reporting requirement of 31 U.S.C.A. § 5313(a). Criminal punishment may be imposed for a violation of this provision under a separate provision, 31 U.S.C.A. § 5322(a). The government's proof at trial established that Ratzlaf learned that banks are required to report cash transactions over $10,000, and that to pay off a $100,000 debt, Ratzlaf purchased multiple cashiers checks in amounts just under the $10,000 reporting requirement. Based on this proof, Ratzlaf was convicted of unlawful structuring. On appeal, Ratzlaf argued unsuccessfully that the trial court had failed to require the government to prove that he had been aware that structuring the transactions was illegal. The Supreme Court reversed the conviction and held that convictions under § 5322(a) required a finding by the jury that the defendant knew that his conduct was unlawful. The Court reasoned, in part, that currency structuring is not "so obviously 'evil' or 'inherently bad' that the 'willfulness' requirement is satisfied irrespective of the defendant's knowledge of the illegality of structuring." Ratzlaf, 114 S.Ct. at 660–61.

neration in exchange for referring patients, in violation of the Medicare Anti–Kickback Statute, 42 U.S.C.A. 1320a–7b(b), as to which question courts of appeal, district courts, and the Departments of Health and Human Services and Justice are all in conflict?" The petition for certiorari was denied.[39]

Another federal court has refused to interpret the anti-kickback statute to contain a "knowledge of the law" proof requirement. In *United States v. Neufeld*,[40] the court declined to adopt the *Ratzlaf* definition of willfulness[41] and rejected the claim of an osteopathic physician that the anti-kickback statute required the prosecutor to prove that he knew that his acceptance of payments from the Caremark home infusion company was unlawful. The court found two significant differences between the currency structuring statute concerned in *Ratzlaf*, and the anti-kickback statute. First, by conditioning punishment on the willful violation of another statutory provision, the currency structuring statute required proof of that a defendant knew his conduct was unlawful. The anti-kickback statute has no analogous provision.[42] Second, the structuring statute targets conduct that could sometimes be innocent. The court was unconvinced that the payment of bribes for referrals could be similarly described.[43]

e. State Court Reaction to *Hanlester*: *Medical Development Network*

A similar decision to *Jain* was reached by a state court presiding over a civil dispute that concerned the validity of an independent contractor agreement that allegedly violated the federal anti-kickback provisions.[44] The suit was brought by Medical Development Network (MDN), a marketing company, against Professional Respiratory Care (PRC), a durable medical equipment (DME) supplier, for breach of contract. PRC and MDN had entered into an agreement whereby PRC agreed to pay MDN a stated percentage of all of the business MDN secured on PRC's behalf from certain residential and health care facilities or providers, and 30% of PRC's reimbursements from the Medicare program for business arranged by MDN. After entering into the contract, PRC was advised by its counsel that the agreement violated the federal anti-kickback provisions. Thereafter, PRC terminated the agreement and MDN sued for breach. PRC defended its termination of the agreement on the

---

39. ___ U.S. ___, 117 S.Ct. 2452, 138 L.Ed.2d 210 (1997).

40. 908 F.Supp. 491 (S.D.Ohio 1995).

41. See id. at 495 ("Ratzlaf's analysis is neither useful nor applicable to the question of the scienter standard for the Anti–Kickback Statute.").

42. See id.

43. See id.

44. See Medical Development Network, Inc. v. Professional Respiratory Care/Home Medical Equipment Services, Inc., 673 So.2d 565 (Fl. Dist. Ct. App. 1996).

ground that it was illegal under the anti-kickback law and thereby void and unenforceable. The trial court agreed. On appeal, relying in part on *Hanlester*, MDN argued that the agreement was not illegal unless it or PRC had known that the statute prohibited the agreement at the time it was entered into. The state appellate court rejected this claim holding that the statute is "directed at punishment of those who perform specific acts and does not require that one engage in the prohibited conduct with the specific intent to violate the statute."[45]

§ 3–14.　The Future of the "Willfulness" Requirement

It remains to be seen which of these conflicting views of the scienter requirement of the statute will prevail. In 1997, the Clinton administration sought to resolve the dispute legislatively by sending to Capitol Hill a bill that would legislatively overrule *Hanlester's* view of the intent requirement.[1] (Congress has previously acted to overrule legislatively judicial decisions interpreting statutes to include a knowledge of the law provision.)[2] The bill proposed to reverse the Ninth Circuit's ruling by amending the statute to require, somewhat confusingly, "the same level of proof needed under other criminal statutes."[3] Since criminal statutes incorporate a host of *mens rea* terms, without a more precise statement of the proposed scienter terms, it is impossible to predict whether the Clinton proposal would resolve or worsen the controversy. One thing is certain, however, the resolution of this controversy will be critical both to the ability of providers to defend themselves against anti-kickback charges and to the government's ability to prove such charges at trial. Given the high stakes involved, the battle over intent is likely to remain the number one issue arising under the statute for some time to come.

§ 3–15.　The "Advice of Counsel Defense"

The controversy surrounding the scienter element of the anti-kickback law may tempt some providers to invoke the so-called "advice of counsel defense" to avoid criminal liability under the statute.[1] The phrase "advice of counsel defense" is, in many ways,

---

45. See id. at 567.

§ 3–14

1. See Medicare and Medicaid Fraud, Abuse and Waste Prevention Amendments of 1997, § 107 (May 16, 1997).

2. Congress legislatively overruled Ratzlaf by passing the Money Laundering Suppression Act of 1994, Pub.L.No. 103–325, Title IV, 108 Stat. 2160, 2243, which denies defendants accused of

structuring transactions the opportunity to pose an ignorance of the law defense.

3. See Medicare and Medicaid Fraud, Abuse and Waste Prevention Amendments of 1997, § 107 (May 16, 1997).

§ 3–15

1. For a helpful discussion of the advice of counsel defense in the context of health care prosecutions, see Michael K. Fee, The Role of the "Advice of Counsel Defense" in the Trial of a Medi-

a misnomer. Unlike a traditional defense, which a health care defendant might invoke to excuse or justify his criminal conduct, the "advice of counsel defense" allows the defendant to deny that he engaged in criminal conduct to begin with, by demonstrating that the government failed to prove that he had the requisite criminal intent.[2] Although a claim of reliance on "advice of counsel" looks like a defense—since it is invoked by the defendant provider who introduces evidence of reliance on counsel to defend himself against a criminal charge—such a claim actually attempts to show that the government has not carried its burden of proving a basic element of its case, i.e., that the defendant "knowingly and willfully" entered into an unlawful kickback arrangement.[3]

Reliance on advice of counsel can be helpful to a health care provider who has taken steps to avoid entering into an unlawful financial arrangement, but nevertheless fails to insulate himself from exposure under the anti-kickback statute. If the provider can establish that he sought the advice of his attorney concerning a particular proposed arrangement, and that the attorney advised the provider that the arrangement complied with the statute or fell within one of the safe harbors, the court may instruct the jury that the provider's reliance on that advice is relevant to whether he "knowingly and willfully" engaged in unlawful kickback activity. This instruction would be particularly helpful to individuals or entities delivering health care in jurisdictions that adopt the view of *Hanlester Network v. Shalala*[4] that the government must prove that a provider had knowledge that he was violating the statute when he acted.[5]

An advice of counsel instruction may be given to a jury if the defendant establishes a sufficient evidentiary basis for the charge.[6] To establish such a basis, most courts require a defendant to produce evidence that he fully disclosed all pertinent facts to his

---

care/Medicaid Kickback Case, Health Care Fraud 1995 at E–35.

2. A classic criminal "defense," essentially concedes that the defendant engaged in criminal conduct, but attempts to excuse or justify that conduct in some way. For example, a defendant charged with murder might admit that he caused the death of another, but then attempt either to justify the killing as an act committed in self-defense, or to excuse the killing as an act committed while the defendant was insane or under duress. By contrast, the health care provider who asserts that he relied on "advice of counsel" is not attempting to justify or excuse conduct that the provider concedes is unlawful. Rather, the provider

is attacking any conclusion that his conduct constituted a crime by using his reliance on his counsel's advice to show that he lacked the requisite criminal intent for the crime.

3. See United States v. Ibarra–Alcarez, 830 F.2d 968, 973 (9th Cir.1987) ("advice of counsel" is not regarded as a separate and distinct defense but rather as a circumstance indicating good faith which the trier of fact is entitled to consider on the issue of fraudulent intent.).

4. 51 F.3d 1390 (9th Cir.1995).

5. See § 3–13b.

6. See Ibarra–Alcarez, 830 F.2d at 973.

counsel before receiving the advice, that he relied in good faith on that advice and acted in strict accordance with it.[7] The defense is not available to a defendant who secures advice simply as a means to facilitate a crime.[8]

The obligation to produce evidence before qualifying for an advice of counsel instruction, can place a defendant in a difficult strategic position. A defendant must divulge all of the facts that were disclosed to the attorney from whom advice was sought, and the nature of the advice received, with no guarantee that the court will grant the request for the instruction.[9] The disclosures made in such a case could provide the government with additional ammunition with which to prove its case, particularly if the disclosures revealed advice given by counsel that the defendant failed to heed. The disclosures would also waive privileged attorney-client communications. Given the potential pitfalls of seeking an advice of counsel instruction, counsel considering invoking the defense should first undertake a careful review of all pertinent facts surrounding the advice to ensure that the request for the instruction will not result in a windfall to the government with no benefit to the defendant.

§ 3–16. Outstanding Enforcement Issues Under the Anti–Kickback Statute

a. Joint Venture Arrangements.[1]

Joint venture arrangements continue to generate some of the most troublesome issues arising under the anti-kickback law. Although some once-popular joint financial arrangements are today acknowledged to be unlawful (e.g., mandatory buy-back agreements under which a joint venture agrees to buy back a physician-investor's interest in the joint venture when the physician leaves

7. See, e.g., United States v. Lindo, 18 F.3d 353 (6th Cir.1994); United States v. Schmidt, 935 F.2d 1440, 1449 (4th Cir.1991); Liss v. United States, 915 F.2d 287 (7th Cir.1990); United States v. Bush, 599 F.2d 72, 72–78 (5th Cir.1979); United States v. Polytarides, 584 F.2d 1350, 1352 (4th Cir.1978) (no instruction warranted where defendant secured the advice after he began the unlawful conduct).

8. See, e.g., United States v. Carr, 740 F.2d 339 (5th Cir.1984) (the defense is unavailable to a defendant who retains counsel "to insure the success" of a criminal scheme, or when an attorney provides advice simply to advance the client's unlawful scheme).

9. For example, a court could deny the request after considering the defendant's proffered evidence if it decides that the defendant failed to disclose all material facts to counsel, or failed to strictly comply with that advice.

§ 3–16

1. Joint ventures in the health care industry commonly involve either a contract under which two or more parties agree to cooperate in providing health care services, or the creation of a separate legal entity (such as a limited partnership or closely held corporation) which provides services. See 59 Fed. Reg. 65,372, 65,373 (1994).

the area or retires),[2] the legality or illegality of other arrangements is less obvious. Many questions continue to perplex the industry. For example, may small physician-owned entities unite to qualify for the shelter provided by the large entity safe harbor?[3] May "earn-out" provisions[4] be utilized by joint venturers without offending the anti-kickback prohibitions? When will financial incentives offered by hospitals to physicians under joint venture agreements violate the anti-kickback rules? Some help with these and other questions relevant to joint ventures may be found in a special fraud alert issued by the OIG in 1989.

In 1989, OIG distributed to over 1.5 million providers, practitioners, suppliers, and others in the industry a special fraud alert on joint venture arrangements which identifies particular practices of limited partnerships and other joint ventures that the OIG considers suspect under the statute.[5] The fraud alert publicizes the OIG's view that a joint venture arrangement may implicate the anti-kickback provisions if it encompasses an agreement by its joint venturers to refer to each other business, items or services for which reimbursement could later be sought under the Medicare or Medicaid programs. Such an arrangement might include, for example, the referral of clinical diagnostic laboratory services, durable medical equipment (DME), or other diagnostic services.[6] The alert warns that a joint venture that channels a stream or referrals from one joint venturer to another in exchange for compensation (either direct or indirect) for those referrals might constitute an unlawful kickback arrangement.

The OIG's concern about the referral activities of independent clinical laboratories (ICLs), independent physiological laboratories, and DME suppliers arose in part from a 1989 study that found "patients of referring physicians who own or invest in clinical laboratories received 45% more clinical laboratory services than all Medicare patients, regardless of the place of service."[7] A second study conducted by the Florida Health Care Cost Containment Board (HCCCB) in 1991 reached similar conclusions. The HCCCB's study showed that in 1989, close to 50% of Florida's ICLs were owned in whole or part by physician referrers, and that 93% of the state's diagnostic imaging centers were physician-owned, and that some services showed a statistically significant increase in utiliza-

2. See Carrie Valient, Legal Issues in Health Care Fraud and Abuse: Navigating the Uncertainties 101 (1994).

3. See supra § 3–11; see also Chapter 4, § 4–5 and 4–6.

4. Under earn-out agreements, the purchase price of a joint venture entity is conditioned on the entity's future earnings.

5. Special Fraud Alert: Joint Venture Arrangements (August 1989), reprinted in 59 Fed. Reg. at 65,373.

6. See id. at 65,373.

7. See OIG, Financial Arrangements Between Physicians and Health Care Business (May 1989).

tion as a result of referral activity. For example, ICLs owned by referring physicians performed almost twice as many diagnostic tests as non-joint venture laboratories.[8]

The special fraud alert on joint venture arrangements reflects the OIG's concern that some physician investors standing to profit from a joint venture referral arrangement may be tempted to order unnecessary tests, procedures or other items from their joint venturers, resulting in overutilization and depletion of program funds. The special fraud alert warns that "questionable features" of "suspect" joint ventures have been detected: 1) within provisions related to the manner in which investors were to be selected and retained; 2) within provisions related to the financing obligations of the investors or their profit distributions; and 3) in the structure of the joint venture itself.[9] A non-exhaustive list of questionable features common to each of these three areas is included in the alert to help providers and their counsel identify problematic features of joint venture arrangements.

(1) Special Fraud Alert—The Manner of Selection and Retention of Investors

The fraud alert dubs "questionable" several selection and retention methods utilized by some joint venturers. Based on this list, the OIG can be expected to take a dim view of the following:

Seeking Rainmakers. Arrangements under which investors are selected because they are able to make referrals.

Perks Conditioned on Volume of Referrals. Arrangements under which physicians who are expected to make a greater number of referrals are offered superior investment opportunities in the joint venture compared to those expected to make fewer referrals.

Low Achievers Get the Boot. Arrangements under which physician investors are encouraged to divest their investment interest in the joint venture if they fail to sustain an "acceptable" level of referrals, or they cease to practice in the service area (e.g., if they move, become disabled or retire).

Keeping and Circulating Scorecards. The joint venture keeps a tally of the referrals made by its investors, and disseminates the tally to the investors.

Nontransferable Investment Interests. The joint venture agreement forbids the transfer of investment interests.[10]

---

8. See Joint Ventures Among Health Care Providers in Florida, Vol. 2 State of Florida HCCCB (Sept. 1991).

9. See 59 Fed. Reg. at 65,374.

10. Id.

(2) Special Fraud Alert—Financing and Profit Distribution Agreements

Also considered suspect are certain financing and profit distribution agreements including the following sweetheart deals:

Lucrative Financing or Inflated Profit Distribution Deals. Agreements under which the amount of capital invested by the physician is disproportionately small and the return on investment disproportionately large when compared to a typical investment in a new business enterprise.

Nominal Investments. Arrangements under which physician investors are asked to invest only nominal amounts in the joint venture.

Joint Venture Advances the Capital for Investment. Arrangements under which physician investors are permitted to "borrow" their initial "investment" from the joint venture entity, and repay it through deductions from profit distributions.

Extraordinary Return on Investment. Investors receive extraordinary returns on the investment given the risk involved in the venture (e.g., in excess of 50 to 100 percent per year).[11]

(3) Special Fraud Alert—The Business Structure of the Joint Venture

Joint ventures that exist or operate essentially as a shell to cloak the profit-making activities of the joint venturers will also be regarded as suspect vehicles for the transfer of unlawful remuneration.[12]

(4) Exclusion Efforts Against Joint Ventures: The Hanlester Network Case

The OIG initiated its first effort to exclude a joint venture in 1989 when it served an exclusion notice on a California partnership known as The Hanlester Network (Hanlester).[13] The OIG alleged that Hanlester had created three shell joint venture limited partnership laboratories to channel laboratory referral business from physician investors to SmithKline Beecham Clinical Laboratories (SmithKline) in exchange for payments to the physicians. Under management contracts with SmithKline, 85% to 90% of all the physician investor's testing was performed on a referral basis by SmithKline laboratories. In December 1989, SmithKline reached a record $1.5 million settlement with the OIG. Shortly thereafter, the OIG filed charges against the joint venture's managing partner, medical director, vice president for marketing, and the partnership

11. See id.
12. See id.

13. 51 F.3d 1390 (9th Cir.1995).

laboratories, under the anti-kickback statute, seeking program exclusions. Not named in the action were the physician investor limited partners, although the OIG did allege that the payments made to the limited partners were unlawful under the statute. After a series of administrative proceedings, an administrative law judge (ALJ) found that the payments to the limited partners and the management contracts with SmithKline violated the anti-kickback statute,[14] and that all of the named defendants were liable for those violations. The ALJ noted that several features of the Hanlester joint venture evidenced its illegality including that the limited partnership interests were marketed only to physicians in a position to refer substantial tests; the physician investors were permitted to invest in the joint venture for minimum amounts (typically $1500); marketing brochures advised the physician investors that failure to refer business would be "a blueprint for failure;" and payments to the physicians were at least indirectly proportional to the limited partners' volume of referrals.[15] On appeal before the United States Court of Appeals for the Ninth Circuit, the court upheld the Secretary's view that the Hanlester joint venture was designed to induce the limited physician partners to refer business to the joint venture laboratories, in violation of the anti-kickback statute.[16] Nevertheless, the court upheld the judgment against only one of the individual defendants (the marketing agent) based on its interpretation of the statute's "knowing and willful" mens rea requirement,[17] discussed above.[18]

b. Routine Waiver of Medicare Part B Copayments and Deductibles

Other financial incentives offered by some health care providers have come under the OIG spotlight, including the practice of waiving copayment responsibilities of Medicare beneficiaries. Although waivers of standard copayment obligations are offered to attract Medicare customers, they function without directly increasing the government's costs. For this reason, several United States Attorneys have taken the position that such waiver practices do not warrant prosecution.[19] The Department of Justice has been reluctant, however, to declare that all waivers of copayment responsibilities are permissible under the statute,[20] and a special fraud alert

---

14. Decision on Remand of the ALJ, The Inspector General v. The Hanlester Network, Dept. of HHS, Departmental Appeals Board; Civil Remedies Division; Doc. No. C–448, Dec. No. CR 181, reprinted in CCH Medicare and Medicaid Guide ¶ 40,064.

15. Id.

16. See id. at 1399.

17. See id.

18. See discussion infra at § 3–13.

19. See Theodore J. McDowell, The Medicare–Medicaid Anti–Fraud and Abuse Amendments: Their Impact on the Present Health Care System, 36 Emory L. J. 691, 750 (Spring 1987).

20. See id. at 749–52.

issued by the OIG suggests that at least some waiver practices will be considered to be suspect.

The special fraud alert focuses on the conduct of "charge-based" practitioners or health care suppliers[21] who routinely decline to bill Medicare beneficiaries for (or waive) Part B copayments and deductibles. Charge-based providers, practitioners or suppliers are paid by Medicare on the basis of an ascertained "reasonable charge" for the item or service provided.[22] The Medicare program generally pays charged-based providers 80% of the reasonable charge of a covered item or service,[23] and requires the Medicare beneficiary to pay the remaining 20% of the charge—that is, the program requires the beneficiary to make a 20% "copayment." In addition, before any payments are made under the program for items or services the Medicare beneficiary is required to pay a "deductible." The special fraud alert cautions that routine waivers of a Medicare beneficiary's copayment and deductible obligations by a charge-based provider may result both in the submission of false claims (by misstating the provider's actual charge)[24] and a violation of the anti-kickback provisions (by offering potential patients something of value, a waiver of financial obligations, to induce them to purchase items or services from the provider). The rationale for the prohibition against routine waivers is that Medicare funds will be conserved if beneficiaries are encouraged to become "better health care consumers, and select items or services because they are medically needed, rather than simply because they are free."[25] The theory is that if a beneficiary is required to pay some portion of the cost of his care, he will police his health care needs more carefully.

To help members of the industry assess the legality of their marketing programs, the alert offers the following non-exhaustive list of marketing practices that the OIG considers to be suspect.

---

21. See Special Fraud Alert: Routine Waiver of Copayments or Deductibles Under Medicare Part B (1991), reprinted in 59 Fed. Reg. 65,372. The alert did not cover similar waivers given by providers, practitioners or suppliers paid on the basis of costs or diagnostic related groups (DRGs).

22. See 42 U.S.C.A. § 1395u(b)(3) (1994); 42 C.F.R. § 405.501.

23. See 42 U.S.C.A. § 13951(a)(1) (1994).

24. See 59 Fed. Reg. at 65,375. The OIG explained why such a waiver might be viewed as a false claim:

[I]f a supplier claims that its charge for a piece of equipment is $100, but routinely waives the copayment, the

actual charge is $80. Medicare should be paying 80 percent of $80 (or $64), rather than 80 percent of $100 (or $80). As a result of the supplier's misrepresentation, the Medicare program is paying $16 more than it should for this item.

Id.

25. See Special Fraud Alert: Routine Waivers of Copayments and Deductibles Under Medicare Part B (1991), 59 Fed. Reg. 65,372, 65,375. The OIG noted that a waiver of copayments and deductibles is lawful when a particular patient suffers from a special financial hardship, but that the hardship exception is not to be used routinely.

Advertising that Waivers or Discounts Will Be Granted. Advertisements publicizing routine waivers (e.g., "Medicare Accepted As Payment in Full," "Insurance Accepted As Payment in Full" or "No Out–Of–Pocket Expense") or that discounts will be given to Medicare beneficiaries are considered suspect.

Practice of Claiming Financial Hardship. A provider's routine use of "Financial Hardship" forms (which state that the beneficiary is unable to pay the coinsurance/deductible) when the provider has made no good faith attempt to determine the beneficiary's actual financial condition, will be considered suspect.

Charging Copayments/Deductibles for Medigap Consumers Only. A provider's practice of collecting copayments and deductibles only if the beneficiary's Medicare supplemental insurance ("Medigap") coverage covers the items or services, is considered suspect.

Inflated Charges to Medicare Beneficiaries to Recoup Waiver Costs. A provider's practice of billing Medicare beneficiaries higher charges for similar services and items than those billed for non-Medicare patients in order to offset waiver of coinsurance costs, will be considered suspect.

Waivers of Copayments/Deductibles for Referrals. A provider's uniform failure to collect copayments or deductibles from a specific group of Medicare patients in exchange for referrals (e.g., a supplier waives coinsurance or deductible for all patients from a particular hospital in order to get referrals from the hospital) will be suspect.

Offering Sham Insurance. Offering "insurance" to cover a beneficiary's copayments or deductibles for items or services provided by the entity, based on the beneficiary's payment of a nominal premium, will be suspect.[26]

Section 231(h) of the Health Insurance Portability and Accountability Act of 1996 (HIPAA),[27] effective January 1, 1997, gave many of these warnings the force of law. Section 231(h) includes within the term "remuneration" any waiver of Medicare copayment obligations that a provider knows or should know is likely to influence a beneficiary to choose it over a competitor.[28] The OIG interpreted this provision to apply to a provider who failed to make reasonable efforts to collect copayments and deductibles from patients, even though the provider contended that the copayment amounts should

26. Id.
27. Pub.L.No. 104–91, 110 Stat. 1936 (1996).
28. See id.

have been paid by the patients' insurer, rather than by the patients themselves.[29]

c. Physician Recruitment and other Hospital Incentive Practices

Physician recruitment practices by hospitals are another subject of investigative and prosecutorial activity. Hospitals have been known to offer a multitude of incentives to convince physicians to join their staffs. The legality of some of these incentives under the anti-kickback provisions is not always clear. At bottom, if an incentive is offered in order to secure a lucrative referral stream, the anti-kickback statute may be violated.

The OIG released a third special fraud alert in May 1992 focusing on hospitals that offer certain economic incentives (also known as "practice enhancements") in order to recruit or retain physicians and boost patient referrals to the hospitals. Practice enhancements vary in form. Some reduce a physician's expenses (e.g., by offering the provider free or rent-reduced office space or an opportunity to become a limited partner in a medical office building), others increase her profits. No matter the form, the fraud alert warns that if a hospital establishes an incentive program that compensates a physician directly or indirectly for the referral of the physician's patients to the hospital, the anti-kickback provisions may be offended, and no safe harbor exists to shelter the program.[30]

To help hospitals identify features in their incentive arrangements that might be suspect, the alert lists as "questionable" a number of compensation practices:

Compensating Referrals. Making payments or providing other incentives to a physician each time the physician refers a patient to the hospital.

Discounts for Referrals. Offering a physician free or significantly discounted use of hospital-owned office space, hospital-owned equipment, billing services, nursing services or other staff services.

Free Staff Training. Offering free training for a physician's staff in such areas as management techniques, CPT coding and laboratory techniques.

Guaranteeing a Floor Income. Offering to supplement a physician's income if the physician's income fails to reach a predetermined level.

---

29. See Advisory Opinion No. 97–3, reprinted in 1 BNA's Health Care Fraud Rptr. 603 (Sept. 10, 1997), and discussed supra at § 3–17.

30. See Special Fraud Alert: Hospital Incentives to Physicians (1992), reprinted in 59 Fed. Reg. at 65,375.

Sweetheart Loans for Referrals. Providing low-interest or interest-free loans, or loans which may be "forgiven" if a physician refers patients to the hospital.

Covering Travel/Conference Costs. Paying the cost of a physician's travel and/or conference expenses.

Covering Continuing Education Costs. Paying the cost of a physician's continuing education courses.

Providing Bargain Insurance. Providing coverage for a physician on hospitals' group health insurance plans at an inappropriately low cost to the physician.

Sham Consulting Agreements. Paying for a physician for "consulting" services when the physician in fact has few, if any, substantive duties, or paying a physician for services in excess of their fair market value.[31]

One reported case provides a helpful example of how a physician recruitment practice that is found to violate the anti-kickback provisions can lead to consequences beyond prosecution or exclusion. In *Polk County v. Peters*,[32] a court held unenforceable a contract between a physician and the hospital that enticed him to join its staff by offering him an income guarantee of $8,500 per month for twelve months, $5,000 in moving expenses, $7,500 for his first year's malpractice insurance premiums, free office space in the hospital for three months, and $6,000 in rental and utilities for six months.[33] The hospital sought to enforce a provision in the contract that required Peters to repay the amounts the hospital advanced to him under the income guarantee. Although no provision in the contract required Peters to refer patients to the hospital, the hospital sought repayment from Peters only *after* it terminated his staff privileges for his failure to use it as his "primary hospital." With this evidence of the hospital's motivation, the court held the contract unenforceable under the anti-kickback statute, writing:

> While the hospital may well have been motivated to a greater or lesser degree by a legitimate desire to make better medical services available to the community, there can be no doubt that the benefits extended to Defendant were, in part, an inducement for him to refer patients to the hospital.[34]

The holding in *Peters* and the OIG's special fraud alert both indicate that where a hospital links particular incentives to a physician's ability to make referrals, the incentive will become suspect under the anti-kickback provision.

31. See 59 Fed. Reg. at 65,376.
32. 800 F.Supp. 1451, 1456 (E.D.Tex.1992).
33. See id.
34. Id.

d. Prescription Drug Marketing Practices

In August 1994, the OIG issued a fourth special fraud alert that targets the aggressive marketing practices employed by some prescription drug companies.[35] Drug companies use a variety of marketing programs to expand their products' distribution. Under these programs physicians, suppliers and patients may be offered a wide array of incentives to choose the prescription drug products of one company over those of its competitors. The alert voices the concern that when such incentives are offered, physicians and pharmacists may be influenced to promote particular brands of drugs based on profits rather than what is in the best medical interests of their patients or customers.[36]

The fraud alert cautions that if one of the purposes underlying an offer of such an incentive is to induce physicians, pharmacists, suppliers or other practitioners to prescribe or recommend medications for which reimbursement may be sought under the Medicaid program, the anti-kickback provisions will apply. The alert reports that the OIG has already investigated of a number drug company marketing plans offering incentives to physicians or pharmacists. Many of the plans did not pass muster. For example, one drug company, under a so-called "product conversion" program, paid pharmacies to help the drug company persuade physicians to prescribe the drug company's products over those of its competitors. The company paid the pharmacies a fee for each physician "converted" to its product. The successful program netted the enterprising drug company 96,000 brand-name conversions.[37]

Other prescription drug companies have employed subtler, but equally violative, tactics. One company adopted a "frequent flier" campaign that offered physicians frequent flier mileage credits each time the physician completed a questionnaire for a new patient on the drug company's product.[38] A third resourceful drug company offered under its "research grant" program sizable payments to

---

35. See Special Fraud Alert: Prescription Drug Marketing Schemes (August 1994), reprinted in 59 Fed. Reg. at 65,376.

36. See id.

37. See id.

38. See id. This example may refer to the government's investigation of the marketing activities of Ayerst Laboratories. Ayerst entered into a consent agreement with the OIG and DOJ's Civil Division on July 29, 1993 under which the company agreed to pay $830,-000 to settle allegations related to a marketing program that enrolled 20,000 physicians to help promote one of the drugs manufactured by Ayerst. See BNA's Health Law Reporter (Aug. 12, 1993). Under the program the physicians were given starter bottles containing 14 capsules of the drug along with questionnaires. Each time one of the physicians filled out a questionnaire indicating that the physician had prescribed Ayerst's product, the physician was awarded points which later could be redeemed for airline certificates or other honoraria. Although the consent agreement concerned civil false claims allegations, Ayerst's conduct could also have been challenged under the anti-kickback statute.

any physician who completed minimal recordkeeping tasks after administering the company's products. Physicians were paid by the company after they had administered the company's products and recorded briefly (often by no more than a word) the outcome of the treatment.[39]

How can a drug company know whether its marketing plan complies with the mandates of the anti-kickback law? The OIG's fraud alert offers some guidance. The alert sets forth a non-exhaustive list of payments or gifts which if offered by a prescription drug company to a physician, pharmacist or other entity might be considered suspect by the OIG:

> *Payments to Rainmakers.* Payments made to a person in a position to generate business for the payor drug company.

> *Proportional Payments.* Payments made proportionate to the volume of business generated by the payee for the drug company.

> *Payments in Excess of Fair Market Value of Services Rendered.* Payments that exceed the fair market value of any legitimate service rendered to the payor drug company, or that are unrelated to any service other than referral of patients.[40]

The special fraud alert warns further that a marketing program with one or more of the following features might become the target of an investigation under the anti-kickback statute:

> *Perks for Prescriptions.* A marketing program that offers a physician and/or supplier (including pharmacies, mail order prescription drug companies and managed care organizations) prizes, gifts, cash, coupons or bonuses (e.g., airline discounts and related travel premiums) in exchange for which the recipient prescribes or provides specific prescription products.[41] These items are particularly suspect if based on value or volume of business generated for the drug company.

> *Product Conversion Agreements.* Marketing materials that offer cash or other benefits to pharmacists (or others in a position to recommend prescription drug products) who agree to help market specific drug products (i.e., contract to perform sales-oriented "educational" or "counseling" services or physician and/or patient outreach).[42]

---

39. See 59 Fed. Reg. 65,372 (1994).

40. See id.

41. See, e.g., Consent Agreement of Ayerst Laboratories, see 2 BNA's Health Law Reporter 32 (August 12, 1993) (agreeing to pay $830,000 to settle allegations that it had induced physicians to prescribe one of its drug products with airline certificates and other honoraria).

42. An example of such a marketing program was featured in the Wall Street Journal on June 1, 1994. The newspaper reported that the OIG was investigating the marketing program of pharmaceutical manufacturer Miles, Inc. Under the

Sham Research Agreements. A marketing program that purports to provide grants to physicians and clinicians to undertake studies of a company's prescription products, when either the study is of questionable scientific value or little or no actual scientific pursuit.[43]

Prescription Conversion Agreements. A program that pays (or provides some other benefit to) a patient, provider or supplier to change a prescription for a competitor's product to its own, or to recommend or request such a change, unless the payment or benefit falls under a "safe harbor" regulation,[44] or complies with some other federal provision governing the reporting of prescription drug prices.[45]

The recent enforcement activities of the OIG and the Department of Justice illustrate how the anti-kickback provisions have affected the marketing programs of pharmaceutical manufacturers. In the well-known *Caremark* litigation, for example, Caremark, Inc., a major drug distribution company, was indicted for paying a physician over $1 million in kickbacks to promote sales of its growth hormone, Protropin.[46] Caremark pleaded guilty to the kickback charges in 1995 and entered into a global settlement of criminal and civil allegations related to its Protropin marketing program. Under the agreement Caremark agreed to pay the federal government and various state agencies $161 million in fines, penalties and restitution.

e. Arrangements for the Provision of Clinical Laboratory Services

In October 1994, the OIG issued its fifth special fraud alert notifying the health care community that certain arrangements for the provision of clinical laboratory services might also be suspect.[47]

program, Miles, Inc. paid participating pharmacists to counsel their customers about Adalat CC, a heart drug manufactured by the Miles, allegedly to encourage those customers to switch from a competing drug manufactured by Pfizer. According to the report, the OIG was investigating whether the fees paid to the pharmacists were unlawful inducements under the anti-kickback statute.

43. See, e.g., Caremark, Inc. global settlement agreement (settling allegations that, under the guise of research and consulting agreements, Caremark had made $1.1 million in kickback payments to a physician to promote the sale of its growth hormone, Protopin). See 4 BNA's Health Law Reporter 953 (June 22, 1995); Settlement Agreement Between Hoffmann–LaRoche and the OIG, settling civil allegations that, under the guise of research grants, Hoffman–LaRoche had paid kickbacks to physicians to promote its drug Rocephin. See 3 BNA's Health Law Reporter 36 (September 15, 1994).

44. See discussion of safe harbor provisions at § 3–11.

45. See 59 Fed. Reg. 65,372 (1994).

46. See In re Caremark Int'l Inc. Derivative Litigation, 1996 WL 549894 at 4 (Del.Ch. Sept.25, 1996). The indictment also charged an executive officer at Genentech, a biotech firm.

47. See Special Fraud Alert: Arrangements for the Provision of Clinical Lab Services (Oct. 1994), reprinted in 59 Fed. Reg. at 65,377.

The alert addresses the validity of arrangements between health care providers and the clinical laboratories to which those providers refer patient specimens for analysis. While recognizing that such arrangements are an important feature of the nation's health care delivery system, the alert indicates that the OIG might consider some to be screens designed to cloak the exchange of remuneration for referrals.[48]

The fraud alert discusses a number of laboratory services arrangements that might violate the anti-kickback statute, including arrangements under which: 1) a laboratory places in a referring physician's office a phlebotomist who not only collects specimens from patients for testing by the laboratory, but performs other clerical or medical tasks normally handled by the physician's office staff; 2) a laboratory offers to perform tests for patients with end stage renal disease (ESRD) (normally compensated according to a standard composite rate)[49] for a price that is less than the fair market value of the tests performed, after securing an agreement from the renal dialysis center that performs the tests that that facility will refer all or most of its non-composite rate tests to the laboratory;[50] 3) a clinical laboratory negotiates a contract with a MCO to provide free laboratory services to a provider affiliated with the plan for the provider's managed care patients, in exchange for the provider's agreement to refer its non-managed care patients' business to the laboratory;[51] 4) a laboratory agrees to pick-up and

48. The fraud alert explains further:

Whenever a laboratory offers or gives to a source of referrals anything of value not paid for at fair market value, the inference may be made that the thing of value is offered to induce the referral of business. The same is true whenever a referral source solicits or receives anything of value from the laboratory. By "fair market value" we mean value for general commercial purposes. However, "fair market value" must reflect an arms length transaction which has not been adjusted to include the additional value which one or both of the parties has attributed to the referral of business between them.

Id.

49. The Medicare program reimburses laboratory services provided to ESRD patients in two different ways. Some ESRD laboratory testing is considered routine. The Medicare program pays a composite rate to the ESRD facility that performs these routine tests, and that facility in turn pays the laboratory. Additional, non-routine tests re-

quired by ESRD patients are billed by the laboratory directly to Medicare and paid according to the usual laboratory fee schedule. See id.

50. See id. See also Chapter 4.

51. The fraud alert explains:

The status of such agreements under the anti-kickback statute depends in part on the nature of the contractual relationship between the managed care plan and its providers. Under the terms of many managed care contracts, a provider receives a bonus or other payment if utilization of ancillary services, such as laboratory testing, is kept below a particular level. Other managed care plans impose financial penalties if the provider's utilization of services exceeds pre-established levels. When the laboratory agrees to write off charges for the physician's managed care work, the physician may realize a financial benefit from the managed care plan created by the appearance that utilization of tests has been reduced. In cases where the provision of free services

dispose of bio-hazardous waste products from a provider free of charge; 5) a laboratory supplies free computers or fax machines to a provider (unless the equipment is integral to, and exclusively used for, performance of the laboratory's work); and 6) a laboratory provides free testing services for its providers, their families and their employees.[52]

f. Fraud in Home Health Care

In June 1995, the OIG issued a sixth special fraud alert separated into two parts. The first part of the alert addresses the problem of fraud in the delivery of home health services.[53] As the cost of home health care has skyrocketed in recent years, so too has the widely-held belief that much of that increase is due to the fraudulent practices of those who deliver home care. The concern about fraud and abuse in home health care reached a high water mark in September 1997 when President Clinton called for a six-month moratorium on the entry of new home health entities into the marketplace.[54] The government's willingness to continue to cover the exploding costs of home health care is also somewhat in doubt. The Balanced Budget Act of 1997[55] cut payments for home health care by $17 billion over five years, called for the implementation of a prospective payment system for home health by 1999, and implemented an interim payment system that is expected to significantly reduce home health payments.[56] Additional prophylactic measures proposed by the administration may require home health agencies in the future to re-enroll every three years and require home health workers to submit to criminal background checks.

The OIG's special fraud alert on fraud in home health care indicates that the OIG has turned its attention as well to this important segment of the health care community. To understand the alert some understanding of the home health care market is needed. Medicare's coverage of home health care permits Medicare patients with restricted mobility to receive care at home, rather than in a hospital. That home care is provided by nurses and aides under a physician-certified plan of care. Home health service costs

results in a benefit to the provider, the anti-kickback statute is implicated.

See 59 Fed. Reg. at 65,377.

52. See id.

53. See Special Fraud Alert: Home Health Fraud, OIG 95–08 (June 1995), reprinted in 60 Fed. Reg. 40,847 (1995).

54. See 1 BNA's Health Care Fraud Rptr. 613 (Sept. 1997). The moratorium was intended to give the HHS time to

promulgate new regulations that will specifically target fraud and abuse in the home health industry. It followed the release of an OIG report that found that 40 percent of all home visits studied were improperly reimbursed by the program. See 1 BNA's Health Care Fraud Rptr. 476.

55. Pub.L.No. 105–33, 111 Stat. 251.

56. See 1 BNA's Health Care Fraud Rptr. 647 (Oct. 8, 1997).

are normally reimbursable under the Medicare program once a beneficiary's physician has certified that the patient is in fact homebound and requires certain services (including physical therapy, speech-language pathology, or intermittent skilled nursing).[57] No co-payments from beneficiaries are required, except for medical equipment.

A number of the Medicare program's distinctive traits may tempt unprincipled home health service providers to engage in fraud and abuse. The program, for example, pays for an unlimited number of home visits for beneficiaries.[58] Some unscrupulous providers have found this to be an irresistible invitation to submit claims for visits never paid to a homebound beneficiary. Because beneficiaries are not required to make co-payments for these fictitious visits, unethical providers have had little fear that their claims for unprovided services would be detected. The program also requires only limited supervision of home health services provided by non-medical personnel. This limits the number of persons who are privy to whether services were actually provided or are aware of the nature of those services. The government has acted recently to curb some of the abuses that are believed to have occurred as a result of the paucity of limits placed on home health care providers. At one time, for example, the program did not even require providers to issue to beneficiaries an explanation of benefits form (EOBs) for the providers' bills for services. Thus a provider could have billed the program for services never rendered without the beneficiary ever being the wiser. Provisions of the Health Insurance Portability and Accountability Act (HIPAA) changed this in 1996. Now home health care providers are required to issue EOBs to homebound beneficiaries.[59]

The OIG's special fraud alert discusses several types of fraud occurring within the home health care field. Most of its investigations have involved home health providers who have committed false claims violations, including providers who had submitted claims for services never provided, double billed for services provided, submitted claims for services provided to ineligible patients, included in their annual cost reports claims for inappropriate expenses, or failed to disclose in their cost reports the identity of related parties with whom they conducted business. The alert also describes a variety of unlawful kickback arrangements, however, involving the exchange of remuneration for referrals between home health care providers and physicians, beneficiaries, hospitals, and nursing homes. According to the alert, kickback activity within the home health care industry may involve a range of parties and commonly takes one of the following forms:

---

57. See 60 Fed. Reg. 40,847 (1995).
58. See id. at 40,848.

59. See HIPAA, Pub.L.No. 104–191, Title II, 110 Stat. 1936 (1996).

Remuneration to Physicians for Certifications. Payments to a physician for each plan of care certified by the physician on behalf of a home health agency.

Remuneration to Physicians for Referrals of Home Health Care Beneficiaries. Attempts to disguise referral fees as payments for services (e.g., paying referring physicians for services not rendered, or in excess of fair market value for services rendered).

Remuneration to Beneficiaries. Free services offered to beneficiaries (e.g., transportation and meals) if they agree to switch home health providers.

Remuneration to Hospitals for Referrals. Providing free services to a hospital (e.g., a discharge planner, home care coordinator, or other home care liaison) to induce home health referrals.

Remuneration to Retirement Homes. Providing free services to a retirement home or adult congregate living facility (e.g., 24 hour nursing coverage) in return for home health referrals, or subcontracting with a retirement home or adult congregate living facility for the provision of home health services, to induce the facility to make referrals to the agency.[60]

g. The Provision of Medical Supplies to Nursing Home Facilities

The second part of the special fraud alert issued by the OIG in June, 1995 addresses the legality of various arrangements between medical supply companies and nursing home facilities.[61] Depending on the circumstances of a resident's stay, skilled nursing facilities may be reimbursed for the cost of the care and services they provide to eligible residents under either the Medicare program (under Part A for the facilities' costs for stays of a limited length, and/or under Part B for medically necessary equipment, prosthetic devices and supplies) or state-administered Medicaid programs (for longer stays). Medicare and Medicaid beneficiaries residing in nursing home facilities make attractive targets for unscrupulous supply companies for a number of reasons: multiple beneficiaries residing in a single facility increase the ill-gained profits that can be made; despite rules to the contrary, some facilities make nursing home patient records available to providers who do not provide direct

---

60. See 60 Fed. Reg. at 40,848–49.

61. See Fraud and Abuse in the Provision of Medical Supplies to Nursing Facilities, OIG 95–09 (June 1995), reprinted in 60 Fed. Reg. at 40,849. One year later the OIG supplemented this with another special fraud alert that dis-

cussed additional ways in which nursing homes and medical equipment suppliers had violated the false claims provisions. See Fraud and Abuse in the Provision of Services in Nursing Facilities (June 1995), reprinted in 61 Fed. Reg. 30,623 (1996).

care to the facilities; and, providers have been permitted to bill the programs directly without verification from the nursing home facility or an attending physician.[62]

The alert identifies a variety of fraudulent schemes the OIG believes have been perpetrated either by suppliers of nursing facilities or the management and staff of the facilities themselves, or both. Although most of the schemes identified in the alert constitute violations of the false claims provisions,[63] some violate the anti-kickback statutes as well, such as where a supplier provides non-reimbursable medical products to a nursing facility free of charge in exchange for which the facility helps the supplier justify claims to Medicare for products that are reimbursable but are not medically necessary or even used by the facility;[64] or a facility solicits unauthorized deliveries, items of value, or rewards from a medical supplier, in exchange for which it offers the supplier access to its patients' medical records and other information needed to bill Medicare.[65]

h. Provision of Services in Nursing Facilities

In 1992, an OIG study reported that the federal government spent approximately $20 billion on nursing care alone.[66] The sheer size of the federal expenditures on nursing facility services, and the Medicare and Medicaid programs' cross-coverage of some nursing patients, have made the facilities a prime target for fraud and abuse.[67]

As larger and larger slices of the health care pie have been swallowed by providers submitting bills for services rendered at nursing facilities, the facilities have come under the scrutiny of the OIG. In a special fraud alert addressing the provision of services in nursing facilities, the OIG has identified a number of nursing facility transactions that it considers fraudulent under the health care laws.[68] Some of the identified transactions, such as claims for services not rendered or claims misrepresenting the services rendered, are uncontroversially unlawful.[69] Other parts of the special fraud alert, however, provide important clues as to where the OIG is likely to focus its investigative efforts in the near future. For example, the alert indicates that some practitioners have submitted false claims to circumvent stringent coverage limitations imposed

---

62. See GAO, Fraud and Abuse: Providers Target Medicare Patients in Nursing Facilities, GAO/HEHS–96–18.

63. See 60 Fed. Reg. at 40,850.

64. See id.

65. See id.

66. See 61 Fed. Reg. at 30,623.

67. See id.

68. See Fraud and Abuse in the Provision of Services in Nursing Facilities, reprinted in 61 Fed. Reg. 30,623 (1996).

69. Common schemes include falsifying bills and medical records to misrepresent the services, or extent of services, provided at nursing facilities. See 61 Fed. Reg. 30,623 (1996) for examples.

by the programs on some specialties, including in particular, podiatry, audiology, and optometry.[70] To assist the self-policing activities of nursing facilities, the alert provides a list of practices for which the facilities should be on guard:

Gang Visits. Visits by one or more medical professionals where a large number of nursing residents are seen in a single day may indicate unnecessary services or raise questions about the quality of services being provided.

Frequent Visits. Recurring "routine visits" by the same professional may indicate the provision of unnecessary medical services.

Free Access to Medical Records. Practitioners who have unlimited access to medical records may be suspected of obtaining information for use in submission of false claims.

Questionable Supporting Documentation. The submission of dubious documentation for medical necessity of services may indicate inappropriate billing.[71]

§ 3–17. The Requirement of Advisory Opinions and Special Fraud Alerts

For the time being it appears that the industry has prevailed in its effort to require the HHS to respond to specific inquiries about the legality or illegality of particular commercial arrangements. The Health Insurance Portability and Accountability Act of 1996 (HIPAA)[1] requires the Department to give formal guidance to health care providers regarding the anti-kickback statute. Specifically, HIPAA directs the Secretary (after consulting with the Attorney General) to issue advisory opinions in response to requests for advice about whether specific business arrangements violate the anti-kickback provisions, including opinions about (1) what constitutes prohibited remuneration under the anti-kickback law; (2) whether an arrangement falls within one of the statutory exceptions to the anti-kickback law; (3) whether an arrangement falls within an applicable safe harbor established by the OIG; (4) what constitutes an inducement to reduce or limit services; and (5) whether a particular activity constitutes grounds for penalties under the anti-kickback law, civil monetary law, or exclusion statutes.[2]

---

70. See id.
71. See id.

§ 3–17

1. Pub.L.No. 104–191, Title II, § 205, 110 Stat. 1936 (1996).

2. HIPAA, Pub.L.No. 104–191, Title II, § 205, 110 Stat. 1936 (1996). The OIG must accept requests for advisory opinions between February 21, 1997 and August 21, 2000.

Advisory opinions must be issued by the Secretary within 60 days of the receipt of a request for guidance, and are binding on both the Secretary and the party requesting the opinion.[3] That period may be tolled in cases in which the requesting party fails to submit complete information about the transaction for which advice is sought, or the OIG finds it necessary to seek the assistance of a nonlegal expert to issue the opinion.[4] A failure to submit a request for an advisory opinion will not be evidence that a provider intended to violate the anti-kickback statute.

The Secretary was directed to issue regulations within six months of the enactment of the HIPAA to announce the procedures by which advisory opinions may be secured by members of the industry.[5] On January 16, 1997, the Inspector General announced the appointment of Washington, D.C. lawyer Kevin G. McAnaney as Chief of the Industry Guidance Branch (IGB) of the Office of Counsel.[6] Under McAnaney's leadership, in February 1997, the OIG released an interim final rule regarding the steps to be followed by providers requesting an advisory opinion, and the procedures that the OIG expects to follow in issuing an opinion. A final rule is expected within nine months of the close of the public comment period (comments were due to the OIG by April 27, 1997).

a. Interim Advisory Opinion Procedures

A party submitting a request for an advisory opinion under the interim procedures must meet various criteria before an advisory opinion will be issued:

> *Actual Parties to Genuine Transactions Only.* Only parties to a genuine transaction are entitled to request an advisory opinion and to use an opinion as a shield to liability. A request for an opinion may not be based on a hypothetical or generalized business arrangement. Accordingly, the arrangement giving rise to the request must either be in existence at the time of the request, or the requestor must have a good faith intention to enter into the described arrangement in the near future.[7] A party requesting an advisory opinion for a prospective arrangement, however, may declare an intention to enter into the arrangement contingent upon the receipt of a favorable advisory opinion.[8]

---

3. See id. If, however, the requesting party fails to disclose all relevant information or provides false information to the OIG, the resulting advisory opinion may not be binding, and the Department may commence any action against the requestor. See 62 Fed. Reg. 7,350, 7,354 (Feb. 1997).

4. See 1 BNA's Health Care Fraud Report 135 (1997).

5. See HIPAA, Pub.L.No. 104–191, Title II, § 205, 110 Stat. 1936 (1996).

6. See 6 BNA's Health Care Fraud Report 44.

7. See 42 CFR § 1008.11.

8. See 42 C.F.R. § 1008.38(b)

Fee Equaling the Cost of Opinion. A party requesting an advisory opinion must pay a fee equal to the cost of issuing the opinion into the United States Treasury.[9] The expected hourly cost for work done on a request is $100.[10] A party concerned with the potential cost of an opinion may designate a "triggering dollar amount."[11] When the cost of processing the opinion reaches this pre-determined ceiling, the requestor will permitted to continue or withdraw the request.

Non-Refundable Filing Fee. A party requesting an opinion must also pay a nonrefundable $250 filing fee at the time the advisory opinion is requested[12] to cover the cost of the initial review of the request and the time needed to accept or reject the request. In the event a party revokes a filed request, the party will be required to pay any cost incurred by the Department above the amount of the filing fee.

Expert Opinion Fee. When a request for an advisory opinion requires the OIG to solicit expert advise on nonlegal matters, the requestor is required to pay the expert's expenses.[13] The OIG will obtain an estimate for the cost of an expert and notify the requestor of the need for expert opinion and the expected fee, at which point the requestor will be given the option to pay the estimated cost for the expert's review or to withdraw the request.[14] The OIG will not issue a completed advisory opinion until the requestor has paid all incurred fees.

Disclosure of all Relevant Facts and Documents. A party requesting an advisory opinion must provide the OIG with a complete, narrative description of the business transaction for which an opinion is requested,[15] a copy of all relevant documents to the transaction (e.g., contracts, leases or court documents), and the name of the requestor and the names of all actual or potential parties to the transaction.[16] In addition, the OIG has published a preliminary list of questions that it encourages requestors to answer in order to expedite the processing of the request.[17]

---

9. See 42 C.F.R. § 1008.31(a) and HIPAA, Pub.L.No. 104–191, § 205(b)(5)(B)(ii), 110 Stat. 1936, 2002 (1996), Social Security Act, § 1128D(b)(5)(B)(ii).

10. See 62 Fed. Reg. at 7353.

11. See id.

12. See 62 Fed. Reg. at 7358.

13. See 42 C.F.R. § 1008.33(b).

14. See 42 C.F.R. § 1008.33(b). The sixty day time period for the issuance of the opinion will be tolled while the expert analyzes the questions.

15. See 42 C.F.R. § 1008.36.

16. See 62 Fed. Reg. at 7352. After the receipt or resubmission of a request for an advisory opinion, the OIG has 10 days to decide to accept or decline the request or to ask for additional information. See id. at 7354; see also 42 C.F.R. § 1009.39.

17. See "Recommended Preliminary Questions and Supplementary Information for Addressing Requests for OIG Advisory Opinions in Accordance with Section 1128D of the Social Security Act

Certifications. Two certifications must be signed by an individual requestor, or the chief executive officer (CEO) or managing partner of a requesting entity, when submitting a request for an advisory opinion:[18] a certification that all of the information included in the request is true and correct and a certification that the request is a complete description of the facts necessary to issue an advisory opinion.[19] In addition, if the requestor seeks an opinion on prospective conduct, the regulations require a declaration of the requestor's good faith intent to enter into the arrangement. A requestor's declaration of good faith intent may be conditioned upon the receipt of a favorable advisory opinion.[20]

Based on these interim rules, non-parties to a transaction are neither entitled to seek an advisory opinion nor entitled to use an issued opinion as a protection against liability or criminal process.[21] Rather, only the actual parties to an advisory opinion may use it as a shield. The reason for this restriction is simple. No two cases investigated under the anti-kickback law are identical. Thus, it would be folly (as well as unfair) to permit a provider who has yet fully to describe her business arrangements to piggyback on a provider who has gone to the time and expense of securing an opinion.

The interim regulations published in February 1997 indicate that industry requests for formal guidance about the anti-kickback statute will undergo rigorous examination by the government.

"Case Specific" Safe Harbors. The OIG will analyze requests for advisory opinions in a manner similar to that used to assess proposals for new safe harbors, by evaluating: (1) access to health care; (2) quality of care services; (3) patient freedom of choice among health care providers; (4) competition among health care providers; (5) cost to federal health care providers; (6) potential overutilization of services; (7) ability of health care facilities to provide services in medically undeserved areas or to undeserved populations; (8) existence of potential benefits to health care professionals or providers that may vary based on decisions to order an item or service or to arrange a referral of health care items or services to a particular practitioner or provider.[22] Because the opinions will relate to particular facts of a specific transaction, only the requesting individual or entity will be entitled to rely on it.

and 42 CFR Part 1008," reprinted in BNA's Health Care Fraud Report, Vol. 1., No. 7, at 244–246 (April 9, 1997); see also 42 C.F.R. § 1008.18.

  18. 42 C.F.R. § 1008.38(c).

19. See 42 C.F.R. § 1008.38(a).
20. See 42 C.F.R. § 1008.38(b).
21. See 62 Fed. Reg. 7350 (1997).
22. See 62 Fed. Reg. 7350 (1997).

Approval of the Department of Justice. A final advisory opinion will be issued only after the OIG has received a completed request, considered all the facts in the request and consulted with the Department of Justice about any legal conclusions it has reached.[23]

Publication of Advisory Opinions. The OIG will publish issued advisory opinions on the DHHS/OIG web site. In addition, copies of the opinions will be available to the public from OIG headquarters. The documents submitted with a request for an advisory opinion will also be available for public inspection subject to Freedom of Information Act (FOIA) restrictions. Health care providers concerned about the public dissemination of confidential trade secrets or other privileged information may identify information it believes to be protected pursuant to 45 C.F.R. 5.65(c) and (d). However, the OIG will be the final arbiter of whether submitted information is protected under the FOIA.

The OIG has reserved the right to rescind an advisory opinion in certain situations, including when it learns after issuing a favorable opinion that the party's conduct will in fact lead to fraud and abuse.[24] In such an event, a requestor will not face sanctions for relying on the opinion provided the requestor did not cause the rescission by submitting false or purposely misleading information with the request materials.[25]

The OIG is not required to issue an advisory opinion every time it receives a request. As explained above, the OIG may reject a request for information submitted by a non-party to a transaction, or by a party who seeks advice about a hypothetical transaction. In addition, the OIG will not accept a request that requires excessive investigation, relates to a pending legal proceeding, or merely seeks a general interpretation of the anti-kickback law.[26] Finally, HIPAA expressly provides that two matters are not subject to the advisory opinion process, including requests concerning (1) what "the fair market value shall be," or whether "the fair market value was paid or received for any goods, services or property;" and (2) "whether an individual is a bona fide employee within the requirements of Section 3121(d)(2) of the Internal Revenue Code of 1986."[27]

---

23. See HIPAA, Pub.L.No. 104–191, § 205(b)(1), 110 Stat. 1936, § 2001 (1996), Social Security Act, § 1128D(b)(1).

24. See 42 C.F.R. § 1008.45; 62 Fed. Reg. 7350 (1997).

25. See 42 C.F.R. § 1008.45; 62 Fed. Reg. 7350 (1997).

26. See 1 BNA's Health Care Fraud Report 259.

27. See 42 C.F.R. § 1008.3(b).

The OIG has already begun to issue advisory opinions[28] giving favorable advice to four of the first six parties to submit requests. The first advisory opinion,[29] sought by the American Kidney Foundation (AKF),[30] concerned the legality of a proposed deal to expand the assistance grants awarded by AKF to needy ESRD patients to help the patients pay the premiums of an insurance program operated by the AKF and other costs. The second concerned a state-supported program to assist ESRD patients with the costs of their care. The OIG concluded with respect to both assistance programs that the grants were unlikely to influence ESRD patients to select certain providers. Thus, the grants were determined to be lawful.

The third request for an advisory opinion concerned whether the application for Medicaid benefits by an elderly nursing home resident violated Section 1320a–7b(a)(6) of the Social Security Act,[31] because the application was filed after the resident had transferred certain assets ($7,785) to her great-nephew.[32] Section 1320a–7b(a)(6) prohibits the disposition of certain assets for the purpose of qualifying for Medicaid benefits. The advisory opinion noted that because the average monthly cost for private nursing home care in the requestor's state was $2,595, retention of the $7,785 would have made the requestor ineligible for Medicaid for a period of three months. Because the requestor applied for benefits more than three months after the disposition of the assets, however, and the state in which she resided indicated that it would not deem her ineligible for benefits due to the transfer, the OIG concluded that the requestor would also not be subject to sanction under federal law.[33]

The HHS's fourth advisory opinion was less favorable to its requestor, an ambulatory surgical center (ACS). The ACS provided endoscopy services to a group of retired workers whose former employer had purchased Medicare supplemental coverage—commonly known as Medigap coverage—from Blue Cross Blue Shield of Michigan (hereinafter Blue Cross). The Medigap policy was de-

28. Advisory Opinion No. 97–1, reprinted in 1 BNA's Health Care Fraud Reporter 399 (June 18, 1997); Advisory Opinion No. 97–2; Advisory Opinion No. 97–3, reprinted in 1 BNA's Health Care Fraud Rptr. 603 (Sept. 10, 1997); Advisory Opinion No. 97–4, reprinted in 1 BNA's Health Care Fraud Rptr. 675 (Oct. 8, 1997); Advisory Opinion No. 97–5, reprinted in 1 BNA's Health Care Fraud Rptr. 728 (Oct. 22, 1997) and Advisory Opinion No. 97–6, reprinted in 1 BNA's Health Care Fraud Rptr. 732 (Oct. 22, 1997). All advisory opinions are posted on the OIG's internet site. See

http://www.sba.gov/ignet/internal/hhs/hhs.html.

29. See Advisory Opinion No. 97–1 (June 10, 1997).

30. The AKF is a charitable foundation partly funded by kidney dialysis providers. See 1 BNA's Health Care Fraud Reporter 395 (June 18, 1997).

31. See 42 U.S.C. § 1320a–7b(a)(6).

32. See Advisory Opinion No. 97–3 (Aug. 21, 1997), reprinted in 1 BNA's Health Care Fraud Rptr. 603 (Sept. 10, 1997).

33. See id. at 604.

signed to cover the retirees' Medicare copayment and deductible obligations. A conflict between the ACS and Blue Cross arose when Blue Cross refused to reimburse the ACS for one of two copayment amounts chargeable to the retirees for endoscopy procedures.[34] The ACS maintained that Blue Cross was obligated to cover both copayment amounts and proposed not to seek payment of the uncollected copayment amounts directly from the retirees. To protect itself against potential criminal, civil and administrative sanctions, however, the ACS requested an advisory opinion that considered whether its plan not to seek copayment from the Medicare beneficiaries would offend the anti-kickback statute and HIPAA's prohibition of routine waivers of coinsurance obligations.[35]

The response was not favorable. After reviewing the proposed waiver policy, the OIG concluded that at least *one purpose* of the ACS's plan was to encourage covered beneficiaries to obtain services at its facilities. The OIG found this intent to violate Section 231(h) of HIPAA which includes within the term "remuneration" any waiver of Medicare copayment obligations that a provider knows or should know is likely to influence a beneficiary to choose it over a competitor.[36] In addition, the advisory opinion noted that the proposed arrangement to forgive the copayment obligations across-the-board would violate Section 231(h)(A)'s requirement that waivers be based on individualized determinations of financial hardship or granted only after the provider has made reasonable efforts to collect the copayment amounts.[37] The OIG was not persuaded that the ACS's unsuccessful efforts to persuade Blue Cross to pay the copayment amounts constituted a "reasonable collection effort" under the statute. The opinion explained:

> Reasonable collection efforts are those that a reasonable provider would undertake to collect amounts owed for items and

---

34. Medicare coverage of ACS services is composed of two fees, a facility fee and a professional fee, both of which are subject to coinsurance and deductible obligations. Blue Cross paid the ACS copayment amounts attributable the professional fees (to cover the fee owed to the physicians who performed the endoscopies) but refused to cover the copayment amounts attributable to the ACS's facility fees.

35. See discussion supra at §§ 3–10d and 3–11g.

36. See id. This view is consistent with the "one-purpose" test enunciated in United States v. Greber, 760 F.2d 68 (3d Cir.1985). See supra § 3–13a.

37. HIPAA, Section 231(h)(A) provides, in pertinent part, that waivers of coinsurance and deductible amounts will constitute unlawful "remuneration" unless:

> (i) the waiver is not offered as part of any advertisement or solicitation;
>
> (ii) the person does not routinely waive coinsurance and deductible amounts; and
>
> (iii) the person—
>
>> (I) waives the coinsurance and deductible amounts after determining in good faith that the individual is in financial need; [or]
>>
>> (II) fails to collect the coinsurance or deductible after making reasonable collection efforts . . .

For a discussion of the waiver of coinsurance and deductibles safe harbor, see supra § 3–11g.

services provided to patients. *These efforts should include a bona fide attempt to bill and collect from the patient if the patient's insurers refuses to pay.* When an insurer has taken a consistent position with the provider that a category of claims are [sic] not covered, the provider's continued submission of such claims, including subsequent appeals, is not a *bona fide* collection effort. In such circumstances, the provider must make reasonable efforts to collect the Medicare copayment from the patient.[38]

The advisory opinion concluded further that because one purpose of the ACS's plan was to offer remuneration (routine waivers of copayment obligations) to induce beneficiaries to purchase services reimbursable under the program, if implemented, the plan might be found to violate the anti-kickback statute as well.[39]

The fifth advisory opinion is the most generous opinion issued by the HHS to date, and may be of particular interest to members of the health care industry contemplating joint venture arrangements.[40] In that opinion the HHS concluded that a proposed agreement between a group of radiologists and a hospital network to establish and operate an outpatient radiology imaging center would not violate the anti-kickback provisions, even though the arrangement did not comply with the requirements of the only safe harbor regulation applicable to the arrangement—the investment interest safe harbor.[41] Although HHS has repeatedly warned that only the actual parties to an advisory opinion will be bound by it, the opinion may shed some light on the legality of a variety of joint venture arrangements currently under contemplation within the marketplace.

The request for the advisory opinion was jointly made by a medical group that specialized in radiologist services and a hospital system comprised of three facilities. The radiology group was partly owned by a physician who also served as the director of the radiology department in one of the hospitals. The radiologist group and the hospitals proposed to establish jointly a radiology imaging center. The physician members of the radiologist group were to be the sole providers of services to the imaging center under a service provider agreement with the center. Under that agreement the radiologists would neither be employees of the imaging center nor be compensated by the center. Rather, the radiologists proposed to

38. See Advisory Opinion No. 97–4 (Sept. 25, 1997) (emphasis added), reprinted in 1 BNA's Health Care Fraud Rptr. 676 (Oct. 8, 1997).

39. See Advisory Opinion 97–4, reprinted in 1 BNA's Health Care Fraud Rptr. at 676.

40. See Advisory Opinion No. 97–5 (Oct. 15, 1997), reprinted in 1 BNA's Health Care Fraud Rptr. 728 (Oct. 22, 1997).

41. For a discussion of the investment interest safe harbor regulation see supra at § 3–11b.

bill patients and third party payors (including the Medicare and Medicaid programs) directly for their professional services, while the imaging center billed patients and third party payors separately for the center's technical support of those services. The question presented by the arrangement was whether the hospitals and the radiology group could make patient referrals to the imaging center while receiving profit distributions from the joint venture.

Although the arrangement did not qualify for the protection afforded by the investment interest safe harbor,[42] the OIG concluded that the described arrangement would not result in the exchange of prohibited remuneration under the anti-kickback statute since neither the radiology group nor the hospital system could channel referrals to the imaging center under the proposed agreement. The advisory opinion noted that radiologists do not normally play a role in ordering the radiological tests that they perform (although they may on occasion recommend additional testing to an attending physician upon consultation) and the hospital system had agreed under the proposal that its physicians would not make referrals to the imaging center, nor would any such referrals be accepted by the center if made. As added precautions, the hospital system had agreed that it would inform its medical staff of the agreement, that it would continue to use its radiology units, and that it would not to encourage its medical staff to use the imaging center or track the volume of the use of the center by its physicians. Because both organizations proposed to put up roughly equal amounts of capital to establish the imaging center, the OIG also concluded that the joint venture was not simply a means to camouflage remuneration flowing from the radiology group to the hospitals for patient referrals to the group, nor remuneration from the radiology group to the hospitals in return for use of space or equipment at one of the hospitals.

By contrast, the sixth advisory opinion was not nearly as favorable to the requesting parties.[43] The advisory opinion concerned the legality of a proposed arrangement under which two acute care hospitals would, free of charge, restock any supplies and medications used by a fleet of local ambulances while transporting patients to one of the two hospitals. Although neither the hospital nor its management company planned to bill any federal health

---

42. Because the radiology group proposed to own 51 percent of the imaging center, the proposed arrangement violated the safe harbor's "60–40 investor rule" which mandates that no more than 40 percent of the investment interests be held by investors who are in a position to make referrals to, or furnish items or services, or otherwise generate business for the joint venture entity. See supra § 3–12a.

43. See Advisory Opinion No. 97–6 (Oct. 16, 1997), reprinted in Vol. 1 BNA's Health Care Fraud Rptr. 732 (Oct. 22, 1997).

care program for the cost of the supplies provided to the ambulances, and thus the restocking proposal would not have resulted in increased costs to the programs, the OIG concluded that the proposal would constitute unlawful remuneration under the anti-kickback statute since the restocking policy could induce the ambulance service to choose to bring federal health care beneficiaries to the two acute care hospitals rather than to one of their competitors. The opinion noted that increased cost to one of the programs is not the sole criterion for determining whether a proposal is abusive, also relevant is whether a proposal will lead to overutilization of items and services, will diminish the quality of care afforded to federal health care beneficiaries, will interfere with patient freedom of choice, will result in unfair competition within the industry. The opinion concluded that because the restocking proposal was essentially a plan "to make payments" (in the form of free supplies) directly related to the delivery of patients to the hospitals, adoption of the proposal could lead to improper patient steering and unfair competition.[44]

b. Efforts to Repeal the Advisory Opinion Requirement

President Clinton recommended the repeal of the rule requiring advisory opinions almost as soon as he signed it into law.[45] Less than a year after its enactment, the administration included a provision in its fiscal 1998 budget proposals that sought to put an end to the advisory opinion process based on the concern that unscrupulous health care providers might misuse the process to obtain opinions under false pretexts and then use the binding opinions as a defense against sanctions.[46] Although the provision did not make it into the final budget agreement, its inclusion in the first place raises some question about the future of the advisory opinion process.[47]

Despite efforts to repeal HIPAA's advisory opinion mandate, as discussed above, the OIG has published a fairly detailed set of procedures for securing an opinion and the Industry Guidance Branch has already begun to issue opinions. Assuming the advisory process does survive, it remains to be seen whether the industry

---

44. See id. at 732–33.

45. See Proposed Offsets for Clinton Administration's New Spending and Tax Proposals, released by White House in Wyandotte, Mich., Aug. 27, 1996, as reprinted in BNA's Daily Report for Executives, L–1 (August 28, 1996).

46. See 1 BNA's Health Care Fraud Report 82 (February 12, 1997).

47. The President's fear is shared by the Department of Justice. In a letter written to former Senate Majority Leader Robert Dole shortly after the passage of HIPAA, Attorney General Janet Reno called advisory opinions "an unprecedented and unwise requirement that would severely undermine our law en-

will find the process to be as helpful as it has long imagined it would be.[48]

The industry's response to the new advisory opinion process has ranged from cautious to skeptical. Although the industry has sought agency guidance about particular transactions for years, many providers are reluctant to invite the scrutiny of the government in order to obtain an advisory opinion.[49] With good reason, some commentators have questioned the government's commitment to the advisory opinion process. Before the enactment of HIPAA, the OIG had taken the position (after considerable nudging by the DOJ) that it could not issue advisory opinions. Even after HIPAA mandated the issuance of advisory opinions, the administration sought to repeal that mandate in its 1998 budget proposals. Thus it can be no surprise that the industry remains skeptical that the advisory opinion process, now underway, will bear the fruit it has desired for so long.[50]

§ 3–18. The State Anti–Kickback Statutes

A clear majority of the states have enacted their own anti-kickback provisions which function independently of the federal anti-kickback statute.[1] State anti-kickback prohibitions typically appear in broad statutes targeting fraud in the Medicaid program.[2] Most of the state provisions parallel the federal statute by carving out certain types of business arrangements (commonly referred to as safe harbors) that are immune from prosecution.[3] Some expressly piggyback on the federal provision. The Texas anti-kickback statute, for example, provides that its anti-kickback rules "shall not be construed to prohibit any payment, business arrangements, or payments practice not prohibited by 42 U.S.C.A. Section 1320a–

---

forcement efforts relating to health care fraud." Id. at 81.

48. See Scott D. Godshall, "Death by Regulation: HHS's Advisory Opinion Guidelines" Andrews Health Care Fraud Litigation Reporter 3–5 (May 1997); Lisa M. Rockelli, "Advisory Opinions: Industry Concerned with Cost, Privacy, IG Rescission Authority" 1 BNΛ's Health Care Fraud Rep. 305–307 (May 7, 1997); Retta M. Riordan "Will New Guidance Mechanisms Provide Needed Clarification to Industry Under Medicare/Medicaid Anti–Kickback Statute?" 1 BNA's Health Care Fraud Rep. 133–136 (February 26, 1997).

49. See Phyllis A. Avery and Andrew B. Wachler, Advisory Opinion Regulations Will Discourage Many Potential Requestors, Vol. 9, No. 6 The Health

Lawyer 24–28 (ABA Health Law Section 1997).

50. See Retta M. Riordan, Will New Guidance Mechanism Provide Needed Clarifications to Industry Under Medicare/Medicaid Anti–Kickback Statute? 1 BNA's Health Care Fraud Rep. 133 (Feb. 26, 1997).

§ 3–18

1. Thirty-eight states now have anti-kickback statutes. See Pamela H. Bucy, Health Care Fraud: Criminal, Civil and Administrative Law § 3.03[2], at 3–63, 3–64 (1996).

2. See Pamela S. Bucy, Health Care Fraud: Criminal, Civil and Administrative Law § 3.03[2] at 3–63 to 3–65 (1996).

3. Id.

7b(b) or any regulations promulgated pursuant thereto."[4]

Conduct that is lawful under the federal anti-kickback statute may be unlawful under state law, or vice versa.[5] While the federal government is likely to be sensitive to state or local concerns, it is not bound by them. Absent some double jeopardy concern,[6] the federal and states' concurrent jurisdiction over conduct proscribed by the anti-kickback laws could result in prosecution in either jurisdiction, or both.

Specialized state Medicaid Fraud Control Units (MFCUs) have piloted numerous investigations and prosecutions of health care providers pursuant to these and other provisions.[7] In addition, many states have established procedures by which providers may seek advisory opinions about the legality of particular business arrangements.[8] Although not necessarily binding on the courts, these opinions may significantly affect a prosecutor's decision to seek an indictment.[9]

§ 3–19. Conclusion

Despite the periodic revision of the anti-kickback provisions, and the promulgation of the safe harbor regulations, disputes over the anti-kickback provisions continue to rage. Central among the disputes is the controversy surrounding the proper interpretation of the statute's scienter requirements. The future promises continued strife over this and other issues as the marketplace pushes toward managed care and providers strive to compete by creating new and innovative ties to other actors doing business in the health care arena.

4. Tex. Health and Safety Code § 161.091.

5. See 56 Fed. Reg. 35,952, 35,957 (1991). In addition to the anti-kickback statutes, the federal government and many states have enacted self-referral laws (discussed separately in Chapter 4). Although the self-referral laws implicate some of the same concerns as the anti-kickback provisions, they typically have different elements of proof and remedies. For example, the federal self-referral law is violated when a "financial relationship" exists between an entity furnishing clinical laboratory services and a physician, and a referral is made or a claim or bill is presented. By contrast, for the anti-kickback statute to be violated, it must be shown that the remuneration between the two parties was intended to induce the referral of busi-

ness payable under Medicare or Medicaid. Further, whereas the anti-kickback statute contains criminal penalties, a violation of Stark will result in a denial of payment and may result in the imposition of civil money penalties and program exclusions.

6. See Chapter 8, § 8–22.

7. For further discussion of the functions performed by the state MFCUs, see Chapter 7, § 7–3.

8. See Adams, Fraud and Abuse Implications of Joint Ventures, in JOINT VENTURES BETWEEN HOSPITALS AND PHYSICIANS: A COMPETITIVE STRATEGY FOR THE HEALTHCARE MARKETPLACE 129, 139 (L. Burns & D. Mancino, eds. 1987).

9. See id.

Chapter 4

SELF–REFERRALS: FEDERAL AND STATE PROHIBITIONS

Table of Sections

WESTLAW Electronic Research

See WESTLAW Electronic Research Guide preceding the Summary of Contents.

Library References:

C.J.S. Social Security and Public Welfare § 126–138.
West's Key No. Digests, Social Security and Public Welfare ⊕18, 241.5–241.110.

§ 4–1. Introduction: The Self–Referral Problem

Statutes that prohibit self-referrals address many of the same concerns and cover much of the same conduct addressed and covered by statutes prohibiting bribes and kickbacks. The federal self-referral prohibition is, however, both narrower and broader than the federal prohibition of bribes and kickbacks. It is, on the

170

one hand, much narrower than the bribe and kickback statute in that it only addresses Medicare and Medicaid payment for certain specifically designated health items and services when those items and services are provided to patients referred by physicians who have ownership or compensation arrangements with the provider. It is also broader in its sweep, however, in that is a strict liability statute: if an ownership or compensation arrangement falls within the statutory proscription, the intent of the parties in forming the arrangement is irrelevant. The bribe and kickback prohibition, of course, is a criminal law statute for which intent is a key consideration.

Congress took its first step toward banning self-referrals when it adopted the Ethics in Patient Referrals Act, usually referred to as the Stark bill after Representative Fortney "Pete" Stark, the Democratic chair of House Ways and Means Committee who fought tenaciously for the passage of this legislation.[1] The bill was adopted as part of the Omnibus Budget Reconciliation Act of 1989.[2] The legislation was extensively amended by the 1993 Omnibus Budget Reconciliation Act, Stark II,[3] and technically amended by the Social Security Act of 1994.

As enacted in 1989, the Stark bill prohibited Medicare payment for services provided to Medicare beneficiaries by clinical laboratories when the physician who referred the beneficiary had an ownership and compensation arrangement with the laboratory. The 1993 amendments extended the law to cover a number of other health law services and to cover services provided to Medicaid recipients as well.[4]

In August of 1995 the Health Care Financing Administration issued final regulations implementing Stark I.[5] Though on their face these rules apply only to Stark I—Medicare billings for self-referred clinical laboratory services—HCFA has indicated that they will be relied on and give guidance in interpreting Stark II as well.[6] As of mid–1997, about a third of the states also have adopted statutes limiting self-referrals, described below.

It is a well-known fact that physicians exercise considerable control over patient access to most health care items and services.

---

§ 4–1

1. See, John K. Iglehart, Congress Moves to Regulate Self–Referral and Physicians' Ownership of Clinical Laboratories, 322 New Eng. J. Med. 1682 (1990) [hereinafter Congress]; John K. Iglehart, The Debate over Physician Ownership of Health Care Facilities, 321 New Eng. J. Med. 198 (1989) [hereinafter Debate]; Robert A. Morse & Renee M. Popovits, Stark's Crusade: The Eth-

ics in Patient Referrals Act of 1989, 22 J. Health & Hosp. L 208 (1989), for legislative history of the Act.

2. 42 U.S.C.A. § 1395nn.

3. Omnibus Budget Reconciliation Act of 1993, Pub. L. No. 103–66, §§ 13,-500–644, 107 Stat. 312, 517–648 (1993).

4. 42 U.S.C.A. § 1396b(s).

5. 60 Fed. Reg. 41,914 (1995).

6. 60 Fed. Reg. at 41,915–16.

Diagnostic tests and therapeutic services must, in most instances, be ordered, prescribed, or certified as necessary by a physician. With respect to many of these items and services there is no gold standard of appropriateness or necessity. There is also no person obviously in a position to contradict the physician's advice. If a treating physician believes that the test, item, or service of a type that is covered by insurance is indicated, the patient will usually seek it, and the insurer will usually pay for it. Though insurers have increasingly tried to control utilization, they still pay for the vast majority of items and services ordered by physicians.[7]

In recent years technologically complex diagnostic and therapeutic services have become increasingly common adjuncts to medical care. These services are more and more frequently being provided by free-standing, for-profit, businesses, such as clinical laboratories, imaging centers, or comprehensive outpatient rehabilitation centers. Much of the money that is to be made in health care is being made by these businesses. This is particularly true in those instances, discussed in earlier chapters, where Medicare pays above-market rates for particular items or services. Physicians who are increasingly squeezed by Medicare, Medicaid, and private managed care programs to deliver their services for lower prices can make up for the lost income by investing or entering into compensation arrangements with these providers.

If the physician has an ownership interest in or compensation arrangement with the entity that provides diagnostic or treatment services, however, the physician not only has the ability but also the motivation to increase patient demand for these services. Physicians who are paid "interpretation" fees every time they order a test for a patient face an obvious incentive to order more tests. Physicians who share in the profits of facilities to which they refer patients are self-evidently in a position to make money every time they refer a patient. There has been a growing concern, therefore, that physicians may be using self-referrals as a means to increasing their own income at the expense of payors and patients.

During the late 1980s a number of studies confirmed the suspicion that self-referrals were becoming quite common, and quite costly. An OIG study issued in 1989 found that of 2690 physicians who responded to its study, 12% had ownership interests and 8% had compensation arrangements with businesses to which they referred patients. It further determined that nationally 25% of

7. During the late 1980s, for example, when the Medicare Peer Review Organization was most powerful, it denied payment retrospectively for less than 2% of the cases it reviewed and prospectively for far less than 1% of the cases subject to prospective review. See Timothy Jost, Policing Cost Containment: The Medicare Peer Review Organization Program, 14 U. Puget Sound L. Rev. 483, 500–01 (1991).

independent clinical laboratories (ICLs), 27% of independent physiological laboratories, and 8% of durable medical equipment suppliers were owned at least in part by referring physicians. Beneficiaries treated by physicians who owned or invested in ICLs received 45% more clinical laboratory services and 34% more services directly from ICLs than beneficiaries in general, resulting in $28 million in additional costs to the Medicare program.[8]

A 1991 Florida study found that nearly 30% of the nine different types of facilities studied were owned entirely or in part by physicians; that physician-owned clinical laboratories averaged 3.3 tests per patient, double the rate of non-physician-owned labs, while generating twice as much in gross revenues per patient; that physician-owned home health agencies provided 27% more home health visits per patient; and that physician-owned physical therapy centers averaged 39% more visits per patient and were more profitable than non-joint venture facilities.[9] The study found that 44% of free-standing facilities providing radiation therapy were physician owned, that none of these were located in inner-city or rural areas, that the frequency and costs of radiation-therapy treatments at free-standing facilities were 40%—60% higher than in the rest of the United States (where 7% of facilities are physician-owned); and that radiation physicists spent 18% less time with each patient over the course of treatment than did their counterparts at non-joint venture facilities.[10]

A California study found that nonradiologists who operate their own diagnostic imaging equipment performed 1.7 to 7.7 times more imaging examinations than physicians who referred cases to radiologists for imaging.[11] Another study looking at California workers' compensation claims found that the program paid more for physician therapy, psychiatric evaluations, and MRI scans for

8. Office of Inspector General Dep't of Health & Human Servs., Financial Arrangements Between Physicians and Health Care Businesses: Report to Congress (1989) described in John K. Iglehart, The Debate over Physician Ownership of Health Care Facilities, 321 New Eng. J. Med. 198, 202 (1989).

9. Jean M. Mitchell & Elton Scott, New Evidence of the Prevalence and Scope of Physician Joint Ventures, 268 JAMA 80 (1992) [hereinafter New Evidence]; Jean M. Mitchell & Elton Scott, Physician Ownership of Physical Therapy Services, 268 JAMA 2055 (1992) [hereinafter Physician Ownership]; 3 Medicare Compliance Alert, Sept. 2, 1991, at 3. The study failed to find abuses with respect to MD–owned hospitals, skilled nursing facilities, or ambulatory

surgical centers. See also, GAO, Medicare, Physicians Who Invest in Imaging Centers Refer More Patients for More Costly Services (GAO/T–HRD–93–14, Apr. 20, 1993); Jean M. Mitchell & Elton Scott, Evidence on Complex Structures of Physician Joint Ventures, 9 Yale J. on Reg. 489 (1992) [hereinafter Complex Structures].

10. Jean M. Mitchell & Jonathan H. Sunshine, Consequences of Physician's Ownership of Health Care Facilities—Joint Ventures in Radiation Therapy, 327 New Eng. J. Med. 1497 (1992).

11. Bruce J. Hillman et al., Physicians' Utilization and Charges for Outpatient Diagnostic Imaging in a Medicare Population, 268 JAMA 2050 (1992).

the patients of self-referring physicians than for the patients of independent-referring physicians.[12] A recent GAO study found that physician investors in Joint–Venture Imaging Centers ordered 54% more MRI scans, 27% more CT scans, 37% more nuclear medicine scans, 27% more echocardiograms; 22% more ultrasounds, and 22% more complex X rays than nonowners, and that physicians with imaging facilities in their offices had even higher rates.[13] A HCFA study, however, found that self-referral rates varied from specialty to specialty and state to state and were not uniformly problematic,[14] and an AMA study found that only about 8% of physicians had an ownership interest in a health care facility.[15]

It has been noted that studies finding high rates of utilization where self-referral is present do not establish that the additional services provided are unnecessary.[16] Higher utilization rates might in fact be appropriate if self-referring physicians treat patients who are sicker, or if they tend to be specialists in treating particular kinds of conditions that required higher levels of intervention. Some of the studies did look beyond simple utilization rates, however. The Florida physical therapy study, for example, found that in facilities owned by referring physicians, physical therapists or therapist assistants spent much less time with patients, and patients received more of their care from non-licensed personnel.[17] The study also found that profits were much higher in facilities owned by referring physicians than in facilities now owned by referring physicians.[18] It is, moreover, difficult to believe that such strong and consistent empirical evidence of higher utilization rates (and of higher cost) where physicians self-refer does not support the notion that physicians maximize their income, as economists predict that they should.

Though apprehension about excessive and inappropriate utilization driven by physician self-interest was probably the primary concern driving the enactment of federal legislation, it was not the only one. Congress was also concerned about physicians referring patients placing their own interest above the patient's "best interests" in deciding where to refer the patient, and about the undercutting of competitive markets in health care if physicians referred

12. Alex Swedlow et al., Increased Costs and Rates of Use in the California Workers' Compensation System as a Result of Self–Referral by Physicians, 327 New Eng. J. Med. 1502 (1992).

13. GAO, Medicare, Referrals to Physician–Owned Imaging Facilities Warrant HCFA's Scrutiny (GAO/HEHS–95–2, Oct. 20, 1994).

14. Medicare Compliance Alert, Apr. 26, 1993 at 3.

15. Medicare Compliance Alert, May 10, 1993 at 8.

16. See Health Care Groups Seek Moratorium, Major Revisions to Stark II Legislation, BNA Health Care Daily, May 5, 1995 (quoting statement by Rep. Nancy Johnson, R–Conn., at House hearings on Stark revisions).

17. Physician Ownership, supra note 9, at 2058.

18. Id.

patients to facilities that they owned rather than to those facilities that offered the best prices and quality.[19]

§ 4–2. Possible Responses to Self–Referrals

There are several possible responses to the self-referral problem.[1] One would be simply to consider the problem as a bribe and kickback issue to be addressed through existing prohibitions against bribes and kickbacks. Most self-referral situations involve remuneration being paid and accepted for a referral, and thus violate 42 U.S.C.A. § 1320a–7b.

This solution is problematic, however. First, some self-referrals may not involve bribes and kickbacks. If a physician refers a patient to a clinical laboratory he or she wholly owns as a sole proprietorship there is, arguably, no remuneration changing hands since the physician is both entities. Second, the bribe and kickback prohibition proscribes knowing and willful offering or accepting of remuneration in exchange for a referral, thus the question is always present as to whether the parties intended to exchange the remuneration for the referral where the remuneration also arguably paid for other services (such as test interpretation[2]) or where it was arguably a return on an investment not directly linked to referrals.[3] Developing and proving intentional violation of the bribe and kickback law requires a substantial commitment of government resources, and most self-referral arrangements would probably go unchallenged if this were the only possible means for challenging them.

A second alternative would be to require or request payors (Medicare carriers or intermediaries or state Medicaid agencies) to require disclosure of facility ownership and then be more diligent in pursuing utilization review when physicians refer patients to facilities that they own.[4] This approach is unrealistic as a global solution, though some payors and insurers have attempted to limit

19. Morse and Popovits, supra note 1 at 209; Timothy Stoltzfus Jost & Sharon Davies, The Fraud and Abuse Statute: Rationalizing or Rationalization, 15 Health Aff. 129 (1996).

§ 4–2

1. See OIG, Financial Arrangements Between Physicians and Health Care Businesses (1989), reprinted in [1989 Transfer Binder] Medicare & Medicaid Guide (CCH) ¶ 37,838 (discussing a number of the options considered below).

2. United States v. Porter, 591 F.2d 1048, 1054–57 (5th Cir.1979).

3. Hanlester Network v. Shalala, 51 F.3d 1390, 1399–1402 (9th Cir.1995). See Morgan R. Baumgartner, Physician Self–Referral and Joint Venture Prohibitions: Necessary Shield Against Abusive Practices or Overregulation?, 19 J. Corp. L. 313, 323–27.

4. See, e.g., E. Haavi Morreim, Conflicts of Interest: Profits and Problems in Physician Referrals, 262 JAMA 390, 392 (1989); Robert Tenery, Should Physicians Abide by a Higher Standard, Am. Med. News Feb. 8, 1993 at 37.

access of their beneficiaries to self-referring physicians.[5] Utilization review is anything but an exact science and at most limits utilization at the margins. It is also very burdensome—Medicare carriers process over four million claims a year for clinical laboratory services alone.[6] Most of the increased utilization attributable to self-referrals would go unchallenged under this option.

Further, this approach also puts the patient in the middle of a conflict between the payor and physician (both of which are pursuing their self-interests), while the patient usually lacks the ability to judge who is in fact serving the patient's interest. A utilization review denial of a self-referral might be an appropriate response by the payor to an inappropriate self-referral, but might be interpreted by the patient as a denial of necessary services motivated by the payor's self-interest. This approach, therefore, unnecessarily heightens the distrust already present between beneficiaries, their doctors, and Medicare.

A third possibility would be to require disclosure to the patient of the fact of the physician's interest in the facility to which the patient is referred at the time of referral. For a time the ethical guidelines of the American Medical Association required disclosure, as some state laws still do.[7] Policing this requirement would be difficult, however, since communications between physicians and their patients would have to be monitored. It is unclear, moreover, what the patient is supposed to do with the information disclosed. Is it realistic to expect the patient to verify independently the need for the item or service once the conflict of interest is disclosed? Is the patient supposed to examine the motives of the treating physician, and if so, how? Will the physician rescind the referral if the patient demands a referral to an alternate facility? If not, will excessive utilization be curtailed? We have the benefit of several decades of experience with physician disclosure to patients in the informed consent to treatment setting, and this experience gives us little reason to be confident that requiring disclosure would have much effect on either physician or patient behavior.[8] Two states that have disclosure laws on the books have experienced the same higher utilization rates among self-referring physicians experienced by other states.[9]

---

5. Peter Kazon, Overutilization and M.D. Self Referrals, Business & Health, July 1991, at 74.

6. 60 Fed. Reg. 41,914, 41,926 (1995).

7. Terri Randall, Despite Some Overlap, Ethical and Legal Issues of Physician Self–Referral Remain Distinct, 255 JAMA 2335 (1991). See, infra, § 4–9.

8. Marc. A. Rodwin, Physicians' Conflicts of Interest: The Limitations of Disclosure, 321 New Eng. J. Med. 1405 (1989); Marc A. Rodwin, The Organized American Medical Profession's Response to Financial Conflicts of Interest: 1980–1992, 70 Milbank Q. 703, 730 (1992) [hereinafter Profession's Response].

9. OIG, Financial Arrangements Between Physicians and Health Care Busi-

Fourth, common law litigation could be relied on to enforce physician obligations.[10] Physicians are often described as fiduciaries, and can be held liable in tort, or perhaps for breach of contract or of fiduciary duty, if the pursuit of self-interest by physicians injures their patients.[11] To successfully pursue common law actions, however, the patient would need both to establish damages and to prove that the damages were caused by breach of contract, fiduciary obligation, or the applicable standard of care. The patient would also need to either pay a lawyer on an hourly basis or find a lawyer willing to take the case on a contingent fee arrangement.

In many cases, the party most injured by self-referrals is the third party payor which pays for the test or therapy. The primary harm caused the patient is the inconvenience and discomfort of undergoing an unnecessary test or procedure. This harm will rarely be of sufficient value to warrant the cost of a lawyer. Only in the case where the patient in fact suffers egregious harm because of unnecessary or substandard care might common law litigation result. These cases, if they exist, are rare enough that they are unlikely to have a significant deterrent effect.[12]

Fifth, the matter could simply be regarded as a question of professional ethics, and left to the bodies that define and enforce professional ethics. Professional organizations have long been concerned with some manifestations of conflicts of interest, most particularly with fee splitting.[13] The medical profession has been less cognizant of the conflicts involved in self-referrals, however, and when self-referrals first became a major public policy concern in the 1980s, the American Medical Association refused to take a position condemning them.[14]

In December of 1991, however, the AMA Council of Ethical and Judicial Affairs issued ethical guidelines holding that it was gener-

nesses (1989), reprinted in [1989 Transfer Binder] Medicare & Medicaid Guide (CCH) ¶ 37,838.

10. See Morreim, supra note 4, at 391–92.

11. See, e.g., Moore v. Regents of Univ. of Cal., 793 P.2d 479, 483, 51 Cal.3d 120, 129, 271 Cal.Rptr. 146, 150 (1990) (physician must reveal financial interest in research involving patient).

12. Self-referral arrangements might also violate the antitrust laws in situations where a significant proportion of the physicians in a geographic and product market acquired and referred to an entity that provided related services. See Brian McCormick, Doctors Ordered to Divest: FTC Breaks New Antitrust Ground in Self-Referrals, Am. Med.

News Nov. 22, 1993, at 2 (FTC consent agreement involving 28 pulmonologists representing 60% of area lung specialists agreeing to divest themselves of their interests in two home oxygen firms so that neither firm is owned by more than 25% of the market's pulmonologists.) The antitrust laws only address a small number of referrals, however.

13. See Marc Rodwin, Medicine, Money and Morals: Physicians' Conflicts of Interest, 19–52 (1993); Profession's Response, supra note 8, at 707–33.

14. American Medical Association, Council on Ethical and Judicial Affairs, Report of the Council on Ethical and Judicial Affairs: Conflicts of Interest (1986).

ally unethical for a physician to refer a patient to health care facilities outside of their office practice in which they had an investment interest, but at which they did not directly provide care or services.[15] These guidelines permitted physicians to invest in facilities to which they referred patients only if they themselves provided care or services to the patient in the facility or if the facility was needed in the community and alternative sources of capital were not available and the investment interest was disclosed to referred patients.[16] The AMA House of Delegates initially rejected this position in June of 1992, voting that self-referral was ethical if disclosed to the patient. Subsequently in December of 1992 the AMA reversed itself and voted to adopt the Council's position.[17]

Even though the AMA has now taken the position that self-referrals are unethical, it only did so after Congress began to take an active interest in the issue. The AMA has continued to call for loosening of self-referral restrictions at the federal level.[18] The AMA has, moreover, only a very limited capacity for enforcing its ethical standards. Its harshest sanction is expulsion from the Association—a power rarely exercised—and it has no power over the majority of American physicians who do not belong to it.[19] Noncompliance with the AMA's prior disclosure policy was widespread and, apparently, did not result in disciplinary action.[20] Although it is significant that the medical profession has taken a stance that self-referrals raise ethical, and not simply economic, issues, professional ethical pronouncements in themselves are unlikely to solve the self-referral problem.[21]

15. Report of the American Medical Association Council on Ethical and Judicial Affairs; Report C (1–91), Dec. 11, 1991, with clarifications published in Council on Ethical and Judicial Affairs, American Medical Association, Conflicts of Interest: Physician Ownership of Medical Facilities, 267 JAMA 2366 (1992).

16. See Thomas S. Crane, The Problem of Physician Self-referral Under the Medicare and Medicaid Antikickback Statute, 268 JAMA 85, 89–90 (1992); Council on Ethical and Judicial Affairs, American Medical Association, Conflicts of Interest: Physician Ownership of Medical Facilities, 267 JAMA 2366 (1992). The AMA also suggested compliance with the OIG's investment safe harbors.

17. See Arnold S. Relman, "Self–Referral"—What's at Stake, 327 New Eng. J. Med. 1522, 1522–23 (1992).

18. See Diane Gianelli, Forecast: Some Relief from Self–Referral Ban, Am.

Med. News, May 22, 1995, at 1. It must be noted that the profession is divided not only ideologically, but also with respect to self-interest, on the self-referral problem. Specialists who rely on referrals from other physicians suffer financially when the referring physicians invest in facilities to provide the services they formerly referred patients out for. See Brian McCormick, Self Referral Bill Divides Florida Physicians, Am. Med. News Feb. 10, 1992, at 1, 31.

19. Profession's Response, supra note 8, at 731.

20. Id. at 730.

21. See, discussing the limitations of professional association self-regulation in medicine generally, David Orentlicher, The Role of Professional Self–Regulation in Regulation of the Health Care Professions, 129 (Timothy S. Jost, ed. 1997).

Sixth, the law could simply ban self-referral arrangements that result in "unearned" remuneration and not worry about arrangements that simply provide a reasonable "earned" return on investment or compensation.[22] If physicians are merely receiving a reasonable return on their investment or reasonable compensation for their services from entities to which they refer patients, the arrangement is not causing harm, since the services would have to be paid for in any event. A physician, arguably, faces no incentive to make unnecessary referrals if the referral will not result in compensation or profit beyond that which is reasonable.

This approach poses several problems. First, there is the problem of who is to determine whether an arrangement is reasonable or not. A requirement that such arrangements be approved prospectively before implementation would require a substantial expansion of the federal or state bureaucracy, flying in the face of the current trend toward shrinking bureaucracy. Retrospective review through criminal, civil, or administrative actions would probably reach only a small fraction of all arrangements. Second, evaluation of reasonableness would be a very difficult, if not impossible, task. Presumably reasonableness would have to be evaluated with respect to some notion of fair market value, but return on investments and compensation for services in markets in which self-referrals are not restricted often reflect the added value of the referrals, and it would be difficult to establish values in the abstract absent these considerations.[23] Just as there is no gold standard for utilization that would make evaluation of medical necessity easy, so there is no gold standard for evaluating the value of capital or services to determine whether they are excessive. At best, only egregiously inappropriate arrangements would be identified.

Seventh, all self-referral arrangement could be banned. On its face this seems like the simplest solution, but it would be very difficult to implement. Physicians normally serve patients in several capacities. For example, they examine the patient; perform and interpret diagnostic tests; diagnose; perform procedures; and prescribe, order, or dispense medication, therapy, or medical devices or supervise the provision of these items or services. Often it is most convenient and economical both for the physician and the patient if one physician or the employees of one physician can perform several of these services for the same patient, even if they are not provided at the same time or in the same office. An absolute

22. See Mark A. Hall, Making Sense out of Referral Fee Statutes, 13 J. Health Pol., Pol'y & L. 623, 628–32 (1988).

23. See David Frankford, Creating and Dividing the Fruits of Collective Economic Activity: Referrals Among Health Care Providers, 89 Colum. L. Rev. 1861, 1889–1900 (1989) (discussing the impossibility of objectively evaluating the cost, efficiency, or necessity of medical care).

prohibition against self-referrals which prohibited a physician from ordering diagnostic tests to be performed in a clinical laboratory owned and operated by the physician in the same building as his practice, would create unnecessary hardships. Similarly, a self-referral law that prohibited referral of patients of a physician member of a group practice to other group members or to a clinical laboratory operated by the group in its own office suite would be impractical and burdensome.

Relationships between hospitals and physicians are often complex and multifaceted. A rule that refused to allow a physician who served on a hospital's utilization review committee in exchange for compensation or who rented an office from the hospital for a reasonable rate to admit patients to that hospital would impose great burdens on physicians, patients, and communities. In some underserved areas, moreover, many health care services might become unavailable if physicians in the community were forbidden from investing in those services. Finally, if our primary concern is to discourage excessive utilization, it makes little sense to prohibit physician investment interests in or compensation arrangements with managed care organizations, which are likely to control excessive utilization by directly or indirectly putting the physicians at risk for the costs of excessive utilization.

Congress ultimately settled on an eighth alternative. It imposed a general ban on self-referrals for particular items or services subject to a host of exceptions. This approach takes advantage of the efficiency of an absolute ban in avoiding case-by-case disputes over the reasonableness of particular arrangements; the adequacy of disclosure of interest conflicts; the necessity of referrals; or the harm caused by referrals. On the other hand, it is much more flexible than an absolute ban, and permits the continuation of arrangements that pose little threat of harm.

This solution, however, is far from perfect. The task of identifying the types of services that are most likely to result in abusive self-referrals, on the one hand, and the contexts in which self-referrals are least likely to be problematic, on the other, has proved difficult. Application of the statute to a nearly infinite variety of continually changing arrangements has proved even more difficult. The rules implementing Stark I did not emerge from HCFA in final form until 1995, six years after the statute was adopted, and the rulemaking notice filled 70 pages of small print in the Federal Register.[24] The rules implementing Stark II have still not emerged three years after its adoption.

24. 60 Fed. Reg. 41,914 (1995). See also, Implementation of "Physician Ownership and Referral" Prohibition, Program Memorandum (Intermediaries/Carriers), HCFA Pub. 60A/B, Transmittal No. AB–95–3, Jan. 1995, repro-

This complexity has resulted in continual agitation among provider groups for the repeal or significant amendment of the statute, which almost came to fruition in the 1995 Republican Budget. This agitation has had one result: the 1997 Balanced Budget Bill requires HHS to issue written advisory opinions upon request concerning whether a referral relating to a health service (other than clinical laboratory services) is covered by the self-referral statute.[25] The advisory opinion process is described in chapter 3.

The exceptions recognized by the Stark law, on the whole, tend to drive physicians into group practice, managed care organizations, and employment relationships with providers that may result in the end in underservice to patients and undermining of the physician-patient relationship.[26] For the moment, however, the federal law continues to ban self-referrals with respect to a considerable number of services subject to an intricate web of exceptions. We next describe this ban, and then these exceptions.

§ 4–3. The Stark Prohibition

The Stark legislation, as amended, generally prohibits a physician from referring a Medicare or Medicaid patient to an entity for the furnishing of the specified services if the physician (or an immediate family member) has a financial relationship with the entity.[1] An entity to which a prohibited referral is made may not present a claim to Medicare, or bill any individual, third party payor or other entity for any service provided pursuant to such a referral.[2] States may not receive federal financial assistance for Medicaid expenditures made for services provided in response to referrals that would be barred by this section if provided under Medicare.[2.5] An entity that does so will be denied payment and must refund within 60 days any amounts collected.[3] Payment is denied even if the referring physician acted in good faith without knowledge or intent that a prohibited referral was being made.[4]

Persons who present or cause to be presented bills under these provisions are also liable for civil penalties of up to $15,000 for each

duced at [1994–1995 Transfer Binder] Medicare & Medicaid Guide (CCH), ¶ 43,078.

25. Pub. L. No. 105–32, adding 42 U.S.C.A. § 1395nn(g)(6).

26. See Frankford, supra note 23; Morreim, supra note 4, at 392–93.

§ 4–3

1. 42 U.S.C.A. §§ 1395nn(a)(1)(A); 1396b(s).

2. 42 U.S.C.A. § 1395nn(a)(1)(B); 42 C.F.R. § 411.353.

2.5 42 U.S.C.A. § 1396b(s).

3. 42 U.S.C.A. § 1395nn(g)(1), (2). The statute requires a refund on a "timely basis" which 42 C.F.R. § 1003.101 defines as 60 days "from the time the prohibited amounts are collected by the individual or the entity."

4. See 60 Fed. Reg. 41,914, 41,924 (1995) (Preamble to Stark I regulations discussing this provision).

service billed or for each failure to make a timely refund where the person knew or should have known of the violation, plus twice the amount claimed for each service that was the basis of a penalty.[5] They may also be excluded from program participation.[6] In addition, physicians or entities that enter into schemes to circumvent the self-referral prohibitions (such as cross-referral schemes, in which two physicians each agree to refer their patients to laboratories owned by the other) are liable for civil money penalties of up to $100,000 and may be excluded from program participation.[7]

There are no explicit criminal nor civil sanctions for violating the self-referral statute, nor is a violation explicitly subject to qui tam litigation. As was noted in chapter 2, however, a claim submitted to Medicare or Medicaid that involves a self-referral which is illegal under the Medicare or Medicaid law, is arguably a false claim. Several district courts have refused to dismiss qui tam cases alleging that claims were for services provided on the basis of referrals that were tainted under the related kickback statute,[8] while the Fifth Circuit has held that a hospital could be held liable for submitting both a false claim and a false statement if it had certified compliance with Medicare statutes and regulations (including the Stark laws) and payment of claims was conditional on such certification.[9] If the courts ultimately uphold this position, the self-referral statute may become even more troublesome to providers.

The "designated services" covered by the prohibition include:

— Clinical laboratory services;

— Physical laboratory services;

— Occupational therapy services;

— Radiology, including magnetic resonance imaging (MRI), computerized axial tomography scans, and ultrasound services;

— Radiation therapy services and supplies;

— Durable medical equipment and supplies;

— Parenteral and enteral nutrients, equipment and supplies;

— Prosthetics, orthotics, and prosthetic devices;

---

5. 42 C.F.R. § 1395nn(g)(3); 42 C.F.R. § 1003.103(b). Rules implementing these provisions were published at 60 Fed. Reg. at 16,850; 60 Fed. Reg. 58,239, 58,241 (1995); 61 Fed. Reg. at 13,430.

6. 42 U.S.C.A. § 1395nn(g)(3).

7. 42 U.S.C.A. § 1395nn(g)(4); 42 C.F.R. §§ 1003.102(b)(10), 1003.106(b).

8. United States ex rel. Roy v. Anthony, 914 F.Supp. 1504, 1506–07 (S.D.Ohio 1994); United States ex rel. Pogue v. American Healthcorp, 914 F.Supp. 1507 (M.D.Tenn.1996).

9. United States ex rel. Thompson v. Columbia/HCA Healthcare Corp., 1997 WL 619314 (5th Cir. 1997).

— Home health services and supplies;[10]

— Outpatient prescription drugs;

— Inpatient and outpatient hospital services.

As regulations have only been issued for Stark I as of this writing, only the term "clinical laboratory services" has been defined in regulations.[11] The clinical laboratory definition has been adopted from the definition used in the Clinical Laboratories Improvement Act.[12] Diagnostic tests that are not subject to CLIA are not considered clinical laboratory services under Stark I.[13]

"Entity" is defined broadly by the Stark I regulations to include a sole proprietorship, trust, corporation, partnership, foundation, not-for-profit foundation, or unincorporated association.[14] This definition is intended to include all possible organizations that can deliver covered services.[15]

The term "physician" is not defined under the statute. The statute presumably, therefore, incorporates the general definition of physician under the Medicare statute, which includes medical doctors, osteopaths, dentists or dental surgeons, podiatrists, optometrists, and chiropractors, operating within the scope of their state licenses, and delivering services they are permitted to provide under the Medicare program.[16] "Referring physician" is defined by the Stark I regulations to include a physician or group practice that

---

10. With respect to home health services, the Medicare statute and regulations also provide that the physician who certified the need for such services may not have a "significant ownership interest" or "a significant financial or contractual relationship" with the home health agency. 42 U.S.C.A. § 1395n(a); 42 C.F.R. § 424.22(d). The regulations define significant ownership interest as a direct or indirect ownership of 5% or more of the agency's capital, stock, or profits or of any secured obligation of the agency if that interest equals 5% or more of the agency's assets. 42 C.F.R. § 424.22(d)(2). A significant financial or contractual relationship exists if the certifying physician receives compensation as an officer or director or has business transactions with the agency that amount to more than $25,000 or 5% of the agency's total operating expenses in a fiscal year. 42 C.F.R. § 424.22(d)(3). Uncompensated officers or directors are not excluded from being certifying physicians, and the limitation does not apply to governmental entities or agencies classified as "sole community HHAs." 42 C.F.R. § 424.22(d)(4), (e).

11. 42 U.S.C.A. § 1395nn(h)(6). The Stark I regulations define clinical laboratory services to include "biological, microbiological, serological, chemical, immunohematological, hematological, biophysical, cytological, pathological, or other examination of materials derived from the human body for the purpose of providing information for the diagnosis, prevention, or treatment of any disease or impairment of, or the assessment of the health of, human beings" including procedures addressing the presence of organisms in the body. They define laboratories as entities providing these services, but not including entities that only collect, prepare, or mail specimens but do not perform tests on them. 42 C.F.R. § 411.351.

12. See 60 Fed. Reg. 41,914, 41,927 (1995).

13. 60 Fed. Reg. at 41,928.

14. 42 C.F.R. § 411.351.

15. 60 Fed. Reg. at 41,930.

16. 42 U.S.C.A. § 1395x(r). See 60 Fed. Reg. 41,942 (discussion of meaning of term in preamble to Stark I regulations).

makes a referral.[17] This definition would seem to indicate that a referral made by a group member is imputed to other group members, a concept expressly adopted in the preamble to the Stark I regulations.[18]

Immediate family member is defined to include husbands; wives; natural or adoptive parents, children or siblings; stepparents, children, brothers and sister; father-in-laws, mother-in-laws, son-in-laws, daughter-in-laws, brother-in-laws, and sister-in-laws; grandparents or grandchildren; and spouses of grandparents or grandchildren.[19] This definition is the definition used by the Medicare program to exclude from Medicare coverage services provided by immediate family members.[20]

"Referral" is defined as the request by a physician for an item or service.[21] This may include a request for a consultation with another physician and any test or procedure ordered by or to be performed by or under the supervision of that other physician.[22] It may also include the request or establishment of a plan of care by a physician when the plan includes furnishing of the designated services.[23] The "plan of care provision" sweeps in many situations not included in the common sense understanding of a referral, and has troubled the commentators.

The statute excepts from the definition of referral, however, a request by a pathologist for clinical diagnostic laboratory tests and pathological examination services; the request by a radiologist for diagnostic radiology services; or the request by a radiation oncologist for radiation therapy if the services are furnished by or under the supervision of the pathologist, radiologist, or radiation oncologist under a consultation requested by another physician.[24]

"Financial relationships" are defined broadly to include both compensation arrangements and ownership or investment interests (including ownership by way of equity, debt, "or other means" and interests in holding companies that hold interests in designated

17. 42 C.F.R. § 411.351.

18. 60 Fed. Reg. at 41,946.

19. 42 C.F.R. § 411.351.

20. 42 U.S.C.A. § 1395y(a)(11).

21. 42 U.S.C.A. § 1395nn(h)(5)(A); 42 C.F.R. § 411.351.

22. 42 C.F.R. § 411.351. The preamble to the Stark I final rules emphasizes the obligation of consultants to be aware of the financial relationships of referring physicians to avoid making prohibited referrals. 60 Fed. Reg. at 41,940.

23. 42 U.S.C.A. 1395nn(h)(5)(B). Under this definition if a physician refers a patient to another physician for consul-

tation, and the consulting physician refers the patient to a clinical laboratory with which the initial physician has a financial relationship, the statute has been violated, even though the consulting physician has no financial relationship with the laboratory. It is prudent, therefore, that physicians notify physicians to whom they refer patients for consultation of any entities with which they have financial relationships. The terms "plan of care" and "referral" are further defined in the regulations. 42 C.F.R. § 411.351.

24. 42 U.S.C.A. § 1395nn(h)(5)(C).

entities) between a physician (or an immediate family member) and the designated entity.[25] The preamble to the Stark I regulations states that the term "other means" was meant to encompass any of the "infinite variety" of interests that might be dreamed up.[26] It does not cover a situation, however, where a physician owns an interest in an entity that is a subsidiary or brother/sister corporation of an entity that delivers designated health services, as long as no remuneration flows from the entity that delivers the services to the physician and the physician does not make referrals for designated services to the entity in which he or she owns an interest.[27] Thus if a physician enters into a joint venture with a hospital for the co-ownership of a physician-hospital organization, the physician is not precluded from referring to the hospital as long as the PHO is not a conduit for remunerating the physician.[28] Also, just because an entity that delivers designated services is owned by certain physician owners of a professional corporation does not mean that other P.C. members who do not own the entity will be barred from referring to it, unless the P.C. is a group practice, in which case the group practice exception must be met for each referral made by a group member.[29]

Compensation arrangements are defined by proposed regulations to include all forms of remuneration, including discounts.[30] The simple fact of compensation brings arrangements within the prohibition, no formal agreement or form of organization is necessary for the prohibition to attach.[31] Remuneration, however, does not include forgiveness of amounts owed for inaccurate or mistakenly performed tests and procedures; the correction of minor billing errors; the provision of items, devices, or supplies used to collect, transport, process, or store specimens or to order or communicate the results of tests or procedures; or the payment by an insurer or self-insured entity on a fee-for-service basis for the fair market value of services provided to an insured where the payment is made

25. 42 U.S.C.A. § 1395nn(a)(2), (h)(1); 42 C.F.R. § 411.351. The holding company prohibition was added by OBRA 1993.

26. 60 Fed. Reg. at 41,931.

27. 60 Fed. Reg. at 41,944–46.

28. See Leonard C. Homer, How New Federal Laws Prohibiting Physician Self–Referrals Affect Integrated Delivery Systems, Health Span, Apr. 1994, at 21, 28, however, observing that if a PHO is created jointly by a hospital and a group of physicians, and the hospital provides a disproportionate share of the capital required to establish the PHO, subsequent payments to physicians by managed care organizations that contract with the PHO may be regarded as compensation flowing from the hospital to the physicians.

29. 60 Fed. Reg. at 41,946.

30. 42 C.F.R. § 411.351 (regulations defining "compensation arrangement" and "remuneration"). Discounts may be permissible if they are offered in the context of otherwise exempt arrangements, as where they are available to health maintenance organizations that meet the statutory exception for HMOs, see 60 Fed. Reg. 41942–43.

31. Homer, supra note 28, at 23.

on behalf of the covered patient and not on a contractual basis.[32] Beyond these specific exceptions, however, there is no general de minimus exception—all other compensation arrangements are prohibited.[33]

§ 4–4. Stark Exceptions Generally

Though the federal self-referral statute starts with a broad and all-inclusive general prohibition of physician referrals to entities from which they receive remuneration, it is subject to a multitude of exceptions. These exceptions tend to fall into several categories, both in terms of their purpose and in terms of their scope.

In terms of the purpose of the exceptions, there are, first, exceptions for situations where the general incentives that self-referrals present for excessive utilization of health care services are controlled in some other way, as with prepaid health plans; or with services for which Medicare pays through a bundled rate that does not increase in size in response to the volume of services used, as with ambulatory surgical centers or hospices. Second are exceptions for situations involving legitimate business arrangements that are unlikely to result in increased utilization: e.g. where the referring physician owns stock in large, publicly traded corporations to which the referral is made; is a bona fide employee of the entity to which the referral is made; has a personal services contract or a space or equipment rental agreement with the entity that meets certain requirements; receives remuneration from a hospital for reasons unrelated to the provision of designated services or under a physician recruitment agreement; pays the market value for designated services; or engages in isolated, one-time, transactions with an entity. The third, and probably most important, category of exceptions involves situations where the referring physician (or a member of the physician's group) is directly involved in the delivery of the service and the service is billed by the physician. This category includes the ancillary services and group practice services exceptions. Fourth, there are situations where a designated service would probably not be available without the exception, as with services in rural areas or in Puerto Rico.

The statute itself categorizes the exceptions differently. It divides them into exceptions that apply 1) to both ownership and compensation arrangements,[1] 2) only to ownership or investment interests,[2] and 3) only to compensation arrangements.[3]

---

32. 42 U.S.C.A. § 1395nn(h)(1)(C).

33. See Homer, supra note 28, at 23.

§ 4–4

1. 42 U.S.C.A. § 1395nn(b).

2. 42 U.S.C.A. § 1395nn(c), (d).

3. 42 U.S.C.A. § 1395nn(e).

The exceptions to the self-referral law, as is true with fraud and abuse law generally, tend to encourage integration of practice, even though it is not completely clear that overutilization is any less of a problem where tests are done within a practice rather than referred outside to an entity owned by the practice.[4]

§ 4–5.   Ownership and Compensation Arrangement Exceptions

The statute first recognizes three general exceptions to both the ownership and compensation arrangement prohibitions. The first exception covers physician's services provided personally by (or under the personal supervision of) another physician in the same group practice as the referring physician.[1]

The second exception covers "in-office" ancillary services furnished personally by the referring physician, by another physician in the same group practice as the referring physician, or by an individual who is directly supervised by the referring physician or another in the group where certain requirements are met.[2] The service must be provided in a building in which the referring physician or another group member furnishes services unrelated to the designated services or in another building used by the group practice for clinical laboratory services or for the centralized provision of other designated services.[3] Services must be billed by the physician performing or supervising the service, the group practice, or another entity wholly owned by the referring physician or group practice.[4] This exception does not apply to durable medical equipment (except infusion pumps) or to parenteral and enteral nutrients, equipment or supplies.[5] A third exception covers services furnished by health maintenance organizations, competitive medical plans (CMPs), and certain other prepaid plans.[6]

The statute also authorizes HHS to make additional exceptions for relationships that do not pose a risk of program or patient abuse.[7] The Stark I rules include one such exception for services furnished by an ambulatory surgical center (ASC), an end stage renal dialysis facility, or a hospice if the services are included in a composite or per diem rate.[8] This exception is based on the Secretary's judgment that there is little likelihood of excessive utilization

4. See David Frankford, Creating and Dividing the Fruits of Collective Economic Activity: Referrals Among Health Care Providers, 89 Colum. L. Rev. 1861, 1910–18 (1989).

§ 4–5

1. 42 U.S.C.A. § 1395nn(b)(1).
2. 42 U.S.C.A. § 1395nn(b)(2)(A)(i).

3. 42 U.S.C.A. § 1395nn(b)(2)(A)(ii).
4. 42 U.S.C.A. § 1395nn(b)(2)(B).
5. 42 U.S.C.A. § 1395nn(b)(2).
6. 42 U.S.C.A. § 1395nn(b)(3).
7. 42 U.S.C.A. § 1395nn(b)(4).
8. 42 C.F.R. § 411.355(d).

where the services ordered by the referring physician are paid out of a bundled rate.[9]

a. The Physicians' Services Exception

The physicians' services exception is a relatively narrow exception that applies to designated health care services that are treated as physicians' services for Medicare purposes.[10] This exception covers physicians' services performed by, or under the supervision of another physician in the same group practice as the referring physician. This exception uses the definition of group practice that is used for the ancillary services exception, which is described below. Under this exception, physicians' services may be performed anywhere, and are not subject to locational limitations.[11]

b. The Ancillary Services Exception

The ancillary services exception is the result of a very controversial exercise in line-drawing. As was acknowledged at the outset, medical practice unavoidably includes self-referrals. If the same physician who examines a patient also performs or interprets diagnostic tests and treats the patient, a self-referral has in a sense occurred. The examining physician has arguably referred to himself or herself the patient for testing and treatment. Even though permitting a physician to both examine and treat a patient creates the possibility for abuse in a fee-for-service system,[12] it is hard to believe that requiring multiple independent and unrelated physicians for each step in patient diagnosis and treatment would result in efficient, cost-effective, medical practice.

Once a single physician is permitted to diagnose and treat a patient, however, it would seem not to make much difference whether the single physician completed the physical examination and laboratory test analysis at the same location or in two separate locations. If we allow the physician to operate a laboratory at a location separate from his or her office, however, why not allow the physician to hire laboratory technicians to analyze the tests, as long as the physician personally supervises their work?

Arguably it is only a small step from allowing a physician to examine in one location and supervise a clinical laboratory in another to allowing one physician member of a group practice who examines and treats patients at one location to refer them for tests to a different physician member of the same group practice at

---

9. 60 Fed. Reg. at 41,939–40, 41,970–71.

10. I.e., services defined as physician's services under 42 U.S.C.A. § 1395x(q) and 42 C.F.R. § 410.20(a).

11. See 60 Fed. Reg. 41,914, 41,947 (1995).

12. See Mark Pauly, The Ethics and Economics of Kickbacks and Fee–Splitting, 10 Bell J. Econ. 344 (1979).

another location. (Of course, to implement this exception, the term "group practice" needs to be defined). The treating physician does not obviously face any greater temptation to refer for unnecessary tests where another group member supervises the laboratory than if the physician supervises it him or herself. Where a group practice bills for all services using a single billing number, moreover, payors are not deceived as to the volume of services being provided to the patient. The group maintains responsibility and control for the quality of care provided the patient. Arguably, therefore, the benefits of permitting intra-group referrals outweigh the dangers.[13]

It is but a small further step, however, from permitting referring physicians to provide ancillary services in their own facilities or referrals within a group practice to permitting shared laboratories, where several sole practitioners or small groups of physicians share the overhead of a laboratory but independently supervise tests performed within the laboratory and bill for these tests. These entities are sometimes referred to as "group practices without walls."[14] In fact, the House Energy and Commerce Committee draft of the 1993 Stark II amendments included an exception for shared laboratories existing as of June 26, 1992 where the services were:

(i) furnished to a shared laboratory patient,

(ii) furnished personally by the referring physician, by an individual supervised by the referring physician,

(iii) furnished by the shared laboratory in a building in which the referring physician furnished services unrelated to the service for which the referral was made and

(iv) billed by the referring physician or by an entity wholly owned by the referring physician.[15]

Neither the House Ways and Means Committee draft nor the Senate included a provision for shared laboratories, however, and the exception was rejected by the final Stark II amendments. Shared laboratories continue to receive vocal support from providers, however, and would have been excepted by the 1995 Republican budget bill had it not been vetoed.

In the end, however, only one step further (one can argue whether it is a small or large step) is necessary to go from shared laboratories to the physician joint venture laboratories that the self-referral legislation was initially aimed at. To be sure, the joint venture laboratory usually lacked the physician supervision and

13. Marc Rodwin, Medicine, Money and Morals: Physicians' Conflicts of Interest, 227–28 (1993).

14. Stephen J. Weiser, Venturing Into the Labyrinth of Stark: Impact of Stark Law and Stark Law Regulations

on Integrated Delivery Systems, 28 J. Health & Hosp. L. 313, 321 (1995).

15. H.R. Conf. Rep. No. 213, 103d Cong., 1st Sess. 809 (1993), reprinted in 1993 U.S.C.C.A.N. 1088, 1498.

personal billing found in a shared laboratory facility, but it is not obvious that the addition of these requirements would solve the overutilization at which the Stark legislation was aimed. For the moment, therefore, the line is drawn between group practices and shared laboratories, not between shared laboratories and other joint ventures, but the line may move.

The ancillary services exception does not cover all designated health services. Specifically it does not apply to durable medical equipment (other than infusion pumps) or parenteral and enteral nutrients, equipment and supplies.[16] These exclusions were presumably included based on a belief that these services were particularly subject to abuse and did not need to be provided directly by referring physicians, but these exceptions have proved quite controversial.

Durable medical equipment is not well defined in the Medicare statute.[17] It has been argued, however, that this provision potentially bars the provision of splints, canes, crutches, and braces by orthopedic surgeons to their patients.[18] It would also seem to prohibit oncologists from providing their patients with nutritional supplements necessary for bone marrow transplants, or for the provision of nutritional supplements in conjunctions with I.V. antibiotics.[19] It is unlikely that either Medicare or its beneficiaries will benefit if patients will need to be referred elsewhere for these services.

The ancillary service exception is subject to locational, supervision, and billing limitations. If designated health services are provided as ancillary services by a sole practitioner, they must be provided in a building in which the physician provides services unrelated to the designated service.[20] The statute does not permit sole practitioners to refer to ancillary laboratories that are not located at the same place as is their office practices.[21] The provision relating to group practices, however, is less restrictive.

First, if the services are provided by a group practice, they must be provided in 1) a building in which one of the members of the group provides unrelated physician's services, 2) in a building in which at least some of the group's clinical laboratory services are provided; or 3) in a building used by the group practice for the

---

16. 42 U.S.C.A. § 1395nn(b)(2).

17. See 42 U.S.C.A. § 1395x(n). The regulatory definition is somewhat more clear, see 42 C.F.R. § 414.202.

18. See testimony of James D. Strickland, American Academy of Orthopaedic Surgeons, House Ways and Means Committee, Subcommittee on Health, May 3, 1995; testimony of Frederick J. Wenzel, Medical Group Manage-

ment, House Ways and Means Committee, Subcommittee on Health, May 3, 1995.

19. Wenzel, supra note 18.

20. 42 U.S.C.A. § 1395nn(b)(2)(A)(ii)(I); 42 C.F.R. § 411.355(b)(2)(i).

21. 60 Fed. Reg. 41,914, 41,950 (1995).

centralized provision of designated health services other than clinical laboratory services.[22] The statute thus permits group practices to operate at several different locations and to refer patients among these locations for laboratory tests and to a centralized facility for other services.

Second, the statute requires that ancillary services be personally provided by the referring physician or by a member of the referring physician's group, or "personally by individuals who are directly supervised by the physician or by another physician in the group practice."[23] Stark I required that the non-physician furnishing the service be employed and "personally supervised" by the referring physician or group, but Stark II eliminated these requirements and substituted for them the "direct supervision" requirement.

The term "direct supervision" has long been used in the Medicare program to identify nonphysician services that physicians can bill as "incident to" their own services.[24] HCFA defined this term in the Stark I regulations in light of this history to mean: "supervision by a physician who is present in the office suite and immediately available to provide assistance and direction throughout the time services are being performed."[25] In doing so, HCFA seemingly rejected the observation found in the Stark II Conference report that the direct supervision requirement could be met "even if the physician is not always on site."[26] It is also clear, however, that under Stark II, the supervised personnel do not need to be employees of the physician or group, and could in fact be employees of an outside laboratory, as long as they were supervised by the referring physician or group.[27]

Third, in-office ancillary services must be billed by the physician or group performing or supervising the service under the physician or group's billing number, or by an entity wholly owned by the physician or group practice.[28] A group practice may also operate an independent laboratory, which provides laboratory services to individuals who are not patients of the group practice, but must bill for these services under a separate independent laboratory number (and cannot bill for these services if the referring physician has a proscribed ownership or compensation relationship with the group or laboratory).[29]

---

22. 42 U.S.C.A. § 1395nn(b)(2)(A)(ii)(II)(aa), (bb); 42 C.F.R. § 411.355(b)(2)(i).

23. 42 U.S.C.A. § 1395nn(b)(2)(A)(i).

24. See 42 C.F.R. § 410.32(a).

25. 42 C.F.R. § 411.351.

26. H.R. Rep. No. 213, 103rd Cong., 1st Sess. 810 (1993). See Fed. Reg. at

41,962 (explaining HCFA's rejection of "direct supervision" by an absent physician).

27. See 60 Fed. Reg. at 41,949.

28. 42 U.S.C.A. § 1395nn(b)(2)(B); 42 C.F.R. § 411.355(b)(3).

29. 60 Fed. Reg. at 41,947–48.

Note that the in-office ancillary services exception in fact permits the continuation of some shared laboratories. As long as the referring physician directly supervises and bills for the designated health services, and provides them in the same building in which the referring physician practices, it is not important that the laboratory is shared by several different physicians. The same is true if the laboratory is shared by several different groups, as long as the locational, supervision, and billing requirements for the in-office ancillary services exception are met with respect to any particular group.

c. The Definition of Group

Both the physician's services and in-office ancillary services exceptions apply to group practices. The term "group practice" is not a term that otherwise has a clear meaning in the Medicare and Medicaid context, thus the self-referral statute and regulations define the term. Group practice is defined by the statute to mean a group of two or more physicians:

> legally organized as a partnership, professional corporation, foundation, not-for-profit corporation, faculty practice plan, or similar association;
>
> (i) in which each physician who is a member of the group provides substantially the full range of services which the physician routinely provides, including medical care, consultation, diagnosis, or treatment, through the joint use of shared office space, facilities, equipment and personnel,
>
> (ii) for which substantially all of the services of the physicians who are members of the group are provided through the group and are billed under a billing number assigned to the group and amounts so received are treated as receipts of the group,
>
> (iii) in which the overhead expenses of and the income from the practice are distributed in accordance with methods previously determined;
>
> (iv) except as provided in subparagraph (B)(i), in which no physician who is a member of the group directly or indirectly receives compensation based on the volume or value of referrals by the physician,
>
> (v) in which members of the group personally conduct no less than 75 percent of the physician-patient encounters of the group practice,

(vi) which meets such other standards as the Secretary may impose by regulation.[30]

Subparagraph (B)(i) permits profit sharing and productivity bonuses based on services personally performed or incident to services personally performed by group physicians as long as the profit sharing or bonus is not directly related to the volume and value of referrals.[31] The statute also provides that, with respect to faculty practice plans in which physician members provide professional services both inside and outside of the faculty practice plan, the requirements need only apply to services provided within the practice plan.[32]

The statute authorizes HHS to clarify and expand on the statutory definition of group practice, and the Stark I regulations attempt to do so. First, the regulations define "member" of the group to include "physician partners and full-time and part-time physician contractors and employees during the time they furnish services to patients of the group practice that are furnished through the group and are billed in the name of the group."[33] This all-inclusive definition avoids manipulation of membership, but makes it easier for groups to meet some requirements, more difficult to meet others. The definition obviates, for example, arguments about whether a physician associated with the group who supervises the furnishing of designated services is a member or not for purposes of the in-office ancillary services exception. It also makes it easy for groups to meet the requirement that at least 75% of the physician-patient encounters of the group must be personally conducted by its members, although it also renders this provision a bit absurd, since by definition all physician-patient encounters of the group are conducted through its members.

An all-inclusive definition of membership, however, makes it more difficult for groups to meet the requirement that "substantially all" of the services of the physicians who are group members must be provided and billed through the group. The Stark I regulations address this problem to some extent by defining "substantially all" to mean 75% of total patient care services delivered by group members.[34] The proposed regulations had defined it as 85%, but the final regulations opted for the lower figure, in part in recognition of the fact that rural groups that depended on contracted specialists might have a hard time meeting the higher number.[35] The regulations further state that the percentage of patient care time allocated to a group practice is to be determined in terms of

30. 42 U.S.C.A. § 1395nn(h)(4)(A).

31. 42 U.S.C.A. § 1395nn(h)(4)(B)(i).

32. 42 U.S.C.A. § 1395nn(h)(4)(B)(ii).

33. 42 C.F.R. § 411.351.

34. 42 C.F.R. § 411.351; see 60 Fed. Reg. at 41,931–32.

35. Id.

time spent on patient care services.[36] The preamble to the regulations includes examples of how the calculation is to be made, such as the following:

> Ten physicians deliver services through a group practice. Eight of them devote 100 percent of their patient care time to the group practice. One devotes 80 percent, and one 10 percent: This can be illustrated as follows:
>
> 8 physicians at 100% each =   800%
> 1 physician at 80% =   80%
> 1 physician at 10% =   10%
>   890% divided by 10 = 89%[37]

In this example the requirement is met.

Groups must make this calculation on a 12 month basis, but can elect whether to do so on a fiscal year, calendar year or immediately-preceding–12–month basis, as long as the group uses the same period consistently.[38] Groups must submit an annual statement in writing to their carrier attesting to their compliance with the requirement.[39] Newly formed groups or groups that have not met the 75% requirement in the past may meet it by attesting to their expectation that they will meet it during the following 12 months, but if they fail to do so, all payments made conditional on the requirement being met will become overpayments.[40]

The "substantially all" test does not apply to group practices located solely within areas designated as health professional shortage areas (HPSAs) under the Public Health Act, nor is time spent by members of group practices located outside of HPSAs in providing services within HPSAs considered in making the "substantially all" calculation.[41]

The requirement that "substantially all" services must be billed through the group effectively forces the group to decide as a whole whether or not to accept assignment or to sign a participation agreement.[42] Group members who do not want to be participating physicians can bill independently, but the services so billed do not count toward the substantially all requirement.

Perhaps the most contentious aspect of the group definition has been the issue of compensation within the group. Group practices have many different approaches to dividing their income, and have become increasingly innovative in recent years as they have

36.   42 C.F.R. § 411.351.

37.   60 Fed. Reg. at 41,932–33.

38.   42 C.F.R. § 411.360(a), (c).

39.   42 C.F.R. § 411.360(a). The attestation was originally to have been filed by Dec. 12, 1995, but the requirement was delayed because of difficulty

HCFA experienced in implementation. 60 Fed. Reg. 53,438 (1995).

40.   42 C.F.R. § 411.360(b).

41.   42 C.F.R. § 411.351.

42.   60 Fed. Reg. at 41,934–35.

tried to use their compensation arrangements to create incentives for quality, cost-effectiveness, or other purposes.[43] Group practices have reacted strongly against what they view as Congress' attempt to micromanage intragroup relationships through Stark's restrictions on compensation arrangements.[44] It is possible, however, to creatively design compensation arrangements that comply with Stark while achieving the operational goals of group practices.[45]

d. Prepaid Health Plans

The federal self-referral prohibition also does not apply to referrals for services provided by prepaid health plans with which the referring physician has an ownership or compensation arrangement. It is widely believed that the incentives created by capitation arrangements militate against overutilization of services, indeed, if anything, encourage underutilization.[46] Congress therefore excepted certain prepaid plans from the ownership and compensation arrangements.[47]

The exception is not an across the board exception for all managed care organizations, however. It only covers specifically identified types of organizations, including:

     a) health maintenance organizations or competitive medical plans with contracts with Medicare under 42 U.S.C.A. § 1395mm and 42 C.F.R. part 417, subpart C, with respect to individuals enrolled in those organizations;[48]

     b) health care prepayment plans that contract for the provision of Part B services under 42 U.S.C.A. § 1395l(a) and 42 C.F.R. part 417, subpart C, with respect to individuals enrolled in those organizations;[49]

     c) organizations receiving payments on a prepaid basis through demonstration projects under section 402(a) of the Social Security Amendments of 1967 or section 222(a) of the Social Security Amendments of 1972, 42 U.S.C.A. § 1395b–1, with respect to individuals enrolled in those organizations;[50] and

---

43. Testimony of Donald C. Balfour, President, American Group Practice Association, House Ways and Means Committee, Subcommittee on Health, May 3, 1995.

44. See id.; testimony of Cecil Wilson, American Society of Internal Medicine, House Ways and Means Committee, Subcommittee on Health, May 3, 1995.

45. See, e.g., Try this Four–Part compensation Formula to Avoid Stark II Problems, Medicare Compliance Alert, Jan. 16, 1995, at 4; Avoid Stark II Prob-

lems with this 3–part compensation formula, Medicare Compliance Alert, Jan. 30, 1995, at 2; Medicare Compliance Alert, Dec. 5, 1994, at 1.

46. See Sharon L. Davies & Timothy Stoltzfus Jost, Managed Care: Placebo or Wonder Drug for Health Care Fraud and Abuse, 31 Ga. L. Rev. 373 (1997).

47. 42 U.S.C.A. § 1395nn(b)(3).

48. 42 U.S.C.A. § 1395nn(b)(3)(A).

49. 42 U.S.C.A. § 1395nn(b)(3)(B).

50. 42 U.S.C.A. § 1395nn(b)(3)(C).

d) federally qualified health maintenance organizations, with respect to individuals enrolled in such organizations.[51]

The exception does not apply to health maintenance organizations that are not federally qualified and do not fall into another exception, or to other kinds of managed care organizations. It also does not apply to individuals who receive services from facilities owned or operated by prepaid organizations but who are not enrolled in those organizations.[52] These limitations have been criticized by commentators who believe that the self-referral limitations make no sense in the context of managed care.[53] The 1995 Republican balanced budget act would have extended the prepaid health plan exception to managed care arrangements generally. The Balanced Budget Act of 1997 creates several new categories of managed care organizations under both the Medicare and Medicaid program,[54] but does not specifically amend the prepaid exception to cover these new categories. Though most will probably fall within another exception, a few may pose problems.

Referrals in managed care arrangements that do not fall within the categories specifically excepted by the statute, however, may well be covered by one of the other statutory exceptions, such as the employment exception or the personal services contract exception, which provides for capitation arrangements or other payment physician incentive plans.[55]

§ 4–6. Ownership and Investment Interest Exceptions

The Stark statute recognizes four general situations in which ownership by a referring physician is not considered an ownership or investment interest within the scope of the self-referral prohibition. First, an exception is recognized for interests in investment securities in publicly traded corporations or mutual funds with total assets exceeding $75 million which were purchased on terms generally available to the public.[1] Second, ownership interests are excepted in entities providing designated health services in rural areas if substantially all of the designated health services provided by the entity are provided to individuals residing in the rural area.[2] A third specific exception exists for hospitals within Puerto Rico.[3] Finally, physicians who have a general ownership interest in hospitals in which they are authorized to perform services may refer to

51. 42 U.S.C.A. § 1395nn(b)(3)(D).
52. See 60 Fed. Reg. at 41,950–51.
53. See Wenzel, supra note 18.
54. Pub. L. No. 105–32, §§ 4001, 4701—4710.
55. See generally Weiser, supra note 14.

§ 4–6

1. 42 U.S.C.A. § 1395nn(c).
2. 42 U.S.C.A. § 1395nn(d)(2); 42 C.F.R. § 411.356.
3. 42 U.S.C.A. § 1395nn(d)(1).

that hospital.[4] There is no exception under the self-referral legislation, as there is under the bribes-and-kickbacks safe harbors,[5] for investments in small entities where referring physicians control only a minority interest, and a request for such an exception under the Stark I regulations was rejected by HHS.[6]

a. Publicly Traded Securities

The publicly traded securities and mutual funds exceptions were included in the statute because income from these sources will obviously vary little based on the referrals generated by a particular physician, and thus ownership of these interests will create little incentive for additional referrals. Further, the idea of imposing federal scrutiny over the investment portfolios of every referring physician in the country is impractical and unpalatable. To be eligible for the exception, investment securities must be traded on the New York or American Stock Exchanges or on another foreign, national, or regional exchange that publishes quotations on a daily basis, or by the National Association of Securities Dealers, and must be securities which may be purchased on terms generally available to the public.[7] Under Stark I (until January 1, 1995) the total assets at the end of the corporation's most recent fiscal year had to exceed $100 million. Under Stark II stockholder equity must exceed $75 million at the end of the corporation's most recent fiscal year or on average during the previous 3 fiscal years.[8] Mutual funds must be administered by related investment companies, as defined under section 851(a) of the Internal Revenue Code, that had at the end of the most recent fiscal year or on average during the past 3 years assets in excess of $75 million.[9]

Stark I provided that securities must have been purchased on terms generally available to the public to qualify for this exception; Stark II amended the requirement to specify that securities had to be those which "may be purchased" on terms generally available to the public.[10] This change arguably permits securities obtained by physicians in trade for their proscribed equity interests in laboratories to qualify for the exception if the securities were otherwise also available to the general public. The proposed Stark I regulations would have imposed an additional requirement that the assets were obtained in the normal course of business to qualify for the exception, but this additional requirement was dropped in the final

---

4. 42 U.S.C.A. § 1395nn(d)(3).

5. 42 C.F.R. § 1001.952(a)(2).

6. 60 Fed. Reg. at 41,971–72.

7. 42 U.S.C.A. § 1395nn(c)(1); 42 C.F.R. § 411.356(a).

8. 42 U.S.C.A. § 1395nn(c)(1)(B); 42 C.F.R. § 411.356(a)(2).

9. 42 U.S.C.A. § 1395nn(c)(2); 42 C.F.R. § 411.356(b).

10. See 60 Fed. Reg. at 41,951.

regulations in the face of enforcement difficulties and adverse comment.[11]

b. Other Ownership and Investment Exceptions

The rural service provider exception was adopted out of a concern that services may not be available in rural areas unless physicians are allowed to invest in the services. The rural exception covers referrals to providers located in areas outside of Metropolitan Statistical Areas.[12] The services referred to the entity must be performed on the premises or, if the services are not performed on the premises, the entity must bill Medicare directly for the services.[13] This provision was added by the regulations to discourage the creation of rural "shell" laboratories that would send most of their work to urban reference laboratories and provide few additional services themselves.[14] Substantially all (defined by the Stark I regulations as 75%) of the services furnished by the provider must be furnished to individuals residing in a rural area.[15] There is no explicit exception covering compensation arrangements with rural service providers, but such arrangements will often fall under other compensation exceptions, such as the employment or personal services exceptions.[16]

The Puerto Rican hospital and general ownership in a hospital exceptions are two of the several exceptions in the self-referral statute relating to hospitals. "Hospital" is defined in 42 U.S.C.A. § 1395x(e) for Medicare purposes, but the Stark I regulations expand on this definition to state that "hospital" means:

> any separate legally organized operating entity plus any subsidiary, related, or other entities that perform services for the hospital's patients and for which the hospital bills. A "hospital" does not include entities that perform services for hospital patients "under arrangements" with the hospital.[17]

This definition recognizes that the modern hospital often consists of several related corporations or other entities, and defines "hospital" to include any entities for whose services the hospital, as more traditionally defined, bills. Thus, if a physician owns an interest in a separately incorporated home health agency through which a hospital serves its patients and for whose services the hospital bills Medicare, the physician owns an interest in the hospital, and cannot refer patients to the hospital for services unless another exception is satisfied.[18]

11. 60 Fed. Reg. at 41,951–52.

12. See 42 U.S.C.A. § 1395ww(d)(2).

13. 42 C.F.R. § 411.356(c)(1)(i)(A), (B).

14. 60 Fed. Reg. at 41,953–54.

15. 42 U.S.C.A. § 1395nn(d)(2); 42 C.F.R. § 411.356(c)(1)(ii).

16. 60 Fed. Reg. at 41,970–71.

17. 42 C.F.R. § 411.351.

18. 60 Fed. Reg. at 41,956.

42 U.S.C.A. § 1395nn(d)(3) permits physicians who own an investment interest in a hospital as a whole (and not merely in a subdivision of the hospital), and who are authorized to perform services at the hospital, to refer to the hospital. This provision was added by the Stark II statute, and is presumably justified by the fact that the referrals of a single physician-investor to the average hospital are unlikely to affect the profit of the hospital sufficiently to influence the referring behavior of the physician-investor.

§ 4–7. Compensation Exceptions

The studies of self-referrals that led to the Stark legislation concerned joint ventures in which the physicians had ownership or investment interests in the entities to which they referred. The Stark legislation, however, covers financial relationships generally, including both ownership and compensation arrangements. By covering compensation arrangements, however, the legislation sweeps in an almost infinite variety of arrangements through which physicians receive some form of compensation from entities to which they might occasionally make referrals. Compensation arrangements are also already addressed, moreover, by the bribes and kickbacks statute if they are intended to induce referrals. It has been argued, therefore, that it was not necessary to include compensation arrangements within the self-referral prohibition, and the vetoed 1995 Republican Balanced Budget Act would have repealed the self-referral law's coverage of compensation arrangements.[1]

As it now stands, the self-referral statute includes eight specific exceptions that apply solely to compensation arrangements. These cover rental of office space and equipment; bona fide employment relationships; personal service arrangements; remuneration by hospitals unrelated to the provision of designated health services; physician recruitment arrangements; isolated transactions; certain group practice arrangements with hospitals; and payments by physicians for certain items and services.[2] These exceptions are generally based on a recognition that the excepted compensation arrangements legitimately provide payment for items or services other than referrals, and that safeguards are present that assure that the payment is not in exchange for referrals.

Several of these exceptions apply only when the compensation received by the referring physician is consistent with the "fair market value" of the item or service, absent consideration of any referrals. "Fair market value" is defined by the statute as:

§ 4–7

1. H.R. 2491, § 8021 (1995).

2. 42 U.S.C.A. § 1395nn(e); 42 C.F.R. § 411.357.

the value in arms length transactions, consistent with the general market value, and, with respect to rentals or leases, the value of rental property for general commercial purposes (not taking into account its intended use) and, in the case of a lease of space, not adjusted to reflect the additional value the prospective lessee or lessor would attribute to the proximity or convenience of the lessor where the lessor is a potential source of patient referrals.[3]

The definition is substantially identical to that used in the bribes and kickbacks safe harbor regulations.[4] The preamble to the Stark I regulations stresses that "fair market value" cannot consider the fact that a "traditional economic factor" considered by the real estate industry in valuing an office for rental to a physician would be the proximity of the office to providers of designated health services to which referrals could be made.[5] How one is to determine fair market value abstracted from considerations important in the real estate market is a mystery that may perhaps be clarified in the future.

a. Rental of Space and Equipment

The first compensation exception permits payment of rental for office space or for equipment. Space and equipment rental agreements are common between physicians and other providers: doctors rent offices from hospitals and rent equipment to hospitals or space to laboratories. But space and equipment rentals have been abused in the past, as in situations where laboratories paid high rents to physicians for space that was too small to use for any useful purpose as disguised kickbacks for referrals. The space and equipment rental exceptions permit reasonable agreements under conditions nearly identical to the bribes and kickbacks rental safe harbors.

These conditions are:

- there must be a written agreement that is signed by the parties that specifies the space or equipment covered;

- the space or equipment must not exceed that which is reasonable for the legitimate business purposes of the lease and must be used exclusively by the lessee when it is being used by the lessee (except that rent may be paid for common areas in a space rental agreement if the rent represents a proportionate share of the expenses of the common areas based on the proportion of the total area other than the common areas used by the lessee);

3. 42 U.S.C.A. § 1395nn(h)(3); 42 C.F.R. § 411.351.

4. 42 C.F.R. § 1001.952(b)(5).
5. 60 Fed. Reg. at 41,930.

- the lease must be for a term of at least one year;

- the rental charges must be set in advance, be consistent with fair market value, and not be determined by taking into account the volume or value of referrals or other business relationships among the parties;

- the lease must be commercially reasonable absent any referrals;

- the lease must meet any other requirements imposed by the Secretary by regulation to protect against patient and program abuse.[6]

b. Bona–Fide Employment Arrangements

A second exception permits physicians to refer to entities with which they or members of their immediate families have bona fide employment arrangements. The arrangement must be for an identifiable service and the remuneration must be consistent with fair market value, not related to the volume or value of referrals, and provided under an agreement that would be commercially reasonable even if no referrals were made to the employer.[7] Amendments made in 1993 also permit productivity bonuses based on personal services performed by the physician or an immediate family member.[8] This employment exception is more detailed, though arguably not more narrow, than the bribes and kickbacks employment relationship exception, which requires bona fide relationships but does not explicitly specify that the agreement must be commercially reasonable and consistent with market value.[9]

The employment exception provides one obvious approach to structuring relationships to avoid Stark problems. If a physician is a bona fide employee of a hospital or of a managed care organization, referrals from the physician to the entity will not be prohibited.[10] Alternatively physicians can enter into independent contractor relationships with entities to which they refer under a third compensation arrangement exception—the personal services exception.

c. Personal Services Contracts

The self-referral statute permits remuneration for specific personal services where:

6. 42 U.S.C.A. § 1395nn(e)(1)(A), (B); 42 C.F.R. § 411.357(a), (b).

7. 42 U.S.C.A. § 1395nn(e)(2); 42 C.F.R. § 411.357(c).

8. 42 U.S.C.A. § 1395nn(e)(2).

9. 42 U.S.C.A. § 1320a–7b(b)(3)(B).

10. See Stephen J. Weiser, Venturing Into the Labyrinth of Stark: Impact of Stark Law and Stark Law Regulations on Integrated Delivery Systems, 28 J. Health & Hosp. L. 313, 321 (1995), noting situations where employment relationships can be used to bring integrated delivery systems into Stark compliance.

1) there is a written arrangement signed by the parties that specifies the services covered;

2) the arrangement covers all of the services provided by the physician or by immediate family members to the entity;

3) the services contracted for are only those reasonable and necessary for legitimate business purposes;

4) the arrangement is for at least a year;

5) the compensation is stipulated in advance, does not exceed fair market value, and does not take into account the value and volume of referrals or of other business between the parties (except where physician incentive plans, described below, are involved);

6) the arrangement does not involve "counseling or promotion of a business arrangement or other activity that violates any State or Federal law", and

7) other terms required by the Secretary are met.[11]

The personal services exception under the 1993 Stark II amendments replaced a more narrow exception under Stark I that was limited to contacts in certain settings or positions (in hospitals, hospices, or non-profit blood centers or as a medical director). It is also somewhat broader than the bribe and kickback safe harbor for personal services. The bribe and kickback safe harbor, for example, requires that the "aggregate compensation" be set in advance, while the Stark exception merely requires that the compensation be set in advance, thus leaving open the possibility of per service compensation, as long as it is not related to referrals.[12]

While the personal services exception protects many types of arrangements, it has a number of problems. First, it is not clear whether it in fact requires that contracts be entered into by referring physicians (and their family members) as individuals, or whether it would also cover contracts entered into by professional corporations or groups. Second, the requirement that there only be a single contract between the referring physician (and immediate family members) and the entity to which referrals are made is very problematic when the complex relationships that exist between physicians and large entities like hospitals are involved. A physician may relate to a hospital in many different capacities, which may be difficult to capture in one contract. Even greater difficulties emerge if the Stark I regulatory definition of "referring physician"—which includes group practices—is applied here. Capturing the entire relationship between all of the members of a group and a hospital in a single contract might be impossible. Finally, it is possible that

11. 42 U.S.C.A. § 1395nn(e)(3).　　**12.** See 42 C.F.R. § 1001.952(d)(5).

contracts that permit termination without cause before the year is up will be found to violate the "one year term" requirement, since they could be terminated and renegotiated several times within a year as referral patterns varied. Such contracts have become quite common in the health care industry.

The requirement of the personal services exception that compensation cannot be tied to the volume of referrals is subject to an exception designed to protect managed care arrangements. Note that this exception extends to managed care arrangements beyond traditional HMOs which are separately and more comprehensively covered by the prepaid health plan general exception. It only extends, however, to payments affecting services provided "with respect to individuals enrolled with the entity," and thus may not cover incentive arrangements established by integrated delivery systems with respect to persons enrolled in insurance plans that contract with the IDS for service delivery.[13]

The physician incentive plan exception provides that compensation can be related to the volume or value of referrals (through withholds, capitation, bonuses or otherwise) if the compensation arrangement meets the physician incentive plan requirements set out in the statute.[14] A physician incentive plan is defined as a compensation arrangement that may reduce or limit services provided to individual enrollees of the entity.[15] Physician incentive plans may not, however, include specific payments made to a physician or group as an inducement to restrict services with respect to a particular individual, and must comply with the 42 U.S.C.A. § 1395mm(i)(8)(A)(ii) and the regulations promulgated pursuant to this statute.[16] Regulations implementing the referenced section, dealing with incentive plans in prepaid health organizations, limit the extent to which physicians can be put at risk and require polling of enrollees for information regarding access and satisfaction.[17] They are discussed in § 1–6(i) above. Entities claiming this exemption must also provide information describing the plan on request to the Secretary.[18]

d. Compensation by Hospitals

A fourth exception permits remuneration by hospitals to physicians where the remuneration is not related to provision of the

---

13. See Leonard C. Homer, How New Federal Laws Prohibiting Physician Self–Referrals Affect Integrated Delivery Systems, Health Span, Apr. 1994 at 21, 29–30.

14. 42 U.S.C.A. § 1395nn(e)(3)(B)(i).

15. 42 U.S.C.A. § 1395nn(e)(3)(B)(ii).

16. 42 U.S.C.A. § 1395nn(d)(3)(B)(i).

17. 61 Fed. Reg. at 13,430, 69,034 (1996) to be codified at 42 C.F.R. § 417.479. See Robert Roth and Barbara Ryland, Physician Incentive Plan Rules' Implications: Throw the Stone, Watch the Ripples, Health Care Fraud Report (BNA), March 26, 1997 at 205, 207–08.

18. 61 Fed. Reg. at 13,430; 42 C.F.R. § 417.479.

designated services.[19] Under the original Stark legislation this exception extended to ownership as well as compensation arrangements, but the ownership exception was eliminated effective January 1, 1995. Note that under the regulatory definition of "hospital," this exception extends to compensation arrangements with organizations that are subsidiary to or related to hospitals if the hospital bills for their services.[20] Compensation arrangements that fit this exception may also meet the requirements of another exception as well, such as the personal services or rental exceptions. In the Stark I regulations, HHS declined a request that it expand this exception to cover non-hospital entities as well, stating that it could not find that such an expansion would be free from patient or program abuse.[21]

A fifth compensation exception permits physician recruitment arrangements that are intended to induce geographic relocation of a physician to become a member of the medical staff of a hospital, where there are no referral requirements and the physician's remuneration does not consider the volume and value of referrals.[22] The Stark I regulations additionally require that the arrangement be in writing and signed by the parties and that the physician not be precluded from establishing staff privileges at another hospital or from referring patients elsewhere.[23] Note that this exception does not cover many situations where recruitment agreements might make sense but geographical relocations are not required, as where a physician is recruited by an inner city hospital or a resident who receives training within a hospital is recruited to remain in the community.

e. Isolated Transactions

The sixth exception permits remuneration for isolated transactions, such as the one time sale of a practice or property.[24] This exception is tremendously important where an integrated delivery system or management-services-only (MSO) entity is attempting to acquire physician practices. Isolated transactions are exempt under the statute only where the amount of remuneration is consistent with fair market value and not affected by the value or volume of referrals and is provided under an agreement that is commercially reasonable without considering referrals.[25] The regulations also define "isolated transaction" as "one involving a single payment between two or more persons. A transaction that involves long-term or installment payments is not considered an isolated transac-

---

19. 42 U.S.C.A. § 1395nn(e)(4).
20. 60 Fed. Reg. at 41,957.
21. 60 Fed. Reg. at 41,958.
22. 42 U.S.C.A. § 1395nn(e)(5).
23. 42 C.F.R. § 411.357(e).

24. 42 U.S.C.A. § 1395nn(e)(6); 57 Fed. Reg. 8588, 8604 (1992) (to be codified at 42 C.F.R. § 411.359(d)) (proposed Mar. 11, 1992).
25. 42 U.S.C.A. § 1395nn(e)(6).

tion."[26] The debt owed by the purchaser to the physician whose practice is purchased in an installment transaction would also constitute a financial interest, proscribed by the law.[27] The regulations also provide that there can be no additional transactions between the parties to an isolated transaction for six months after the transaction unless they qualify under another exception, like the personal services or employment exception.[28]

It often makes sense for integrated delivery systems (IDSs) to purchase physician practices on an installment basis rather than through a single lump sum. This is commonly true because the IDS lacks the capital up front to make a lump sum purchase, but also because the IDS wants to assure the continued diligent support of the physician for the plan.[29] It has been argued that physicians may be able to refer to an entity that is purchasing their practice on an installment basis if their relationship also falls within another exception.[30] But it would seem that if the payment being made under a proscribed installment purchase is not excepted, the fact that other forms of remuneration (employment compensation) are permitted would not make a difference. It has also been suggested that installment payments may be possible in the form of deferred compensation, but an attempt to set this up may be treated as a an attempt at illegal circumvention, subject to heavy penalties.[31]

f. Group Practice Arrangements with Hospitals

A seventh exception covers designated health services provided by a group practice and billed in the name of a hospital if the arrangement began prior to December 19, 1989 and has continued without interruption since that date; the group furnishes substantially all of the services furnished to patients of the hospital; the arrangement is set out in a writing that specifies the service and compensation; the compensation is consistent with fair market value and the compensation per unit is fixed in advance and is not determined in a manner that takes into account the volume and value of referrals; and the compensation is provided pursuant to an arrangement that is commercially reasonable without considering referrals.[32]

g. Physician Purchases of Services

A final exception permits physicians to pay laboratories or other service-providers for services where the price paid is consis-

26. 42 C.F.R. § 411.351.
27. 60 Fed. Reg. at 41,960.
28. 42 C.F.R. § 411.357(f).
29. See Weiser, supra note 10, at 318–19.

30. Id.
31. Id. at 323.
32. 42 U.S.C.A. § 1395nn(e)(7).

tent with fair market value.[33] While payments by physicians to other providers are not technically remuneration paid by the other provider to the physician, these payments may in fact constitute remuneration if they are significantly less than the fair market value of the services the physician receives in return. This provision focuses consideration on the central issues in these transactions: did the physician pay for what he or she received?

§ 4–8. Reporting Requirements

Finally, the Act imposes two reporting requirements. All entities providing Medicare or Medicaid reimbursed services must report the covered items and services that they provide and the names and physician identification numbers of physicians who (or whose immediate relatives) have an ownership or investment interest in the entity.[1] This information must be submitted initially within 30 days of a request by a carrier or intermediary and within 60 days of any subsequent change in the information.[2] It need not be submitted by entities that provide 20 or fewer Medicare services a year or that provide services outside of the United States.[3] The information submitted in public information.[4] Failure to comply with this requirement can result in civil penalties of up to $10,000 per day per violation.[5]

Second, the Act requires all entities submitting Medicare claims, where the entity knows or has reason to believe there has been a referral by a referring physician, to include on each claim the name and provider number of the referring physician, and to specify whether or not the referring physician has an ownership interest in or compensation arrangement with the entity submitting the claim. The penalty for violating this provision is denial of payment if the claim is submitted on an assignment basis or a $2000 per violation civil money penalty and exclusion for up to five years if the claim is not submitted on an assignment basis and the information is knowingly and willfully withheld.[6]

§ 4–9. State Self–Referral Laws

The federal self-referral statute currently only covers referrals by physicians for designated health care services insofar as those services are paid for by Medicare or Medicaid. In addition to this federal prohibition, however, about two-thirds of the states have

33. 42 U.S.C.A. § 1395nn(e)(8).

§ 4–8

1. 42 U.S.C.A. §§ 1395nn(f)(1), (2); 1396b(s).

2. 42 C.F.R. § 411.361(e).

3. 42 C.F.R. § 411.361(b).

4. 42 C.F.R. § 411.361(g).

5. 42 U.S.C.A. §§ 1395nn(g)(5); 1396b(s).

6. 42 U.S.C.A. § 1395l(q)(2)(B). The information must also be repeatedly withheld before an exclusion can be imposed.

also adopted their own self-referral prohibitions. These statutes are important because they often cover referrals not reached by the federal prohibition, most significantly referrals paid for by payors other than Medicare and Medicaid, referrals by practitioners other than physicians, and referrals for services other than those designated by the federal law.

The self-referral statutes of some states, moreover, include requirements additional to those imposed by the Stark legislation. It may be necessary under some of these laws, for example, for a referring physician to disclose to referred patients the fact that the physician has a financial relationship with the entity to which a referral is made, even though the entity would fit within an exception under the federal self-referral statute, and thus the referral would be legal without disclosure in the absence of the state law. Finally, the sanctions imposed by state self-referral laws may be more onerous than those found in the federal law. The federal self-referral law in most instances simply forbids payment for services resulting from a self-referral, but under state law the self-referral may result in loss of professional licensure or even criminal penalties. A few of the state statutes, however, explicitly provide that they do not apply in situations where the federal law applies.[1]

As is explained in detail below, the terms of state self-referral laws vary dramatically from state to state. Specifically, they vary in terms of

— which referring professionals they cover;

— the referred services and facilities to which they pertain;

— whether they apply to all referrals for designated services or only those financed by certain payors (such as workers' compensation);

— whether they prohibit self-referrals or simply require that self-referrals be disclosed;

— whether they just extend to investment interests or also to compensation arrangements, and how these interests and arrangements are defined;

— under what circumstances they recognize exceptions and permit referrals; and

— what sanctions they impose if impermissible referrals are made and which state agency is responsible for enforcement.

§ 4–9

1. See, e.g., Ga. Code Ann. § 43–1B–8.

Several of the statutes follow quite closely the wording of the Stark legislation.[2] Most, however, are home-grown creations. Many are more flexible than the federal statute—particularly in providing broader exceptions for facilities which are needed in the community[3]—but some have fewer or narrower exceptions than the federal statute. Several of the state self-referral statutes only cover investment interests.[4] It is important to remember, however, that states that do not prohibit compensation arrangements often also have statutes prohibiting bribes and kickbacks, and that these statutes reach most compensation arrangements. The fact, therefore, that a self-referral statute does not reach compensation arrangements may not make much difference in the end.

Several helpful surveys of state-self referral statutes are available. James C. Dechene and Karen P. O'Neill, " 'Stark II' and State Self–Referral Restrictions"[5] provides a good general overview of state self-referral statutes and includes a complete state-by-state description of self-referral laws in an appendix. Professor Thomas Mayo provided a comprehensive fifty-state survey of both self-referral and anti-kickback statutes at the 1997 National Health Lawyer's Association Fraud and Abuse Conference. A student comment, "The Physician as Entrepreneur: State and Federal Restrictions on Physician Joint Ventures," provides a thoughtful discussion of state self-referral laws as they existed in 1994.[6] Another Student note, "Implications of the Georgia Patient Self–Referral Act of 1993,"[7] describes the statute of one particular state—Georgia.

As of mid–1997, seventeen states had adopted free standing statutes that prohibit self-referrals.[8] The professional licensure

---

2. See, e.g., N.Y. Pub. Health Law §§ 238 to 238–d. A hazard with this approach is that the state law must be regularly amended if it is to continue to resemble the federal law. The Ohio statute, for example, was modeled after Stark I and only covers clinical laboratory referrals. See Ohio Rev. Code Ann. § 4731.65–68. A new Washington statute takes another approach, essentially incorporating the federal law by reference. Wash. Rev. Code § 74.09.240(3).

3. See, infra, text accompanying notes 72–76.

4. See infra note 26.

5. James C. Dechene & Karen P. O'Neill, "Stark II" and State Self–Referral Restrictions, 29 J. Health & Hosp. L. 65 (1996).

6. Jennifer Herndon Puryear, Comment, The Physician as Entrepreneur: State and Federal Restrictions on Physi-

cian Joint Ventures, 73 N.C.L. Rev. 293, 313–28 (1994).

7. Charles F. Fenton III, Notes and Comments, Implications of the Georgia Patient Self–Referral Act of 1993, 11 Ga. St. U. L. Rev. 543 (1995).

8. Cal. Bus. & Prof. Code §§ 650–54; Fla. Stat. ch. 455.654; Ga. Code Ann. § 43–1B–1 to 43–1B–8; Ill. Rev. Stat. ch. 225, ¶ ¶ 47/1 to 47/160; La. Rev. Stat. Ann. § 37:1744–37:1745; Me. Rev. Stat. Ann. tit. 22, §§ 2081–2086; Md. Code Ann., Health Occ. §§ 1–301 to 1–306; Nev. Rev. Stat. §§ 439B.420–439B.425; N.J. Stat. §§ 45:9–22.4 to 45:9–22.9; N.Y. Pub. Health Law §§ 238 to 238–d; N.C. Gen. Stat. §§ 90–405 to 90–408; Ohio Rev. Code Ann. §§ 4731.66–4731.68; 35 Pa. Cons. Stat. § 449.22; S.C. Code Ann. §§ 44–113–20 to 44–113–40; Tenn. Code Ann. §§ 63–6–502, 63–6–601 to 63–6–608; Va. Code Ann.

statutes of several of the states with free-standing statutes, as well as those of a number of other states, also provide that self-referral or self-referral without disclosure is a ground for disciplinary action.[9] The free standing statutes often rival the Stark legislation in their length and complexity,[10] while the disclosure statutes tend to be shorter.[11]

The free standing statutes usually prohibit both self-referrals and the presentation of claims and the payment by third party payors for services provided pursuant to a self-referral.[12] Also common is a requirement that an entity that collects a payment in violation of the section must promptly refund it.[13] Specific prohibitions also commonly extend to cross-referral or circumvention schemes.[14]

In addition to these standard requirements, a few statutes impose idiosyncratic additional requirements. The Tennessee disclosure statute requires that the physician not "exploit the patient in any way, as by inappropriate or unnecessary utilization."[15] Several statutes prohibit hospitals from penalizing health care

§§ 54.1–2410 to 54.1–2413; Wash. Rev. Code § 74.09.240(3).

9. Ariz. Rev. Stat. Ann. §§ 32–1854 (disclosure required for osteopaths), 32–1401(ff) (disclosure required for physicians and surgeons); Ark. Code. Ann. § 20–77–804 (prohibition of payment for self-referred services limited to home intravenous drug therapy); Conn. Gen. Stat. § 20–7a; Haw. Rev. Stat. § 431:10C–308.7(c); Kan. Stat. Ann. § 65–2837(b)(29); Mass. Gen. L. ch. 112, § 12AA; Mo. Rev. Stat. § 334.253; Mont. Code Ann. § 39–71–1108; N.H. Rev. Stat. Ann. § 125:25–b; Okla. Stat. tit. 59, § 725.4; S.D. Codified Laws Ann. § 36–2–19; Utah Code Ann. § 58–12–44; Va. Code Ann. § 54.1–2964; Wash Rev. Code § 19.68.010; W. Va. Code § 30–3014(c)(7).

The Michigan health professional licensure statute defines unprofessional conduct to include "directing or requiring an individual to purchase or secure a drug, device, treatment, procedure, or service from another person, place, facility, or business in which the licensee has a financial interest." Mich. Comp. Laws § 333.16221(e)(iv). See Indenbaum v. Michigan Board of Medicine, 539 N.W.2d 574, 584–85, 213 Mich.App. 263, 283–84 (Ct.App.1995) (interpreting this provision to prohibit self-referrals, even

with disclosure), app. denied, 562 N.W.2d 198 (1997).

10. See, e.g., Cal. Bus. & Prof. Code §§ 650–654; Fla. Stat. ch. 455.654; N.Y. Pub. Health Law §§ 238 to 238–d.

11. See, e.g., Conn. Gen. Stat. § 20–7a; Haw. Rev. Stat. § 431.10C–308.7(c); Okla. Stat. tit. 59, § 725.4 .

12. See, e.g., Cal. Bus. & Prof. Code § 650.01(a), (d), (e); Ga. Code Ann. § 43–1B–4(3); Ill. Rev. Stat. ch. 225, §§ 47/20(a), 47/25; Me. Rev. Stat. Ann. tit. 22, §§ 2085(1), 2086; Md. Code Ann., Health Occ. § 1–302(a), (b); N.Y. Pub. Health Law § 238–a(1); N.C. Gen. Stat. § 90–406.

13. See, e.g., Fla. Stat. ch. 455.654(4)(d). The Maryland and New York statutes provide that the referring physician, the entity to which the referral is made, or any other person who collects any money pursuant to a prohibited referral is jointly and severally liable for repayment. Md. Code Ann., Health Occ. § 1–305; N.Y. Pub. Health Law § 238–a(7).

14. See, e.g., N.Y. Pub. Health Law § 238–a(9); N.C. Gen. Stat. § 90–406; Ohio Rev. Code Ann. § 4731.66(C).

15. Tenn. Code Ann. § 63–6–502(b)(2).

workers that comply with the self-referral prohibition.[16]

The free-standing statutes commonly provide for civil fines for knowing violation of the statute,[17] and often provide higher fines for circumvention schemes.[18] Many of the statutes make a prohibited self-referral grounds for professional discipline.[19] A few statutes also make violation of the prohibition a criminal offense.[20]

State self-referral prohibitions or disclosure requirements often apply to a broader range of practitioners than the federal prohibition. The narrowest apply only to physicians (as does the federal law),[21] but the statutes usually apply more broadly to other independent practitioners.[22] Maine's statute, one of the broadest, applies to "acupuncturists, chiropractors, dentists, dental hygienists,

16. Ill. Rev. Stat. ch. 225, § 47/20(d); S.C. Code Ann. § 44–113–30(H); Va. Code. Ann. § 54.1–2413(A).

17. See, e.g., Fla. Stat. ch. 455.654(4)(e) ($15,000 per violation); Ga. Code Ann. § 43–1B–4(5) ($15,000 per violation); Ill. Rev. Stat. ch. 225, § 47/25 ($20,000 per violation); Me. Rev. Stat. Ann. tit. 22, § 2086 ($2000 per violation); Nev. Rev. Stat. § 439B.420 ($5000 per violation or the value of the illegal transaction, whichever is higher plus the costs of enforcement); N.C. Gen. Stat. § 90–407 ($20,000 per violation); Okla. Stat. tit. 59 § 725.4(B) (fine of not less than $100 or more than $1000); 35 Pa. Cons. Stat. § 449.22(b) (fine not to exceed $1000); S.C. Code Ann. § 44–113–30(E) (civil penalty of not more than $5000). The Nevada statute also provides that the money recovered is to be used for health care as directed by the legislature.

18. See, e.g., Fla. Stat. ch. 455.654(4)(f) ($100,000 per violation); Ga. Code Ann. § 43–1B–5(6) ($50,000 per violation); N.C. Gen. Stat. § 90–407(c) ($75,000); S.C. Code Ann. § 44–113–30(F).

19. See, e.g., Fla. Stat. ch. 455.645(g); Ga. Code Ann. § 43–1B–4(8); Md. Code Ann., Health Occ. § 1–306; S.C. Code Ann. § 44–113–30(G).

20. Cal. Bus. & Prof. Code § 650.01(g).

21. See, e.g., Ariz. Rev. Stat. Ann. § 32–1401(25)(ff) (medical doctors); Ariz. Rev. Stat. Ann. § 32–1854(35) (osteopaths); Mass. Gen. L. ch. 112, § 12AA (physicians and surgeons); Mo. Rev. Stat. § 334.252 (physicians); Ohio Rev. Code Ann. § 4731.66 (medical doc-

tors, osteopaths, and podiatrists); Tenn. Code Ann. § 63–6–602 (physicians).

22. See, e.g., Cal. Lab. Code § 3209.3, as incorporated by Cal. Bus. & Prof. Code § 650.01(b)(4); Conn. Gen. Stat. § 20–7a ("practitioners of the healing arts"); Fla. Stat. ch. 455.654 ("health care provider"); Ga. Code Ann. § 43–1B–3(6) ("health care provider" defined to include physicians, chiropractors, podiatrists, optometrists, pharmacists, and physical therapists); Ill. Rev. Stat. ch. 225, § 47/15(d) ("health care worker" defined to include all persons licensed in the state to provide health services); La. Rev. Stat. Ann. § 37:1744 ("health care provider" defined to include licensed personnel including "a physician, dentist, chiropractor, podiatrist, optometrist, physical therapist, psychologist, licensed professional counselor, registered or licensed practical nurse, pharmacist, and any officer, employee, or agent thereof acting in the course and scope of his employment"); Md. Code Ann., Health Occ. § 1–301(g) ("health care practitioner" defined as anyone licensed to provide health care services); N.H. Rev. Stat. Ann. § 125:25–a ("health care practitioner" defined as person licensed to provide health services); N.J. Rev. Stat. § 49:9–22.4 ("practitioner" defined to include physicians, chiropractors, or podiatrists); N.C. Gen. Stat. § 90–405 ("health care provider" including persons licensed to practice "medicine, dentistry, optometry, osteopathy, chiropractic, nursing, podiatry, psychology, physical therapy, occupational therapy, or speech and language pathology and audiology"); Okla. Stat. tit. 59, § 725.4(A) ("health or mental health care professional or health care provider").

nurses, occupational therapists, optometrists, pharmacists, physical therapists, physicians including allopathic and osteopathic physicians, physician assistants, podiatrists, psychologists, clinical social workers, speech therapists, and audiologists or hearing aid dealers and examiners."[23]

Under some statutes, the prohibition attaches specifically to referrals that originate from particular institutions. A California statute requires disclosure when members of the medical staff of hospitals or nursing homes refer patients in those facilities to ancillary health service providers in which the hospital or nursing home has a significant beneficial interest.[24] A Virginia statute prohibits hospitals from referring patients to their affiliates without disclosure.[25]

States that require disclosure or prohibit referrals are divided as to whether the requirement or prohibition only applies when the referring physician has an investment interest in the facility to which the referral is made,[26] or whether they also apply to situations where there is a compensation arrangement between the referring physician and referred-to entity, or to other situations in which remuneration is present.[27] Some of the statutes are even more narrow, only covering "significant investment interests"[28] or "substantial financial interests."[29]

The self-referral statutes of a minority of states only prohibit referrals for a few specific services. The Arkansas statute, for example, only applies to referrals to home intravenous drug therapy providers in which the referring physician has an ownership or investment interest.[30] The Massachusetts and Missouri disclosure

23. Me. Rev. Stat. Ann. tit. 22, § 2084(4).

24. Cal. Health & Safety Code § 1323. Florida has a similar statute, Fla. Stat. ch. 400.518(1).

25. Va. Code Ann. § 32.1–125.2.

26. See, e.g., Fla. Stat. ch. 455.654(4)(a); Ga. Code Ann. § 43–1B–4; Ill. Rev. Stat. ch. 225, § 47/20(a).

27. See, e.g., Cal. Bus. & Prof. Code § 650.01(b)(2) (covering situations involving a "financial interest" defined comprehensively to include a wide range of ownership and compensation interests, including ownership interests in entities that lease property to the referral recipient); Conn. Gen. Stat. § 20–7a(c) (ownership or investment interests or compensation arrangements); La. Rev. Stat. Ann. § 37:1744(A)(3) (significant ownership or investment interest

or any form of direct or indirect remuneration for the referral); Md. Code Ann., Health Occ. § 1–302(a); Mo. Rev. Stat. § 334.253(1) (financial relationship, including ownership or investment interests and compensation arrangements); N.Y. Pub. Health Law § 238(3) (ownership or investment interests and compensation arrangements); Ohio Rev. Code Ann. § 4731.66(A) (ownership or investment interests and compensation arrangements); Utah Code Ann. § 58–12–44 (incorporating definition of "financial relationship" from 42 U.S.C.A. § 1395nn).

28. Kan. Stat. Ann. § 65–2837(h) (defined as a 10% ownership interest).

29. S.D. Codified Laws Ann. § 36–2–19 (defined as an ownership, direct creditor's or direct lessor's interest of 25% or more).

30. Ark. Code Ann. § 20–77–804.

statutes only apply to physical therapy referrals.[31] New York limits its prohibition to referrals for clinical laboratory services, pharmacy services and X-ray or imaging services.[32] The Oklahoma statute only covers referrals to a "testing center or laboratory."[33]

More common, however are broader prohibitions that are at least as broad, and often broader, than Stark II. The California statute, for example, covers "laboratory, diagnostic nuclear medicine, radiation oncology, physical therapy, physical rehabilitation, psychometric testing, home infusion therapy, or diagnostic imaging goods and services"[34] and the Florida statute: "clinical laboratory services, physical therapy services, comprehensive rehabilitation services, diagnostic imaging services, and radiation therapy services."[35] Some statutes are even broader, comprehensively prohibiting referrals for "diagnostic or therapeutic services,"[36] "diagnosis, treatment, and rehabilitative services,"[37] "diagnostic, treatment, therapy, or rehabilitation service,"[38] or "testing for or diagnosis or treatment of human disease or dysfunction; or dispensing of drugs or medical devices for the treatment of human disease or dysfunction."[39] The Illinois statute covers all health procedures and services that can be provided by a health care worker,[40] and the North Carolina statute any service that is covered by a health insurance plan, ERISA plan, federal or state employee benefit plan, Medicare or Medicaid.[41]

Some state statutes, however, specifically do not cover referrals by specific providers for specific services. The Florida statute, for example, excludes from coverage a dozen specific types of referrals—generally referrals by specialists for specialty services, such as

31. Mass. Gen. L. ch. 112, § 12AA; Mo. Rev. Stat. § 334.252.

32. N.Y. Pub. Health Law § 238–a(a).

33. Okla. Stat. tit. 59, § 725.4.

34. Cal. Bus. & Prof. Code § 650.01(a).

35. Fla. Stat. ch. 455.654(3)(c). See also Ga. Code Ann. § 43–1B–3(2) (clinical laboratory services, physical therapy services, rehabilitation services, diagnostic imaging services, pharmaceutical services, durable medical equipment, home infusion therapy services, home health services, and outpatient surgical services).

36. Conn. Gen. Stat. § 20–7a(c)(2) (therapeutic services are defined to include physical therapy, radiation therapy, intravenous therapy, rehabilitation services, occupational therapy, or speech pathology); N.H. Rev. Stat. Ann. § 125:25–b (diagnostic and therapeutic services are defined in N.H. Rev. Stat. Ann. § 125:25–a). The Louisiana statute covers "health care goods and services, including but not limited to . . . clinical laboratory services, diagnostic service, medical suppliers, and therapeutic services. . . ." La. Rev. Stat. Ann. § 37:1744.

37. Me. Rev. Stat. Ann. tit. 22, § 2084(5).

38. Tenn. Code Ann. § 63–6–601(3).

39. N.J. Rev. Stat. § 45:9–22.4.

40. Ill. Rev. Stat. ch. 225, § 47/15(c). See also the South Carolina statute, which covers "any health care procedure, service or item provided by a health care provider." S.C. Code Ann. § 44–113–20(4).

41. N.C. Gen. Stat. § 90–405(3).

radiologists for diagnostic imaging services; cardiologists for cardiac catheterization services; or urologists for lithotripsy services.[42] More common are exceptions for a few specific types of referrals by specific specialists found within the exception section of the statute.[43]

Free-standing prohibition statutes that prohibit billing for such self-referred services commonly cover bills submitted to all or virtually all payors—including patients, insurers, self-insurers, government payors and other payors—for self-referred services.[44] They thus expand considerably on the federal law, which is limited to services paid for by Medicare and Medicaid. Where the prohibition is more limited, it is usually specifically addressed to self-referral for services paid for by workers' compensation programs.[45] Statutes attempting to prohibit payment for self-referred services by ERISA plans might well be preempted by federal law as laws that "relate to" an employee benefits plan.[46] Professional disciplinary actions based on prohibited referrals would probably not be preempted, however.[47]

Statutes that require disclosure of financial interests vary dramatically in terms of the specificity and scope of their requirements. Most require disclosure to the patient in writing, signed by the patient,[48] and some require that the disclosure be on a form developed by a state licensure board,[49] or on a form set out in the statute.[50] Some statutes, however, permit as an alternative in certain situations the posting of a conspicuous disclosure, as where the service is provided by members of the professional corporation to which the referring physician belongs and on the same premises

---

42. Fla. Stat. ch. 455.654(3). The Georgia and New York statutes contain similar, though shorter, lists. Ga. Code Ann. § 43–1B–3(10)(C); N.Y. Pub. Health Law § 238–a(6)(c).

43. See, e.g., N.J. Rev. Stat. § 45:9–22.5(c)(2) (referrals for radiation therapy pursuant to an oncological protocol, lithotripsy and renal dialysis); Ohio Rev. Code Ann. § 4731.67(B) (pathology services provided under supervision of a pathologist).

44. See, e.g., Cal. Bus. & Prof. Code § 650.01(e); Fla. Stat. ch. 455.654(4)(c); Ohio Rev. Code Ann. § 4731.66(B).

45. Cal. Lab. Code § 139.2; 1995 Mass. H.B. 3303 § 16 (1995); Mont. Code Ann. § 39–71–1108; N.H. Rev. Stat. Ann. § 281–A:23; 77 Pa. Cons. Stat. § 531(3)(iii).

46. See 29 U.S.C.A. § 1144(a).

47. See New York State Conference of Blue Cross & Blue Shield Plans v. Travelers Insurance Co., 514 U.S. 645, 649–61, 115 S.Ct. 1671, 1674–80, 131 L.Ed.2d 695 (1995) (ERISA did not preempt state hospital rate regulation scheme which had only a remote connection with benefit plans).

48. See, e.g., Haw. Rev. Stat. § 431:10C–308.7(d). The Maryland statute requires a written disclosure statement unless the referral is made orally over the telephone. Md. Code Ann., Health Occ. § 1–303(b)(1). The New Hampshire statute also permits oral disclosures for telephone referrals, but requires a prompt written follow-up. N.H. Rev. Stat. Ann. § 125:25–b.

49. Ariz. Rev. Stat. Ann. § 32–1401(24)(ff) (physician must use form developed by state licensure board which must be signed and dated by patient).

50. N.J. Rev. Stat. Ann. § 45:9–22.6,

as the referring physician practices.[51] A third alternative is found in Connecticut, which requires verbal or posted disclosure.[52] Finally, the South Dakota statute simply requires a disclosure of the "general nature" of the financial interest, without specifying the form of disclosure.[53] Where written permission is required, some of the statutes require that the forms be retained by the provider for a certain period of time,[54] others require that it be documented in the referred patient's medical record.[55]

While disclosure statutes uniformly require disclosure of financial interests to the referred patient, they often also require disclosure to third party payors, usually on request, of the investment interests of providers.[56] Some statutes also require practitioners to disclose their ownership interests in specified providers to their own licensure boards.[57] The New Hampshire statute requires both referring physicians and entities that receive referrals from interested referrers to file regular reports of referrals with the state.[58] The New York statute requires entities that provide covered services to disclose the names of practitioners who have ownership or investment interests in them.[59]

With respect to the content of the disclosure, the simplest disclosure statutes require only that the physician disclose that he or she has a financial interest in the entity to which the patient is referred and that the service is otherwise available on a competitive basis.[60] Where posted disclosure is required, the statute may require that the notice list the entities in which the referring physician has an ownership or investment interest and to note that alternative referrals will be provided on request.[61] The Florida statute requires both the referring provider and referred-to service entity to give the patient written disclosure forms. The referring provider must disclose the existence of the financial interest, the right of the patient to get services elsewhere, and the names and addresses of at least two alternate sources of services.[62] The referred-to service provider must provide the same information, plus a schedule of typical fees or a patient-specific fee estimate.[63] Disclosure statutes often provide that in certain situations, such as

---

51. Cal. Bus. & Prof. Code § 650.01(f).

52. Conn. Gen. Stat. § 20–7a(c).

53. S.D. Codified Laws Ann. § 36–2–19.

54. See, e.g., Haw. Rev. Stat. § 431:10C–308.7(d) (2 years).

55. Md. Code Ann., Health Occ. § 1–303(b)(2).

56. See, e.g., Ill. Rev. Stat. ch. 225, ¶ 47/20(b)(8); Me. Rev. Stat. Ann. tit. 22, § 2085(2)(D)(8).

57. See, e.g, Mass. Gen. L. ch. 112, § 12AA.

58. N.H. Rev. Stat. Ann. 125:25–c.

59. N.Y. Pub. Health Law § 238–c.

60. See, e.g., Ariz. Rev. Stat. Ann. § 32–1401(24)(ff); Kan. Stat. Ann. § 65–2837(b)(29); 35 Pa. Cons. Stat. § 449.22(a).

61. Conn. Gen. Stat. § 20–7a(c).

62. Fla. Stat. ch. 455.701(1).

63. Fla. Stat. ch. 455.701(2).

referrals to another physician practicing within the same group, disclosure of financial interest is not necessary.[64]

Free standing self-referral prohibition statutes commonly include a list of exceptions to the general prohibition.[65] Where they provide for exceptions, however, they also often require that the referring physician disclose any financial interest in an entity to which he or she refers a patient when the referral falls within a statutory exception.[66]

The exceptions found within free standing statutes often bear some resemblance to the exceptions found in the federal statute, though they often diverge in both the number and precise delineation of the exception. One of the most common exceptions is for referrals within a group practice.[67] "Group practice" is usually defined as it was under Stark I: a group exists if group members provide their full range of services through the group, the group bills for services in the name of the group, and the group divides income and expenses in accordance with a previously determined method.[68] In-office ancillary services are also commonly excepted.[69]

Another common exception covers investments in publicly traded securities where payments are not related to referrals, other safeguards are satisfied, and the corporation has assets of a specified value.[70] Still another exception found in most statutes covers

64. Ariz. Rev. Stat. Ann. § 32–1401(24)(ff).

65. See Cal. Bus. & Prof. Code § 650.02.

66. Cal. Bus. & Prof. Code § 650.01(f); Fla. Stat. ch. 455.654(4)(j); Ga. Code Ann. § 43–1B–5(b); Nev. Rev. Stat. § 439B.420(9); N.Y. Pub. Health L. § 238–d(1); S.C. Code Ann. § 44–113–40(A).

67. See, e.g., Cal. Bus. & Prof. Code § 650.02(h); Ga. Code Ann. § 43–1B–3(10)(c)(iii); Md. Code Ann., Health Occ. § 1–302(d)(2).

68. Cal. Bus. & Prof. Code § 650.01(b)(6); Fla. Stat. ch. 455.654(3)(f); Ga. Code Ann. § 43–1B–3(5); Ill. Rev. Stat. ch. 225, ¶ 47/15(c); Me. Rev. Stat. Ann. tit. 22, § 2084(3); Md. Code Ann., Health Occ. § 1–301(f). The Nevada statute requires additionally that health care services must be provided in one building or group of buildings. Nev. Rev. Stat. § 439B.425(4). The New York statute provides that for faculty practice plans meeting certain conditions the requirements only apply with respect to service provided within the plan. N.Y. Pub. Health Law § 238(5).

69. See, e.g., Conn. Gen. Stat. § 20–7a(c); Md. Code Ann., Health Occ. § 1–302(d)(4) (ancillary services, however, are defined in Maryland so as not to include MRI, radiation therapy services, or CT scans provided by radiologist groups, Md. Code Ann., Health Occ. § 1–301(k)(2)); N.Y. Pub. Health Law § 238–a(2)(b); Ohio Rev. Code Ann. § 4731.67(C). The Ohio statute contains a separate provision for in-office ancillary services where a third-party payer is aware of the financial arrangement and has agreed in writing to pay for the service. Ohio Rev. Code Ann. § 4731.67(D).

70. See, e.g., Cal. Bus. & Prof. Code § 650.02(b)(3) ($75 million); Fla. Stat. ch. 455.654(4)((b)(1) ($50 million); Ga. Code Ann. § 43–1B–3(8)(E) ($50 million); Ill. Rev. Stat. ch. 225, ¶ 47/20(c) ($30 million); Me. Rev. Stat. Ann. tit. 22, § 2085(3)(b) ($50 million); Md. Code Ann., Health Occ. § 1–301(b)(2) (no minimum); N.Y. Pub. Health Law § 238(3)(b). As recently amended Nev. Rev. Stat. § 439B.425(2)(f) permits referrals to corporations with a shareholder equity of more than $100 million re-

referrals to a health maintenance organization where the referring provider has an interest in the entity or where the patient is referred pursuant to an HMO contract.[71]

Most statutes provide an exception for referrals by investors to entities established to serve underserved populations. Some statutes define the entities covered by this exception in terms of their remoteness from alternate providers of service;[72] others follow the federal lead in excepting facilities in rural areas;[73] still others permit a referral if "there is no entity or facility of reasonable quality, price, or service in the community" and additional requirements are met.[74] The Illinois, Maine, North Carolina and Virginia statutes permit referrals to entities in which the referring health care worker has an investment interest if a designated state agency determines that there is a "demonstrated need in the community," as defined in the statute, for the entity, and if additional listed precautionary requirements are met.[75] The statutes commonly require disclosure of the self-referral when the underserved population exception is claimed.[76]

State statutes also, however, incorporate idiosyncratic investment exceptions not found in the federal Stark legislation. Referrals to ambulatory surgical centers are excepted by several statutes.[77] The California statute excepts referrals to hospitals and nursing homes when no compensation is paid for the referral; nonprofit corporations controlled by health facilities or health facility systems; emergency referrals; referrals by university-affiliated physicians to university facilities; referrals for cardiac rehabilita-

gardless of whether the securities of the corporation are publicly traded.

71. See, e.g., Cal. Bus. & Prof. Code § 650.02(i); Haw. Rev. Stat. § 431:10C–308.7(c); Ill. Rev. Stat. ch. 225, ¶ 40/20(h); N.Y. Pub. Health Law § 238–a(2)(c) (HMO, managed care organizations or prepaid health service plans operating under various statutes).

72. See, e.g., Cal. Bus. & Prof. Code § 650.02(a) (25 miles or 40 minutes traveling time); Nev. Rev. Stat. § 439B.425(2)(a) (30 miles).

73. See, e.g., Fla. Stat. ch. 455.654(3)(i)(1); Ga. Code Ann. § 43–1B–3(8)(A); Mo. Rev. Stat. § 334.253(2)(1).

74. See, e.g., Ga. Code Ann. § 43–1B–6(a).

75. Ill. Rev. Stat. ch. 225, ¶ 47/20(b); Me. Rev. Stat. Ann. tit. 22, § 2085(2). N.C. Gen. Stat. § 90–408(a); Va. Code Ann. § 54.1–2411(B). The Maryland statute also provides for determination of community need, but does not de-

scribe in detail how it is to be determined. Md. Code Ann., Health Occ. § 1–302(d)(5). The Montana statute provides an exception for investment interests where there is a "demonstrated need" in the community for a facility and no alternative financing available, but does not define these terms. Mont. Code Ann. § 39–71–1108. The Tennessee statute, on the other hand, sets out detailed requirements for showing "demonstrated need" in detail, but does not specify who will determine it. Tenn. Code Ann. § 63–6–603.

76. See, e.g., Cal. Bus. & Prof. Code § 650.02(a); Ga. Code Ann. § 43–1B–6(a)(3); Ill. Rev. Stat. ch. 225, ¶ 47/20(b)(4)(7); Me. Rev. Stat. Ann. tit. 22, § 2085(2)(D)(7); N.C. Gen. Stat. § 90–408(c); Va. Code Ann. § 54.1–2411(C).

77. See, e.g., N.Y. Pub. Health Law § 238–a(4)(c). This exception exists under the federal regulations, but not under the federal statute.

tion services; or referrals where the financial relationship is a commercially reasonable loan.[78]

The Florida and South Carolina statutes contain an exception for entities other than publicly held corporations where not more than 50% of the value of investment interests held in the entity are held by investors who can make referrals to the entity, the return on investment is not related to the volume of referrals, the investor is not required to make referrals to the entity, and other conditions are met.[79] The Georgia statute excepts referrals to a hospital by health care providers who have staff privileges at that hospital.[80] The Illinois, Maine, and Virginia statutes permit referrals where the health care worker "directly provides health services within the entity and will be personally involved with the provision of care to the referred patient."[81] The Missouri statute permits referrals where the only ownership interest is a bona fide debt and the terms of the debt comply with fair market value and the debt is not disguised compensation for referrals.[82] The North Carolina statute exempts investment interests owned through a stock purchase, savings, pension, profit sharing or other similar benefit plan in which the investor does not direct investments.[83] The South Carolina Code excepts investment interests in entities that own or lease and operate hospitals or nursing facilities.[84]

Several states establish procedures under which licensure boards can issue advisory opinions or declaratory statements determining whether a financial relationship precludes self-referrals under the statute.[85] The New Hampshire workers' compensation statute provides an exception for referrals that are "ethically appropriate and medically indicated," and permits the Commissioner to confirm that referrals fit into this exception.[86] The New York statute permits exceptions for financial relationships that the Public Health Council determines do not pose a risk of abuse, as

---

78. Cal. Bus. & Prof. Code § 650.02(b)(1), (c)(1), (d), (e), (g). The Georgia statute also contains exceptions for emergency referrals. Ga. Code Ann. § 43–1B–3(10)(C)(vii).

79. Fla. Stat. ch. 455.654(4)(b)(2); S.C. Code Ann. § 44–113–30(A)(3).

80. Ga. Code Ann. § 43–1B–3(10)(v). See also Me. Rev. Stat. Ann. tit. 22, § 2084(7) (investment interests in licensed hospitals excepted from coverage of statute); Md. Code Ann., Health Occ. § 1–302(d)(6), (7) (permitting practitioners and single specialty groups employed by or affiliated with hospitals to refer to entities owned by those hospitals or under common ownership and control with the hospital if the referrer does not have a direct beneficial interest in the re-

ferred-to entity); N.Y. Pub. Health Law § 238–a(2)(d), (e) (referrals for inpatient hospital services excepted, as are inpatient, outpatient or emergency services provided by the hospital).

81. Ill. Rev. Stat. ch. 225, ¶ 47/20; Me. Rev. Stat. Ann. tit. 22, § 2085(1); Va. Code Ann. § 54.1–2411(A).

82. Mo. Rev. Stat. § 334.253(2)(4).

83. N.C. Gen. Stat. § 90–405(9)(c).

84. S.C. Code Ann. § 44–113–20(10(c).

85. Ga. Code Ann. § 43–1B–4(2); Ill. Rev. Stat. ch. 225, ¶ 47/20(g); Me. Rev. Stat. Ann. tit. 22, § 2085(7).

86. N.H. Rev. Stat. Ann. § 281–A:23(IV).

consistent with exceptions provided in the federal self-referral regulations.[87]

Specific exceptions for compensation arrangements are less common than general or investment interest exceptions. Where compensation arrangement exceptions are found, however, they resemble federal exceptions, including exceptions for bona fide employment relationships,[88] personal services contracts,[89] physician recruitment arrangements involving a geographic relocation,[90] isolated transactions,[91] or space rentals.[92] A few additional compensation exceptions are found in some state statutes, as the exceptions in the Ohio statute for remuneration for medical director services or physician's services in hospices or non-profit blood centers.[93]

There have to date been only a handful of cases involving state self-referral laws. Indenbaum v. Michigan Board of Medicine[94] held that the Michigan statute prohibiting physicians from "directing or requiring" individuals to purchase a service from a facility in which the physicians held a financial interest was violated when the physicians referred patients to a facility they owned, even though they disclosed the fact of their ownership and offered to make alternative referrals.[95] A Florida case, Agency for Health Care Administration v. Wingo,[96] held that a group practice forfeited the benefit of a narrow exception from the general prohibition of MRI self-referrals which permitted referrals "solely" for the group's own patients when it also accepted referrals who were not group members for its MRI. Finally, a Pennsylvania case held that an employer was not obligated to pay for physical therapy services provided under the workers' compensation services to an employee in a facility solely owned by the physician who referred the employee because payment was excused under the state self-referral statute.[97]

87. N.Y. Pub. Health Law § 238–a(2)(g), (5)(b)(vii).

88. See, e.g., Md. Code Ann., Health Occ. § 1–301(c)(2)(ii); N.Y. Pub. Health Law § 238a(5)(b)(ii).

89. See, e.g., Md. Code Ann., Health Occ. § 1–301(c)(2)(iii); N.Y. Pub. Health Law § 238–a(5)(b)(iii); Ohio Rev. Code Ann. § 4731.68(C).

90. See, e.g., Md. Code Ann., Health Occ. § 1–301(c)(2)(v); N.Y. Pub. Health Law § 238–a(b)(iv); Ohio Rev. Code Ann. § 4731.68(D).

91. N.Y. Pub. Health Law § 238–a(5)(v); Ohio Rev. Code Ann. § 4731.68(F).

92. See, e.g., Md. Code Ann., Health Occ. § 1–301(c)(2)(vi); N.Y. Pub. Health Law § 238–a(5)(b)(i); Ohio Rev. Code Ann. § 4731.68(B).

93. Ohio Rev. Code Ann. § 4731.68(E)(1).

94. Indenbaum v. Michigan Board of Medicine, 539 N.W.2d 574, 584–85, 213 Mich.App. 263, 283–85 (Ct.App.1995).

95. See also State v. Physical Therapy Rehabilitation Ctr. of Coral Springs, Inc., 665 So.2d 1127 (Fla.Ct.App.1996) involving the constitutionality under the Florida Constitution of an unrelated provision of the Florida statute.

96. 22 Fla. L. Weekly D1577, No. 95–1971, 1997 WL 352894 (Fla.Ct.App. 1997).

97. Eighty–Four Mining Co. v. Three Rivers Rehabilitation, 688 A.2d 239 (Pa. Commwlth. Ct. 1997).

There have also been a few state Attorney General Opinions interpreting the statutes.[98] The paucity of litigation is undoubtedly due to the fact that most of these statutes are quite recent in origin, but might also indicate that they are not being vigorously enforced.[99]

98. See, e.g., Maryland Attorney General Opinion No. 94–062 (Dec. 12, 1994), reported at 4 BNA Health Law Reporter 66 (1995) (providing neutral information about physician-owned facility along with other alternatives without recommending that patient use it probably not violation of prohibition).

99. See, e.g., Conn. Gen. Stat. Ann. § 20–7a; Fla. Stat. Ann. §§ 458.327(c), .331(gg); Ga. Code Ann. § 43–1B; Md. Health Occ. § 1–206; Minn. Stat. Ann. § 147.091(p)(3); Mo. Ann. Stat. § 334.253; N.J. Rev. Stat. Ann. § 45:9–22.5; N.Y. Pub. Health Law § 238–a; Nev. Rev. Stat. Ann. §§ 616.690, 630.305(3), (4). See generally, Effectiveness of State Efforts to Restrict Referrals is Questioned, 2 BNA Health Law Reporter 494 (1993).

Chapter 5

ADMINISTRATIVE PENALTIES
AND EXCLUSIONS

Table of Sections

WESTLAW Electronic Research

See WESTLAW Electronic Research Guide preceding the Summary of Contents.

Library References:

C.J.S. Social Security and Public Welfare § 136.
West's Key No. Digests, Social Security and Public Welfare ⚷241.110.

§ 5–1. Introduction

Earlier chapters have examined criminal prosecution and civil litigation as alternative approaches for attacking health care fraud. Federal law and the laws of some states also provide a third approach: administrative program exclusions and civil penalties. This approach has resulted in a large and growing administrative caseload. Reference has been made in chapters 2, 3 and 4 above to administrative penalties and program exclusions in false claims, bribe and kickback, and self-referral cases. This chapter will further explore these sanctions.

The original Medicare and Medicaid fraud and abuse statute, adopted in 1972, provided only for criminal penalties. These penalty provisions were supplemental, of course, to the general false claims, false statements, and mail fraud provisions of the federal criminal law, as well as the provision for civil litigation under the federal False Claims Act. Criminal prosecutions require, however, proof beyond a reasonable doubt and proof of intentional conduct. Both criminal prosecution and civil litigation also require a substantial commitment of resources on the part of the Department of Justice to mastering the complexities of Medicare and Medicaid law and to understanding practices that violate that law. Given other demands on their resources, prosecutions were relatively infrequent through the 1970s.

In 1981, therefore, Congress amended the statute to permit the Department of Health and Human Services Office of Inspector General (OIG) authority to impose civil money penalties for violation of the Medicaid fraud laws.[1] Authority was also added for the OIG to exclude from program participation persons who violated various program obligations.[2] Both the civil money penalty and exclusion authorities were substantially expanded by the Medicare and Medicaid Patient and Program Protection Act of 1987 (MMPPPA).[3] Additional grounds for OIG administrative sanctions have been added with virtually every annual budget reconciliation act since.

The basic provisions for fraud and abuse civil money penalties are found at 42 U.S.C.A. § 1320a–7a, and the basic provisions for exclusions at 42 U.S.C.A. § 1320a–7. Additional provisions for exclusions and civil money penalties are found, however, throughout the Social Security Act. Regulations implementing the civil money penalty authority are found at 42 C.F.R. Part 1003; Medicare exclusions at 42 C.F.R. Part 1001, and Medicaid exclusions at 42 C.F.R. Part 1002.[4] Finally, regulations governing OIG investigations are found at 42 C.F.R. Part 1005. These provisions are discussed in detail in this chapter.[5]

While this chapter is primarily concerned with sanctions available under the Medicare and Medicaid statutes, it should be noted that civil penalties of $5000 per claim plus assessments of double

§ 5–1

1. Medicare and Medicaid Amendments of 1981, Pub. L. No. 97–35, § 2105, 1981 U.S.C.C.A.N. (95 Stat.) 396, 1311–12. See Travers v. Sullivan, 801 F.Supp. 394, 399–400 (E.D.Wash. 1992), aff'd., 20 F.3d 993 (9th Cir.1994) (upholding this transfer of authority); Greene v. Sullivan, 731 F.Supp. 835, 837 (E.D.Tenn.1990).

2. Amendments to the Social Security Act in 1977 had already required exclusion of providers "convicted of a criminal offense related to such individual's involvement in Medicare or Medicaid" or who had failed to disclose requested information relating to business arrangements. H.R. Rep. No. 393, 95th Cong., 1st Sess. 50–52, 69–70 (1977), reprinted in 1977 U.S.C.C.A.N. 3039, 3052–54, 3071–73.

3. MMPPPA of 1987, Pub. L. No. 100–93, §§ 2–3, 7, 1987 U.S.C.C.A.N. (101 Stat.) 682, 685–702.

4. Final regulations implementing the MMPPPA were adopted on January 29, 1992, and appear at 57 Fed. Reg. 3298 (1992). These regulations are not applied retroactively to limit the rights of persons threatened with exclusion. Bassim v. Inspector General, [1992 Transfer Binder] Medicare & Medicaid Guide (CCH) ¶ 40,457 (DAB May 28, 1992).

5. For an excellent overview of these provisions, see Pamela Bucy, Civil Prosecution of Health Care Fraud, 30 Wake Forest L. Rev. 693 (1993).

the amount of the false claim can also be imposed administratively for false claims under the general federal Program Fraud and Civil Remedies Act.[6] This statute permits greater penalties than those available under the more specific Medicare and Medicaid false claims statute and permits penalties for statements that omit material facts as well as false statements.[7] On the other hand, it also requires proof that the claimant "knows or has reason to know" that a statement is false.[8] Perhaps most importantly, the general federal program fraud act requires approval by an assistant attorney general of any penalty actions before they are filed.[9] Because of these limitations, the Program Fraud Act has not been used in practice for prosecuting Medicare and Medicaid false claims, and will not be discussed further here.

§ 5–2. Exclusions, Denials, and Terminations

a. Generally

Exclusion from participation in the Medicare or Medicaid programs is one of the most serious sanctions that can be experienced by a health care professional or institution. It can be a professional or institutional death sentence for a practitioner or entity that depends heavily on such programs for income. Nonetheless, the administrative sanction of exclusion from program participation is used with steadily increasing frequency. In 1994, 1265 providers were excluded from the Medicare program.[1]

The effects of an exclusion are wide ranging. Neither Medicare nor a state health care program may pay for services rendered by a person or entity subject to a program exclusion or for services rendered by the order of, or under the supervision of, an excluded person.[2] This is true regardless of whether the claim in question is

---

6. 31 U.S.C.A. §§ 3801–3812.
7. 31 U.S.C.A. § 3802(a)(1).
8. Id.
9. 31 U.S.C.A. § 3803.

§ 5–2
1. GAO, Medicare, Adapting Private Sector Techniques Could Curb Losses to Fraud and Abuse (GAO/T–HEHS–95–211, July 19, 1995) (471 of these were mandatory and 794 were permissive). Almost half (566) of the exclusions were for failure to pay student loans, however, and only 289 for program-related convictions.
2. 42 U.S.C.A. §§ 704(b)(6), 1395u(j)(2), 1395y(e), 1396b(i)(2), 1397d(a)(9); 42 C.F.R. § 1001.2. If a beneficiary submits a claim for services provided by an excluded person, HCFA

will pay the first claim and immediately notify the beneficiary that the person is excluded. It will not pay for services provided more than 15 days after the date of the notice. 42 C.F.R. § 1001.1901(c). Payment may also be made to patients admitted to a hospital before the exclusion or hospice or home health agency patients receiving care under a plan or care established before the exclusion for up to 30 days after an exclusion becomes effective unless the Secretary determines that the exclusion should take effect earlier. 42 U.S.C.A. § 1320a–7(c)(2)(B). Payments may also be made under limited circumstances for emergency services rendered by excluded persons. 42 C.F.R. § 1001.1901(c)(4).

an assigned or non-assigned claim (i.e., whether the provider bills Medicare directly or bills the beneficiary who in turn bills Medicare). A hospital that renders services to a beneficiary admitted by an "excluded" physician may not receive Medicare payment for the stay unless it can show that it did not know or have reason to know of the exclusion.[3] A person who submits a claim for which payment cannot be made because of an exclusion is also liable for a civil penalty;[4] as is a person, other than an organization, agency, or entity, who retains a direct or indirect ownership or control interest, or is an officer or managing employee or an entity that participates in Medicare or a state health program;[5] or an entity that contracts (by employment or otherwise) with an entity that the person knows or should know is excluded.[6] In promulgating regulations implementing the exclusion authority, HHS also considered permitting exclusions against manufacturers or other entities that do not directly receive Medicare or Medicaid payments but that furnish items or services to persons or entities that do. HHS initially rejected the idea, deciding that implementing exclusions against these parties would be too difficult to administer.[7] HHS is currently reconsidering this position and has proposed rules that would permit exclusion to be imposed on such indirect providers and refusal of payment for services provided by indirect suppliers.[7.5]

While criminal sanctions, civil money penalties, and exclusion are often available for the same conduct, the focus of the sanctions is different. Criminal penalties are imposed to punish and deter deviant conduct. Civil money penalties (whether imposed administratively or through civil litigation) are intended to make the wrongdoer recompense the government for the misconduct and to deter future misconduct, in particular where the motivation for the misconduct is primarily financial. Exclusion, on the other hand, is designed to remove the sanctioned individual or entity from the program, and is particularly appropriate when the continued participation of an individual or entity who has demonstrated lack of trustworthiness poses a risk to the program or its beneficiaries.[8] If, however, a person successfully defends against imposition of a criminal or civil penalty, the OIG will not subsequently institute exclusion proceedings for the same offense.

3. 42 U.S.C.A. § 1395y(e)(1)(B).

4. 42 U.S.C.A. § 1320a–7a(a)(1)(D).

5. 42 U.S.C.A. § 1320a–7a(a)(4).

6. 42 U.S.C.A. § 1320a–7a(a)(6).

7. 57 Fed. Reg. 3298, 3300 (1992).

7.5 Proposed rule 42 C.F.R. § 1000.10 at 62 Fed. Reg. 47,182, 47,-185, 47,189 (1997).

8. Manocchio v. Kusserow, 961 F.2d 1539 (11th Cir.1992); Harman v. Inspector General, [1989–1990 Transfer Bind-

The issue of when it is appropriate to exclude a provider was considered recently in the *Hanlester* case.[9] *Hanlester* was one of the first court of appeal cases applying the bribes and kickbacks prohibition of 42 U.S.C.A. § 1320a–7b(b) and is discussed at length in chapter 3 which considers the bribe and kickback prohibition. It involved a number of institutional and individual respondents with varying alleged degrees of involvement in the sanctioned conduct—kickbacks offered by biomedical laboratories to physicians who invested in them. The *Hanlester* litigation generated a number of reported decisions at both the administrative and judicial levels, several of which considered the exclusion issue.

Though the administrative law judge (ALJ) ultimately held that all of nine of the respondents had violated the law, he held that exclusion of three of the respondents would serve no purpose because there was no evidence that they would violate the law again in the future.[10] The Departmental Appeals Board (DAB) reversed. Though the DAB did not endorse the OIG's position that exclusion should be automatic whenever an excludable offense is found, it did hold that the respondent bears the burden of proving trustworthiness once a violation is found, a burden it found had not been met in the *Hanlester* case.[11] The DAB further noted that, although the primary purpose of exclusion was remedial, incidental deterrent or punitive effects did not invalidate a remedial sanction.[12] The DAB held that "willingness to flirt" with a violation was enough to ground the sanction, even though the exact reach of the bribe and kickback law was unclear before the decision in the case.[13] It ultimately excluded all respondents.

Though the *Hanlester* DAB decision was affirmed on appeal to the district court,[14] the Court of Appeal reversed, addressing both the substance of the violation and the question of exclusion. The court first reversed the decision of the DAB with respect to all but one of the individual respondents (Hitchcock) on the merits, thus mooting the exclusion issue with respect to the other individual respondents.[15] The court did find, however, that the corporate respondents were vicariously liable for the acts of the one individual respondent who had violated the statute, and thus went on to address the issue of exclusion of those respondents.[16] It reversed the exclusion of these corporate respondents, finding that there was

er] Medicare & Medicaid Guide (CCH) ¶ 38,453 (DAB Mar. 5, 1990).

9. Hanlester Network v. Shalala, 51 F.3d 1390 (9th Cir.1995).

10. Inspector General v. Hanlester, [1992 Transfer Binder] Medicare & Medicaid Guide (CCH) ¶ 40,064 (DAB Mar. 10, 1992).

11. Inspector General v. Hanlester, [1992 Transfer Binder] Medicare &

Medicaid Guide (CCH) ¶ 40,406B at 31,-799–801 (DAB July 24, 1992).

12. Id. at 31,801.

13. Id. at 31,803.

14. Hanlester Network v. Sullivan, No. CV92–4552–LHM, 1993 WL 78299 (C.D.Cal.1993), aff'd in part & rev'd in part, 51 F.3d 1390 (9th Cir.1995).

15. 51 F.3d at 1402.

16. 51 F.3d at 1400–02.

no evidence that they had "caused harm to the Medicare or Medicaid programs."[17] Because the liability of the corporate respondents was wholly vicarious, the court held, any potential untrustworthiness on their part was cured by the exclusion of the individual respondent whose conduct had violated the statute.[18] Exclusion of the corporate respondents, therefore, was not necessary to serve the remedial purposes of the Act.[19]

The position taken by the Court of Appeals in *Hanlester* obviously places much greater restrictions on the authority of the OIG to exclude providers from the Medicare and Medicaid program than either the position urged by the OIG or adopted by the DAB below. It clearly identifies the purpose of exclusion as remedial. It could be read to rule out exclusion as a sanction against any institutional provider that purges itself of employees who engage in wrongful conduct. On the other hand, the court emphasized its belief that the corporate respondents had not harmed the Medicaid program. Perhaps if the court had perceived the corporate respondents to have been infected more pervasively by the wrongful conduct or the wrong as more serious, it would have been willing to countenance corporate exclusion, despite the fact that Hitchcock was no longer with them. It remains to be seen, of course, whether other appellate courts will follow *Hanlester* in this respect.

Exclusion is a particularly harsh sanction in situations where the practitioner or provider is almost totally dependent on Medicare and Medicaid for its business. Some have argued, therefore, that mandatory exclusion is a cruel and unusual punishment, violative of the Eighth Amendment. The Eighth Amendment, however, applies only to criminal punishments and not to civil sanctions.[20] At least one court has held that civil sanctions disqualifying individuals from receiving certain benefits based on prior convictions do not violate the Eighth Amendment, even when they apply automatically to all offenders without regard to the circumstances of the offense.[21] It has also been held at the administrative level that Medicare exclusions do not violate the Eighth amendment.[22]

b. Mandatory Exclusions

Exclusion from program participation for at least five years is mandatory under four circumstances. The first is conviction of a

---

17. 51 F.3d at 1402.

18. Id.

19. Id.

20. See, e.g., Powell v. Texas, 392 U.S. 514, 531–32, 88 S.Ct. 2145, 2153–54, 20 L.Ed.2d 1254 (1968); Stamp v. Commissioner, 579 F.Supp. 168, 171 (N.D.Ill.1984); Popow v. City of Margate, 476 F.Supp. 1237, 1242 n.2 (D.N.J. 1979).

21. See Blount v. Smith, 440 F.Supp. 528, 533 (M.D.Pa.1977).

22. Strausbaugh v. Inspector General, [1992 Transfer Binder] Medicare & Medicaid Guide (CCH) ¶ 40,244 at 30,-702 (DAB Sept. 16, 1991).

criminal offense related to the delivery of an item or service reimbursed under Medicare or a state health care program.[23] Conviction is defined broadly to include nolo contendere pleas or entrance into diversion programs, even if state law would not consider the disposition of the case to be a criminal conviction.[24] Exclusions can be imposed based on *Alford* pleas, in which the defendant pleads not guilty but accepts the conviction to avoid a trial.[25] They may be imposed even though the underlying conviction is still on appeal in the state courts,[26] or is subsequently expunged,[27] as the statutory standard is simply conviction. The broad interpretation is consistent with Congressional intent, which was to permit exclusion whenever "individuals have admitted that they engaged in criminal abuse against a Federal health program" even though the state may ultimately choose not to impose criminal penalties for the offense.[28]

An exclusion can be imposed on a physician based on a criminal plea even though the plea purported to settle all civil and criminal claims, as a Medicare exclusion is neither a civil nor a criminal claim.[29] It may also be imposed where the conviction is for

---

23. 42 U.S.C.A. § 1320a–7(a)(1); 42 C.F.R. § 1001.101(a). Though these exclusions are mandatory, they may be waived at the request of a state where the excluded individual or entity is a sole community physician or the sole source of essential specialized services in a community. 42 U.S.C.A. § 1320a–7(c)(3)(B); 42 C.F.R. § 1001.1801(b).

24. 42 U.S.C.A. § 1320a–7(i); Travers v. Shalala, 20 F.3d 993, 996 (9th Cir.1994).

25. Hein v. Inspector General, [1993 Transfer Binder] Medicare & Medicaid Guide (CCH) ¶ 41,366 (DAB Feb. 26, 1993); Baisley v. Inspector General, [1991 Transfer Binder] Medicare & Medicaid Guide (CCH) ¶ 39,191 (DAB Apr. 26, 1991). It does not, however, include deferred prosecutions, see Travers v. Shalala, 20 F.3d at 997; or bond forfeitures, see Reeder v. Inspector General, [1995 Transfer Binder] Medicare & Medicaid Guide (CCH) ¶ 43,605 (DAB May 12, 1995).

26. In Erickson v. United States ex rel. Dep't of Health & Human Servs., 67 F.3d 858 (9th Cir.1995), the district court had held that a doctor and clinic had been denied due process when the OIG excluded them based on a state court conviction that was on appeal. The Ninth Circuit reversed, upholding the original exclusion. It held that the plaintiffs had no property interest in continued participation in Medicare, but that they did have a liberty interest. Id. at 862–63. It proceeded to find, however, that the state jury trial had provided ample process for the defendants to assert their innocence, and that a mandatory exclusion could be boot-strapped to the state conviction without the requirement of an additional plenary administrative hearing. Id. The court also held that the plaintiffs had to exhaust administrative remedies with respect to the question of whether the conviction "related to the delivery of an item or service" under Medicare. Id. at 864.

27. Howle v. Bowen, No. Civ. A. 86–1495SSH, 1987 WL 19007 (D.D.C.1987); Mathews v. Inspector General, [1997–1 Transfer Binder] Medicare & Medicaid Guide (CCH) ¶ 45,066 (DAB Jan. 3, 1997); White v. Inspector General, [1993 Transfer Binder] Medicare & Medicaid Guide (CCH) ¶ 40,994 (DAB July 23, 1992); Hebert v. Inspector General, [1992 Transfer Binder] Medicare & Medicaid Guide (CCH) ¶ 40,362 (DAB May 11, 1992).

28. See H.R. Rep. No. 727, 99th Cong., 2d Sess. 74–75, reprinted in 1986 U.S.C.C.A.N. 3607, 3664–65.

29. United States v. Potrocky, No. 92–6392, 1993 WL 69537, at *2–3 (4th Cir.1993). Similarly, the OIG is not bound by a plea agreement between a

a strict liability criminal offense.[30] Many ALJ and DAB decisions have held that a respondent may not collaterally challenge a conviction in the exclusion proceedings, and that mandatory exclusions based on convictions can be disposed of summarily.[31] The courts have uniformly upheld this position.[32]

For a mandatory exclusion to be imposed, there must not only be a conviction, but this conviction must also relate "to the delivery of an item or service" reimbursed by Medicare or a state health program. The OIG's determination on this matter is reviewable by the ALJ in a subsequent administrative hearing, but the issue is frequently disposed of summarily based on the pleadings in the criminal proceeding.[33] The standard is interpreted quite broadly to cover a wide range of dishonest conduct relating to the Medicare or Medicaid programs.[34] Persons may be excluded under this provision even though they are not health care professionals if they engage in the business of providing health care items or services.[35]

The second grounds for mandatory exclusion is conviction of a crime relating to neglect or abuse of patients in connection with the delivery of health care.[36] The term patient is defined in proposed

provider and a state Medicaid Fraud Control Unit that did not contemplate a settlement. Accaputo v. Inspector General, [1993 Transfer Binder] Medicare & Medicaid Guide (CCH) ¶ 41,600 (DAB June 3, 1993). See, discussing settlement issues generally, James M. Becker et al., Avoiding Multiple Sanctions and Collateral Consequences When Settling Fraud and Abuse Cases, in 1993 Health Law Handbook 187 (Alice G. Gosfield ed., 1993).

30. Franzen v. Inspector General, [1992 Transfer Binder] Medicare & Medicaid Guide (CCH) ¶ 38,570 (DAB June 13, 1990).

31. See, e.g., Philips v. Inspector General, [1993 Transfer Binder] Medicare & Medicaid Guide (CCH) ¶ 40,992 (DAB Nov. 12, 1991); Edmonson v. Inspector General, [1993 Transfer Binder] Medicare & Medicaid Guide (CCH) ¶ 40,-993 (DAB May 21, 1992). See also, Howard v. Inspector General, HHS DAB Dec. No. CR 459, Feb. 7, 1997 (mental state of provider in committing crime irrelevant in mandatory exclusion proceeding).

32. Travers v. Shalala, 20 F.3d 993, 998 (9th Cir.1994).

33. See, e.g., Nagy v. Inspector General, [1992 Transfer Binder] Medicare & Medicaid Guide (CCH) ¶ 40,132 (DAB Mar. 11, 1992).

34. See, e.g., Hirsch v. Inspector General, [1995 Transfer Binder] Medicare & Medicaid Guide (CCH) ¶ 43,606 (DAB June 2, 1995) (false claims submitted to Arhizonga Health Care Cost Containment System, which administers Arizona Medicaid program under 1115 waiver); Schram v. Inspector General, [1993 Transfer Binder] Medicare & Medicaid Guide (CCH) ¶ 41,308 (DAB Nov. 24, 1992) (false billings related to delivery of item or service even though they occurred afterwards); Orlando Ariz and Ariz Pharmacy Inc. v. Inspector General, [1990 Transfer Binder] Medicare & Medicaid Guide (CCH) ¶ 38,451 (DAB Feb. 22, 1990) (false Medicaid billings tied to delivery of drugs to Medicaid patient); Wheeler & Todd v. Inspector General, [1990 Transfer Binder] Medicare & Medicaid Guide (CCH) ¶ 38,388 (DAB Jan. 17, 1990) (falsifying Medicaid cost reports related to delivery of services).

35. Afeonyi v. Inspector General, [1993 Transfer Binder] Medicare & Medicaid Guide (CCH) ¶ 41,663 (DAB May 7, 1993).

36. 42 U.S.C.A. § 1320a–7(a)(2); 42 C.F.R. § 1001.101(b). Here again, the excluded provider is not permitted to challenge the underlying conviction collaterally in the exclusion proceedings. Jones v. Inspector General, [1993 Trans-

regulations to include "any individual who is receiving health care items or services, including any item or service provided to meet his or her physical, mental or emotional needs, whether or not the item or service is reimbursed under Medicare or a State health care program and regardless of the location in which it is provided." The intent of this definition is to broaden this category to include residents of non-medical institutions or others not normally thought of as "patients."[36.5] The neglect and abuse need not involve patients who are Medicare beneficiaries or Medicaid recipients.[37]

This provision covers not only convictions for actual neglect or abuse, but also convictions for failure to report patient abuse.[38] It encompasses convictions "relating to" neglect, whether or not they result in patient injury.[39] Neglect can include failing to attend to the needs of nursing facility residents.[40] Abuse can include unauthorized treatment.[41] In some cases, the OIG has looked behind corporate structures, excluding providers for neglect occurring in their facilities, even though the nolo contendere plea was entered by the corporate parent of the actual operator of the facility in which the neglect occurred rather than by the operator itself.[42] Under proposed regulations, HHS would consider in determining length of sanction under this provision whether the conduct was

fer Binder] Medicare & Medicaid Guide (CCH) ¶ 41,645 (DAB Apr. 16, 1993).

36.5 Proposed rule 42 C.F.R. § 1001.2 at 62 Fed. Reg. 47,182, 47,185, 47,189 (1997).

37. Westin v. Shalala, 845 F.Supp. 1446, 1451–52 (D.Kan.1994); S. Rep. No. 109, 100th Cong., 1st Sess. 5–6 (1987), reprinted in 1987 U.S.C.C.A.N. 686–87.

38. Westin v. Shalala, 845 F.Supp. 1446 (D.Kan.1994); Barrett v. Dep't of Health & Human Servs., 14 F.3d 26 (8th Cir.1994); Cantu v. Inspector General, HHS DAB No. CR462 (Feb. 24, 1997); Bandel v. Inspector General, [1993 Transfer Binder] Medicare & Medicaid Guide (CCH) ¶ 41,662 (DAB May 6, 1993).

39. Balos v. Inspector General [1996–1 Transfer Binder] Medicare & Medicaid Guide (CCH) ¶ 44,035 (DAB June 2, 1995).

40. Small v. Inspector General, [1992 Transfer Binder] Medicare & Medicaid Guide (CCH) ¶ 39,443 (DAB June 12, 1991) (failure to administer medication).

41. Tommasiello v. Inspector General, [1994 Transfer Binder] Medicare &

Medicaid Guide (CCH) ¶ 41,932 (DAB Aug. 20, 1993) (nurse excluded based on assault conviction, which in turn was based on nurse administering injection without physician authorization).

42. Summit Care–California Inc. v. Newman, 705 F.Supp. 36 (D.D.C.1989). In a subsequent decision in the same case, the court held that this provision could be applied to exclude a corporate provider for a conviction entered before the effective date of the 1987 amendments, which clarified the power of the OIG to exclude such entities. Summit Care–California Inc. v. Newman, No. CIV. A. 89–0169, 1989 WL 44058 (D.D.C.1989). On remand, the DAB concluded that the subsidiary corporation did not have standing to appeal the exclusion of the parent corporation, even though the facility was bound by the exclusion, Summit Health Ltd. v. Inspector General, [1990 Transfer Binder] Medicare & Medicaid Guide (CCH) ¶ 38,-653 (DAB June 29, 1990). The DAB observed: "Obviously, a large parent corporation should not be able to avoid the effects of an exclusion though paper charades involving its subsidiaries."

premeditated, repeated, or sexual in nature.[42.5]

Third, the statute, as amended by the Health Insurance Portability and Accountability Act of 1996 (HIPAA), provides that individuals and entities may be excluded, after the date of enactment of that statute for any felony conviction under federal or state law:

> in connection with the delivery of a health care item or service or with respect to any act or omission in a health care program * * * operated or financed in whole or in part by any Federal, State or local government agency, of a criminal offense consisting of a felony relating to fraud, theft, embezzlement, breach of fiduciary responsibility, or other financial misconduct.[43]

Fourth, the HIPAA also amended the statute to provide that a person who is convicted under federal or state law after the enactment of the HIPAA of a felony "relating to the unlawful manufacture, distribution, prescription, or dispensing of controlled substances," must also be excluded from the program.[44]

Mandatory exclusions can be imposed for a period in excess of five years where there are aggravating circumstances. In determining whether to extend a mandatory exclusion beyond 5 years, the OIG may consider certain aggravating factors including the fact that the loss to Medicare and the state health care programs equaled or exceeded $1500 (including amounts resulting from similar acts not adjudicated and regardless of whether full or partial restitution had been made for improper billings); that the acts that resulted in the conviction, or similar acts, were committed over a period of one year or more; that the acts that resulted in the conviction, or similar acts, had a significant adverse physical, mental or financial impact on program beneficiaries or others; that the sentence imposed by the court included incarceration;[44.5] or that the convicted individual or entity has a prior criminal, civil or administrative sanction record.[45]

42.5 Proposed rule 42 C.F.R. § 1001.102(b)(4) at 62 Fed. Reg. 47,182, 47,185, 47,190 (1997).

43. 42 U.S.C.A. § 1320a–7(a)(3).

44. 42 U.S.C.A. § 1320a–7(a)(4). Under proposed rules, this exclusion authority would apply only to persons who are health care providers, their owners or employees. Proposed rule 42 C.F.R. § 1001.101(d), at 62 Fed. Reg. 47,182, 47,189–47,190 (1997).

44.5 A new proposed rule defines "incarceration" to include community confinement (as in a work release center) or house arrest, recognizing that many white collar criminals are in fact not jailed. Proposed rule 42 C.F.R. § 1001.2, at 62 Fed. Reg. 47,182, 47,185, 47,189 (1997).

45. 42 C.F.R. § 1001.102(b). See, e.g., Patel v. Inspector General [1997–1 Transfer Binder] Medicare and Medicaid Guide (CCH) ¶ 45,034 (DAB Nov. 26, 1996); Amro v. Inspector General Koh v. Inspector General [1997–1 Transfer Binder] Medicare and Medicaid Guide (CCH) (DAB Dec. 13, 1996); HHS App. Bd., No. CR466 (Mar. 5, 1997) (10 year exclusions based on length of fraudulent activities and amount of money involved).

HHS has also proposed consideration of an additional aggravating factor: whether the individual or entity has been convicted of any other offenses prior to, at the time of, or subsequent to the conviction for which the exclusion is being imposed.[45.5]

Mitigating factors that may be considered include the facts that the individual or entity was convicted of three or fewer misdemeanor offenses, and the entire amount of financial loss to Medicare and the state health care programs due to the acts that resulted in the conviction, and similar acts, was less than $1500; that the record in the criminal proceedings, including sentencing documents, demonstrates that the court determined that the individual had a mental, emotional or physical condition that reduced the individual's culpability; or that cooperation with federal or state officials resulted in others being criminally convicted for Medicare or Medicaid fraud or in the imposition of civil money penalties against others.[46] A proposed rule would add as a mitigating factor consideration of whether cooperation from the defendant resulted in new cases being opened or reports being issued, or in system vulnerabilities being identified.[46.5] The ALJs and the DAB will sustain lengthy exclusions if the evidence shows the presence of aggravating factors,[47] but will also reduce the length of exclusion without hesitation if evidence of aggravating factors is not sufficiently present or if mitigating factors were convincingly argued.[48] Mitigating factors may not, of course, reduce the exclusion below the mandatory five year period in any event.[49]

45.5 Proposed amendment to rule 42 C.F.R. § 1001.201(b)(8), and related sections, at 62 Fed. Reg. 47,182, 47,186, 47,190 (1997).

46. 42 C.F.R. § 1002.102(c). See Stern v. Shalala, 14 F.3d 148, 149 (2d Cir.1994) (upholding a HHS Appeals Council decision substituting a five for a twenty year exclusion because of "legitimate differences of opinion" as to whether claims which formed the basis of a false claims plea agreement were in fact false).

46.5 Proposed addition to 42 C.F.R. § 1001.102(c)(3) and related rules, at 62 Fed. Reg. 47,182, 47,186, 47,190 (1997).

47. Payne v. Inspector General, [1992 Transfer Binder] Medicare & Medicaid Guide (CCH) ¶ 39,619 (DAB July 16, 1991) (10 years); Cooper v. Inspector General, [1990 Transfer Binder] Medicare & Medicaid Guide (CCH) ¶ 38,-619 (DAB July 24, 1990)(15 years). See generally, Steven Kessel, Criteria for Determining the Length of Exclusions and Their Effect on Civil Remedy Adminis-

trative Hearings, in ABA, Health Care Fraud, 1997, F–55.

48. Donaldson v. Inspector General, [1993 Transfer Binder] Medicare & Medicaid Guide (CCH) ¶ 41,073 (DAB Oct. 9, 1992) (15 years reduced to 10); Herlich v. Inspector General, [1992 Transfer Binder] Medicare & Medicaid Guide (CCH) ¶ 40,360 (DAB May 11, 1992) (20 year exclusion reduced to 10); Thomas v. Inspector General, [1994 Transfer Binder] Medicare & Medicaid Guide (CCH) ¶ 41,935 (DAB Aug. 18, 1993) (10 year exclusion reduced to 5 where mental illness shown as mitigating factor).

49. Prakash v. Inspector General, [1993 Transfer Binder] Medicare & Medicaid Guide (CCH) ¶ 41,667 (DAB May 24, 1993); Escalante v. Inspector General, [1990 Transfer Binder] Medicare & Medicaid Guide (CCH) ¶ 38,620 (DAB July 27, 1990). A mandatory exclusion will also not be shortened to recognize time that the provider has already been excluded from program par-

The Balanced Budget Act of 1997 modifies previous sanction provisions by adding a "three strikes and you're out" provision. It provides that if an individual is convicted of a crime that could form the basis for a mandatory exclusion after the effective date of the statute, and had earlier (before or after the effective date of the new statute) been convicted of an offense that could have resulted in an exclusion, the exclusion must last at least ten years.[50] If the convicted individual had on two or more previous occasions been convicted of such offenses, the individual shall be permanently excluded.[51]

Since 1993, the OIG has focused its exclusion efforts primarily on mandatory exclusions because of resource constraints.[52] Because these exclusions are targeted at the behavior of most concern to Congress and because they can be imposed in summary proceedings based on criminal convictions without extensive additional investigation, they tend to in fact represent an efficient use of resources.

Because exclusions are civil and remedial (as opposed to punitive) sanctions, the OIG has taken the position, supported by the courts, that exclusions do not present double jeopardy problems.[53] Where the federal exclusion is imposed pursuant to a state conviction, the "dual sovereignty" doctrine also precludes double jeopardy problems.[54] Under this doctrine, states are considered to be a "separate sovereign" from the federal government, because a state's power to prosecute is derived from its own inherent sovereignty, and not from the powers of the Federal government.[55] Prosecution by one does not, therefore, preclude prosecution by the other. In any event, a double jeopardy claim can only be raised after administrative remedies have been exhausted, because it is dependent upon the exclusion being in fact valid and is thus not collateral

ticipation under state exclusion provisions. Jain v. Inspector General, [1993 Transfer Binder] Medicare & Medicaid Guide (CCH) ¶ 41,601 (Mar. 23, 1993).

50. Pub.L. No. 105–32, § 4301, to be codified at 42 U.S.C.A. § 1320a–7(c)(3)(G)(i).

51. Pub.L. No. 105–32, § 4301, to be codified at 42 U.S.C.A. § 1320a–7(c)(3)(G)(ii).

52. See Office of Inspector General, Semi-annual Report, Apr. 1, 1993–Sept. 30, 1993, [1994 Transfer Binder] Medicare & Medicaid Guide (CCH) ¶ 42,009.

53. See 57 Fed. Reg. 3298, 3300–01 (1992). Erickson v. United States Dep't of Health & Human Servs., 67 F.3d 858, 864 n.2 (9th Cir.1995); Manocchio v. Kusserow, 961 F.2d 1539, 1541–42 (11th Cir.1992); Kahn v. Inspector General,

848 F.Supp. 432, 437–38 (S.D.N.Y.1994); Westin v. Shalala, 845 F.Supp. 1446, 1452–54 (D.Kan.1994); Greene v. Sullivan, 731 F.Supp. 835, 838 (E.D.Tenn. 1990).

54. Kahn v. Inspector General, 848 F. Supp. at 437; United States v. Anthony, 727 F.Supp. 792, 794 (E.D.N.Y. 1989). See also, Abbate v. United States, 359 U.S. 187, 193–94, 79 S.Ct. 666, 669–70, 3 L.Ed.2d 729 (1959); United States v. Lanza, 260 U.S. 377, 382, 43 S.Ct. 141, 142, 67 L.Ed. 314 (1922); Chapman v. United States Dep't of Health & Human Servs., 821 F.2d 523, 529 (10th Cir.1987).

55. See United States v. Wheeler, 435 U.S. 313, 320, 98 S.Ct. 1079, 1084, 55 L.Ed.2d 303 (1978).

to the exclusion proceeding.[56]

c. Discretionary Exclusions

The basic exclusion statute also authorizes permissive or discretionary exclusion under a variety of circumstances. In situations where either a mandatory or discretionary exclusion might be appropriate, the OIG must impose the mandatory exclusion.[57]

In determining the length of permissive exclusions, the aggravating and mitigating factors considered in determining the length of mandatory exclusions are generally considered, when appropriate. In addition the availability of alternative sources of health care in the community and other circumstances specifically applicable to the particular violation are considered.[58]

Five of the permissive exclusion authorities are derivative, i.e. they are based on the actions of another. These include exclusions for providers who:

> 1) have been convicted of misdemeanor crimes relating to fraud, theft, embezzlement, breach of fiduciary duty or other financial misconduct in the delivery of health care in general or of any financial offenses in non-health care governmental programs;[59]

> 2) have been convicted of obstruction or interference with a criminal investigation related to Medicare or state health care program fraud, patient neglect or abuse, or fraud in the delivery of health care or in a governmental program;[60]

56. Erickson v. United States, 67 F.3d at 863–64.

57. Leung v. Inspector General, [1990 Transfer Binder] Medicare & Medicaid Guide (CCH) ¶ 38,577 (DAB June 25, 1990); 55 Fed. Reg. 12,005, 12,207 (57 Fed. Reg. 3298).

58. The mere fact that some of the excluded provider's patients may have some difficulty in immediately finding another physician is not sufficient to affect the exclusion, however, where other doctors are in fact available. Rad v Inspector General, [1995 Transfer Binder] Medicare & Medicaid Guide (CCH) ¶ 42,974 (DAB Apr. 14, 1994); Holmes v. Inspector General, [1993 Transfer Binder] Medicare & Medicaid Guide (CCH) ¶ 41,714 (DAB June 7, 1993). It is also not enough to show that the provider offers services not offered by others in the area if it is not shown that these services are used by Medicare and Medicaid recipients. Renick v. Inspector General, [1995 Transfer Binder] Medicare & Medicaid Guide (CCH) ¶ 42,975 (DAB Apr. 22, 1994).

59. 42 U.S.C.A. § 1320a–7(b)(1); 42 C.F.R. § 1001.201. The offense only needs to be "in connection with the delivery of a health care item or service," and need not be directly related to Medicare or Medicaid. Kachoria v. Inspector General, Medicare & Medicaid Guide (CCH) ¶ 41,936 (ALJ Jan. 13, 1993). Prior to 1996, the provision covered all health care financial crimes, including felonies, not committed against Medicare or Medicaid.

60. 42 U.S.C.A. § 1320a–7(b)(2); 42 C.F.R. § 1001.301.

3) have been convicted of misdemeanor crimes relating to the unlawful manufacture, distribution, prescribing or dispensing of a controlled substance;[61]

4) have had their licenses revoked or suspended or have otherwise lost their licenses, or have surrendered such a license while a disciplinary proceeding was pending, for reasons bearing on professional competence or performance or financial integrity;[62] and

61. 42 U.S.C.A. § 1320a–7(b)(3); 42 C.F.R. § 1001.401. Prior to the HIPAA 1996 amendments, requiring exclusion for felony controlled substance convictions, exclusion was permissive for all controlled substance convictions. The provision also covers convictions for failure to keep records of controlled substances. Wilkinson v. Inspector General, [1990 Transfer Binder] Medicare & Medicaid Guide (CCH) ¶ 38,452 (DAB Feb. 12, 1990). When controlled substance violations are at issue, ALJs were, prior to 1993, often willing to reduce the length of the exclusion if they believed that the provider was being rehabilitated and posed little ongoing threat to the integrity of federal and state health care programs in determining the length of exclusion. Compare Krickenbarger v. Inspector General, [1993 Transfer Binder] Medicare & Medicaid Guide (CCH) ¶ 41,363 (DAB Jan. 13, 1993); Keil v. Inspector General, [1990 Transfer Binder] Medicare & Medicaid Guide (CCH) ¶ 38,455 (DAB Mar. 16, 1990); and Behymer v. Inspector General, [1990 Transfer Binder] Medicare & Medicaid Guide (CCH) ¶ 38,-433 (DAB Mar. 16, 1990) (reducing the length of exclusion); with Reiner v. Inspector General, [1991 Transfer Binder] Medicare & Medicaid Guide (CCH) ¶ 38,-803 (DAB Aug. 8, 1990) (refusing to do so where ongoing threat to program). Since January 22, 1993, however, 42 C.F.R. § 1001.1(b) has required ALJs to exclude persons convicted for controlled substance offenses for at least three years unless mitigating factors specifically identified in the regulations are established. Rodriguez v. Inspector General, [1995 Transfer Binder] Medicare & Medicaid Guide (CCH) ¶ 43,188 (DAB Mar. 18, 1994). Under proposed rules only health care providers, their owners or employees would be subject to exclusion. Proposed rule 42 C.F.R. § 1001.101(a), at 62 Fed. Reg. 47,182, 47,191.

62. 42 U.S.C.A. § 1320a–7(b)(4); 42 C.F.R. § 1001.501. See Bennett v. Inspector General, [1990 Transfer Binder] Medicare & Medicaid Guide (CCH) ¶ 38,-390 (DAB Jan. 24, 1990) (defining "formal disciplinary proceeding"). An exclusion can be imposed when the provider's license has been revoked for reasons "bearing on" professional competence or performance, even if the problem is arguably a medical disability. Pousma v. Inspector General, [1993 Transfer Binder] Medicare & Medicaid Guide (CCH) ¶ 41,710 (DAB July 16, 1993) (revocation based on psychosexual disorder); Saini v. Inspector General, [1993 Transfer Binder] Medicare & Medicaid Guide (CCH) ¶ 41,327 (DAB Nov. 23, 1992) (psychotic episode). In such a situation, the OIG has only the option of excluding or not excluding the provider. Even if permitting the provider to continue to participate in the program subject to restrictions (the presence of a chaperon) such limitations are not an option for the IG. Pousma v. Inspector General, Medicare & Medicaid Guide (CCH) ¶ 41,710.

While an exclusion may be imposed even though judicial review of the licensure action has not been completed, 57 Fed. Reg. at 3305, the exclusion may not be imposed where the licensure revocation has been stayed pending state court review. King v. Inspector General, [1991 Transfer Binder] Medicare & Medicaid Guide (CCH) ¶ 39,141 (DAB Mar. 19, 1991).

The "otherwise lost" the license language was added to assure broad coverage of state disciplinary actions, regardless of the names particular jurisdictions apply to their actions. The provisions that permit exclusion based on surrender of a license while disciplinary actions were pending were added, of course, to address the situation where a provider under threat of sanction in one state surrenders his or her license and moves to another. Exclusion is not appropriate for minor infractions such as failure to pay licensure fees or advertising violations. See S. Rep. No. 109, 100th Cong., 1st Sess. 7–8 (1987), reprinted in 1987 U.S.C.C.A.N. 682, 688.

5) have been excluded or suspended or otherwise sanctioned from participation in another federal health care program, including Veteran's Administration programs or CHAMPUS, or a state health care program for reasons related to professional competence, professional performance or financial integrity.[63]

The Act, as amended in 1996 by the HIPAA, also provides that:

Any individual–

(i) who has a direct or indirect ownership or control interest in a sanctioned entity and who knows or should know * * * of the action constituting the basis for [a conviction that should result in a mandatory exclusion under one of the first three grounds listed above] or exclusion [from Medicare or a state health program]; or

(ii) who is an officer or managing employee * * * of such an entity,

may also be excluded from program participation.[64]

While the OIG has the discretion not to impose an exclusion even though one of these grounds exist, once the OIG decides to exclude, the provider may not collaterally attack the underlying action on which the exclusion is based in the exclusion proceedings.[65]

Under the 1996 HIPAA amendments, exclusions under paragraphs 1, 2, and 3 above must be for 3 years, unless HHS determines in accordance with published regulations that aggravating or mitigating factors indicate a longer or shorter period of exclusion.[66]

---

63. 42 U.S.C.A. § 1320a–7(b)(5); 42 C.F.R. § 1001.601. The "or otherwise sanctioned" language "is intended to cover all actions that limit the ability of a person to participate in the program at issue regardless of what such action is called." 42 C.F.R. § 1001.601(a)(2); see Ibrahim v. Inspector General [1997–1 Transfer Binder] Medicare and Medicaid Guide (CCH) ¶ 45,039 (DAB Nov. 20, 1996) (based on state action limiting doctor to hospital practice for Medicaid patients). Exclusions under this provision can be based on state Medicaid exclusions that predate the effective date of the MMPPPA. Harman v. Sullivan, No. Civ. A. 89–6089, 1990 WL 2188 (E.D.Pa.1990). Voluntary withdrawal from Medicaid participation as part of the settlement of criminal charges, however, may not in itself be a sanction supporting exclusion. Korins v. Inspec-

tor General, [1990 Transfer Binder] Medicare & Medicaid Guide (CCH) ¶ 38,-457 (DAB Feb. 8, 1990). But voluntary withdrawal in the face of proposed termination may be, 42 C.F.R. § 1001.601(a)(2). See Shusman v. Inspector General, [1992 Transfer Binder] Medicare & Medicaid Guide (CCH) ¶ 39,-441 (DAB May 24, 1991).

64. 42 U.S.C.A. § 1320a–7(b).

65. Iturralde v. Inspector General, [1993 Transfer Binder] Medicare & Medicaid Guide (CCH) ¶ 41,309 (DAB Dec. 9, 1992); Friedman v. Inspector General, [1992 Transfer Binder] Medicare & Medicaid Guide (CCH) ¶ 40,460 (DAB Nov. 18, 1991).

66. 42 U.S.C.A. § 1320a–7(c)(3)(D). Proposed rules implementing this authority have been published at 62 Fed. Reg. 47,182 (1997).

The statute also provides that exclusions under paragraphs 4 and 5 should last as long as the individual or entity's license is suspended, revoked, or surrendered, or the person is excluded or suspended.[67]

The term conviction is defined as broadly and inclusively with respect to permissive exclusions as it is with respect to mandatory exclusions.[68] Permissive exclusions may be imposed not only for convictions for fraud against the Medicare or Medicaid programs (which are grounds for mandatory exclusion) but also for fraud against private health care programs or against governmental programs other than health care programs. The regulations implementing the MMPPPA set a benchmark of three years for exclusions derived from criminal convictions, with flexibility to increase or decrease the period.[69] Exclusion will not be delayed merely because post-judgment motions are pending, though the individual or entity excluded will be reinstated if the conviction is overturned.[70]

Though it has always been necessary for providers to be licensed under state licensing laws to be eligible for Medicare or Medicaid payment, the provision permitting exclusion of unlicensed providers was added to address the problem of providers who had lost a license in one state but obtained or retained a license in another.[71] Exclusions based on actions taken by licensing boards or by other federal and state health care programs will normally last at least as long as the period of the prior licensure or other sanction, and can be for a longer period of time if there are aggravating circumstances or if a longer exclusion is necessary to prevent harm to the Medicare or Medicaid programs.[72] An agreement to surrender a license in one state by a physician who is also licensed and resides in another may result in exclusion, despite the physician's argument that he surrendered the license because he no

---

67. 42 U.S.C.A. § 1320a–7(c)(3)(E).

68. See also 42 U.S.C.A. § 1320a–7(i); 42 C.F.R. § 1001.2. For purposes of permissive exclusions, however, a nolo contendere plea is not treated as an admission of the underlying charges even though it is treated as a conviction. Kranz v. Inspector General, [1993 Transfer Binder] Medicare & Medicaid Guide (CCH) ¶ 40,096 (DAB Dec. 19, 1991).

69. 42   C.F.R.   §§ 1001.201(b), .301(b), .401(c). See, e.g., Castro v. Inspector General, Medicare & Medicaid Guide (CCH) ¶ 41,642 (Apr. 28, 1993) (three year exclusion for controlled substance exclusion).

70. 42 C.F.R. § 1001.3005.

71. 55 Fed. Reg. 12,205, 12,207; S. Rep. No. 109, 100th Cong., 1st Sess. 7 (1987), reprinted in 1987 U.S.C.C.A.N. 682, 688.

72. 42 U.S.C. § 1320a(7)(c)(3)(D) & (E). 42 C.F.R. §§ 1001.501(b), .601(b) and 57 Fed. Reg. 3298, 3305. See, e.g., Bhatti v. Inspector General, [1993 Transfer Binder] Medicare & Medicaid Guide (CCH) ¶ 41,602 (DAB June 1, 1993) (upholding IG's imposition of indefinite exclusion in licensure revocation case). Prior regulatory authority permitting the Secretary to impose an exclusion for a shorter period of time where a professional obtained a license in another state was invalidated by 1996 statutory amendments. See 62 Fed. Reg. 47,-182, 47,186, 47,190 (1997).

longer intended to practice in the first state.[73] Normally a request for reinstatement by a person excluded based on the sanction of another agency will not be considered until the person is reinstated by the program that originally imposed the sanction.[74]

The statute also authorizes a number of "nonderivative" grounds for exclusions, including:

1) filing of claims with Medicare or a State health care program including charges or costs substantially in excess of usual claims or costs. Under proposed HHS amendments to this provision, language would be added specifying that exclusion could be imposed on providers for charging Medicare or state health programs charges in excess of the usual charges charged to "any of their customers, clients or patients," effectively creating a "most favored nations" provision for Medicare and Medicaid.[75] This proposal reflects an important change in federal policy, and will provoke considerable controversy. The regulations establish a three year benchmark for this exclusion.[76]

2) furnishing health care to any patient (whether or not eligible for services under Medicare or a State health care program) substantially in excess of the needs of such patients or of a quality that fails to meet professionally recognized standards.[77] An exclusion under this provision must last at

---

73. Wilson v. Inspector General, [1992 Transfer Binder] Medicare & Medicaid Guide (CCH) ¶ 39,623 (DAB July 31, 1991).

74. 42 C.F.R. § 1001.601. If the state or federal action is reversed or vacated on appeal, the individual or entity will be reinstated unless there are other grounds for exclusion. 42 C.F.R. § 1001.3005(a).

75. Proposed amendments to 42 C.F.R. § 1001.701, at 62 Fed. Reg. 47,-182, 47,186, 47,192 (1997).

76. 42 U.S.C.A. § 1320a–7(b)(6)(A); 42 C.F.R. § 1001.701. HHS has declined to define "usual charges" or "substantially in excess," stating that it will analyze billing patterns on a case-by-case basis. This provision only applies to services paid for on a cost or charge basis, not to services paid for on a prospective payment basis, where the charges are fixed by Medicare or its intermediaries or carriers. See S. Rep. No. 109 at 8, reprinted in 1987 U.S.C.C.A.N. at 689.

77. 42 U.S.C.A. § 1320a–7(b)(6)(B). Professionally recognized standards of health care are defined as "Statewide or national standards of care, whether in writing or not, that professional peers of the individual or entity whose provision of care is an issue, recognize as applying to those peers practicing or providing care within a State. Where the Food and Drug Administration (FDA), the Health Care Financing Administration (HCFA) or the Public Health Service (PHS) has declared a treatment modality not to be safe and effective, practitioners who employ such a treatment modality will be deemed not to meet professionally recognized standards of health care." 42 C.F.R. § 1001.2 The OIG rejected comments on the proposed rule suggesting that a local or regional standard of care be adopted in implementing this position, accepted rather a state or national standard recognizing local resource limitations. See 57 Fed. Reg. 3298 at 3301; Lahiri v. Inspector General, [1995 Transfer Binder] Medicare & Medicaid Guide (CCH) ¶ 43,461 (DAB Dec. 12, 1994) (applying this provision to exclude an oncologist who had billed for $172,-000 in unnecessary services).

least a year.[78] This provision substantially overlaps the authority of the OIG to exclude providers, practitioners or suppliers upon the recommendation of a Medicare Peer Review Organization for utilization or quality related problems. This provision and the preceding provision authorizing exclusion for excessive costs or charges do not authorize exclusion where the excess charges or care are attributable to unusual circumstances or medical complications, or where the provider furnishes items or services ordered by a physician or other authorized provider and is not in a position to question the necessity of the services.[79] The regulations establish a three year benchmark for this exclusion.[80]

3) in the case of a Medicaid HMO, a primary care case-management system, a specialty physician services arrangement, or Medicare HMO or CMP, failing substantially to provide medically necessary services, where the failure adversely affects a plan member or is substantially likely to do so.[81] The regulations establish a three year benchmark for this exclusion;[82]

4) committing an act which is a criminal offense under the criminal provisions of the fraud and abuse laws,[83] including false claims and kickbacks,[84] or for which a fraud and abuse civil penalty can be imposed.[85] A provider can be excluded under this provision even though it has not actually been convicted of a crime or had a civil money penalty levied against it, and liability need merely be proved by a preponderance of the evidence,[86] but, unless there is a threat to health or safety of individuals receiving services, the sanction cannot take effect until the provider has had the opportunity for an ALJ hearing.[87] In deciding whether or not to impose a permissive exclusion under this authority the OIG considers the following factors:

1) the circumstances of the misconduct and seriousness of the offense (including whether a criminal sanction was imposed

---

78. 42 U.S.C.A. § 1320a–7(c)(3)(F).

79. 42 C.F.R. § 1001.701(c).

80. 42 C.F.R. § 1001.701(d).

81. 42 U.S.C.A. § 1320a–7(b)(6)(C)-(D). Congress recognized in adopting this provision that managed care organizations tend to practice conservative medicine. This provision is intended to address, however: "serious failures to abide by acceptable standards of medical practice, rather than isolated cases of inadvertent omissions" including instances where there is a "deliberate omission or a pattern of failing to pro-

vide necessary items and services," as determined by "generally accepted HMO practice standards." S. Rep. No. 109 at 9, reprinted in U.S.C.C.A.N. at 690.

82. 42 C.F.R. § 1001.801(c).

83. 42 U.S.C.A. § 1320a–7b

84. 42 C.F.R. § 1001.901, .951.

85. 42 U.S.C.A. §§ 1320a–7a, 1320a–7(b)(7).

86. See S. Rep. No. 109 at 9–10, reprinted in U.S.C.C.A.N. at 690.

87. 42 U.S.C.A. § 1320a–7(f)(2).

and its extent, evidence of fiscal or mental harm to patients or financial harm to the program, whether the conduct was intentional or repeated, and whether the defendant's involvement was active or passive);

2) the defendant's response to the allegations or determination of unlawful conduct (Has the defendant cooperated with investigators and prosecutors, made restitution, paid fines, taken steps to undo the conduct or its effects, or acknowledged the wrongdoing and changed its behavior?);

3) the likelihood that the offense or similar abuse will occur again (Has prior or subsequent conduct been exemplary or improper? Had prior measures been taken to ascertain whether the conduct complied with the law or to assure that it would? Did the defendant have a compliance plan in place and did it work? Has the defendant subsequently implemented an effective compliance plan?); and

4) financial responsibility (If permitted to continue in the program, can the defendant assure solvency and quality of care?).[88] There is no benchmark for this exclusion, the length of which will be determined on a case by case basis;

5) being owned or managed by a person, or having a person as an officer, director, agent, or managing employee who has been convicted criminally of Medicare or Medicaid fraud and abuse or been subjected to a fraud and abuse exclusion or civil penalty.[89] Entities may also, under the Balanced Budget Act of 1997, be excluded if they were transferred from a sanctioned person, in anticipation or following the sanction, to an immediate family member or household member.[90] This exclusion will correspond in length to the period of the exclusion of the person whose relationship with the entity is the basis for the exclusion.[91] The OIG will, prior to imposing

88.   62 Fed. Reg. 55,410 (1997).

89.   42 U.S.C.A. § 1320a–7(b)(8). The ownership or control interest must be at least a 5% share. Ownership of a whole or part interest in a mortgage, deed or trust, note or other obligation secured by 5% or more of the total assets of the entity also qualifies as ownership or control. The provision also covers indirect ownership of an entity if the excluded individual owns indirectly a share of at least 5% (as where the excluded individual owns 10% of an entity that controls 50% of the entity). 42 C.F.R. § 1001.1001.

90.   42   U.S.C.A.   § 1320a–7(b)(8)(A)(iii). The statute, at 42 U.S.C.A. § 1320a–7(j), defines "immediate family member" to include spouses; natural or adoptive parents, children or siblings; stepparents, children, or siblings; parent-, children-or sibling-in-laws; grandparents or grandchildren; or spouses of grandchildren or grandparents. "Member[s] of household" include domestic employees or others living with the individual in a common abode as part of a family unit, not including roomers or boarders.

91.   42 C.F.R. § 1001.1001(b).

this sanction, notify the entity of its intent to do so, and will generally not impose the exclusion if the entity promptly terminates its relationship with the sanctioned individual;

6) failing to make disclosures required by law[92] concerning the identity of individuals with an ownership or control interest in the entity or who act as officers, directors, agents or managing employees of the entity.[93] As to this and the next two authorities dealing with failure to provide required information, exclusions will not be imposed for isolated or unintentional violations unless they have a significant impact on the program or its beneficiaries. Generally exclusion will not occur until the entity or individual has been given thirty days notice of the OIG's intention to exclude and opportunity to comply with the disclosure request;

7) failing when requested to do so to make statutorily required disclosures[94] regarding the ownership of subcontractors with whom the entity has had business transactions within the preceding twelve months in excess of $25,000 or significant business transactions between the entity and any subcontractor or wholly owned supplier within the preceding five years;[95]

8) failing when requested to do so to supply information (such as medical records or x-rays) necessary to determine whether Medicare or Medicaid payments are due or their amount, or to permit examination of records to verify the information;[96]

9) failing to grant immediate (on the spot) access for HHS or appropriate state agencies to certain facilities for the purposes of performing reviews or surveys or determining compliance with conditions of participation, or, access for the OIG or for State Medicaid Control units upon twenty-four hours notice to records and documents.[97] If there is reason to believe that records are about to be altered or destroyed, the OIG or MFCUs can insist on immediate access. On the other hand, entities can be granted more than twenty-four hours to comply where unusual situations require a longer period of time. Exclusions under this authority may last only for the length of time during which access was denied plus an additional period of up to ninety days;[98]

92. 42 U.S.C.A. §§ 1320a–3, 1320a–5.

93. 42 U.S.C.A. § 1320a–7(b)(9).

94. 42 U.S.C.A. § 1320a–3.

95. 42 U.S.C.A. § 1320a–7(b)(10).

96. 42 U.S.C.A. 1320a–7(b)(11).

97. 42 U.S.C.A. § 1320a–7(b)(12); 42 C.F.R. § 1001.1301(a)(3).

98. 42 U.S.C.A. § 1320a–7(c)(3)(C).

10) in the case of a hospital, failing to comply substantially with a corrective action plan required under 42 U.S.C.A. § 1395ww(f)(2) to correct actions taken by the hospital to circumvent DRG-prospective payment, such as inappropriate or multiple admissions or improper practice patterns.[99] In reviewing exclusions under these provisions, only information regarding compliance with the corrective action plan may be considered;

11) defaulting on a health education loan or scholarship obligation where all reasonable steps have been taken to secure repayment.[100] Exclusion is only to be imposed in these cases as a last resort, after HHS has taken all reasonable steps otherwise available to collect the debt.[101] This is one of the most common grounds for program exclusion. Exclusion based on loan default is not to be imposed if the physician is a sole community physician or sole source of essential specialized services in a community and the state requests that the physician not be excluded. HHS must also take into account the impact that an exclusion will have on access to services under Medicare and Medicaid.[102]

The civil money penalty provisions of the Medicare and Medicaid fraud and abuse laws (discussed below) permit HHS to exclude a person from participation in Federal health care programs.[103] The OIG may also exclude a practitioner, provider or supplier on the recommendation of a Medicare Peer Review Organization for certain standard of care violations. Exclusions may also be based on knowing and willful violation of certain billing and charging requirements, noted above in chapter 2.[104]

---

99. 42 U.S.C.A. § 1320a–7(b)(13); 42 C.F.R. § 1001.1401.

100. 42 U.S.C.A. § 1320a–7(b)(14); 42 C.F.R. § 1001.1501.

101. 42 U.S.C.A. § 1320a–7(b)(14). Under the regulations, if the Public Health Service has offered the provider a Medicare offset arrangement (see 42 U.S.C.A. § 1395ccc), it has met its obligations to exhaust otherwise reasonable collection efforts.

102. 42 U.S.C.A. § 1320a–7(b)(14). See also 42 U.S.C.A. § 1395cc(a)(3)(B). The OIG will rely on the Public Health Service to take the required reasonable actions to collect, but will find that all reasonable steps have been taken if the PHS offers a Medicare offset agreement.

103. 42 U.S.C.A. § 1320a–7a(a); 42 C.F.R. §§ 1003.105, .107.

104. See, e.g., 42 U.S.C.A. §§ 1395m(b)(5)(C), 1395u(j)(2), 1395w–4(g)(1) and 42 C.F.R. 1001.601 (violation of limitations on physician charges); 42 U.S.C.A. § 1395u(k)(1) and 42 C.F.R. § 1001.1701 (violation of limitations on use of assistants in cataract surgery); 42 U.S.C.A. § 1395l(h)(5)(D) (billing for clinical diagnostic laboratory test on other than an assignment basis); 42 U.S.C.A. § 1395m(a)(11) (failing to furnish durable medical equipment without charge when the equipment is furnished on a rental basis and rental payments may no longer be made by Medicare); 42 U.S.C.A. § 1395u(l), (m) (failing to refund on a timely basis charges paid by a beneficiary for services determined by a PRO to have not been reasonable or necessary or to disclose specified information on charges to beneficiaries); 42 U.S.C.A. § 1395u(n) (improper charges for diagnostic tests); 42 U.S.C.A. § 1395w–4(g)(3) (billing on other than

d.   Consequences of Exclusion

If the OIG excludes an individual or entity from Medicare program participation, state Medicaid agencies must also exclude that individual or entity from participation in Medicaid for the same period of time.[105] States may, however, request that exclusion from state health programs be waived.[106] States may also at their own initiative exclude an individual or entity from participation in Medicaid for any of the reasons that the individual or entity could have been excluded from participation under Medicare under 42 U.S.C.A. §§ 1320a–7, 1320a–8a, or 1395cc(b)(2), or may impose exclusions for longer periods of time than those imposed by the OIG.[107] States must also exclude from their Medicaid programs HMOs or primary case management or specialty physician service arrangements that are owned or managed by or that have substantial contractual relationships with individuals who have been convicted of certain crimes or sanctioned by Medicare, or who employ or contract with individuals excluded from Medicare participation.[108] Under Executive Orders 12549 and 12689, Medicare exclusions are also given government-wide effect to bar participation in any other federal program.[109]

Exclusions may result in exclusion of parent, subsidiary or other affiliated entities, particularly if the penalized conduct was undertaken for or on behalf of the affiliate or with the knowledge of the affiliate, unless the exclusion is limited to the original entity.[110] It also may result in exclusion of entities controlled by the sanctioned individual, or entities transferred by the sanctioned individual to an immediate family member or household member to avoid sanction.[111]

The OIG must notify appropriate state or local licensing or certification agencies of exclusion decisions, request that an appropriate investigation be made and sanctions invoked, and request that the agency inform the OIG of any action it takes in response to

an assignment basis for Medicare beneficiaries who are also eligible for Medicaid); 42 U.S.C.A. § 1395w–4(g)(4) (submitting bills on improper claim forms); 42 U.S.C.A. § 1395w–4(b)(3) (billing for interpretation of ECGs performed or ordered as part of a physician visit).

105. 42 U.S.C.A. §§ 1320a–7(d), 1396a(a)(39). The OIG does not, however, have authority to exclude a provider from a state health care program, but rather must direct the state to exclude the provider. Inspector General v. Romero, [1996–1 Transfer Binder] Medicare &

Medicaid Guide (CCH) ¶ 44,034 (June 5, 1995).

106. 42 U.S.C.A. § 1320a–7(d)(3)(B).

107. 42 U.S.C.A. §§ 1320a–7(d)(3)(B)(ii), 1396a(p)(1).

108. 42 U.S.C.A. § 1396a(p)(2).

109. 42 C.F.R. § 1001.1901.

110. See 45 C.F.R. §§ 76.105, 76.325; Hope Foster, Defending a Nationally Orchestrated, Multi–Provider, Federal Health Task Force Investigation, in ABA, Health Care Fraud, 1997, at M–1, M–12 to M–14.

111. 42 U.S.C.A. § 1320a–7(b)(8).

the request.[112] The OIG also gives notice of the program exclusion to the public; entities where the person excluded is employed or serves in some capacity; state Medicaid Fraud Control Units; PROs; hospitals, skilled nursing facilities, home health agencies and health maintenance organizations; medical societies and other professional organizations; contractors, health care prepayment plans, private insurance companies and other affected agencies and organizations; State and Area Agencies on Aging; other Departmental operating divisions, Federal agencies, and other agencies or organizations, as appropriate; and the Attorney General in the case of a mandatory exclusion for a program related crime to which 21 U.S.C.A. § 824(a)(5) (involving controlled substances) applies.[113]

In addition to the statutory provisions permitting the OIG to exclude providers and practitioners entirely from program participation, various authorities exist elsewhere in the Medicare and Medicaid statutes for denying payment for particular services or for terminating providers from eligibility to receive Medicare or Medicaid payments. Thus, HHS may deny payment in whole or in part for the implantation or replacement of pacemaker devices or leads manufactured by a manufacturer determined to have violated provisions requiring the registering of pacemakers and the returning to the manufacturer and testing of removed pacemakers.[114] It may also deny payment after the twentieth day of hospitalization or after a time period prescribed by regulations for individuals where there has been a substantial failure of the hospital or nursing facility to comply with requirements for timely review of long-term-stay cases.[115] Denial of payment is further authorized for hospital admissions (including multiple admissions of the same patient) determined to be medically unnecessary and undertaken to circumvent DRG prospective payment.[116]

The Medicare statute also permits HHS to refuse to enter into or to renew, or to terminate provider agreements that fail to meet the requirements of provider status.[117] Legislation adopted in 1997 specifically permits HHS to refuse to enter into provider agreements or to enter into agreements with physicians or suppliers, or to refuse to renew or to terminate such agreements where the individual or entity has been convicted of a felony under federal or state law and HHS determines that contracting with the individual would be "detrimental to the best interests of the program or

---

112.   42 U.S.C.A. § 1320a–7(e); proposed rule 42 C.F.R. § 1001.2005, at 62 Fed. Reg. 47,182, 47,187, 47,194 (1997).

113.   42 C.F.R. § 1001.2006. Under proposed rules implementing HIPAA, notice will also be given to the newly established Adverse Action Data Bank.

62 Fed. Reg. at 47,182, 47,187, 47,194 (1997).

114.   42 U.S.C.A. § 1395y(h)(4).

115.   42 U.S.C.A. § 1395cc(d).

116.   42 U.S.C.A. § 1395ww(f)(2)(A).

117.   42 U.S.C.A. § 1395cc.

program beneficiaries."[118] Special provisions also exist authorizing termination of other entities, including hospital providers of extended care services,[119] risk-share contract organizations (HMOs & CMPs),[120] end stage renal disease facilities or providers, and end stage renal disease network administrative organizations.[121]

Amendments to the Medicare statute adopted as part of the HIPAA provide that, in lieu of termination of HMOs and CMPs, HHS may impose intermediate sanctions on the entity, consisting of civil money penalties of no more than $25,000 for each deficiency in the entity's compliance with its contract or with conditions imposed on HMOs and CMPs where the deficiency has a direct adverse effect on a recipient or is substantially likely to have such an effect.[122] Additional civil money penalties of $10,000 per week and suspension of new enrollments can be imposed if the deficiency persists.[123] The 1997 Balanced Budget Act authorizes states to use similar sanctions against Medicaid managed care entities.[124]

The Medicaid statute or regulations provide for termination of intermediate care facilities for the mentally retarded,[125] psychiatric facilities,[126] nursing facilities,[127] home and community care settings for functionally disabled elderly individuals,[128] and rural health clinics,[129] and of drug manufacturers and wholesalers who do not comply with drug rebate requirements.[130] In addition, exclusion of a provider may result in termination of the provider agreement.[131]

§ 5–3. Procedures for Imposing Exclusions

The exclusion statute provides persons excluded from participation with a right to notice, a hearing, and judicial review.[1] If the

118. 42 U.S.C.A. §§ 1395cc(b)(2)(D), 1395u(h)(8).

119. 42 U.S.C.A. § 1395tt(c).

120. 42 U.S.C.A. § 1395mm(i)(1). See also provisions for suspending payment to HMOs with risk contracts and for requiring them to suspend enrolling Medicare beneficiaries or marketing to them at 42 C.F.R. § 417.500.

121. 42 U.S.C.A. § 1395rr(c)(1)(A)(ii)(II), (c)(3).

122. 42 U.S.C.A. § 1395mm(i)(6)(C)(i).

123. 42 U.S.C.A. § 1395mm(i)(6)(C)(ii), (iii).

124. Pub.L. No. 105–32, § 4706, to be codified at 42 U.S.C.A. § 1396v(e).

125. 42 U.S.C.A. §§ 1396r–3(e)(2), 1396a(i)(1). This statute also provides for intermediate sanctions, including denial of payment prospectively for future admissions. HHS has concurrent "look behind" authority to decertify ICF–MRs, 42 U.S.C.A. § 1396i(b).

126. 42 U.S.C.A. § 1396a(y).

127. 42 U.S.C.A. § 1396r(h)(1). This provision also provides for intermediate sanctions, discussed in chapter 1. HHS also has concurrent "look behind" authority to cancel the certification of nursing facilities. 42 U.S.C.A. § 1396r(h)(6)(B).

128. 42 U.S.C.A. § 1396u. This statute also provides for intermediate sanctions.

129. 42 U.S.C.A. § 1396i(a); 42 C.F.R. § 405.2404(b).

130. 42 U.S.C.A. § 1396r–8(b)(4)(B).

131. 42 U.S.C.A. § 1395cc(b)(2)(C).

§ 5–3

1. 42 U.S.C.A. § 1320a–7(f).

proposed exclusion is for false claims, bribes and kickbacks, charges in excess of limiting charges, or billing for an unapproved assistant in a cataract surgery, the OIG sends a "Notice of Proposal to Exclude," from which the person threatened by exclusion can request a hearing within sixty days.[2] If no request is received, the exclusion goes into effect after sixty days. If a request is received, the exclusion does not go into effect until the conclusion of the hearing, unless the OIG determines that the health and safety of beneficiaries will be threatened unless it takes effect sooner.[3]

For other offenses, the OIG will initiate an exclusion action with a "Notice of Intent to Exclude," to which the individual or entity threatened with exclusion may respond within 35 days with documentary evidence and written argument.[4] If the threatened exclusion is for excessive care or care that does not meet professional standards, or for failure of an HMO or CMP to provide medically necessary services, a request to present evidence or oral argument in person is also permitted.[5]

If the OIG decides thereafter to proceed with the exclusion, it must send a written notice to the affected individual or entity, stating the basis for the exclusion; its length, and, where appropriate, factors considered in setting the length; its effect; the earliest date on which the OIG will consider a request for reinstatement; the requirements and procedures for reinstatement; and the appeal rights available to the excluded individual or entity.[6] The exclusion takes effect 20 days from the date of the notice.[7] A proposed rule would permit the OIG to amend the notice based on information

2. 42 C.F.R. § 1001.2003. The hearing request must set forth the specific issues or statements in the notice with which the individual or entity disagrees, the basis for that disagreement, the defenses which will be argued, any reasons why the proposed length of exclusion should be modified, and reasons why the health or safety of individuals receiving services under Medicare or any of the State health care programs does not warrant the exclusion going into effect prior to the completion of an ALJ proceeding. Id.

3. 42 U.S.C.A. § 1320a–7(f)(2); 42 C.F.R. § 2003.

4. 42 C.F.R. § 1001.2001(a). Notice and an opportunity to present evidence is not offered where the exclusion is based on failure to comply with a DRG circumvention corrective action plan, or default on a student loan. The OIG determined that a notice and an opportunity to present evidence requirement

was not appropriate for these authorities since violation of these provisions was determined by HCFA or the PHS and not the IG. Notice and an opportunity to present evidence is also not required for denial of access for an investigation, survey, or audit, since the denial of access rule permits the person denying access to give a reason for doing so at the time access is requested. 42 C.F.R. § 1001.2001(c).

5. 42 C.F.R. § 1001.2001(b). The OIG has proposed eliminating this opportunity for oral presentation as inefficient, as most of these cases simply involve review of medical records. 62 Fed. Reg. 47,182, 47,187 (1997).

6. 42 C.F.R. § 1001.2002(a), (c). This notice is not necessary where the exclusion is based on denial of access to records or facilities. 42 C.F.R. § 1001.2002(d).

7. 42 C.F.R. § 1001.2002(b).

that subsequently comes to its attention.[7.5]

The OIG has control over the date on which the exclusion takes effect, and the ALJ cannot change the date the exclusion begins as long as the OIG operates within the discretion permitted by the statute.[8] The OIG's control over the beginning of the date of the exclusion may be subject to one significant exception, however. In Richmond Paramedical Services, Inc. v. United States Department of Health & Human Services,[9] the provider threatened with exclusion was involved in bankruptcy proceedings. It argued to the court that if it could delay exclusion for sixty days, it could successfully complete a merger, creating a financially viable surviving entity. If it were excluded, it argued, it would have no choice but to go into Chapter 7 proceedings. The bankruptcy court delayed the exclusion long enough to permit the merger. On appeal, the district court rejected arguments that exhaustion was necessary, as the OIG's decision was not challenged on the merits, and held that equitable grounds in fact existed to support an injunction. The court noted that the OIG might have succeeded had it claimed immunity from an injunction based on its sovereign immunity, though this argument is weaker after the 1994 amendments to the Bankruptcy Act.[10] The case underscores one of the most significant limitations on the exclusion remedy. Entities that are excluded from Medicare and Medicaid often disappear immediately upon exclusion, resurfacing under another name and getting back on the Medicare roles.

An excluded individual or entity has a right to request a hearing within sixty days of service of the notice letter.[11] For exclusions based on authorities other than those mentioned in the first paragraph of this section,[12] the hearing is provided post-exclusion. The OIG has taken the position that due process does not require a pre-exclusion hearing.[13] The courts have consistently

7.5 Proposed rule 42 C.F.R. § 1001.2002(e), at 62 Fed. Reg. 47,182, 47,187, 47,194 (1997).

8. DeFries v. Inspector General, [1992 Transfer Binder] Medicare & Medicaid Guide (CCH) ¶ 40,453 (DAB Mar. 24, 1992); Chang v. Inspector General, [1991 Transfer Binder] Medicare and Medicaid Guide (CCH) ¶ 38,899 (DAB Oct. 3, 1990); Guberman v. Inspector General, Medicare & Medicaid Guide (CCH) ¶ (Nov. 30, 1990).

9. In re Richmond Paramedical Servs., Inc., No. Civ. A. 89–0081–R, 1989 WL 149144 at *2 (E.D.Va.1989).

10. It should be noted, however, that the pendency of bankruptcy proceedings does not automatically stay exclusion proceedings, Chappel v. Inspector General, [1991 Transfer Binder] Medicare & Medicaid Guide (CCH) ¶ 38,990 (DAB Nov. 8, 1990).

11. 42 C.F.R. § 1005.2(c). This time limit is strictly observed. See, e.g., Ramirez–Golzalez v. Inspector General, [1992 Transfer Binder] Medicare & Medicaid Guide (CCH) ¶ 40,125 (DAB Jan. 28, 1992) (denying hearing where request one day late).

12. I.e., for false claims, bribes and kickbacks, charges in excess of limiting charges, or billing for an unapproved assistant in a cataract surgery.

13. See, e.g., Ram v. Heckler, 792 F.2d 444, 447 (4th Cir.1986); Gellman v.

supported HHS in this position and refused to excuse exhaustion of post-exclusion administrative remedies before reviewing exclusion decisions,[14] though HHS may waive application of the requirement of exhaustion of all levels of administrative review once a claim has been presented.[15] Administrative delay in reviewing an appealed exclusion is also not, in itself, a violation of due process.[16]

Where the failure to provide a pre-exclusion hearing has been attacked as denying due process, courts have generally held that a liberty interest (if not a property interest) is implicated by an exclusion,[17] but have found that the process meets the demands of the due process clause when evaluated under the Mathews v. Eldridge calculus.[18] Other courts have refused to even reach the question of whether there was a colorable collateral constitutional claim in cases where administrative remedies had not yet been exhausted, holding that the plaintiff had failed to show that exhaustion would cause irreparable harm or to show that requiring exhaustion would not serve the cause of the exhaustion requirement.[19] In light of the Supreme Court's historic reluctance to

Sullivan, 758 F.Supp. 830, 833–34 (E.D.N.Y.1991).

14. See, e.g., Doe v. Bowen, 682 F.Supp. 637, 640–41 (D.Mass.1987). See also, Hilst v. Bowen, 874 F.2d 725, 726–27 (10th Cir.1989) (refusing to permit Bivens action challenging constitutionality of suspension of Medicare payments where administrative remedy was available).

15. Mathews v. Eldridge, 424 U.S. 319, 328–31, 96 S.Ct. 893, 899–900, 47 L.Ed.2d 18 (1976).

16. Hall v. Bowen, 830 F.2d 906 (8th Cir.1987).

17. See Erickson v. United States Dep't of Health & Human Servs., 67 F.3d 858, 862–63 (9th Cir.1995) (liberty interest in loss of provider status, no property interest in continued Medicare participation where mandatory exclusion imposed based on conviction still on appeal); but see Doe v. Bowen, 682 F. Supp. at 641–43 (finding both liberty and property interest); Gellman v. Sullivan, 758 F. Supp. at 833–34 (no property interest in continued participation in Medicare, liberty issue not presented). See also, Kahn v. Inspector General, 848 F.Supp. 432, 438 (S.D.N.Y.1994) (holding that exclusion cannot violate the Takings Clause because there is no property right in continued participation in Medicare).

18. See Erickson v. United States Dep't of Health & Human Servs., 67 F.3d at 863; Ram v. Heckler, 792 F.2d at 447; Doe v. Bowen, 682 F. Supp. at 642–43. The federal appellate courts have also consistently upheld challenges to pre-hearing exclusions under 42 U.S.C.A. § 1320c–5 (based on Peer Review Organization determinations) against due process challenges. Anderson v. Sullivan, 959 F.2d 690, 693 (8th Cir.1992); Thorbus v. Bowen, 848 F.2d 901, 903–04 (8th Cir.1988); Doyle v. Secretary of Health & Human Servs., 848 F.2d 296, 301–02 (1st Cir.1988); Cassim v. Bowen , 824 F.2d 791, 798 (9th Cir.1987); Varandani v. Bowen, 824 F.2d 307, 310–11 (4th Cir.1987); Koerpel v. Heckler, 797 F.2d 858, 863 (10th Cir. 1986); Ritter v. Cohen, 797 F.2d 119, 123 (3d Cir.1986).

19. Barrett v. Dep't of Health & Human Servs., 14 F.3d 26, 27 (8th Cir. 1994). See also Doe v. Bowen, 682 F. Supp. at 644–46 (plaintiff had not suffered irreparable harm as services provided during the exclusion could be paid for later if it was not upheld); Gross v. Dep't of Health & Human Servs., No. 89–72542, 1989 WL 223038 at *3–4 (E.D.Mich.1989) (waiver of the exhaustion requirement would defeat its purpose of allowing the agency an opportunity correct any errors it may have made).

excuse exhaustion in the Medicare program,[20] it is likely that the Court would accept the position of the lower courts were this issue to reach it.

The request for a hearing must contain a statement as to the specific issues or findings of fact and conclusions of law in the notice letter with which the petitioner or respondent disagrees, and the basis for his or her contention that the specific issues or findings and conclusions are incorrect.[21] All parties to the hearing may be accompanied, represented and advised by an attorney; carry out permitted discovery of documents; present evidence relevant to the issues at the hearing; submit and cross-examine witnesses; present oral arguments at the hearing as permitted by the ALJ; and submit written briefs and proposed findings of fact and conclusions of law after the hearing.[22]

The ALJ has authority to conduct the hearing, including authority to subpoena witnesses or documents, supervise discovery, and decide cases by summary judgment where there is no dispute of material fact.[23] The ALJ is required to hold at least one prehearing conference to arrange for the expeditious disposition of the case, including arranging for, where possible, stipulations, simplification of issues, or settlement.[24] Though the ALJ cannot compel settlement, the ALJ may encourage the parties to discuss settlement, and may, if the parties agree, refer the parties to the Departmental Appeals Board alternative dispute resolution staff.[25] Discovery is limited to requests for production of documents, which do not include investigative material that will not be presented at the hearing.[26] The parties may file a motion for a protective order within ten days of a request for the production of documents, and are not required to file a motion for a protective order as a condition precedent for withholding documents under a claim of privilege.[27] Witness lists, prior statements of witnesses, and hearing exhibits must be exchanged at least fifteen days before the hearing.[28] Requests for subpoenas must be submitted thirty days before the hearing.[29] The ALJ may summarily dispose of cases in which

20. See, e.g., Heckler v. Ringer, 466 U.S. 602, 614, 104 S.Ct. 2013, 2021, 80 L.Ed.2d 622 (1984); Weinberger v. Salfi, 422 U.S. 749, 757–59, 95 S.Ct. 2457, 2462–63, 45 L.Ed.2d 522 (1975).

21. 42 C.F.R. § 1005.2(d).

22. 42 C.F.R. § 1005.3(a).

23. 42 C.F.R. § 1005.4(b).

24. 42 C.F.R. § 1005.6.

25. See Steven Kessel, Administrative Hearings in Civil Remedies—Enforcement Cases Before the United States Department of Health and Human Services, in American Bar Association, Health Care Fraud, 1996, F–31, F–35. Judge Kessel is one of the ALJs who hear exclusion cases, and this article provides an excellent overview of practice in these cases.

26. 42 C.F.R. § 1005.7(c).

27. 42 C.F.R. § 1005.7(e)(1).

28. 42 C.F.R. § 1005.8. Unless extraordinary circumstances are present, witnesses or documents not listed cannot thereafter be presented in a party's case in chief. Id.

29. 42 C.F.R. § 1005.9(d).

there is no genuine issue of material fact and frequently does so, particularly where mandatory exclusions are at issue.[30]

The ALJ is not permitted to

— find federal statutes or regulations or Secretarial delegations of authority to be invalid;

— enter an order in the nature of a directed verdict;

— compel settlement negotiations;

— enjoin any act of the Secretary;

— review the exercise of discretion by the OIG to exclude an individual or entity in imposing permissive exclusions or to determine the scope or effect of the exclusion; or

— to reduce a period of exclusion to zero in any case where the ALJ finds that an individual or entity committed an act described in the provisions of the law authorizing permissive exclusions.[31]

The only issues that can be raised at the ALJ hearing are whether a basis for the exclusion exists and—except where a mandatory five year exclusion has been imposed—whether the length of the exclusion is unreasonable.[32] ALJs review the length of exclusion quite freely, reducing the length when they believe that the equities favor the provider.[33] In making the determination to reduce an exclusion period, the ALJ is not bound by the OIG's prior

---

30. See, e.g., Brown v. Inspector General, [1991 Transfer Binder] Medicare & Medicaid Guide (CCH) ¶ 38,958 (DAB Nov. 15, 1990).

31. 42 C.F.R. § 1005.4(c). Jain v. Inspector General, [1993 Transfer Binder] Medicare & Medicaid Guide (CCH) ¶ 41,- 601 (DAB Mar. 23, 1993); Fishman v. Inspector General, [1991 Transfer Binder] Medicare & Medicaid Guide (CCH) ¶ 38,842 (DAB Sept. 19, 1990) (no authority to find statute unconstitutional); Reife v. Inspector General, [1993 Transfer Binder] Medicare & Medicaid Guide (CCH) ¶ 41,396 (DAB Apr. 28, 1989) (no authority to review delegation of authority to OIG or Secretary's obligation to promulgate rules); Willig v. Inspector General, [1992 Transfer Binder] Medicare & Medicaid Guide (CCH) ¶ 40,357 (DAB Apr. 30, 1992) (no authority to review reasonableness of IG's decision to impose discretionary exclusion). But see Baratta v. Inspector General, [1990 Transfer Binder] Medicare & Medicaid Guide (CCH) ¶ 38,600 (DAB June 29,

1990) (questioning whether the ALJ does have authority, despite these regulations, to review the IG's exercise of discretion in imposing permissive exclusions).

32. 42 C.F.R. § 1001.2007(a)(1).

33. See, e.g., Barranco v. Inspector General, [1992 Transfer Binder] Medicare & Medicaid Guide (CCH) ¶ 40,246 (DAB Mar. 30, 1992); Bilang v. Inspector General, [1992 Transfer Binder] Medicare & Medicaid Guide (CCH) ¶ 40,097 (DAB Jan. 27, 1992); Kranz v. Inspector General, [1992 Transfer Binder] Medicare & Medicaid Guide (CCH) ¶ 40,096 (DAB Dec. 19, 1991); Craven v. Inspector General, [1992 Transfer Binder] Medicare & Medicaid Guide (CCH) ¶ 39,- 621 (DAB July 17, 1991); Hughey v. Inspector General, [1991 Transfer Binder] Medicare & Medicaid (CCH) ¶ 39,088 (DAB Jan. 25, 1991); Haney v. Inspector General, [1990 Transfer Binder] Medicare & Medicaid Guide (CCH) ¶ 38,571 (DAB June 7, 1990).

exclusion decision.[34] Prior to 1993, a number of ALJ decisions had also held that the ALJs were not bound by the regulations that govern the OIG's exercise of discretion in setting the period of exclusion.[35] On January 22, 1993, however, HHS modified these regulations to make clear that they also govern the ALJs.[36]

When the exclusion is derivative, the underlying action may not be attacked procedurally or substantively.[37] The standard of proof is preponderance of the evidence,[38] in keeping with standard administrative practice. The regulations authorize the ALJ to allocate the burden of proof as is deemed appropriate.[39] In fact, the ALJs always allocate the burden of proving the grounds for exclusion to the OIG.[40] Proposed regulations that would have shifted to the excluded party the burden of negating liability were not implemented.

The hearing is recorded and transcribed and transcripts are available after the hearing.[41] Administrative rules of evidence are followed. The parties may offer expert testimony, but experts must explain the meaning of technical terms that they use, since the ALJ may not look beyond the record to find the meaning of technical language.[42] The parties may file (or the ALJ require) post-hearing briefs.[43] The ALJ must issue an initial decision, including findings of fact and conclusions of law, based on the record.[44] The decision may be appealed within thirty days to the Departmental Appeals Board (DAB), which reviews the record and briefs submitted to it, and may decline to review the case, or may affirm, increase, reduce, reverse or remand any penalty, assessment or exclusion determined by the ALJ.[45] The decision becomes final if it is not appealed or if a request is not made for reconsideration within 30 days.[46] The

34. Davids v. Inspector General, [1992 Transfer Binder] Medicare & Medicaid Guide (CCH) ¶ 40,095 (DAB Dec. 11, 1991) (ALJ applies a reasonableness standard in reviewing the length of the period of exclusion, and is not bound by IG's exercise of discretion).

35. Willig v. Inspector General, Medicare & Medicaid Guide (CCH) ¶ 40,-357; Herlich v. Inspector General, [1992 Transfer Binder] Medicare & Medicaid Guide (CCH) ¶ 40,360 (DAB May 11, 1992). In any event, the regulations do not apply retroactively where they would limit the rights of a provider, Harrison v. Inspector General, [1993 Transfer Binder] Medicare & Medicaid Guide (CCH) ¶ 40,996 (DAB Oct. 16, 1992); Barranco v. Inspector General, Medicare & Medicaid Guide (CCH) ¶ 40,-246.

36. 42 C.F.R. § 1001.1(b), published at 53 Fed. Reg. 5618. See Walley v. Inspector General, [1993 Transfer Binder] Medicare & Medicaid Guide (CCH) ¶ 41,643 (DAB Mar. 18, 1993).

37. 42 C.F.R. 1001. Iturralde v. Inspector General, [1993 Transfer Binder] Medicare & Medicaid Guide (CCH) ¶ 41,-309 (DAB Dec. 9, 1992).

38. 42 C.F.R. § 1001.2007(c).

39. 42 C.F.R. § 1005.15(c).

40. Kessel, supra note 25 at F–38.

41. 42 C.F.R. § 1005.18(a).

42. Kessel, supra note 25 at F.39.

43. 42 C.F.R. § 1005.19.

44. 42 C.F.R. § 1005.20(a).

45. 42 C.F.R. § 1005.21.

46. Harmon v. Inspector General [1996—2 Transfer Binder] Medicare & Medicaid Guide (CCH) ¶ 44,777 (CRD Sept. 3, 1996).

standard of review on a disputed issue of fact before the DAB is whether the initial decision is supported by substantial evidence on the whole record.[47] The standard of review on a disputed issue of law is whether the initial decision is erroneous.[48] An excluded individual who succeeds in overturning the OIG's judgment in an administrative hearing may be entitled to attorney's fees under the Equal Access to Justice Act.[49]

An action for judicial review must be filed within sixty days of the DAB decision.[50] The federal courts must uphold HHS's final decision if it is supported by substantial evidence.[51] The courts will defer to the ALJ's resolution of credibility issues.[52] As was noted earlier, judicial review of exclusion is only available if and after administrative remedies are exhausted.[53] Further, one district court has held that an exclusion was moot and unreviewable where the exclusion was based on a state licensure proceeding and the excluded individual was subsequently reinstated.[54] The court believed that individual was unlikely to be excluded again and that the exclusion did not impose any stigma on the doctor beyond that resulting from the state proceeding.

An excluded entity or individual can request reinstatement only after the minimum period of exclusion specified in the exclusion notice has ended.[55] A provider continues to be excluded until officially reinstated by the OIG. Procurement of a provider number prior to reinstatement has no effect on the continuation of the exclusion.[55.5] Reinstatement is not guaranteed, even though the OIG has set a fixed exclusion period. In determining whether reinstatement should be granted, the OIG must determine that the period of exclusion has expired; that there are reasonable assurances that the types of actions that formed the basis for the original exclusion have not recurred and will not recur; and that there is no

47. Matesic v. Inspector General, [1992 Transfer Binder] Medicare & Medicaid Guide (CCH) ¶ 40,296 (DAB Apr. 22, 1992).

48. 42 C.F.R. § 1005.21(h).

49. Godreau v. Inspector General, [1993 Transfer Binder] Medicare & Medicaid Guide (CCH) ¶ 40,825 (DAB Feb. 14, 1992).

50. 42 C.F.R. § 1005.21(k).

51. 42 U.S.C.A. §§ 405(g), 1320a–7(f)(1); Bonebrake v. United States, No. 94–6296, 1995 WL 321930 at *1 (10th Cir.1995); Travers v. Shalala, 20 F.3d 993, 995 (9th Cir.1994); Kahn v. Inspector General, 848 F.Supp. 432, 436 (S.D.N.Y.1994).

52. Bonebrake, 1995 WL 321930 at *2.

53. 42 C.F.R. § 1003.127; Gellman v. Sullivan, 758 F.Supp. 830, 832–33 (E.D.N.Y.1991).

54. Friedman v. Shalala, 46 F.3d 115, 115–18 (1st Cir.1995).

55. 42 U.S.C.A. § 1320a–7(g)(1); 42 C.F.R. § 1001.3001(a). Exceptions are made for exclusions based on license revocation, suspension from other state or federal health care programs, ownership or control by an excluded individual, or default on student loans, where actions by other entities may justify reinstatement.

55.5 See proposed rules clarifying this policy at 62 Fed. Reg. 47,182, 47,186–87, 47,193–95 (1997).

additional statutory basis for continuation of the exclusion.[56] Though a person denied reinstatement may request reconsideration within thirty days, a determination not to grant reinstatement is otherwise nonreviewable.[57] If reinstatement is granted, the OIG must notify the relevant state Medicaid agency (which must automatically reinstate the entity or individual unless a longer exclusion was imposed by the state or state law precludes reinstatement), and, to the extent possible, the other agencies and persons to whom notice of the exclusion was sent.[58]

§ 5–4. Civil Money Penalty Authorities

Provisions authorizing civil money penalties and assessments for false claims and other improper billing practices have been discussed in chapter 2; for bribes and kickbacks in chapter 3, and for prohibited self-referrals in chapter 4. The Medicare and Medicaid statutes create a host of other miscellaneous civil money penalty authorities, which are discussed here.[1]

First, the basic federal health care program civil money penalty statute, 42 U.S.C.A. § 1320a–7a, has several provisions in addition to its false claims civil penalty provisions discussed in chapter 2 and its bribe and kickback provisions discussed in chapter 3. First, it authorizes civil money penalties of up to $15,000 for giving any person information that the person giving the information knows or should know to be false or misleading when the information could reasonably be expected to influence a decision as to when to discharge the person who was given the information or another person from the hospital.[2] Second, it provides civil penalties against persons that contract (by employment or otherwise) with an individual or entity that the person knows or should know was excluded from program participation.[3]

Third, another provision, adopted in 1986, authorizes civil money penalties of up to $2000 per patient against hospitals or rural primary care hospitals that knowingly make a payment, directly or indirectly, to a physician to reduce or limit services to a Medicare or Medicaid patient under the care of the physician or against physicians who accept such payments.[4] This provision addresses the reverse situation from that addressed by the antikick-

---

56. 42 U.S.C.A. § 1320a–7(g)(2); 42 C.F.R. § 1001.3002.

57. 42 C.F.R. § 1001.3002(e).

58. 42 U.S.C.A. § 1320a–7(g)(3); 42 C.F.R. § 1001.3003(b).

§ 5–4

1. See 42 C.F.R. § 1003.102 for a further partial listing of Medicare and Medicaid civil penalty authorities.

2. 42 U.S.C.A. § 1320a–7a(a)(3).

3. 42 U.S.C.A. § 1320a–7a(a)(6).

4. 42 U.S.C.A. § 1320a–7a(b)(1), (2).

back and self-referral provisions discussed in chapters 3 and 4 above. The antikickback law is concerned with the incentives for overutilization presented by fee-for-service reimbursement, where various compensation or ownership arrangements can generate additional income for physicians who order additional tests and procedures. Payment on a DRG-prospective payment basis, however, creates incentives for underservice: the faster a patient is discharged and the fewer tests and procedures that are ordered for the patient while hospitalized, the better the financial situation of the hospital will be. The decision to discharge a patient or to order a test or procedure is generally the decision of a physician, not of the hospital. The hospital may be able to influence physician behavior, however, through offering incentives for underservice. This provision makes such incentives illegal, thus protecting patients from underservice.

Until 1990 this provision also extended to HMOs and CMPs with risk contacts, which face similar incentives for underservice. The HMO situation was more difficult, however, since managed care is based on the notion of controlling utilization and financial relationships between HMOs and their physicians are much more complex. For this reason, Congress first delayed implementation of this provision, and then repealed it. In its place Congress adopted provisions prohibiting HMOs and CMPs from making specific payments to induce physicians to withhold or limit services from particular enrollees and requiring HMOs and CMPs to provide "adequate and appropriate" stop-loss insurance for physicians or physician groups who are at "significant" financial risk for services they provide.[5] These provisions are discussed in chapter 1.

Other civil money penalty provisions addressing a wide variety of concerns relating to managed care are found throughout the Medicare and Medicaid statutes. HMOs and CMPs with Medicare risk-sharing contracts are liable for civil money penalties for substantially failing to provide medically necessary items or services to a beneficiary where the failure adversely affects the beneficiary; imposing premiums in excess of those permitted; expelling or refusing to reenroll a beneficiary in violation of the Medicare law; engaging in practices that would reasonably be expected to have the effect of denying or discouraging enrollment by eligible beneficiaries whose medical condition or history indicates a need for substantial medical services; misrepresenting or falsifying information to HHS or to other individuals or entities; failing to comply with prompt payment requirements or with membership requirements;

5. 42 U.S.C.A. § 1395mm(i)(8).

or employing or contracting with an individual or entity excluded from Medicare.[6]

The statute provides for penalties of up to $25,000 per violation, with $100,000 penalties for each determination of misrepresentation of information to HHS or of practices to discourage enrollment of high-risk individuals (plus, for each individual denied or discouraged, $15,000).[7] HMOs or CMPs that overcharge beneficiaries may also be assessed an amount equal to twice the excess amount charged, and the excess amount shall be deducted from the penalty and returned to the beneficiary.[8] Identical provisions also apply to Medicaid HMOs.[9]

Civil money penalties may be imposed against insurers that violate Medicare supplement insurance requirements.[10] Civil money penalties may be also imposed by the OIG upon the recommendation of Medicare Peer Review Organizations for utilization or quality violations.[11] Finally, fines may be imposed for violation of the Emergency Medical Treatment and Active Labor Act.[12] Under assorted other provisions of the Medicare and Medicaid statutes, HHS may assess civil penalties of:

> 1) up to $5000 against employers or other sponsors of group health plans that would be primary payers under the Medicare as Secondary Payor provisions if they offer individuals eligible for group health care coverage incentives not to enroll in the plan when those incentives are not available to all persons eligible to enroll;[13]

> 2) up to $1000 per incident against employers who willfully and repeatedly fail to provide information regarding the insured status of employees or their dependents for determination of Medicare's secondary payer status;[14]

> 3) up to $1000 per assessment for willfully and knowingly certifying a material and false statement in an assessment of a

---

6. 42 U.S.C.A. § 1395mm(i)(6)(A); 42 C.F.R. § 417.500. See, discussing the application of these provisions in some detail, 59 Fed. Reg. 36,072–36,083 (1994). Similar provisions apply under the 1997 Balanced Budget Act to Medicare+Choice managed care organizations. Pub. L. No. 105–32, § 4001, new Social Security Act § 1857(g), and for Medicaid managed care organizations, § 4707(e), to be codified at 42 U.S.C.A. § 1396v(e).

7. 42 U.S.C.A. § 1395mm(i)(6)(B); 42 C.F.R. § 1003.103(f). Similar penalties apply under the 1997 Balanced Budget Act, Pub. L. No. 105–32, § 4001, new Social Security Act § 1857(g), to

Medicare+Choice managed care organizations; and under § 4707(e), to be codified at 42 U.S.C.A. § 1396v(e) for Medicaid managed care plans.

8. Id.

9. 42 U.S.C.A. § 1396b(m)(5)(A), (B); 42 C.F.R. § 434.67.

10. 42 U.S.C.A. § 1395ss(s)(3) (Medicare Gap policy sales practices).

11. 42 U.S.C.A. § 1320c–5(b)(3).

12. 42 U.S.C.A. § 1395dd(d)(1). See Barry Furrow et al., 1 Health Law §§ 12–2—12–12 (1995).

13. 42 U.S.C.A. § 1395y(b)(3).

14. 42 U.S.C.A. § 1395y(b)(5)(C)(ii).

nursing facility resident's functional capacity and up to $5000 for willfully and knowingly causing another to do so;[15]

4) up to $2000 for giving advance notice of a state or federal survey to a nursing facility or community care setting for functionally disabled elderly individuals;[16]

5) up to $5000 for use in an advertisement or other communication or production (or $25,000 for use in a broadcast or telecast) the words "Department of Health and Human Services", "Health and Human Services", "Medicaid", "Medicare", "Health Care Financing Administration", "DHHS", "HHS", or similar words or the symbols or emblems of the Department or HCFA, including the Medicare card, in a manner that could be reasonably interpreted or construed as conveying a relationship with the Department or HCFA;[17]

6) up to $10,000 per payment for failure of an insurer or self-insured entity to report a payment made in settlement or in satisfaction of judgment of a malpractice case under the Health Care Quality Improvement Act;[18]

7) up to $10,000 per violation for improper disclosure of information reported under the Health Care Quality Improvement Act;[19]

8) the greater of $5000 or three times the amount of payments made for home health services where a physician executes a certificate that an individual needs home health services where the physician knows that the eligibility requirements for home health services have not been met;[20]

9) $100 for each failure to furnish an itemized statement when requested in writing by a beneficiary to do so with respect to a furnished item or service.[21]

---

15. 42 U.S.C.A. §§ 1395i–3(b)(3)(B)(ii), 1396r(b)(3)(B)(ii).

16. 42 U.S.C.A. §§ 1395i–3(g)(2), 1396r(g)(2).

17. 42 U.S.C.A. § 1320b–10; 42 C.F.R. § 1003.102(b)(7). State agencies are exempt from this prohibition. In group mailings, each letter constitutes a separate violation. The use of disclaimers of affiliation is not a mitigating factor in determining penalties. See, on the amount of penalties imposed under this provision, 42 C.F.R. § 1003.103(d), and, regarding factors to consider in imposing a penalty under this section, 42

C.F.R. § 1003.106(a)(3). This provision was amended in the Social Security Improvements Act of 1994, which separated out the SSA from HHS. Prior to that act, this provision also permitted penalties for the use of references to "Social Security" in advertising. Those prohibitions are now enforced by the Social Security IG.

18. 42 U.S.C.A. § 11131(c); 42 C.F.R. §§ 1003.102(b)(5), .106(a)(2).

19. 42 U.S.C.A. § 11137(b)(2); 42 C.F.R. §§ 1003.102(b)(6), .106(a)(2).

20. 42 U.S.C.A. § 1320a–7a(b)(3).

21. Pub.L. No. 105–32, § 4311(b).

Finally, 42 U.S.C.A. § 1320a–7a(a) also permits exclusion of providers in civil money penalty proceedings, as noted above.[22] This provision gives HHS the flexibility to either exclude a provider under 42 U.S.C.A. § 1320a–7a with civil penalties or under 42 U.S.C.A. § 1320a–7 without civil penalties in a number of situations where either provision might apply.[23]

Where more than one person is held liable for presenting false claims, civil money penalties may be imposed against any one such person or against all jointly and severally, but the total collected may not exceed the amount that could be assessed if only one person were liable.[24] Where more than one person is held liable for improper presentation of requests for payment or for giving false or misleading information, each may be held liable for the prescribed penalty.[25] Where more than one person is held liable for offenses related to National Practitioner Data Bank requirements, each may be held liable for the penalty.[26] Each responsible physician may also be separately penalized for violations of the Emergency Medical Treatment and Active Labor Act.[27] Under implementing regulations, principals are liable for penalties and assessments for the acts of their agents acting within the scope of their agency, though there is authority antedating the regulations holding that employers cannot be subjected to punitive penalties where their liability is solely vicarious.[28]

The civil money authorities generally grant the OIG considerable discretion in determining the proper amount of a civil money penalty or assessment to impose. ALJs also exercise considerable discretion in reviewing assessments.[29] The amount of civil penalties is determined by statute and is not limited to damages in fact provable by the government.[30] Factors considered in imposing civil money penalties for false claims were discussed above. The regulations also list factors considered in imposing other penalties and assessments.[31] Generally, where there are substantial aggravating factors the amount should be set sufficiently close to the maximum amount to reflect this fact, and where there are substantial mitigating factors the penalty or assessment must be correspondingly reduced.[32] Absent extraordinary mitigating factors, however, the

22. See also 42 C.F.R. §§ 1003.105, .107.

23. See S. Rep. No. 109, 100th Cong., 1st Sess. 16 (1987), reprinted in 1987 U.S.C.C.A.N. 682, 696–97.

24. 42 C.F.R. § 1003.102(d)(1).

25. 42 C.F.R. § 1003.102(d)(2).

26. 42 C.F.R. § 1003.102(d)(3).

27. 42 C.F.R. § 1003.102(d)(4).

28. Inspector General v. Silver, [1993 Transfer Binder] Medicare & Medicaid Guide (CCH) ¶ 40,977 (DAB Mar. 8, 1988).

29. See, e.g., Inspector General v. Anesthesiologists Affiliated, [1990 Transfer Binder] Medicare & Medicaid Guide (CCH) ¶ 38,554 (DAB Feb. 5, 1990).

30. Chapman v. United States Dep't of Health & Human Servs., 821 F.2d 523, 528 (10th Cir.1987).

31. 42 C.F.R. § 1003.106.

32. 42 C.F.R. § 1003.106(c)(1), (2). See, e.g., Inspector General v. Portoghese, [1993 Transfer Binder] Medicare & Medicaid Guide (CCH) ¶ 40,786

amount should never be less than twice the amount of damages and costs incurred by the United States or any state, including costs attributable to the investigation, prosecution and administrative review of the case.[33] Doubling this amount assures that less tangible costs, such as the diversion of scarce resources from and the erosion of public confidence in the integrity of federal and state health care programs, are also considered.[34]

Imposition of penalties substantially in excess of this amount, however, may result in a punitive sanction, raising constitutional problems under United States v. Halper,[35] which recognizes that double jeopardy problems arise if a punitive sanction is applied in addition to a criminal conviction. An ALJ imposing a civil sanction, therefore, must independently consider whether the sanction imposed results in an unconstitutional punitive sanction.[36] Civil penalties may also not be imposed where they would contravene a plea bargain entered into by the defendant in a federal criminal case that waives or limits collection of civil penalties.[37]

§ 5–5. Procedures for Imposing Civil Money Penalties and Assessments

Civil money penalty actions for Medicare false claims are initiated by the Office of Inspector General. Civil money penalties with respect to claims paid by other federal programs are brought by the relevant department and its inspector general.[1] Under a memorandum of understanding between the Office of Inspector General and the Department of Justice, the OIG must normally refer the case to the United States Attorney with jurisdiction over the case or to the Attorney General, which must complete or

(DAB Aug. 12, 1992); Inspector General v. Schoettle, [1986 Transfer Binder] Medicare & Medicaid Guide (CCH) ¶ 35,-393 (DAB Feb. 26, 1986); Matter of George G. Griffon, [1986 Transfer Binder] Medicare & Medicaid Guide (CCH) ¶ 34,893 (DAB Aug. 14, 1985) (assessing maximum amount due to aggravating circumstances); Inspector General v. Hobbs, [1990 Transfer Binder] Medicare & Medicaid Guide (CCH) ¶ 38,294 (DAB Dec. 5, 1989); Inspector General v. Livingston, [1993 Transfer Binder] Medicare & Medicaid Guide (CCH) ¶ 41,629 (DAB Apr. 19, 1993) (reducing penalties because of mitigating circumstances).

33. 42 C.F.R. § 1003.106(c)(3), (d)(2).

34. See, Chapman v. Dep't of Health & Human Servs., 821 F.2d at 528; Mayers v. United States, Dep't of Health & Human Servs., 806 F.2d 995, 999 (11th Cir.1986).

35. United States v. Halper, 490 U.S. 435, 446, 448–49, 109 S.Ct. 1892, 1900–02, 104 L.Ed.2d 487 (1989).

36. 42 C.F.R. § 1003.106(e)(1). See, e.g., Matter of Mayers & Mayers, [1985 Transfer Binder] Medicare & Medicaid Guide (CCH) ¶ 34,892 (DAB Aug. 11, 1985).

37. Stern v. Shalala, 14 F.3d 148, 149–50 (2d Cir.1994).

§ 5–5

1. 42 U.S.C.A. § 1320a–7(m)(1). Where more than one agency or department has been defrauded, the agency or department which was primarily defrauded can bring the action, but should give notice to other agencies and departments that have also suffered the fraud. 42 U.S.C.A. § 1320–7(m)(2).

decline prosecution before the OIG can proceed with a civil money penalty case.[2]

To initiate a civil money penalty action, the OIG sends a notice of the proposed penalty or assessment in a manner authorized by Rule 4 of the Federal Rules of Civil Procedure.[3] The notice must include reference to the statutory basis for the penalty or assessment; a description of the claims, requests for payment, or incidents with respect to which the penalty, assessment or exclusion are proposed;[4] the reason why such claims, requests for payment or incidents subject the respondent to a penalty or assessment; the amount of the proposed penalty or assessment; any mitigating or aggravating circumstances that were considered when determining the amount of the proposed penalty or assessment; and instructions for responding to the notice.[5] Such an action must be initiated within six years of the alleged claim, request for payment, or incident.[6] The person or entity must request a hearing within sixty days of the penalty or assessment is imposed without right of appeal.[7] If the respondent fails to appear for the hearing, the full amount proposed by the OIG can be assessed, essentially by default.[8]

The procedures followed in a civil money penalty or assessment appeal are basically the same as those followed in an exclusion appeal, discussed above. A final determination in another proceeding concerning a false claim or other criminal offense involving the same party and the same transactions that are at issue in the civil penalty proceeding may be relied on in the civil penalty proceeding

---

2. This memorandum of understanding was entered into pursuant to 42 U.S.C.A. § 1320a–7a(c)(1) and is subject to certain exceptions.

3. 42 C.F.R. § 1003.109(a).

4. In cases where the Inspector General is relying upon statistical sampling in accordance with 42 C.F.R. § 1003.133, the notice must describe those claims and requests for payment comprising the sample upon which the Inspector General is relying and must also briefly describe the statistical sampling technique utilized.

5. 42 C.F.R. § 1003.109(a).

6. 42 U.S.C.A. § 1320a–7a(c)(1). Prior to the 1987 amendments the limit was five years. See Bernstein v. Sullivan, 914 F.2d 1395, 1399 (10th Cir.1990) (upholding retroactive application of six year statute). The statute begins to run at the time the claim is received for processing by the agency responsible for payment. Inspector General v. Frazier, [1990 Transfer Binder] Medicare & Medicaid Guide (CCH) ¶ 38,559 (DAB May 31, 1990). An action is initiated, for purposes of determining whether the limitations period has been exceeded, when the OIG sends a notice of proposed sanctions. Inspector General v. Petrus, [1992 Transfer Binder] Medicare & Medicaid Guide (CCH) ¶ 39,600 (DAB July 5, 1991).

7. 42 U.S.C.A. § 1320a–7a(g); 42 C.F.R. § 1003.109(a)(6)(ii).

8. Inspector General v. Anthony, [1993 Transfer Binder] Medicare & Medicaid Guide (CCH) ¶ 41,323 (DAB Nov. 15, 1988). If the provider can show, however, that she never received the OIG's notice, she may be able to obtain a hearing subsequently. Tomasevic v. Inspector General, [1989 Transfer Binder] Medicare & Medicaid Guide (CCH) ¶ 37,609 (DAB Jan. 17, 1989).

under the doctrine of collateral estoppel, if the party had an opportunity to be heard at the earlier proceeding.[9]

Administrative proceedings reviewing civil penalties are governed by the same rules as govern exclusion proceedings, and are virtually identical with two important exceptions. First, a hearing is available for civil money penalty cases before imposition of the sanction, in contrast to some exclusion cases, where only a post-sanction hearing may be available.[10] Second, in civil money penalty cases, the OIG clearly bears the burden of going forward and of persuasion on all issues except for affirmative defenses and mitigating circumstances.[11] Under appropriate circumstances, the OIG may need to present expert testimony to establish liability.[12]

An appeal of a civil money penalty or assessment can be taken within sixty days by an affected party to the Court of Appeals for the circuit in which the person resides or in which the claim was presented.[13] No objection can be considered in that proceeding that was not considered in the administrative proceedings, except where the failure to raise the issue is excused by extraordinary circumstances.[14] Review of factual issues is on a substantial evidence basis.[15] Where it is shown that new material factual evidence is available and that there were reasonable grounds for failing to produce the evidence at the administrative hearing, the court may remand for consideration at the administrative level.[16]

Notice of a final imposition of civil penalties or assessments must be given to the appropriate state or local medical or professional association; the appropriate Peer Review Organization; as appropriate, the state agency responsible for the administration of state health care programs; the appropriate Medicare carrier or intermediary; the appropriate state or local licensing agency or organization (including the Medicare and Medicaid state survey agencies); and the long-term care ombudsman.[17]

9. 42 U.S.C.A. § 1320a–7a(c)(3); 42 C.F.R. § 1003.114.

10. Further imposition of civil penalties is stayed pending review by the Departmental Appeals Board, and may be stayed further by the ALJ with the posting of bond pending judicial review. 42 C.F.R. § 1005.22.

11. 42 C.F.R. 1005.15. Inspector General v. Anesthesiologists Affiliated, [1990 Transfer Binder] Medicare & Medicaid Guide (CCH) ¶ 38,554 (DAB Feb. 5, 1990). The OIG need only prove its case by the preponderance of the evidence, not beyond a reasonable doubt. Scott v. Bowen, 845 F.2d 856, 856–57 (9th Cir.1988).

12. Inspector General v. Livingston, [1993 Transfer Binder] Medicare & Medicaid Guide (CCH) ¶ 41,630 (DAB July 15, 1993).

13. 42 U.S.C.A. § 1320a–7a(e).

14. Id.

15. Id. See Frazier v. Secretary, Dep't of Health & Human Servs., No. 90–4121, 1991 WL 148735 at *3–4 (6th Cir.1991) (applying substantial evidence review to uphold ALJ decision in CMP case).

16. 42 U.S.C.A. § 1320a–7a(e).

17. 42 C.F.R. § 1003.129.

Civil money penalties or assessments can be collected by deducting them from amounts owed by Medicare, Medicaid or other state programs to the person against whom the penalty was imposed, or by a civil action brought in the district court in the district in which the person resides or the claim was presented.[18] Matters that could have been raised in an ALJ hearing challenging the penalty or in an appeal of an ALJ decision may not be raised in a subsequent civil collection action.[19] The HHS General Counsel, in consultation with the IG, may compromise such claims.[20] Amounts collected are paid to states in an amount proportionate to their share of the original improper claim in Medicaid cases. Amounts collected in cases involving federal health care programs that are attributable to payments made by those programs are repaid to the relevant program, while any excess funds collected are paid to the Medicare Hospital Insurance Trust Fund.[21]

§ 5–6. Other Sanctions and Administrative Remedies

Though exclusions and civil money penalties are the most significant sanctions available for dealing with Medicare and Medicaid fraud, a variety of interim and lesser administrative remedies can also be used by HCFA, the OIG, or the carriers or intermediaries that administer the Medicare program.[1]

First, in cases not involving life-threatening or harmful care or practices, a carrier may initiate educational contacts to advise a provider that it is engaged in questionable or improper practices, inform it of correct practice, and warn it of consequences that may follow if the practice continues.[2]

Second, a regional office of HCFA may revoke a provider's assignment privileges (privileges to receive payment directly from Medicare) or deny payment to a provider if the provider violates assignment of benefits regulations or when a criminal prosecution is being considered or is in progress.[3] The Regional Office initiates these proceedings by giving the provider 15 days notice of its intended action.[4] The provider may submit a statement explaining why the proposed action is incorrect, including pertinent evidence, within the 15 days. After receiving the statement, or if the 15 days expires without a provider response, the Regional Office decides

---

18. 42 U.S.C.A. § 1320a–7a(f).

19. 42 C.F.R. § 1003.128(d).

20. 42 U.S.C.A. § 1320a–7a(f); 42 C.F.R. § 1003.128(b).

21. 42 U.S.C.A. § 1320a–7a(f)(3).

§ 5–6

1. See Gabriel Imperato, Federal Administrative Sanctions for Health Care Fraud and Abuse, in American Bar Association, Health Care Fraud, 1996, reviewing these sanctions.

2. Medicare Carrier's Manual, §§ 14032.1(A), 14033.2.

3. 42 C.F.R. § 424.82(c); Medicare Carrier's Manual § 14032.1(B).

4. 42 C.F.R. § 424.82(d); Medicare Carrier's Manual § 14025(F).

whether to revoke the provider's right to receive payment.[5] If the Regional Office decides to revoke the provider's right to receive payment, it notifies the carrier to withhold payment on all assigned claims after the effective date of the revocation, and notifies the provider of the revocation.[6] The provider may then request a hearing within 60 days from HCFA.[7] If the hearing officer upholds the regional office determination, the carrier is instructed not to make further payments to the provider and to notify other carriers to not pay the provider, but rather to make payments directly to the beneficiary who received the service or to others authorized to receive the payment.[8] The decision remains in effect until the regional office determines that the reason for the revocation has been removed and there are reasonable assurances that it will not recur.[9]

Third, the Medicare regulations authorize carriers or intermediaries to suspend or recoup payment under certain circumstances. An intermediary or carrier may suspend payment when it determines that a provider has been overpaid or when it has reliable evidence that such overpayment exists, or that fraud or willful misrepresentation has occurred, or that incorrect payments have been made, even though additional evidence may be needed for a final determination, and that a suspension is necessary to protect the program from financial loss.[10] The intermediary or carrier may also offset or recoup payments when the intermediary, carrier or HCFA determines that an overpayment has been made.[11] The provider is usually given 15 days to submit a rebuttal statement as to why the suspension should not be put into effect, though the carrier or intermediary may shorten or extend the response period for cause.[12] The carrier or intermediary must review the rebuttal statement and evidence submitted by the provider and provide a written notice of its determination, explaining the facts on which the decision is based.[13] A suspension is normally limited to 180 days, but may be extended for an additional 180 days where additional time is necessary to investigate cases of suspected fraud, and for even longer at the request of the Justice Department.[14] If a case is referred to or is being considered by the OIG for administrative action, the time limits do not apply.[15] A suspension is not

5. 42 C.F.R. § 424.82(e)(1); Medicare Carrier's Manual § 14025(F).

6. 42 C.F.R. § 424.82(e)(2); Medicare Carrier's Manual § 14025(F).

7. 42 C.F.R. §§ 424.82(e)(2)(v); 424.83; Medicare Carrier's Manual § 14925(F).

8. 42 C.F.R. §§ 424.82(e)(2)(vi), 424.84(a)-(b); Medicare Carrier's Manual § 14025(F).

9. 42 C.F.R. § 424.84(c)(2); Medicare Carrier's Manual § 14025(F).

10. 42 C.F.R. § 405.371(a).

11. 42 C.F.R. § 405.371(a)(2).

12. 42 C.F.R. §§ 405.372(a), 405.373, 405.374(a).

13. 42 C.F.R. § 405.375(b).

14. 42 C.F.R. § 405.372(d).

15. 42 C.F.R. § 405.372(d)(3).

stayed by the filing of bankruptcy proceedings by the provider.[16] Suspended payments, upon release, are first applied to reduce or eliminate overpayments, including interest and then to any other obligations owed to HCFA and HHS, with the remainder released to the provider or supplier.[17]

The carrier or intermediary may suspend payment immediately, without prior notice in cases where the provider or supplier has failed to submit information required to determine amounts due, where the Medicare Trust Fund would be harmed by prior notice because prior notice would hinder the possibility of recovering money, or when HCFA determines that prior notice is not appropriate because of suspected fraud or abuse.[18] The provider or supplier must be given the opportunity in these cases to submit a rebuttal statement explaining why the suspension should be removed.[19] As a practical matter, suspension can continue for the duration of the fraud and abuse investigation, imposing severe hardships on providers or suppliers who are dependent on Medicare payments for cash flow for meeting their obligations.

HCFA charges interest on overpayments and pays interest on underpayments from the date of final determination of the amount due for each 30 day period that payment is delayed, with periods of less than 30 days treated as 30 day periods.[20] Interest continues to accrue during periods of administrative or judicial appeal.[21]

The Courts have upheld suspension without a hearing pending resolution of fraud and abuse charges against due process challenges.[22] Indeed, temporary suspension of Medicare payment may not even be a final determination subject to judicial review.[23] If the suspension continues indefinitely, without resolution, however, due process might be denied.[24]

Finally, HHS has authority to bring an action in federal district court to enjoin any person who has engaged, is engaging or is about to engage in any activity subject to a civil money penalty from "concealing, removing, encumbering, or disposing of assets"

---

16. In re Orthodontic Ctr. Inc., 193 B.R. 832 (N.D.Ohio 1996).

17. 42 C.F.R. § 405.372(e).

18. 42 C.F.R. § 405.372(a).

19. 42 C.F.R. § 405.372(b)(2).

20. 42 C.F.R. § 405.376.

21. 42 C.F.R. § 405.376(e)(1).

22. Peterson v. Weinberger, 508 F.2d 45, 50 (5th Cir.1975); Neurological Assocs. v. Bowen, 658 F.Supp. 468, 472–73 (S.D.Fla.1987). See also Levin v. Childers, 101 F.3d 44 (6th Cir.1996) (rejecting due process challenge against prehearing suspension of Medicaid payments).

23. Homewood Professional Care Ctr., Ltd. v. Heckler, 764 F.2d 1242, 1248 (7th Cir.1985), Neurological Assocs. v. Bowen, 658 F. Supp. at 471. See also, Integrated Generics, Inc. v. Bowen, 678 F.Supp. 1004, 1009 (E.D.N.Y.1988) (action challenging suspension stayed pending outcome of investigation of provider).

24. See Krebsbach v. Heckler, 617 F.Supp. 548, 551 (D.Neb.1985).

that may be necessary to pay a civil penalty.[25] The OIG has secured broad and Draconian orders freezing the assets of individuals and corporations under this provision.[26]

§ 5–7.   State Exclusion and Civil Money Penalty Statutes

As was noted above, federal law requires that in most instances state Medicaid programs withhold payment from providers who have been excluded from Medicare participation by the Office of Inspector General.[1] Federal law also permits suspension of payments to providers where there is reliable evidence of fraud or intentional misrepresentation.[2] Most states also have their own statutes authorizing the state to "suspend," "terminate," or "revoke"[3] the Medicaid participation of providers who commit certain offenses, including fraud and abuse.[4] A few states also authorize alternative sanctions, such as imposition of limits, conditions or controls on a provider,[5] or requiring prior authorization before a provider may deliver a service.[6] In some states, provisions governing Medicaid suspension or termination are found in the public or medical assistance code, in other states they are found in specific Medicaid fraud statutes.

Most commonly, state statutes permit—or require—state Medicaid programs to suspend or terminate providers who are found guilty of Medicaid fraud either through a criminal prosecution or civil penalty proceedings.[7] Several state statutes additionally list a

---

25.   42 U.S.C.A. § 1320a–7a(k).

26.   But see, United States v. Brown, 988 F.2d 658, 662–63 (6th Cir.1993) (frozen assets must be related to the alleged fraud).

§ 5–7

1.   42 C.F.R. § 455.23.

2.   42 C.F.R. § 455.23(a). See Levin v. Childers, 101 F.3d 44 (6th Cir.1996) (upholding such a pre-hearing suspension against a due process challenge).

3.   The term used in the federal statute, "exclude," is rarely found in state statutes, but suspend, revoke, or terminate seems to have basically the same meaning. "Suspend" is commonly used to refer to short-term expulsions, "termination" or "revocation" to longer term expulsions. The Florida statute, for example authorizes suspensions of up to a year, and terminations lasting from 1 to 20 years. Fla. Stat. Ann. § 409.913(15)(a), (b). The Illinois statute indicates that suspensions are for up to a year. The provider is automatically reinstated at the end of the suspension. Providers who are terminated are ex-

cluded from the program for a period in excess of a year and must apply for reinstatement. Ill. Rev. Stat. ch. 305, para. 5/12–4.25(D).

4.   See, e.g., Ark. Code Ann. § 20–77–910; Cal. Welf. & Inst. Code § 14123; Fla. Stat. Ann. § 409.913; Ga. Code Ann. § 49–4–146.1(f); Ill. Rev. Stat. ch. 305, para. 5/12–4.25(A); Mich. Comp. Laws Ann. §§ 400.111d, 400.111e; Minn. Stat. Ann. § 256B.48; Miss. Code Ann. § 97–19–71(6)(d); Mo. Rev. Stat. § 208.164(2); Nev. Rev. Stat. Ann. § 422.2345(1)(c); N.H. Stat. Ann. § 167:60; Ohio Rev. Code Ann. § 5111.03(C); Okla. Stat. tit. 56, § 1007(C); 62 Pa. Stat. § 1407(b)(3), (c)(1); R.I. Gen. Laws §§ 40–8.2–11, 40–8.2–19; Tenn. Code Ann. § 71–5–118; Tex. Hum. Res. Code § 36.009; Utah Code Ann. § 26–18–3(4).

5.   Mich. Comp. Laws § 400.111d(d), (e).

6.   Mo. Rev. Stat. § 208.164(3).

7.   See Ark. Code Ann. § 20–77–910 (permissive suspension or revocation); Cal. Welf. & Inst. Code § 14123 (di-

number of other grounds for suspension or termination. The Florida statute, among the most complex, lists sixteen grounds for administrative sanctions, including exclusion from Medicare participation; license revocation by the state licensing agency; refusal to grant access to Medicaid-related records to the Department or to a state auditor, investigator or attorney; provision of goods or services that are unnecessary or of inferior quality; false claims or statements; illegal supplementation; or being found liable for neglect of patients resulting in death or injury.[8] The Illinois and Michigan statutes include lists of grounds for suspension or termination that are equivalent in length and in content to the Florida statute.[9] Other state statutes simply permit the agency head or designee to suspend or terminate providers for any violation of program regulations,[10] or permit termination from program participation with reasonable notice.[11]

The statutes often reach beyond the specific provider that committed an offense and provide for suspension or termination of providers that are owned or operated by individuals convicted of program related crimes.[12] These requirements are not always abso-

rector must suspend or revoke provider for conviction of felony or misdemeanor involving fraud or patient or program abuse); Ga. Code Ann. § 49–4–146.1(f) (permissive termination); Mich. Comp. Laws Ann. § 400.111e (Department must terminate provider participation if the provider is convicted of violating the Medicaid false claims act. The statute lists several other grounds for which termination is mandatory, and others for which termination is permissive or for which some sanction is mandatory, but sanctions other than termination may be considered). Mo. Rev. Stat. § 198.158 (provider shall be terminated, but can be reinstated for good cause shown); N.H. Rev. Stat. Ann. § 167:60 (director shall suspend provider found guilty of fraud); Okla. Stat. Ann. tit. 56, § 1007(C) (Authority may suspend provider for up to five years upon a judgment of Medicaid fraud); 62 Pa. Cons. Stat. § 1407(b)(3) (person convicted for Medicaid fraud shall be terminated for five years, Department may also terminate providers that it determines have committed fraud, § 1407(c)(1)); Tex. Hum. Res. Code Ann. § 36.009 (permissive termination for Medicaid fraud). The Nevada statute permits the Administrator to suspend or exclude providers whom he determines to have committed fraud without having to bring a criminal action. Nev. Rev. Stat. § 422.2345. The

Rhode Island statute permits the judge in a criminal proceeding to order the suspension of program participation. R.I. Gen. Laws § 40–8.2–11.

8. Fla. Stat. Ann. § 409.913(14).

9. Ill. Rev. Stat. ch. 305, para. 5/12–4.25(A), (B); Mich. Comp. Laws Ann. §§ 400.111d, 400.111e. The Michigan statute is more detailed than any of the others in attempting to specify the appropriate sanction for a variety of offenses.

10. Cal. Welf. & Inst. Code § 14123(a); R.I. Gen. Laws § 40–8.2–19; Utah Code Ann. § 26–18–3(4). See also, Tenn. Code Ann. § 71–5–118, permitting suspension or termination of providers for, inter alia, violating their provider contracts or any Medicaid statute or regulation.

11. See Fla. Stat. Ann. § 409.907(2).

12. See Cal. Welf. & Inst. Code § 14123(a) (Director may suspend clinic, group, corporation or other association if officer, director, or shareholder with more than 10% interest is convicted of fraud or abuse and Director believes suspension would be in best interests of Medicaid program. The California statute also provides for suspension or termination of government facilities if the person in charge of the facility is convicted of fraud or abuse.); Ill. Rev. Stat.

lute, however. The Ohio statute provides for termination of persons with a more than five percent ownership interest in an offending provider, but permits providers or owners to escape termination by demonstrating that they did not directly or indirectly authorize actions taken by their agents or employees.[13]

While several of the statutes specify that the suspension and termination actions are subject to the state's administrative procedures act,[14] this is likely to be true whether or not the statute specifically says so. Some states provide for temporary suspensions prior to the administrative hearing when necessary to protect the program,[15] or suspension of payment to providers who refuse to cooperate in investigations.[16]

The statutes generally provide little guidance with respect to the length of the sanctions.[17] The Florida statute is unusual in specifying considerations that the Department must take into account in determining the type appropriate sanction.[18] These include the seriousness and extent of the violation; prior history of offenses; evidence of continued violation after written notification of violation; licensing action; pain and suffering inflicted on recipients; the extent to which a lesser sanction might be sufficient to remedy the violation; and the impact of the proposed action on access to services by Medicaid recipients.[19] The Illinois statute provides that terminations for a first offense shall last at least one year, terminations for second or subsequent offenses shall last at least two

ch. 305, para. 5/12–4.25(A)(f) (Department may suspend or terminate provider if person with management responsibility or with 5% or more ownership interest, or partner in partnership was previously terminated or had a management or ownership interest in previously terminated provider or has engaged in practices that violate federal or state Medicaid law or had a management or ownership interest in a provider that violated federal or state Medicaid law).

13. Ohio Rev. Code Ann. § 5111.03(C).

14. Cal. Welf. & Inst. Code § 14123(c); Ill. Rev. Stat. ch. 305, para. 5/12–4.25; Mich. Comp. Laws Ann. § 400.111e(4).

15. Cal. Welf. & Inst. Code § 14123(c).

16. Miss. Code Ann. § 43–13–229(2).

17. The courts will uphold a reasonable exercise of discretion in setting the length of exclusion under these statutes. See Zimmerman v. Brian, 116 Cal.Rptr.

211, 216, 41 Cal.App.3d 563, 569–70 (1974) (three month suspension for overcharging Medicaid for drugs upheld); Girard Prescription Ctr. v. Department Pub. Wel. 90 Pa.Cmwlth. 488, 496 A.2d 83 (1985) (two year suspension for permitting unlicensed and untrained employee to practice pharmacy upheld); Schaubman v. Blum, 49 N.Y.2d 375, 426 N.Y.S.2d 230, 402 N.E.2d 1133 (permanent disqualification for substitution of generic equivalent for brand name drug while billing for brand name not excessive even though only $3.39 involved).

18. Fla. Stat. Ann. § 409.913(16).

19. Id. These factors apply in considering whether a fine is appropriate, and, presumably, the amount of the fine. The Florida statute also provides that the Department may sanction only one particular group member or office rather than an entire group if it determines that this action is in the best interests of Medicaid recipients. Fla. Stat. ch. 409.913(17).

years.[20]

State statutes permitting imposition of administrative fines for fraud and abuse are less common than statutes authorizing suspension or termination.[21] The Florida statute permits administrative fines of up to $5000 per violation.[22] The statute additionally permits the Department to recover investigative and expert costs of up to $15,000 if its charges against a provider are not contested or the Department prevails.[23] Fines can be imposed under this statute for any of the sixteen grounds mentioned above for which suspensions or terminations can be imposed.[24] The statute defines what a single violation means in the context of several of these offenses—e.g., each day of refusing access to Medicaid-related records is considered a separate violation.[25] In determining the amount of the penalty, the Department is directed to consider the factors listed above with respect to determining the appropriate sanction.[26]

New Jersey also has a statute permitting administrative penalties.[27] The penalties consist of the interest on any excess payments, an amount not to exceed three times the amount of excess payments, and payments of up to $200 for each excessive payment.[28] If an impermissible claim is unintentional, only interest can be assessed.[29] Penalties are reviewable under the New Jersey Administrative Procedures Act, and can be collected through a civil action or by withholding funds otherwise due the provider.[30] The New Jersey courts have held that penalties under this statute are remedial rather than punitive, and not subject to constitutional provisions limiting criminal prosecutions, such as the double jeopardy clause.[31]

The District of Columbia civil money penalty statute permits civil money penalties to be assessed for up to $2000 plus twice the amount claimed for false claims.[32] The provider must be given an opportunity for an administrative hearing. The Director must take

20. Ill. Rev. Stat. ch. 305, para. 5/12–4.25(D). Similarly, the Kentucky statute provides for suspensions of 2 to 6 months for a first offense, 6 months to a year for a second offense, 1–5 years for a third offense. Ky. Rev. Stat. Ann. § 205.8467(e).

21. State civil penalty provisions are much more common, and are discussed below at chapter 6. Also common are state provisions for imposition of administrative fines on nursing facilities for violation of participation requirements under the federal nursing home reform law. 42 U.S.C.A. § 1396r(h)(2)(A)(ii).

22. Fla. Stat. § 409.913(15)(c). See Medicaid Program Integrity, Dep't of Health & Rehabilitative Servs. v. Conval Care Inc., 636 So.2d 117, 117–18 (Fla. Dist.Ct.App.1994) (claim for overpayments must be pursued through administrative action, not through civil suit).

23. Fla. Stat. ch. 409.913(22)(a).

24. Fla. Stat. ch. 409.913(14).

25. Fla. Stat. ch. 409.913(15)(c).

26. See text supra at note 18.

27. N.J. Rev. Stat. § 30:4D–17(e).

28. Id.

29. N.J. Rev. Stat. § 30:4D–17(f).

30. N.J. Rev. Stat. § 30:4D–17(H), (i).

31. Matter of Garay, 89 N.J. 104, 111, 444 A.2d 1107, 1110 (1982).

32. D.C. Code Ann. § 3–703.

into account in assessing the penalty the nature of the claims, the circumstances in which they were submitted, the culpability and financial condition of the provider, any history of prior offenses, and "other matters as justice may require."[33] Civil money penalties assessed under this statute may be recovered in a civil action, but matters that could have been raised in the administrative action or in an appeal of that action may not be raised in the collection proceeding.[34]

The Georgia Code permits administrative assessment of fines of the greater of three times the amount claimed or $1000 for each false claim.[35] If the provider fails to request a hearing on the assessment, it can be entered by the court clerk as a docketed judgment of the superior court and collected accordingly.[36] The Kentucky statute permits assessment of restitution, civil penalties equalling three times the excess payment, a civil payment of $500 per false claim, and payment of legal fees and the cost of investigation and enforcement pursuant to an administrative finding of fraud and abuse.[37] The state has a lien against all property of the provider to collect this penalty.[38]

A recent Texas statute permits civil penalties to be assessed for Medicaid false claims and also against managed plans that fail to provide services they are obligated to provide by contract, fail to provide required information to the government, engage in fraudulent marketing or enrollment practices, or engage in a pattern of denying or delaying treatment.[39] The Texas statute provides for penalties of twice the amount paid plus $2000 for each item or service falsely claimed, $15,000 for each violation that results in the injury of an elderly person, disabled person, or person under 18, and $10,000 for other violations.[40] The statute provides for three year exclusions for providers who violate the statute, which shall be extended to ten years where the violation injured an elderly or disabled person or a person under 18 years.[41] Finally, the statute provides that the Department may by rule require providers of types that have "demonstrated significant potential for fraud or abuse" to file a surety bond with the Department to cover potential fraud and abuse damages or penalties.[42]

Finally, states generally possess the authority to recover over-

33. D.C. Code Ann. § 3–703(b), (c).
34. D.C. Code Ann. § 3–703(e), (f).
35. Ga. Code Ann. § 49–4–146.1(d).
36. Ga. Code Ann. § 49–4–146.1(e)(3).
37. Ky. Rev. Stat. Ann. § 205.8467.
38. Ky. Rev. Stat. Ann. § 205.8471(1).

39. Tex. Hum. Res. Code 32.039(b).
40. Tex. Hum. Res. Code § 32.039(c).
41. Tex. Hum. Res. Code § 32.039(u), (v).
42. Tex. Hum. Res. Code § 32.0321.

payments from providers through administrative action.[43] Several cases have upheld the use of statistical sampling for determining the amount of overpayment.[44]

Medicaid providers regularly seek judicial review of administrative sanction decisions, and occasionally challenge state proceedings in federal court. Courts have generally upheld pre-termination administrative hearings as providing adequate due process.[45] Suspensions or terminations without an opportunity for a hearing have been held by some courts to violate due process,[46] though some courts have held that a posttermination hearing is adequate.[47] In the absence of state authority on these issues, courts are likely to look to federal Medicare law, which in a variety of contexts—including not only program exclusions,[48] but also actions under the Peer Review Organization program[49] or nursing home decertification—[50] have shown little inclination to closely scrutinize agency actions dealing with providers for due process violations.

43. See Enrico v. Bane, 623 N.Y.S.2d 25, 213 A.D.2d 784, 785–86 (1995).

44. Mercy Hosp. v. New York State Dep't of Soc. Servs., 79 N.Y.2d 197, 204–07, 590 N.E.2d 213, 217–19, 581 N.Y.S.2d 628, 632–34 (1992); Del Borrello v. Commonwealth Dep't of Pub. Welf., 96 Pa. Commw. 507, 512–13, 508 A.2d 368, 371 (Commw. Ct. 1986).

45. Augustin v. Quern, 461 F.Supp. 441, 443 (N.D.Ill.1978), aff'd 611 F.2d 206 (7th Cir.1979). But see Medical Servs. Admin. v. Duke, 378 So.2d 685, 686–88 (Ala.1979) (notice of hearing was insufficiently detailed to meet due process standards).

46. MEDCARE HMO v. Bradley, 788 F.Supp. 1460, 1468–70 (N.D.Ill.1992).

47. Rockland Medilabs, Inc. v. Perales, 719 F.Supp. 1191, 1200–01 (S.D.N.Y.1989). See also Margulis v. Myers, 122 Cal.App.3d 335, 343–44, 175 Cal.Rptr. 787, 791 (Ct. App. 1981) (physician has no statutory or constitutional right to a hearing before being subjected to prior authorization requirement for providing Medicaid services).

48. See supra section 6–3.

49. See Thorbus v. Bowen, 848 F.2d 901, 902 (8th Cir.1988); Doyle v. Secretary of Health & Human Servs., 848 F.2d 296, 297–98 (1st Cir.1988); Cassim v. Bowen, 824 F.2d 791, 797–99 (9th Cir.1987).

50. Americana Healthcare Corp. v. Schweiker, 688 F.2d 1072, 1082–83 (7th Cir.1982); Wayside Farm, Inc. v. United States Dep't of Health & Human Servs., 863 F.2d 447, 449–50 (6th Cir.1988).

Chapter 6

THE CIVIL FALSE CLAIMS ACT
AND QUI TAM ACTIONS

Table of Sections

WESTLAW Electronic Research

See WESTLAW Electronic Research Guide preceding the Summary of Contents.

Library References:

C.J.S. United States § 174.
West's Key No. Digests, United States ☞122.

§ 6–1. Introduction

While the possibility of criminal prosecution and administrative sanctions for fraud and abuse is of very real concern to providers, potential civil liability under the federal Civil False Claims Act, 31

U.S.C.A. § 3729 (FCA), is in some respects even more of a threat. This is, first, because of the extensive liability faced by a FCA defendant: three times the amount of actual damages sustained by the government plus a penalty of not less than $5000 or more than $10,000 per claim. Because health care providers, who normally bill on a per-service basis, submit large numbers of small claims, these penalties may rapidly reach astronomical proportions. Although there are constitutional boundaries to liability (see infra, section 6–6), false claims settlements and recoveries for millions of dollars are becoming increasingly common.[1]

A second cause for concern are the qui tam provisions of the FCA. Only the government can initiate criminal prosecutions and administrative sanctions, and the limited resources of federal and state prosecutors compel them to focus their resources on a relatively small number of usually egregious cases. Under 31 U.S.C.A. § 3730(b)(1), however, any private person (subject to several exceptions explored below) can bring a qui tam action on behalf of the government to enforce the Civil FCA. The potential for recovery of bounties of up to 25–30% of the false claim recovery creates a significant incentive for private litigants to bring such cases, and the potential for statutory attorney's fees (plus possible contingency fees) makes these cases very attractive to attorneys as well. Qui tam actions are often brought by disgruntled current or former employees, (a fact that employers should be acutely aware of) but can also be brought by competitors, beneficiaries, or even corporate officers or directors. Because qui tam actions are filed under seal, and often remain sealed for a considerable period of time while the government is investigating the claim, qui tam actions can be time bombs, waiting to go off, of which the defendant may be completely unaware. Qui tam filings are increasing exponentially in the health care area, and every health care provider should be attentive to this threat.

This chapter will begin with a examination of the qui tam provisions of the FCA. As already noted, qui tam actions in health care are very important and are becoming more so, thus this consideration will be rather detailed, with a focus on issues that arise commonly in health care litigation. This Treatise does not purport to provide an exhaustive exploration of qui tam litigation generally, however. Several excellent sources are available that

§ 6–1

1. See United States v. Caremark, Inc., No. CR. 4–94–95, 1995 WL 422157 (D.Minn.1995) (FCA case settled for payment of $81,854.594 plus interest to United States); United States ex rel. Wagner v. Allied Clinical Labs., No. C–1–94–092, 1995 WL 254405 (S.D.Ohio1995) (qui tam FCA case settled for payment of $4.9 million to the United States and $833,458 to the qui tam relator).

accomplish this.[2] After qui tam actions are explored, the chapter briefly considers procedural and remedial issues raised by FCA cases, including the double jeopardy issue that arises when civil penalties are sought after a criminal prosecution has been completed. This chapter does not address substantive false claims issues, which were explored in chapter 2.

§ 6–2. Qui Tam Actions—Introduction

Qui tam is an abbreviated version of "qui tam pro domino rege quam pro se ipso in hac parte sequitur"—he who litigates for himself as well as for the king.[1] The doctrine has English origins, and qui tam provisions were enacted into United States law by the first federal Congress. When the federal FCA was adopted in 1863 to combat defense contractor fraud during the civil war, it included qui tam provisions. Congress amended the statute to sharply limit who could serve as a qui tam plaintiff in 1943 in response to an expansive Supreme Court interpretation of qui tam jurisdiction earlier that year.[2] In 1986, however, Congress amended the statute again, significantly expanding jurisdiction over qui tam complaints.

Since the 1986 amendments, qui tam litigation has blossomed. Whereas only 33 qui tam cases were filed in 1987 (the year following the amendments) 333 were filed in FY 1996 (178 of which were health care fraud related).[3] Qui tam recoveries grew from $2 million in FY 1988 to 379 million in FY 94.[4] Moreover, while on average 7% of total FCA recoveries (about one third of which are attributable to qui tam actions) were from health care fraud cases during the period FY 1987—FY 1990, an average of 40% of fraud recoveries were health care-based between FY 1993 and FY 1995.[5]

§ 6–3. Standing to Bring Qui Tam Actions

a. Introduction

A federal qui tam action is brought in the name of the United States and for the United States.[1] As will be described more fully below, the United States retains significant control over qui tam

---

2. Among the best is John Boese, Civil False Claims and Qui Tam Actions (1995).

§ 6–2

1. See David Ryan, The False Claims Act: An Old Weapon with New Firepower Is Aimed at Health Care Fraud, 4 Annals of Health L. 127, 150 (1995).

2. See Robert Salcido, Screening out Unworthy Whistleblower Actions: An Historical Analysis of the Public Disclo-

sure Jurisdictional Bar to Qui Tam Actions Under the False Claims Act, 24 Pub. Cont. L. J. 237, 240–50 (1995).

3. BNA Health Care Daily, Oct. 4, 1996; Department of Justice News Release, Oct. 18, 1995.

4. Id.

5. Id.

§ 6–3

1. 31 U.S.C.A. § 3730(b)(1).

litigation. The key characteristic of qui tam actions, however, is that they are also brought by and for private persons.

Under 31 U.S.C.A. § 3730(b)(2), any private person may bring a qui tam action. In fact, qui tam actions are brought by a wide range of plaintiffs. Among the most common qui tam relators are current and former employees.[2] The protections of § 3730(h), which bars retaliatory actions against employees who engage in conduct in furtherance of qui tam actions (see below), enhance the attractiveness of these actions to employees. Qui tam actions are also brought by program beneficiaries,[3] competitors and their employees,[4] state governments,[5] public interest groups,[6] attorneys and law firms,[7] and government employees.[8] Qui tam actions have even been brought by in-house counsel and corporate insiders of the defendants.[9]

The universe of persons who can bring qui tam actions is, however, subject to significant limitations. Section 3730(e) bars qui tam jurisdiction over actions brought by private persons fitting into a number of categories. Some of these categories have little importance in the health care arena. Sections 3730(e)(1) and (2), for example, bar actions by members of the armed forces against other members of the armed forces and actions against high government officials. Other sections are quite relevant in health care litigation, however.

Section 3730(e)(3), for example, prohibits qui tam actions based on allegations or transactions that are already the subject of a civil suit or administrative civil penalty action in which the government is a party. Section 3730(b)(5) prohibits persons from intervening in or bringing actions based on pending qui tam actions. These provisions have occasionally resulted in disputes regarding the question of whether or not a qui tam action is based upon the same

---

2. See, e.g., United States ex rel. Pogue v. American Healthcorp, Inc., 914 F.Supp. 1507 (M.D.Tenn.1996); United States ex rel. Ramseyer v. Century Healthcare Corp., No. Civ–92–2192–B, 1994 WL 746694 (W.D.Okla.1994), order rev'd, 90 F.3d 1514 (10th Cir.1996).

3. Cooper v. Blue Cross & Blue Shield of Florida, 19 F.3d 562 (11th Cir. 1994); United States ex rel. Glass v. Medtronic, Inc., 957 F.2d 605 (8th Cir. 1992).

4. See Federal Recovery Servs. Inc. v. United States, 72 F.3d 447 (5th Cir. 1995).

5. United States ex rel. Woodard v. Country View Care Ctr., 797 F.2d 888 (10th Cir.1986).

6. United States ex rel. Public Integrity v. Therapeutic Technology, 895 F.Supp. 294 (S.D.Ala.1995) (these groups are often formed for the purpose of qui tam litigation).

7. United States ex rel. Stinson, Lyons, Gerlin & Bustamante v. Blue Cross, Blue Shield of Georgia, Inc., 755 F.Supp. 1055 (S.D.Ga.1990).

8. United States ex rel. Fine v. Chevron, U.S.A., Inc., 72 F.3d 740 (9th Cir. 1995) (en banc), cert. denied, __ U.S. __, 116 S.Ct. 1877, 135 L.Ed.2d 173 (1996).

9. United States ex rel. Doe v. X Corp., 862 F.Supp. 1502 (E.D.Va.1994).

allegations as another proceeding.[10] The most important provision limiting qui tam jurisdiction, however, is § 3730(e)(4), the public disclosure limitation.

b. The Public Disclosure Limitation and Original Source Exception

Section 3730(e)(4) provides:

(A) No court shall have jurisdiction over an action under this section based upon the public disclosure of allegations or transactions in a criminal, civil, or administrative hearing, in a congressional, administrative, or Government Accounting Office report, hearing, audit, or investigation, or from the news media, unless the action is brought by the Attorney General or the person bringing the action is an original source of the information.

(B) For purposes of this paragraph, "original source" means an individual who has direct and independent knowledge of the information on which the allegations are based and has voluntarily provided the information to the Government before filing an action under this section which is based on the information.

The intended effect of these provisions is to limit qui tam plaintiffs to those persons who in fact have first-hand, direct personal knowledge of fraudulent claims and to bar opportunistic "parasitical" suits based on information already publicly-known. These provisions have also been interpreted to bar at least some suits brought by current or former government employees who learned of fraud in the course of their employment, and thus to serve the public policy of limiting litigation for private gain brought by public servants.[11] The interpretation of these provisions has proved to be the most difficult and contested problem presented by the qui tam sections of the FCA.[12]

---

10. A subsequent action is barred if it is based on "the same material elements of a fraudulent transaction which are alleged in the pending action," even if the claims in the actions are not identical. United states ex rel. Merena v. SmithKline Beecham Corp., No. 93–5974 (E.D.Pa. 1997). See also United States ex rel. Dorsey v. Dr. Warren E. Smith Community Mental Health/Mental Retardation & Substance Abuse Ctrs., No. CIV. A. 95–7446, 1997 WL 381761 (E.D.Pa.1997); United States ex rel. S. Prawer & Co. v. Fleet Bank, 24 F.3d 320, 328 (1st Cir.1994).

11. See, e.g., Chevron, U.S.A., Inc., 72 F.3d at 740.

12. See Robert Salcido, Screening out Unworthy Whistleblower Actions: An Historical Analysis of the Public Disclosure Jurisdictional Bar to Qui Tam Actions Under the False Claims Act, 24 Pub. Cont. L. J. 237, 241; Robert L Vogel, The Public Disclosure Bar Against Qui Tam Suits, 24 Pub. Cont. L. J. 477 (1995); Note, The False Claims Act—Finding Middle Ground Between Opportunity and Opportunism: The "Original Source" Provision of 31 U.S.C.A. § 3730(e)(4), 17 W.New Eng. L. Rev. 255 (1995).

This subsection was added to the qui tam statute by the 1986 amendments, and must be understood in the context of those amendments. The original 1863 qui tam provisions imposed no limits on who could serve as a qui tam relator. The opportunities presented by the 1863 statute were largely neglected, however, until the late 1930s when enterprising relators began filing "parasitic" suits based on criminal indictments or congressional investigations.[13] In United States ex rel. Marcus v. Hess,[14] the Supreme Court permitted a relator to bring an action based solely on a criminal complaint he had copied from a court file. Congress reacted to this situation by revising the statute in 1943 to deny courts jurisdiction over cases in which the suit was based on "evidence or information in the possession of the United States . . . at the time such suit was brought," even if the information had been supplied by the relator. In 1984 the Seventh Circuit interpreted this provision to bar a qui tam action brought by the state of Wisconsin in a Medicaid fraud case because the state had disclosed the information to the federal government prior to filing the suit, even though the state had been solely responsible for uncovering and investigating the fraud.[15] In response, Congress again amended the qui tam provisions of the FCA in 1986, significantly expanding the class of persons who can bring qui tam actions, by enacting the provisions reproduced above.

The 1986 amendments generally deny courts jurisdiction over qui tam actions "based on" allegations or transactions publicly disclosed. The statute then presents a list, apparently exhaustive, of "public" sources of allegations. The amendments go on to provide, however, that if the qui tam relator is an "original source" of the publicly disclosed allegations, the court has jurisdiction over the case. An "original source" is further defined as a person who has "direct" and "independent" knowledge of the information, and who "voluntarily" discloses the information to the government before filing the qui tam action. The statute further stipulates, moreover, that courts have jurisdiction over actions in which the Attorney General intervenes, even if the information on which the action was based was public prior to the filing of the action. In such cases, the relator's share of the proceeds is significantly reduced.[16]

---

13. Salcido, supra note 12, at 241.

14. 317 U.S. 537, 63 S.Ct. 379, 87 L.Ed. 443 (1943).

15. United States ex rel. Wisconsin v. Dean, 729 F.2d 1100 (7th Cir.1984).

16. 31 U.S.C.A. § 3730(d). It may not equal more than 10% of the proceeds. If the federal government chooses to sue the defendant in a separate action rather than to intervene in a case brought by a relator who is not an original source, the relator cannot later sue in the Court of Claims to recover a share of the proceeds the government recovers. Stinson, Lyons & Bustamante, P.A. v. United States, 79 F.3d 136 (Fed.Cir. 1996).

The first question raised by these requirements is what disclosures of allegations qualify as "public" disclosures within the meaning of the statute. The courts have defined a "public" disclosure as one "placed in the 'public domain,' "[17] that is, disclosed to one or more persons who are "strangers to the fraud."[18] Several courts have interpreted the publicity requirement liberally to include not only openly published material, but also information potentially accessible to the public in court files.[19] Information disclosed to the government under a voluntary disclosure program, for example, may be considered to be public, barring subsequent qui tam actions based on the disclosed information.[21] On the other hand, other courts have held that mere potential availability of information in government files is not enough to establish "public disclosure" if the information is not in fact made public.[22] Some courts have also interpreted the "allegations or transactions" requirement narrowly, so that the mere availability of some evidence of fraud is not enough, if allegations of fraud were not disclosed, or if critical elements of the fraud remained concealed.[23]

Courts have also generally held that only public disclosure through the sources listed in the statute result in the jurisdictional bar.[24] That list includes disclosure through criminal, civil, or administrative hearings; congressional, administrative or GAO investigations, audits or reports; or through the news media. A relator who files a qui tam action after having filed another action involving the same facts (under a state whistleblower protection act, for example) may be barred under the public disclosure provision as

17. United States ex rel. Doe v. John Doe Corp., 960 F.2d 318, 322 (2d Cir. 1992).

18. United States ex rel. Stinson, Lyons, Gerlin & Bustamante, P.A. v. Prudential Ins. Co., 944 F.2d 1149, 1155–56 (3d Cir. 1991).

19. United States ex rel. Kreindler & Kreindler v. United Techs. Corp., 985 F.2d 1148, 1158 (2d Cir.1993); United States ex rel. Stinson, Lyons, Gerlin & Bustamante, P.A. v. Prudential Ins. Co., 944 F.2d at 1149.

21. See Robert S. Ryland, The Government Contractor's Dilemma: Voluntary Disclosures as a Source of Qui Tam Litigation, 22 Pub. Cont. L. J. 764, 777 (1993).

22. United States ex rel. Ramseyer v. Century Healthcare Corp., 90 F.3d 1514 (10th Cir.1996); United States ex rel Schumer v. Hughes Aircraft Co., 63 F.3d 1512, 1519–20 (9th Cir.1995), rev'd on other grounds., ___ U.S. ___, 117 S. Ct. 187, 138 L.Ed.2d 135 (1997); United States ex rel. Springfield Terminal v. Quinn, 14 F.3d 645, 652–53 (D.C.Cir. 1994).

23. United States ex rel. Springfield Terminal Ry. Co. v. Quinn, 14 F.3d 645, 654 (D.C.Cir.1994); United States ex rel. Cooper v. Blue Cross & Blue Shield of Fla., Ind., 19 F.3d 562, 567 (11th Cir. 1994) (per curiam).

24. United States ex rel. Rabushka v. Crane Co., 40 F.3d 1509, 1513 n.2 (8th Cir.1994); United States ex rel. Williams v. NEC Corp., 931 F.2d 1493, 1499–1500 (11th Cir.1991). But see United States ex rel. Stinson, Lyons, Gerlin & Bustamante, P.A. v. Prudential Ins. Co., 736 F.Supp. 614, 621 (D.N.J. 1990), aff'd on other grounds, 944 F.2d 1149 (3d Cir. 1991).

the facts are disclosed by the original lawsuit.[25] Courts have generally interpreted the term "hearing" broadly to encompass not just oral evidentiary hearings, but judicial or administrative proceedings in general, so that allegations disclosed in a complaint or during discovery are included.[26] The "investigation" disclosure bar has been used to block cases brought by former government investigators who obtained information in the course of a government investigation.[27] The "investigation" provision has also been relied on to bar a suit where information had been disclosed during employee interviews in the course of an agency investigation.[28]

The next issue presented by the statute is what is meant by a qui tam complaint being "based upon" publicly disclosed allegations. This issue arises when there has been a public disclosure, but the relator claims that the allegations he or she raises were obtained from a different source. The obvious meaning of "based upon" would seem to be "derived from": a qui tam suit would be "based upon" a publicly disclosed source if the publicly disclosed information formed the basis and was the source of the allegations in the qui tam suit.[29] This interpretation of the term would seem to meet the concern of Congress that qui tam cases not be parasitical suits, merely parroting publicly available information. While one court of appeals decision has adopted this interpretation of the statute,[30] this interpretation has been rejected by most other courts. Most courts have interpreted the provision to mean that a qui tam action is barred if there is a "substantial identity" between the publicly disclosed material and the allegations of the complaint, regardless of the causal relationship between the two, unless the

25. Jones v. Horizon Healthcare Corp, No. 94–CV–71573–DT (E.D. Mich. March 11, 1997), reported in Health Care Fraud Reporter [BNA], May 21, 1997 at 335.

26. See Prudential Ins. Co., 944 F.2d at 1158; United States ex rel. Siller v. Becton Dickinson & Co., 21 F.3d 1339, 1350 (4th Cir.). But see United States ex rel. Stinson, Lyones, Gerlin & Busta-mante, P.A. v. Blue Cross Blue Shield of Ga., Inc., 755 F.Supp. 1040, 1049–50 (S.D.Ga.1990) (rejecting this position).

27. United States ex rel. LeBlanc v. Raytheon Co., 913 F.2d 17, 20 (1st Cir. 1990).

28. United States ex rel. John Doe v. John Doe Corp., 960 F.2d 318, 323–24 (2d Cir.1992). Interpreting the provision in this way effectively restores the 1943 bar against suits based on "information in the possession of the United States"

in that virtually any allegations known to the government because of an investigation could not form the basis of a subsequent qui tam case. Because the public disclosure requirement is subject to the "original source" exception under the 1986 amendments, however, the current statute would still permit suits not possible prior to 1986.

29. See Vogel, supra note 12, at 499–501.

30. Becton Dickinson & Co., 21 F.3d at 1347–49. See also, United States ex rel. Kusner v. Osteopathic Medical Ctr. of Philadelphia Co., No. CIV. A. 88–9753, 1996 WL 287259 (E.D.Pa.1996); United States ex rel. LaValley v. First Nat'l Bank of Boston, 707 F.Supp. 1351, 1366–67 (D.Mass.1988); United States ex rel. LeBlanc v. Raytheon, 874 F.Supp. 35, 40–41 (D.Mass.1995), aff'd 62 F.3d 1411 (1st Cir.1995).

qui tam relator fits within the original source exception.[31] Though this interpretation is somewhat unusual, it is supported by Congressional interest in barring suits that do not uncover information not already publicly known.[32]

A second issue raised by the "based upon" language is whether the qui tam complaint must be fully or only partially "based upon" publicly disclosed information to meet the jurisdictional bar. Here again the bar has been interpreted broadly, with most courts holding that if any part of the qui tam allegations are based on publicly disclosed material, the suit is barred.[33] This is consistent with the tendency of the courts not to linger long over the "based upon" requirement, but rather to see it as a "quick trigger to get to the more exacting original source inquiry"[34] once it is clear that there has been a public disclosure.

Because the courts have broadly interpreted the "based upon" requirement, they frequently reach the next statutory inquiry: whether the qui tam relator is an "original source." This provision permits persons with personal first-hand knowledge of fraud to bring qui tam actions, even if the fraud has become publicly known prior to the filing of the qui tam action. On its face the "original source" provision contains three requirements: the "original source" must have 1) "direct" knowledge and 2) "independent" knowledge "of the information on which the allegations are based" and must 3) "voluntarily" disclose this information to the government prior to filing a qui tam action.[35]

"Direct" knowledge is information gained through the plaintiff's own experience or investigation.[36] This knowledge must be something more than a mere hunch or suspicion, even if such suspicion triggers a government investigation that in fact subsequently reveals fraud.[37] The "independent" requirement assures

31. United States ex rel. Findley v. FPC–Boron Employees' Club, 105 F.3d 675 (D.C.Cir.1997); United States ex rel. Precision Co. v. Koch Indus., Inc., 971 F.2d 548, 553–54 (10th Cir.1992); Wang v. FMC Corp., 975 F.2d 1412, 1419 (9th Cir.1992); United States ex rel. Doe v. John Doe Corp., 960 F.2d 318, 324 (2d Cir.1992); Houck on behalf of United States v. Folding Carton Admin. Comm., 881 F.2d 494, 504 (7th Cir.1989).

32. Salcido, supra note 12, at 278–79.

33. See also FPC–Boron Employees Club, 105 F.3d at 682–88; United States ex rel. Fine v. Sandia Corp., 70 F.3d 568,

572 (10th Cir.1995); United States ex rel. Precision Co., 971 F.2d at 552–53; Cooper v. Blue Cross & Blue Shield of Fla., 19 F.3d 562, 567 (11th Cir.1994); United States ex rel. Kreindler & Kreindler, 985 F.2d at 1158.

34. Precision, 971 F.2d at 552; Cooper, 19 F.3d at 568, n.10.

35. 31 U.S.C.A. § 3730(e)(3), (4)(B).

36. United States ex rel. Barth v. Ridgedale Elec., Inc., 44 F.3d 699, 703 (8th Cir.1995).

37. United States ex rel. Detrick v. Daniel F. Young, Inc., 909 F.Supp. 1010, 1021–23 (E.D.Va.1995).

that the information is not derived from the publicly disclosed source.[38]

The direct and independent requirements are particularly important in two types of cases. The first group of cases involve government employees, who learn of fraud in the course of their government employment and then seek to file qui tam actions based on this knowledge. Several courts faced with this situation have barred these relators from proceeding with the litigation, holding that their knowledge is not independent, but was rather gained on behalf of the government.[39] The problem of government employee whistleblowers is complex, however, as they may serve a useful role in cases where responsible government officials refuse to take action.[40] A second group of cases involves qui tam actions brought by organizations formed for the purposes of qui tam litigation, which have been barred because a corporation cannot be an individual with direct knowledge.[41]

The requirement that the relator voluntarily disclose the information to the government as a condition of qualifying as an original source has generated less controversy, though it has also been relied on to bar qui tam cases brought by government employees (who arguably disclose the information as part of their employment obligations and thus not voluntarily)[42] or relators who first disclosed the information when interviewed during a government investigation.[43]

The most litigated condition of the original source requirement is one that does not appear on the face of the statute. In early interpretations of the "original source" exception, both the Second and Ninth Circuits held that the original source, in addition to meeting the three requirements noted above, must also be the source of the allegations released to the public.[44] Thus, in cases where information was released to the public prior to the filing of qui tam litigation, a relator who had first hand knowledge of the

38. Houck on behalf of United States v. Folding Carton Administration Comm., 881 F.2d 494, 505 (7th Cir. 1989).

39. United States ex rel. LeBlanc v. Raytheon Co., 913 F.2d 17, 20 (1st Cir. 1990). See also, United States ex rel. Fine v. MK–Ferguson Co., 861 F.Supp. 1544, 1553–54 (D.N.M.1994) (relator who is government investigator cannot sue on the basis of information learned from government investigation), aff'd 99 F.3d 1538 (10th Cir.1996).

40. See, discussing this issue, Elletta Callahan, Double Dippers or Bureaucracy Busters? False Claims Act Suits by Government Employees, 49 Wash. U. J. Urb. & Contemp. L. 97 (1996).

41. United States v. Crescent City EMS, Inc., No. Civ. A. 91–4150, 1994 WL 518171, at *6 (E.D.La.1994), aff'd, 72 F.3d 447 (5th Cir.1995).

42. United States ex rel. Fine v. Chevron, U.S.A., Inc., 72 F.3d 740, 741 (9th Cir.1995) (en banc), cert. denied, ___ U.S. ___, 116 S.Ct. 1877, 135 L.Ed.2d 173 (1996).

43. Ridgedale Elec., Inc., 44 F.3d at 703.

44. United States ex rel. Dick v. Long Island Lighting Co., 912 F.2d 13, 16 (2d Cir.1990); Wang ex rel. United States v. FMC Corp., 975 F.2d 1412, 1418 (9th Cir.1992).

fraud completely independently of the public source could still not proceed unless the relator was also the "original source" of the entity that made the information public. More recently, however, the Fourth and Eleventh and District of Columbia Circuits have rejected this interpretation of the original source requirement, holding that the qui tam relator who can prove that he or she possessed direct knowledge independently of that information publicly disclosed need not additionally show that he or she was the source of the public disclosure.[45] While the earlier interpretation finds some support in the legislative history and assures that suits are only brought that in fact bring new evidence of fraud to light, the latter interpretation is more consistent with the general policy of encouraging private persons who have first hand knowledge of fraud to assist the government in prosecuting that fraud.[46] Finally, the D.C. Circuit has also added an additional requirement, that the "original source" must disclose the information to the government before it is publicly disclosed.[47]

c. Potential Plaintiffs

Section 3730(e) does not on its face bar current or former government employees from bringing qui tam actions based on knowledge they gained in the course of their employment. Though some courts have permitted government employees to proceed as qui tam plaintiffs in some circumstances, noting that such suits are not explicitly barred by the statute,[48] other courts have found grounds to bar such suits in the "original source" or "voluntary disclosure" requirements.[49] Permitting government employees to file qui tam actions may assist in ferreting out fraud in instances where government resources are limited or where the government is reluctant to take action because of inappropriate influence. On the other hand, the specter of federal employees using their power and position for their own private benefit at the government's expense, while potentially compromising criminal inquiries and deterring potential defendants from cooperating with government

---

45. United States ex rel. Findley v. FPC–Boron Employees' Club, 105 F.3d 675, 690 (D.C.Cir.1997); Becton Dickinson & Co., 21 F.3d at 1351–53; Cooper v. Blue Cross & Blue Shield of Fla., 19 F.3d 562, 568 n.13 (11th Cir.1994). See supra note 12 (supporting this position).

46. The commentators generally support the latter position for these reasons. See Vogel, supra note 12, at 479.

47. FPC–Boron Employees' Club, 105 F.3d. at 690–91.

48. United States ex rel. Williams v. NEC Corp., 931 F.2d 1493, 1501–04 (11th Cir.1991); United States ex rel. Hagood v. Sonoma County Water Agency, 929 F.2d 1416, 1419–20 (9th Cir. 1991), aff'd 81 F.3d 1465 (9th Cir.1996), cert. denied, ___ U.S. ___, 117 S. Ct. 175, 136 L.Ed.2d 116 (1996).

49. See United States ex rel. Fine v. Chevron, U.S.A., Inc., 72 F.3d 740 (9th Cir.1995) (en banc), cert. denied, ___ U.S. ___, 116 S.Ct. 1877, 135 L.Ed.2d 173 (1996).

investigations, prompts courts to try to find some way to bar government employees from qui tam relator status.[50]

The statute does not bar plaintiffs from bringing qui tam actions merely because they themselves participated in the fraud, except in the situation where the plaintiff has been criminally convicted of his or her role in the fraud on which the action is based.[51] Neither have the courts permitted employer-defendants to claim indemnification from a relator who participated in the fraud on which the qui tam action is based.[52] The share of the proceeds that the relator would otherwise have received in a qui tam action may be reduced, however, if the relator participated in the fraud.[53]

A settlement or release agreement under which an employee or former employee agrees not to pursue a qui tam action is unenforceable.[54] Neither is an in-house counsel barred from bringing a qui tam action against his or her client under federal law, though state law governing the attorney-client relationship may bar the disclosures necessary to bring such a suit.[55]

A qui tam action is remedial in nature, and therefore survives the death of the relator.[56] The personal representative of the relator should be substituted as plaintiff at the relator's death.

§ 6–4. Procedural and Remedial Issues in Qui Tam Actions

a. Filing Requirements

A qui tam action is filed in camera under seal, and is not served on the defendant until the court so orders.[1] The complaint remains sealed for 60 days while the government considers whether or not to intervene.[2] The seal provision allows the government to investigate the allegations confidentially, prevents wrongdoers from being tipped off before such an investigation can be completed, and

---

50. See generally, Dorthea Beane, Are Government Employees Proper Qui Tam Plaintiffs?, 14 J. Legal Med. 279 (1993); Patrick Hanifin, Qui Tam Suits by Federal Government Employees Based on Government Information, 20 Pub. Cont. L. J. 556 (1991).

51. 31 U.S.C.A. § 3730(d)(3).

52. Mortgages Inc. v. District Court, 934 F.2d 209, 212–14 (9th Cir.1991). But counterclaims not based on the qui tam defendant's potential liability may, in some circumstances, be brought in a qui tam action. See United States ex rel. Madden v. General Dynamics Corp., 4 F.3d 827, 830–31 (9th Cir.1993).

53. 31 U.S.C.A. § 3730(d)(3).

54. United States ex rel. Green v. Northrop Corp., 59 F.3d 953, 969 (9th Cir.1995), cert. denied, ___ U.S. ___, 116 S.Ct. 2550, 135 L.Ed.2d 1069 (1996).

55. United States ex rel. Doe v. X Corp., 862 F.Supp. 1502, 1508 (E.D.Va. 1994).

56. United States ex rel. Semtner v. Medical Consultants d/b/a Emergency Physicians Billing Servs. Inc., No. CIV–94–617–C, 170 F.R.D. 490 (W.D.Okla. 1997), reported in Health Care Fraud Report [BNA], May 7, 1997 at 298.

§ 6–4

1. 31 U.S.C.A. § 3730(b)(2).

2. Id.

protects the defendant's reputation while the government is reviewing the merits of the case.[3] Disclosure of the case prior to the
unsealing can result in dismissal of the case, though the requirement is not jurisdictional and the court does have discretion to
permit the case to proceed despite the disclosure.[4] The government
can move, on good cause shown, for an extension of the time that
the case remains sealed and routinely does so.[5] Though the government must substantiate the reason why it seeks an extension,[6]
cases often remain under seal for months after they are filed.

A copy of the complaint and a written disclosure of "substantially all material evidence and information" the relator possesses
must be served upon the government.[7] The disclosure statement
enables the court to examine the extent of the plaintiff's knowledge
for application of the "original source" exception.[8] Though the
statement need not necessarily contain all of the evidence known to
the plaintiff,[9] the plaintiff will usually try to provide the government with as much information as possible to attempt to convince
the government to intervene. Several courts have held that disclosure statements are subject to discovery in subsequent litigation.[10]

Qui tam complaints raise allegations of fraud, and thus must
comply with the particularity requirements of Rule 9(b) of the
Federal Rules of Civil Procedure. Although the courts have permitted some flexibility in pleading, given the fact that information in
these cases is less available to the plaintiff than to the defendant,
they normally require "allegations of the particulars of the time,
place and contents of the false representations, as well as the
identity of the person making the representations and what he

---

3. Erickson ex rel. United States v.
American Institute for Biol. Sciences,
716 F.Supp. 908, 912 (E.D.Va.1989), citing S. Rep. No. 345, 99th Cong., 2d Sess.
24, reprinted in 1986 U.S.C.C.A.N. 5266,
5289.

4. United States ex rel. Lujan v.
Hughes Aircraft Co., 67 F.3d 242, 245–
47 (9th Cir.1995); United States ex rel.
Pilon v. Martin Marietta Corp., 60 F.3d
995, 1000 (2d Cir.1995); United States
ex rel. Kusner v. Osteopathic Medical
Ctr., No. CIV. A. 88–9753, 1996 WL
287259 (E.D.Pa.1996); Erickson, 716 F.
Supp. at 912; Anthony DeWitt, Badges?
We Don't Need No Stinking Badges! Citizen Attorney Generals and the False
Claims Act, 65 U.M.K.C.L. Rev. 30, 41
(1996).

5. 31 U.S.C.A. § 3730(b)(3).

6. United States ex rel. McCoy v.
California Medical Review, Inc., 715
F.Supp. 967, 968–69 (N.D.Cal.1989).

7. 31 U.S.C.A. § 3730(b)(2). See De-
Witt, supra note 4, at 44–45.

8. See John Boese, Civil False
Claims and Qui Tam Actions 4–74 to 4–
75 (1995).

9. See United States ex rel. Woodard
v. Country View Care Ctr., Inc., 797
F.2d 888, 892 (10th Cir.1986) (relator
was not required to include all documentary evidence of fraud that was in its
possession in the disclosure statement as
information provided was sufficient to
permit United States to assess case and
to decide whether or not to intervene).

10. United States ex rel. Stone v.
Rockwell Intern. Corp., 144 F.R.D. 396,
399 (D.Colo.1992); United States ex rel.
Burns v. A.D. Roe Co., Inc., 904 F.Supp.
592, 593–94 (W.D.Ky.1995). These cases
reject arguments that the statement is
protected by the attorney-client privilege, work project immunity, or the FCA
itself.

obtained from thereby."[11] The court may at its discretion permit the plaintiff, moreover, to amend the complaint to meet the particularity requirement when 9(b) issues are raised.

At the close of the sixty day period and any extensions thereof, the government must decide whether to intervene—and thus to take over the case—or to decline intervention.[12] It may also dismiss the case or attempt to settle it.[13] If the government investigation reveals criminal conduct, it may seek a criminal indictment and negotiated plea. Since a guilty plea estops the defendant from denying civil liability, an indictment frequently results in a global settlement of both the criminal and qui tam action, with a rapid recovery for the plaintiff.[14]

The decision to intervene is a portentous one for qui tam plaintiffs. The government only intervenes in about one quarter of qui tam cases,[15] but as of late 1995, cases in which the government had intervened had resulted in judgements and settlements of over one billion dollars since the 1986 amendments went into effect, cases declined by the government had only amounted to $15.6 million.[16] The government decision may reflect its assessment of the strength of the case or of the amount it is likely to recover compared to the costs of litigation. If the government declines intervention, the entire cost of litigating rests on the plaintiff, while the defendant may fight more vigorously, believing it can exhaust the resources of the private plaintiff.[17] The plaintiff should present as strong a case as possible to the government to encourage intervention. If the government declines to intervene, it may do so at a later date upon a showing of good cause.[18]

If the government chooses to intervene, the plaintiff's attorney becomes co-counsel with the Department of Justice (DOJ). This may mean that the DOJ effectively takes over the case, though the government may alternatively allow the qui tam plaintiff largely to manage the case or may work together as a partner.[19] Under the

11. United States v. Crescent City, E.M.S. Inc., 151 F.R.D. 288, 289–91 (E.D.La.1993). See also United States ex rel. Thompson v. Columbia/HCA Healthcare Corporation, 1997 WL 619314 (5th Cir. 1997); United States ex rel. Stinson, Lyons, Gerlin & Bustamante, P.A. v. Blue Cross, Blue Shield of Ga., 755 F.Supp. 1040, 1051–53 (S.D.Ga.1990), aff'd on reconsideration, 755 F.Supp. 1055, 1058–59 (S.D.Ga.1990); United States ex rel. Mikes v. Straus, 853 F.Supp. 115, 118 (S.D.N.Y.1994).

12. 31 U.S.C.A. § 3730(b)(4)(A), (B).

13. 31 U.S.C.A. § 3730(c)(2)(A), (B).

14. John Philips & Janet Goldstein, The False Claims Act in Practice in PLI, Qui Tam: Beyond Government Contracts, (PLI Litig. & Admin. Practice Course Handbook Series No. H4–5154, 1993).

15. Richard C. Reuben, Ferreting Out Fraud, 13 Dec. Cal. Law. 39 (1993).

16. News Release, Justice Dep't Recovers Over $1 Billion in Qui Tam Awards and Settlements, Oct. 18, 1995.

17. Philips & Golstein, supra note 14.

18. 31 U.S.C.A. § 3730(c)(3).

19. Philips & Golstein, supra note 14.

statute, the government may ask the court to limit the qui tam plaintiff's participation in the trial—including specifically the plaintiff's calling, interrogation, and cross-examination of witnesses—if the plaintiff's conduct interferes with the litigation.[20] The defendant may also ask the court to limit the plaintiff's participation, if it would result in harassment or unnecessary burden or expense.[21]

One strategy open to some qui tam defendants who learn that a qui tam action has been filed is to launch a preemptive strike: to file a separate declaratory action in a separate (hopefully more favorable) court while the qui tam action is still under seal to establish that they have not defrauded the government; for example by declaring a rule the defendant was alleged to have violated to be invalid. In one such case, the Ninth Circuit upheld a district court's refusal to allow the qui tam relator to intervene, holding that the qui tam relator had no interest in the case independent of the government's interest, and that the government would adequately represent that interest.[21.5] It also refused to dismiss the declaratory judgment action under the "first to file" rule.[21.10] The court went on, however, to observe that even if the challenged Rule were held to be improperly promulgated, the hospital could still be found liable for filing a false claim if the claim was filed for goods or services not covered by the rule.[21.15] The action may, therefore, prove futile in the end.

b. Dismissal and Settlement

A qui tam suit may be dismissed on the motion of the qui tam plaintiff, defendant, or government. The defendant may move to dismiss on any grounds generally available in civil actions. Under 31 U.S.C.A. § 3730(c)(2)(A) the government may dismiss the action over the relator's objection "if the person has been notified by the government and the court has provided the person with an opportunity for a hearing on the motion." The relator may move to dismiss the action, but the statute requires that the Attorney General give "written consent to the dismissal and their reasons for consenting."[22] In a number of cases the government has refused to intervene, but then objected when the qui tam plaintiff and defendant settled the case with the settlement structured so as to maximize the amounts the plaintiff recovered as attorneys' fees or under pendant claims and to minimize the FCA recovery, which would have to be shared with the government. Although the

---

20. 31 U.S.C.A. § 3730(c)(2)(C).

21. 31 U.S.C.A. § 3730(c)(2)(D).

21.5 Cedar–Sinai Medical Center v. Shalala, Medicare & Medicaid Guide (CCH) ¶ 45,621 (9th Cir. 1997).

21.10 Id.

21.15 Id.

22. 31 U.S.C.A. § 3730(b)(1).

decisions in this area are not consistent, recent precedent seems to recognize the government's right to raise questions about the allocation of settlement funds without intervening, but not an absolute government right to block the proposed settlement.[23]

The relator may also object if the government settles the case. The relator's objections might concern the amount of the settlement, the realtor's share, the allocation of the settlement between FCA recoveries and collateral government claims,[24] or the government's willingness to accept restitution from the defendant outside of the FCA and not subject to the relator's claim.[25] It is generally believed that the relator has little to lose from objecting to a settlement, and may be able to gain a larger recovery or share by objecting. The government may settle the case over the objections of the relator only "if the court determines, after a hearing, that the proposed settlement is fair, adequate, and reasonable under all the circumstances."[26] For example, in one case where the government settled the dispute without including the relator in the negotiations or conducting an investigation of the relator's allegations, the court set aside the settlement on the objection of the relator.[27] The relator may also be granted limited discovery regarding the settlement when the relator is excluded from settlement negotiations.[28] In most cases, however, the court treats a settlement negotiated by the government with considerable deference.[29]

c. The Relator's Share

The 1986 amendments significantly increased the potential awards to be gained by successful relators. In the standard qui tam case where the government intervenes, the relator is entitled to "at least 15 but not more than 25 percent of the proceeds of the action or settlement of the claim, depending upon the extent to which the person substantially contributed to the prosecution of the action."[30] From 1986 through FY 1995, qui tam relators were awarded $184,470,378 in cases where the government intervened, an average of 17.87 percent of the proceeds in cases where shares had been

23. See United States ex rel. Killingsworth v. Northrop Corp., 25 F.3d 715, 720 (9th Cir.1994); United States v. Texas Instruments Corp., 25 F.3d 725, 728 (9th Cir.1994). See Mark Troy, Qui Tam Settlements: Is the Government Being Short–Changed?, Health Care Fraud Litig. Rptr., Dec. 1996 at 3.

24. See, e.g., United States ex rel. Burr v. Blue Cross & Blue Shield of Fla., Inc., 882 F.Supp. 166 (M.D.Fla.1995) (percentage of settlement proceeds and attorney's fees litigated).

25. See, e.g., Covington v. Sisters of 3d Order of St. Dominic, 61 F.3d 909 (9th Cir. 1994).

26. 31 U.S.C.A. § 3730(c)(2)(B).

27. Gravitt v. General Elec. Co., 680 F.Supp. 1162 (S.D.Ohio 1988).

28. United States ex rel. McCoy v. California Medical Review, Inc., 133 F.R.D. 143, 148–49 (N.D.Cal.1990).

29. See United States ex rel. Burr v. Blue Cross & Blue Shield of Fla., Inc., 882 F. Supp. at 166.

30. 31 U.S.C.A. § 3730(d).

determined.[31] Qui tam awards in health care cases have been as high as 15 million dollars. The government usually argues for the minimum relator's share, contending that the 25% award should be limited to fully litigated cases where the relator plays a major role.[32] Courts reviewing award amounts also consider whether the relator made a substantial and independent contribution to the case and the extent of the personal risk incurred by the relator in bringing the case.[33]

Where the government declines to intervene in a qui tam case, the relator is entitled to 25 to 30 percent of the proceeds.[34] If the relator "planned or initiated" the FCA violation, on the other hand, the court may reduce the relator's award.[35] If the action is based primarily on publicly disclosed information, and the Government elects to proceed with the case, the relator may recover an award of not more than 10 percent.[36]

A prevailing relator is also entitled to recover "reasonable expenses which the court finds to have been necessarily incurred, plus reasonable attorneys' fees and costs."[37] These expenses are recoverable whether the case goes to verdict or is settled. In determining attorneys' fees, courts apply the "lodestar" methodology, beginning with the number of hours reasonably spent on the litigation multiplied times a reasonable rate.[38] Unusually difficult or novel cases may warrant a higher rate. On the other hand, time spent litigating with the government over the plaintiff's share of the recovery or litigating unsuccessful claims may not be recoverable.[39] Although a qui tam case may be pursued on a contingency fee basis, the court may either reduce the fee recovery or strike the contingency fee agreement if the combination would result in too high a fee for the relator's attorney.[40]

The successful qui tam defendant may also recover reasonable attorneys' fees and expenses from the relator in an action where the government declines to intervene and the defendant prevails, if the plaintiff's claim was "clearly frivolous, clearly vexatious, or brought primarily for the purpose of harassment."[41] Certain prevailing defendants may also be able to recover from the government

---

31. Department of Justice Press Release, October 18, 1995.

32. Boese, supra note 8, at 4–106.

33. Blue Cross & Blue Shield of Fla., 882 F. Supp. at 169.

34. 31 U.S.C.A. § 3730(d)(2).

35. 31 U.S.C.A. § 3730(d)(3). If the relator is criminally convicted of the fraud, the relator may not recover any award.

36. 31 U.S.C.A. § 3730(d)(1). See United States ex rel. Precision Co. v. Koch Indus., 971 F.2d 548, 553 n.3 (10th Cir.1992).

37. 31 U.S.C.A. § 3730(d)(1), (2).

38. United States ex rel. Burr v. Blue Cross & Blue Shield of Fla., 882 F.Supp. 166, 169–70 (M.D.Fla.1995).

39. See United States ex rel. Taxpayers Against Fraud v. General Elec. Co., 41 F.3d 1032, 1045–46 (6th Cir.1994).

40. Id. at 1046–48.

41. 31 U.S.C.A. § 3730(d)(4).

under the Equal Access to Justice Act where the government's position was not "substantially justified."[42] The government is never liable for the relator's costs.[43]

§ 6–5. Whistleblower Protection Provisions

The qui tam statute recognizes that the most knowledgeable potential qui tam relators are often employees, and that employees may often be deterred from revealing the wrongdoing of their employers because of fear of retaliation. Section 3730(h) provides:

> Any employee who is discharged, demoted, suspended, threatened, harassed, or in any other manner discriminated in the terms and conditions of employment by his or her employer because of lawful acts done by the employee on behalf of the employee or others in furtherance of an action under this section, shall be entitled to all relief necessary to make the employee whole. Such relief shall include reinstatement with the same seniority status such employee would have had but for the discrimination, 2 times the amount of back pay, interest on the back pay, and compensation for any special damages sustained as a result of the discrimination, including litigation costs and reasonable attorneys' fees.

It is generally held that the employee need not have actually filed an action to claim the protection of the statute.[1] It is necessary, however, that the employee be able to demonstrate actions in furtherance of a qui tam action which formed the basis of the retaliatory conduct.[2] The requirement that the retaliation be against "lawful acts" raises interesting issues when the employee is disciplined for copying or removing confidential documents of the employer to serve as evidence for the qui tam case.[3] The provision also raises questions when an employer takes action against a qui tam relator/employee who was personally involved in the fraud, an action which itself may be indicated by a corporate compliance program designed to comply with the Federal Sentencing Guidelines.[4]

---

42. 31 U.S.C.A. § 3730(g), referring to 28 U.S.C.A. § 2412(d).

43. 31 U.S.C.A. § 3730(f).

§ 6–5

1. Childree v. UAP/GA AG Chem, Inc., 92 F.3d 1140 (11th Cir.1996); United States ex rel. Dorsey v. Dr. Warren E. Smith Community Mental Health/Mental Retardation and Substance Abuse Ctrs., No. CIV. A. 95–7446, 1997 WL 381761 (E.D.Pa.1997); Neal v. Honey-well, Inc., 33 F.3d 860, 863–65 (7th Cir. 1994).

2. United States ex rel. Ramseyer v. Century Healthcare Corp., 90 F.3d 1514 (10th Cir.1996); Robertson v. Bell Helicopter Textron, Inc., 32 F.3d 948, 950–52 (5th Cir.1994).

3. See John Boese, Civil False Claims and Qui Tam Actions 4–135 to 4–136 (1995).

4. 28 U.S.C.A. § 994. See infra, chapter 8.

§ 6–6. Constitutionality of the Qui Tam Statute

The constitutionality of the qui tam statute has been attacked repeatedly in qui tam litigation.[1] While arguments that the qui tam statute violates the Constitution are of considerable academic interest,[2] they are consistently rejected by the courts and thus are of little practical relevance. Among these arguments are:

1) the qui tam statute violates the separation of powers doctrine because it delegates to private persons prosecutorial functions that are delegated by the Constitution to the executive branch;

2) the qui tam statute violates the appointments clause[3] by "appointing" private persons to litigate on behalf of the United States while the Constitution vests authority to appoint prosecutorial officers exclusively in the executive branch;

3) the qui tam statute permits relators to have standing despite the fact that they are not personally injured by the defendants, in violation of the "case or controversy" standing requirement imposed by Article III.

The courts commonly reject these constitutional arguments, arguing that the Attorney General in fact controls qui tam litigation, and that injury to the Government is sufficient to permit constitutional standing. The constitutional issues that have most troubled the courts are those raised by retroactive application of the 1986 amendments in qui tam cases and the double jeopardy and excessive penalty issues raised by large False Claim Act penalties. As these issues apply not just to qui tam litigation but in all FCA litigation, they will be considered in the context of the FCA below.

§ 6–7. Procedural Issues in Civil False Claims Litigation

a. Introduction

Chapter 2 of this book discussed the substantive law standard of civil false claims liability. The first part of this chapter examined procedural and remedial issues unique to qui tam actions. This section considers procedural and remedial issues that apply to CFA

§ 6–6

1. See, e.g., United States ex rel. Taxpayers Against Fraud v. General Elec. Co., 41 F.3d 1032, 1040–42 (6th Cir.1994); United States ex rel. Kelly v. Boeing Co., 9 F.3d 743, 747–60 (9th Cir. 1993); United States ex rel. Truong v. Northrop Corp., 728 F.Supp. 615 (C.D.Cal.1989); United States ex rel. Stillwell v. Hughes Helicopters, Inc., 714 F.Supp. 1084 (C.D.Cal.1989).

2. See John D. Bessler, The Public Interest and the Unconstitutionality of Private Prosecutors, 47 Ark. L. Rev. 511 (1994); Note, 1001 Attorneys General: Executive–Employee Qui Tam Suits and the Constitution, 62 Geo.Wash. L. Rev. 609 (1994); Note, The False Claims Act, Qui Tam Relators, and the Government: Which is the Real Party in Interest, 43 Stan. L. Rev. 1061 (1991).

3. U.S. Const. art. II, § 2.

actions generally: retroactive application of the 1986 amendments; the statute of limitations, venue, jurisdiction, and pleading for CFA actions; discovery; calculation of damages and penalties under the FCA; and constitutional issues raised by CFA penalties.

b. Retrospective Application of the 1986 Amendments

As has already been noted several times in this chapter and in chapter 1, the 1986 FCA amendments significantly changed the FCA as it had existed prior to their adoption. The 1986 amendments expanded qui tam jurisdiction, the share of the FCA recovery available to the qui tam relator, and the role of the qui tam relator in the case, and provided protection against retaliation for qui tam relators. The amendments also expanded the FCA statute of limitations to permit cases to be brought after six years under certain circumstances. They specified that using a false record to decrease an obligation to the United States, a so-called "reverse false claim," was a violation of the statute. They expansively defined the term "claim," rejecting more restrictive interpretations of the prior law. They clarified, and arguably changed the level of intent that must be proved in a false claims case, defining the term "knowingly" to make clear that proof of specific intent to defraud was not necessary, rejecting the decisions of some courts that it was. The amendments also made it clear that FCA liability only need be proved by the preponderance of the evidence. Finally, the 1985 amendments increased the damage multiplier from double to treble and penalties from $2000 per claim to $5000 to 10,000 per claim.

The retrospective application of various of these amendments has been much litigated in the years following 1986.[1] While this issue will obviously diminish in importance as time goes on, it is still very much alive in the mid–1990s as this book is written. The early court decisions addressing retrospectivity problems were somewhat confused, mirroring confusion in Supreme Court precedents. Two Supreme Court decisions in 1994[2] clarified the law limiting retroactive application of statutes, holding that statutes that "impair rights a party possessed when he acted, increase a party's liability for past conduct, or impose new duties with respect to transactions already completed" should not be imposed retroactively absent clear congressional intent.[3] Jurisdictional and proce-

---

§ 6–7

1. See Hughes Aircraft Co. v. United States ex rel. Schumer, ___ U.S. ___, 117 S.Ct. 1871, 138 L.Ed.2d 135 (1997); Robert Metzger & Robert Goldbaum, Retroactivity of the 1986 Amendments to the False Claims Act, 22 Pub. Cont. L. J. 684 (1993); Michael Waldman, 1986 Amendments to the False Claims Act, 18 Pub. Cont. L. J. 469 (1989).

2. Landsgraf v. USI Film Prods., 511 U.S. 244, 280, 114 S.Ct. 1483, 1505, 128 L.Ed.2d 229 (1994); Rivers v. Roadway Express Inc., 511 U.S. 298, 309–313, 114 S.Ct. 1510, 1518–20, 128 L.Ed.2d 274 (1994).

3. Landsgraf, 114 S.Ct. at 1504.

dural amendments, however, that do not limit substantive rights, can be applied in current cases challenging pre-amendment conduct.[4] Finally, a 1997 Supreme Court decision, Hughes Aircraft Company v. United States, applied this law to the problem of retroactive application of the 1986 amendments to the FCA.[5]

The Supreme Court in *Hughes* held that the provision of the 1986 amendments permitting original source qui tam plaintiffs to bring suit in cases where the government knew of the fraud before the suit was filed could not be applied in cases challenging pre–1986 conduct, since these amendments effectively create a new cause of action.[6] The Court held that, even though the amendments did not extend liability to conduct not previously penalized, they did effectively create a new cause of action, because they extended the ability of qui tam relators to bring suit where they could not do so previously, but that Congress had not clearly indicated its intent to apply the provisions retroactively.[7] Recognizing that qui tam relators face different incentives and are driven by different motives than the government, and that the 1986 amendments permitted qui tam relators to bring suit who would otherwise have been barred from doing so, the court held that the amendments exposed defendants to liability they would not have otherwise faced.[8] The Court rejected arguments that the statute simply regulated the secondary conduct of litigation, but rather held that it created jurisdiction where none had existed before.[9]

In reaching this result, the court overruled earlier lower court decisions, which had generally held that qui tam suits could be brought under the 1986 amendments by "original source" relators based on prior conduct because the amendments did not affect the legality of the defendant's conduct, but only the question of who was a proper plaintiff to challenge that conduct.[10] Other pre-*Hughes* cases are called into question, though not expressly overruled, by *Hughes*. The increased relator's share in the bounty had been held, for example, to be a procedural change that did not affect the defendant's rights, and thus was applied retrospectively.[11] The 1986 amendments providing for attorneys' fees in qui tam actions had also been applied retrospectively, since *Landsgraf* expressly refused to overrule precedent on this issue, finding attor-

---

4. Landsgraf, 114 S.Ct. at 1501.

5. ___ U.S. ___, 117 S.Ct. 1871, 138 L.Ed.2d 135 (1997).

6. Id.

7. Id. at 1876–77.

8. Id.

9. Id. at 1867–78.

10. United States ex rel. Lindenthal v. General Dynamics Corp., 61 F.3d 1402, 1406–08 (9th Cir.1995); United States ex rel. Newsham v. Lockheed Missiles & Space Co., Inc., 907 F.Supp. 1349 (N.D.Cal.1995).

11. Lockheed, 907 F. Supp. at 1349.

neys' fees "collateral to the main cause of action."[12] Insofar as these provisions increase the incentives for qui tam relators to bring suits, they could be interpreted as effectively "creating a new cause of action," under *Hughes*, though they may still fall within the "secondary conduct of litigation" exception of Hughes.

As to other issues, courts had refused to apply the 1986 amendments retrospectively even before *Hughes*. Retrospective application of the enhanced damages and penalty provisions, for example, was rejected as increasing the defendant's burden impermissibly.[13] The 1986 clarifications of the law with respect to the level of scienter (the meaning of "knowing") and the burden of proof, have also not been applied retrospectively in jurisdictions where they would change the law to make it less favorable to the defendant.[14] In jurisdictions where they did not change the former law, there is, of course, no question of retrospective application of the amendments.[15] Finally, the statute of limitations provisions cannot be applied retrospectively to revive claims that became stale under the old law (i.e. claims based on conduct occurring prior to October 27, 1980).[16]

c. Statute of Limitations, Venue and Jurisdiction

The statute of limitation for FCA actions is six years from the date on which the violation of the FCA was committed.[17] Additionally, under the 1986 amendments, an action may be brought within 3 years of the date when "facts material to the right of action are known or reasonably should have been known by the official of the United States charged with responsibility to act in the circumstances" up to 10 years after the date of the violation of the act.[18] This amendment reflected law that was developing prior to 1986, which recognized that the statute of limitations was tolled when the defendant concealed its violation of the FCA.[19] The extended period is available to qui tam relators, but runs from the time the qui tam relator knew or should have known about the fraud.[20]

The majority of courts have held that the statute begins to run on the date government payment is made,[21] though a minority of

12. See Lockheed, 907 F. Supp. at 1360 (citing Landsgraf, 114 S.Ct. at 1503).

13. United States v. TDC Mgmt. Corp., Inc., 24 F.3d 292, 298 (D.C.Cir. 1994); United States v. Incorporated Village of Island Park, 888 F.Supp. 419, 444 (E.D.N.Y.1995).

14. Lockheed, 907 F. Supp. at 1359.

15. TDC Management, 24 F.3d at 298.

16. Lockheed, 907 F. Supp. at 1358–59.

17. 31 U.S.C.A. § 3731(b)(1).

18. 31 U.S.C.A. § 3731(b)(2).

19. See United States v. Uzzell, 648 F.Supp. 1362, 1367–68 (D.D.C.1986).

20. See United States ex rel. Hyatt v. Northrop Corp., 91 F.3d 1211 (9th Cir.1996).

21. See, e.g., United States ex rel. Kreindler & Kreindler v. United Techs. Corp., 985 F.2d 1148, 1157 (2d Cir. 1993).

cases hold that the period begins to run when the defendant in fact submits a claim to the Government.[22] The latter result is more in accord with the legislative history and purpose of the statute.[23] The cases tend to hold that the "official of the United States" referred to in the tolling provision is responsible official in the Department of Justice,[24] though the statute will not be tolled despite the Justice Department's lack of knowledge of the violation if it "should have known" of the violation through the exercise of due diligence.[25] One recent case has held that qui tam relators can claim the benefit of the three year tolling period as well as the government.[26]

Under 31 U.S.C.A. § 3732(a), a false claims action may be brought "in any judicial district in which the defendant or, in the case of multiple defendants, any one defendant can be found, resides, transacts business, or in which any act proscribed by section 3729 occurred." False claims actions can also be interposed as counterclaims in court of claims actions brought by government contractors. The section further provides that process under the FCA may be served "at any place within or outside the United States."[27] Finally, the FCA confers upon the district courts jurisdiction to hear any state law action for recovery of funds by a state or local government that "arises from the same transaction or occurrence" as a FCA action.

As noted above, F.R.C.P. Rule 9(b), requiring that fraud claims in false claims actions be stated "with particularity," is applied in FCA actions.[28] Some courts, however, have allowed the government and qui tam plaintiffs in FCA actions to particularize sketchy pleadings during discovery or in a pretrial order, particularly when the necessary facts are more accessible to the defendant than plaintiff.[29]

The Eleventh Amendment does not bar qui tam actions brought against state institutions, since the suit is brought on behalf of the United States, even if the United States chooses not to

---

22. See, e.g., United States v. Entin, 750 F.Supp. 512, 517 (S.D.Fla.1990).

23. See John Boese, Civil False Claims and Qui Tam Actions 5–17 to 5–18 (1995).

24. United States ex rel. Condie v. Board of Regents of Univ. of Cal., No. C893550–FMS, 1993 WL 740185 (N.D.Cal.1993); United States v. Incorporated Village of Island Park, 791 F.Supp. 354, 361–63 (E.D.N.Y.1992).

25. Island Park, 791 F. Supp. at 363–64.

26. United States ex rel. Hyatt v. Northrop Corp., 91 F.3d 1211 (9th Cir. 1996).

27. 31 U.S.C.A. § 3732(a).

28. Gold v. Morrison–Knudsen Co., 68 F.3d 1475, 1476–77 (2d Cir.1995), cert. denied, __ U.S. __, 116 S.Ct. 1836, 134 L.Ed.2d 939 (1996).

29. See United States v. Kensington Hosp., 760 F.Supp. 1120, 1125–26 (E.D.Pa.1991). See also Wilkins ex rel. United States v. Ohio, 885 F.Supp. 1055, 1060–61 (S.D.Ohio 1995); United States v. Warning, No. Civ.A. 93–4541, 1994 WL 396432 (E.D.Pa.1994).

intervene.[30] Recent district court opinions, however, have split on the question of whether a state is a "person" subject to being sued under the FCA.[30.5]

Third party claims for contribution and indemnification, either against a qui tam plaintiff or against another party who is responsible in part for the alleged fraud, are generally not available in FCA actions.[31]

d. Discovery

In general a FCA action proceeds like any other civil action, and any means of discovery available in civil actions generally are also available in FCA actions. There are, however, several additional means of discovery available to the federal government in developing FCA actions that are not generally available in civil litigation.

First, prior to the filing of an action the Department of Justice may issue a Civil Investigative Demand to aid in the investigation of possible FCA violations.[32] Section 3733 sets out in great detail the procedure through which CIDs are issued and enforced. A CID may be served upon any person whom the Attorney General has reason to believe may be in possession, custody or control of documentary material or information relevant to a FCA violation, and may demand that person:

> (A) to produce such documentary material for inspection and copying;

> (B) to answer in writing interrogatories with respect to such documentary material or information;

> (C) to give oral testimony concerning such documentary material or information; or

> (D) to furnish any combination of such material, answers, or testimony.[33]

The CID must specify the nature of the conduct under investigation and the law alleged to have been violated.[34] It may not require information that would be protected from disclosure under the law governing grand jury subpoenas or the discovery standards

---

30. United States ex rel. Sanders v. East Ala. Healthcare Auth., 953 F.Supp. 1404 (M.D.Ala.1996); United States ex rel. Milam v. University of Texas, 961 F.2d 46 (4th Cir. 1992); United States ex rel. Foulds v. Texas Tech. Univ., No 5:95–CV–135–C (N.D. Tex. 1997).

30.5 See, holding that a state is a "person," United States ex rel. Foulds v. Texas Tech. Univ. No. 5:95–CV–135–C (Oct. 3, 1997). See, rejecting this position, United States v. Regents of the University of Minnesota, No. 3–95–168 (D.Minn. July 23, 1997).

31. For an extensive analysis of this issue, see Thomas O'Neil III et al., The Buck Stops Here: Preemption of Third-Party Claims for the False Claims Act, 12 J. Contemp. Health L. & Pol'y 41 (1995).

32. 31 U.S.C.A. § 3733(a)(1).

33. 31 U.S.C.A. § 3733(a)(1).

34. 31 U.S.C.A. § 3733(a)(2)(A).

applicable under the Federal Rules of Civil Procedure.[35] Information obtained under a CID is only available to a false claims law investigator or other officer or employee of the DOJ, Congress, and, with court permission, to other federal agencies.[36] Petitions to enforce, modify, or set aside CIDs may be made to the federal district court.[37] Though CIDs are only available prior to the filing of an FCA action, there is some authority supporting the government's being able to use a CID during the period after a qui tam action has been filed but before the government intervenes.[38]

Inspectors General may issue pre-litigation subpoenas under the Inspectors General Act.[39] Information obtained through OIG subpoenas is often shared with the DOJ in preparation of FCA cases. Attorneys with the Civil Division of the DOJ may not normally obtain access to grand jury evidence, but may do so if they can show a "particularized need" under Fed.R.Crim.Proc. 6(e)(3)(C)(i).[40] Finally, it may be possible for providers fearing a FCA suit to "discover" information possessed by the government relevant to their claims through the Freedom of Information Act.[41]

§ 6–8. Damages and Penalties in Civil False Claims Litigation

The FCA provides that a person found to have violated its terms is liable for "a civil penalty of not less than $5,000 and not more than $10,000, plus 3 times the amount of damages which the Government sustains because of the act of that person" plus costs.[1] Determination of damages and penalties is often a key issue in an FCA case, particularly in cases where liability is established based on a prior criminal conviction through collateral estoppel.

Damages in FCA actions are based on the actual damages sustained by the government. In a case in which the claim is submitted for a service that was not provided, or for services that were provided but not in a form qualifying for reimbursement, the government is entitled to recover the full amount it paid.[2] In many cases, however, the amount of damages will be less than the

---

35. 31 U.S.C.A. § 3733(b)(1). See chapter 7, infra.

36. 31 U.S.C.A. § 3733(i)(C). Material obtained through a CID is not available under the Freedom of Information Act, 31 U.S.C.A. § 3733(k).

37. 31 U.S.C.A. § 3733(j).

38. Avco Corp. v. Department of Justice, 884 F.2d 621 (D.C.Cir.1989).

39. 5 U.S.C.A. App. 3, § 6(a).

40. See United States v. John Doe, Inc. I, 481 U.S. 102, 107 S.Ct. 1656, 95 L.Ed.2d 94 (1987).

41. 5 U.S.C.A. § 552.

§ 6–8

1. 31 U.S.C.A. § 3729(a). This provision is subject to an exception, discussed below, when there is voluntary disclosure and certain requirements are met. In such cases, only double damages are assessed.

2. See, e.g., Peterson v. Weinberger, 508 F.2d 45, 49 (5th Cir.1975); United States ex rel. Fahner v. Alaska, 591 F.Supp. 794, 801 (N.D.Ill.1984).

amount of the false claim.[3] When the defendant overcharges the government for an otherwise appropriate service, for example, the government is damaged only to the extent of the overcharge.[4] Where cost-based claims are submitted that include fraudulent as well as validly claimed costs, the government's damages are measured by the extent of the excess costs it paid.[5] When the FCA charge is based upon the payment of a bribe or kickback, some courts have awarded the amount of the payment;[6] others, more sensibly, have required the government to prove the extent of its actual damages caused by the bribe or kickback.[7] In a Medicaid FCA case, the damages due the United States are based on the federal share of the payment made.[8]

Once actual damages are calculated, the statute requires that they be trebled.[9] However, section 3729(a) provides that damages may be merely doubled, rather than tripled:

> [I]f the court finds that—
>
> (A) the person committing the violation . . . furnished officials of the United States responsible for investigating false claims violations with all information known to such person about the violation within 30 days after the date on which the defendant first obtained the information;
>
> (B) such person fully cooperated with any Government investigation of such violation; and
>
> (C) at the time such person furnished the United States with the information about the violation, no criminal prosecution, civil action, or administrative action had commenced under this title with respect to such violation, and the person did not have actual knowledge of the existence of an investigation into such violation.

If these requirements are met, a penalty also need not be assessed. These provisions are, it should be noted, permissive rather than mandatory. Voluntary disclosure thus is not risk free. The advan-

---

3. In this respect the measure of damages varies from that applied under the Medicare Civil Money Penalties law, which measures damages at the outset by the amount claimed. See Chapman v. United States Dep't of Health & Human Servs., 821 F.2d 523, 526–28 (10th Cir. 1987).

4. United States v. Halper, 490 U.S. 435, 437, 109 S.Ct. 1892, 1895, 104 L.Ed.2d 487 (1989).

5. See United States v. Education Dev. Network, Inc., No. Civ. A. 89–7780, 1993 WL 533218 (E.D.Pa.1993).

6. Id.

7. United States v. Killough, 848 F.2d 1523, 1532 (11th Cir.1988).

8. United States ex rel. Woodard v. Country View Care Ctr., 797 F.2d 888, 892–93 (10th Cir.1986).

9. 31 U.S.C.A. § 3729(A). Prior to the 1986 amendments the damages were doubled. Though the statute indicates that the trebling is non-discretionary, in one case a bankruptcy court refused to triple the damages since to do so would only damage other creditors, In re Bicoastal Corp., 134 B.R. 50, 54–55 (Bankr.M.D.Fla.1991).

tages and disadvantages of voluntary disclosure are discussed in chapter 8.

While damages under the FCA are extensive, they are also limited. Consequential damages seem not to be available under the act.[10] The government's costs of investigating violations are also not recoverable.[11] Where the government has already recovered money from the defendant through restitution in a criminal case or otherwise, the amount must be subtracted from the damages, though usually this is done after the original damages have been trebled.[12] Where the government concludes that the defendant did not "knowingly" defraud the government, however, there is no violation of the CFA, and the defendant can repay an overpayment without the multiplier being applied.[13]

The statute, as amended in 1986, provides for penalties of $5000 to $10,000 per claim. The statute does not specify the circumstances under which the higher or lower penalty is appropriate, and courts imposing penalties have offered little additional guidance. The statute seems to require a penalty for each "request or demand" submitted to the government for payment.[14] Courts would seem to have no discretion as to either the counting of claims or as to whether a penalty less than the minimum may be imposed.[15] If the penalties calculated under this provision are too great, however, they may raise constitutional issues, discussed in the next section.

Damages paid in FCA actions to compensate the government for its losses are tax deductible as business expenses, while amounts paid as penalties to punish or deter illegal conduct are not.[16] Whether a particular payment (including double damage payments) are compensatory or punitive is a question of fact.[17]

---

10. See John Boese, Civil False Claims and Qui Tam Actions 3–38 to 3–40 (1995) (discussing legislative history of 1986 amendments rejecting attempts to amend FCA to permit recovery of consequential damages).

11. Id. at 3–41 to 3–42.

12. United States v. Bornstein, 423 U.S. 303, 317, 96 S.Ct. 523, 531, 46 L.Ed.2d 514 (1976); United States v. Education Dev. Network, Inc., No. Civ. A. 89–7780, 1993 WL 533218 (E.D.Pa. 1993).

13. See Covington v. Sisters of 3d Order of St. Dominic, 61 F.3d 909 (9th Cir. 1995).

14. 31 U.S.C.A. § 3729(c). See United States v. Krizek, 111 F.3d 934, 938–40 (D.C.Cir.1997) (holding that relevant

unit for determining liability is entire claim form submitted by physician, not each separate code for which payment is claimed entered on form).

15. See, e.g., United States v. Killough, 848 F.2d 1523, 1533 (11th Cir. 1988); United States ex rel. Fahner v. Alaska, 591 F.Supp. 794, 799–800 (N.D.Ill.1984). Although Peterson v. Weinberger, 508 F.2d 45 (5th Cir.1975) would seem to recognize some discretion in the court in calculation of penalties, it is more appropriately understood as a recognition of the constitutional limits on imposition of penalties, discussed below.

16. Talley Indus. v. Commissioner, 116 F.3d 382 (9th Cir.1997).

17. Id.

§ 6–9.　Constitutional Limitations on False Claims Act Penalties

While the basic purpose of the FCA is to recover money improperly taken from the United States government by its contractors, the damage multiplier and penalties imposed by the statute can on occasion result in exceedingly large recoveries in relationship to the actual damages suffered by the United States.

One such case was United States v. Halper,[1] in which a physician who had been criminally convicted of overcharging the Medicare program through 65 claims at $9.00 a claim for a total of $585, was sued under the pre–1986 FCA for $130,000 in penalties ($2000 a claim). The Supreme Court, reviewing a district court judgment rejecting this proposed sanction, held that if a civil sanction is sufficiently disproportionate to the injury it is intended to remedy, it could have "either a retributive or deterrent purpose," and thus constitute a "punishment."[2] It further held that, where a civil penalty is in fact a "punishment," the Double Jeopardy clause of the Fifth Amendment would preclude the imposition of such civil punishments against a defendant who had already been subjected to criminal prosecution.[3] The Supreme Court, therefore, remanded Halper for the district court to determine if the penalty imposed was in fact so disproportionate to the total costs in fact incurred by the government (including their investigative costs) as to invoke the double jeopardy clause.[4]

In a subsequent case, Austin v. United States, the Court held that civil in rem forfeitures were reviewable for their reasonableness under the Excessive Fines Clause of the Eighth Amendment.[5] This holding permits an excessive civil recovery on the part of the government to be set aside, whether or not there was a prior criminal prosecution. While Austin did not involve a FCA case, its holding has subsequently been applied in a FCA case.[6]

Following Halper and Austin, courts are routinely called upon to determine whether FCA fines are excessive.[7] Where this issue is raised, courts commonly require the government to account for costs it has incurred in the criminal and/or civil investigation and prosecution of the particular defendant.[8] The courts are normally reluctant to hold damages and penalties imposed pursuant to the formulas set out in the FCA to be constitutionally defective, recognizing that Halper itself cautioned that its rule was a rule of reasonableness "for the rare case . . . where a fixed-penalty provi-

§ 6–9

1.　490 U.S. 435, 109 S.Ct. 1892, 104 L.Ed.2d 487 (1989).

2.　Id. at 448.

3.　Id. at 448–49.

4.　Id. at 452.

5.　509 U.S. 602, 113 S.Ct. 2801, 2802, 125 L.Ed.2d 488 (1993).

6.　United States ex rel. Smith v. Gilbert Realty, 840 F.Supp. 71, 73 (E.D.Mich.1993).

7.　See James Deverl, Double Jeopardy, False Claims and United States v. Halper, 20 Pub. Cont. L. J. 56, 56–86 (1990).

8.　See United States v. Fliegler, 756 F.Supp. 688, 696–97 (E.D.N.Y.1990).

sion subjects a prolific but small-gauge offender to a sanction overwhelmingly disproportionate to the damages he has caused."[9]

Thus in United States v. Pani the court approved a recovery of $32,460 for three false claims totaling $1280.[10] In United States v. Education Network Development, Inc., the court held that the amount of $2,344,530.94 sought by the government was reasonably related to the $204,376.98 that the defendant conceded it owed the government, and thus violated neither the double jeopardy nor the excessive fines clauses.[11] And in United States v. Barnette the court approved a recovery of up to $50.5 million on proved losses of $15,750,153, holding that the 3.2 to 1 ratio was not excessive, reasoning that the ratio, not the amount, was the key consideration.[12]

The courts do, however, from time to time reject penalties as excessive. In United States v. Kanelos, for example, the court required the government to prove its actual losses, reasoning that the possible ratio of 17.7 to 1 of the amount demanded by the government to its actual costs might be constitutionally excessive if found to be true.[13] And in United States ex rel. Smith v. Gilbert Realty,[14] the court found a penalty of $290,000 for a $1630 loss to be excessive. Prosecutors also, no doubt, limit the number of claims that they include in false claims actions to avoid confronting courts with absurdly great penalty claims.

Halper reserved the question of whether excessive recoveries in qui tam actions would raise double jeopardy problems.[15] The Double Jeopardy clause only pertains to cases brought by the government, and qui tam actions are in part private suits. If qui tam cases are to avoid constitutional problems under the appointments and separation of powers clauses, however, they must be understood as cases brought by the government, and thus subject to constitutional constraints on their recoveries. At least one case has so held.[16]

§ 6–10.   State False Claims Acts and Qui Tam Actions

a. Introduction

Many states have statutes permitting civil or administrative actions for Medicaid fraud and abuse. Statutes authorizing civil

---

9. 490 U.S. 435, 449, 109 S.Ct. 1892, 1902, 104 L.Ed.2d 487 (1989).

10. 717 F.Supp. 1013, 1019 (S.D.N.Y. 1989).

11. No. CIV. A. 89–7780, 1993 WL 533218 (E.D.Pa.1993).

12. 10 F.3d 1553, 1558–60.

13. No. 93 C 2251, 1994 WL 148655 (N.D.Ill.1994), vacated pursuant to set-

tlement, No. 93 C 251, 1994 WL 507796 (N.D. Ill.1994).

14. 840 F.Supp. 71, 75 (E.D.Mich. 1993).

15. 490 U.S. 435, n.11, 109 S.Ct. 1892, 104 L.Ed.2d 487 (1989).

16. United States ex rel. Smith v. Gilbert Realty, 840 F.Supp. 71, 74 (E.D.Mich.1993).

false claims remedies are discussed in chapter 2; statutes authorizing administrative recoveries in chapter 5. These statutes often parallel their federal equivalents in providing for multiple damages and monetary penalties for false claims. State statutes prohibiting bribes and kickbacks or self-referrals, discussed in chapters 3 and 4, also often provide for civil penalties.

Fewer states have statutes authorizing qui tam actions. As of this writing, California, Florida, Illinois, Oklahoma, Tennessee, and Texas have statutes authorizing qui tam actions for fraud committed against the state, including Medicaid or other state health care fraud.[1] Most of these statutes are modeled after the federal act, though there are important differences between the state acts and the federal acts, which are discussed below.[2]

b. California

The California qui tam statute permits persons (including business entities as well as natural persons) to bring qui tam actions to enforce the state false claims statute.[3] The California False Claims Act itself subjects persons who commit various acts, including the submission of false claims or false statements to treble damages plus fines of up to $10,000 for each false claim.[4] The act, and thus its qui tam provisions, only apply to false claims totaling in aggregate $500 or more.[5] Actions must be brought within three years of the discovery of the fraud by the official responsible to act in the circumstances, but in any event not later than 10 years after the violation.[6]

In a significant departure from the federal law, a qui tam relator under the California law may not bring an action that is based on information that was discovered by a present or former state or local government employee in the course of employment,

---

§ 6–10

1. Cal. Gov't Code §§ 12650—12655 (West 1995); Fla. Stat. Ann. §§ 68.081—68.089 (West 1995); Ill. Ann. Stat. ch. 740 para. 175/2—175/4 (Smith–Hurd 1995) Okla. Stat. Ann. tit. 62, § 373 (West 1995); Tenn. Code Ann. §§ 56–26–401 to 56–26–402, 71–5–181 to 71–5–186 (1995); Tex. Hum. Res. § 36.101.

2. An excellent discussion of the state qui tam statutes is found in John Boese, Civil False Claims and Qui Tam Actions (1995). This book contains a section-by-section analysis of the California False Claims Act prepared by the Center for Law in the Public Interest as an appendix.

3. Cal. Gov't Code §§ 12650(e); 12652(c)(1) (West 1995).

4. Id. at § 12651. If a person voluntarily disclosed a violation of the act within 30 days of discovering it, fully cooperates with the investigation, and discloses before a criminal, civil, or administrative action is commenced and without actual knowledge of an investigation, a penalty will not be assessed and damages of two to three times actual damages will be assessed. Id. at 12651(b). A person who inadvertently benefits from a false claim, and subsequently discovers but fails to disclose it within a reasonable time is also liable under the Act. Id. at 12651(a)(8).

5. Id. at § 12651(d). It also does not cover false claims or statements relevant to workers' compensation or to taxation. Id. at 12651(e),(f).

6. Id. at § 12654(a).

unless the employee first in good faith exhausted internal procedures to report and recover the falsely claimed money and the government failed to act within a reasonable period of time.[7] Like the federal statute, the California statute prohibits successive actions based on the same underlying facts and actions based upon allegations already the subject of civil or administrative proceedings brought by the state or based on information already publicly disclosed unless the relator is an original source of the information.[8] Significantly, the statute requires an original source to be a person whose directly and independently obtained information provided the "basis or catalyst" for the public disclosure.[9]

Under the California statute, the complaint is filed in camera and remains under seal for up to 60 days.[10] The relator must serve the Attorney General with the complaint and the information on which it is based.[11] The Attorney general must within 15 days notify the prosecuting authority of any political subdivision whose funds were involved in the fraud.[12] The Attorney General or local prosecuting authority must decide whether or not to intervene within 60 days.[13] While this period can be extended for good cause, the complaint may not in any event remain under seal for more than 45 days beyond the initial 60 day period, a significant departure from federal practice where complaints commonly remain under seal for more than a year.[14] If the Attorney General or prosecuting attorney elects not to intervene, it may intervene at a later stage of the proceeding if the interest of the state is not adequately protected by the qui tam plaintiff.[15] The government may settle or dismiss the case after the relator is given a hearing on any objections.[16]

A qui tam relator is entitled to 15 to 33 percent of the proceeds of an action or settlement if the Attorney General or a prosecuting attorney intervenes; 25 to 50 percent if the Attorney General or prosecuting attorney elects not to intervene or intervenes at a later stage of the proceeding.[17] If the relator is a present or former government employee, there is no minimum recovery, though the court may grant up to the maximum recovery considering the significance of the information provided by the relator, the role of the qui tam plaintiff in the litigation, and the extent of the relator's effort to secure government action initially.[18] Similar provisions apply with respect to relators who are present or former employees of the defendant and actively participated in the fraudulent activi-

7. Id. at § 12652(d)(4).
8. Id. at § 12652(c)(8), (d)(2), (3).
9. Id. at § 12652(d)(3)(B).
10. Id. at § 12652(c)(2).
11. Id. at § 12652(c)(3).
12. Id. at § 12652(c)(7)(a).
13. Id. at § 12652(c)(8)(B).
14. Id. at § 12652(c)(7)(D).
15. Id. at § 12652(f)(2)(A).
16. Id. at § 12652(e)(2).
17. Id. at § 12652(g)(2), (3).
18. Id. at 12652(g)(4).

ty.[19] Prevailing plaintiffs may recover their attorneys' fees and costs, as may prevailing defendants in actions where the state did not join and where the action was clearly frivolous, vexatious or brought solely for harassment.[20]

The California statute prohibits employers from adopting rules or policies preventing employees from cooperating with government investigations or enforcement activities and from taking retaliatory actions against persons who cooperate in fraud investigations or file qui tam actions.[21] It only protects an employee who participated in a fraud, however, if the employee voluntarily cooperated with the government and was coerced into engaging in the fraudulent activity in the first place.[22]

c. Florida

The Florida False Claims Act provides that persons who engage in forbidden conduct, including the knowing making of false claims or statements, are liable for treble damages and penalties of from $5000 to $10,000 per claim.[23] Innocent mistake is a defense under the Act.[24] The Act can be enforced through civil actions brought by the Department of Legal Affairs, the Department of Banking and Finance (where the action arises from one of its investigations) or by qui tam relators.[25] Under the Florida statute, actions must be brought within five years after the date of the violation plus up to two years from the date of the discovery of the violation by the responsible government official.[26]

The broad standing granted by the Florida statute to qui tam relators is subject to a public disclosure exception (which in turn is subject to the original source exception), which closely tracks its federal cognate.[27] The Act also, however, bars from bringing actions persons who are acting as attorneys for the state or employees or former employees of the state where the action is based on information obtained during the course of their employment, or by persons who have obtained information from present or former state employees not acting in the scope of their employment.[28] Actions may not be brought under the Act against local governments or against

---

19. Id. at § 12652(g)(5).

20. Id. at § 12562(g)(8), (9).

21. Id. at § 12653(a), (b). See Southern California Rapid Trans. Dist. v. Laster, 30 Cal.App.4th 713, 36 Cal. Rptr.2d 665 (1994).

22. Cal. Gov't Code § 12653(d) (West 1995).

23. Fla. Stat. Ann. § 68.082(2) (West 1995). Persons who voluntarily disclose violations that they discover within 30 days or before an action against them begins and before they become aware of an investigation, or who fully cooperate with a government investigation, may only be liable for double damages. Id. at § 68.082(3).

24. Id. at § 68.082(3).

25. Id. at § 68.083(1), (2).

26. Id. at § 68.089(1),(2).

27. Id. at § 68.087(3).

28. Id. at § 68.087(4), (5).

members of the legislature or judiciary or senior executive branch officials based upon information known to the state government.[29]

Under the Florida statute, a qui tam complaint is filed under seal and must be served immediately, with supporting information on the Attorney General and the head of the Department of Banking and Finance.[30] The government has up to 90 days to decide whether to intervene, and may seek extensions of this period.[31] The government may dismiss the claim even though the qui tam relator objects,[32] but may not settle the case without court permission.[33]

Provisions of the Florida False Claims Act governing the amount of the plaintiff's recovery closely track the federal statute. Qui tam plaintiffs may be awarded 15 to 25% of the recovery if the government intervenes or 25–30% if it does not, subject to reductions if the action is based in part on public disclosures or if the plaintiff participated in the fraud.[34] Prevailing public and qui tam plaintiffs may be awarded attorneys' fees and costs.[35] Prevailing defendants are also entitled to reasonable attorneys' fees and costs in actions where the state does not intervene, without any requirement that the action be frivolous or vexatious.[36] Employees who bring false claims actions or cooperate in false claims investigations are protected under the act from retaliation.[37]

d. Other States

The provisions of the Illinois statute are virtually identical to those of the Federal False Claims Act, including its civil investigative demand and retaliation provisions.[38] It deviates from the federal act only in 1) excluding actions related to the Illinois Income Tax Act or against the National Guard;[39] 2) not providing for reduced damages where the defendant voluntarily discloses and cooperates; 3) not providing for the payment of the costs of prevailing defendants by the government; 4) not extending collateral estoppel effect to nolo contendere pleas; and 5) providing for allocation of recoveries among state departments and enforcement agencies.[40]

Similarly, the Tennessee qui tam statutes bear a strong resemblance to the federal statute, though they are very different in two respects. First, they apply only to health care claims. (Tennessee in fact has two virtually identical qui tam statutes, one which applies

---

29. Id. at § 68.087(1), (6).
30. Id. at § 68.083(2),(3).
31. Id. at § 68.083(5), (6).
32. Id. at § 68.084(2)(a).
33. Id. at § 68.084(2)(b).
34. Id. at § 68.085.
35. Id. at § 68.086(1) & (2).

36. Id. at § 68.086(3).
37. Id. at § 68.088.
38. Ill. Ann. Stat. ch. 740, para. 175/1—175/8 (Smith–Hurd 1995).
39. Id. at 175/3(d), 175/4(e)(1).
40. Id. at 175/8.

to Medicaid claims,[41] the other which applies to other health insurance claims.[42]) Second, the statutes only authorize actions brought by qui tam relators, not by the state itself. Beyond these two major differences, the statute also deviates from the federal statute in other less significant respects. It does not provide for civil investigative demands, it includes a shorter list of conduct subject to penalty;[43] it prohibits the making of claims and statements knowing that they are false rather than the knowing making of false claims or statements;[44] it does not prohibit actions against public officials; it does not permit prevailing defendants to recover attorneys' fees against the government.

The Texas statute also provides only for qui tam actions for Medicaid fraud, but otherwise closely resembles the federal statute.[45] The statute permits the state to be represented by a private attorney in qui tam actions,[46] and to request a stay of discovery for 60 days subject to extension while it is investigating the allegations.[47] The statute allows the state to elect to proceed in administrative rather than court proceedings, with findings of fact and conclusions of law made in the administrative proceedings binding in the court proceedings if they are not appealed, not subject to judicial review, or affirmed on appeal.[48] The relator has the same rights in the administrative proceedings as he or she would have in court.[49] Under the statute the state may recover restitution of any payments or benefits provided, interest, and a civil penalty of $5000 to $15,000 if the violation results in injury to an elderly or disabled person or person under 18; $1000 to 10,000 for other violations, plus two times the value of the benefit.[50] A qui tam relator may be awarded costs and attorneys' fees plus 10% to 25% of the proceeds of the action, but not more than 7% if the action is based primarily on disclosures of specific information other than that provided by the relator.[51] The court may also reduce the award, to the extent the court considers appropriate, if the relator planned or initiated the violation.[52] The statute also prohibits retaliation by employers against persons bringing actions.[53] Separate provisions of the recent Texas legislation permit the state to award persons who report fraud, abuse or overcharges to the state not less than 10% of the savings to the state that result from the disclosure where the

---

41. Tenn. Code Ann. §§ 71–5–181 to 71–5–186 (1995).

42. Id. at §§ 56–26–401 to 56–26–406.

43. Id. at 71–5–182, 56–26–403.

44. Id. at 71–5–182(a)(1)(A), 56–26–403(a)(1)(A).

45. Tex. Hum. Res. Code § 36.101.

46. Tex. Hum. Res. Code § 36.105.

47. Tex. Hum. Res. Code § 36.108.

48. Tex. Hum. Res. Code § 36.109.

49. Tex. Hum. Res. Code § 36.109(a).

50. Tex. Hum. Res. Code § 36.052(a).

51. Tex. Hum. Res. Code § 36.110.

52. Tex. Hum. Res. Code § 36.111.

53. Tex. Hum. Res. Code § 36.115.

disclosure results in the recovery or an overcharge or in the termination of fraud and abuse.[54]

In contrast to the other statutes discussed above, the Oklahoma qui tam statute is aimed more at corrupt government than at false claims, and only covers money paid by the state for claims known to be fraudulent or void or pursuant to "unauthorized, unlawful, or fraudulent" contracts.[55] This prohibition could conceivably cover some health care claims, however. The Act provides for treble damages against the government official and any other participants in the fraud.[56] It further provides that a taxpayer may demand that a responsible government official take action in response to the fraud. If no action is forthcoming, the taxpayer may file a qui tam action.[57] A prevailing qui tam plaintiff in such an action may claim half of the recovery.[58]

e. Issues in State False Claims and Qui Tam Actions

On the whole these state statutes are quite new and have not yet been the subject of reported litigation. Since most of the statutes closely parallel the federal qui tam statute, the state courts will presumably draw on the extensive federal caselaw for precedents interpreting their own statutes, though they are of course not bound to do so. In particular, though challenges to the constitutionality of the Federal False Claims Act and its qui tam provisions have been uniformly rejected, challenges to state qui tam statutes under state constitutional provisions may enjoy greater success.[59] For example, state qui tam statutes may be vulnerable to challenges based on constitutional provisions giving exclusive authority to litigate for the state to the state attorney general.[60]

Since the Medicaid program is jointly funded by both the federal and state government, Medicaid false claims violate both the federal and state false claims laws, and could be pursued by either federal or state false claims actions. This raises a number of obvious issues of choice of courts and laws.

The first is whether an action alleging both federal and state claims should be brought in federal or state court. Although 28 U.S.C.A. § 1335 would seem to give exclusive jurisdiction to the federal courts for actions involving a fine or penalty, the qui tam statute itself says simply that a false claims action may be brought

---

54. Tex. Gov't Code § 531.101.

55. Okla. Stat. Ann. tit. 62, § 372 (West 1995).

56. Id.

57. Id. at § 373.

58. Id.

59. See Boese, supra note 2, at 6–20 to 6–22.

60. See, e.g., Ill. Const. art 5, § 15. Under which the Illinois Environmental Protection Act was declared unconstitutional for authorizing the prosecution of actions on behalf of the state by persons other than the Attorney General. People ex rel. Scott v. Briceland, 65 Ill.2d 485, 3 Ill.Dec. 739, 359 N.E.2d 149 (Ill. 1976).

in federal court,[61] and a couple of district court cases have found jurisdiction for deciding federal false claims disputes in state courts.[62] Section 3732(b) gives the federal district courts pendant jurisdiction over state law claims to recover state funds in federal false claims actions. The California statute, however, states that a qui tam claim "shall be filed in superior court in camera,"[63] and the Florida statute specifies that a qui tam action "shall be filed in the circuit court of the Second Judicial Circuit, in and for Leon County."[64] It may be, therefore, that these actions could not be brought in federal court. Failure to raise related claims under both federal and state statutes in a single forum may preclude subsequent litigation under the other statute in the other forum.[65]

Presumably whichever court is chosen will apply state law to state claims and federal law to federal claims. Where both laws apply, however (as with retaliatory discharges in some states), this may be problematic.

Both the federal and state governments may claim restitution, multiple damages, and penalties for Medicaid false claims under both federal and state law, both of which are violated by false Medicaid claims. Presumably the state could only recover for its share of the Medicaid payments (plus penalties under state law) and the federal government for its share (plus penalties under federal law).[66] A Medicaid provider faced with false claims charges is well advised to deal with both sovereigns to avoid multiple recoveries.

---

61. 31 U.S.C.A. § 3732(a).

62. United States ex rel. Hartigan v. Palumbo Bros., Inc., 797 F.Supp. 624 (N.D.Ill.1992); United States ex rel. Paul v. Parsons, Brinkerhoff, Quade & Douglas, Inc., 860 F.Supp. 370 (S.D.Tex. 1994), aff'd 53 F.3d 1282 (5th Cir.1995), cert. denied, ___ U.S. ___, 116 S.Ct. 817, 133 L.Ed.2d 762 (1996). See, criticizing these decisions, Boese, supra note 2, at 5–48 to 5–49.

63. Cal. Gov't Code § 12652(c)(2) (West 1995).

64. Fla. Stat. Ann. § 68.083(3) (West 1995).

65. See Parsons, Brinkerhoff, Quade & Douglas, Inc., 860 F.Supp. 370.

66. See United States ex rel. Woodard v. Country View Care Ctr., 797 F.2d 888 (10th Cir. 1986).

Chapter 7

INVESTIGATIONS

Table of Sections

WESTLAW Electronic Research

See WESTLAW Electronic Research Guide preceding the Summary of Contents.

Library References:

C.J.S. Social Security and Public Welfare § 126–138.
West's Key No. Digests, Social Security and Public Welfare ☞18, 241.5–241.115.

§ 7–1. Introduction

The investigation of Medicare and Medicaid fraud has become a national priority. The United States Attorney General has named health care fraud her number one white collar crime priority,[1] and a veritable army of federal, state and private entities and individuals has joined the fight against fraud and abuse in the health care industry. On the front line in this battle are private insurance companies known as carriers and intermediaries. Carriers and intermediaries, under contract with HCFA, process claims for payment under the Medicare program, and thus are frequently first to detect the improper billing practices of a health care provider. These private contractors also receive and investigate consumer complaints about the services provided by, or billing practices of, members of the health care industry. State and federal agencies, departments and offices with oversight and prosecutorial responsibilities, make up the next enforcement regiment. This diverse group includes the Department of Health and Human Services, HHS's Office of the Inspector General (OIG), the Health Care

§ 7–1

1. See BNA Health Care Daily d3 (August 14, 1997) (the Attorney General announced this priority at a conference of United States Attorneys in Washington, D.C. in late 1993).

Financing Administration (HCFA), the Department of Justice, the Federal Bureau of Investigation, the United States Attorneys' Offices, the state Medicaid Fraud Control Units (MFCUs) and more. State Medicaid Fraud Control Units (MFCUs), now in place in almost every state, patrol disbursements under the Medicaid program with a combined staff of over one thousand employees. Peer Review Organizations (PROs), state licensing boards, *qui tam* relators and other whistle-blowers comprise the rear guard against fraud and abuse within the federal health care programs.

This chapter examines the role played by each of these important participants in the fight against Medicare and Medicaid fraud and abuse, and the increasing coordination among these players. The chapter describes the investigative tools preferred by regulators and investigators, including: the operation of the grand jury and the issuance of grand jury subpoenas, the execution of search warrants as a tool for collecting evidence, and the use of administrative subpoenas and search warrants. Also considered are the defenses most frequently employed by health care providers either to resist grand jury or administrative demands for documents or testimony, or to recapture documents or other items confiscated in a search pursuant to warrant. Challenges based on the Fourth and Fifth Amendments to the United States Constitution are specifically addressed, as are a host of common law and statutory privileges that are raised in this context, such as the attorney-client privilege, the physician-patient privilege and the psychotherapist-patient privilege.

§ 7–2. The Investigators—Carriers and Intermediaries

The Medicare program is divided into two parts: Part A, covering services furnished by hospitals, home health agencies, hospices and skilled nursing facilities, and Part B, covering physician services and a host of other noninstitutional supplies and services, including durable medical equipment (DME), diagnostic laboratory tests and x-rays.[1] As discussed in Chapter 1,[2] HCFA, the agency within the Department of Health and Human Services (HHS) responsible for administering the Medicare program, contracts with approximately 73 private companies (such as Blue Cross and Blue Shield, Travelers, Mutual of Omaha and Aetna), commonly referred to as "carriers" and fiscal "intermediaries" to process and review claims and approve appropriate claim payments under the Medicare program.[3] Carriers process, review and issue payment

§ 7–2

1. See 42 U.S.C.A. § 1395i and 42 U.S.C.A. § 1395k.

2. See § 1–3.

3. See GAO, Medicare and Private Payers Are Vulnerable to Fraud and Abuse at 1 (GAO/T–HRD–92–95 Sept. 10, 1992). The Health Insurance Portability and Accountability Act of 1996

on Part B claims, while intermediaries process, review and issue payment on Part A claims. One intermediary received considerable attention recently when its special investigative unit reported that it had saved the Medicare program more than $172 million and referred 167 cases to law enforcement officials in a single year.[4]

Carriers and intermediaries are expected not only to process claims in a timely and efficient manner, but to utilize payment safeguards to prevent improper program expenditures. Carriers and intermediaries are permitted to establish local criteria by which medical services are to be reimbursed in particular geographical areas. This arrangement is designed to account for locality-based differences that exist between medical practices and billing rates. An outgrowth of this accommodation has been that significant variations in payment practices have developed between different geographic areas. These differences sometimes make it difficult for investigators to detect fraud, waste and abuse within the Medicare program.[5]

Carriers and intermediaries employ a variety of controls to carry out their payment safeguard responsibilities. Software packages perform edits and audits of providers' claims for payment while private contractors conduct utilization reviews, cost report and physician audits, facility inspections and complaint investigations to prevent improper disbursements.[6] Each carrier and intermediary has a Special Investigative Unit (SIU) to explore reports of suspected fraud which come from a variety of sources including consumers, data entry personnel, auditors, medical review teams and HCFA. If the SIU determines that a particular claim or a pattern of claim activity is suspicious, the matter will be referred to the OIG for further investigation.[7]

Although carriers and intermediaries are uniquely positioned to guard against improper claims for payment under the Medicare program, the task of identifying suspicious claims is fraught with difficulty. To understand why, it is important to know how the claims processing and payment safeguard system works. Claims processing is performed through a combination of human and

(hereinafter HIPAA) authorizes the Secretary to enter into contracts with entities other than the current carriers and intermediaries to safeguard the Medicare program. See HIPAA, Pub.L.No. 104–191, § 202. The Secretary has yet to award such a contract, however. See Medicare: Control Over Fraud and Abuse Remains Elusive, GAO/T–HEHS–97–165 at 3, n. 1 (June 1997).

4. See Ursula Himali, Mutual of Omaha Recovers $5 Million In Fraud, Saving $11 for Every Dollar Spent, 1 BNA's Health Care Fraud Report, 439, 439–40 (1997).

5. See GAO, Medicare and Private Payers Are Vulnerable to Fraud and Abuse, GAO/T–HRD–92–56 (Sept. 10, 1992).

6. The states are required to implement similar controls to guard against waste, fraud and abuse in the Medicaid program.

7. See Medicare Carrier's Manual § 14,000.

computer effort. Claims for payment are analyzed first by a computer under an automated payment system. Carriers and intermediaries receive claims either in paper form (in which case data entry personnel manually enter, or scan, the information on the claim form into the computer) or in electronic form. No matter how the claim is submitted, after entry into the computer system, each claim will undergo an automated edit—which searches the claim for data entry errors—and a series of automated audits—which assess whether the claim should be paid. When operational,[8] the computerized audits probe each claim to test: (1) whether the claim data entered is accurate and complete; (2) whether prior authorization was required, and if so, obtained for the procedure; (3) whether the entered procedure code appropriately corresponds to the diagnosis; (4) whether the provider is enrolled in the program, is approved to perform the procedure, needs to submit supporting documentation, and whether the provider's rates have been approved; (5) whether the consumer is enrolled in the program, is covered for the procedure, and is subject to a deductible; (6) whether the provider's charge for the procedure falls within the range of acceptable charges; (7) whether the consumer is covered for the procedure in light of earlier claims for procedures undergone by the consumer; (8) whether a possible duplicate claim for the procedure has been submitted by another provider; and (9) whether the claim improperly bundles procedure codes.[9]

Carriers and intermediaries are required to authorize payment for the provision of any covered service or supply that is medically necessary. Thus, claims that maneuver through this computerized series of edits and audits without incident are passed on for automatic payment. Payment will be made to the physician, supplier or Medicare beneficiary, as appropriate, and an Explanation of Medicare Benefits (EOMB) letter will be issued to the beneficiary.[10]

Claims that raise a red flag for one reason or another, however, will either be automatically rejected (with a notice sent to the provider explaining the basis for the denial of payment), automatically adjusted and paid (e.g., the data entry error or the improper charge will be corrected and the proper rate for the procedure paid)

8. See Malcom K. Sparrow, License to Steal: Why Fraud Plagues America's Health Care System 82 (Westview Press 1996) (noting that carriers and intermediaries sometimes disengage their audit software packages to limit their claims-suspension rates because HCFA will compensate the carrier for a maximum suspension rate of approximately 9% of the claims).

9. For a thorough discussion of the inquiries involved in the computerized

auditing process, see Sparrow, supra note 8, at 78.

10. An EOMB is an important payment safeguard. Many fraud and abuse investigations begin when a beneficiary questions a payment made by the program for a service reflected on an EOMB form. See GAO, Medicare: Control Over Fraud and Abuse Remains Elusive at 6, GAO/T–HEHS–97–165 (June 26, 1997).

or suspended for further investigation. Thus, typically, only suspended claims are routed to a claims examiner or a medical review team for manual review and investigation.

Existing automated payment system controls work reasonably well in weeding out claims for payment that are based on flawed billing procedures. Thus, if a provider submits a claim that improperly bundles certain procedures resulting in a higher cost to the program, the automated auditing programs should deny the inflated claim for payment either by rejecting it outright, or by reducing it to what it should have been absent the improper bundling. Similarly, if the provider submits a claim that includes a charge for a procedure not covered by the program, automated payment system controls should send the provider a notice denying payment and explaining the basis of the denial.[11] The implementation of these control mechanisms has resulted in significant savings to the government.

Automated edit and audit controls are less adept at identifying fraud within the Medicare program. The computerized controls assume the truthfulness of the data submitted on claims for payments. Thus, if a provider submits a claim for payment based upon a particular diagnosis and procedure, the software will probe the claim for certain things, such as whether the procedure was appropriate for the diagnosis, whether the provider is an eligible participant in the program, whether the beneficiary and the particular procedure are covered by Medicare, and so on. The automated auditing functions will assume, however, that the diagnosis was actually given, the procedure was actually performed, the consumer actually received the provider's services, etc. In other words, computerized auditing controls are not designed to consider the possibility that information on claims for payment may be fraudulent.[12]

In addition to pre-payment claims review, carriers and intermediaries conduct a variety of post-payment reviews, including "focused medical reviews" which examine the billings of particular providers, comprehensive audits of the claims of suspect providers and audits of cost reports.[13] Focused medical reviews look for

11. See id.

12. See id. at 95.

13. See GAO, Medicare: Control Over Fraud and Abuse Remains Elusive at 6, GAO/T–HEHS–97–165 (June 1997). Cost reports are submitted by providers reimbursed on a cost basis, i.e., for the reasonable cost of providing the service, rather than on the basis of a fee schedule or the charge for a service. Intermediaries process "interim" payments for the services provided by cost-based providers (including hospital outpatient departments, skilled nursing facilities and home health agencies) based on the providers' historical costs and current cost estimates. See id. at 7. Adjustments to those payments are made by intermediaries on the basis of the providers' end-of-the-year cost reports which set forth the providers' actual costs. Unscrupulous providers may inflate the costs reflected in these reports to receive larger payments.

unusual billing patterns by comparing the claims submitted by a provider to the bills of the provider's peers. If irregularities are detected, the provider's claims may be subjected to a claims audit. Claims audits carefully examine a sample of a provider's claims to determine whether the services were medically necessary and otherwise in compliance with billing procedures. Because claims audits involve time- and resource-intensive reviews of documents and beneficiary interviews, the abusive billing practices of many providers and suppliers go undetected. Recent budget allocations for claims review and post-payment auditing have not kept pace with the escalating number of Medicare claims processed by the private contractors, thus weakening their ability to detect and deter fraud and abuse.[14]

In 1992, Congress held hearings to study the quality of carriers' claim processing procedures.[15] Thereafter, in response to legislation, HCFA moved to curb disturbing levels of fraud found common among DME suppliers by reducing the number of Medicare carriers that processed DME claims from 32 to 4. The remaining carriers, located in four separate regions, are commonly referred to as Durable Medical Equipment Regional Carriers, or DMERCs.

Even with this change, concerns about the ability of private contractors to detect fraudulent billing practices milking the Medicare program remain. A frequently voiced complaint is that carriers and intermediaries have not made use of available commercial software to detect abusive claims.[16] A study conducted in 1995 compared the claims that would have been approved by four commercial firms using such computer software technology to those actually approved by Medicare. The firms were asked to reprocess (without compensation) over 200,000 selected claims that the Medicare paid in 1993. The findings revealed that had Medicare used the same computer technology used by the firms, the program would have saved approximately $640 million in fiscal year 1994 alone.[17]

A more fundamental concern is that the efficient automated payment system controls employed by carriers and intermediaries

---

14. See GAO, Medicare: Control Over Fraud and Abuse Remains Elusive, GAO/T–HEHS–97–165 (June 1997).

15. See GAO, HCFA Monitoring of the Quality of Part B Claims Processing (Sept. 23, 1992). GAO, Health Insurance: Medicare and Private Payers Are Vulnerable to Fraud and Abuse, GAO/T–HRD–92–56 (Sept. 10, 1992).

16. See GAO, Medicare: Control Over Fraud and Abuse Remains Elusive at 10–11, GAO/T–HEHS–97–165 (June 1997).

17. See GAO, Medicare Claims Billing Abuse: Commercial Software Could Save Hundreds of Millions Annually at 3, GAO/T–AIMD–95–133 (May 5, 1995); GAO, Medicare Claims: Commercial Technology Could Save Billions Lost to Billing Abuse at 23, GAO/AIMD–95–135 (May 5, 1995); GAO, Reducing Fraud and Abuse Can Save Billions at 6, GAO/T–HEHS–95–157 (May 16, 1995).

are not designed to identify and prevent fraud.[18] One commentator has observed that although the edit and auditing software programs guarantee that Medicare will "pay the right amount to the right person for the service claimed," the programs do not "verify that the service was in fact provided as claimed, or that the diagnosis is genuine, or that the patient knows anything at all about the alleged treatment."[19] Thus, without more frequent post-payment reviews for patterns of billing irregularities, or the use of more sophisticated computer programs designed to compare claims "on line,"[20] carriers and intermediaries will never be able fully to protect the Medicare program against losses due to fraud and abuse.

In the future, fraud control activities may no longer be the responsibility of carriers and intermediaries currently under contract with HCFA. Under the Medicare Integrity Program[21] established by the Health Insurance Portability and Accountability Act of 1996 (HIPAA),[22] the Secretary is authorized to enter into contracts with private eligible entities other than its current contractors to review the services or items supplied by health care providers or other individuals for which payment may be sought under the Medicare program; conduct medical, utilization and fraud reviews; audit cost reports; determine whether payments should or should not be (or have been) made under the program; educate providers, beneficiaries and others about payment integrity and benefit quality assurance; and develop a list of durable medical equipment subject to preauthorization controls.[23] HCFA has yet to award any of these contracts, however.

§ 7–3. State Investigators—Medicaid Fraud Control Units (MFCUs)

Although the problem of fraud and abuse within the health care programs has recently become a priority of the United States Department of Justice, the states have been vigilant protectors

---

18. See Sparrow, supra note 8, at 79–83.

19. See id. at 79.

20. For an interesting discussion of HCFA's now abandoned plan to replace the contractors' current automated systems with the Medicare Transaction System (MTS) to enhance their fraud and abuse detection capabilities, see GAO, Medicare: Control Over Fraud and Abuse Remains Elusive at 10, GAO/T-HEHS–97–165 (June 1997).

21. See HIPAA, Pub.L.No. 104–191, § 202, 110 Stat. 1936, 1996–98 (1996)(adding Social Security Act § 1816(l), 1842(c)(6) & 1893, 42 U.S.C.A. § 1395h(l), 1395u(c)(6) & 1395ddd).

22. Pub.L.No. 104–191, 110 Stat. 1936 (1996).

23. See HIPAA, Pub.L.No. 104–191, § 202(a), 110 Stat. 1936, 1996 (1996), 42 U.S.C.A. § 1395ddd (West Supp.1997), Social Security Act § 1893.

against fraud in the Medicaid program for nearly twenty years.[1] In 1977, after a series of congressional hearings revealed that theft and patient abuse were running rampant in the Medicaid program, Congress passed legislation which authorized the creation of state Medicaid Fraud Control Units (MFCUs) to combat abuse of the system.[2] The Medicare–Medicaid Anti–Fraud and Abuse Amendments conferred broad authority upon the MCFU's to investigate and prosecute both fraud and abuse in the Medicaid program, and patient abuse and neglect in health care facilities funded by the Medicaid program.[3] State MFCUs operate independently of the agencies that administer the Medicaid programs.[4] They are normally housed in the offices of the state Attorneys' General and are manned by squads of lawyers, investigators and auditors specially trained in the complexities of health care fraud.[5] The responsibilities of the state MFCUs were significantly expanded in 1995, when the National Association of Medicaid Fraud Control Units (NAMFCU), the National Association of Attorneys General, HHS and the United States Attorney General agreed to expand the jurisdiction of the units to permit their investigation of suspected fraud and abuse occurring within the Medicare and other federally funded health care programs.

Since the inception of the State Medicaid Fraud Control Unit Program in 1977, the MFCUs have grown in number and stature due to legislative mandates and an assortment of financial incentives created to encourage the states both to set up MFCUs and to ensure that the units vigilantly police Medicaid program expenditures. With the passage of the Omnibus Reconciliation Act of 1980, each state was required to institute a MFCU as a prerequisite for receiving federal Medicaid funds, unless the state could certify that only a minimum of Medicaid fraud and abuse occurred within the state which it could address through other effective means.[6] As a result, as of 1996, all but three states had established a MFCU to

§ 7–3

1. See Health Care Fraud: Milking Medicare and Medicaid: Hearings S.Hrg. 104–434 before the Senate Special Comm. on Aging, 104th Cong., 1st Sess., 49–50 (1995)(testimony of New York Attorney General Dennis Vacco).

2. See the Medicare–Medicaid Anti-Fraud and Abuse Amendments, Pub. L.No. 95–142, 91 Stat. 1175 (1977), which established the state MFCU program. The program was patterned after a program established in New York in 1975. 42 U.S.C.A. § 1396b(q)(3) (1994); see also H.R. Rep. No. 95–393(II), 79 (1977), reprinted in 1977 U.S.C.C.A.N. 3039, 3082.

3. See id.; see also People v. Baghai-Kermani, 605 N.Y.S.2d 19, 199 A.D.2d 36 (N.Y.App.Div.1993).

4. See Medicare–Medicaid Anti-fraud and Abuse Amendments, Pub.L.No. 95–142, 91 Stat. 1175 (1977).

5. See Health Care Fraud: Milking Medicare and Medicaid: Hearings on S.Hrg. 104–434 before the Senate Special Comm. on Aging, 104th Cong., 1st Sess., 49–50 (1995)(testimony of New York Attorney General Dennis Vacco).

6. The Omnibus Reconciliation Act of 1980, Pub.L.No. 96–499, 94 Stat. 2599 (1980). See also Pedroso v. Florida, 450 So.2d 902, 903 (Fla.Dist.Ct.App.1984) (state must have a MFCU as a prerequisite to receiving federal Medicaid funds).

scout out incidents of fraud and abuse within the Medicaid program.

In addition, important financial incentives encourage MFCUs to police the Medicaid programs aggressively. Increased Medicaid payments from the federal government are tied to each state's fraud and abuse recoveries. The costs and expenses of state MFCUs are also federally subsidized.[7]

The state units execute the same investigatory functions on the state level as the OIG executes on a federal level. By 1995, the state MFCUs deployed a combined staff of approximately 1,150,[8] and in addition to state funding, received $62 million in federal support.[9] The units vary in size in proportion to the size of their states' Medicaid programs. Near the close of 1995, the state MFCUs were responsible for the successful prosecution of over 7,000 errant providers, vendors and other abusers of the state health care program.[10]

The state MFCUs have developed uniform procedures to coordinate their efforts with those of their federal counterparts through the National Association of Medicaid Fraud Control Units (NAMFCU). These procedures have eased the resolution of Medicaid-related claims against interstate providers,[11] and more recent coop-

---

7. For the first three years of a unit's operation, the federal government provides 90% of the unit's costs. See Omnibus Reconciliation Act of 1980, Pub.L.No. 96–499, 94 Stat. 2599. Thereafter each unit receives 75% its funding from the federal government, with a 25% state matching rate. See A Review of the State Medicaid Fraud Control Unit Program, Medicaid Fraud and Patient Abuse at 81 n.1 and n.9 (National Association of Medicaid Fraud Control Units).

8. See Health Care Fraud: Milking Medicare and Medicaid: Hearings on S.Hrg. 104–434 before the Senate Special Comm. on Aging, 104th Cong., 1st Sess., 49 (1995)(testimony of New York Attorney General Dennis Vacco).

9. See John R. Munich, The Medicaid Anti–Fraud Amendments of 1994: Attorney General's Weapon in the Fight Against White Collar Crime, 52 J.Mo.B. 26, 27 (Jan./Feb. 1996) (citing Daniel R. Anderson, State Fraud Initiatives: The Role of Medicaid Fraud Control Units at 4 (1994)).

10. See A Review of the State Medicaid Fraud Control Unit Program, Medicaid Fraud and Patient Abuse at 1 (National Association of Medicaid Fraud

Control Units). In addition to the MFCUs, many states have Bureaus of Utilization Review which conduct civil investigations by inspecting providers' bills and other records to determine if the providers' bills accurately reflect the services rendered and whether the providers are adhering to practice standards. Although utilization review bureaus do not conduct criminal investigations, they do refer suspected criminal activity to state MFCUs and other investigative bodies. See, e.g., Commonwealth v. Wu, 343 Pa.Super. 108, 110, 494 A.2d 7, 8 (Pa.1985) (dentist suspected of medicaid fraud referred by Bureau of Utilization Review to MFCU).

11. See Health Care Fraud: Milking Medicare and Medicaid: Hearings on S.Hrg. 104–434 before the Senate Special Comm. on Aging, 104th Cong., 1st Sess., 45–46 (1995)(testimony of New York Attorney General Dennis Vacco). In one of the largest multistate settlements to date, 27 state MFCUs and the District of Columbia negotiated a $16.3 million settlement with NME Psychiatric Hospitals, Inc. NME was charged to have paid kickbacks to physicians who referred patients to NME hospitals. See id. at 46.

erative efforts between state and federal investigators of health care fraud have resulted in large settlements.

In summary, state MFCUs have led the fight against fraud and abuse in the Medicaid program for the last twenty years. Recently, the role played by these state investigative units has been broadened to cover fraud in other federally funded health care programs as well. The developing interest of the United States Department of Justice in health care fraud cases promises that formidable investigative and prosecutorial resources will be devoted to Medicare and Medicaid fraud in the years to come. State and federal investigators hope that their increased coordination will result in more effective policing of the federally funded health care programs and ultimately deter misconduct within the health care industry.

§ 7–4. The Department of Health and Human Services

a. The Office of Inspector General (OIG)

The Office of the Inspector General (OIG) for the Department of Health and Human Services (HHS) is the principal federal investigatory agent of fraud and abuse in the federal health care programs. The Inspector General is appointed by the President on the advice and consent of Congress, and serves at the discretion of the President under the supervision of the Secretary of HHS. The OIG recommends policy to improve the economy and efficiency of HHS entitlement programs, and keeps Congress abreast of flaws in the programs.

The OIG's duties and responsibilities are substantial. It conducts fraud and abuse investigations independent of those conducted by the United States Department of Justice and oversees the investigations undertaken by state MFCUs into fraud and abuse in the Medicaid program. The Health Insurance Portability and Accountability Act of 1996 (HIPAA)[1] provided increased funding for the OIG's investigative efforts. For fiscal year 1997, HIPAA allocated $70 million to the OIG alone. The office plans to use this money to hire 250 additional investigators, auditors, attorneys and other experts to expose fraud and abuse within the programs. It also plans to establish a field office in every state by the year 2003.[2] Dramatic increases in the size of the OIG's staff have already been realized. As a result of the HIPAA funding, the number of federal health care fraud investigators increased by 31 percent in just two years,[3] and many of those investigators make up part of the OIG's

§ 7–4

1. Pub.L.No. 104–191, 110 Stat. 1936 (1996).

2. See While Fraud–Fighting Efforts Increase, Chances of Being Caught Said to be Slim, BNA Health Care Daily d2 (August 21, 1997).

3. See 1 BNA's Health Care Fraud Rptr. 690 (Oct. 22, 1997).

burgeoning staff. The OIG's full time employees (FTEs) grew from slightly over 900 to 1,143 in fiscal year 1996 alone.[4]

Between May 1996 and October 1997, the OIG was divided into an assortment of divisions, including the Office of Audit Services, the Office of Evaluation and Inspections, the Office of Investigations, the Office of Enforcement and Compliance, the Office of Litigation and Coordination and the Office of Management and Policy. In October 1997, however, the OIG disbanded the Office of Enforcement and Compliance, following the resignation of that division's Deputy Inspector General, Eileen Boyd. The tasks formerly assigned to the Office of Enforcement and Compliance will now be shared by the Office of Investigations and the OIG's Office of Counsel. The OIG divisions enjoy wide-reaching powers to audit HHS programs for fraud, abuse and waste, to conduct inspections and formulate policies designed to stem fraudulent and abusive practices, to conduct investigations, to suspend, exclude or impose civil monetary penalties upon errant health care providers, to develop corporate compliance programs, to coordinate state, federal and private investigations and litigation related to fraud within the health care programs, and to issue fraud alerts.

To perform these myriad duties, the divisions of the OIG enjoy broad access to records, reports, audits, reviews, documents, papers, recommendations, and other material that relate to the Medicare, Medicaid or other federally funded health care programs. The OIG can demand access to facilities or documents maintained by health care providers, and access must be granted within twenty-four hours, or immediately if there is reason to believe that records are about to be altered or destroyed.[3] In addition, the OIG has access to provider and beneficiary data maintained by carriers and intermediaries under contract with HCFA.

Once alerted to the possibility of fraudulent activity, as explored more fully below,[4] the OIG has the power to issue subpoenas for documents, take testimony under oath and conduct searches.[5] Administrative subpoenas issued by the OIG are enforceable in federal district court.[6] Special Agents of the OIG also conduct undercover surveillance, interview "whistleblowers,"[7] and follow up on leads from anonymous tipsters over the OIG hotline.[8]

---

4. See id.

3. 42 C.F.R. § 1001.1301.

4. See § 7–20.

5. 42 U.S.C.A. § 1320a–7a(j)(1994).

6. See 5 U.S.C.App. § 6(a)(4) (1994).

7. Quick Start Key to Defense of Fraud Allegations, Defense Attorney Says, 2 BNA Health Law Reporter 564 (fertile source of information about health care fraud is discontented whistleblowers).

8. See K. DeBry et al., Eleventh Survey of White Collar Crime, Health Care Fraud, 33 Am. Crim. L. Rev. 815, 836 (1996).

Although the OIG is not empowered to prosecute suspected criminal activity, it is authorized to share evidence that it has gathered with the Department of Justice, which may use that information to file criminal charges. Claims that the OIG is not authorized to conduct criminal investigations have failed. In the leading case *United States v. Medic House*,[9] a federal district court rejected the claim that the OIG was obligated to refer suspected criminal violations to the United States Attorney General for investigation, and held that the OIG has broad powers to carry out its function "to prevent and detect fraud and abuse."[10]

The consequences of an OIG investigation are daunting. In addition to the possibility of criminal prosecution, OIG's civil and administrative proceedings may result in the imposition of sanctions similar to criminal penalties—civil monetary penalties and exclusion. Sanctions may be imposed against either individuals or entities who engage in fraud or abuse, or against those whose behavior poses a risk to the integrity of the federal health care programs or the programs' beneficiaries. Sanctioned individuals or entities are not permitted to participate in the health care programs while sanctions are in effect. From the government's perspective, pursuit of civil and administrative remedies may be the preferred course given the more favorable discovery rules, the less onerous standard of proof that adheres to such proceedings, and parties who are more apt to settle.

b. Health Care Financing Administration (HCFA)

The Health Care Financing Administration (HCFA) is responsible for administering the federal entitlement programs for HHS. As discussed above, HCFA contracts with private insurance companies known as carriers and intermediaries to perform claims processing and payment safeguarding functions under the Medicare program, and with peer review organizations (PROs) to monitor physicians' services for medical necessity and quality of care under the Medicare and Medicaid programs. HCFA has developed criteria, standards and procedures by which to evaluate the claims processing and payment safeguard performance of carriers and intermediaries. Carriers and intermediaries that fail adequately to perform these dual functions are subject to termination.

HCFA has come under fire for its slow pace in improving the detection capabilities of its contractors.[11] HCFA received one of the

9. 736 F.Supp. 1531 (W.D.Mo.1989).

10. Id. at 1535.

11. See GAO, Medicare: Control Over Fraud and Abuse Remains Elusive, GAO/T–HEHS–97–165 at 18 (June 1997) ("weak monitoring, poor coordination, and delays have characterized HCFA's past efforts to oversee fee-for-service contractors, the MTS acquisition process, and Medicare managed care plans").

smallest grants of all of the government agencies involved in the fight against health care fraud and abuse. For fiscal year 1997, HIPAA earmarked for HCFA only $1.8 million of the $104 million granted to the DOJ and HHS.

c. Peer Review Organizations (PROs)

Private organizations commonly known as Peer Review Organizations (PROs) contract with HCFA and state Medicaid agencies to conduct independent reviews of physician services that are provided primarily as a part of in-patient hospital care. PROs attempt to identify physicians who fail to furnish services that satisfy prevailing professional standards of conduct. PRO investigations emanate from a number of sources including referrals from the OIG, HCFA, a PRO subcontractor or a Medicare contractor.[12] If a PRO determines that a physician has failed to comply with her obligations in a substantial number of cases, or that the physician has "grossly and fragrantly violated" her professional obligations, the PRO will notify the OIG[13] with a recommendation of the sanction and period of exclusion to be imposed,[14] which the OIG may accept or reject in its discretion.[15] Practitioners are entitled to reasonable notice of a negative PRO finding, and an opportunity to be heard on a proposed PRO recommendation.[16] Depending on the circumstances, some may even be given the opportunity to initiate or complete a corrective action plan.[17] If the matter is not resolved to the satisfaction of the PRO, however, a report will be submitted to the OIG with the PRO's recommendation of appropriate sanctions.

Upon receipt of a negative PRO finding and recommendation, the OIG will review the PRO's report to ensure that the PRO followed proper procedures in formulating the recommendation, to determine whether the physician in fact committed a violation, and to establish whether the physician's conduct demonstrated an unwillingness or inability to comply with her professional obligations.[18]

---

12. See Peer Review Organization Manual § 6005.

13. See 42 C.F.R. § 1004.30.

14. See 42 C.F.R. § 1004.70. A "substantial violation in a number of cases" will be found where the professional has engaged in a "pattern of care ...that is inappropriate, unnecessary, or does not meet recognized professional standards of care as required by the PRO." See 1004.1(b) (1996). A "gross and flagrant violation" where the professional has violated an obligation "in one or more instances" presenting "an imminent danger to the health, safety, or well-being of a Medicare beneficiary or places the beneficiary unnecessarily in high risk situations." Id.

15. See 42 U.S.C.A. § 1320c–5 (1994), Social Security Act § 1156.

16. See Social Security Act § 1154; 42 U.S.C.A. § 1320c–3 (1994 & Supp. 1995).

17. See 42 C.F.R. §§ 1004.40 and 1004.50.

18. See id.

§ 7-5. The United States Department of Justice (DOJ)

The United States Department of Justice is another major player in the criminal investigation and prosecution of health care fraud and in the civil enforcement of the civil False Claims Act. Over the past decade the Department of Justice (DOJ) has significantly strengthened its response to the problem of fraud and abuse within the nation's health care programs by assigning more Special Agents of the Federal Bureau of Investigation to work on health care fraud teams, creating a health care fraud unit within the DOJ's Criminal Division, increasing the resources available to the DOJ's Civil Division staff to commence civil actions for health care fraud, and hiring new prosecutors to work out of the United States Attorney's offices.

The DOJ recently received increased funding to support its efforts to investigate and prosecute health care fraud. HIPAA earmarked $24 million for the DOJ for fiscal year 1997 alone. The DOJ plans to use this money to hire an additional 120 new prosecutors who will work exclusively on health care fraud cases.[1]

Health care fraud cases investigated and prosecuted by the Department of Justice more than tripled between fiscal year 1992 and fiscal year 1996.[2] During that period, the Department's investigations (conducted by the FBI) rose from 657 to 2,200 cases, prosecutions grew from 83 to 246 cases,[3] and convictions jumped from 90 defendants (out of 116 prosecuted) to 307 defendants (out of 450 prosecuted). An even more dramatic increase was seen in the number of civil health care fraud investigations undertaken by the Department. Such investigations rose from 270 cases in fiscal year 1992 to 2,500 cases in fiscal year 1996.[4] The Department's Civil Division recovered more than $274 million in health care fraud cases resolved in fiscal years 1995 and 1996; this amount comprised one-third of the Department's total civil recoveries during that time period.[5]

a. The Federal Bureau of Investigation (FBI)

Special Agents of the Federal Bureau of Investigation (FBI), working in conjunction with the Department of Justice's United States Attorneys Offices, are now among the primary investigators of fraud and abuse in the Medicare and Medicaid programs. The commitment of FBI personnel to health care fraud investigations

---

§ 7-5

1. See Medicare: Control Over Fraud and Abuse Remains Elusive, GAO/T–HEHS–97–165 at 16 (June 1997).

2. See Fraud Investigations, Prosecutions Up, Recoveries Top $274 Million, DOJ Says, BNA Health Care Daily d3 (August 14, 1997) (citing the DOJ's Health Care Fraud Report, Fiscal Years 1995–1996).

3. See id.

4. See id.

5. See id.

has exploded in the last decade. Between 1992 and 1994 alone, the number of FBI agents assigned to investigate health care offenses jumped from 97 to 249. The financial resources made available to the FBI to fund health care fraud investigations also soared. In fiscal year 1997, $47 million was appropriated to the Health Care Fraud and Abuse Control Account[6] to fund the enforcement and investigative activities of the FBI devoted to health care fraud. That amount is expected to increase to $114 million in fiscal year 2003.

According to FBI Director Louis J. Freeh, work performed by his agents helped to attain 353 criminal health care fraud convictions in 1994. In addition, FBI health care fraud investigations reportedly resulted in the collection of $480 million in fines, civil recoveries and restitution orders, and nearly $32 million in forfeitures.[7]

The FBI has plenary authority to investigate any felony offense cognizable under federal law,[8] whether the offense victimizes one of the federal entitlement programs, a private insurance company, a business entity or a private individual. Although, unlike the OIG, the FBI lacks independent authority to issue grand jury subpoenas, its agents are empowered to serve subpoenas issued by a federal grand jury, carry firearms, execute search warrants, and make arrests.[9] In addition, Special Agents of the FBI swear out affidavits in federal court in support of the issuance of search warrants, appear before the grand jury to give testimony about the results of investigations, conduct interviews, and engage in authorized electronic monitoring and undercover operations. The Health Insurance Portability and Accountability Act of 1996 (HIPAA)[10] added to the tools available to the FBI by conferring upon the bureau's Special Agents the authority to issue administrative subpoenas. This new investigative demand authority permits the FBI to bypass involvement of a United States Attorney, who is needed to issue a grand jury subpoena.

Once an investigation conducted by the FBI is complete, a request will be made to one of the United States Attorneys Offices either to prosecute the case or to defer prosecution. If the United States Attorney decides to seek an indictment, and an indictment is returned by the grand jury, the FBI will typically continue to investigate the case until the charges are resolved, by following up on leads, conducting interviews, and assisting the prosecutor at trial.

6. See § 7–5a.

7. See Gaming the Health Care System: Trends in Health Care Fraud: Hearings on S.Hrg. 104–110 before Senate Special Comm. On Aging, 104th Cong., 1st Sess., 12–13 (March 21, 1995) (statement by Hon. Louis J. Freeh, Director, Federal Bureau of Investigation).

8. See 18 U.S.C.A. § 3052 (1994).

9. See id.

10. HIPAA, Pub.L.No. 104–91, 110 Stat. 1936 (1996).

b. The United States Attorneys' Offices (USAOs)

The United States Attorneys, whose offices are located in every major city in the country, are the primary prosecutors of criminal federal health care offenses. The United States Attorney's Offices (USAOs) also bring civil actions under the provisions of the False Claims Act. USAOs receive their cases from a slew of sources, including primarily the DOJ, the OIG, the FBI, the DEA, the Postal Service, *qui tam* relators and the general public. Although the OIG enjoys independent authority to conduct investigations, to suspend or exclude providers, and to impose civil money penalties (CMPs),[11] the OIG field offices refer suspected criminal activity to one of the USAOs for evaluation and possible prosecution. United States Attorneys make frequent use of federal grand juries to conduct investigations into allegations of fraud. As described more fully below, Assistant United States Attorneys (AUSAs) present evidence to grand juries before seeking the return of a criminal indictment. AUSAs also have primary responsibility for prosecution of health care fraud charges, including putting on the government's evidence at trial, and representing the government on appeal before any one of the federal circuit Courts of Appeal.

§ 7–6. Other Federal Investigative Agencies

An assortment of other federal investigative agencies contribute to the investigative efforts of the OIG and the FBI in the fight against health care fraud and abuse, including the United States Drug Enforcement Administration (DEA), the Defense Department's Criminal Investigative Service (DCIS), the United States Postal Inspection Service, the Inspector General for the Department of Labor (IG/Labor), the Inspector General for Amtrak (IG/Amtrak), the Inspector General for the Railroad Retirement Board (IG/RRB) and the Inspector General for the Office of Personnel Management (IG/OPM). The DEA, for example, oversees and investigates individuals and entities authorized by law to distribute certain controlled substances, including physicians, pharmacists, pharmacies and drug manufacturers and wholesalers. DEA agents are authorized to issue and serve administrative subpoenas, execute search warrants, conduct undercover surveillance, carry firearms, and make arrests.[1] Inspectors of the United States Postal Inspection Service also play an important role. Because essentially every claim for payment under the Medicare or Medicaid programs involves some use of the mails, agents of the Postal Inspection

---

11. See § 5–4 for a discussion of civil monetary penalty authorities.

§ 7–6

1. See 21 U.S.C.A. § 878 (1994).

Service are frequently involved in criminal investigations of health care fraud.[2]

§ 7–7. Licensing Boards, Private Insurance Companies and Whistleblowers

a. State Medical and Licensing Boards

State medical and licensing boards also play an important role in the fight against fraud and abuse within the federally funded health care programs. These boards have the authority to issue licenses to and discipline health care professionals. A false claims enforcement action, exclusion proceeding or a criminal conviction of a health care fraud offense will normally be enough to trigger an independent investigation by the medical board of the hospital and the licensing board of the state in which the targeted physician practices.

b. Private Insurance Companies

In addition to official law enforcement authorities, most private insurance companies now house enforcement bureaus to search for fraudulent medical claims. These bureaus operate under authority granted to them by their contracts with health care providers. After detecting suspected fraudulent conduct, private fraud bureaus will commonly relay the results of their investigations to either the OIG, a United States Attorney's Office, or the local field office of the FBI.

The successful detective activities of private payors have increasingly gained the government's attention and support. Several provisions of HIPAA[1] call for greater cooperation and information sharing between governmental investigators and representatives of health plans. HIPAA also added to the arsenal of criminal fraud provisions the new crime of health care fraud[2] which makes it unlawful for any person to knowingly and willfully execute a scheme to defraud any health care benefit program in connection with the delivery of, or payment for, health care benefits, or to obtain by false representations any property belonging to such a program. This new offense is expected to fill a gap in health care fraud investigations and prosecutions, since it will authorize punishment of activity designed to defraud a health care payor, irrespective of whether the fraud utilized the mails or wires.

---

2. The Postal Inspection Service is authorized to investigate any criminal matter related to the mails.

§ 7–7

1. HIPAA, Pub.L.No. 104–191, 110 Stat. 1936 (1996).

2. HIPAA, Pub.L.No. 104–191, § 204(a), 110 Stat. 1936, 1999 (1996), 42 U.S.C.A. § 1320a–7b (1994), Social Security Act § 1128B.

Notwithstanding the increasingly visible role played by private payors against health care fraud, some argue that the government continues to undervalue the important anti-fraud work being performed by private health plans.[3] The HIPAA provisions may forecast, however, a growing appreciation for the contributions being made by private health plans in the fight against fraud. Expanded coordination between official and private anti-fraud activity in the future may well be the result.

c. Whistleblowers

As discussed in Chapter 6,[4] the False Claims Act permits a private citizen who has evidence that a health care provider has submitted a false claim under the Medicare or Medicaid programs to bring a *qui tam* action on behalf of the United States.[5] These private attorneys general, encouraged by the prospect of recouping up to 30 percent of any recovery made as a result of the action, have played a critical role in informing official law enforcement authorities about fraud within the HHS entitlement programs. Indeed, in kickback investigations in particular, *qui tam* relators are one of the most common sources of information for federal and state investigators. These "insiders" have proven to be critical to such investigations because they have had access to information about kickback arrangements that would not easily be detected through a routine document review.[6]

§ 7–8. Operation Restore Trust (ORT)

On May 3, 1995, HHS unveiled a pilot voluntary disclosure program titled Operation Restore Trust[1] which was initially proposed to last two years but has since been extended. ORT is designed to forge new partnerships in the fight against Medicare and Medicaid fraud and abuse[2] and to study and implement new approaches to detect and combat fraud and abuse within the programs. Operation Restore Trust initially targeted home health

---

3. See, e.g., The New Legislative Environment for Anti–Fraud Activity—The Private Payer Perspective, Health Care Fraud 1997 (ABA, Chicago, Il.) 1997, at A–12 to A–15.

4. See § Chapter 6.

5. See 31 U.S.C.A. § 3730 (1994).

6. See supra § Chapter 6.

§ 7–8

1. See CCH Medicare and Medicaid Guide, New Developments ¶ ¶ 43,213–43,214 (May 18, 1995).

2. To carry out the objectives of Operation Restore Trust, HHS designated an team of investigators from federal and state agencies to work on the project, including representatives of three agencies within HHS itself (the Office of Inspector General, the Health Care Financing Administration, and the Administration on Aging), the state MFCUs and the United States Department of Justice. See ˙Operation Restore Trust Objectives and First–Year Accomplishments, Office of Inspector General Fact Sheet at 7 (Dept. of Health and Human Services, Wash. D.C., May 13, 1996).

agencies,[3] nursing homes[4] and durable medical equipment suppliers[5] doing business in five states (New York, Florida, Illinois, Texas and California).[6] After sizable recoveries were made under the program, the initiative was expanded to target additional providers and services (including hospices, partial hospitalization, psychiatric hospitals, and independent physiological laboratories,[7] clinical labs, community health centers and some rural health clinics),[8] and to cover twelve more states (Arizona, Colorado, Georgia, Louisiana, Massachusetts, Missouri, New Jersey, Ohio, Pennsylvania, Tennessee, Virginia and Washington[9]).

Central among Operation Restore Trust's stated objectives were the following goals: 1) identifying and punishing willful defrauders of the Medicare and Medicaid programs; 2) identifying problems with existing statutes and regulations, systemic problems and special vulnerabilities to fraud and abuse within the programs; 3) alerting the public and the health care community to particular health care fraud schemes; and 4) establishing a program that encouraged voluntary disclosure of fraudulent conduct.[10] On the first year anniversary of Operation Restore Trust, HHS issued a press release trumpeting the pilot program's accomplishments, including an analysis of the progress made by the program toward these objectives.[11] As to its first objective—identifying and punish-

3. The Medicare program reimburses home health agencies for certain services provided to homebound beneficiaries. In 1995, the program's payments totalled approximately $14.5 billion (an $2 billion increase over payments in the preceding year); $5.3 billion of that amount was paid for home health care delivered in Operation Restore Trust states. See id. at 8.

4. In 1994 alone, Medicaid spent an estimated $27 billion for services to nursing facility beneficiaries, $9.5 billion of that amount went to nursing facilities located in the five originally-targeted Operation Restore Trust states. In 1995, Medicare paid skilled nursing facilities $7.3 billion for care provided under the Medicare skilled nursing facility benefit, $2.7 billion of that amount was paid in the five targeted Operation Restore Trust states. See id. at 8.

5. Medicare reimburses medical equipment suppliers for specified items that are medically necessary for the health care needs of Part B beneficiaries, including durable medical equipment, prosthetic devices, and orthotic devices, supplies used with durable medical equipment or prosthetics and certain other supplies. Five regional car-

riers under contract with HCFA pay suppliers for covered items. In 1995, Medicare allowed an estimated $4.5 billion in payments for medical equipment and supplies. $1.6 billion of that total was paid in the five targeted Operation Restore Trust states. Id. at 8–9.

6. Id. at 7. At the time these five states housed 38.5 percent of all Medicaid beneficiaries and 34 percent of all Medicare beneficiaries. Id. at 7.

7. See Administration Expands Health Fraud Effort to 12 More States, 6 BNA's Health Law Reporter at 807 (May 22, 1997).

8. See HCFA Official Says Expanded ORT Will Target More Providers, States, BNA's Health Care Fraud Report, Vol. 1, No. 6 (March 26, 1997).

9. See Administration Expands Health Fraud Effort to 12 More States, 6 BNA's Health Law Reporter 807 (May 22, 1997).

10. Operation Restore Trust Objectives and First–Year Accomplishments, Office of Inspector General Fact Sheet at 1 (Dept. Of Health and Human Services, Wash. D.C. May 13, 1996).

11. See id.

ing willful defrauders of the Medicare and Medicaid programs—the government announced considerable success. According to the press release, over the course of the year the courts had ordered offenders to pay upwards of $24.5 million in criminal fines, restitution and civil awards into the Medicare Trust Fund,[12] an additional $14.1 million would be paid into the Trust Fund as a result of civil judgements, settlements and civil monetary penalties,[13] and hundreds of new investigations were underway, the vast majority of which were opened as a result of the Operation Restore Trust initiative.

A second objective of the initiative—identifying problems with existing statutes and regulations, systemic problems and special vulnerabilities to fraud and abuse within the programs—has also yielded demonstrable results. According to HHS, substantial savings in Trust Fund monies can be effected by the adoption of certain legislative, regulatory and administrative proposals. The agency is testing new ways to involve state and local enforcement authorities in identifying and reporting fraud, waste and abuse.[14] The press release also reported a variety of systemic problems observed in home health agency and DME supplier practices through the use of new audit[15] and survey[16] techniques.

In an effort to meet its third objective—alerting the public and the industry to particular health care fraud schemes—HHS issued two special fraud alerts and a consumer advisory, established a satellite office in Miami, Florida to perform outreach to the public about health care fraud, and created a hotline which members of the public and the health care community were encouraged to use to report known or suspected incidents of fraud or abuse.[17] Within the first year, over 30,000 calls were received on the hotline,

---

12. See id. at 2. It is unclear precisely how much of this success is actually attributable to Operation Restore Trust. The government reported that 35 criminal convictions, 18 civil judgements, and 93 program exclusions of individuals and corporations had taken place since March 1, 1995. However, many of those cases already underway before the start of the Operation Restore Trust initiative, were simply "folded into the ORT project." Id. at 2.

13. See id. at 2.

14. See id. at 3–4. For example, over 500 newly trained state and local ombudsmen had already begun to identify and report suspected fraud, waste and abuse to the OIG for investigation. See id. at 5.

15. Audits of three Florida home health agencies revealed disturbing incidences of fraud, to the tune of $3.7 million in potential disallowances. In the audit of one of those agencies, investigators reviewed 100 randomly selected claims submitted by the agency to Medicare and determined that 40% of the claims were for services not covered by Medicare guidelines. See id. at 4.

16. HHS utilized a new survey procedure to study the compliance of five home health agencies in New York. Fifty of the agencies' patients were visited and interviewed. Of that number, nine of the patients were found not to be homebound and twenty had received unnecessary or overutilized services. See id. at 4–5.

17. See id. at 5.

although not all relating to Operation Restore Trust matters.[18]

The fourth and most controversial prong of the Operation Restore Trust initiative was its implementation of a program to encourage providers to voluntarily disclose evidence of fraud uncovered in their own organizations. The voluntary disclosure program allows certain eligible providers[19] to disclose existing or potential fraud or abuse within their own organizations in return for possible reduced penalties. For those eligible to participate in the program, precise procedures have been established for reporting disclosures. An eligible provider must first apply for admission into the pilot program in writing, fully describing the facts and circumstances of the matter being disclosed (including an estimate of the cost to Medicare or Medicaid program caused by the matter disclosed). The provider must agree to continue to cooperate throughout the course of any subsequent investigation and to fully disclose all relevant matters throughout its participation in the program.[20]

In return for a voluntary disclosure under the program, the government offers the self-disclosing entities "the opportunity to minimize the potential cost and disruption of a full scale audit and investigation; to negotiate monetary settlements to the Medicare and Medicaid programs based upon the matter disclosed; and, to reduce or avoid an OIG permissive exclusion under 42 U.S.C.A. § 1320(a)–7(2b), as appropriate."[21]

From the industry's perspective, the program's significance may be less what it does do, than what it does not do. Unlike an amnesty program, Operation Restore Trust does not offer immunity to providers who decide to make voluntary disclosures. Indeed, providers who disclose evidence of wrongdoing in their own organizations may be subject to civil and criminal penalties, or even exclusion, and at the very least should expect to make restitution for the full cost of the fraud. Further, a provider's protection under the program applies only to the entity itself, it does not eliminate the potential exposure of senior management or other employees, directors, officers, or agents to prosecution. For this reason, some have suggested that the benefits being offered in return for self-disclosures are illusory, and should be accepted by a provider only

---

18. See id. at 5.

19. In its initial form, the voluntary disclosure program was targeted at home health agencies and nursing home industries in the five target states. However, some "ineligible" organizations were permitted to use the program's procedures as a guide, and it appears that new procedures may be applied to providers that do not fall within the region or type of company covered by the program. Id. at 6.

20. See Operation Restore Trust Voluntary Disclosure Program, Office of Inspector General Fact Sheet at 2 (Dept. Of Health and Human Services, Wash. D.C. May 3, 1995).

21. Id. at 1.

after careful reflection and consultation with counsel.[22]

§ 7–9. Increased Funding and Coordination of Fraud and Abuse Enforcement Activities

Provisions of the Health Insurance Portability and Accountability Act of 1996 (HIPAA) are designed to strengthen the hand of state and federal investigators of health care fraud by providing investigators with increased funds for enforcement activity[1] and establishing a national database which will collect reports of any final adverse action taken against a health care provider, supplier or practitioner.[2] The OIG and the DOJ are in the process of developing programs that will coordinate federal, state, local and private enforcement activity. Increasingly stressed is the need for improved coordination between public and private enforcement controls. To help solidify the working relationship between the public and private sectors, the OIG issued guidelines in January 1997[3] urging private health plans to coordinate their investigative efforts and share their intelligence with state and federal officials. In return, government agencies are designing mechanisms by which their studies, evaluations and profiles of health care fraud and abuse will be shared with private plans. Certain information about ongoing investigations and enforcement efforts will also be exchanged, as will information to be conveyed to victims of fraud and abuse. "Information coordinators" are being designated to facilitate these exchanges of information.[4]

a. The Health Care Fraud and Abuse Control Account

To provide a stable source of funding for future enforcement activities, HIPAA also called for the establishment of a "Health Care Fraud and Abuse Control Account" which is housed within the Federal Hospital Insurance Trust Fund.[5] Congress authorized an appropriation up to $104 million to this account to cover the

---

22. See, e.g., Operation Restore Trust—Should a Provider Participate In It's Voluntary Disclosure Program?, Health Care Cytes (Crummy, Del Deo, Dolan, Griffinger & Vecchione, A Professional Corporation 1995). Hospice Issues Under Operation Restore Trust, Health Law Trends Vol. 1, No.1 (Arent Fox Kintner Plotkin & Kahn, Wash. D.C. 1996).

§ 7–9

1. HIPAA, Pub.L.No. 104–191, § 201(b), 110 Stat. 1993 (1996), 42 U.S.C.A. § 1395i (1994), Social Security Act § 1817.

2. HIPAA, Pub.L.No. 104–191, § 221(a), 110 Stat. 1936, 2009 (1996), 42 U.S.C.A. § 1320a–7e (West Supp.1997), Social Security Act § 1128E.

3. The Guidelines were released by the Inspector General for HHS on January 24, 1997 and are reprinted in the Fraud and Abuse Control Program as mandated by the Health Insurance Portability and Accountability Act of 1996. See Vol.1 No.2 BNA Health Care Fraud Report 59 (1997).

4. See id.

5. HIPAA, Pub.L.No. 104–191, 110 Stat. 1936, 1993 (1996), 42 U.S.C.A. § 1395i (1994), Social Security Act § 1817.

costs of audits, investigations, and civil and criminal prosecutions brought under the Fraud and Abuse Control Program. That appropriation may be increased by 15% each year through fiscal year 2003. The coffers of the account will be further enhanced by fines, penalties, forfeiture awards, and other recoveries collected in criminal and civil health fraud proceedings.

A large percentage of these funds has been earmarked specifically for use by the OIG. The OIG is due to receive between $60 and $70 million of the 1997 appropriation to fund its Medicare and Medicaid enforcement activities. That amount will increase each year until fiscal year 2003 when the OIG will be entitled to between $150 and $160 million of the Control Account funds. The legal staff of the OIG is expected eventually to triple in size in order to handle the increased enforcement activity caused by HIPAA's infusion of funds into the Control Account.[6] Additional monies, beginning at $47 million in fiscal year 1997 and increasing to $114 in fiscal year 2003, have been promised to the account to fund FBI fraud and abuse enforcement activities. These increased financial resources demonstrate the seriousness of the government's resolve to combat health care fraud, and promise increasing regulatory and investigatory activity within the industry in the years to come.

b. The Health Care Fraud and Abuse Data Collection Program

Congress has recognized that greater coordination among the many investigators of health care fraud is necessary to adequately protect the programs. Thus, HIPAA required the establishment of a national Health Care Fraud and Abuse Data Collection Program, to which federal and state government agencies and health plans must report any "final adverse action (not including settlements in which no findings of liability have been made) taken against a health care provider, supplier, or practitioner."[7] Health plans that fail to report adverse actions are subject to a $25,000 civil penalty for each adverse action not reported, and the Secretary is to publish a report identifying government agencies that fail to report.[8] Adverse actions are defined as criminal convictions, civil judgments, government licensure or certification actions, exclusions, publicly available negative findings or actions by government agencies, or other adjudicated actions or decisions, as established by regulations, but not malpractice claims.[9] Though private health plans are required

6. See Health Care Fraud and Abuse Control Account, The Health Lawyer, Vol. 9, No. 2, at 12 (ABA Health Law Section Newsletter, Chicago, Ill. Winter 1996).

7. 42 U.S.C.A. § 1128E(a).

8. 42 U.S.C.A. § 1320a–7e(b).

9. 42 U.S.C.A. § 1128E(g)(1).

by the law to report final adverse actions, the statute does not state what adverse actions they are required to report, and all of the enumerated adverse actions are those taken by public agencies. The disclosure must include the name and taxpayer identification number of the person or entity subject to the action, the name of entities with which the person or entity subject to the action is affiliated or associated, the nature of the action, and a description of the acts or omissions and injuries on which the action was based.[10] The report must be disclosed to the person or entity about whom the report was made, and an opportunity must be given for correction of the information.[11] Any person or entity who reports to the data bank is immune from liability for the report unless the report was made with knowledge of the falsity of information contained in it.[12] The information in the data bank can be disclosed to federal and state government agencies and to health plans that request it (and pay fees for it, if they are not federal agencies).[13]

§ 7–10. Common Investigative Methods

Federal and state investigators make use of an array of investigative tools and resources to ferret out fraud and abuse within the programs. As described above, much help is received from carriers and intermediaries who pour through records looking for billing irregularities and suspect billing patterns. Valuable assistance has also been provided by *qui tam* relators. There are, however, important investigative instruments frequently used in health care fraud investigations available only to certain federal, state and administrative actors. One of the most lethal of these investigative weapons is the power to subpoena documents and testimony. Individuals and entities on the receiving end of a criminal or administrative subpoena or subject to a full-scale search may have difficulty defending themselves.

Federal and state grand juries[1] and administrative agencies[2] wield wide authority to issue subpoenas to gather information about suspected fraudulent activity. Only in an exceptional case will the courts intervene to prevent or limit the use of this broad investigatory tool. The secrecy rules surrounding grand jury proceedings add to the anxiety experienced by any target or subject of a grand jury investigation, and the possibility of an order of exclusion from participation in the programs (sometimes referred to as "economic death" for a health care provider) makes the receipt

10. 42 U.S.C.A. § 1128E(b)(2).
11. 42 U.S.C.A. § 1128E(c).
12. 42 U.S.C.A. § 1128E(e).
13. 42 U.S.C.A. § 1128E(d).

§ 7–10

1. See § 7–12b.
2. See § 7–20.

of an administrative or grand jury subpoena for testimony or documents a very serious matter indeed.

Another powerful tool brandished by these investigators is the authority to conduct searches for evidence of criminal or other wrongful activity. Although employed less frequently than the subpoena power, many investigations of health care fraud and abuse have been built upon evidence seized pursuant to search. Being the subject of a search is much more unsettling and disruptive than being the recipient of a subpoena. It is not uncommon for a team of FBI agents armed with a search warrant to show up at a provider's door, either at home or the office, without notice, demanding full and immediate access to desk drawers, file cabinets, computers, documents and more. The subject of the search is left to stand by and watch (interference with a search could give rise to additional criminal charges) as the agents haul out boxes and boxes of patient files, financial books and other records and items.

Both of these investigative techniques, and the most common defenses raised against them, are discussed more fully below.

§ 7–11. The Subpoena Power

The subpoena power is one of the most effective devices employed by federal and state investigators to obtain evidence in Medicare and Medicaid fraud investigations. The government principally employs two types of subpoenas to investigate fraud and abuse, grand jury subpoenas and administrative subpoenas. Grand jury subpoenas may only be issued in connection with a criminal investigation, while administrative subpoenas may be used to collect evidence related to either criminal or civil violations.

§ 7–12. Grand Jury Investigations

a. The Grand Jury Power to Indict

In the federal and state systems, the grand jury serves the "dual function of determining if probable cause exists to believe that a crime has been committed and of protecting citizens against unfounded criminal prosecutions."[1] Because the bulk of the statutes criminalizing health care fraud are felonies, in the absence of a waiver of indictment, the grand jury will have to be involved in any criminal charges brought against a health care provider. The Fifth Amendment guarantees that "[n]o person shall be held to answer for a capital, or otherwise infamous crime, unless on a presentment or indictment of a Grand Jury."[2] Although this constitutional

---

§ 7–12

1. Branzburg v. Hayes, 408 U.S. 665, 686–87, 92 S.Ct. 2646, 2659, 33 L.Ed.2d 626 (1972).

2. U.S. CONST. amend. V.

requirement of an indictment does not apply to the states,[3] most state criminal prosecutions of Medicare and Medicaid fraud also proceed by indictment.

The grand jury alone is empowered to decide whether to return an indictment, but the grand jury is heavily dependent upon the prosecutor in reaching its decisions. In most cases, the prosecutor decides which witnesses to call, issues subpoenas on the grand jury's behalf, and drafts proposed indictments. Although the familiar adage, "the grand jury will indict a ham sandwich," is perhaps an overstatement, it is fair to say that in the average case the prosecutor will exercise a powerful influence over the grand jury's decision to return an indictment or to vote no true bill.

In the federal system, the grand jury consists of at least sixteen and not more than twenty three persons[4] selected from a pool of prospective jurors drawn from the surrounding community.[5] Grand jurors serve for a term of up to eighteen months,[6] or until discharged by the court.[7] Some very active federal districts have a grand jury in session at all times, while other districts will empanel the grand jury as the need arises.

Grand jury proceedings are shrouded in secrecy. Once impaneled, the grand jury operates in seclusion, generally without judicial involvement. To maintain this secrecy, grand jury proceedings are conducted *ex parte*, and persons who appear before the grand jury do so without assistance of counsel in the grand jury room.[8] Only the prosecutor, the witness under examination, the grand jurors, and certain limited authorized persons (stenographers who transcribe the proceedings or, as needed, interpreters) are permitted to be in the grand jury room while it conducts its investigation.[9] Thus, if counsel for a subpoenaed health care provider accompanies her client to a grand jury proceeding, the attorney must remain outside the room while her client is questioned. In addition, no one save the

---

3. See Hurtado v. People of State of California, 110 U.S. 516, 538, 4 S.Ct. 111, 122, 28 L.Ed. 232 (1884); Alexander v. Louisiana, 405 U.S. 625, 633, 92 S.Ct. 1221, 1226–27, 31 L.Ed.2d 536 (1972) (due process clause of the Fourteenth Amendment does not require indictment by grand jury for fair trial).

4. See Fed.R.Crim.P. 6(a).

5. See The Jury Selection and Service Act of 1968, Pub.L.No. 90–274, 82 Stat. 53 (1968), 28 U.S.C.A. § 1861 (1994), which provides that "all litigants in Federal courts entitled to trial by jury shall have the right to grand and petit juries selected at random from a fair cross-section of the community in the district or division wherein the court convenes." The Act further provides

that "[n]o citizen shall be excluded from service as a grand or petit juror in the district courts of the United States ... on account of race, color, religion, sex, national origin, or economic status." 28 U.S.C.A. § 1862 (1994).

6. Fed.R.Crim.P. 6(g).

7. The grand jury's term is sometimes extended in the public interest for a term of up to six months. See Fed. R.Crim.P. 6(g).

8. Witnesses may consult with counsel outside the grand jury room, however. See United States v. Mandujano, 425 U.S. 564, 581, 96 S.Ct. 1768, 1779, 48 L.Ed.2d 212 (1976).

9. Fed.R.Crim.P. 6(d).

witness under examination is permitted to disclose any matter that transpires before the grand jury,[10] and only the grand jurors are permitted to remain in the room while it deliberates and votes upon a proposed indictment.[11]

b. The Grand Jury Power to Investigate

The grand jury has extensive power to investigate possible criminal activities. The grand jury operates on the notion that "the public has a right to every man's evidence,"[12] and thus is entrusted with exceedingly broad investigative authority. It can issue *subpoenas ad testificandum*, which compel witness testimony, as well as *subpoenas duces tecum*, which compel the production of records and other physical evidence. Moreover, once underway, a grand jury investigation will normally be permitted to proceed without outside interference until it is satisfied that every avenue has been fully explored.

Although technically grand jury subpoenas issue under the jurisdiction and authority of the grand jury, the prosecutor overseeing an investigation will normally decide whether a subpoena should issue, to whom it will be addressed, and what it will call for. It is extremely unusual, for example, for the grand jury itself to direct the issuance of a subpoena calling for witness testimony or the production of documents. Rather, blank grand jury subpoena forms are kept in prosecutors' offices where they are filled out and signed by the prosecutor on the grand jury's behalf, in most cases, without the grand jury's knowledge.[13] Typically, the grand jury will be advised by the prosecutor that a witness is present to give testimony or to produce documents, or both, moments before that testimony or production occurs.

In addition to the breadth of its investigative authority, there are few limits on what may serve as the impetus for a grand jury investigation. The grand jury may decide to investigate based on "tip, rumors, evidence proffered by the prosecutor, or the personal

---

10. See Fed.R.Crim.P. 6(e)(2).

11. See Fed.R.Crim.P. 6(d).

12. Branzburg v. Hayes, 408 U.S. 665, 688, 92 S.Ct. 2646, 2660, 33 L.Ed.2d 626 (1972). Based on this ideal, any personal sacrifice suffered as a result of compliance with a subpoena is considered to be the citizenry's contribution to the public welfare. See United States v. Dionisio, 410 U.S. 1, 10, 93 S.Ct. 764, 769, 35 L.Ed.2d 67 (1973); Blair v. United States, 250 U.S. 273, 281, 39 S.Ct. 468, 471, 63 L.Ed. 979 (1919).

13. The courts have repeatedly acknowledged that the group of prosecutors authorized to issue grand jury subpoenas in health care fraud cases includes those housed within the offices of state Attorneys General and the MFCUs. See, e.g., Doe v. Kuriansky, 91 A.D.2d 1068, 1068, 458 N.Y.S.2d 678, 679 (N.Y.App.Div.1983) (MFCU); Neuman v. Lefkowitz, 77 A.D.2d 588, 589, 430 N.Y.S.2d 14, 15 (N.Y.App.Div.1980) (Deputy Attorney General); Landau v. Hynes, 49 N.Y.2d 128, 400 N.E.2d 321, 424 N.Y.S.2d 380 (N.Y.1979) (Deputy Attorney General).

knowledge of the grand jurors,"[14] none of which need amount to probable cause.[15] No threshold showing need be made to a court to justify an investigation,[16] rather, the grand jury is authorized to "investigate merely on suspicion that the law is being violated, or even just because it wants assurance that it is not."[17] Thus, a grand jury investigating a possible kickback scheme need not demonstrate nor even have cause to believe that the objects or testimony sought by its subpoenas will in fact constitute evidence of such criminal activity.[18]

Once underway, the grand jury conducts its investigations without significant restriction. The grand jury functions largely unencumbered by evidentiary or other restraints applicable at trial due to the belief that such restraints would bog the grand jury down in a quagmire of "minitrials and preliminary showings."[19] In the federal system, for example, the grand jury may rely on hearsay evidence in its deliberations.[20] Similarly, the exclusionary rule is not generally applicable to grand jury proceedings.[21] Thus, a sub-

---

14. Branzburg v. Hayes, 408 U.S. 665, 701 92 S.Ct. 2646, 2666, 33 L.Ed.2d 626 (1972). Accord In re Special Investigation No. 281, 192, 299 Md. 181, 473 A.2d 1, 6 (Md.1984).

15. See, e.g., Counseling Services, Inc. v. Wisconsin, 95 Wis.2d 670, 675, 291 N.W.2d 631, 634–35 (Wis.Ct.App. 1980) (no finding of probable cause or reason to believe crime has been committed is required to require witness to produce records and give testimony in medicaid fraud investigation).

16. See, e.g., In re Special Investigation No. 249, 296 Md. 201, 461 A.2d 1082 (Md.1983) (grand jury investigating possible Medicaid fraud is not required to make preliminary showing of relevance, jurisdiction or purpose before subpoena may be enforced).

17. United States v. Morton Salt Co., 338 U.S. 632, 642–643, 70 S.Ct. 357, 364, 94 L.Ed. 401 (1950).

18. See People v. Dorr, 47 Ill.2d 458, 462–463, 265 N.E.2d 601, 603 (Ill.1970) ("Unless the effectiveness of the grand jury in the administration of criminal law is to be drastically impaired, the most that can be required as a standard of materiality is as precise a statement of the subject matter under investigation as the circumstances permit."); People v. Allen, 410 Ill. 508, 103 N.E.2d 92, 96–97 (Ill.1951) ("The very purpose of such an inquiry is to uncover matters previously unknown to the investigating agency. It is not necessary that a 'cause' or 'specific charge' be pending before the

grand jury as a condition to its right to command production of the documents."). Compare People v. Lurie, 39 Ill.2d 331, 336–337, 235 N.E.2d 637, 640 (Ill. 1968) (requests for production of documents that best have a tenuous relationship with the instant investigation is considered unreasonable and overbroad and is a violation of constitutional standards).

19. United States v. Dionisio, 410 U.S. 1, 17, 93 S.Ct. 764, 773, 35 L.Ed.2d 67 (1973). United States v. R. Enterprises, Inc., 498 U.S. 292, 298–99, 111 S.Ct. 722, 727, 112 L.Ed.2d 795 (1991).

20. Costello v. United States, 350 U.S. 359, 363, 76 S.Ct. 406, 408, 100 L.Ed. 397 (1956). Not all states agree with this approach. Some states permit the grand jury to consider only evidence admissible under controlling rules of evidence. See N.M. Stat. Ann. § 31–6–11; Nev. Rev. Stat. § 172.135; N.Y. McKinney's Crim. Proc. Law § 190.30.

21. United States v. Calandra, 414 U.S. 338, 349, 94 S.Ct. 613, 620–21, 38 L.Ed.2d 561 (1974). There is one exception. A witness may oppose a grand jury subpoena that was based on evidence obtained through illegal electronic surveillance. See 18 U.S.C.A. § 2518 (1968) and Gelbard v. United States, 408 U.S. 41, 92 S.Ct. 2357, 33 L.Ed.2d 179 (1972). In addition, although the Supreme Court has sanctioned the practice, the Department of Justice opposes the intro-

poenaed party may not properly refuse to testify or to produce evidence on the ground that a subpoena was the fruit of some earlier unlawful police conduct.[22]

Providers who have challenged grand jury subpoenas on constitutional or other grounds have faced formidable obstacles. A grand jury subpoena for testimony or documents is presumed to be valid.[23] Thus, a provider who seeks to avoid compliance with a subpoena bears the burden of establishing that it was issued in bad faith or is otherwise invalid.[24] Claims that the grand jury lacks jurisdiction to investigate have not been well received by the courts.[25]

Providers who fail to comply with an order enforcing a subpoena may expect to be held in contempt of court.[26] Indeed, an unsuccessful motion to quash a subpoena generally is not appealable until the provider fails first to comply with an order enforcing the subpoena and is adjudged to be in contempt.[27] Most state courts have similarly declined to permit a recalcitrant witness to appeal a denial of a motion to quash absent a contempt citation.[28]

duction of evidence obtained in violation of a party's constitutional rights during grand jury proceedings. 7 DOJ Manual § 9–11.231 (1989–2).

22. See, e.g., In re a Special Investigation No. 227, 55 Md.App.Ct. 650, 652, 466 A.2d 48, 49 (Md. Ct. Spec. App. 1983), (denying motion predicated upon a claim that the subpoena sought documents that were the fruit of an earlier assertedly unconstitutional search of a hospital and nursing home in light of Calandra).

23. United States v. Dionisio, 410 U.S. 1, 93 S.Ct. 764, 35 L.Ed.2d 67 (1973); In re Special Investigation No. 281, 299 Md. 181, 193, 473 A.2d 1, 7 (Md.1984); In re Special Investigation No. 249, 296 Md. 201, 205, 461 A.2d 1082, 1085 (Md.1983).

24. United States v. R. Enterprises, Inc., 498 U.S. 292, 301, 111 S.Ct. 722, 728, 112 L.Ed.2d 795 (1991).

25. Blair v. United States, 250 U.S. 273, 282–83, 39 S.Ct. 468, 471, 63 L.Ed. 979 (1919). See also In re Special Investigation No. 249, 296 Md. 201, 461 A.2d 1082, (Md.1983) (grand jury investigating Medicaid fraud has power to summon records of corporate landlord and nursing home provider of medical assistance services located beyond the confines of the city).

26. See, e.g., In re Special Investigation No. 281, 299 Md. 181, 473 A.2d 1 (Md.1984) (custodian of subpoenaed records of Medicaid patients held in contempt); Pedroso v. Florida, 450 So.2d 902 (Fla.Dist.Ct.App.1984), motion denied, 456 So.2d 1302 (Fla.Dist.Ct.App. 1984) (per curiam) (records custodian of a medical center in contempt for refusing to comply with subpoena duces tecum); Stornanti v. Massachusetts, 389 Mass. 518, 451 N.E.2d 707 (Mass.1983) (affirming order holding pharmacist in civil contempt of court for refusing to comply with subpoena duces tecum).

27. See United States v. Ryan, 402 U.S. 530, 532, 91 S.Ct. 1580, 1581–1582, 29 L.Ed.2d 85 (1971). See also United States v. Fesman, 781 F.Supp. 511, 515 (S.D.Ohio 1991) (Medicare provider seeking to contest trial court's order enforcing a subpoena must refuse to comply and be found in contempt which order is then appealable).

28. See, e.g., State v. Threet, 294 Or. 1, 653 P.2d 960 (Or.1982) (en banc); but see In re Special Investigation No. 249, 296 Md. 201, 212, 461 A.2d 1082, 1088 (Md.1983) (Murphy. C.J., dissenting) (permitting a corporate landlord and nursing home provider to appeal immediately after motion to quash was denied without requiring a contempt citation).

§ 7–13. Limitations on the Grand Jury's Investigative Powers

Despite the breadth of the grand jury's investigative powers, some important limitations on the use of those powers remain. The primary limitations spring from the Fifth Amendment's privilege against self-incrimination, the Fourth Amendment's guarantee against unreasonable searches and seizures,[1] and certain evidentiary privileges, such as the attorney-client privilege,[2] the physician-patient privilege,[3] and the psychotherapist-patient privilege.[4]

§ 7–14. The Fifth Amendment Privilege Against Self-Incrimination

The Fifth Amendment privilege against self-incrimination offers health care providers one safeguard against an abusive use of the subpoena power. Expecting the Fifth Amendment privilege to provide a substantial barrier to the evidence gathering activities of state and federal investigators, however, would be a mistake. While some providers subpoenaed in connection with Medicare or Medicaid investigations have successfully invoked the privilege to secure a measure of protection against the compulsory authority of the grand jury, the privilege against compelled self-incrimination offers limited protection in the context of grand jury proceedings.

According to the Fifth Amendment, "no person ... shall be compelled in any criminal case to be a witness against himself."[1] This privilege is applicable to any *testimonial communication* (but not nontestimonial acts[2]) and applies whether that communication occurs before the grand jury or at trial.[3] The question of "whether a compelled communication is testimonial ... depends on the facts and circumstances of the particular case."[4] As the phrase suggests, however, the privilege primarily protects incriminating oral state-

§ 7–13

1. See § 7–15.
2. See § 7–16c.
3. See § 7–16a.
4. See Jaffee v. Redmond, ___ U.S. ___, 116 S.Ct. 1923, 135 L.Ed.2d 337 (1996); see also § 7–16b.

§ 7–14

1. U.S. CONST. amend. V.
2. Only testimonial communication is protected. Thus, a subpoena may compel a person to produce a blood sample, see Schmerber v. California, 384 U.S. 757, 765, 86 S.Ct. 1826, 1833, 16 L.Ed.2d 908 (1966), a voice exemplar, see United States v. Dionisio, 410 U.S. 1, 7, 93 S.Ct. 764, 768, 35 L.Ed.2d 67 (1973), a handwriting specimen, see

United States v. Euge, 444 U.S. 707, 718, 100 S.Ct. 874, 881–882, 63 L.Ed.2d 141 (1980), fingerprints, see State v. Sheppard, 350 So.2d 615 (La.1977), and to participate in a line-up, see United States v. Wade, 388 U.S. 218, 222–23, 87 S.Ct. 1926, 1929–1930, 18 L.Ed.2d 1149 (1967), even though such acts may provide the state or federal government with incriminating evidence against the complying party.

3. See Schmerber v. California, 384 U.S. 757, 761 n. 5, 86 S.Ct. 1826, 1831, 16 L.Ed.2d 908 (1966).

4. Doe v. United States, 487 U.S. 201, 214–15, 108 S.Ct. 2341, 2350, 101 L.Ed.2d 184 (1988).

ments made by a witness under oath in response to questioning,[5] though it may also apply to personal records,[6] and to admissions that are implicit in the production of documentary evidence.[7] The party invoking the privilege must demonstrate that risk of incrimination is "substantial and real" not "trifling or imaginary."[8]

If one puts aside the question of subpoenaed records, the Fifth Amendment does provide a targeted health care provider with an important protection—the provider may not be compelled to verbally incriminate himself before the grand jury. Thus, while the grand jury's authority to compel the provider's attendance before it is virtually unlimited, it cannot make him speak if to do so would make the provider a witness against himself. Should a provider receive a subpoena calling for his testimony before the grand jury, therefore, provider's counsel will need to weigh carefully whether that testimony might furnish law enforcement authorities with incriminating evidence against the provider. If so, the Fifth Amendment privilege will supply the provider with the means to avoid the testimony (although he may have to appear before the grand jury to assert the Fifth) in the absence of a grant of immunity from prosecution.

Health care providers involved in administrative or civil proceedings should take special precautions not to inadvertently waive their Fifth Amendment privilege. Although technically the Fifth Amendment privilege against compelled self-incrimination applies only to criminal, and not civil, proceedings, the privilege can be invoked in a civil or administrative proceeding if there is reason to believe that the statements made there might incriminate the provider in a subsequent criminal proceeding.[9] If it is not invoked, the provider will have little defense against the introduction of

---

5. United States v. Mandujano, 425 U.S. 564, 572, 96 S.Ct. 1768, 1774, 48 L.Ed.2d 212 (1976) (plurality opinion); Fisher v. United States, 425 U.S. 391, 409, 96 S.Ct. 1569, 1580, 48 L.Ed.2d 39 (1976).

6. Schmerber v. California , 384 U.S. 757, 764, 86 S.Ct. 1826, 1832, 16 L.Ed.2d 908 (1966); see also Boyd v. United States, 116 U.S. 616, 622, 6 S.Ct. 524, 527, 29 L.Ed. 746 (1886). More recently, however, the Court has suggested that the incriminating content of personal documents *voluntarily* created may not be entitled to Fifth Amendment protection, because the author of the documents was not compelled by state or federal authorities to create them. See Andresen v. Maryland, 427 U.S. 463, 471–77, 96 S.Ct. 2737, 2744–47, 49 L.Ed.2d 627 (1976); Fisher v. United States, 425 U.S. 391, 409–10, 96 S.Ct.

1569, 1580, 48 L.Ed.2d 39 (1976) and United States v. Doe, 465 U.S. 605, 618, 104 S.Ct. 1237, 1245, 79 L.Ed.2d 552 (1984) (O'Connor, J., concurring) (The Fifth Amendment "provides absolutely no protection for the contents of private papers of any kind.").

7. See Fisher v. United States, 425 U.S. 391, 410–13, 96 S.Ct. 1569, 1581–82, 48 L.Ed.2d 39 (1976), and the discussion regarding the act of production doctrine at § 7–14a.

8. United States v. Doe, 465 U.S. 605, 614 n. 13, 104 S.Ct. 1237, 1243, 79 L.Ed.2d 552 (1984) (quoting Marchetti v. United States, 390 U.S. 39, 53, 88 S.Ct. 697, 705, 19 L.Ed.2d 889 (1968)).

9. See Lefkowitz v. Turley, 414 U.S. 70, 77, 94 S.Ct. 316, 322, 38 L.Ed.2d 274, 281 (1973).

damaging statements during a later criminal trial.[10] Invoking the privilege against self-incrimination in a civil proceeding may be costly, however, because, unlike criminal juries, civil fact-finders are permitted to draw an adverse inference from an invocation of the privilege.[11]

Grand jury investigations of health care fraud frequently involve the issuance of grand jury *subpoenas duces tecum* which call for the production (and perhaps authentication) of corporate or other documents relating to the business of a provider or supplier. The Fifth Amendment shield available to health care providers for use against a subpoena for documents is considerably weaker than the shield available to ward off demands for testimony. This is particularly so in light of the fact that most of the documents that will be sought be are likely to belong to a corporate or other organizational entity.

Unlike individuals, corporations[12] and other "collective entities"[13] enjoy no Fifth Amendment privilege whether at trial or before the grand jury. Because a corporation is a creature of the state, whose powers the state may limit, a demand that corporate records be produced to the grand jury presents no Fifth Amendment problem.[14] Furthermore, since an artificial entity may not itself invoke the privilege against compulsory self-incrimination, neither may an individual acting on its behalf invoke a personal privilege over the documents to protect corporate documents from disclosure.[15] This principle applies to individuals doing business in a

---

10. See, e.g., Commonwealth v. Wu, 343 Pa.Super. 108, 494 A.2d 7 (Pa.1985) (incriminating statements made by dentist during an administrative investigation could be introduced at later criminal trial); United States v. Vecchiarello, 187 U.S.App.D.C. 1, 569 F.2d 656, 664 (D.C.Cir.1977) (statements made by defendant during civil deposition may be used at later trial for impersonating a physician); State v. Carr, 861 S.W.2d 850, 853 (Tenn.Crim.App.1993) (statements made by pharmacist in civil audit admissible during later criminal fraud prosecution).

11. See Baxter v. Palmigiano, 425 U.S. 308, 316–18, 96 S.Ct. 1551, 1557–58, 47 L.Ed.2d 810, 820–21 (1976).

12. See Hale v. Henkel, 201 U.S. 43, 74, 26 S.Ct. 370, 379, 50 L.Ed. 652 (1906).

13. See United States v. White, 322 U.S. 694, 699, 64 S.Ct. 1248, 1251, 88 L.Ed. 1542 (1944) (announcing collective entity rule and holding the officer of unincorporated labor union could not re-

fuse to produce records belonging to the union even if they incriminated the officer). See also Bellis v. United States, 417 U.S. 85, 88, 94 S.Ct. 2179, 2183, 40 L.Ed.2d 678 (1974) (rejecting argument of a member of a defunct three-partner law firm that the small size of the partnership made it unrealistic to consider the firm as an "entity" independent of the three partners).

14. See Hale v. Henkel, 201 U.S. 43, 75, 26 S.Ct. 370, 379, 50 L.Ed. 652 (1906); Braswell v. United States, 487 U.S. 99, 105, 108 S.Ct. 2284, 2288, 101 L.Ed.2d 98 (1988).

15. See Bellis v. United States, 417 U.S. 85, 97, 94 S.Ct. 2179, 2187, 40 L.Ed.2d 678 (1974). See also Moe v. Kuriansky, 502 N.Y.S.2d 221, 222, 120 A.D.2d 594, 595–96 (N.Y.App.Div.1986) (corporate entity under investigation for Medicaid fraud has no Fifth Amendment privilege and thus corporate agent cannot rely on the privilege to avoid producing corporate records held in his representative capacity).

variety of organizational structures including a person who is the sole owner and shareholder of the corporation,[16] or a partner in a partnership,[17] and to any organization serving a group interest regardless of whether the entity is a professional corporation that lacks the attributes of an ordinary business corporation,[18] a Sub–Chapter S corporation,[19] the mere business alter ego of the individual owner or shareholder,[20] an unincorporated association,[21] or a tenancy in common.[22] It is of no moment whether the subpoena for corporate documents is issued to the custodian of records of the corporation or to a specific individual within the corporation.[23] The privilege against self-incrimination is "purely personal" belonging solely to "the natural individual"[24] who is compelled to give some testimonial communication. It has no application to a corporate entity, no matter its size or professional character, and whether it is closely held or family owned.

With no Fifth Amendment privilege to protect the contents of records of a collective entity, an officer or any other custodian of records of a health care organizational entity has no privilege to refuse to produce records belonging to the entity even if that production will incriminate the officer, custodian or the entity

---

16. See, e.g., In re Grand Jury Subpoenas Duces Tecum Dated January 30, 1986, 638 F.Supp. 794, 800–02 (D.Me. 1986) (rejecting motion to quash filed by psychiatrist, sole owner of corporation, where subpoena duces tecum was addressed to the corporation and not the movant, and holding that if the act of producing the documents would incriminate the psychiatrist, another agent of the corporation must produce them to the grand jury).

17. Bellis v. United States, 417 U.S. 85, 94 S.Ct. 2179, 40 L.Ed.2d 678 (1974).

18. Reamer v. Beall, 506 F.2d 1345, 1346 (4th Cir.1974), cert. denied, 420 U.S. 955, 95 S.Ct. 1338, 43 L.Ed.2d 431 (1975).

19. United States v. Mid–West Business Forms, Inc., 474 F.2d 722, 723 (8th Cir.1973).

20. United States v. Rosenstein, 474 F.2d 705 (2d Cir.1973).

21. See Rogers v. United States, 340 U.S. 367, 371–72, 71 S.Ct. 438, 441, 95 L.Ed. 344 (1951) (records of a political party not privileged).

22. See In re Grand Jury Proceedings (Shiffman), 576 F.2d 703 (6th Cir. 1978), cert. denied, 439 U.S. 830, 99 S.Ct. 106, 58 L.Ed.2d 124 (1978).

23. See Braswell v. United States, 487 U.S. at 108, 108 S.Ct. at 2290.

24. United States v. White, 322 U.S. 694, 699, 64 S.Ct. 1248, 1251, 88 L.Ed. 1542 (1944). Justice Murphy, writing for a unanimous court, explained this principle as follows:

Since the privilege against self-incrimination is purely a personal one, it cannot be utilized by or on behalf of any organization, such as a corporation. Moreover, the papers and effects which the privilege protects must be the private property of the person claiming the privilege, or at least in his possession in a purely personal capacity. But individuals, when acting as representatives of a collective group, cannot be said to be exercising their personal rights and duties nor to be entitled to their purely personal privileges. Rather they assume the rights, duties and privileges of the artificial entity or association of which they are agents or officers and they are bound by its obligations. In their official capacity, therefore, they have no privilege against self-incrimination.

Id. at 699, 64 U.S. at 1251 (citations omitted).

itself.[25] For example, a federal circuit court of appeals rejected the argument of an osteopathic physician convicted of submitting false Medicare claims that records required by a grand jury subpoena were his personal papers and thus entitled to protection.[26] The subpoena was addressed to the clinic with which the appellant was affiliated, a professional corporation under Colorado state law. The court held that although the subpoena sought the files of patients treated by the physician individually, the records were held by the doctor in a representative capacity and thus were not protected by the Fifth Amendment.[27] The same principles have been adopted by state courts under state constitutions.[28]

By contrast, a sole proprietor is considered to be the equivalent of an individual, who may invoke the privilege against self-incrimination in response to a subpoena demanding testimony, or perhaps documents,[29] since he would not appear before the grand jury in any representative capacity.[30] Some courts have severely restricted even this modest protection, however. For example, one state appellate court upheld a trial court order denying a motion to quash filed by a dentist who received a grand jury subpoena that demanded the production of all of the appellant's patient records, even those created while the dentist was a sole practitioner.[31] The record on appeal established that the dentist had changed his business from a solo practice to a professional corporation and that the subpoena sought both files created prior to and after incorpo-

25. See, e.g., In the Matter of Moe v. Kuriansky, 120 A.D.2d 594, 595–596, 502 N.Y.S.2d 221, 222 (N.Y.App.Div. 1986) (because corporate entity has no Fifth Amendment protection, corporate agent must comply with subpoena for corporate records); In re Grand Jury Subpoena Duces Tecum Dated December 14, 1984, 113 A.D.2d 49, 51–52, 495 N.Y.S.2d 365, 366–67 (N.Y.App.Div. 1985) (Fifth Amendment does not apply to corporate records maintained by custodian relating to services provided by psychiatrists to patients).

26. See United States v. Radetsky, 535 F.2d 556, 569 (10th Cir.1976), cert. denied, 429 U.S. 820, 97 S.Ct. 68, 50 L.Ed.2d 81 (1976).

27. See id. at 568–69.

28. See, e.g., State v. Cote, 95 N.H. 108, 58 A.2d 749 (N.H.1948) (the state privilege against self-incrimination is purely personal and has no application to organizations, whether incorporated or not, whose characters are essentially impersonal).

29. Again, the continuing viability of Fifth Amendment protection for person-

al documents is unclear. See United States v. Doe, 465 U.S. 605, 618, 104 S.Ct. 1237, 1245, 79 L.Ed.2d 552 (1984) (O'Connor, J., concurring); see also discussion regarding act of production below at § 7–14a.

30. See Doe v. United States, 465 U.S. at 608, 104 S.Ct. at 1239 (the production of records of a sole proprietorship may in effect constitute a testimonial act protected by the Fifth Amendment). This is so because a sole proprietor does not hold records in a representative capacity. See Braswell v. United States, 487 U.S. at 110, 108 S.Ct. at 2292. See also In the Matter of Grand Jury Subpoena Duces Tecum Served Upon John Doe, 126 Misc.2d 1010, 484 N.Y.S.2d 759 (N.Y.Sup.Ct. 1984) (sole proprietor operator of consulting firm that served hospitals and nursing homes could not be required by the grand jury to produce books, documents and records of the firm without grant of immunity).

31. See In re Special Investigation No. 281, 299 Md. 181, 473 A.2d 1 (Md. 1984).

ration. Appellant argued that the pre-incorporation files were covered by his personal Fifth Amendment privilege against incrimination. The state appellate court rejected the claim holding that title to the files had passed from the solo practice to the corporation at the time of incorporation, and hence were not protected by the Fifth Amendment.[32] Other courts have held that even documents created by a solo practitioner may properly be sought by the grand jury because the "required records doctrine"[33] mandates their maintenance and disclosure.[34]

a. Act of Production as Testimonial Communication

Although the contents of subpoenaed documents are not protected by the Fifth Amendment, in certain circumstances, the *act of producing* the documents may be. As the Supreme Court held in *Fisher v. United States*,[35] the act of producing documents subpoenaed by the grand jury may sometimes have "communicative aspects." If so, that act (though not the contents of the documents)[36] may be privileged and production will be excused. When does an act of production have communicative aspects? When the person who complies with the demand for documents would, by producing the documents, implicitly admit that the documents exist, that the documents were in her possession or under her control, or that she believes that the documents produced are those described by the subpoena.

Troubles have sometimes arisen from subpoenas seeking documents in the hands of a third party custodian, such as an attorney.[37] The question of whether the Fifth Amendment can be invoked by a custodian to prevent the disclosure of documents

---

32. See id. See also In re Criminal Investigation No. 465, 80 Md.App. 347, 563 A.2d 1117 (Md.Ct.Spec.App.1989) (physician's records became corporate property when he incorporated his medical practice and could be sought by the grand jury).

33. See discussion infra at § 7–14b.

34. See, e.g., Stornanti v. Commonwealth, 389 Mass. 518, 451 N.E.2d 707 (Mass.1983) (president, sole pharmacist and director of drug store could be required to produce records sought by subpoena duces tecum under the required records doctrine); In re Morris Thrift Pharmacy, 397 So.2d 1301 (La.1981) (sole owner and operator of a pharmacy had no Fifth Amendment privilege protecting disclosure of his pharmaceutical records due to required records rule).

35. 425 U.S. 391, 96 S.Ct. 1569, 48 L.Ed.2d 39 (1976).

36. See United States v. Doe, 465 U.S. 605, 612–13, 104 S.Ct. 1237, 1242, 79 L.Ed.2d 552 (1984) (holding that although the *contents* of business records held by a sole proprietor were not protected by the Fifth Amendment, the act of producing the documents to the grand jury was, if the production necessitated an admission that the documents existed, were authentic, or were in the proprietor's possession).

37. See Fisher v. United States, 425 U.S. 391, 96 S.Ct. 1569, 48 L.Ed.2d 39 (1976) (attorney required to produce papers of taxpayer's accountant); Couch v. United States, 409 U.S. 322, 93 S.Ct. 611, 34 L.Ed.2d 548 (1973) (accountant required to produce books and records of his client, as subpoena compelled nothing on the part of the taxpayer).

depends foremost on the nature of the documents themselves—that is, whether the documents are private records or the records of an artificial entity. As discussed above, since a collective entity can act only through its representatives, the effect of permitting a custodian of partnership or corporate records to avoid production would be to extend the privilege against self-incrimination to the collective entities. For this reason the Supreme Court has held that a custodian of corporate or partnership records acts only in a representative capacity, not as an individual, and hence the production of such records cannot constitute a testimonial act of the custodian,[38] even if the act of producing the records would incriminate the custodian personally. A subpoenaed corporation must "find some means by which to comply" and may not defeat a subpoena for documents simply by selecting an agent who will assert a personal privilege,[39] such as by designating an agent who is able to respond without incriminating himself. Failure to do so will subject the corporation to contempt proceedings and may even lead a court to appoint an agent for the corporation to produce the records.[40]

Where, however, the records sought are the private records of an individual or sole proprietor, the Fifth Amendment may permit the custodian to refuse to comply with the subpoena calling for their production if it is established that an act of production would entail a testimonial admission that the records existed, were in his possession, or were authentic.[41] Such a custodian would be relying on his personal Fifth Amendment privilege, which would be available only if he was able to demonstrate that the grand jury would inevitably conclude that he was the person who produced the records, because, for example, he was the sole employee and officer of the corporation or entity.[42]

In the final analysis, the act of production doctrine is not likely to confer much protection to health care providers resisting subpoe-

---

38. Braswell v. United States, 487 U.S. 99, 108 S.Ct. 2284, 101 L.Ed.2d 98 (1988) (president and sole shareholder of two corporations could not interpose Fifth Amendment objection to production of corporate records).

39. See id. at 116, 108 S.Ct. at 2294 (quoting In re Sealed Case, 266 U.S.App. D.C. 30, 44 n.9, 832 F.2d 1268, 1282 n.9 (1987)).

40. See, e.g., In re Grand Jury Subpoenas Duces Tecum Served Upon 22nd Avenue Drugs, Inc., 633 F.Supp. 419, 423 (S.D.Fla.1986).

41. United States v. Doe, 465 U.S. 605, 104 S.Ct. 1237, 79 L.Ed.2d 552 (1984).

42. See Braswell v. United States, 487 U.S. 99, 101, 118, 119, 108 S.Ct.

2284, 2286, 2295, 2296, 101 L.Ed.2d 98 (1988) which held that while the custodian of records of any "collective entity" may not claim privilege on behalf of the corporation against a compelled act of production, the government may not inform the jury who produced the documents in order to ensure that the compelled act of production of corporate records does not violate the custodian's personal Fifth Amendment privilege. As long as the jury is not told that the custodian produced the records, the act of production will simply imply possession and authentication by the corporation, not the custodian, thus the production will not incriminate the custodian.

nas duces tecum for several reasons. First, even if a provider is able to show that an act of production would have incriminating aspects, the provider may not be able to avoid producing the documents if the existence and authenticity of the documents is "a foregone conclusion."[43] Second, the doctrine itself is extremely narrow in scope—it applies only to demands for personal documents or documents of a sole proprietorship, not to documents belonging to a corporation or other collective entity.[44] Third, the required records doctrine[45] severely limits, and indeed may destroy altogether, the act of production rule in the context of health care fraud investigations. Finally, prosecutors can dispose of act of production claims simply by naming another custodian to deposit the sought-after records in the grand jury, or by granting immunity to the resisting provider for the act of producing the documents. Such a grant of immunity would apply only to the provider's act of production and would not immunize the provider for the contents of the documents themselves. Since in most cases the government will be able to authenticate the documents without the provider's testimony, the price of granting immunity for an act of production to the government is minimal.

b. The Required Records Exception

A major limitation on the Fifth Amendment's protection against compelled self-incrimination in the context of a Medicare or Medicaid fraud investigation is the so-called "required records" rule. Numerous state[46] and federal[47] courts have looked to the

---

43. Fisher, 425 U.S. at 411, 96 S.Ct. at 1581 (holding that a taxpayer's production of his accountant's workpapers was not testimonial because their existence and authenticity were a foregone conclusion). The rationale of the foregone conclusion doctrine is that there is nothing testimonial about a party's act of production if the existence and authenticity of the records are already known to the government.

44. See Braswell, 487 U.S. at 104, 108 S.Ct. at 2288 (1988).

45. See § 7–14b.

46. See, e.g., In the matter of Grand Jury Subpoenas Served on Progressive Labs, 132 Misc.2d 695, 505 N.Y.S.2d 787 (N.Y.Sup.Ct.1986) (no Fifth Amendment protection for pharmacy's prescription forms required by Medicaid program to be maintained and disclosed); In the Matter of Grand Jury Subpoena Duces Tecum Dated December 14, 1984, 69 N.Y.2d 232, 505 N.E.2d 925, 513 N.Y.S.2d 359 (N.Y.1987) (psychiatrists must comply with subpoena for docu-

ments in light of fact that Medicaid investigators have been given an unqualified right to review all records needed for their investigation of possibly fraudulent conduct); Matter of Shoe Ring Ltd., 1986 WL 75882 (N.Y.Sup.Ct.1986) (manufacturer of orthopedic shoes must comply with subpoena issued by state MFCU seeking corporate books and records which were records required to be kept by law); Stornanti v. Commonwealth, 389 Mass. 518, 451 N.E.2d 707 (Mass.1983) (upholding order of civil contempt imposed on pharmacist president of drug company who refused to comply with subpoena demanding production of Medicaid prescription documents); People v. Herbert, M.D., 108 Ill.App.3d 143, 438 N.E.2d 1255, 63 Ill. Dec. 892 (Ill.App.Ct.1982) cert. denied, 459 U.S. 1204, 103 S.Ct. 1190, 75 L.Ed.2d 436 (1983)(physician cannot assert the privilege against self-incrimination in refusing to produce certain medical records because of application of the required records exception); In re Morris

required records doctrine as a basis for rejecting Fifth Amendment challenges to subpoenas seeking documents from providers or other professionals in the health care industry.

Under the required records doctrine, if a person or entity is required by law to maintain certain written records—even personal records belonging to a non-corporate entity—the grand jury will be able to compel the production of those records without offending the Fifth Amendment's privilege against self-incrimination, provided the record requirement is part of a regulatory scheme or governmental program.[48] To qualify as a required record and thus be subject to disclosure, a document must satisfy the three-part test set out in *Grosso v. United States*.[49] First, the purpose of the government's requirement that the records be kept must be regulatory, rather than criminal in nature. Second, the records sought must contain the type of information that the regulated party would ordinarily keep. And third, the records must have assumed "public aspects" which render them analogous to public documents.[50] Once these three prongs are satisfied, the required records rule mandates disclosure of the documents, even if such disclosure would incriminate the party producing the documents, and regard-

Thrift Pharmacy, 397 So.2d 1301 (La. 1981) (pharmacist subpoenaed in connection with kickback investigation had no reasonable expectation of privacy in prescription drug records which he had agreed to maintain and disclose as a part of his Medicaid Provider Agreement); In the Matter of People v. Doe (Hospital Investigation), 107 Misc.2d 605, 435 N.Y.S.2d 656 (N.Y.Sup.Ct.1981) (long term care center for children with disabling mental health problems investigated for overbilling Medicaid must comply with grand jury subpoena for documents required to be kept by law); In the Matter of an Offense Under Investigation in re Rozas Gibson Pharmacy of Eunice, Inc., 382 So.2d 929 (La. 1980) (pharmacy suspected of charging name brand price for generic substitute could have no reasonable expectation of privacy in records due to its agreement to maintain and disclose records as part of the Medicare Provider Agreement).

47. See, e.g., In re Grand Jury Subpoena Duces Tecum, 1997 WL 12126 (6th Cir.1997) (unpublished) (per curiam) (a podiatrist's patient files, records of patient visits, operative notes and billing information are required records and thus not covered by Fifth Amendment); In re Grand Jury Proceed-ings, 867 F.2d 562, 565 (9th Cir.1989) (per curiam) (psychiatric records of grand jury target not within scope of Fifth Amendment privilege because not voluntarily kept business records), cert. denied, 493 U.S. 906, 110 S.Ct. 265, 107 L.Ed.2d 214 (1989); In re Grand Jury Proceedings, 801 F.2d 1164 (9th Cir. 1986) (because federal and state law required physician target to maintain for 3 years all records of manufacture, sale, purchase, or disposition of dangerous drugs, a subpoena that sought target's purchase, sale and prescription records was covered by required records exception).

48. See Shapiro v. United States, 335 U.S. 1, 33, 68 S.Ct. 1375, 1392, 92 L.Ed. 1787 (1948) ("The privilege which exists as to private papers cannot be maintained in relation to 'records required by law' in order to ensure that there is suitable information about transactions which are the appropriate subjects of governmental regulation"), quoting Wilson v. United States, 221 U.S. 361, 380, 31 S.Ct. 538, 544, 55 L.Ed. 771 (1911).

49. 390 U.S. 62, 67–68, 88 S.Ct. 709, 713, 19 L.Ed.2d 906 (1968).

50. Id. at 67–68, 88 S.Ct. at 713.

less of whether it is state or federal law that requires that the records be kept.[51]

Turning to the first *Grosso* factor, health care providers have had little success avoiding the required records doctrine by claiming that the record-keeping obligations imposed on the industry are criminal in nature, rather than regulatory.[52] Both the Medicare and Medicaid programs are heavily regulated and health care providers are required by federal and state law to maintain and disclose upon request a vast array of records related to the provision of professional services or medical supplies for which payment is sought under the programs.[53] The Social Security Act, for example, provides in pertinent part:

> (a) A State plan for medical assistance must * * * (27) provide for agreements with every person or institution providing services under the State plan which such person or institution agrees (A) to keep such records as are necessary fully to disclose the extent of the services provided to individuals receiving assistance under the State plan, and (B) to furnish the State agency or the Secretary with such information, regarding any payments claimed by such person or institution for providing services under the State plan, as the State agency or the Secretary may from time to time request . . . [54]

Under this provision, in order to obtain federal funding for a percentage of the costs of their Medicaid programs, each state must have a plan for medical assistance approved by the Secretary of HHS. Approval will only be granted if the state agrees to require health care providers within the state to maintain and make available records relating to services for which reimbursement may be sought under the program. The Secretary has promulgated additional regulations to the same effect.[55] To secure federal funding each state has complied with this federal mandate, and many have enacted their own required records statutes.[56] In addition,

---

51. See Shapiro, 335 U.S. at 17–18 & n.25, 68 S.Ct. at 1384–85 & n.25.

52. See, e.g., In re Grand Jury Proceedings, 801 F.2d 1164, 1168 (9th Cir. 1986).

53. See 42 C.F.R. § 413.20(c) (1996) (Medicare); 45 C.F.R. § 250.80 (1996) (Medicaid).

54. See 42 U.S.C.A. § 1396a (1994).

55. See 42 C.F.R. § 431.107(b), which provides:

> (b) Agreements—A state plan must provide for an agreement between the Medicaid agency and each provider or organization furnishing services under

the plan in which the provider or organization agrees to—

> (1) Keep any records necessary to disclose the extent of services the provider furnishes to recipients . . .

56. See, e.g., Illinois Rev. Stat., ch. 23, ¶ 5–5 (1979) ("All dispensers of medical services shall be required to maintain and retain business and professional records sufficient to fully and accurately document the nature, scope, details and receipt of the health care provided to persons eligible for medical assistance under this Code . . ."); N.Y. Pub. Health Law §§ 3322, 3338(2), 3331(6) & 3333(4) (McKinney 1977) (re-

forms filled out by a provider to bill the Medicaid program for goods or services contain a certification that acknowledges the provider's obligation to maintain records.[57] These extensive record-keeping and disclosure obligations have frequently enabled prosecutors to invoke the required records doctrine to fend off Fifth Amendment privilege claims.

Courts reviewing Medicare, Medicaid and other record-keeping statutes and regulations have found them to be regulatory efforts to monitor the publicly funded fisc of the programs, notwithstanding that records required to be kept under the provisions are often sought in connection with grand jury investigations of possible criminal activity. As explained by one court:

> Respondent argues that because his records are sought by a grand jury investigating him for possible criminal violations, the reason for which his records are sought is not regulatory. Respondent is improperly attempting to shift the focus away from the purpose for which the records are required to be kept to the purpose for which they are sought. The purpose of the record keeping obligations here is to monitor the operation of the Medicaid program, not to catch criminals.[58]

Prosecutors have had even less trouble meeting the second *Grosso* requirement—that the required records be of a kind customarily kept by health care providers. The courts have recognized that health care providers ordinary keep a wide assortment of documentary evidence frequently sought by the grand jury, including patient files,[59] examination and treatment records,[60] prescription records,[61] a physician's W–2 forms,[62] records of patient visits,[63] billing information,[64] and more. These conclusions seem unremarkable. Federal and state provisions impose stiff record-keeping obligations, and under many state laws, health care providers who fail to keep

quiring practitioners to prepare an official prescription form for any dispersement of a Schedule II drug, to retain copies thereof for 5 years, and to forward a copy of all prescription forms to the New York State Department of Health).

57. For example, the form filled out by New Hampshire health care providers reads:

> I hereby agree to keep such records as are necessary to disclose fully the extent of services provided and to furnish such information regarding any payments claimed as the state agency may request for a period of six years from the date the claim is received.

Reprinted in Records, Grand Juries and the Privilege Against Self-Incrimination, Health Care Fraud 1993 at J–1 (ABA, Chicago, Ill. 1997).

58. See People v. Herbert, 108 Ill. App.3d 143, 148, 438 N.E.2d 1255, 1258, 63 Ill.Dec. 892, 895 (Ill.App.Ct.1982), cert. den., 459 U.S. 1204, 103 S.Ct. 1190, 75 L.Ed.2d 436 (1983).

59. See id.

60. See id.

61. See, e.g., In re Doe, 711 F.2d 1187, 1191 (2d Cir.1983).

62. See id. at 1191.

63. See, e.g., In re Grand Jury Subpoena Duces Tecum, 105 F.3d 659, 1997 WL 12126 (6th Cir.1997) (per curiam) (unpublished).

64. See id.

certain treatment records breach additional professional responsibility standards.[65]

In theory, the most troublesome requirement of *Grosso* for a prosecutor is the last requirement: that records (and particularly patient files) have "public aspects" which render them analogous to public documents. Subpoenas issued in connection with Medicare and Medicaid fraud investigations frequently seek patient files which record patients' medical conditions, or prescription records which indicate the nature of patient medication. Some providers have argued that even if state or federal laws require such records to be kept, confidential patient records have no "public aspects" in light of patients' expectations of privacy in matters relating to their health. The courts have rejected such claims, however, finding that patients' expectations of privacy do not negate the public aspect of such records under applicable regulatory schemes.[66]

The courts have struggled with the question of whether the required records doctrine requires disclosure of the records of a sole proprietor covered by the act of production doctrine.[67] That is, if subpoenaed records meet the *Grosso* required records test, may a party refuse personally to produce them based on an act of production privilege claim? Although it was not always so, the courts now appear to agree that the required records doctrine wins out in a fight with an act of production claim.[68] In *Doe v. United States*,[69] for example, the United States Court of Appeals for the Second Circuit considered an act of production claim asserted by a psychiatrist who had received a grand jury subpoena demanding his W–2 forms, schedule II prescription forms, and assorted patient files in connection with the grand jury's investigation concerning the medical clinic with which the psychiatrist was affiliated. The government believed the clinic operated as a front for the illegal sale of quaa-

---

65. See, e.g., Fla. Stat. § 458.331(1)(m) (1996).

66. See In re Grand Jury Proceedings, 801 F.2d 1164, 1168 (9th Cir.1986); In re Kenny, 715 F.2d 51, 53 (2d Cir. 1983); In re Doe, 711 F.2d 1187, 1192 (2d Cir.1983). The same result has been reached by several state courts. See, e.g., People v. Herbert, 108 Ill.App.3d 143, 147, 438 N.E.2d 1255, 1258, 63 Ill.Dec. 892, 895 (1982) cert. den. 459 U.S. 1204, 103 S.Ct. 1190, 75 L.Ed.2d 436 (1983); Stornanti v. Commonwealth, 389 Mass. 518, 523–24, 451 N.E.2d 707, 711–12 (Mass. 1983) (records kept as condition of participation in Medicaid program have public aspects, particularly since Commonwealth uses taxpayers' dollars to fund reimbursements under the program); In re Morris Thrift Pharmacy, 397 So.2d 1301 (La.1981) (because of federal regulations and disclosure agreements signed by owner-operator of pharmacy, the records sought by grand jury had acquired public aspects).

67. See § 7–14a.

68. See, e.g., United States v. Spano, 21 F.3d 226 (8th Cir.1994); In re Grand Jury Duces Tecum Served Upon Underhill, 781 F.2d 64, 70 (6th Cir.1986) (the required records doctrine is an exception to the Fifth Amendment which presupposes that compliance with a subpoena may be incriminating; to have meaning, the exception must apply to the act of production as well as to the contents of the documents requested); Doe v. United States, 711 F.2d 1187, 1191–92 (2d Cir. 1983).

69. 711 F.2d 1187 (2d Cir.1983).

ludes. Although the court agreed that testimony elicited from the psychiatrist in connection with his production of the demanded documents might tend to incriminate him (since it could implicitly admit his affiliation with the target clinic and the inordinate number of patients he treated there) the court nonetheless held the records could be compelled under the required records exception.[70]

Under this view, the required records doctrine threatens to consume what little remaining protection the privilege against self-incrimination may afford documentary evidence belonging to health care providers. The federal government and most states heavily regulate the industry, requiring participating providers to maintain voluminous documentation of their health care services for lengthy periods of time. These records must not only be maintained, they must be disclosed to regulators upon request. Although in theory the Fifth Amendment outweighs an individual's statutorily-imposed reporting obligations if the obligations are penal, rather than regulatory,[71] no court has found the reporting obligations of health care providers to be penal in nature. Thus, prosecutors have had few problems demonstrating that the records most often sought by grand jury subpoenas duces tecum in connection with a Medicare or Medicare fraud or abuse investigations pose no Fifth Amendment problem.

c. Grants of Immunity

If it is determined that testimony compelled by a subpoena *ad testificandum* would incriminate the testifying party, or that the act of producing documents compelled by a subpoena duces tecum is protected by the Fifth Amendment, only a grant of immunity (typically use immunity) will overcome the privilege.[72] Testimony given under a grant of use immunity, and evidence derived directly or indirectly from such testimony, may not subsequently be used against the witness in any criminal case (except in a prosecution for perjury or a contempt proceeding) and the government will bear the burden of showing that the evidence came from an independent source.[73] Once immunized, however, a subpoenaed party has no choice but to testify truthfully before the grand jury or to deliver

---

70. See id. at 1191–92.

71. See Whiteside & Co. v. SEC, 883 F.2d 7, 9 (5th Cir.1989) (per curiam).

72. See Pillsbury Co. v. Conboy, 459 U.S. 248, 254–55, 103 S.Ct. 608, 612–13, 74 L.Ed.2d 430 (1983) (grant of immunity sufficient to compel testimony over claim of Fifth Amendment privilege); Kastigar v. United States, 406 U.S. 441, 458–59, 92 S.Ct. 1653, 1664, 32 L.Ed.2d 212 (1972), reh'g denied, 408 U.S. 931, 92 S.Ct. 2478, 33 L.Ed.2d 345 (1972).

73. 18 U.S.C.A. § 6002 (1994); Kastigar v. United States, 406 U.S. 441, 461–62, 92 S.Ct. 1653, 1665, 32 L.Ed.2d 212 (1972), reh'g denied, 408 U.S. 931, 92 S.Ct. 2478, 33 L.Ed.2d 345 (1972) ("One raising a claim under [the federal immunity] statute need only show that he testified under a grant of immunity in order to shift to the government the heavy burden of proving that all of the evidence it proposes to use was derived from legitimate independent sources.").

the documents.[74] In at least one state case, a prosecutor has been forced to confer separate grants of immunity to cover testimony and the act of producing documents and other items.[75]

§ 7–15. The Fourth Amendment Prohibition Against Unreasonable Searches and Seizures

Health care providers have looked to the Fourth Amendment as another basis for quashing or limiting the scope of grand jury subpoenas for testimony or documents. The Fourth Amendment guarantees "the right of the people to be secure in their persons, houses, papers and effects against unreasonable searches and seizures."[1] Although Fourth Amendment jurisprudence primarily concerns limits on the right of government agents to obtain evidence by search, many have argued that the Amendment should apply to evidence obtained by subpoena as well. While some Fourth Amendment limitations on the scope of subpoenas remain, the protection afforded by the Amendment has been significantly reduced over time.

Although over a century ago the Supreme Court announced in *Boyd v. United States*[2] that a grand jury subpoena for documents could constitute a search under the Fourth Amendment, that view was relatively short-lived. Twenty years after *Boyd*, in *Hale v. Henkel*,[3] a closely divided Court once again considered whether the Fourth Amendment applied to grand jury subpoenas. By a 5–4 vote, the Court held that although a subpoena duces tecum "might constitute a forbidden search *if* its terms were 'unreasonable,'" as a general matter, the Fourth Amendment's search and seizure clause was not intended to impede "the power of courts to compel * * * the production * * * of documentary evidence."[4] The Court suggested that questions of Fourth Amendment reasonableness would depend on the breadth of a subpoena's demand.[5]

---

74. See also United States v. Silkman, 543 F.2d 1218, 1220 (8th Cir.1976) (per curiam) cert.denied, 431 U.S. 919, 97 S.Ct. 2185, 53 L.Ed.2d 230 (1977).

75. See, e.g., In re Grand Jury Subpoena Duces Tecum Served Upon Doe, 484 N.Y.S.2d 759, 763–64, 126 Misc.2d 1010, 1015 (N.Y.Sup.Ct.1984) (dentist must receive dual grants of immunity to cover his oral responses and his act of producing and identifying books and records before the grand jury).

§ 7–15

1. U.S. CONST. amend. IV.

2. 116 U.S. 616, 621–22, 630, 6 S.Ct. 524, 527–28, 532, 29 L.Ed. 746, 748, 751 (1886).

3. 201 U.S. 43, 26 S.Ct. 370, 50 L.Ed. 652 (1906).

4. See id. at 76, 73, 26 S.Ct. at 379–380, 378 (emphasis added).

5. See id. at 76–77, 26 S.Ct. at 379–380. For the next twenty years the judicial battleground over subpoenas was littered with overbreadth claims. See, e.g., Consolidated Rendering Co. v. Vermont, 207 U.S. 541, 553–54, 28 S.Ct. 178, 181–82, 52 L.Ed. 327 (1908); Wilson v. United States, 221 U.S. 361, 375–76, 31 S.Ct. 538, 542, 55 L.Ed. 771 (1911); Wheeler v. United States, 226 U.S. 478, 489, 33 S.Ct. 158, 162, 57 L.Ed. 309 (1913); Brown v. United States, 276 U.S. 134, 142–43, 48 S.Ct. 288, 289–90, 72 L.Ed. 500 (1928).

The Supreme Court revisited the issue again in 1946 when it decided *Oklahoma Press Publishing Co. v. Walling*,[6] a case involving an administrative subpoena for documents. The Court held that unlike the execution of a search, the compulsive force of a subpoena duces tecum does not amount to a search or seizure within the meaning of the Fourth Amendment. The Court reiterated, however, that subpoenas duces tecum must be "reasonable" to be constitutionally valid (though the Court left unclear whether this was due to the Fourth Amendment or the due process clause)[7] and to be reasonable a subpoena duces tecum must meet three criteria.[8] First, the subpoena must seek documents or other records for "a lawfully authorized purpose, within the power of Congress to demand." Second, the information sought must be relevant to the authorized inquiry. Third, the subpoena must include an adequate specification of the documents to be produced, and must not be excessive, for the purposes of the relevant inquiry.[9]

"Relevance" in the grand jury context has been given a very broad meaning. A motion to quash a grand jury subpoena based on relevance grounds will be denied unless "there is no reasonable possibility that the category of materials the Government seeks will produce information relevant to the general subject of the grand jury's investigation."[10] In addition, the burden of persuading a court that a subpoena seeks documents or other items irrelevant to a lawfully authorized purpose is on the party resisting compliance.[11]

The reasons for this broad understanding of relevance are clear. A strict view of the relevance requirement would severely hamper grand jury investigations. Typically such challenges are made just after receipt of a subpoena, before the government has had a chance to receive and review the sought-after documents. The

---

6. 327 U.S. 186, 66 S.Ct. 494, 90 L.Ed. 614 (1946).

7. Writing for the majority, Justice Rutledge explained:

The short answer to the Fourth Amendment objections is that the records in these cases present no question of actual search and seizure.... No officer or other person has sought to enter petitioners' premises against their will, to search them, or to seize or examine their books, records or papers without their assent.... Only in [an] analogical sense can any question related to search and seizure be thought to arise in situations which, like the present ones, involve only the validity of authorized judicial orders.

Id. at 195, 202, 66 S.Ct. at 498, 502.

8. The Court subsequently made clear that these requirements apply to

grand jury subpoenas duces tecum as well as administrative subpoenas, which were the subject of *Oklahoma Press*.

9. Oklahoma Press, 327 U.S. at 208–09, 66 S.Ct. 505–06.

10. See United States v. R. Enterprises, 498 U.S. 292, 301, 111 S.Ct. 722, 727–28, 112 L.Ed.2d 795 (1991), on remand 955 F.2d 229 (4th Cir.1992).

11. See United States v. R. Enterprises, Inc., 498 U.S. 292, 300, 111 S.Ct. 722, 727–28, 112 L.Ed.2d 795 (1991), on remand 955 F.2d 229 (4th Cir.1992). See also In re Grand Jury Subpoena Duces Tecum Served Upon John Doe, 126 Misc.2d 1010, 484 N.Y.S.2d 759, 761 (N.Y.Sup.Ct.1984); In re Special Investigation No. 281, 299 Md. 181, 191–92, 473 A.2d 1, 6–7 (Md. 1984); State v. Washington, 83 Wis.2d 808, 843–45, 266 N.W.2d 597, 614–15 (Wis. 1978).

government, therefore, may need to establish the relevance of documents without having seen them.[12] Motions to quash subpoenas on relevance grounds create difficulties for courts as well. Because a court is likely to be faced with a relevance challenge during the infancy of a grand jury or administrative investigation, before the grand jury or agency has focused on any particular target or transaction, determining the ultimate relevance of the subpoenaed information is difficult.[13] In addition, in light of the closely-guarded secrecy of grand jury proceedings, a court called upon to review a subpoena for relevance will likely be reluctant to order the government to disclose many details about its investigation.

Thus, a grand jury subpoena that seeks documents even minimally germane to an investigation of bribes, kickbacks or false statements is likely to be enforced. In one case for example, a court refused to quash a subpoena issued in connection with an investigation of one health care provider's possible false billing activity which called for the provider's investigation records of other insurers.[14] In another case, the subpoenaed records of a dentist's Blue Shield patients were deemed relevant because the records *"might shed some light on whether the dentist engaged in fraudulent conduct with respect to the billing of his Medical Assistance patients."*[15]

Attacks on subpoenas due to vagueness (i.e., on the ground that the subpoena inadequately describes the documents or items demanded) have also rarely been successful.[16] Although the rule of *Oklahoma Press/Walling* requires that a subpoena sufficiently describe the documents to be produced by a subpoenaed provider, the courts will not require the government to recite with mathematical precision every document it wishes to review. No more is required than that the wording of the subpoena sufficiently identify the documents sought to enable the witness to know in good faith what she is being asked to produce. If a subpoena meets this minimum specificity standard it will be upheld.

12. To deal with this problem, of course, the government could take a conservative approach and seek only those records that are certain to be relevant to its administrative or grand jury inquiry. Such a conservative approach, however, raises the possibility that the government's demand could miss information that could later turn out to be relevant, or even critical, to the grand jury inquiry.

13. Frank E. Cooper, Federal Agency Investigations: Requirements for Production of Documents, 60 Mich.L.Rev. 187, 191 (1961).

14. See In re Special Investigation No. 281, 299 Md. 181, 473 A.2d 1 (Md. 1984).

15. In re Special Investigation, 299 Md. 181, 194, 473 A.2d 1,7 (Md.1984).

16. See John Benton, Administrative Subpoena Enforcement, 41 Tex.L.Rev. 874, 889 (1963).

Challenges based on grounds of a subpoena's breadth or burdensomeness have had more success in the courts.[17] A subpoena that places an undue burden on the party responsible for producing the documents may be found constitutionally defective, resulting either in an order to quash, or in an order narrowing the subpoena's scope.[18] As with the relevance requirement, however, the burden of persuasion of establishing a subpoena's excessiveness is on the party challenging the subpoena.[19]

Several factors are relevant to the question of whether a subpoena is overly broad or places an unreasonable burden on a subpoenaed party: (1) whether the subpoena could be more selective; (2) the volume of documents sought; (3) the time period covered by the subpoena; (4) the disruption caused to the subpoenaed party's ongoing operations; (5) the financial cost of collecting the documents; and (6) the relation of the subpoenaed party to the subject matter of the investigation.[20] Although no single factor is determinative,[21] where a challenging party is able to establish that the relationship of the subpoenaed records to the investigation is negligible, or that the records cover an unreasonably long period of time, the subpoena may be quashed or at least narrowed in its scope.[22]

§ 7-16. Privilege Claims

Assorted common law and statutory privileges act as an important buffer between official attempts to obtain testimony and

17. See Benton, Administrative Subpoena Enforcement, 41 Tex. L. Rev. 874, 890 (1963). Perhaps the best known example of such a claim is that in F.T.C. v. American Tobacco, 264 U.S. 298, 44 S.Ct. 336, 68 L.Ed. 696 (1924), an antitrust case in which the FTC subpoenaed virtually all of American Tobacco's business records. Referring to the FTC's subpoena as a "fishing expedition," the Supreme Court declined to enforce the demand. See id. at 306, 44 S.Ct. at 337. ("It is against the first principles of justice to allow a search through all the [company's] records, relevant or irrelevant, in the hope that something will turn up.")

18. See D'Alimonte v. Kuriansky, 144 A.D.2d 737, 535 N.Y.S.2d 151, 152 (3d Dep't 1988) (quashing a grand jury subpoena that contained no time limitation).

19. In re Grand Jury Subpoenas Duces Tecum Addressed to Certain Executive Officers of the M.G. Allen & Assocs., Inc., 391 F.Supp. 991 (D.R.I. 1975).

20. See In re Grand Jury Subpoena Duces Tecum, 203 F.Supp. 575 (S.D.N.Y. 1961).

21. For example, attacks based on the volume of a request, without more, may be rejected. See, e.g., In re Borden Co., 75 F.Supp. 857 (N.D.Ill.1948) (non-health care fraud case declining to quash a subpoena for records relevant to a grand jury investigation despite proof that an earlier investigation had demanded documents that weighed fifty tons, took ten truckloads to deliver, and required the reinforcement of the courthouse floor to store).

22. See, e.g. Hale v. Henkel, 201 U.S. 43, 76–7, 26 S.Ct. 370, 379–80, 50 L.Ed. 652 (1906) (subpoena requiring company to produce records from the date of its organization was excessive); Application of Certain Chinese Family Benevolent and District Ass'ns, 19 F.R.D. 97, 98, 101 (N.D.Cal.1956) (quashing subpoenas that required associations to produce records for the entire period of the associations' existence).

documents on the one hand, and interests in the confidentiality of certain communications on the other. Health care providers have laid claim to a number of privileges as a means to defend against official probes for evidence, including the physician-patient privilege, the psychotherapist-patient privilege, the attorney-client privilege, the work-product privilege and the joint-defense privilege. Successful invocation of one of these privileges can preclude the government's use of covered materials before the grand jury or at trial. However, because privilege claims frustrate the venerated principle that the public has a right to every man's evidence, and operate "in derogation of the search for truth," privileges are neither "lightly created nor expansively construed."[1]

a. The Physician–Patient Privilege

Physician-patient privilege rules date from the early nineteenth century.[2] Although no such privilege existed at common law,[3] many state legislatures have passed statutes expressly providing protection for doctor-patient communications.[4] These privilege rules are designed to provide repose to, and encourage frank communication from, patients who might be reluctant to disclose essential information about their symptoms or medical conditions to their physicians out of fear that the information might later be disclosed to others. Accordingly, approximately two-thirds of the states and the District of Columbia have passed statutes that permit a patient to prevent a physician from testifying about or otherwise disclosing information revealed by a patient to a physician in her professional capacity.[5]

The federal government has not followed suit. Although Rule 501 of the Federal Rules of Evidence permits a court to preclude the disclosure of any information it deems advisable "in the light of reason and experience,"[6] Congress has enacted no express federal

§ 7–16

1. United States v. Nixon, 418 U.S. 683, 710, 94 S.Ct. 3090, 3108, 41 L.Ed.2d 1039 (1974).

2. See 8 J. Wigmore, Evidence in Trials at Common Law § 2380, at 819–20 (J. McNaugton ed. 1961).

3. See Whalen v. Roe, 429 U.S. 589, 602, 97 S.Ct. 869, 877, 51 L.Ed.2d 64 (1977) (there was no physician-patient privilege at common law).

4. New York was the first state to pass such a statute in 1828. See 2 N.Y.Rev.Stat. pt. 3, ch. 7, § 73, at 406 (1828).

5. See McNaughton, Wigmore on Evidence § 2380 (1961 rev., Supp.1994); see also Pamela H. Bucy, The Poor Fit of Traditional Evidentiary Doctrine and Sophisticated Crime: An Empirical Analysis of Health Care Fraud Prosecutions, 63 Fordham L. Rev. 383, 470–71 (1994).

6. The Fed.Evid.R. 501 reads in pertinent part:

"[T]he privilege of a ... person ... shall be governed by the principles of the common law as they may be interpreted by the courts of the United States in the light of reason and experience."

Most of the federal courts have declined to recognize the doctor-patient privilege, although some have done so in limited circumstances. See Pamela H. Bucy, Litigating Health Care Fraud, From

physician-patient privilege provision, and the courts have been reluctant to construe the Rules to provide one.[7] Thus, to date, the federal courts have spurned the claims of health care providers who have refused to produce patient files or other medical records on the basis of the physician-patient privilege.[8] A single exception to this relatively free federal access to medical documents exists: if the records relate to treatment for substance abuse in a federally funded program, a court order is required to obtain patient records.[9]

In most instances, even state doctor-patient privilege rules have not shielded health care professionals from demands for testimony or documents related to patient treatment. As a rule, state courts are reluctant to allow health care providers to hide behind the physician-patient privilege in order possibly to conceal their own wrongdoing.[10] Efforts to restrict the scope of the investigators' access, for example by retracting certain information (such as the names of patients whose files are subpoenaed or other medical information) from the records have also been rejected.[11] Thus, despite the prevalence of state patient-physician privilege rules, state courts have repeatedly given grand juries and other investigators the green light to subpoena medical records or to require provider testimony about patient treatment. Over time, several rationales have been used to justify disclosure of this arguably confidential information.

Quackery to Computers, 10 Crim. Just. 20, 55 (Spring 1995).

7. See United States v. Mancuso, 444 F.2d 691 (5th Cir.1971) (there is no federal common law physician-patient privilege to cover medical or hospital records); Robinson v. Magovern, 83 F.R.D. 79 (W.D.Pa.1979) (same); In re Grand Jury Subpoena, 460 F.Supp. 150 (W.D.Mo.1978) (same); In re Verplank, 329 F.Supp. 433 (C.D.Cal.1971) (same); United States v. Kansas City Lutheran Home & Hospital Ass'n, 297 F.Supp. 239 (W.D.Mo.1969) (same).

8. See e.g., United States v. Colletta, 602 F.Supp. 1322, 1327 (E.D.Pa.1985) aff'd without op., 770 F.2d 1076 (3d Cir.1985); United States v. Witt, 542 F.Supp. 696, 697–98 (S.D.N.Y.1982) aff'd without op., 697 F.2d 301 (2d Cir. 1982); In re Verplank, 329 F.Supp. 433, 438 (D.C.Cal.1971); Hardy v. Riser, 309 F.Supp. 1234, 1236–37 (N.D.Miss.1970).

9. See 42 U.S.C.A. § 290dd–2 (West Supp.1994). See also In re the August 1993 Regular Grand Jury (Hospital Sub-

poena), 854 F.Supp. 1380, 1382 (S.D. Ind. 1994) (hospital grounding motion to suppress on government's failure to obtain court order authorizing release of drug and alcohol abuse treatment records); Mulholland v. Dietz Co., 896 F.Supp. 179, 179 (E.D.Pa.1994) (order memorandum) (records of patients who participate in federally sponsored substance abuse programs are statutorily confidential).

10. See, e.g., In re Grand Jury Proceeding (Doe), 56 N.Y.2d 348, 351, 452 N.Y.S.2d 361, 362, 437 N.E.2d 1118, 1120 (N.Y.1982); People v. Doe, 107 Misc.2d 605, 607–08, 435 N.Y.S.2d 656, 658–59 (N.Y.Sup.Ct.1981). See also State v. Chenette, 151 Vt. 237, 248, 560 A.2d 365, 373 (Vt.1989) ("To allow the defendant to gain any advantage from the privilege would make the privilege a protector of fraud rather than a privacy shield.").

11. See, e.g., Doe v. Kuriansky, 91 A.D.2d 1068, 1068–69, 458 N.Y.S.2d 678, 679–80 (N.Y.App.Div.1983).

To begin with, the privilege belongs to the patient, not the provider. Although providers are permitted by most state privilege laws to invoke the privilege on behalf of their patients, once it is determined that the provider does not speak for the patient, the privilege claim will normally expire.[12]

The Supremacy Clause[13] provides another important rationale frequently relied on by state courts for refusing to block disclosure: state-created privilege rules are trumped by conflicting reporting obligations imposed by the federal Medicaid statute and other federal provisions. For example, a Rhode Island court rejected a claim advanced by two private physicians that a state-enacted doctor-patient privilege rule prevented their compliance with a grand jury subpoena demanding patient treatment records from a period of alleged Medicaid fraud.[14] The court held that the state privilege could not be applied if it conflicted with a federal law such as the Social Security Act, which, as discussed above, conditions federal funding of state Medicaid programs on a requirement that all physicians participating in the Medicaid program maintain and disclose records of goods and services paid for by the program during state fraud investigations.[15] Reasoning that "full priority must be given" to federal law under the Supremacy Clause, the court concluded that the state physician-patient privilege rule had to give way.[16] Several other state courts have reached similar conclusions.[17] In light of these decisions it is apparent that even if a state has adopted a rule which purports to shield medical records from disclosure, in truth, a health care provider may be compelled to produce such records to a grand jury investigating health care fraud allegations. Given the breadth of the record-keeping and disclosure obligations mandated by federal law, essentially any patient treatment record would appear to be fair game for the grand jury or other authorized party investigating criminal fraud.

---

12. See, e.g., State v. Chenette, 151 Vt. 237, 248, 560 A.2d 365, 373 (Vt. 1989) (patient records of physician investigated for false billing practices could be disclosed where patients had waived privilege after the documents were obtained by subpoena).

13. See U.S. CONST. art. VI.

14. See In re Grand Jury Investigation, 441 A.2d 525 (R.I.1982).

15. See Social Security Act, § 1901, 1902(a)(1), 42 U.S.C.A. §§ 1396, 1396a(a)(1) (1994).

16. See In re Grand Jury Investigation, 441 A.2d 525, 531 (R.I.1982).

17. See, e.g., Brillantes v. Superior Court, 51 Cal.App.4th 323, 58 Cal. Rptr.2d 770 (Cal.Ct.App.1996); In re People v. Bhatt, 160 Misc.2d 973, 981, 611 N.Y.S.2d 447, 452 (N.Y.Sup.Ct. 1994); People v. Ekong, 221 Ill.App.3d 559, 164 Ill.Dec. 25, 26, 582 N.E.2d 233, 234 (1991) (rejecting claim that Illinois physician-patient privilege protected from disclosure to grand jury a physician's medical records due to conflict with congressional objectives requiring disclosure); In Matter of Camperlengo v. Blum, 56 N.Y.2d 251, 255–56, 451 N.Y.S.2d 697, 699, 436 N.E.2d 1299, 1301 (N.Y.1982); State v. Latta, 92 Wash.2d 812, 819–21, 601 P.2d 520, 525–26 (Wash.1979).

Some state courts have cited additional, albeit less persuasive, reasons for evading the preclusive impact of state doctor-patient privilege provisions. Under these cases, state doctor-patient privileges have been found inapplicable to health care fraud investigations due to the disclosure obligations accepted by health care providers at the time they joined the program. According to these courts, the physician-patient privilege "simply does not arise under these circumstances"[18] because disclosure agreements signed by providers eliminate any expectation of privacy the providers might have in keeping the information secret. Because providers must agree to abide by applicable federal and state statutes and regulations which require them to keep "such records as are necessary to fully disclose" the extent of the Medicaid-related services provided, no such privilege can be said to exist.

The notion that a physician-patient privilege rule will not shelter otherwise confidential communications once a *provider* has become a signatory to a disclosure agreement with the state is dubious. The purpose of the physician-patient privilege is to encourage free and full disclosure between a patient and a doctor, and to protect the patient from the embarrassment and invasion of privacy that disclosure might involve. Indeed, it is widely acknowledged that the privilege exists for and belongs to the patient.[19] If the true holder of the privilege is the patient, it is difficult to see how the physician may properly waive that privilege, whether that be by entering into a disclosure agreement with the state, or by being aware generally of federal or state disclosure requirements.

Other courts clearly concerned with the interest in confidentiality that is lost when medical records are broadcast to grand juries and other investigators have permitted disclosure only after employing a balancing analysis which pits the patient's interest in confidentiality against the public's interest in "maintaining the breadth of the grand jury's power to conduct investigations regarding criminal violations."[20] Although this approach seems better reasoned than an approach that denies the patient interest altogether, it too is questionable. In health care fraud cases, patients' interests in confidentiality have repeatedly been found outweighed by society's interest in fighting fraud and abuse. As the Supreme Court has stated elsewhere, "Making the promise of confidentiality contingent upon a trial judge's later evaluation of the relative importance of the patient's interest in privacy and the evidentiary need for disclosure would eviscerate the effectiveness of the privi-

---

18. Department of Social and Health Services v. Latta, 92 Wash.2d 812, 820–21, 601 P.2d 520, 525–26 (Wash.1979).

19. 81 Am. Jur. 2d Witnesses § 438 (1992).

20. Illinois v. Herbert, 108 Ill.App.3d 143, 149–50, 438 N.E.2d 1255, 1259, 63 Ill.Dec. 892, 895 (1982) cert.den. 459 U.S. 1204, 103 S.Ct. 1190, 75 L.Ed.2d 436 (1983).

lege."[21] Perhaps in recognition of the cost incurred by patients in this balancing process, some courts have sanctioned disclosure of patient treatment records only after the state demonstrated that it had taken steps to secure written waivers from the patients themselves.[22]

In summary, there is no federally recognized doctor-patient privilege and despite the existence of doctor-patient privilege rules in most states, grand juries, MFCUs and other investigators of fraud and abuse have been granted relatively free access to records of Medicaid patients. One possible exception to this wide wielding access is when a privilege claim is advanced during a civil or administrative investigation, as opposed to a criminal investigation. Some courts have suggested that physician-patient confidentiality is entitled to greater weight when documents are sought in conjunction with a civil investigation.[23]

b. The Psychotherapist–Patient Privilege

In addition to doctor-patient rules, some health care providers—namely, psychiatrists, psychologists and other mental health specialists—subpoenaed for testimony or documents have sought refuge under the shelter of state and federal psychotherapeutic privilege rules. The federal government, all fifty states and the District of Columbia now recognize the psychotherapist-patient privilege in one form or another. The privilege has been longstanding in the states and the District of Columbia. By contrast, the federal government is a relative newcomer to the privilege. The Supreme Court recognized the privilege for the first time in 1996 in *Jaffee v. Redmond*.[24]

(1) The Federal Privilege

Prior to the Supreme Court's decision in *Jaffee*, the federal courts of appeals disagreed whether Rule 501 of the Federal Rules of Evidence required recognition of a psychotherapist-patient privilege.[25] The Supreme Court resolved the dispute in *Jaffee* when it

---

21. See Jaffee v. Redmond, __ U.S. __, __, 116 S.Ct. 1923, 1932, 135 L.Ed.2d 337 (1996).

22. See State v. Chenette, 151 Vt. 237, 560 A.2d 365 (Vt.1989) (although patient waivers were obtained after the state received records from custodian pursuant to subpoena and reviewed the records, physician-patient privilege not violated because patients participated fully in the investigation and did not object to discussing with MFCU investigators their consultation with physician-defendant).

23. See, e.g., Division of Medical Quality, Board of Medical Quality v. Gherardini, 93 Cal.App.3d 669, 680–81, 156 Cal.Rptr. 55, 61–62 (Cal.Ct.App. 1979).

24. __ U.S. __, 116 S.Ct. 1923, 135 L.Ed.2d 337 (1996).

25. Compare Jaffee v. Redmond, 51 F.3d 1346, 1355–56 (7th Cir.1995); In re Doe, 964 F.2d 1325, 1328–29 (2d Cir. 1992); In re Zuniga, 714 F.2d 632, 636–37 (6th Cir.1983), cert. denied, 464 U.S. 983, 104 S.Ct. 426, 78 L.Ed.2d 361 (1983); Covell v. CNG Transmission

held that confidential communications between a licensed psychotherapist and her patients in the course of diagnosis or treatment are protected from compelled disclosure under Rule 501.

The case involved a wrongful death claim brought against Illinois Police Officer Mary Lu Redmond, who shot and killed a man while responding to a "fight in progress" call at an apartment complex. On several occasions after the shooting, Redmond sought the counsel of a licensed social worker concerning the shooting incident. Notes taken during those sessions were subsequently sought by the decedent's estate for use in a wrongful death action against Redmond. Both Redmond and her psychotherapist refused to produce the notes on the basis of psychotherapist-patient privilege. At trial, the court instructed the jury that Redmond's refusal to produce the notes was not supported by law and that the jury could infer from her refusal that the notes were damaging to the defense. The United States Court of Appeals for the Seventh Circuit reversed and remanded for a new trial holding that the notes were privileged under the psychotherapist-patient privilege,[26] and the Supreme Court affirmed.[27]

Under *Jaffee*, the psychiatrist-patient privilege will bar the disclosure of certain communications in order to "facilitate the provision of appropriate treatment for individuals suffering the effects of a mental or emotional problem."[28] The privilege extends not only to licensed psychiatrists and psychologists, but to licensed social workers as well.[29] In addition, in deciding future psychotherapist-patient privilege claims, federal courts must not balance the patient's interest in nondisclosure against the state's need for the protected information—an approach employed by some state and federal courts prior to *Jaffee*.[30]

Corp., 863 F.Supp. 202, 205 (M.D.Pa. 1994) (memorandum decision); In re Grand Jury Subpoena (Psychological Treatment Records), 710 F.Supp. 999, 1010 (D.N.J.1989); In re Doe, 97 F.R.D. 640, 643–44 (S.D.N.Y.1982) (memorandum decision); Lora v. Board of Educ., 74 F.R.D. 565, 574 (E.D.N.Y.1977), which recognized the privilege, with United States v. Burtrum, 17 F.3d 1299, 1302 (10th Cir.1994), cert. denied, 513 U.S. 863, 115 S.Ct. 176, 130 L.Ed.2d 112 (1994); In re Grand Jury Proceedings, 867 F.2d 562, 565 (9th Cir.1989) (per curiam), cert. denied sub nom. Doe v. United States, 493 U.S. 906, 110 S.Ct. 265, 107 L.Ed.2d 214 (1989); United States v. Corona, 849 F.2d 562, 567 (11th Cir.1988), cert. denied, 489 U.S. 1084, 109 S.Ct. 1542, 103 L.Ed.2d 846 (1989); United States v. Meagher, 531

F.2d 752, 753 (5th Cir.1976), cert. denied, 429 U.S. 853, 97 S.Ct. 146, 50 L.Ed.2d 128 (1976), which declined to do so.

26. 51 F.3d 1346 (7th Cir.1995).

27. See ___ U.S. ___ , 116 S.Ct. 1923, 135 L.Ed.2d 337 (1996).

28. See Jaffee, 116 S.Ct. at 1929.

29. See id. at 1931.

30. The Court concluded that parties to confidential conversations "must be able to predict with some degree of certainty whether particular discussions will be protected," and that an approach that balanced patients' interest in confidentiality against a need for disclosure after the fact would be "little better than no privilege at all." Jaffee, 116 S.Ct. at 1932, quoting Upjohn, 449 U.S. at 393, 101 S.Ct. at 684.

Precisely what the new federal privilege will mean to psychiatrists and other covered mental health workers in the context of health care fraud investigations is not yet known. Prior to *Jaffee*, even the courts that recognized the psychotherapist-patient privilege routinely refused to apply it to preclude documents subpoenaed in connection with a fraud and abuse investigation.[31] These "privilege friendly" courts were able to recognize the psychotherapist-patient privilege and still rule in favor of the government by using a balancing approach that weighed patient privacy interests against the government's need to investigate suspected fraudulent conduct. The Supreme Court in *Jaffee* specifically disparaged this balancing approach, at least in the factual context of that case, writing:

> We reject the balancing component of the privilege implemented by that court and a small number of States. Making the promise of confidentiality contingent upon a trial judge's later evaluation of the relative importance of the patient's interest in privacy and the evidentiary need for disclosure would eviscerate the effectiveness of the privilege. As we explained in Upjohn, if the purpose of the privilege is to be served, the participants in the confidential conversation "must be able to predict with some degree of certainty whether particular discussions will be protected. An uncertain privilege, or one which purports to be certain but results in widely varying applications by the courts, is little better than no privilege at all."[32]

Mental health professionals could rely on this language to fend off subpoenas seeking documents in the connection with health care fraud investigations. How far the federal courts will extend this language, however, is unclear. The Supreme Court's misgivings about the balancing approach were expressed in a case easily distinguished from cases involving psychotherapists under investigation for fraud or abuse.[33] Moreover, a footnote in *Jaffee* recognizes that there will be situations in which the federal privilege will

31. See, e.g., In re Grand Jury Subpoena (Psychological Treatment Records), 710 F.Supp. 999, 1010, 1014 (D.N.J.1989) (recognizing the privilege but declining to apply it where grand jury was investigating whether psychotherapist had engaged in billing fraud); In re Doe, 711 F.2d 1187, 1193 (2d Cir. 1983) (recognizing the privilege but declining to apply it in favor of psychiatrist who saw 70 patients a day and prescribed quaaludes for over 90% of his patients); United States v. Witt, 542 F.Supp. 696, 699 (S.D.N.Y.1982), aff'd by oral opinion, 697 F.2d 301 (2d Cir. 1982) (recognizing privilege but refusing to quash subpoena directed at a counseling center believed to be operating as a "scrip mill" for the illegal distribution of quaaludes).

32. See Jaffee, 116 S.Ct. at 1932 (footnote omitted), quoting Upjohn, 449 U.S. at 393, 101 S.Ct. at 684.

33. Redmond was a patient attempting to keep her own confidences to a licensed social worker secret. This contrasts sharply with a psychotherapist who attempts to use a patient's privacy expectations as a shield to protect the therapist from investigation.

have to "give way."[34] Although the Court refused to speculate about when such an accommodation would have to be made, given the tenor of decisions predating *Jaffee*,[35] it seems prudent to expect that at least some of those situations may involve psychotherapists resisting the production demands of grand juries in Medicare and Medicaid fraud and abuse investigations.

(2) State Privileges

All of the states and the District of Columbia have adopted some form of psychotherapist-patient privilege.[36] The homogeneity ends there, however. Although the states unanimously agree on the need for a psychotherapist-patient privilege to protect certain communications, there is considerable disagreement among the states concerning the types of psychotherapeutic relationships that war-

34. See Jaffee, 116 S.Ct. at 1932 n.19.

35. See, e.g, In re Grand Jury Subpoena (Psychological Treatment Records), 710 F.Supp. 999, 1015 (D.N.J. 1989) ("[I]t may well be that the privilege should give way in any case where there is a showing that the relationship . . . may have been used to work a fraud upon other litigants or a court of law or administrative agency."). Other courts restricted the application of the privilege on other grounds. See In re August 1993 Regular Grand Jury (Hospital Subpoena), 854 F.Supp. 1380, 1391 (S.D.Ind. 1994) (even assuming a federal psychotherapist privilege exists, a hospital would not have standing to invoke the privilege on behalf of patients treated by a psychotherapist affiliated with the hospital); In re Grand Jury Subpoenas Duces Tecum Dated January 30, 1986, 638 F.Supp. 794, 799 (D.Me.1986) (memorandum decision) (As to Medicaid and Medicare patients, the psychotherapist privilege does not cover records reflecting the identity of a patient, the time of the patient's appointment, the length of the appointment, fees paid, diagnoses, treatment plans, medical recommendations or somatic therapies; it only covers documents reflecting a patient's "thoughts, feelings, and impressions . . . or the substance of any psychotherapeutic dialogue.").

36. For state psychotherapist-patient privilege laws, see Ala. Code § 34–26–2 (Supp.1996); Alaska Evid.R. 504; Ariz. Rev.Stat. § 32–2085 (1996); Ark.Evid.R. 503; Cal.Evid. Code Ann. §§ 1010, 1012, 1014; Colo.Rev.Stat. § 13–90–107(g) (Supp.1996); Conn.Gen.Stat. § 52–146c (1997); Del. Uniform Rule Evid. 503; D.C. Code Ann. § 14–307 (Supp.1997); Fla.Stat. § 90.503 (1996); Ga. Code Ann. § 24–9–21 (Supp.1997); Haw.Evid.R. 504, 504.1; Idaho Evid.R. 503; Ill.Comp. Stat., ch. 225 § 15/5 (1994); Ind. Code § 25–33–1–17 (1993); Iowa Code § 622.10 (1996); Kan.Stat.Ann. § 74–5323 (1996); Ky.Evid.R. 507; La. Code Evid.Ann., Art. 510 (West 1997); Me. Evid.R. 503; Md.Cts. & Jud.Proc. § 9–109 (1996); Mass.Gen. Laws § 233:20B (1995); Mich.Comp. Laws Ann. § 333.18237 (Supp.1996); Minn.Stat. § 595.02 (1996); Miss.Evid.R. 503; Mo. Rev.Stat. § 491.060 (1996); Mont. Code Ann. § 26–1–807 (1995); Neb.Rev.Stat. § 27–504 (1996); Nev.Rev.Stat.Ann. § 49.209 (Supp.1995); N.H.Evid.R. 503; N.J.Stat.Ann. § 45:14B–28 (West 1995); N.M.Evid.R. 11–504; N.Y.Civ.Prac. Law § 4507 (McKinney 1992); N.C.Gen.Stat. § 8–53.3 (Supp.1996); N.D.Evid.R. § 503; Ohio Rev. Code Ann. § 2317.02 (Banks–Baldwin 1994, Supp.1997); Okla. Stat., Tit. 12 § 2503 (Supp.1996); Ore. Evid.R. 504, 504.1; 42 Pa.Cons.Stat. § 5944 (Supp.1996); R.I.Gen. Laws §§ 5–37.3–3, 5–37.3–4 (Supp.1996); S.C. Code Ann. § 19–11–95 (Supp.1996); S.D. Codified Laws §§ 19–13–6 to 19–13–11 (Supp.1997); Tenn. Code Ann. § 24–1–207 (Supp.1996); Tex. Rules Civ.Evid. 509, 510; Utah Evid.R. 506; Vt.Evid.R. 503; Va. Code Ann. § 8.01–400.2 (Supp. 1997); Wash. Rev.Code § 18.83.110 (1994); W.Va.Code § 27–3–1 (Supp. 1997); Wis.Stat. § 905.04 (1995–1996); Wyo.Stat. § 33–27–123 (Supp.1995).

rant protection[37] and the breadth of the communications covered.[38]

Despite their many variations, state psychotherapist-patient privilege statutes can be categorized into three basic groups. The statutes comprising the first and largest group contain multiple subsections which exhaustively describe the scope of protection afforded by the privilege and the universe of parties protected by the rule. These statutes commonly include provisions that define the parties and types of communications covered, delineate the scope of the protection offered, identify the parties entitled to assert the privilege, and set out a host of exceptions to the rule.[39] The second most common type of psychotherapist-patient privilege statute, used by approximately 20% of the states, consists of a less elaborate provision stating that confidential relations and communications between psychotherapists and their patients are protected in the same way as are communications between attorneys and their clients.[40] The final and smallest group of psychotherapist-patient privilege provisions simply includes psychotherapists among a list of persons who are either deemed incompetent to testify, or

37. For example, a few states limit the privilege to psychiatrists and psychologists only. See, e.g., Haw.Evid.R. 504, 504.1 and N.D.Evid.R. 503. However, most state provisions cover additional relationships. See, e.g., Ariz.Rev.Stat. Ann. § 32–3283 (1992) ("certified behavioral health professional"); Tex. Rule Civ. Evid. 510(a)(1) (any person "licensed or certified . . . in the diagnosis, evaluation or treatment of any mental or emotional disorder" or "involved in the treatment or examination of drug abusers"); Utah Evid.R. 506 (any marriage and family therapist, professional counselor or psychiatric mental health nurse specialist).

38. Some statutes define the privilege broadly and brook few exceptions. See, e.g., Ark. Code Ann. § 17–46–107 (1996); Haw.Evid.R. 504, 504.1. Others include a laundry list of exceptions that permit relatively liberal disclosure. See., e.g., Cal. Evid.Code Ann. §§ 1016–1027; R.I. Gen. Laws § 5–37.3–4 (1996).

39. See Alaska Evid.R. 504; Cal. Evid. Code. Ann. §§ 1010, 1012, 1014; Del. Uniform Evid.R. 503; Fla. Stat. § 90.503 (1996); Haw. Evid.R. 504, 504.1; Idaho Evid.R. 503; La. Code Evid. Ann. Art. 510; Me. Evid.R. 503; Miss. Evid.R. 503; Neb. Rev. Stat. § 27–504 (1995); N.M. Evid.R. 11–504; N.D. Evid.R. § 503; Okla. Stat., Tit. 12 § 2503 (1991); Ore. Evid.R. 504, 504.1;

S.D. Codified Laws §§ 19–13–6 to 19–13–11 (1995); Tex. Rules Civ. Evid. 509, 510; Utah Evid.R. 506; Vt. Evid.R. 503; Wis. Stat. § 905.04 (1995–1996).

Some minor variations exist among these statutes. For example, while most of the statutes combine the psychotherapist-patient privilege with the physician-patient privilege, see Alaska Evid.R. 504; Cal. Evid. Code. Ann. §§ 1010, 1012, 1014; Del. Uniform Evid.R. 503; Idaho Evid.R. 503; La. Code Evid. Ann. Art. 510; Me. Evid.R. 503; Miss. Evid.R. 503; Neb. Rev. Stat. § 27–504 (1995); N.M. Evid.R. 11–504; N.D. Evid.R. § 503; Okla. Stat., Tit. 12 § 2503 (1991); S.D. Codified Laws §§ 19–13–6 to 19–13–11 (1995); Utah Evid.R. 506; Vt. Evid.R. 503; Wis. Stat. § 905.04 (1995–1996), others do not. In addition, a few of the statutes contain no provision that identifies the parties entitled to claim the privilege. See Conn. Gen. Stat. § 52–146c (1997); Ky. Evid.R. 507; Md. Cts. & Jud. Proc. § 9–109 (1996).

40. See Ala. Code § 34–26–2 (1996); Ariz. Rev. Stat. § 32–2085 (1996); Ark. Evid.R. 503; Ga. Code Ann. § 24–9–21 (1996); Kan. Stat. Ann. § 74–5323 (1996); Mont. Code. Ann. § 26–1–807 (1995); N.H. Evid.R. 503; N.J. Stat. Ann. § 45:14B–28 (West 1995); N.Y. Civ. Prac. Law § 4507 (McKinney 1992); 42 Pa. Cons. Stat. § 5944 (1982); Wash. Rev. Code § 18.83.110 (1994).

who are prohibited from testifying without the consent of their patients.[41]

Psychotherapists under investigation for Medicare or Medicare fraud and abuse may be particularly concerned about the long list of exceptions included in many of these privilege statutes. The exceptions are numerous and varied.[42] These include provisions which exempt from the coverage of the privilege: communications occurring between a psychotherapist and patient communications sought, used or obtained to enable another to commit or plan a crime or fraud, or to escape apprehension after the commission of a crime or fraud;[43] communications sought in connection with a criminal or civil action brought against a psychotherapist suspected of engaging in Medicaid fraud;[44] information that psychotherapists are required to report to a public employee or state agency, or to record in a public office,[45] and communications related to an unlawful effort to obtain a controlled substance or a prescription for a controlled substance.[46]

In addition, many state legislatures have acted to minimize the obstacles that psychotherapist-patient privilege rules can present to criminal investigators. In Washington, for example, disclosure of treatment information required "[i]n response to a subpoena from a court of law" is expressly exempted from the coverage of the state's privilege rule.[47] In Missouri, information that pertains to a criminal act may be disclosed.[48] In Texas, the privilege is suspended when the information is sought in any criminal prosecution.[49] In Kansas and Oklahoma, information that pertains to "violations of

---

41. See Colo. Rev. Stat. § 13–90–107(g)(1) (1996); Minn. Stat. Ann. § 595.02 (1996); Miss. Evid.R. 503 (1996); and Ohio Rev. Code. § 2317.02 (Banks–Baldwin 1994, Supp.1997).

42. Among the most common exceptions are communications occurring in cases where a court has ordered that a witness or party submit to a mental health examination; where the mental health of the witness or party is an element of a claim or defense raised in a proceeding; where the mental condition of the patient is relevant to a court's determination of whether to hospitalize the patient for mental illness; in a homicide trial, where disclosure relates to the fact of, or circumstances surrounding, the crime; and where the communications are relevant to an issue concerning the physical, mental or emotional condition of, or injury to, a child. See, e.g., Idaho Evid.R. 503(d)(4).

43. See, e.g., Alaska Evid.R. 504(d)(2).

44. For example, D.C. Code § 14–307(b)(4) (1996) excludes from its privilege any "evidence in criminal or civil cases where a person is alleged to have defrauded the District of Columbia or federal government in relation to receiving or providing services under the District of Columbia medical assistance program authorized by title 19 of the Social Security Act ..." See also S.C. Code Ann. § 19–11–95(D)(2) and (3).

45. See, e.g., Alaska Evid.R. 504(d)(5); N.M.Evid.R. 11–504(D)(4); Vt. Evid.R. 503(d)(6).

46. See, e.g., R.R.S. Neb. § 27–504(4)(e) (1996).

47. See Wash. Rev. Code § 18.19.180 (1997).

48. See Mo. Rev. Stat. § 337.636(2) (1989, Supp.1997).

49. See Tex. Rule Crim. Evid. 501 et seq.

any law" may be disclosed notwithstanding the privilege.[50] In Rhode Island, confidential health care information may be released to peer review boards, state licensing boards, and grand juries (pursuant to a subpoena or subpoena duces tecum) without the consent of the patient, and to the state's MFCU "for investigation or prosecution of criminal or civil wrongdoing by a health care provider."[51] Information that reveals either a "violent crime or act"[52] or a "serious harmful act"[53] may be disclosed in some states, while others require privilege claims by mental health care providers to be balanced against the need for the information being sought. If the need for otherwise confidential treatment records outweighs the interest in keeping them private, disclosure may be ordered.[54] Under these laws, a mental health professional subpoenaed to produce treatment records to the grand jury in connection with a Medicare or Medicaid investigation may have trouble staving off an order to disclose the records. For example, in *Commonwealth v. Kobrin*[55] a psychiatrist who refused to disclose certain patient records to a grand jury investigating false claims allegations was held in contempt, despite his claim that disclosure would violate the state's psychiatrist-patient rule. The court held that the information contained within patient files sought by the grand jury was not protected notwithstanding an existing state privilege rule. A similar conclusion was reached by the Iowa Supreme Court in *Chidester v. Needles*,[56] a case involving a contempt proceeding brought against the custodian of records of a mental health clinic who refused to produce patient treatment records to the grand jury. The custodian argued that the records were covered by the state's psychotherapist-patient privilege which prohibited a psychotherapist from giving testimony that would disclose confidential information entrusted to the psychotherapist in his professional capacity.[57] The court found the provision inapplicable since the custodian was not required to give testimony in order to produce the documents.[58]

c. The Attorney–Client Privilege

Health care providers subpoenaed for documents or testimony have sometimes relied upon a third privilege—the attorney-client privilege—to avoid compliance with grand jury demands. The attor-

---

50. See Kan. Stat. Ann. § 65–6315(a)(2) (1996); Okla. Stat., Tit. 59, § 1261.6(2) (1996).

51. See R.I. Gen. Laws § 5–37.3–4(b)(1), (2), (15) and (19) (1996).

52. See Del. Code Ann., Tit. 24, § 3913(2) (1996); Idaho Code § 54–3213(2) (1997).

53. See Ind. Code Ann. § 25–23.6–6–1(2) (1997).

54. See, e.g., Me. Rev. Stat. Ann., Tit. 32, § 7005 (1996); N.H. Rev. Stat. Ann. § 330–A:19 (1996); N.C. Gen. Stat. § 8–53.7 (1996); Va. Code Ann. § 8.01–400.2 (1997).

55. 395 Mass. 284, 479 N.E.2d 674 (Mass.1985).

56. 353 N.W.2d 849 (Iowa 1984).

57. See Iowa Code § 622.10 (1996).

58. See Chidester v. Needles, 353 N.W.2d 849 (Iowa 1984).

ney-client privilege is "the oldest of the privileges for confidential communications known to the common law,"[59] and is recognized by both the federal government and the states. The central purpose of the privilege is to promote full and uninhibited communication between attorneys and their clients in order to serve broader societal interests "in the observance of law and administration of justice."[60] The premise of the privilege is that able advice and advocacy can only be secured if the lawyer is kept fully informed by the client of all facts relevant to the legal representation. It is feared that a client will only be so forthcoming if his disclosures will not later be used against him. Thus, the privilege shields from disclosure communications of wrongdoing by a client to his attorney to encourage the client to seek "the aid of persons having knowledge of the law and skilled in its practice."[61]

As with any privilege, an application of the attorney-client privilege is not without cost. As an exception to the general duty to disclose information to the grand jury, the privilege obstructs the search for truth. To limit this cost the privilege is strictly construed against its holder.[62] The burden of proving the applicability of the attorney-client privilege is borne by the party who seeks to withhold information from the grand jury.[63] Thus, the privilege applies only where:

(1) the purported holder of the privilege was a client (or was seeking to become one) of the attorney to whom the communication was made;

(2) the communication was made to an attorney (or her subordinate) acting in her capacity as an attorney;

(3) the communication related to a fact of which the attorney was informed by her client, outside the presence of others, for the purpose of securing an opinion on law, or legal services, or assistance in some legal proceeding, and not for the purpose of committing a crime or tort; and

(4) the client has claimed, and has not in some way waived, the privilege.[64]

As this list of prerequisites suggests, only certain communications between a client and attorney are covered by the privilege. The attorney-client privilege does not apply, for example, to fee arrangements or to information concerning the identity of a

---

59. Upjohn Co. v. United States, 449 U.S. 383, 389, 101 S.Ct. 677, 682, 66 L.Ed.2d 584 (1981).

60. See id. at 389, 101 S.Ct. at 682.

61. Hunt v. Blackburn, 128 U.S. 464, 470, 9 S.Ct. 125, 127, 32 L.Ed. 488, 491 (1888).

62. 8 J. Wigmore, Evidence § 2290 at 554 (McNaughton rev. 1961).

63. See United States v. Jones, 696 F.2d 1069, 1072 (4th Cir.1982).

64. See United States v. United Shoe Machinery Corp., 89 F.Supp. 357, 358–59 (D.C.Mass.1950). See also United States v. Bay State Ambulance and Hospital Rental Service, Inc., 874 F.2d 20, 27–28 (1st Cir.1989).

client.[65] Nor does it apply to communications made in the presence of, or to, third persons (*i.e.*, where the privileged has been waived), unless the presence of those third persons was needed to assist the attorney or the legal services to be provided.[66] The privilege may cover, however, communications made to agents hired to assist an attorney in rendering legal advice, such as investigators hired by an attorney, accountants, paralegals, secretaries and others.[67] A helpful illustration can be found in *Commonwealth v. Edwards*.[68] There, owners of a nursing home sought the advice of their attorney concerning cost reports. The attorney hired an accountant to review the nursing home's books, and based on work performed by the accountant, rendered advice about the cost reports. In a subsequent investigation, the state MFCU issued a subpoena duces tecum to the accountant for all documents pertaining to the nursing home's cost report adjustments. The nursing home opposed the subpoena on the basis of the attorney-client privilege, and the trial court agreed. The court held that the nursing home's voluntary submission of data to the accountant did not waive its attorney-client privilege, since the nursing home had communicated with the accountant only in order to obtain its attorney's advice about potential cost report adjustments.[69]

The importance of establishing a nexus between the communication and an existing legal relationship cannot be overemphasized. Health care providers who have been unable to demonstrate the existence of such a concrete relationship have been unable to keep secret documents sought in connection with an official investigation. Such were the problems of John Felci, an official of Quincy City Hospital (QCH), in the well-known kickback case, *United States v. Bay State Ambulance and Hospital Rental Service, Inc.*[70] The case grew out a lucrative ambulance service contract awarded by QCH to Bay State Ambulance. The hospital awarded Bay State the contract upon the recommendation of John Felci, who failed to inform the hospital that he was a paid consultant of Bay State's at the time and had accepted various forms of remuneration from the ambulance company. During a subsequent investigation of the award of the contract, the FBI requested Bay State to produce any documents in its possession that might corroborate its contention

65. See In re Grand Jury Subpoena Served Upon Doe, 781 F.2d 238, 247–48 (2d Cir.), cert. denied, 475 U.S. 1108, 106 S.Ct. 1515, 89 L.Ed.2d 914 (1986); People of the State of New York v. Crean, 115 Misc.2d 526, 529 454 N.Y.S.2d 231, 234 (Sup. Ct. 1982) (extending the rule to matters involving awards and settlements).

66. See Commonwealth of Virginia v. Edwards; Medicaid Fraud Control Unit v. Doe, 235 Va. 499, 509, 370 S.E.2d 296, 301 (1988).

67. See, e.g., Westinghouse Electric Corp. v. Republic of the Philippines, 951 F.2d 1414, 1424 (3d Cir.1991) (collecting citations). See also MFCU v. Doe, 235 Va. 499, 509 370 S.E.2d 296, 301 (1988).

68. 235 Va. 499, 370 S.E.2d 296 (1988).

69. See id. at 512–13, 303–304.

70. 874 F.2d 20 (1st Cir.1989).

that its payments to Felci were for actual services rendered, as opposed to remuneration paid in exchange for business reimbursable under the Medicare program. One of the documents produced by the ambulance company was a list of the projects on which Felci had worked for Bay State. Felci had prepared the list at the request of Bay State's in-house counsel, without the knowledge of his own attorney. The government introduced the list at trial, over Felci's objections, to highlight the payments that had flowed from the ambulance company to Felci before Bay State was awarded the ambulance service contract. On appeal, Felci argued that the list should have been excluded as attorney-client privileged material, because he had prepared the list at the request of an attorney—Bay State's counsel. The First Circuit rejected this claim holding that no attorney-client relationship existed between Felci and Bay State's counsel.[71] The court also rejected Felci's claim that the document was privileged because it was prepared as a part of a joint defense.[72]

It is important to note that the attorney-client privilege applies only to *communications* between the attorney (and other necessary personnel) and the client, it does not apply to underlying facts or documents which comprise the subject of the communication. A simple hypothetical may help to illustrate this important distinction. Suppose a health care entity discovers in its files a document that contains evidence of an arrangement that might violate the anti-kickback provisions. The president of the entity then takes the document to its corporate counsel and requests the counsel's advice about whether arrangement is or is not lawful. Although the resulting communication that occurs between the attorney and the entity may be protected by the attorney-client privilege, the underlying document is not.

Another important consideration for health care providers is that the attorney-client privilege may be waived by the disclosure of otherwise protected communications to a party outside the privileged relationship. This is of great concern to counsel for health care providers who may waive the privilege inadvertently by complying with reporting obligations or otherwise cooperating with an official investigation. In one case, for example, the vice-president of a corporation being investigated for Medicaid fraud was found to have waived the corporation's attorney-client privilege by authorizing the corporate attorney to cooperate with the investigation.[73] In

---

71. See id. at 28.

72. See id. at 29; see also discussion regarding privilege claims in the context of joint defense agreements, infra at § 7–16e.

73. See In re Grand Jury Proceedings, Detroit, Michigan, August, 1997, 570 F.2d 562 (6th Cir.1978). See also In re Grand Jury Proceeding October 12, 1995, 78 F.3d 251, 254–55 (6th Cir.1996) (laboratory waived its privilege with re-

this regard, pervasive reporting obligations may place health care providers in a Catch–22 situation vis-a-vis claims of attorney-client privilege. On the one hand, as discussed above,[74] multiple statutory and regulatory provisions require providers fully to disclose to the OIG and state MFCUs any requested information related to patient care and program disbursements. Cooperation with an OIG or MFCU investigation may also be critical in reducing a provider's sentencing exposure,[75] civil monetary penalties,[76] and avoiding or limiting an order of exclusion.[77] On the other hand, disclosures made to the government may affect a provider's ability to assert a subsequent attorney-client privilege claim.

It may be possible, however, to waive the privilege with respect to some communications made to an attorney, but not others. This tactic is sometimes referred to as a "partial waiver." In one Medicare fraud case, for example, in an effort to cooperate with an official investigation, a laboratory informed government investigators about the advice it had received from its attorney concerning some, but not all, aspects of a plan to market the laboratory's services to surrounding nursing homes.[78] The owner and president of the laboratory informed the investigators that the laboratory sought legal counsel concerning a proposed twenty-four point marketing plan and that the attorney had advised the laboratory that several elements of the plan were lawful.[79] The laboratory did not disclose, however, other aspects of the marketing plan which the attorney had considered potentially unlawful. The government subsequently sought to compel the disclosure of the legal advice that had been rendered concerning the omitted aspects of the marketing plan on the ground that any privilege claim over the materials had been waived by the laboratory's earlier disclosures. The district court ordered the disclosure of the additional advice rendered by the attorney, but the Sixth Circuit reversed. The court held that although the laboratory had partially waived its privilege, it had not opted to reveal to the federal agents the legal advice it had received on several other aspects of the marketing plan. As to that advice no waiver had occurred, and thus the district court's order compelling disclosure of that advice was erroneous.[80]

---

spect to advice received from its attorney concerning parts of a marketing plan by disclosing the advice it had received to government investigators).

74. See § 7–14b.

75. The federal sentencing guidelines consider cooperation to be a mitigating factor that can lead to the reduction of a provider criminal sentencing exposure. See Chapter 8, § 8–7.

76. See Chapter 5, § 5–4.

77. See Chapter 5, § 5–2.

78. See In re Grand Jury Proceedings October 12, 1995, 78 F.3d 251, 254–55 (6th Cir.1996).

79. See id. at 252.

80. See id. at 256.

A close cousin of partial waivers, is the so-called "selective waiver." Unlike partial waivers (where the holder discloses some privileged information to another while withholding other privileged information), a selective waiver occurs when the holder seeks to selectively disclose privileged information to one party, while denying the same information to another party. The federal circuit courts are currently split on the question of whether a party may selectively choose the parties to whom it will waive the attorney-client privilege, while retaining the privilege as to others.[81] The Third and D.C. Circuits have emphatically rejected the suggestion that the attorney-client privilege may be selectively waived.[82] In *Westinghouse Electric Corp. v. The Republic of the Philippines*, for example, the United States Court of Appeals for the Third Circuit held that a voluntary disclosure of privileged information to any governmental agency or representative results in a complete loss of any attorney-client or work product claim concerning the same material. Once confidential information is disclosed to a governmental agency or official, the privilege is waived and may not be re-invoked either in the context of a later investigation by another governmental body or in private litigation. By contrast, the Eighth Circuit has permitted a party to selectively waive the privilege as to one party, while retaining it as to another. In *Diversified Industries, Inc. v. Meredith*,[83] the Eighth Circuit Court of Appeals held that privileged communications selectively disclosed to the SEC in the course of a formal investigation could remain privileged in subsequent litigation.

The debate over selective waivers of the attorney-client privilege has important implications for health care providers who are not only subject to myriad reporting and disclosure obligations as a condition of participation in the Medicare and Medicaid programs, but who have recently been invited by ground-breaking provisions of HIPAA[84] to seek advisory opinions from the OIG concerning the legality of proposed business transactions under the anti-kickback provisions.[85] The plight of a provider who wishes to seek an advisory opinion from the newly formed Industry Guidance Branch can illustrate the dilemma. In order to obtain an advisory opinion, a

81. For a helpful discussion of this ongoing debate see Note, Internal Corporate Investigations: The Waiver of Attorney–Client Privilege and Work–Product Protection Through Voluntary Disclosures to the Government, 34 Am. Crim. L. Rev. 347 (Winter 1997).

82. See Westinghouse Electric Corp. v. The Republic of the Philippines, 951 F.2d 1414, 1425 (3d Cir.1991); Permian Corp. v. United States, 665 F.2d 1214, 1220 (D.C.Cir.1981). See also United States v. Massachusetts Institute of Technology, 957 F.Supp. 301, 304 (D.Mass.1997) (disclosure of detailed billing summaries to one government agency waived any privilege claim over the summaries when they were later sought by the IRS).

83. 572 F.2d 596, 611 (8th Cir.1977).

84. Pub. L. No. 104–191, Title II, § 205, 110 Stat. 1936 (1996).

85. For a discussion of the anti-kickback provisions see Chapter 3.

provider is required to make a number of disclosures to the IGB, including disclosures about its own identity and the parties involved in the transaction. The provider is also required to certify that the proposed transaction is genuine—that is, that the provider either has entered into, or intends to enter into, the deal, subject to the receipt of the IGB's blessing. Should the IGB decide that such a transaction would violate the fraud and abuse provisions, by seeking the opinion not only will the provider have succeeded in focusing the government's attention on itself, in some federal circuits, it may also have waived any applicable attorney-client privilege respecting the subject matter disclosed to the IGB. Similar waiver concerns are raised whenever a provider receives a grand jury or administrative subpoena for documents or testimony. Before complying with any such demand, the provider and counsel should undertake a careful review of all documents responsive to the request in order to determine if an attorney-client privilege claim could be asserted.

d. The Work Product Privilege

Closely related to the attorney-client privilege is the work product doctrine. The purpose of the work product privilege is to allow an attorney to perform her duties "with a certain degree of privacy, free from unnecessary intrusion by opposing parties and their counsel."[86] Thus, unlike the attorney client privilege, the work product doctrine protects only material "prepared by an adversary's counsel with an eye toward litigation."[87] Although this restriction does not require that litigation actually be pending, it does require that the prospect of litigation be more than simply a remote possibility. If this can be established, the privilege will protect from disclosure an attorney's interviews, statements, memoranda, correspondence, briefs, mental impressions, legal theories or personal beliefs concerning the litigation.[88]

Unlike the attorney-client privilege, work product claims do not belong solely to the client; an attorney may assert a work product claim even when the client has already waived the privilege.[89] The work product doctrine can be overcome, however, by a showing of sufficient need for the documents. Where the party seeking disclosure demonstrates a substantial need for the information and establishes that the she cannot obtain the information (or its equivalent) by alternative means without undue hardship, dis-

---

86. Hickman v. Taylor, 329 U.S. 495, 511, 67 S.Ct. 385, 394, 91 L.Ed. 451 (1947).

87. Hickman, 329 U.S. at 510, 67 S.Ct. at 393.

88. See id.

89. See In re Sealed Case, 676 F.2d

closure of the documents may be ordered.[90]

A court may be more receptive to a request for documents based on such a need where the sought-after information concerns "fact" work product materials, as opposed to "opinion" work product materials. Fact work product materials encompass documents comprised of factual information rather than the mental impressions of an attorney. A prime example of fact work product would be a memorandum prepared by an attorney of a witness interview. By contrast, opinion work product materials—those that contain the opinions, mental impressions, legal strategies or personal beliefs of the attorney—are entitled to greater protection. To overcome the protection conferred upon opinion work product, the government must demonstrate an extraordinary need for the material.[91]

e. The Joint Defense Attorney–Client Privilege

Over time, the courts have recognized an extension of the attorney-client privilege, the so-called joint defense privilege.[92] The joint defense privilege protects communications between an individual and the attorney of another when the communications are part of an on-going and joint effort to set up a common defense.[93] Under this privilege, communications made to another's attorney in order to establish a common defense are entitled to protection, even if the clients' interests are in some respect adverse.[94]

As with any attorney-client privilege claim, the joint defense privilege covers only communications made in confidence,[95] and questions about the expected confidential nature of particular communications are resolved by determining whether the client reasonably understood at the time the communication occurred that the

---

793, 809 n. 56 (D.C.Cir.1982).

90. See, e.g., Fed. R. Civ. Pro. 26(b)(3); Hickman v. Taylor, 329 U.S. 495, 509, 67 S.Ct. 385, 392, 91 L.Ed. 451 (1947); In re Sealed Case, 676 F.2d 793, 809 n. 59 (D.C.Cir.1982); In re Grand Jury Subpoena Dated November 9, 1979, 484 F.Supp. 1099, 1103 (S.D.N.Y. 1980).

91. See Hickman v. Taylor, 329 U.S. at 513 67 S.Ct. at 394. See also Upjohn Co. v. United States, 449 U.S. 383, 401, 101 S.Ct. 677, 688, 66 L.Ed.2d 584, 598–99 (1981).

92. The federal courts broadly recognize the privilege, as do a sizeable number of state courts. See David Lugert, "Joint Defense Agreements: A Prosecutor's View," Health Care Fraud 1996, at G–1, G–4.

93. See United States v. Bay State Ambulance and Hospital Rental Service, Inc.; United States v. Felci, 874 F.2d 20, 28 (1st Cir.1989), citing In re Bevill, Bresler & Schulman Asset Management Corp., 805 F.2d 120, 126 (3d Cir.1986).

94. See Eisenberg v. Gagnon, 766 F.2d 770, 787–88 (3d Cir.), cert. denied, 474 U.S. 94, 106 S.Ct. 3426, 88 L.Ed.2d 290 (1985). The work product doctrine is similarly extended to protect documents created and distributed to joint defense members in anticipation of litigation.

95. See United States v. Keplinger, 776 F.2d 678, 701 (7th Cir.1985), cert. denied, 476 U.S. 1183, 106 S.Ct. 2919, 91 L.Ed.2d 548 (1986); United States v. Friedman, 445 F.2d 1076, 1085 n. 4 (9th Cir.), cert. denied 404 U.S. 958, 92 S.Ct. 326, 30 L.Ed.2d 275 (1971).

information would remain private.[96] Although the joint defense privilege may be waived, a waiver normally requires the consent of all of the parties to the agreement.[97] Thus, should a party to a joint defense agreement decide to withdraw from the agreement in order to cooperate with the government, the party will be permitted to waive the privilege only as to himself.[98] Absent an explicit waiver, a joint defense privilege will be considered terminated when and if the parties to the joint defense agreement become opponents.[99] Confidential communications that occur prior to the termination of joint defense arrangement, however, will remain protected from disclosure.[100]

Similarly situated co-defendants in criminal or civil cases are not automatically entitled to the protection of the joint defense privilege. A party asserting such a privilege claim must first make a threshold showing that (1) the communications were made in the course of a joint defense effort, (2) the statements were designed to further that effort, and (3) the privilege has not been waived.[101] Health care providers laying claim to the joint defense privilege will find it easier to meet these prerequisites if they have memorialized their intentions surrounding their communications in a written agreement. Indeed, although a joint defense agreement may be oral,[102] most are written to forestall any question that communications between co-defendants occurred in the context of a joint defense strategy and were made to further that strategy.[103] Such a written agreement will usually include several paragraphs confirming that: the parties share common interests; those interests will best be served by sharing facts, documents and mental impressions; any shared information is privileged from disclosure to adverse parties; no signatory to the agreement will disclose information shared pursuant to the agreement with any other person without the consent of all of the other signatories; any signatory may withdraw from the agreement by providing express notification to all other signatories, but that any withdrawing party will continue to protect communications covered by the agreement; withdrawing parties must return or destroy confidential documents upon with-

96. Kevlik v. Goldstein, 724 F.2d 844, 849 (1st Cir.1984) (quoting McCormick on Evidence, § 91 at 189 (1972)).

97. See Polycast Technology Corp. v. Uniroyal, Inc., 125 F.R.D. 47, 50 (S.D.N.Y.1989).

98. See, e.g., In re Grand Jury Subpoenas, 902 F.2d 244, 248 (4th Cir. 1990); John Morrell & Co. v. Local Union 304A, 913 F.2d 544, 556 (8th Cir. 1990); Medcom Holding Co. v. Baxter Travenol Laboratories, Inc. 689 F.Supp. 841, 845 (N.D.Ill.1988).

99. See In the Matter of Grand Jury Subpoena Duces Tecum Dated November 16, 1974, 406 F.Supp. 381, 394 (S.D.N.Y.1975).

100. See id. at 388.

101. See id.

102. See Continental Oil Company v. United States, 330 F.2d 347 (9th Cir. 1964).

103. For a helpful sample joint defense agreement, see David Lugert, Joint Defense Agreements: A Prosecutor's View, at G–9 to G–11, Health Care Fraud 1996.

drawal from the agreement.[104] Joint defense agreements also frequently include (and perhaps should always include) waiver of conflict language.[105]

United States v. Bay State Ambulance and Hospital Rental Service[106] demonstrates the difficulties one defendant confronted when he attempted to invoke the privilege in the absence of a written joint defense agreement. The case concerned allegations that the hospital for which John Felci, the defendant, worked awarded a lucrative ambulance service contract to Bay State Ambulance after Bay State had made several alleged kickbacks to Felci, in the form of "consulting payments." The proof at trial showed that the hospital awarded Bay State the contract upon Felci's positive recommendation, and that Felci had failed to inform the hospital that he was providing paid consulting services to Bay State at the time. During an investigation that targeted Felci and Bay State, the FBI asked counsel for Bay State for proof that its payments to Felci were for actual services rendered. To comply with this request, in-house counsel for Bay State asked Felci to prepare a list of the projects he had performed for the ambulance company. Felci did so, without seeking the advice of his own separate counsel. Bay State later voluntarily delivered Felci's list to the FBI. Over Felci's objections, the government introduced the list at trial to highlight the payments that had flowed from the ambulance company to Felci before Bay State was awarded the ambulance service contract. On appeal, Felci argued both that the list should have been excluded as attorney-client privileged material,[107] and that the list was protected by the joint defense privilege. With respect to the latter claim, Felci contended that he had prepared the list as a part of a common defense strategy with the ambulance company. The First Circuit disagreed. While acknowledging that Felci "had many interests in common" with Bay State, and thus much of the communication that had passed between them could have been privileged, the court concluded that Felci had not prepared the outline as a part of a joint defense strategy. The court found it significant that Felci had failed to seek his attorney's advice about Bay State's request for the list when he first received that request, that he had turned over that list without seeking his counsel's advice, and that he first mentioned the list to his own counsel months after delivering the list to Bay State. These facts, the court held, made it impossible to find that the list had been prepared as a part of a joint defense.[108] The court also rejected the suggestion that Felci could have had a reasonable expectation that

---

104. See id. at G–9 to G–10.

105. For a sample of such language see Joint Defense Agreements, 55 BNA Crim. Prac. Manual 21,651 to 21,660.

106. 874 F.2d 20 (1st Cir.1989).

107. See § 7–16c.

108. See Bay State, 874 F.2d at 29.

Bay State would keep the list confidential since Bay State's counsel had advised Felci that the company wanted the list to respond to the FBI's request.[109]

Any decision to enter into a joint defense agreement carries advantages and disadvantages that should be carefully weighed. The foregoing discussion makes the advantages perhaps the more obvious. Parties who feel free to exchange information with others similarly situated, gain greater access to information and the ability to coordinate and present a unified defense. As put by one commentator, "[I]f knowledge is power in litigation, then shared knowledge is power multiplied."[110] Joint defense agreement participants may also achieve substantial cost savings by being able to pool their resources and avoid duplicative defense efforts. In addition, with a joint defense agreement in place, attorneys who desire to trade client information to gather a better understanding of the government's (or other opponent's) case, will be able to do so without fear of breaching client confidentiality rules. A joint defense agreement may also give its signatories early warning when one signatory has decided to "turn state's witness."

There may be significant drawbacks to entering into a joint defense agreement, however. Joint defense agreements may make it more difficult for attorneys to meet their duty to zealously represent their client's interests to the best of their abilities. In some cases, for instance, it may be in a health care provider's best interest to cooperate with the government in order to reduce the provider's sentencing exposure and the possibility of exclusion. If the provider is a signatory to a prior joint defense agreement, however, the government may be reluctant to accept the provider's cooperation, since the provider will be bound by the agreement to keep confidential certain communications about which the government may wish to know. The DOJ appears particularly suspicious of joint defense agreements and has attempted in at least one case to disqualify counsel who entered into such an agreement.[111] As explored more fully below, such a conflict of interest may hamper an attorney's ability to cross examine a damaging witness with information that was acquired by the attorney within the context of a joint defense agreement.[112] At minimum, the pros and cons of

109. See id.

110. See McSweeney & Brody, "Defending the Multi–Party Civil Conspiracy Case," Litigation at 8 (Spring 1986).

111. See e.g., United States v. Anderson, 790 F.Supp. 231 (W.D.Wash. 1992) (declining to disqualify counsel where defendant entered into joint defense agreement informed of the possibility that a conflict could arise).

112. But see Joint Defense Participants Oppose Conflicts Inquiry, 6 BNA Crim. Prac. Manual 473 (Sept. 30, 1992) (arguing that cross examination is not hampered since counsel would not have had access to the information in the absence of the agreement).

entering into a joint defense agreement must be carefully considered by counsel for all parties. Although the advantages of such an arrangement to a health care defendant may outweigh the potential risks involved, the final determination is likely to depend on the factual circumstances of each particular case.

§ 7–17. The Crime–Fraud Exception

The attorney-client, work product and joint-defense privileges protect from compelled disclosure only communications that concern *past* fraudulent or criminal activity. No shield is conferred by the privilege upon communications concerning future or ongoing criminal conduct. This important limitation—known as the crime-fraud exception—subjects to disclosure any otherwise privileged communication concerning a pending or future crime, even if the communication was made with the expectation that it would remain confidential or in anticipation of litigation.

Increasingly, the government has relied on the crime-fraud exception as a means to expose communications occurring within the context of an attorney-client relationship. In order to justify such a disclosure, the government bears the burden of showing by prima facie evidence that the subject communication was made to further criminal or fraudulent conduct.[1] A district court may exercise its discretion to conduct an *in camera* review to determine whether the crime-fraud exception applies once the government has made a minimal showing that the exception could apply.[2] However, an *in camera* review of potentially privileged materials is justified only where the government has proffered "a factual basis sufficient to support a reasonable, good faith belief that in camera inspection may reveal evidence that information in the materials is not privileged."[3] In other words, although a *prima facie* showing of crime or fraud is not required to justify an *in camera* inspection, some showing that the communication may have concerned a present or future crime or fraud is necessary. The question of whether such an evidentiary showing is sufficient to allow an *in camera* review is a mixed question of law and fact subject to de novo review on appeal.[4]

One court held that such a showing was not made out where the government simply pointed to the fact that a target laboratory sought and received the advice of counsel before instituting a

---

§ 7–17

1. See United States v. Zolin, 491 U.S. 554, 572, 109 S.Ct. 2619, 2631, 105 L.Ed.2d 469, 490 (1989); In re Sealed Case, 754 F.2d 395, 399 (D.C.Cir.1985).

2. See Zolin, 491 U.S. at 572, 109 S.Ct. at 2631, 105 L.Ed.2d at 491. See also In re Grand Jury Investigation;

United States v. The Corporation, 974 F.2d 1068, 1071 (9th Cir.1992).

3. See United States v. The Corporation, 974 F.2d at 1072, citing Caldwell v. District Court, 644 P.2d 26, 33 (Colo. 1982).

4. See United States v. The Corporation, 974 F.2d 1068, 1071 (9th Cir.1992).

testing program. In *United States v. The Corporation*,[5] the grand jury subpoenaed an unnamed laboratory (widely believed to be National Health Laboratories) for documents. The laboratory produced some documents, but declined to produce others on the ground of the attorney-client privilege. One of the undisclosed documents had been prepared by the laboratory's counsel before it initiated the suspect testing program. The government moved the district court to examine the undisclosed documents *in camera* to determine whether the crime-fraud exception applied. The court declined to do so finding that the laboratory had introduced unrefuted *prima facie* evidence of the privilege's application. The Ninth Circuit affirmed, rejecting the government's argument that the mere fact that the laboratory had solicited and received legal advice about the testing program prior to its commencement was enough to support a reasonable, good faith belief that an in camera examination of the withheld documents might reveal that the crime-fraud exception was applicable.[6]

§ 7–18. Conflicts of Interest

Counsel for health care providers may find themselves confronting questions about potential conflicts of interest more often than practitioners in other areas of the law. This is particularly so for an attorney who represents a large corporate health care entity, or a vertically integrated organization, where several officers and employees of the entity or organization may find themselves targets, subjects or witnesses in a single health care fraud investigation. In such a case it will be difficult for corporate counsel to represent the entity and its employees conflict-free. Although the same attorney may be able to represent both the entity and its employees during the very early stages of an investigation, before long the appearance of a conflict or the danger of a potential conflict is likely to require that separate counsel be secured. Certainly, before agreeing to provide legal services to any person or entity, an attorney must first consider whether the representation will give rise to a conflict with other potential or existing clients. Attorneys must also be on the look out for conflicts that may arise as the representation proceeds.

Important constitutional and professional ethical restrictions limit when an attorney may represent multiple clients implicated in a single case, or when an attorney may take on a client whose representation may impair the attorney's professional obligations to another. The Sixth Amendment to the United States Constitution guarantees the right to effective assistance of counsel in all criminal prosecutions. This right has been read to encompass a right to

---

5. 974 F.2d 1068 (9th Cir.1992).   **6.** See id. at 1074–75.

counsel unimpaired by conflicting obligations to other clients.[1] In addition, a host of professional ethical standards are similarly designed to ensure that clients receive legal services free of conflicts of interest. Disciplinary Rule 5–105(A) of the Model Code of Professional Responsibility, for example, requires an attorney to decline any employment opportunity that will, or is likely to, "adversely affect" the exercise of her independent professional judgment on behalf of another client, or that will, or is likely to, involve her in "representing differing interests."[2] Disciplinary Rule 5–105(B) provides further that an attorney shall not continue multiple representation if such a conflict arises.[3] Similarly, Rule 1.7 of the Model Rules of Professional Conduct prohibits an attorney from representing a client "if the representation of the client will be directly adverse to another client" or the representation will be "materially limited by the lawyer's responsibilities to another client."[4] Other ethical standards limit an attorney's ability to represent a client if that representation will be impaired by the attorney's obligation to respect the confidences of a former client or where the interests of the current and former client conflict.[5]

Exceptions to these ethical rules are countenanced only where the attorney harbors a reasonable belief that the conflict will not in fact harm her clients, the attorney discloses the conflict to each affected client, and the clients waive their right to unconflicted counsel. For example, under the ABA Disciplinary Rules of Professional Responsibility, an attorney is permitted to represent clients with conflicting interests or potentially conflicting interests if "it is obvious that" the attorney can represent each client's interests adequately, and each client "consents to the representation after full disclosure of the possible effect of such representation on the exercise of [the attorney's] independent professional judgment on behalf of each."[6] The Model Rules of Professional Conduct carve out a similar exception, allowing an attorney to represent a client where that representation will be directly adverse or may be materially affected by the lawyer's responsibilities to another, only

---

§ 7–18

1. See Strickland v. Washington, 466 U.S. 668, 692, 104 S.Ct. 2052, 2067, 80 L.Ed.2d 674, 696 (1984); Wheat v. United States, 486 U.S. 153, 159, 108 S.Ct. 1692, 1697 100 L.Ed.2d 140, 148–49 (1988) . .

2. See ABA Code of Professional Responsibility, D.R. 5–105(A). See also id., Ethical Consideration 5–15 which requires a lawyer who represents "multiple clients having potentially differing interests" to "weigh carefully the possibility that his judgment may be impaired or his loyalty divided if he accepts

or continues the employment," and to "resolve all doubts against the propriety of the representation."

3. See ABA Code of Professional Responsibility, D.R. 5–105(B); see also id., Canon 6.

4. Model Rule of Professional Conduct, Rule 1.7(a) and (b).

5. See Canon 9 of the ABA Code of Professional Responsibility; Model Rules of Professional Conduct, Rule 1.9.

6. ABA Code of Professional Conduct, D.R. 5–105(C).

if "the lawyer reasonably believes the representation will not be adversely *affected*" and "the client consents after consultation."[7]

Although these provisions impose self-policing responsibilities upon all attorneys, other procedural rules require the courts to oversee the conflict judgments that are made by private counsel. In the federal criminal system, for example, the courts will evaluate, prevent or remedy potential conflict problems, either *sua sponte*, or on a prosecutor's motion to disqualify counsel. The Federal Rules of Criminal Procedure require the court independently to inquire about potential conflicts and to advise each jointly-represented defendant of his or her right to separate representation, in order to prevent post-conviction claims that defendants in a criminal case were deprived of their Sixth Amendment right to effective counsel by being jointly-represented at trial. Under Rule 44(c), the court must take appropriate measures to protect each defendant's right to effective counsel unless there is "good cause to believe no conflict of interest is likely to arise" as a consequence of continued joint representation.[8] Although the rule does not define what particular measures must be taken, one common approach is to secure a knowing, intelligent and voluntary waiver of the right to separate representation.[9]

Even if jointly-represented health care defendants are willing to waive their right to separate counsel, a court may refuse to allow the joint representation, particularly in a criminal prosecution.[10] The Sixth Amendment guarantee of the undivided loyalty of counsel has been found to be paramount to the right to select one's own attorney,[11] thus, in the exercise of its supervisory powers, a court may disqualify counsel if it determines that joint representation will cause the attorney to violate professional ethical standards or

---

7. Model Rule of Prof. Conduct Rule 1.7(a)(1), (a)(2), (b)(1) and (b)(2). See also ABA Standards Relating to the Defense Function § 3.5(b) (Approved Draft, 1971) which provides that:

[The] potential for conflict of interest in representing multiple defendants is so grave that ordinarily a lawyer should decline to act for more than one of several co-defendants except in unusual situations when, after careful investigation, it is clear that no conflict is likely to develop and when the several defendants give an informed consent to such multiple representation.

8. Fed. R. Crim. P. 44(c). Some states have adopted similar positions. See, e.g., State v. Olsen, 258 N.W.2d 898 (Minn.1977).

9. See Holloway v. Arkansas, 435 U.S. 475, 483 n. 5, 98 S.Ct. 1173, 1178 n. 5, 55 L.Ed.2d 426, 433 n. 5 (1978) (the right to assistance of unconflicted counsel may be waived). See also United States v. Migliaccio, 34 F.3d 1517, 1526–28 (10th Cir.1994) (physician's waiver of right to separate counsel was properly the subject of a Rule 44(c) pretrial proceeding at which defendant chose to proceed to trial with counsel despite a known conflict).

10. See, e.g., United States v. RMI Co., 467 F.Supp. 915, 921–22 (W.D.Pa. 1979) (disqualifying RMI's counsel from representing both RMI and its employees despite their decision to waive conflict-free counsel).

11. See Wheat v. United States, 486 U.S. 153, 159, 108 S.Ct. 1692, 1697, 100 L.Ed.2d 140, 148–49 (1988).

that the parties' willingness to accept joint representation is otherwise outweighed by their interest in conflict-free representation.[12] An order of disqualification may preclude not only an attorney's representation of certain clients, but the attorney's participation in the case altogether. An attorney who opts to continue to represent multiple clients whose interests conflict, therefore, may risk being involuntarily disqualified from the entire matter.[13]

§ 7–19. Search Warrants

Another major weapon stored in the health care fraud investigator's arsenal is the power to search. Historically, government investigators have preferred the use of grand jury subpoenas over search warrants as a means of collecting evidence in Medicare and Medicaid fraud investigations. There are several possible explanations for this preference. Unlike search warrants, grand jury subpoenas need not be supported by probable cause and may be issued without the involvement of a judge.[1] They can also be used to compel testimony as opposed to simply seeking the production of documents or other physical evidence. Fewer governmental resources are needed to serve a subpoena than are needed to execute a search, and the subpoenas themselves can be prepared more expeditiously than can a search warrant application. They also provide a less intrusive means by which to obtain documents from third parties.

Despite the relative ease by which evidence can be gathered by use of a subpoena, search warrants have become a popular tool of both state and federal investigators of health care fraud and abuse. One study indicates that search warrants have been the investigative weapon of choice in 13% of reported health care fraud prosecutions,[2] and the list of health care providers that have been subjected to search since the beginning of this decade alone is indeed quite lengthy.[3] It appears then that prosecutors have been willing to

---

12. See id. at 162; United States v. Dolan, 570 F.2d 1177, 1184 (3d. Cir. 1978); United States v. Gotti, 771 F.Supp. 552, 558–59 (E.D.N.Y.1991).

13. See, e.g., United States v. DeLuna, No. 81–00107/11–CR–8 (W.D. Mo. Dec. 28, 1981).

§ 7–19

1. See United States v. Dionisio, 410 U.S. 1, 9–10, 15, 93 S.Ct. 764, 769–70, 772, 35 L.Ed.2d 67, 76–77, 80 (1973). For a discussion regarding the use of grand jury subpoenas, see § 7–12b.

2. See Pamela H. Bucy, The Poor Fit of Traditional Evidentiary Doctrine and Sophisticated Crime: An Empirical Analysis of Health Care Fraud Prosecutions [hereinafter "Health Care Fraud"], 63 Fordham L. Rev. 383, 450 (1994).

3. Providers subjected to search by federal law enforcement authorities mentioned in cases decided between 1990 and 1997 include: United States v. Rutgard, 108 F.3d 1041 (9th Cir.1997); F.E.R. v. Valdez, 58 F.3d 1530 (10th Cir.1995); United States v. Singh, 54 F.3d 1182 (4th Cir.1995); United States v. Grewal, 39 F.3d 1189, 1994 WL 587395 (9th Cir.1994); Krol v. Owens, 35 F.3d 566, 1994 WL 487333 (6th Cir. (Ohio) 1994) (unpublished disposition); United States v. Gomez, 31 F.3d 28 (2d Cir.1994); United States v. Nichols, 977

shoulder the additional burdens involved in seeking search warrants. What can explain this tolerance? The answer may lie in the unique advantages inherent in the power to search itself. Although a health care provider is never likely to be pleased to receive a grand jury subpoena for documents, the recipient will normally have an opportunity to digest the official demand, discuss the implications and scope of the subpoenas with her counsel, attempt to negotiate the scope of the demand with the government, and even attempt to quash the request before complying. By contrast, once a search team has arrived at a provider's door with a warrant, the search will be almost impossible to stop, and the scope of the search will be out of the provider's hands. Relative to a search, therefore, the amount of time a provider has to decide whether and how to comply with a subpoena seems luxurious. An additional reason for choosing a warrant over a subpoena relates to the element of surprise that attends a search. Persons subjected to search are given no forewarning, and thus have no opportunity to conceal or destroy incriminating evidence that may be found on the

F.2d 583, 1992 WL 238264 (6th Cir. 1992) (unpublished disposition); Quality Clinical Laboratories, Inc. v. Hyndman, 959 F.2d 235, 1992 WL 68332 (6th Cir. (Mich.) 1992) (unpublished); Pembaur v. City of Cincinnati, 947 F.2d 945, 1991 WL 216875 (6th Cir.1991) (unpublished); United States v. Malloch, 936 F.2d 574, 1991 WL 114449 (6th Cir. 1991) (unpublished); United States v. Hooshmand, 931 F.2d 725 (11th Cir. 1991); United States v. East Side Ophthalmology, 1996 WL 384891 (S.D.N.Y.1996); Psychiatric Care Day Hosp. Center in Birmingham, Inc. v. Shalala, 876 F.Supp. 260 (N.D.Ala. 1994); In re Medicar Ambulance Co., 174 B.R. 804 (N.D.Cal.1994); United States v. Piacentile, 1994 WL 176973 (S.D.N.Y.1994); United States v. Hughes, 823 F.Supp. 593 (N.D.Ind. 1993); United States v. Fesman, 781 F.Supp. 511 (S.D.Ohio 1991); United States v. Enriquez, 1991 WL 236502 (S.D.Fla.1991); In re Black & White Cab Co., 175 B.R. 24 (Bkrtcy.E.D. Ark. 1994).

Providers subjected to search who are mentioned in state court decisions between 1990 and 1997 include: Commonwealth v. Sbordone, 424 Mass. 802, 678 N.E.2d 1184 (Mass. 1997); State v. Baker, 78 Ohio St.3d 108, 676 N.E.2d 883 (1997); Brillantes v. Superior Court, 51 Cal.App.4th 323, 58 Cal.Rptr.2d 770 (2d Dist. 1996); Dickerson v. Gynecological Associates, Inc., 1996 WL 751461 (Wash. App. Div. 1 1996); People v. Singh, 37 Cal.App.4th 1343, 44 Cal.Rptr.2d 644 (1st Dist. 1995); In re Search Warrant No. 5077/91, 96 Ohio App.3d 737, 645 N.E.2d 1304 (10th Dist. 1994); State v. Lamson, 640 A.2d 1076 (Maine 1994); Demetracopoulos v. Wilson, 138 N.H. 371, 640 A.2d 279 (N.H. 1994); Commonwealth v. Litke, 873 S.W.2d 198 (Ky. 1994); People v. Hepner, 21 Cal.App.4th 761, 26 Cal.Rptr.2d 417 (2d Dist. 1994); State v. Dolce, 92 Ohio App.3d 687, 637 N.E.2d 51 (6th Dist. 1993); Morris v. State, 622 So.2d 67 (Fla.App. 4th Dist. 1993); People v. Fiorillo, 195 Mich.App. 701, 491 N.W.2d 281 (1992); Ex parte Key Management Co., 598 So.2d 1386 (Ala.1992); State v. Medibus–Helpmobile, Inc., 481 N.W.2d 86 (Minn.App. 1992); People v. Ekong, 221 Ill.App.3d 559, 582 N.E.2d 233, 164 Ill.Dec. 25 (3d Dist. 1991); State v. DeBlanco, 1991 WL 151225 (Ohio App. 10th Dist. 1991); State v. Krivitskiy, 70 Ohio App.3d 293, 590 N.E.2d 1359 (10th Dist. 1990); Wisconsin v. DeSmidt, 155 Wis.2d 119, 454 N.W.2d 780 (1990); State ex rel. McGee v. Ohio State Bd. of Psychology, 49 Ohio St.3d 59, 550 N.E.2d 945 (1990); State v. Deutsch, 1990 WL 252919 (Ohio App. 10th Dist. 1990).

For an excellent collection and discussion of search warrants contested in earlier cases, see Pamela H. Bucy, Health Care Fraud, supra note 2, at 449–465.

premises. In cases in which the government is concerned that a provider might try to hide or destroy evidence of her wrongdoing, a search warrant may be the prosecutor's weapon of choice.

Armed with search warrants, qualified federal and state law enforcement officers, and certain others,[4] have been permitted to enter homes,[5] offices,[6] clinics,[7] laboratories,[8] pharmacies,[9] and other specified areas[10] in search of evidence of wrongdoing. With the authority conferred by a search warrant, searching parties are able to search for and seize any item specified on the warrant's face. In health care fraud cases, this has resulted in the seizure of patient files,[11] billing records,[12] medical charts,[13] pharmaceutical records,[14] prescription drugs,[15] computer files, equipment and software,[16] and more.[17] As might be expected, such a search can be not only professionally disruptive but personally traumatic as well.

4. See discussion infra at § 7–19c concerning the use of private parties in the execution of search warrants.

5. See, e.g., United States v. Grewal, 39 F.3d 1189, 1994 WL 587395 (9th Cir. (Cal.) 1995); United States v. Gomez, 31 F.3d 28 (3d Cir. 1994). See also Ohio v. Dolce, 92 Ohio App.3d 687, 693, 637 N.E.2d 51, 54 (1993).

6. See, e.g., United States v. East Side Ophthalmology, 1996 WL 31843 (S.D.N.Y.1996) (unpublished) (physician's office); Dickerson v. Gynecological Associates, Inc., 1996 WL 751461 (Wash. App. Div. 1 1996) (unpublished) (same); Krol v. Owens, 35 F.3d 566, 1994 WL 487333 (6th Cir. (Ohio) 1994) (unpublished) (business offices of search oxygen supply business). See also Ohio v. Dolce, 92 Ohio App. 3d at 693, 637 N.E.2d at 54; Morris v. State So.2d 67 (Fla. App. 4th Dist. 1993) (same); The State ex rel. McGee v. Ohio State Board of Psychology, 49 Ohio St.3d 59, 550 N.E.2d 945 (1990) (psychologist's office).

7. See, e.g., Commonwealth v. Sbordone, 424 Mass. 802, 678 N.E.2d 1184 (Mass. 1997) (three searches conducted pursuant to warrants at chiropractic clinic); Ex parte Key Management Co. v. Alabama, 598 So.2d 1386 (Ala.1992) (family clinic).

8. See, e.g., Quality Clinical Laboratories, Inc. v. Hyndman, 959 F.2d 235, 1992 WL 68332 (6th Cir. (Mich.) 1992).

9. See, e.g., Ohio v. Baker, 78 Ohio St.3d 108, 676 N.E.2d 883 (1997); In re Search Warrant No. 5077/91, 96 Ohio App.3d 737, 645 N.E.2d 1304 (10th Dist. 1994).

10. See, e.g., Psychiatric Care Day Hosp. Ctr. in Birmingham, Inc. v. Shalala, 876 F.Supp. 260 (N.D.Ala.1994) (center providing mental health services); Commonwealth v. Sbordone, 424 Mass. 802, 678 N.E.2d 1184 (Mass. 1997) (storage areas); United States v. Hughes, 823 F.Supp. 593 (N.D.Ind.1993) (safe deposit box); Ohio v. Dolce, 92 Ohio App. 3d at 693, 637 N.E.2d at 54 (car).

11. See, e.g, United States v. East Side Ophthalmology, 1996 WL 31843 (S.D.N.Y.1996) (unpublished). See also Dickerson v. Gynecological Associates, Inc., 1996 WL 751461 (Wash.App. Div. 1 1996); California v. Hepner, 21 Cal. App.4th 761, 26 Cal.Rptr.2d 417 (1994); Wisconsin v. DeSmidt, 155 Wis.2d 119, 454 N.W.2d 780 (1990) (patient dental records).

12. See, e.g, United States v. East Side Ophthalmology, 1996 WL 31843 (S.D.N.Y.1996) (unpublished). See also Wisconsin v. DeSmidt, 155 Wis.2d 119, 454 N.W.2d 780 (1990).

13. See, e.g, Wisconsin v. DeSmidt, 155 Wis.2d 119, 454 N.W.2d 780 (1990).

14. See, e.g., Ohio v. Baker, 78 Ohio St.3d 108, 676 N.E.2d 883 (1997).

15. See, e.g., United States v. Gomez, 31 F.3d 28 (2d Cir. 1994).

16. See, e.g., Ohio v. Baker, 1995 WL 783664 (Ohio App. 2d Dist. 1995) (unpublished); Psychiatric Care Day Hosp. Ctr. in Birmingham, Inc. v. Shalala, 876 F.Supp. 260 (N.D.Ala.1994).

17. See, e.g., Wisconsin v. DeSmidt, 155 Wis.2d 119, 454 N.W.2d 780 (1990) (x-ray negatives, daily business summaries and remittance forms); Common-

Because of the seriousness of the privacy interest lost as a result of this type of governmental conduct, the Fourth Amendment[18] and similarly worded state constitutional provisions[19] erect an important buffer between the citizenry and the federal and state power to search. For example, the Supreme Court has read the Fourth Amendment to prefer that searches be conducted pursuant to warrant,[20] and searches conducted without a warrant are presumptively unconstitutional. The Amendment also describes when a search warrant may issue and specifies some limits on its scope. For instance, before a search warrant may be issued the government is required to demonstrate to a neutral and detached magistrate[21] that there is probable cause to believe that evidence of a crime will be found in the place the government wishes to search.[22] If probable cause exists, the warrant must also particularly describe the items to be seized in the place to be searched.[23]

a. Challenges Based on Lack of Probable Cause

Health care providers frequently challenge searches conducted pursuant to warrant by attacking the issuing judge's decision to authorize the search in the first place. Unlike a grand jury subpoena, a search warrant may not be utilized in cases of mere suspicion.

---

wealth v. Sbordone, 424 Mass. 802, 804, 678 N.E.2d 1184, 1187 (1997) (sign-in sheets, logs and appointment books).

18. The Amendment provides:

The right of the people to be secure in their persons, houses, papers and effects, against unreasonable searches and seizures, shall not be violated, and no Warrants shall issue, but upon probable cause, supported by Oath or affirmation, and particularly describing the place to be searched, and the persons or things to be seized.

U.S. CONST. amend. IV.

19. Many state constitutions include provisions identical or virtually identical to the Fourth Amendment to the United States Constitution. See, e.g., Wisconsin Constitution, Art. I, Sec. 11, and the state courts have traditionally interpreted these state provisions consistent with their federal counterpart. See also Wisconsin v. DeSmidt, 155 Wis.2d 119, 130, 454 N.W.2d 780, 784 (1990).

20. See Johnson v. United States, 333 U.S. 10, 13–14, 68 S.Ct. 367, 369, 92 L.Ed. 436 (1948).

21. Johnson v. United States, 333 U.S. 10, 13–14, 68 S.Ct. 367, 368–69, 92 L.Ed. 436 (1948); Shadwick v. City of Tampa, 407 U.S. 345, 350, 92 S.Ct. 2119,

2123, 32 L.Ed.2d 783, 788 (1972). See also Wisconsin v. DeSmidt, 155 Wis.2d 119, 131, 454 N.W.2d 780, 785 (1990).

22. Warrantless searches are proper only when conducted incident to a valid arrest, United States v. Robinson, 414 U.S. 218, 235, 94 S.Ct. 467, 477, 38 L.Ed.2d 427, 440–41 (1973), or in certain "exigent situations" such that it is impracticable to secure a warrant before conducting the search. Arkansas v. Sanders, 442 U.S. 753, 759, 99 S.Ct. 2586, 2590, 61 L.Ed.2d 235 (1979). Such exigencies have been found when the search is of an automobile which may readily be moved beyond the reach of government investigators. Sanders, 442 U.S. at 760 n. 7, 761. Even in such cases, the police must have probable cause to believe that contraband or other evidence of a crime will be found in the car before it may be searched without a warrant. In the normal case, however, an investigatory search for evidence must be made pursuant to a warrant issued by a neutral and detached magistrate.

23. The Fourth Amendment requires that warrants "shall issue ... particularly describing the place to be searched and the person or things to be seized." U.S. Const. Amend. IV.

The Fourth Amendment expressly provides that a warrant may be issued "only upon probable cause, supported by oath or affirmation." Thus, only upon such a showing of probable cause is a magistrate able properly to issue a warrant authorizing a search for criminal evidence in a particular place. Moreover, where a provider is able to establish that an affiant made false statements in the application for a warrant, intentionally or with reckless disregard for the truth, and that the inclusion of the statements was necessary for the demonstration of probable cause, the search warrant will be voided and the fruits of the search excluded.[24]

In Medicare and Medicaid fraud and abuse cases, the government's showing of probable cause is typically based on information contained in the sworn affidavit of an authorized law enforcement officer, such as a Special Agent of the Federal Bureau of Investigation,[25] an Investigator of a state MFCU,[26] or certain others.[27] Probable cause is a fluid concept not readily reduced to a mathematical formula.[28] It is sometimes described as the quantum of facts and circumstances known to the law enforcement affiant seeking the warrant that would lead a reasonably prudent person to conclude that particular items related to criminal activity will be found in a particular place.[29] The facts and circumstances described

24. See, e.g., In re Search Warrants Served on Home Health and Hospice Care, Inc., 121 F.3d 700, 1997 WL 545655 (4th Cir. 1997) (unpublished) (upholding district court decision to void a search warrant and order the forthwith return of property to defendant).

25. See, e.g., United States v. Gomez, 31 F.3d 28 (2d Cir.1994); United States v. Nichols, 977 F.2d 583, 1992 WL 238264 (6th Cir. (Ky.) 1992) (unpublished); Psychiatric Care Day Hosp. Ctr. in Birmingham, Inc. v. Shalala, 876 F.Supp. 260 (N.D.Ala.1994).

26. See, e.g., F.E.R. v. Valdez, 58 F.3d 1530 (10th Cir.1995) (search warrant obtained by agents of the Utah Bureau of Medicaid Fraud); In re Search Warrant #5077/91, 96 Ohio App.3d 737, 645 N.E.2d 1304 (10th Dist. 1994) (search warrant affidavit filed by Special Agent of the Ohio Attorney General's Division of Medicaid Fraud Control); Key Management Co. v. Alabama, 598 So.2d 1386 (Ala.1992) (application filed by investigators of the state MFCU); Ohio v. DeBlanco, 1991 WL 151225 (Ohio App. 10 Dist. 1991) (unpublished) (warrant application filed by Ohio Division of Medicaid Fraud Control); In re Search Warrant for 2045 Franklin, Denver, Colorado, 709 P.2d 597 (Colo. Ct. of App., Div. II, 1985) (warrant application filed by the Colorado MFCU); In re Search Warrant on 5000 Northwind Drive, 128 Mich.App. 564, 341 N.W.2d 141 (1983) (warrant obtained by Division of Michigan Attorney General's Office); McKirdy, M.D. v. Superior Court for the City and County of San Francisco, 138 Cal.App.3d 12, 188 Cal.Rptr. 143 (1st Dist. 1982) (warrant obtained by state Attorney General's Medi-Cal Fraud Unit).

27. See, e.g., United States v. Singh, 54 F.3d 1182, 1185 (4th Cir.1995) (warrant obtained by Drug Diversion Investigative Unit of the state police); Krol v. Owens, 35 F.3d 566, 1994 WL 487333 (6th Cir. (Ohio) 1994) (unpublished) (warrant application filed by Sheriff's Department); Quality Clinical Laboratories, Inc. v. Hyndman, 959 F.2d 235, 1992 WL 68332 (6th Cir. (Mich.) 1992) (warrant obtained by Economic Crime Division of state Attorney General's office). Administrative search warrants are addressed separately below. See § 7-20.

28. See Illinois v. Gates, 462 U.S. 213, 231-32, 103 S.Ct. 2317, 2328-29, 76 L.Ed.2d 527, 544 (1983).

29. See id.

in an affidavit may derive either from information provided by reliable sources, or information collected by the affiant herself based on her own personal observations. Disgruntled past or current employees are perhaps the most common source of information for these agents and investigators.[30] Other familiar sources of information are customers, competitors and concerned citizens.

Some health care providers have sought to suppress evidence collected in a search by arguing that the search warrant application failed to demonstrate probable cause to believe that criminal evidence would be found in the place to be searched at the time the warrant was issued.[31] Because evidence of criminal activity is both transportable and destructible, a probable cause showing must demonstrate not only that criminal evidence was once kept in a particular spot, but that there is probable cause to believe that the items are still present in that place at the time the warrant is sought. In other words, the information contained in an affidavit about sought-after evidence must not be stale. This requirement can cause great difficulty to a law enforcement officer who has solid information that a crime has been committed, but less than solid information about where evidence of the crime might presently be found. In such a case, government officials might choose to issue a grand jury subpoena for the evidence rather than face a later challenge to a warrant based on staleness grounds.

Staleness problems are of special concern to law enforcement authorities involved in white collar criminal investigations, such as health care fraud investigations. These investigations tend to be largely "paper cases." Much of the most damaging evidence of a routine practice of false billing, for instance, will come from patient and billing records, appointment books, claim forms, etc. Medical records can be stored in a facility off-site, some distance from a provider's office. This possibility may make it difficult for the government to obtain a warrant. In a case where the information about a provider's alleged false billing practices stems from a former employee, a probable cause challenge may be brought on the ground that the employee had no ability to know where those

---

30. See, e.g., United States v. Nichols, 1992 WL 238264 at 1 (former employee of dentist who provided FBI with documents evidencing false claims); Wisconsin v. DeSmidt, 155 Wis. 2d at 125–26 454 N.W.2d at 782–83 (former employee of dentist who was fired after she confronted the dentist about false billing practices); Dickerson v. Gynecological Associates, Inc., 1996 WL 751461 at 1 (former receptionist and medical assis-

tant who was fired after she questioned doctor about billings); California v. Hepner, 21 Cal. App. 4th at 765, 26 Cal. Rptr. 2d at 419 (former and current employees); Ohio v. Dolce, 92 Ohio App.3d at 693, 637 N.E.2d at 54 (tip given by chiropractor's former employee to local police department).

31. See, e.g., Kentucky v. Litke, 873 S.W.2d 198 (1994).

records would be found at the time the search warrant application was filed.

An example of this type of claim (albeit an unsuccessful one) can be found in *Kentucky v. Litke*.[32] There, a Medicaid provider sought to suppress records collected in a search of his business premises. Prior to the search, an investigator of the state Attorney General's office received a tip from an anonymous caller asserting that the defendant had billed the state Medicaid program for unperformed services. To confirm the caller's information, the investigator interviewed a former employee of Litke's who had performed billing services for the defendant. The former billing clerk estimated that during the period of her employ (which ended more than five years before the search) approximately half of Litke's Medicaid billings were fraudulent. Based on this information, the investigator prepared an affidavit in support of an application for a search warrant that recounted the information he had received from the anonymous tipster and the former billing clerk. Attached to the affidavit was a seven-page list of patient files to be seized. Based on this affidavit, a warrant was issued and executed, resulting in the seizure of numerous treatment records. Dr. Litke subsequently moved to suppress the records on the ground that the information in the affidavit was insufficient to establish probable cause to believe that the allegedly fraudulent records would still be on the premises. Although the trial court and the court of appeals agreed and ordered the documents suppressed, the Supreme Court of Kentucky reversed. The court found significant that Medicaid regulations require providers to retain documentation of services provided for a least five years. The court further ruled that even had the warrant been issued on insufficient evidence, under a state analog to the good faith exception established in *United States v. Leon*,[33] exclusion of the evidence was not required since a reasonably trained officer could have believed that the affidavit sufficient and the warrant valid.[34]

Other challenges have been premised on the ground that the probable cause showing made out in the government's affidavit was sufficient to warrant the seizure of only *some* of the items named on the face of the warrant, and because the warrant authorized the seizure of other items for which there was no probable cause, the resulting search was unreasonable, warranting the suppression of all of the evidence seized. Most courts have been reluctant to

---

32. See 873 S.W.2d 198 (1994).

33. 468 U.S. 897, 104 S.Ct. 3430, 82 L.Ed.2d 677 (1984). Leon established that the exclusionary rule will not apply in cases where a searching agent acts in the objectively reasonable belief that his conduct complies with the Fourth Amendment, such as where the agent reasonably relies on a warrant issued by a neutral and detached magistrate.

34. See id. at 199.

suppress the fruits of a search conducted pursuant to a warrant on such grounds.[35]

b. Challenges Based on Insufficient Particularity

A common challenge brought by health care providers to suppress the fruits of search warrants executed at their places of business and elsewhere has been based upon the Fourth Amendment's particularity requirement. As noted above, the Fourth Amendment expressly requires that all search warrants particularly describe the place to be searched and things to be seized there. This requirement is designed to ensure that searching agents will be able to ascertain with reasonable ease the precise location they are entitled to search and the items for which they have authorization to look. The particularity requirement cabins the scope of a search within precisely identified and pre-established boundaries in an effort to prevent the occurrence of long-disdained "general searches."

Yet, notwithstanding the oft-quoted phrase—"As to what can be taken, nothing is left to the discretion of the officer executing the warrant"[36]—in general, the courts have not required warrants to furnish an *exact* list of all seizable items. Rather, warrants are required to provide a precise enough description of the property to be seized to avert the seizure of property as to which there is no probable cause.[37] In other words, searching agents are to be guided, not hamstrung, by the terms of a warrant. Some discretion to determine whether an item falls under the scope of the warrant is conferred upon searching agents, and even an erroneous decision to seize an item not covered by the warrant will generally be condoned so long as the agents' behavior is not flagrantly abusive.[38]

---

35. Compare United States v. Abrams, 615 F.2d 541, 542 (1st Cir. 1980) (affidavit based on information provided by 3 former employees alleging approximately 50 false billing incidents could not provide probable cause to believe all of defendant's patients' billings were inflated) and Wisconsin v. De-Smidt, 155 Wis.2d 119, 454 N.W.2d 780 (1990) (authorizing seizure of all of the files in a dentist's office on the theory that the allegations in the search warrant affidavit indicated that the dentist's practice was "permeated with fraud"); Hayes, 794 F.2d at 1356 (information in affidavit that specified 58 illegal prescriptions by defendant could be fairly considered as representative of more pervasive violations of federal law and justify seizure of other prescription records).

36. Marron v. United States, 275 U.S. 192, 196, 48 S.Ct. 74, 76, 72 L.Ed. 231, 237 (1927).

37. See W. LaFave, Search and Seizure § 4.6, Vol. II, p. 96 (noting that a literal reading of the language from Marron would cause few warrants to pass muster).

38. For examples of searches upheld against particularity challenges see United States v. Hooshmand, 931 F.2d 725 (11th Cir.1991); United States v. Lamport, 787 F.2d 474, 476 (10th Cir. 1986), cert. denied, 479 U.S. 846, 107 S.Ct. 166, 93 L.Ed.2d 104 (1986); United States v. Hershenow, 680 F.2d 847, (1st Cir.1982); United States v. Hughes, 823 F.Supp. 593, 603 (N.D.Ind.1993); State v. Dorn, 145 Vt. 606 496 A.2d 451 (Vt. 1985); Wisconsin v. DeSmidt, 155 Wis.2d 119, 454 N.W.2d 780 (Wis. 1990); State v. Hughes, 433 So.2d 88 (La.1983); State v. Ruud, 259 N.W.2d 567 (Minn.1977).

Nevertheless, health care professionals have on occasion moved to suppress the fruits of a search on the ground that the searching agents wrongfully took custody of items that they were not authorized by the warrant to seize.[39] As stated above, the particularity requirement seeks to ensure that searching officers will not engage in general searches for evidence. Part of this requirement ensures that only records and other items specifically named on the face of the warrant will be seized. When searching agents go beyond the boundaries set by the magistrate and seize an item not delineated on the face of the warrant, a motion to suppress will often result.

The test most frequently applied to such suppression motions is not whether the agents in fact seized an item outside the scope of the warrant, but whether the agents flagrantly disregarded the limitations imposed by the warrant. In one case, for example, officers arrived at a pharmacy armed with a search warrant that authorized the seizure of any "illegally possessed controlled substances, drug paraphernalia, receipts, business records, ledgers, vouchers, prescription forms, computer files and software, and/or any documentation pertaining to or associated with the sale of controlled substances and/or medicaid billing."[40] While executing the warrant the officers seized, among other things, $1,000 in cash, firearms, an article of women's underwear and a sexual device. At a later hearing held to determine whether the evidence should be suppressed, all parties acknowledged that the officers had acted beyond the scope of their authorization. Nevertheless, both the trial and the appellate courts concluded that there was enough of a nexus between illegal drug trafficking (one of the counts brought against the pharmacist defendant) and the seized items to prevent a finding that the officers flagrantly disregarded the limits of their charge.[41] Thus, suppression was not required.[42]

Prosecutors have not always fared so well, however. A claim based on particularity grounds was successfully advanced in *United States v. Abrams*,[43] one of the few cases in which evidence seized pursuant to a warrant has been suppressed in a health care fraud

---

39. See, e.g., Ohio v. Baker, 1995 WL 783664 (Ohio App. 2d Dist. 1995).

40. See id. at 3.

41. See id. at 3–4. The case involved allegations that the defendant had traded drugs for sexual favors which gave rise to the nexus identified by the court.

42. A similar result was reached in State v. Dorn, 145 Vt. 606, 496 A.2d 451 (Vt. 1985) (non-Medicaid prescriptions seized under a search warrant which authorized the seizure of only Medicaid-related prescriptions and prescription records, although outside the scope of

the warrant, were properly seized under the "plain view" exception, since it was immediately apparent that the non-Medicaid records were also evidence of a crime). See also United States v. Hughes, 823 F.Supp. 593, 604 (N.D.Ind. 1993) (agents could properly seize records that they suspected, but were not certain, would be evidence of a fraud, since otherwise agents' review of the documents while conducting the searching would have taken several days).

43. 615 F.2d 541, 542 (1st Cir.1980).

case. In *Abrams,* several former employees of two physicians advised federal authorities that the physicians had filed Medicare claim forms for laboratory tests that had never been performed. The employees described approximately fifty false billing incidents that had occurred during the periods of their employ. Based largely on this information, the government sought and obtained a search warrant that broadly authorized the seizure of "certain business and billing and medical records of patients of [the defendants] which show actual medical services performed and fraudulent services claimed to have been performed in a scheme to defraud the United States and to submit false medicare and medicaid claims for payment ...."[44] Armed with the warrant, FBI agents seized all of the Medicare and Medicaid records in the doctors' offices and approximately twenty medical records of non-Medicare or non-Medicaid patients. After a lengthy hearing following the search, the district court suppressed all of the records seized in the search. The court of appeals affirmed, holding that the warrant insufficiently particularized the items that could appropriately be seized. The court explained as follows:

> The warrant as drawn left it entirely up to the discretion of the officers to determine what records to seize. Since they had no guidance at all, they seized them all. This may have been prudent, but it was also unconstitutional. Even if there were probable cause to seize all of the doctors' Medicare and Medicaid files, the mere fortuity that the officers seized records that could have been within the permissible scope of an adequately drafted warrant cannot rehabilitate this particular warrant.[45]

According to the court, by bestowing upon the agents the unfettered discretion to distinguish between bona fide and fraudulent records, the warrant sanctioned "exactly the kind of investigatory dragnet that the fourth amendment was designed to prevent."[46] *Abrams* suggests that it may be easier to prevail on a particularity challenge that is based on the imprecise wording of a warrant, than it is to succeed on a particularity claim that searching officers acted outside the scope of the authorization conferred by a warrant. Indeed, the latter claim appears to be less of a particularity challenge (since the warrant particularly described the items to be seized, but the officers failed to heed that description) than a challenge based on probable cause. A better argument in such a case might be that the officers lacked justification for seizing the items since they had neither probable cause to believe the items were evidence of a crime nor probable cause to believe that the items would be found in the place to be searched.

44. Id. at 542.
45. Id. at 544.

46. Id. at 543.

c. Challenges Based on Unauthorized Party Involved in a Search

Other constitutional attacks have been brought to challenge search warrants where searching agents have permitted civilians to help execute the warrants. Federal agents are expressly authorized to utilize the assistance of civilian agents in the execution of warrants under certain circumstances.[47] Difficulties have arisen, however, where state law enforcement officers have carried out a search with a civilian agent in tow,[48] or permitted civilians to carry out the search altogether.[49] For example, in *Commonwealth v. Sbordone*,[50] an investigator for a Massachusetts insurance fraud bureau was allowed to actively participate in the execution of several search warrants on the offices of a chiropractor who was suspected of submitting false claims. After the searches were completed the defendant moved to suppress all items taken from his clinic based on the ground that the state had failed adequately to limit the involvement of a civilian in the execution of the warrant. The motions court agreed and ordered the evidence suppressed holding that the executing officers had exceeded the limits of using civilian assistance because they had not sufficiently supervised the insurance bureau investigator, and instead had granted the investigator complete license to search patient files. The suppression order was short-lived. While agreeing that certain restrictions are rightfully placed on the role that civilians may play in the execution of a warrant, the Supreme Judicial Court reversed the lower court's ruling. In its decision the court acknowledged that sound public policy supports requiring law enforcement officers, and not civilians, to be the parties primarily responsible for executing lawfully issued warrants. Such officers have both a sworn duty to uphold and enforce the law, as well as the training to conduct searches lawfully. Nevertheless, the court ruled there are times when civilians can properly provide needed expertise in a search.[51] In such a case, the civilian's presence and assistance during the search will be lawful provided the civilian is adequately supervised by an officer authorized to conduct the search.[52] The court found it significant

---

47. See 18 U.S.C.A. § 3105 (1994).

48. A civilian agent would include any person not specifically named on the face of the warrant as authorized to conduct or to assist the search. See, e.g., Commonwealth v. Sbordone, 424 Mass. 802, 678 N.E.2d 1184 (1997).

49. See, e.g., Morris v. State, 622 So.2d 67, 68–69 (Fla.App. 4th Dist.1993) (invalidating a search where Medicaid fraud investigators displaced the police officer who was authorized to execute the warrant).

50. 424 Mass. 802, 678 N.E.2d 1184 (1997).

51. See id. at 807, 678 N.E.2d at 1188, citing (Harris v. State, 260 Ga. 860, 401 S.E.2d 263 (1991) (upholding search where dentist was allowed to execute a search warrant for dental x-rays and dental impressions); United States v. Schwimmer, 692 F.Supp. 119, 126–27 (E.D.N.Y.1988) (search upheld where civilian computer expert was permitted to assist search).

52. See id. at 810.

that the civilian in question was the chief investigator for a statutorily created entity that often worked in tandem with the Attorney General's office, that at least one police officer had been in close physical proximity to the bureau investigator throughout the search,[53] that the investigator had confined his searching activities to the area in which the officers were authorized to search, and that he had not performed any other law enforcement functions, such as presenting the warrant, preparing the inventory return on the warrant, or taking official custody of the seized records.[54]

Although, as *Sbordone* reflects, assistance provided by a civilian will not always invalidate a search, it may lead to suppression in some instances. As one court succinctly put it, "[a]ssistance is one thing, displacement is another."[55] If an officer completely relinquishes to a civilian assistant his duty to search, suppression may result. For example, in *Morris v. Florida*,[56] suppression was deemed to be the appropriate remedy where a police officer abdicated his responsibility to conduct a search of a doctor's office by standing outside the office while employees of the state Auditor General's Office inspected, boxed and removed records to the Auditor General's headquarters.

d.   Motions for the Return of Seized Documents

As might be expected, the execution of a search warrant on the office of a health care provider or entity can significantly interfere with the ability of the provider or entity to carry on its business. Searches generally involve the forcible seizure and removal of many, if not all of a provider's patient files, computer records, appointment books, and other important items needed to conduct a health care practice.[57] To avoid the potentially crippling effect of such seizures, health care providers subject to search have frequently sought the immediate return of items seized on the ground that the government's continued possession of the items threatened the providers' professional livelihoods. Although not unsympathetic to such claims, the courts rarely order the return of documents seized pursuant to warrant. The courts will, however, routinely order authorities to provide health care providers with a photocopy of any document taken during a search to aid providers' ongoing

---

53. Compare Morris, 622 So.2d at 68–69 (police officer waited outside while six Medicaid fraud investigators conducted the search unsupervised for the entire duration of the search).

54. See Sbordone, 424 Mass. at 812.

55. Morris, 622 S.2d at 69.

56. 622 So.2d 67 (Fla.App. 4th Dist. 1993).

57. See, e.g., Wisconsin v. DeSmidt, 155 Wis.2d 119, 454 N.W.2d 780 (1990) (agents seized 22 boxes of materials including all of dentist's active patient files and the office's appointment books).

operations.[58]

The facts of *Wisconsin v. DeSmidt* [59] illustrate. After a search of his office, Dr. DeSmidt filed a motion seeking the return of all of the documents seized. The officers who searched the office had seized all of DeSmidts' active patient files, his appointment book and much more.[60] DeSmidt argued that the state's retention of his active files was constitutionally unreasonable due to its impact on his professional livelihood and his patients' welfare, and requested the immediate return of all the items taken.[61] The trial court rejected the request, but ordered the state to return any record that it did not intend to use as evidence at trial and to provide DeSmidt with a photocopy of any record that it did intend to retain for trial. On DeSmidt's appeal of this decision, the appellate court affirmed, and held further that even if the state wrongly retained some of the defendant's records, the remedy for such conduct was not suppression of relevant evidence at trial, but a contempt citation.[62]

e. Public versus Private Searches—The Threshold Requirement of Governmental Action

It is important to bear in mind that the Fourth Amendment (and its state counterparts) is triggered by governmental action only.[63] It is only when a federal, state or local law enforcement officer conducts a search of a person or property, that the Amendment's protections come into play. The Amendment is not triggered by a search or seizure of evidence that is conducted by a non-governmental party. That is, where a private party *acts on his own* to gather evidence against another, and subsequently turns that evidence over to governmental authorities, the Fourth Amendment is not implicated, and there is no constitutional bar to the government's use of the evidence before the grand jury or at trial.

The critical issue raised in cases involving evidence gathered by a private party (e.g., a former or current employee suspicious of her boss's billing practices) is whether the individual in fact acted on her own, as opposed to at the behest of the government. The courts are not willing to condone the government's use of a private party

---

58. See, e.g., In re Medicar Ambulance Co., 174 B.R. 804 (N.D.Cal.1994); Wisconsin v. DeSmidt, 155 Wis.2d 119, 454 N.W.2d 780 (1990); State ex rel. McGee v. Ohio State Bd. of Psychology, 49 Ohio St.3d 59, 550 N.E.2d at 945 (1990).

59. 155 Wis.2d 119, 454 N.W.2d 780 (1990).

60. The officers had permitted Dr. DeSmidt to photocopy the medical charts of the patients he expected to treat within the next day, as well as several pages of his appointment book reflecting scheduled appointments in the near future. See id. at 127, 454 N.W.2d at 783.

61. See id. at 141, 454 N.W.2d at 789.

62. See id. at 142, 454 N.W.2d at 790.

63. See Burdeau v. McDowell, 256 U.S. 465, 475, 41 S.Ct. 574, 576, 65 L.Ed. 1048, 1051 (1921).

to circumvent the warrant and probable cause requirements of the Fourth Amendment. Hence, if it appears that a private party conducted a search outside the physical company of governmental officials, but at their urging, the Fourth Amendment will be implicated. Where, however, a private party searches for and/or seizes criminal evidence without the knowledge of the government,[64] or after receiving and disregarding contrary instructions from a governmental official,[65] the results of the search may be used, no matter how egregious the private searcher's actions.

f. Conclusion

As the foregoing illustrates, the power to search has proven to be a formidable weapon in the hands of state and federal investigators of Medicare and Medicaid fraud and abuse. Health care providers, increasingly on the receiving end of such searches, have struggled, very often in vain, for the return or suppression of documents seized pursuant to a warrant. Given the distinct advantages inherent in the power to search, and the courts' reluctance to interfere with that power absent some egregious conduct on the part of the government, it is safe to predict that forcible searches will continue to be one of the government's preferred evidence gathering techniques in health care fraud cases in the near future.

§ 7–20. Administrative Investigations

Prior to the New Deal, the courts closely confined the role played by administrative agencies in the investigation of criminal activity. Administrative subpoenas were stuck down by the courts as unwarranted "fishing expeditions" and administrative agencies were expected to respond reactively, rather than proactively, to suspected incidents of fraud and abuse.[1] With the advent of the New Deal, however, the courts' attitude toward the powers of the administrative state underwent a dramatic shift. Subsequent to the New Deal the court abandoned its earlier sentry role guarding against the encroaching administrative state and began to permit administrative agencies to exercise broader and broader investigative powers.[2]

---

64. See, e.g., United States v. Lamport, 787 F.2d 474, 475–76 (10th Cir.), cert. denied, 479 U.S. 846, 107 S.Ct. 166, 93 L.Ed.2d 104 (1986); United States v. Ziperstein, 601 F.2d 281, 289 (7th Cir. 1979), cert. denied, 444 U.S. 1031, 100 S.Ct. 701, 62 L.Ed.2d 667 (1980); United States v. Mekjian, 505, F.2d 1320, 1326–28 (5th Cir. 1975).

65. See, e.g., United States v. Cella, 568 F.2d 1266, 1271–77 (9th Cir.1977).

§ 7–20

1. A helpful discussion of the evolving judicial tolerance of administrative activities can be found in Note, Revoking the "Fishing License:" Recent Decisions Place Unwarranted Restrictions on Administrative Agencies' Power to Subpoena Personal Financial Records, 49 Vand. L. Rev. 395, 398–99 (1966).

2. See id.

As the administrative state has mushroomed to regulate an ever increasing segment of the commercial industry, so too has the authority granted to agencies and departments to investigate breaches of regulations and to impose civil and administrative penalties for their breach. Administrative officials, including the Inspector General for HHS, have been statutorily empowered to make civil investigative demands similar to demands made historically only by the grand jury. The Supreme Court has nourished the OIG's investigative authority by comparing its subpoena power to the broad detective powers of the grand jury.[3] Although it is clear that the right to issue an administrative subpoena exists only by statute, the OIG for the HHS enjoys such a statutory grant of authority.[4]

Although many similarities exist between the evidentiary demands posed by administrative and grand jury subpoenas, health care providers who receive administrative subpoenas may fare better than their counterparts who receive grand jury demands. As discussed above,[5] persons subpoenaed to give testimony before the grand jury must do so alone, without the presence of counsel. In addition, because grand jury's proceedings are shrouded in secrecy, apart from a witness's own testimony, the witness may have very little knowledge of the grand jury's mission and the scope of its investigation. A grand jury witness will not be provided with even a copy of the transcript of his or her own testimony. By contrast, a witness subpoenaed to testify before an administrative agency may do so with counsel present, may pose objections during that testimony, may clarify his answers on the record, may review the transcript of the proceeding, and may submit written errata.[6] In addition, unencumbered by grand jury secrecy rules, an administrative agency may be more willing to give the recipient of an administrative subpoena a sense of the scope of the agency's investigation, including whether the investigation is likely to remain civil or administrative, as opposed to criminal. There may be other procedural advantages as well.[7]

---

3. United States v. Morton Salt Co., 338 U.S. 632, 642–43 70 S.Ct. 357, 364, 94 L.Ed. 401, 410–411 (1950).

4. See United States v. Medic House, Inc., 736 F.Supp. 1531, 1535 (W.D.Mo. 1989) (affirming the Inspector General's power to conduct criminal investigations).

5. See § 7–12a.

6. See 42 C.F.R. § 1006.4.

7. One scholar has argued that a party challenging an administrative subpoena may enjoy yet another procedural advantage not available in the context of a grand jury subpoena challenge: the right to appeal the denial of a motion to quash an administrative subpoena. See G. Hughes, "Administrative Subpoenas and the Grand Jury: Converging Streams of Criminal and Civil Compulsory Process," 47 Vand. L. Rev. 573, (1994) (citing Reisman v. Caplin, 375 U.S. 440, 449, 84 S.Ct. 508, 513, 11 L.Ed.2d 459 (1964)). Because the denial of a motion to quash a grand jury subpoena is not considered a final judgment, no such interlocutory appeal is available. United States v. Ryan, 402 U.S. 530, 532, 91 S.Ct. 1580, 1582, 29

§ 7–21. Challenging Administrative Subpoenas—Overview

Although the OIG's authority to issue administrative subpoenas is quite broad, some important limitations on the agency's investigative powers remain. A party or witness may challenge an administrative subpoena "on any appropriate ground"[1] including that it violates the Fifth Amendment's privilege against self-incrimination;[2] the Fourth Amendment's protection against unreasonable searches and seizures,[3] or the law of privileges.[4] With the exception of challenges brought under the Fourth Amendment, there appears to be very little difference between how the courts handle challenges to administrative subpoenas and challenges to grand jury subpoenas.

In practice, health care providers have had little success in challenging administrative subpoenas issued by the OIG. Although early in this century the Supreme Court denounced administrative "fishing expeditions" seeking the production of private papers that might or might not disclose evidence of crime,[5] in 1943, the Court embraced the need for broader administrative access to information when it held that a civil subpoena is enforceable so long as the "evidence sought ... [is] not plainly incompetent or irrelevant to any lawful purpose."[6] The Court refined this view a short time later in the now famous cases of *Oklahoma Press Publishing Co. v. Walling*[7] and *United States v. Morton Salt Co.*[8]

In *Oklahoma Press*, the Supreme Court drew a distinction between searches and seizures conducted by law enforcement officers (as to which the Fourth Amendment requires a showing of probable cause) and subpoenas that call for the production of

L.Ed.2d 85, 88 (1971). Professor Hughes argues that this difference may cause the government to use the grand jury over an administrative alternative in some cases.

§ 7–21

1. Reisman v. Caplin, 375 U.S. 440, 449, 84 S.Ct. 508, 513, 11 L.Ed.2d 459, 465–66 (1964).

2. See § 7–14.

3. See § 7–15.

4. See § 7–16.

5. FTC v. American Tobacco Co., 264 U.S. 298, 306, 44 S.Ct. 336, 337, 68 L.Ed. 696, 670 (1924); see also Jones v. SEC, 298 U.S. 1, 26, 56 S.Ct. 654, 662, 80 L.Ed. 1015, 1026 (1936) (declining to enforce an SEC subpoena for books and

records connected to its investigation of a suspected registration statement on ground that once the corporate entity withdrew the statement, the SEC could no longer show a proper purpose for the inquiry).

6. Endicott Johnson v. Perkins, 317 U.S. 501, 509, 63 S.Ct. 339, 343, 87 L.Ed. 424, 429 (1943); see also FTC v. Texaco, Inc., 555 F.2d 862, 871–73 (D.C.Cir.1977) (en banc) (tracing the evolving judicial acceptance of administrative subpoenas).

7. 327 U.S. 186, 66 S.Ct. 494, 90 L.Ed. 614 (1946).

8. 338 U.S. 632, 70 S.Ct. 357, 94 L.Ed. 401 (1950); see also 1 Kenneth C. Davis & Richard J. Pierce, Jr., Administrative Law Treatise §§ 4.1, 4.2, 4.5 (3d ed. 1994).

documents (which, at most, constitute "constructive" searches requiring no showing of probable cause).[9] The Court concluded that 1) persons who are called upon to produce corporate records are entitled to no Fifth Amendment protection under the self-incrimination clause (whether for the corporation or its officers) and 2) the Fourth Amendment, if applicable, shields a subpoenaed person only from a demand that is either too indefinite or too broad, provided the subpoena is issued by an agency authorized by law to make such a demand, and the materials specified in the subpoena are relevant to the agency's inquiry.[10]

The Court pressed this analysis even further in *Morton Salt*. There, the Court declared that an administrative agency "has a power of inquisition" akin to that of the grand jury, which the agency may wield "merely on suspicion that the law is being violated, or even just because it wants assurance that it is not."[11] To pass constitutional muster, "it is sufficient if the inquiry is

---

9. Oklahoma Press, 327 U.S. at 202–08, 66 S.Ct. at 502–05, 90 L.Ed. at 625–629. In the words of Justice Rutledge:

The short answer to the Fourth Amendment objections is that the records in these cases present no question of actual search and seizure, but raise only the question whether orders of court for the production of specified records have been validly made; and no sufficient showing appears to justify setting them aside. No officer or other person has sought to enter petitioners' premises against their will, to search them, or to seize or examine their books, records or papers without their assent, otherwise than pursuant to orders of court authorized by law and made after adequate opportunity to present objections, which in fact were made.

327 U.S. at 195 n.12, 66 S.Ct. at 498 n.12, 90 L.Ed. at 622 n.12. See also United States v. Dionisio, 410 U.S. 1, 8–10, 93 S.Ct. 764, 768–70, 35 L.Ed.2d 67, 75–77 (1973) (grand jury subpoena is not a "seizure"); United States v. Doe (Schwartz), 457 F.2d 895, 898 (2d Cir. 1972) (Friendly, J.) (same), cert. denied, 410 U.S. 941, 93 S.Ct. 1376, 35 L.Ed.2d 608 (1973).

10. See Oklahoma Press, 327 U.S. at 208, 66 S.Ct. at 505, 90 L.Ed. at 629; see also In re Grand Jury Subpoena Duces Tecum Dated October 29, 1992, 1 F.3d 87, 93 (2d Cir.1993) (Fifth Amendment does not protect the contents of voluntarily prepared documents, regardless of

their business or personal nature), cert. denied, 510 U.S. 1091, 114 S.Ct. 920, 127 L.Ed.2d 214 (1994).

11. The Morton Salt Court wrote:

The only power ... involved here is the power to get information from those who best can give it and who are most interested in not doing so. Because judicial power is reluctant if not unable to summon evidence until it is shown to be relevant to issues in litigation, it does not follow that an administrative agency charged with seeing that the laws are enforced may not have and exercise powers of original inquiry. It has a power of inquisition, if one chooses to call it that, which is not derived from the judicial function. It is more analogous to the Grand Jury, which does not depend on a case or controversy for power to get evidence but can investigate merely on suspicion that the law is being violated, or even just because it wants assurance that it is not. When investigative and accusatory duties are delegated by statute to an administrative body, it, too, may take steps to inform itself as to whether there is probable violation of the law.

338 U.S. 632, 642–43, 70 S.Ct. 357, 364, 94 L.Ed. 401, 410–411; see also United States v. Powell, 379 U.S. 48, 53, 85 S.Ct. 248, 252, 13 L.Ed.2d 112, 117 (1964) (like the grand jury, an agency need not show probable cause to justify civil summons).

within the authority of the agency, the demand is not too indefinite and the information sought is reasonably relevant."[12] A final ingredient in this mix, added by *United States v. Powell*,[13] requires that an administrative subpoena seek only those documents or items not already be in the agency's possession. Considered together, the *Oklahoma Press*, *Morton Salt* and *Powell* standards embody the modern-day test for the enforcement of an administrative subpoena.[14]

As might be predicted, efforts to avoid compliance with an OIG subpoena under these standards have rarely succeeded. Once the OIG is able to produce *prima facie* evidence justifying its issuance of an administrative subpoena, the agency will be entitled to an enforcement order. The OIG normally attempts to make out its *prima facie* case by submitting an affidavit to the court establishing its authority and attesting that the investigation will be conducted pursuant to a legitimate purpose, that the subpoena seeks information relevant to that purpose, and that the information sought is not already within its possession.[15] If the affidavit is deemed sufficient, a heavy burden will shift to the provider to rebut the showing.[16] Only by demonstrating that enforcement would be an abuse of the court's process will the provider fend off an order to comply,[17] and the courts will recognize such an abuse only upon proof that the agency issued the challenged subpoena in bad faith for an improper purpose, such as where the subpoena was issued simply to harass the provider.[18] The courts have rejected bad faith claims based on evidence that an OIG agent made "friendly overtures" toward a target provider or failed to disclose that the provider was the target of a formal OIG investigation.[19] An administrative agency may act with an improper purpose, however, if it issues a subpoena or summons solely for the purpose of gathering evidence for a criminal investigation *after* it has recommended to the DOJ that a criminal prosecution related to the subject matter of the subpoena be undertaken, or it delays its recommendation

---

12. Id.

13. 379 U.S. 48, 57–58, 85 S.Ct. 248, 255, 13 L.Ed.2d 112, 119 (1964).

14. For applications of these standards, see, e.g., United States v. Stuart, 489 U.S. 353, 359, 109 S.Ct. 1183, 1188, 103 L.Ed.2d 388, 400 (1989); United States v. Arthur Young & Co., 465 U.S. 805, 813 n. 10, 104 S.Ct. 1495, 1500–01 n. 10, 79 L.Ed.2d 826, 83 n. 10 (1984); In re McVane, 44 F.3d 1127, 1136–37 (2d Cir.1995).

15. See, e.g., United States v. Stuart, 489 U.S. 353, 359, 109 S.Ct. 1183, 1188, 103 L.Ed.2d 388, 400 (1989).

16. See E.E.O.C. v. Children's Hosp. Medical Ctr. of Northern California, 719 F.2d 1426, 1428 (9th Cir.1983) (en banc).

17. United States v. Stuart, 489 U.S. at 360, 109 S.Ct. at 1188, 103 L.Ed.2d at 400; United States v. Powell, 379 U.S. at 58, 85 S.Ct. at 255, 13 L.Ed.2d at 120; Medic House, 736 F.Supp. at 1536.

18. See, e.g., E.E.O.C. v. Children's Hospital Medical Center, 719 F.2d 1426, 1428 (9th Cir.1983) (en banc).

19. See Medic House, 736 F. Supp. at 1538.

simply to gather additional evidence for the prosecution.[20]

Even if a provider is able to establish that the OIG issued a subpoena in bad faith, it is not clear that denial of an enforcement order will be the remedy for the misconduct. Some courts have suggested that, demonstrable official misconduct notwithstanding, the question of whether to enforce an administrative subpoena "requires that the court evaluate the seriousness of the violation under all the circumstances, including the government's good faith and the degree of harm imposed by the unlawful conduct."[21]

a. Challenges Based on the OIG's Lack of Authority

There is little question that the OIG for HHS has been authorized to issue administrative demands for documents or testimony. The Inspector General Act of 1978,[22] as amended in 1988, confers broad powers upon the Office of Inspector General "to prevent and detect fraud and abuse"[23] within the Medicare and Medicaid programs.[24] To carry out these duties, OIG is authorized "to require by subpoena the production of all information, documents, reports, answers, records, accounts, papers, and other data and documentary evidence" necessary to perform its assigned functions.[25] Unlike the investigative authority of some administrative agencies,[26] the subpoena power of the Inspector General for HHS is not confined to issuing subpoenas for documents. OIG investigators are expressly authorized to compel testimony under oath as well. Moreover, relative to the grand jury, the OIG enjoys wide freedom to share

---

20. See United States v. LaSalle Natl. Bank, 437 U.S. 298, 317–18, 98 S.Ct. 2357, 2367–68, 57 L.Ed.2d 221, 236 (1978).

21. United States v. Bank of Moulton, 614 F.2d 1063, 1066 (5th Cir.1980); SEC v. ESM Govt. Securities, 645 F.2d 310, 317 (5th Cir.1981). See also Medic House, 736 F. Supp. at 1539 (citing ESM approvingly).

22. 5 U.S.C.A. App. 3 §§ 1–11.

23. See also 5 U.S.C.App. 3 § 2(2)(B).

24. See the Inspector General Act of 1978, 5 U.S.C.A. App. 3 § 2. The Act was enacted to address concerns that fraud, waste, and abuse in federal departments and agencies were "reaching epidemic proportions." S. Rep. No. 1071 1, 4, 95th Cong., 2d Sess. (1978), reprinted in 1978 U.S. Code Cong. & Admin. News 2676, 2676. To investigate such fraud and abuse, Congress established fifteen "independent and objective" Offices of Inspector General who were authorized to:

"conduct and supervise audits and investigations relating to the programs and operations of the [specified departments and agencies]; (2) to provide leadership and coordination and recommend policies for activities designed (A) to promote economy, efficiency, and effectiveness in the administration of, and (B) to prevent and detect fraud and abuse in, such programs and operations; and (3) to provide a means for keeping the head of the establishment and the Congress fully and currently informed about problems and deficiencies relating to the administration of such programs and operations and the necessity for and progress of corrective action. 5 U.S.C.A. App. 3 § 2.

25. 5 U.S.C.A. App. 3 § 6(a).

26. Inspector General Act of 1978, S.Rep. No. 95–1071, 95th Cong., 2d Sess 2679 (1978); 5 U.S.C.A. app. §§ 2–3, 9. See also United States v. Iannone, 610 F.2d 943, 945 (D.C.Cir.1979) (Department of Energy Inspector General may not compel the attendance of witnesses).

the substance of any such testimony with other government agencies, including United States Attorneys, who may use it as a basis for initiating a criminal investigation.[27] In the event that a subpoenaed party refuses to comply with an administrative demand for documents or testimony, an order of enforcement may be sought from "any appropriate United States district court."[28]

While it is not improper for the OIG to issue a subpoena when a criminal proceeding is likely, or to refer a case to the Department of Justice for prosecution while continuing to use its own subpoena power to investigate further for civil and administrative investigatory purposes, an abuse of the court's process might be found if the OIG continued to exercise its subpoena power to collect evidence of criminal activity after it had referred the case to the Department of Justice.[29] Health care providers who have challenged the OIG's authority to issue an administrative subpoena in connection with an investigation of criminal wrongdoing before such a referral, however, have been unsuccessful.[30]

b. Challenges Based on Relevance

To be valid an administrative subpoena duces tecum must call for records that are reasonably relevant to the agency's investigation.[31] The OIG enjoys wide latitude in determining questions of relevancy, and its power to issue subpoenas will not readily be restricted by forecasts of the probable result of its investigations.[32] Like those issued by the grand jury,[33] administrative subpoenas are presumed to be valid, and the burden to demonstrate irrelevance is on the person challenging the subpoena.[34] Because an agency can-

---

27. See Medic House, 736 F.Supp. at 1537 ("While Rule 6(e) prevents disclosure of what is presented to the grand jury, it does not prevent an OIG agent from disclosing to prosecutors, other agencies or a grand jury what the agent has discovered."). See also 5 U.S.C.A. App. 3 § 4(d) (West Supp. 1995) (directing the OIG to report to the Attorney General whenever the Inspector General has reasonable grounds to suspect a violation of federal criminal law).

28. 5 U.S.C.A. App. 3 § 6(a).

29. United States v. LaSalle National Bank, 437 U.S. 298, 312, 98 S.Ct. 2357, 2365, 57 L.Ed.2d 221, 233 (1978).

30. See Medic House, 736 F. Supp. at 1535 (the Inspector General is authorized to conduct criminal investigations and issue subpoenas in conjunction with those investigations); United States v. Educational Dev. Network Corp., 884 F.2d 737, 740–44 (3d Cir. 1989) (same);

United States v. Aero Mayflower Transit Co., 831 F.2d 1142, 1145 (D.C.Cir.1987) (the Inspector General enjoys coextensive civil and criminal subpoena power).

31. Medic House, 736 F. Supp. at 1535.

32. Oklahoma Press Publishing Co. v. Walling, 327 U.S. 186, 209, 216, 66 S.Ct. 494, 506, 509, 90 L.Ed. 614, 630, 634 (1946) (quoting Blair v. United States, 250 U.S. 273, 282, 39 S.Ct. 468, 471, 63 L.Ed. 979 (1919).

33. See §§ 7–12b and 7–13.

34. Civil Aeronautics Bd. v. Hermann, 353 U.S. 322, 323, 77 S.Ct. 804, 805, 1 L.Ed.2d 852 (1957). In addition, some courts have held that their role in a proceeding to enforce an administrative subpoena is "extremely limited," In re McVane, 44 F.3d 1127, 1135 (2d Cir. 1995) (quoting NLRB v. C.C.C. Assoc., Inc., 306 F.2d 534, 538 (2d Cir.1962); FTC v. Rockefeller, 591 F.2d at 182 (2d

not be expected to know the precise nature of a target's wrongful conduct (if any) at the time it issues a subpoena for documents or testimony, relevance is construed broadly in the agency's favor.[35] Indeed, some courts have gone so far as to hold that an administrative subpoena that seeks "required records" (records a business is required by law to keep) cannot be questioned on grounds of relevancy.[36]

c. Challenges Based on Breadth and Burdensomeness

Unlike relevancy claims, overbreadth and burdensomeness claims challenge the reasonableness of the *number* of documents demanded by the government, rather than the reasonableness of the nature of the documents sought. A motion to quash based on burdensomeness will normally allege that compliance with the agency's voluminous demand for documents will cripple or otherwise unduly impede the subpoenaed party's ability to continue to operate,[37] while a motion based on an overbreadth claim will allege that the demanded documents span an unreasonable period of time.[38] Both challenges are evaluated by the courts under the Fourth Amendment's reasonableness requirement.

If it can be shown that a subpoena deposits an oppressive and unjustified burden on the shoulders of a subpoenaed party, or that the demand appears excessive relative to its justification, a court may either refuse to issue an enforcement order, or alternatively, may order that the request be modified.[39]

Cir. 1979), and that an agency's appraisal of relevancy "must be accepted so long as it is not obviously wrong." In re McVane, 44 F.3d at 1135.

35. See, e.g., In re McVane, 44 F.3d at 1135; United States v. Arthur Young & Co., 677 F.2d 211, 216 (2d Cir.1982) ("[b]efore the IRS knows where the issues lie, it has no choice but to utilize a general summons"), aff'd in part and rev'd in part on other grounds, 465 U.S. 805, 104 S.Ct. 1495, 79 L.Ed.2d 826 (1984), cert. denied, 466 U.S. 936, 104 S.Ct. 1906, 80 L.Ed.2d 456 (1984); United States v. Noall, 587 F.2d 123, 125 (2d Cir.1978) (standard for relevance satisfied where the documents "might have thrown light upon" the object of the investigation), cert. denied, 441 U.S. 923, 99 S.Ct. 2031, 60 L.Ed.2d 396 (1979).

36. Cf. Craib v. Bulmash, 49 Cal.3d 475, 485, 261 Cal.Rptr. 686, 693, 777 P.2d 1120 (1989).

37. See, e.g., In re Grand Jury Subpoenas Duces Tecum Dated January 30, 1986, 638 F.Supp. 794, 795–96 (D. Maine 1986); Wisconsin v. Hazel Washington, 83 Wis.2d 808, 844, 266 N.W.2d 597, 615 (Wis. 1978); New York v. Doe, 126 Misc.2d 1010, 484 N.Y.S.2d 759, 761 (Sup. Ct. Queens County 1984); In re Special Investigation No. 281, 299 Md. 181, 473 A.2d 1, 6–7 (Md.Ct.App.1984).

38. Cf. D'Alimonte v. Kuriansky, 144 A.D.2d 737, 535 N.Y.S.2d 151, 152 (3d Dep't 1988) (finding overbroad a grand jury subpoena that contained no time limitation). But see Medic House, 736 F. Supp. at 1535–36 (rejecting argument that administrative subpoena duces tecum issued to provider of diabetic supplies to nursing homes was vague, unduly burdensome and would disrupt the provider's business operations).

39. Cf. D'Alimonte, 535 N.Y.S.2d at 152 (quashing grand jury subpoena that contained no time limitation).

§ 7–22. Administrative Subpoenas for Personal Records

The *Morton Salt* standard[1] has been applied to administrative subpoenas seeking personal as well as corporate records.[2] Some courts have been reluctant, however to enforce an agency subpoena that seeks the personal records of a person who is not the target of the agency's investigation.[3] In such a case, the agency may be required to demonstrate some need for the material.[4] In drawing a distinction between corporate and personal records, the courts will generally look to "who prepared the document, the nature of its contents, its purpose or use, who maintained possession and who had access to it, whether the corporation required its preparation, and whether its existence was necessary to the conduct of the corporation's business."[5] With this fairly limited exception, there appears to be little difference between the standards used to examine the validity of administrative subpoenas and the standards used to determine the validity of grand jury subpoenas for the purposes of enforcement.

§ 7–23. Administrative Searches

In addition to being the unhappy recipients of grand jury and administrative subpoenas, from time to time health care providers have also been the subjects of administrative searches commonly referred to as "administrative inspections." Administrative searches within the health care industry generally occur pursuant to state[1] or federal statute.[2] A health care provider may challenge

---

§ 7–22

1. United States v. Morton Salt Co., 338 U.S. 632, 70 S.Ct. 357, 94 L.Ed. 401 (1950)

2. Cf. United States v. Stuart, 489 U.S. 353, 109 S.Ct. 1183, 103 L.Ed.2d 388 (1989) (applying relevance test to IRS investigation of individuals' tax returns); Resolution Trust Corp. v. Walde, 18 F.3d 943, 946–47 (D.C.Cir.1994) (applying test to subpoena for personal financial information of former directors of failed saving and loan institutions).

3. In re McVane, 44 F.3d at 1137.

4. See id. ("[W]e conclude that administrative subpoenas issued pursuant to an agency investigation into corporate wrongdoing, which seek personal records of persons who are not themselves targets of the investigation and whose connection to the investigation consists only of their family ties to corporate participants, must face more exacting scrutiny than similar subpoenas seeking records solely from corporate partici-

pants. With regard to subpoenas seeking such material, we conclude, 'an administrative agency is not automatically entitled to obtain all material that may in some way be relevant to a proper investigation. Rather ... the agency must make some showing of need for the material sought beyond its mere relevance to a proper investigation.' ") (quoting Federal Election Comm'n v. Larouche Campaign, 817 F.2d 233, 234 (2d Cir. 1987) (per curiam)).

5. In re Grand Jury Subpoena Duces Tecum Dated April 23, 1981, Witness v. United States, 657 F.2d 5, 8 (2d Cir. 1981); see also United States v. Wujkowski, 929 F.2d 981, 984 (4th Cir.1991).

§ 7–23

1. See, e.g., Section 1, Act. 105, Session Laws of the State of Hawaii, amending Chap. 346 of Hawaii Rev. Stat. See also Hawaii Psychiatric Society v. Ariyoshi, 481 F.Supp. 1028 (D.Hawaii 1979) (enjoining enforcement of the statute).

such a search either on the ground that the statute that authorized the search is unconstitutional on its face,[3] or that the search itself violated some constitutional or other right.[4]

The Supreme Court has drawn an important distinction between searches conducted for criminal purposes, discussed above,[5] and searches conducted for noncriminal or regulatory purposes. When the government conducts a search for traditional law enforcement purposes—to gather evidence of the commission of a crime—a warrant is presumptively required, the warrant will be issued only upon a showing of probable cause, and the Fourth Amendment's particularity requirement will limit the warrant's reach.[6] Where, however, a search is conducted for administrative purposes—"to curtail various other types of conduct considered to be against the public interest"[7]—less stringent standards apply. As governmental regulation of particular industries has expanded, so too has the need for official entry upon and inspection of commercial property to ensure compliance with those regulatory standards. In recognition of this need, the courts have upheld administrative inspections of business establishments operating within certain "pervasively regulated" industries,[8] such as the health care system.[9] The loss of privacy that results from these routine inspections has been justified by the idea that persons who choose to participate in such a highly regulated industry do so with the knowledge that they will be subject to routine, periodic inspection, and therefore have a

2. See, e.g., 21 U.S.C.A. § 880(d) of Federal Drug Abuse Prevention and Control Act of 1970, which permits the issuance of a warrant authorizing an administrative inspection and seizures.

3. See, e.g., Hawaii Psychiatric Society v. Ariyoshi, 481 F.Supp. 1028, 1035 (action to enjoin enforcement of state statute that authorized the issuance of administrative inspection warrants to search records of Medicaid providers). See also United States v. Schiffman, 572 F.2d 1137, 1139–41 (5th Cir.1978) (challenging constitutionality of federal provision that authorized the issuance of administrative warrant to inspect and seize pharmaceutical records).

4. See, e.g., United States v. Prendergast, 585 F.2d 69 (3d Cir.1978) (pharmacist seeks suppression of evidence taken pursuant to administrative warrant on ground that no probable cause existed to justify the warrant).

5. See § 7–19.

6. See § 7–19a–e.

7. C. Whitebread & C. Slobogin, Criminal Procedure 267 (2d ed. 1986).

8. See, e.g., New York v. Burger, 482 U.S. 691, 107 S.Ct. 2636, 96 L.Ed.2d 601 (1987) (automobile junkyard dealers); United States v. Biswell, 406 U.S. 311, 92 S.Ct. 1593, 32 L.Ed.2d 87 (1972) (firearms dealers); Colonnade Catering Corp. v. United States, 397 U.S. 72, 90 S.Ct. 774, 25 L.Ed.2d 60 (1970) (liquor industry).

9. See, e.g., United States v. Voorhies, M.D., 663 F.2d at 30 (6th Cir. 1981) (upholding inspection and seizure of physician's patient medication cards pursuant to an administrative warrant); Schiffman, 572 F.2d at 1142 (the pharmaceutical industry is a pervasively regulated industry subject to administrative inspections to ensure that drugs are distributed only through accepted channels and not diverted to unlawful uses). But see Hawaii Psychiatric Society v. Ariyoshi, 481 F.Supp. 1028, 1050 (D.Hawaii 1979) (administrative searches of psychiatrists' confidential files may not be justified as regulation of pervasively regulated industry).

diminished expectation of privacy in their businesses and their business trappings.[10]

As a general matter, although an administrative search does implicate the Fourth Amendment, it need not proceed solely upon the existence of probable cause, a standard "peculiarly related to criminal investigations,"[11] nor even upon a showing of suspicious activity.[12] Rather, most courts have relaxed the individualized suspicion requirement that attends criminal searches, and allowed administrative inspections to take place where there is a "valid public interest" to conduct the inspection.[13]

§ 7–24.   The Problem of Subterfuge

Difficulties may arise, however, if it appears that the government is attempting to do an end run around the Fourth Amendment, by calling a criminal search an administrative inspection. A statutory scheme conferring authority to carry out administrative inspections will be valid only if its primary purpose is regulatory and not criminal,[1] and the courts have repeatedly considered allegations that governmental agents have taken advantage of the lesser threshold requirements of administrative warrants to conduct what are in fact searches for evidence of criminality.

Determining whether a purported administrative inspection is in truth a search for criminal evidence, is a difficult task, as both the state[2] and federal[3] courts have discovered. The facts of *Commonwealth v. Slaton*[4] illustrate. In *Slaton*, the Supreme Court of Pennsylvania considered the propriety of a warrantless search of a pharmacy conducted by narcotics agents designated by the Secretary of the state's Department of Health. After the search, Slaton, the proprietor of the pharmacy, moved the trial court to suppress all of the evidence taken in the search on the ground that the warrantless search violated the Fourth and Fourteenth Amend-

---

10. See New York v. Burger, 482 U.S. at 701, 107 S.Ct. at 2643, 96 L.Ed.2d at 613.

11. Colorado v. Bertine, 479 U.S. 367, 371, 107 S.Ct. 738, 741, 93 L.Ed.2d 739, 745 (1987) quoting South Dakota v. Opperman, 428 U.S. 364, 370 n. 5, 96 S.Ct. 3092, 3097 n. 5, 49 L.Ed.2d 1000, 1006 n. 5.

12. See United States v. Voorhies, 663 F.2d at 33.

13. See, e.g., Prendergast, 585 F.2d at 70 ("Probable cause in the criminal law sense is not required to support the issuance of an administrative warrant."); United States v. Schiffman, 572 F.2d at 1140 (federal law permits the issuance of an administrative search warrant where there is a valid public interest to do so).

§ 7–24

1. See New York v. Burger, 482 U.S. at 702 (an administrative inspection scheme must be designed to further regulatory objectives in order to be constitutionally valid); Donovan v. Dewey, 452 U.S. 594, 600, 101 S.Ct. 2534, 2539, 69 L.Ed.2d 262, 270 (1981) (same).

2. See, e.g., Commonwealth v. Slaton, 530 Pa. 207, 608 A.2d 5 (1992).

3. See, e.g., United States v. Nechy, 827 F.2d 1161 (7th Cir.1987) (Posner, J.).

4. 530 Pa. 207, 608 A.2d 5 (1992).

ments. In defense of the search, the Commonwealth argued that the agents had acted under authority of a statute that permitted warrantless administrative entries and inspections by designated officers at any reasonable time.[5] The state court rejected this characterization of the agents' conduct in light of the fact that the agents had "never claimed to have any administrative purpose, but instead, declared at the outset that their desire was to gather additional information for an ongoing criminal investigation."[6] The court concluded that, unlike an administrative inspection conducted on a regular basis, the agents had intended to conduct a search for criminal evidence, which, in the absence of Slaton's consent, violated traditional Fourth Amendment warrant requirements.[7]

Slaton rightly suggests that where it can be shown that a purported administrative inspection is carried out for criminal, rather than civil or regulatory purposes, all of the protections of the Fourth Amendment should apply, including the warrant requirement, the requirement of probable cause and compliance with the particularity requirement. However, the court may have been too quick to conclude that an agent's desire to find evidence of criminal activity in and of itself converts an otherwise proper administrative inspection into an improper search for criminal evidence.

In a case involving similar facts,[8] the United States Court of Appeals for the Seventh Circuit reached the opposite conclusion. In *United States v. Nechy*, a DEA compliance investigator (responsible for the civil enforcement of federal narcotics provisions in Wisconsin and Illinois) obtained an administrative warrant to inspect and seize records found in a Milwaukee pharmacy.[9] Before seeking the warrant, the investigator had participated in a criminal investigation of the pharmacy and had recommended criminal prosecution, although no prosecution ensued. Upon receipt of the warrant, several federal compliance investigators searched the pharmacy and seized numerous items including prescription records, receipts and other documents related to the pharmacy's purchase and distribution of Talwin, an analgesic sometimes unlawfully used as a substitute for heroin. After the search, pharmacist Michael Nechy moved

---

5. See id. at 211, 608 A.2d at 7.

6. Id. at 214, 608 A.2d at 8.

7. See id. at 213–15, 608 A.2d at 8–9.

8. See United States v. Nechy, 827 F.2d 1161 (7th Cir.1987).

9. The warrant was issued under 21 U.S.C.A. § 880, which authorizes entry into premises where controlled substances or records thereof are maintained, (see § 880(a)), "for the purpose of inspecting, copying, and verifying the correctness of records, reports, or other documents required to be kept or made"

under Title 21. See id. at 1163, 21 U.S.C.A. § 880(b)(1). Federal magistrates are authorized to issue warrants authorizing such an entry and seizure upon a showing of "a valid public interest in the effective enforcement of [Title 21] or regulations thereof sufficient to justify administrative inspections of the area, premises, building, or conveyance, or contents thereof." 21 U.S.C.A. § 880(d)(1). Probable cause to believe that the search will reveal evidence of a crime is not required.

to suppress the items taken during the search on the ground that the investigators' so-called inspection was simply a subterfuge for a search for criminal evidence.[10] While acknowledging that the investigators' "ulterior purpose" was to search for evidence of a crime,[11] the Seventh Circuit nonetheless upheld the search. The court reasoned that, as long as the principal violators of Title 21's record-keeping obligations are pharmacies engaged in illegal drug trafficking activities, investigators will always have such a motive.[12] Hence, where "a search is objectively reasonable, the motives of the officers conducting it will not turn it into a violation of the Fourth Amendment."[13] Upon this reasoning, the Seventh Circuit upheld the trial court's denial of the motion to suppress.

The reasoning in *Nechy* is consistent with the current approach of the United States Supreme Court to claims of pretextual motivation in law enforcement. In several notable decisions, the Supreme Court has indicated that it will not scrutinize the internal thought-processes of law enforcement agents if their conduct is objectively reasonable.[14] Thus, as long as officers act within the bounds of their authority, their subjective motivations will be considered largely irrelevant.

In the final analysis, the most important difference between the *Slaton* and *Nechy* may come down to the fact that in the former, the agents conducted the search without seeking a warrant, whereas in the latter, the statute imposed a duty to obtain a warrant first. A warrant requirement is significant even if the prerequisites for an administrative warrant are not as onerous as the prerequisites for a criminal search warrant. In both scenarios a neutral magistrate uninvolved in the enterprise of ferreting out crime or other wrongdoing will be interposed between the citizen and the agent seeking the authority to search. Even if the standard for issuing the warrant is less than probable cause (as is the case for administrative warrants), the potential subject will benefit from having an impartial eye consider whether a valid public interest for the search is supported by the facts known to the agent. Because

---

10. See id. at 1164.

11. Id. at 1166.

12. The court wrote:

The purpose of the requirement makes it inevitable that the government agencies that enforce it will be hoping to obtain evidence for use in criminal proceedings; but since Nechy does not question the lawfulness of the record-keeping requirement, he can hardly insist that it be enforced only against pharmacists not suspected of illegal conduct.

Id. at 1167.

13. Id.

14. See Whren v. United States, ___ U.S. ___, 116 S.Ct. 1769, 1774, 135 L.Ed.2d 89 (1996) ("subjective intentions play no role in ordinary, probable-cause Fourth Amendment analysis"); Horton v. California, 496 U.S. 128, 138, 110 S.Ct. 2301, 2308–09, 110 L.Ed.2d 112, 124 (1990) ("[E]venhanded law enforcement is best achieved by the application of objective standards of conduct, rather than standards that depend upon the subjective state of mind of the officer.").

the statute in *Slaton* authorized warrantless inspection, agents were excused from having to submit to such a prophylactic review. Thus, a better reasoned justification for the *Slaton* suppression order would be that the agents' were wrongly permitted to forego necessary pre-search review.[15]

15. See Camara v. Municipal Court, 387 U.S. 523, 87 S.Ct. 1727, 18 L.Ed.2d 930 (1967) (although the meaning of probable cause can vary with the context, a statute that authorizes city inspectors to conduct warrantless administrative inspections of buildings lacked traditional safeguards which the Fourth Amendment guarantees). See also United States v. Lawson, 502 F.Supp. 158, 165 (D. Maryland 1980) (federal law mandating warrants for administrative inspections of pharmacy records was enacted in response to *Camara*).

Chapter 8

SENTENCING CONSIDERATIONS
FOR HEALTH CARE FRAUD
OFFENDERS

Table of Sections

WESTLAW Electronic Research

See WESTLAW Electronic Research Guide preceding the Summary of Contents.

Library References:

West's Key No. Digests, Social Security and Public Welfare ⚷18.

§ 8–1.　Introduction

The criminal, civil and administrative liability of a Medicare or Medicaid fraud offender, particularly an organizational offender, can wreak havoc on the provider's ability to continue to operate within the health care marketplace. Fines and civil monetary penalties can quickly add up to the millions of dollars. If followed by an order of exclusion, often referred to within the industry as "economic death," the blow suffered by a provider can be fatal. In addition, state and federal criminal sentencing provisions will frequently place individual offenders behind bars, sometimes for years. In light of these severe sentencing realities, health care providers will be well advised to take steps to protect themselves against burgeoning and potentially lethal sentencing exposures.

This chapter addresses the serious sentencing concerns that any target of a health care fraud investigation or prosecution is likely to have. The chapter begins with a discussion of the Federal Sentencing Guidelines. It examines how the Guidelines have changed the way in which the courts fashion the sentences of providers prosecuted federally. The Guideline provisions relevant to individual health care providers and organizational defendants are considered separately. Examples of the application of the Guidelines are included, as well as a review of recent caselaw reflecting how the courts have resolved particular disputes arising under the Guidelines in health care fraud cases.

The chapter also explores the steps a defendant can take to minimize the defendant's sentencing exposure. For individual defendants, reductions based on role in the offense, acceptance of responsibility and cooperation with law enforcement authorities are considered. Also discussed is the dramatic sentencing reducing effect an effective corporate compliance program can have on the sentencing exposure of an organizational defendant.

Finally considered are the multitude of sanctions that can accumulate in health care fraud cases where parallel criminal and civil proceedings are the frequently the norm. The chapter examines the protection that may be afforded by the Double Jeopardy Clause of the Fifth Amendment to providers who are forced to defend themselves on a multitude of fronts. The constitutional shield provided by the Eighth Amendment's Ex Post Facto Clause is also considered.

§ 8–2. The Federal Sentencing Guidelines—An Overview

In the Sentencing Reform Act of 1984,[1] Congress mandated the creation of the United States Sentencing Commission to propose guidelines for a comprehensive federal sentencing scheme which would further the four recognized purposes of criminal punishment: deterrence, incapacitation, just punishment and rehabilitation. The Sentencing Reform Act directed the Sentencing Commission to create categories of offense and offender characteristics, and to prescribe guideline ranges specifying the sentence that should be imposed on a defendant who engages in specific offense conduct in light of the defendant's particular offender characteristics. The Sentencing Commission promulgated its first set of guidelines, known as the United States Sentencing Guidelines, in April 1987. Initially, the guidelines were adopted to guide the sentencing decisions of federal judges as to individual defendants convicted in the federal courts. The Guidelines for individual defendants took effect on November 1, 1987.[2] Four years later, the Sentencing Commission enacted a second set of guidelines, effective November 1, 1991, to address the sentencing of organizational defendants convicted of federal offenses.[3] Together, these guidelines govern the sentencing options available to a federal sentencing judge who presides over the sentence of a convicted health care provider or entity.

§ 8–3. The Federal Sentencing Guidelines for Individuals

The basic philosophy of the Federal Sentencing Guidelines for individuals is deceptively straightforward. The Guidelines are premised on the notion that appropriate criminal sentences can be fashioned only after taking two things into account: the nature of a defendant's conduct and the defendant's past (if any) criminal history. In practice, the Guidelines are far from straightforward. Indeed, the proper application of the guideline provisions has the

§ 8–2

1. See The Sentencing Reform Act of 1984, (Title II of the Comprehensive

Crime Control Act of 1984), 28 U.S.C. § 994(a).

2. See U.S.S.G., ch. 1 through 7.

3. See U.S.S.G. ch. 8.

subject of uninterrupted, heated dispute.[1] Since the adoption of the Guidelines, the federal courts of appeal have devoted increasing portions of their dockets to resolve Guideline disputes. Notwithstanding this controversy, it certainly appears that the Guidelines are here to stay. Thus, counsel who represent or advise persons or entities with possible federal criminal exposure are well advised themselves to master the guideline provisions, and to keep abreast of the mounting caselaw interpreting those provisions.[2]

Although an in depth treatment of the Guidelines is outside the scope of this treatise, a basic understanding of the Guidelines (what they are and how they apply) may be helpful to a health care provider who is being investigated or prosecuted for a federal health care offense.

The Federal Sentencing Guidelines seek the imposition of determinative, uniform and proportional sentences. The Guidelines restrict the discretion of federal sentencing judges by requiring judges to utilize a formulaic sentencing approach and to impose upon a defendant a prison term and criminal fine that falls within a pre-determined range, subject only to applicable statutory maximums.[3] As might be expected, prescribed sentence ranges have not

§ 8–3

1. See, e.g., Frank O. Bowman, III, The Quality of Mercy Must be Restrained, and Other Lessons in Learning to Love the Federal Sentencing Guidelines, 1996 Wis.L.Rev. 679 (1996); William J. Powell and Michael T. Cimino, Prosecutorial Discretion Under the Federal Sentencing Guidelines: Is the Fox Guarding the Hen House? 97 W.Va. L.Rev. 373 (1997); Note, The Ills of the Federal Sentencing Guidelines and the Search for a Cure: Using Sentencing Entrapment to Combat Governmental Manipulation of Sentencing, 49 Vand. L.Rev. 197 (January 1996).

2. Many resources are available for further study in this area. Every year the Mercer Law Review surveys additions to the guideline provisions and important Eleventh Circuit cases addressing myriad issues arising under the Guidelines. See e.g., Andrea Wilson, Federal Sentencing Guidelines, 46 Mercer L. Rev. 1395 (Spring 1996). Another very helpful resource is the Federal Sentencing Guideline Reporter which summarizes case law related to the Guidelines. In addition, several excellent articles address particular provisions of the Sentencing Guidelines in great depth. See e.g., Dana H. Freyer, Corporate Compliance Programs for

FDA–Regulated Companies: Incentives for Their Development and the Impact of the Federal Sentencing Guidelines for Organizations, 51 Food and Drug L. J. 225 (1996); Karla R. Spaulding, "An Ounce of Prevention is Worth a Pound of Cure" Federal Sentencing Guidelines for Organizations, 42 Fed. Law. 35 (Sept. 1995); Charles H. Roistacher and Catherine M. Cook, Federal Sentencing Guidelines and Organizational Defendants, 41 Fed. B. News & J. 416 (July 1994).

3. Most of the statutes under which persons accused of health care fraud or abuse are prosecuted prescribe a maximum imprisonment term of five years. See e.g., 18 U.S.C. § 287 (false claims); 18 U.S.C. § 1001 (false statements); 18 U.S.C. § 371 (conspiracy); 18 U.S.C. §§ 1341 and 1343 (mail and wire fraud) and 42 U.S.C. 1320a–7b (kickbacks). There are important exceptions, however. Providers convicted of money laundering are subject to a maximum imprisonment term of 20 years, per count. See 18 U.S.C. §§ 1956 and 1957. The health care fraud statute enacted in 1996 carries a 10–year maximum prison term. See HIPAA, Pub. L. No. 104–191, 110 Stat. 1936, Title II, § 242, codified at 18 U.S.C. § 1347. These statutes also permit the imposition of a fine on an indi-

received a warm welcome in all circles. In particular, the loss of sentencing discretion caused by the Guidelines has evoked the ire of many federal jurists.[4]

As they have with all federal offenders, the Guideline's restrictions on sentencing discretion have had a noticeable effect on the sentences imposed on health care offenders. The following passage contained within the sentencing memorandum decision of one judge illustrates the difference in outcome a health care provider might experience if sentenced by a post-Guidelines court from that which he might have experienced pre-Guidelines.

> Prior to the Federal Sentencing Guidelines, a judge could have taken the position that eight months is a substantial sentence for a defendant like Dr. Skodnek. He is, after all, a first offender, much of whose life had been spent caring for patients as a psychiatrist. He is charged with a non-violent crime. In days past, this Court would have been able to focus solely on Skodnek as an individual offender. This judge could have decided that for this defendant, whose career as a psychiatrist had been ruined, walking into a penal institution for the first time, hearing the doors clank shut behind him, would be devastating, and further, that it would not take nearly seven years of taxpayers' money to effect his rehabilitation or to deter others from the sort of misconduct of which Skodnek was convicted. However, these are not pre-Guidelines days.[5]

In addition to setting pre-determined sentencing ranges, the Guidelines abolished the system of parole that formerly existed in the federal criminal justice system. Under the (now defunct) parole system, a parole board would decide how much of the sentence imposed by a federal judge the defendant would actually serve. The Guidelines did away with the operation of the parole board, leaving sentencing decisions in the (somewhat tied) hands of federal sentencing judges. Without the possibility of parole, any term of imprisonment imposed upon a defendant at sentencing, is the sentence the defendant will serve,[6] giving meaning to the now familiar phrase "truth in sentencing."

vidual defendant of up to $250,000 per count, and on an organizational defendant of up to $500,000 per count. See 18 U.S.C. § 3571(c).

4. See, e.g., United States v. Skodnek, 933 F.Supp. 1108, 1110–1111 (D.Mass.1996) ("In order to homogenize sentencing, courts are obliged to apply rigid categories to what is or should be an individualized decision, rather than to exercise broad discretion and judgment.").

5. Id. at 1110. The court sentenced Skodnek to a 46 month prison term. Id. at 1122.

6. The only exception to this determinate sentencing scheme is that the defendant may be eligible to reduce any prison term by approximately fifteen percent for good behavior (after the defendant served one year of that term).

In the "silver lining" department, health care providers facing possible criminal sentences under the Federal Sentencing Guidelines should be able to predict their criminal exposure with greater certainty. For all of the Guidelines' alleged faults, the provisions do make it easier for informed counsel to foretell the sentence that will be imposed upon a provider for a particular offense. The ability to predict sentencing outcomes may in turn assist the development of effective defense strategies. With this greater ability to predict the outcome, however, comes the realization that post-Guidelines health care offenders may face steeper fines and penalties and a greater chance of serving some term of incarceration than ever before.

§ 8–4. Calculating an Individual Defendant's Offense Level

Formulaic sentencing calculations, now a routine matter throughout the federal courts, find their genesis in the Federal Sentencing Guidelines Manual. The Guidelines Manual has become a necessary component of any criminal lawyer's library. Counsel for health care providers as well have increasing added the annually updated manual to their collections. With the help of the Guidelines Manual, a provider's criminal exposure becomes fairly knowable.

a. Finding the Applicable Base Offense Level

To determine a particular individual defendant's sentence, a federal sentencing court will look first to the provisions set forth in Chapter 2 of the Federal Sentencing Guidelines Manual to determine the category (or categories) of offense conduct most applicable to the defendant's count (or counts) of conviction. Chapter 2 is divided into several parts, each of which pertains to a particular category of offense, including, for example, offenses against the person,[1] offenses against property,[2] offenses involving public officials,[3] offenses involving drugs,[4] offenses involving criminal enterprises and racketeering,[5] offenses involving fraud and deceit,[6] and so forth. Once the sentencing court determines the category of offense under which the defendant's count of conviction falls, it will apply the prescribed guideline provisions that pertain to that offense category.

A simple hypothetical may be useful to illustrate how this process works. Let us suppose that a physician stands convicted of submitting a false claim to the Medicare program, a violation of 18 U.S.C. § 287. To begin its guidelines calculation process, the sen-

§ 8–4

1. See U.S.S.G. Ch.2, Pt.A.
2. See U.S.S.G. Ch.2, Pt.B.
3. See U.S.S.G. Ch.2, Pt.C.
4. See U.S.S.G. Ch.2, Pt.D.
5. See U.S.S.G. Ch.2, Pt.E.
6. See U.S.S.G. Ch.2, Pt.F.

tencing court will first determine the category of offense that best fits the physician's false claims conviction—this will almost certainly be the category of "offenses involving fraud and deceit."[7] Next, the court will ascertain the "base offense level" (BOL) that has been prescribed by the Sentencing Commission for offenses involving fraud or deceit.[8] The base offense level for offenses involving fraud or deceit is a level 6.[9]

b.   Accounting for Specific Offense Characteristics

After determining the applicable base offense level, the court will decide whether an upward adjustment of the BOL is warranted. The court will adjust an offender's BOL upwards if something about the crime, commonly referred to as a "specific offense characteristic," makes the BOL worthy of enhancement. Each category of offense carries its own possible specific offense characteristics. Under the fraud or deceit guideline a number of specific offense characteristics may lead to an increase in an offender's offense level. For instance, the court might upwardly adjust our hypothetical physician's BOL in proportion to the extent of the loss caused by the offense.[10] It might also add additional levels if the crime involved "more than minimal planning" or more than one victim,[11] if the physician violated a judicial or administrative order, injunction, decree, or other process,[12] or if the offense involved a con-

---

7. See U.S.S.G. Ch.2, Pt.F.

8. See U.S.S.G. § 2F1.1. The Guidelines Manual includes a BOL for each category of offense. Thus, the process of determining the BOL for a particular offense category is a simple exercise in turning to the page in the Manual that relates to that category, and reading the BOL that has been pre-determined by the Sentencing Commission.

9. See U.S.S.G. § 2F1.1(a).

10. See U.S.S.G. § 2F1.1(b)(1). Adjustments based on the amount of the loss involved in the offense can significantly enhance an offender's offense level. Pursuant to a table set forth in the guideline, see id., additional levels may be added to the base offense level depending on the amount of the loss.

11. See U.S.S.G. § 2F1.1(b)(2)(A) and (B). The phrase "more than minimal planning" is satisfied "in any case involving repeated acts over a period of time, unless it is clear that each instance was purely opportune." See U.S.S.G. § 1B1.1, Application Note 1(f). The inherent complexity of fraudulent billing schemes and unlawful kickback arrange-

ments have resulted in frequent application of the "more than minimal planning" provision to health care providers. See, e.g., United States v. Adam, 70 F.3d 776, 779 (4th Cir.1995) (upholding minimal planning adjustment imposed on internist who accepted kickbacks for referrals from a cardiologist with whom he shared office); United States v. Henry, 12 F.3d 215, 1993 WL 492302 at 9 (6th Cir.1993) (approving more than minimal planning enhancement for administrator of a home health agency who engaged in repeated acts to make and conceal false statements contained within a Medicare cost report); United States v. Abud–Sanchez, 973 F.2d 835, 837 (10th Cir.1992) (upholding more than minimal planning points imposed on physician convicted of false claims violation); United States v. Romano, 970 F.2d 164 (6th Cir.1992) (operator of three medical clinics convicted of conspiracy, and multiple counts of Medicaid fraud, kickbacks, mail fraud and the unlawful distribution of controlled substances) United States v. Skodnek, 933 F.Supp. 1108, 1119 (D.Mass.1996) (psychiatrist).

12. See U.S.S.G. § 2F1.1(b)(3)(B).

scious or reckless risk of death or serious bodily injury.[13]

The facts of *United States v. Abud–Sanchez*,[14] illustrate how adjustments for specific offense characteristics can quickly lead to substantially increased sentencing exposure. In that case, Dr. Danilo Abud–Sanchez was named in a thirty-five count indictment on charges of filing false claims to the Medicare program. After the doctor pleaded guilty to one of those counts, the sentencing court added to the doctor's BOL of 6, a total of 8 additional levels—6 levels to account for the amount of loss caused by the offense, and 2 levels to account for the amount of planning involved in the offense.[15] Facing a significantly longer prison term as a result of the adjustments,[16] the doctor appealed, and the Tenth Circuit reversed and remanded for resentencing. The court agreed that the record demonstrated that the doctor's offense had involved "more than minimal planning," thereby warranting an upward adjustment by 2 levels of his BOL.[17] The court disagreed, however, that the government had sufficiently proven the amount of the actual or intended loss involved in the offense, since the government could not establish what percentage of the loss calculation stemmed from Abud–Sanchez's criminal, as opposed to civil, violations.[18]

---

13. See U.S.S.G. § 2F1.1(b)(4). See also United States v. Laughlin, 26 F.3d 1523, 1530 (10th Cir.1994) (conscious or reckless risk of serious bodily injury adjustment added where physician performed a medically unnecessary tubal ligation).

14. 973 F.2d 835 (10th Cir.1992).

15. See United States v. Abud–Sanchez, 973 F.2d 835, 837–40 (10th Cir. 1992).

16. The sentencing range for a first offender with an offense level of 6 (assuming no further adjustments or reductions) is 0–6 months imprisonment, which may be substituted by a probationary term. The sentencing range for a first offender with an offense level of 14 (assuming no further adjustments or reductions) is 15–21 months imprisonment, which may not be substituted by a term of probation. See U.S.S.G. Sentencing Table. Although unreflected in the published decision, the 4 month prison sentence actually imposed on Dr. Abud–Sanchez must have resulted from downward adjustments made by the sentencing court, such as a downward reduction for acceptance of responsibility to acknowledge Abud–Sanchez's plea. See § 8–4c(4).

17. 973 F.2d at 837. The following proof added up to more than minimal planning by the industrious doctor:

The record shows that Abud–Sanchez submitted numerous false billings involving many different patients, and that his fraudulent practices were aimed at three different federal programs with distinct billing procedures, different regulations, and coverage for different services. Moreover, the nature of the fraud varied: some billings were for services not performed at all; some for services done by a provider other than Dr. Abud–Sanchez; and some for services claimed to be performed when in fact other services were performed. Dr. Abud–Sanchez's staff was instructed to file fraudulent claims and threatened with job loss if they did not do so. He used the services of a friend to bring people in off the streets and from housing projects who were then hospitalized if they were eligible for an federal benefits program.

Id. at 837.

18. See id. at 839.

c. Chapter 3 Adjustments

Additional adjustments may be made to a defendant's offense level pursuant to the provisions of Chapter 3 of the Guidelines. These adjustment provisions seek to account for the characteristics of the victim (or victims) of the offense, the defendant's role in the offense, whether the defendant obstructed justice in any way in connection with the offense or its investigation, and whether the defendant accepted responsibility for the offense.

(1) Victim–Related Adjustments

The victim-related adjustment provisions of the Guidelines permit 2 levels to be added to an individual defendant's offense level if the defendant knew or should have known that the victim was unusually vulnerable due to age, physical or mental condition, or that the victim was otherwise unusually susceptible to the criminal conduct.[19] This provision can lead to an increased offense level for the health care provider who is shown to have victimized persons suffering an impaired ability to detect or prevent the provider's crime.[20]

(2) Role in the Offense Adjustments

Under the adjustment provisions for role in the offense,[21] a defendant's offense level may be increased by 4 levels if the defendant was an organizer or leader of a criminal scheme that involved five or more participants or was otherwise extensive;[22] by 3 levels if the defendant was a manager or supervisor of such a criminal venture;[23] or by 2 levels if the defendant was an organizer, leader, manager or supervisor of a less extensive criminal scheme.[24] Conversely, a defendant's offense level may be reduced by 4 levels if

---

19. See U.S.S.G. § 3A1.1.

20. See, e.g., United States v. Gill, 99 F.3d 484, 486–88 (1st Cir.1996) (upholding two level increase for victim vulnerability where defendant who falsely presented himself as a psychologist for mental health patients); United States v. Echevarria, 33 F.3d 175, 180–81 (2d Cir. 1994) (unlicensed doctor); United States v. Sims–Robertson, M.D., 16 F.3d 1223, 1994 WL 12212 at 16 (6th Cir.1994) (drug abusing or drug selling patients of medical clinic were vulnerable victims where the clinic dispensed prescriptions and controlled substances to the patients in exchange for blood samples billed to Medicaid); United States v. Bachynsky, 949 F.2d 722, 735–36 (5th Cir. 1991) (physician making false diagnoses), cert. denied, 506 U.S. 850, 113 S.Ct. 150, 121 L.Ed.2d 101 (1992).

21. See U.S.S.G. Ch.3, Pt.B.

22. See U.S.S.G. § 3B1.1(a).

23. See U.S.S.G. § 3B1.1(b). The courts consider a host of factors to determine whether a defendant was an organizer or leader (as opposed to a manager or supervisor) including "the exercise of decision making authority, the nature of participation in the commission of the offense, the recruitment of accomplices, the claimed right to a larger share of the fruits of the crime, the degree of participation in planning or organizing the offense, the nature and scope of the illegal activity, and the degree of control and authority exercised over others." Commentary to id., Application Note 4.

24. See U.S.S.G. § 3B1.1(c).

she was a minimal participant in the criminal venture,[25] or by 2 levels if she was a minor participant.[26]

The courts are currently divided on the question of whether an offender may receive an upward adjustment for both "more than minimal planning" under § 2F1.1(b)(2) and playing a primary role in the offense under § 3B1.1(a). At least one health care provider has successfully argued that a sentencing court may choose one or the other, but not both, when calculating an offender's offense level under the Guidelines.[27] In *United States v. Romano*, the United States Court of Appeals for the Sixth Circuit reversed a guidelines calculation that enhanced the sentence imposed upon the owner of three Detroit medical clinics both for being an organizer and manager of criminal activity with control over five or more participants and for committing an offense involving more than minimal planning. The court held that the dual enhancements constituted impermissible double counting since the aggravating role enhancement provision "already takes into account the conduct penalized in [the more than minimal planning provision] because, by its very nature, being an organizer or leader of more than five persons necessitates more than minimal planning."[28]

Not all courts agree. Some courts outside the Sixth Circuit have taken the view that double counting occurs only when the Guidelines expressly prohibit the application of two or more offense level adjustments to the same conduct.[29]

(3) Abuse of a Position of Trust, Use of Special Skill, and Obstruction of Justice

In addition to an enhancement for aggravating role, a health care provider's offense level may be subject to a 2–level upward

---

25. See U.S.S.G. § 3B1.2(a). The Commentary to § 3B1.2(a) indicates that a defendant will be considered a minimal participant if she is "plainly among the least culpable of those involved in the conduct of a group," as perhaps demonstrated by her "lack of knowledge or understanding of the scope and structure of the enterprise and of the activities of others." Id., Application Note 1.

26. See U.S.S.G. § 3B1.2(b). The definition of a minor participant is not a study in precision. The Commentary simply states "a minor participant means any participant who is less culpable than most other participants, but whose role could not be described as minimal." Id. at Application Note 3. See also United States v. Gomez, 31 F.3d 28 (2d Cir.1994) (defendant claiming he

played a minor role in drug diversion scheme had burden to prove by preponderance of evidence entitlement to the reduction); United States v. Henry, 12 F.3d 215 (Table), 1993 WL 492302 at 9 (6th Cir.1993) (home health agency administrator who made false statements on at least two cost reports, signed sham promissory notes to support non-existent bonuses, and accepted bogus consulting fees, not entitled to minimal or minor participant reduction).

27. See United States v. Romano, 970 F.2d 164, 166–67 (6th Cir.1992).

28. Id. at 167 (citing as support United States v. Werlinger, 894 F.2d 1015, 1017 (8th Cir.1990)).

29. See, e.g., United States v. Curtis, 934 F.2d 553, 556 (4th Cir.1991).

adjustment if the record demonstrates that the defendant abused a position of public or private trust when committing the offense conduct,[30] used some special skill that significantly facilitated or concealed the offense,[31] or willfully obstructed or impeded (or attempted to wilfully obstruct or impede) the investigation, prosecution or sentencing of his offense conduct.[32]

The courts have sometimes disagreed about when an offender providing medical or mental health services will be found to have abused a position of trust sufficient to warrant an adjustment to his offense level. Special difficulties are presented in cases in which the provider falsely holds himself out to be a licensed physician or mental health professional. Some courts have held that the abuse of a position of trust enhancement can be meted out only where the offender legally or legitimately occupies a position of trust.[33] Other courts have been less forgiving of errant impostors, holding that such an enhancement is appropriate where an imposter assumes a position of trust relative to his patients and uses that ostensible position to commit the crime.[34]

In a case involving a bona fide internist charged with receiving unlawful kickbacks, one circuit court held broadly that the authority to make claims for public funds conferred upon an internist by virtue of his professional role, placed him in a position of trust vis-a-vis the nation's taxpayers.[35] An abuse of trust enhancement has also been approved in a case involving a health care provider who engaged in various schemes to defraud a private insurance carrier and the Medicare program by requesting payment for professional services not rendered.[36] Such broad applications of the abuse of trust provision would seem to place any health care professional at risk of having his offense level enhanced once it is shown that the professional engaged in criminal wrongdoing.

---

30. See U.S.S.G. § 3B1.3.

31. See id. See also United States v. Garfinkel, 29 F.3d 1253, 1261 (8th Cir. 1994); United States v. Custodio, 39 F.3d 1121, 1125–26 (10th Cir. 1994); United States v. Gandy, 36 F.3d 912, 914 (10th Cir.1994).

32. See U.S.S.G. § 3C1.1. See also United States v. Harpster, 951 F.2d 1261 (10th Cir.1991) (unpublished opinion, No. 90–20048–1) (affirming the addition of 2 levels to a physician's offense level tally where the defendant instructed his wife not to turn over documents in compliance with a grand jury subpoena duces tecum).

33. See, e.g., United States v. Echevarria, 33 F.3d at 181–82 (reversing abuse of trust enhancement on defen-

dant who falsely held himself out to be a physician).

34. See, e.g., United States v. Gill, 99 F.3d 484, 488–89 (1st Cir.1996) ("The threat is equally present whether the lawyer or doctor is fully licensed or is a pretender sporting a vest or white coat and displaying a fake diploma.").

35. See United States v. Adam, 70 F.3d 776, 782 (4th Cir.1995).

36. See United States v. Skodnek, 933 F.Supp. 1108, 1119 (D.Mass.1996) ("Billing systems depend upon trust, and [defendant] plainly took advantage of whatever honor system exists in the systems currently used for professional billings directed to insurance carriers for reimbursement.").

In addition to fighting off abuse of trust enhancements, health care offenders have struggled to avoid additional enhancements for the use of a special skill.[37] Precisely when the presence of a special skill will lead to an enhancement of a provider's offense calculation has been the subject of some dispute. A broad interpretation of the provision would subject virtually all convicted health care professionals to the enhancement, a reality that has caused the courts some consternation. In *United States v. Gandy*,[38] for example, the United States Court of Appeals for the Tenth Circuit remanded a district court's decision to enhance a podiatrist's offense level for his purported use of a special skill, holding that "the mere fact that a defendant possesses a special skill is not enough to warrant his sentence being enhanced." To be subject to the adjustment, the court held, the record had to show that the podiatrist used his skill as a podiatrist in some way to facilitate the billing fraud scheme for which he was convicted.[39] Because the record was devoid of any reference about how the podiatrist had used his special skills to further the offense, the case was remanded for further factual findings.

The *Gandy* court's judgment that a medical or other professional license alone should not automatically result in an enhancement for use of a special skill seems plainly correct. A contrary conclusion would justify an upward adjustment in any case involving a health care professional, even though the professional's skills were entirely ancillary to the commission of the offense in question.[40] Despite its cautious approach to the applicability of the special skill provision, the court's description of the government's burden to proof to show that a special skill was used to facilitate the crime may strike some as surprising light. The court opined that facts showing that the podiatrist had used his diagnostic skills to falsify the claims forms and operative reports might be enough.[41] The implicit suggestion being that the government will able to secure a special skill enhancement simply by demonstrating that a doctor used his diagnostic skills in constructing a false claim, a showing that should be fairly readily made in any false claims prosecution.

Additional unwanted level increases may be accumulated by a convicted health care offender who wilfully obstructs or impedes, or

---

37. See U.S.S.G. § 3B1.3.

38. 36 F.3d 912, 915–16 (10th Cir. 1994).

39. Id. at 916. See also United States v. Garfinkel, 29 F.3d 1253, 1261 (8th Cir.1994) (no enhancement for use of special psychiatric skills where psychiatrist did not use those skills to submit false claims to the government).

40. Compare United States v. Fairchild, 940 F.2d 261, 266 (7th Cir.1991) (use of special skill adjustment appropriate where defendant uses his knowledge of chemistry to manufacture methamphetamine).

41. 36 F.3d at 916.

attempts to obstruct or impede, the administration of justice during an investigation, prosecution or sentencing.[42] Although fleeing or otherwise attempting to avoid arrest will not amount to obstruction of justice under this provision,[43] furnishing false or misleading information to a law enforcement officer or court will suffice, as will efforts to conceal or destroy evidence of criminal activity.[44]

(4) Acceptance of Responsibility

Under Guideline § 3E1.1, a health care offender will be entitled to a 2–level reduction in his offense level if the provider has clearly demonstrated acceptance of responsibility for his criminal conduct.[45] This provision recognizes that society gains where a defendant admits his culpability, terminates his association with a criminal enterprise, voluntarily surrenders to law enforcement authorities, assists authorities in the recovery of the fruits or instrumentalities of an offense, or undertakes post-offense rehabilitative efforts, in a timely fashion.[46]

Although many seek the acceptance of responsibility reduction, not all do so successfully. The commentary accompanying the acceptance of responsibility guideline makes clear that the reduction was not intended to benefit the defendant "who puts the government to its burden of proof at trial by denying the essential factual elements of guilt, is convicted, and only then admits guilt and expresses remorse."[47] Although it possible for a defendant who goes to trial to receive the acceptance of responsibility reduction, such awards will be rare, such as where the defendant went to trial to contest something other than factual guilt (e.g., to preserve a legal attack on the statute under which she is charged).[48]

---

42. See U.S.S.G. § 3C1.1

43. See Commentary to § 3C1.1.

44. See United States v. Grewal, 39 F.3d 1189 (Table), 1994 WL 587395 at 2–3 (9th Cir.1994) (upholding obstruction adjustment imposed on sole proprietor of a mobile laboratory convicted of false claims and structuring violations where defendant provided false information to the court and probation officer, lied to federal agents about his whereabouts, opened new bank accounts after the I.R.S seized certain of his accounts, assumed an alias, and attempted to conceal or destroy incriminating evidence).

45. See U.S.S.G § 3E1.1. An additional 1–level may be subtracted from the defendant's offense level if greater than a level 16 and the defendant actively assists law enforcement authorities in their investigation and prosecution of the offense by either providing them timely information about his involvement in the offense, or by giving them timely notice of his intention to enter a guilty plea. See U.S.S.G. § 3E1.1(b)(2). See also United States v. Gomez, 31 F.3d 28, 30 (2d Cir.1994) (defendant convicted of drug diversion who pleaded guilty awarded 2–level reduction for acceptance of responsibility); United States v. Grewal, 39 F.3d 1189, 1994 WL 587395 at 4 (9th Cir.1994) (no acceptance of responsibility reduction where provider engages in conduct that results in enhancement of offense level under the obstruction of justice provision).

46. See id., Application Note 1.

47. U.S.S.G. § 3E1.1, Application Note 2.

48. See id.

Courts struggling to avoid imposing a prison term on health care providers have sometimes gone too far in granting an acceptance of responsibility reduction. Such was the case in *United States v. Jaramillo*[49] where a psychiatrist was convicted after a trial by jury of Medicare fraud, 95 counts of Medicaid fraud, and 15 counts of filing false claims with the CHAMPUS program. A jury convicted Jaramillo after he maintained his innocence throughout trial. Despite the defendant's decision to put the government to its proof, the district judge informed Jaramillo at sentencing that Jaramillo could reduce his sentence for acceptance of responsibility if he made a sufficient statement of remorse. When Jaramillo stiltedly complied,[50] the court awarded the defendant a 2–level decrease. On appeal, the government argued successfully that the decrease was clear error. The Tenth Circuit found it significant that Jaramillo had contested his criminal intent from the outset of the case, and that the sentencing court had been forced to call a recess to permit Jaramillo the chance to devise an acceptable statement of remorse after he had failed miserably to do so when first given the chance in open court. Concluding that Jaramillo's predicament was "hardly the sort of 'rare situation' involving a defendant convicted by a jury that warrants an acceptance of responsibility reduction,"[51] the court reversed and remanded the case for resentencing.

Even a defendant who pleads guilty may be denied a decrease in his offense level. The defendant bears the burden of demonstrating that such a reduction is warranted.[52] Such a demonstration is not made simply by the entry of a plea of guilt. Rather, before awarding an acceptance of responsibility deduction, the courts will scrutinize a multiplicity of factors, including "the offender's recognition of the wrongfulness of his conduct, his remorse for the harmful consequences of that conduct, and his willingness to turn away from that conduct in the future."[53]

Accepting responsibility often proves to be harder than it looks, particularly for white collar crime defendants who deny any intentional wrongdoing from the outset of a case. Indeed, even those seeking the obvious advantages of the acceptance reduction have had trouble mouthing the necessary words to qualify for it. In one

49. 98 F.3d 521, 526 (10th Cir.1996).

50. After a recess, Jaramillo stated on the record, "The jury has found me guilty and I accept the jury's findings and therefore I am remorseful and I will accept the responsibility." Id. at 526. Not all courts would have deemed this statement sufficient to qualify for an acceptance of responsibility reduction, even had the timing of the statement been better and less promoted by the sentencing judge.

51. Id.

52. See United States v. Calhoon, 97 F.3d 518, 531 (11th Cir.1996) (citing cases).

53. Id. at 531, quoting United States v. Scroggins, 880 F.2d 1204, 1215 (11th Cir.1989), cert. denied, 494 U.S. 1083, 110 S.Ct. 1816, 108 L.Ed.2d 946 (1990).

case, for example, a hospital employee who prepared false Medicare cost reports, was denied a § 3E1.1 reduction despite his claim that he had cooperated fully with the authorities and had not denied any of the alleged overt acts in the indictment, where he declined to accept responsibility at sentencing when offered the chance to do so, and instead maintained that the acts underlying his conviction were not improper.[54]

§ 8-5. Determining an Individual Defendant's Criminal History Category

After a sentencing court has calculated an individual provider's offense level, it will turn its attention to the provider's prior criminal history (if any) to determine his "criminal history category."[1] Not surprisingly, a defendant with a prior criminal history is treated more severely under the guidelines than a defendant with no "priors." Thus, a sentencing court will add to a convicted provider's criminal history score, 3 points for each prior term of imprisonment exceeding 13 months imposed upon the provider,[2] 2 points for each prior prison term longer than 60 days but less than 13 months,[3] and 1 point for each prior sentence not falling under the foregoing.[4] In addition, 2 points will be added to a provider's criminal history score if he committed the offense while on probation, parole, supervised release or work release, while incarcerated, or while engaged in an escape.[5] An additional 2 points will be added to the criminal history tally of a provider who commits the health care offense within two years of release from a term of imprisonment greater than 60 days.[6]

A provider's criminal history category is determined by the total criminal history points attributable to the provider. To illustrate, if a provider has no prior criminal history, the provider will have zero criminal history points and will concomitantly fall within the lowest criminal history category (Criminal History Category I). Conversely, a more serious prior criminal history will yield a greater number of criminal history points, and a greater criminal history category.[7]

---

54. See id. at 531–32.

§ 8-5

1. U.S.S.G. § 4A1.1.
2. See U.S.S.G. § 4A1.1(a).
3. See U.S.S.G. § 4A1.1(b).
4. See U.S.S.G. § 4A1.1(c).
5. See U.S.S.G. § 4A1.1(d).
6. See U.S.S.G. § 4A1.1(e).
7. A sentencing table in Chapter 5 of the Guidelines specifies the criminal history category that corresponds to certain criminal history points: Criminal History Category I for defendants with between 0 and 1 criminal history points; Category II for defendants with between 2 and 3 criminal history points; Category III for defendants with between 4 and 6 criminal history points; Category IV for defendants with between 7 and 9 criminal history points; Category V for defendants with between 10 and 12 criminal history points; and Category VI for all others. See U.S.S.G. Ch. 5, Pt. A.

§ 8–6. Determining the Sentence of an Individual Defendant

Once a sentencing court has determined an offender's adjusted offense level and the offender's criminal history category, it will refer to the Sentencing Table set forth in Chapter 5 of the Guidelines Manual to determine the guideline range (range of months of imprisonment) within which the defendant must be sentenced, absent an appropriate upward or downward departure.

§ 8–7. Upward and Downward Departures for Individual Defendants

A final matter of consideration for any federal sentencing judge imposing sentence under the Guidelines is the question of departures. The Guidelines authorize sentencing judges to impose a sentence outside of the applicable guideline range if it finds "that there exists an aggravating or mitigating circumstance of a kind, or to a degree, not adequately taken into consideration by the Sentencing Commission in formulating the guidelines."[1] As this language suggests, a departure from the Guidelines may be upward or downward. Because the Guidelines themselves are so comprehensive, most courts have held that conclusions that the Commission did not adequately consider a factor will be rare.[2] Nevertheless, such departures have occurred, not always to the advantage of health care offenders.[3]

Although it is impossible to foresee all of the circumstances that might give rise to a departure, several enumerated situations have been expressly recognized in the Guidelines themselves as possibly warranting an upward[4] or downward[5] departure.

§ 8–7

1. 18 U.S.C. § 3553(b); U.S.S.G. § 5K2.0.

2. See, e.g., United States v. Weinberger, 91 F.3d 642, 643–44 (4th Cir. 1996) (district court did not err when it refused to depart downward in sentence of podiatrist convicted of defrauding Medicaid and Medicare programs).

3. See, e.g, United States v. Khan, 53 F.3d 507, 518–19 (2d Cir.1995) (upholding finding that guidelines failed to adequately account for the enormous health risks posed by clinic that performed medical exams and dispensed drugs without regard to need, and the effect the scheme on public's confidence in Medicaid program); United States v. Bachynsky, 949 F.2d 722, 733 (5th Cir. 1991) (granting upward departure to account for the vulnerability of physician defendant's patients).

4. See U.S.S.G. §§ 5K2.1 (death occurs as result of offense); 5K2.2 (physical injury); 5K2.3 (extreme psychological injury); 5K2.4 (person is abducted or unlawful restrained to facilitate the offense); 5K2.5 (property damage or loss not otherwise taken into account); 5K2.6 (weapons or dangerous instrumentality used or possessed in the commission of the offense); 5K2.7 (offense causes a significant disruption of a governmental function); 5K2.8 (defendant's conduct was unusually heinous, cruel, brutal or degrading to victim); 5K2.14 (offense significantly endangers national security, public health or safety); 5K2.15 (offense committed to further terrorism).

5. See U.S.S.G. §§ 5K2.10 (victim's wrongful conduct contributed significantly to provoking the offense); 5K2.11 (offense committed to avoid perceived greater harm); 5K2.12 (offense commit-

The facts of *United States v. Khan*[6] illustrate the serious ramifications of an upward departure for a defendant convicted of defrauding the Medicaid program. In that case, Mohammed Sohail Khan was convicted of conspiring to participate in, and participating in, a racketeering enterprise designed to defraud the New York state Medicaid program. The trial record established that four clinics operated by Khan had submitted approximately $8 million in false claims to the program. The clinics' patients were overwhelmingly indigent Medicaid recipients. Many were alcoholics or drug addicts. The clinics provided these patients with prescriptions for drugs for which they had no medical need, in return for which the patients underwent unnecessary tests and procedures which the clinics could then bill to the program. At Khan's sentencing, the trial court departed upward by 9 levels from the applicable guideline range. Khan had an original offense of 23, which called for a 46 to 57 month prison term. The court increased that to an offense level of 32, which authorized a 121 to 151 month prison term. The court based the upward departure on three grounds not adequately taken into account by the Sentencing Commission, all of which were upheld on appeal. First, Khan's clinics posed a substantial risk to the health of persons who were in particular need of able medical treatment. Second, the scheme disrupted the government's ability to efficiently operate the Medicaid program and undermined public confidence in the program. Third, in addition to being an organizer or leader of the unlawful enterprise,[7] Khan induced doctor's to abuse their positions of trust with their patients.[8] But for the "5K1.1 motion" filed by the prosecutor in the case,[9] which convinced the court to depart downward to a 60–month prison term, the defendant would have faced a term of imprisonment of at least 121 months.

---

ted under coercion or duress); 5K2.13 (defendant's diminished capacity contributed to offense); 5K2.16 (defendant voluntarily discloses offense to authorities). See also U.S.S.G. § 5K1.1 which, upon the motion of the government, allows a court to depart downward from the applicable guidelines range to account for a defendant's substantial assistance in the investigation, or prosecution of another person.

   6.   53 F.3d 507 (2d Cir.1995).

   7.   Khan received a role adjustment under § 3B1.1(a) for his leadership role. See discussion at § 8–4c(2).

   8.   See Khan, 53 F.3d at 8.

   9.   A 5K1.1 motion, is a motion filed by the government that states that a defendant has provided the government with substantial assistance in the prosecution or investigation of another person or persons, which authorizes the court to depart downward from the otherwise

§ 8–8. The Federal Sentencing Guidelines for Organizations—An Overview

Chapter Eight of the Federal Sentencing Guidelines[1] (the Organizational Guidelines) sets forth the guideline provisions for organizational defendants convicted of a federal offense. These provisions took effect on November 1, 1991, four years after the effective date of the guidelines for individual defendants. The Organizational Guidelines are designed to guide the discretion of federal sentencing courts in fashioning an appropriate sentencing package for convicted corporate or other organizational[2] defendants. Any organizational defendant convicted of a federal felony or Class A misdemeanor is subject to the Organizational Guideline provisions.[3] As a result, the sentence of any health care entity convicted under the federal False Claims statute, the anti-kickback provisions, or any other federal health care criminal statute, will be determined in accordance with the Organizational Guideline mandates.

§ 8–9. The Organizational Guidelines at Work

Because, unlike an individual defendant, a corporation or other organizational defendant cannot be sentenced to prison, the Organizational Guideline provisions channel the discretion exercised by a sentencing court in constructing non-incarceratory sanctions for the unlawful conduct of a corporate defendant. The Organizational Guidelines emphasize foremost redressing the harm done by an organizational defendant. Thus, whenever possible, sanctions imposed upon a convicted corporation or entity will be fashioned to remedy the harm caused by the offense and to make the victim or victims whole.[1] An appropriate sanction package may include an order of restitution to the victim, a criminal fine, and a term of probation conditioned upon compliance some other appropriate remedial order. Each of these sanctions is explored more fully below.

§ 8–10. Restitution Orders

A federal sentencing court will order a convicted organizational defendant to remedy the harm caused by its offense "whenever

applicable guideline range. See U.S.S.G. § 5K1.1.

§ 8–8

1. See U.S.S.G. §§ 8A1.1 through 8E1.3.

2. The term "organization" includes "corporations, partnerships, associations, joint-stock companies, unions, trusts, pension funds, unincorporated organizations, governments and political subdivisions thereof, and non-profit organizations." See U.S.S.G. § 8A1.1, application n.1.

3. See U.S.S.G. § 8A1.1.

§ 8–9

1. See Introductory Commentary, U.S.S.G. Ch. 8; see also U.S.S.G. § 8B1.2 (restitution orders), § 8B1.2 (remedial orders) and § 8B1.3 (community service orders as a condition of probation).

practicable."[1] To this end, the court will order the convicted organization to pay restitution to the victim or victims of the offense.[2] Restitution is not considered to be a form of punishment, it is simply a means by which the court attempts to make the victim or victims of the offense whole.[3] Thus, the restitution amount will not be credited against a criminal fine also imposed upon the defendant. If an order of restitution is imposed at sentencing, the organization's payment of the restitution amount will be a condition of its probation.

§ 8–11. The Imposition of a Criminal Fine

Other provisions in the Organization Guidelines are designed to punish organizations that commit criminal acts, and to deter similar misconduct in the future.[1] Thus, in addition to orders of restitution, a sentencing court may impose a criminal fine upon a convicted organization to punish the organization for its wrongful conduct.

The sentencing court will determine the amount of a criminal fine based upon the seriousness of the defendant's offense and the organization's culpability in the offense. Where an organization has "operated primarily for a criminal purpose or by criminal means"—that is, as a front for engaging in criminally fraudulent activity—a sentencing court may impose a fine sufficient to divest the organization of the totality of its net assets.[2] Some commentators refer to this extreme sanction as the corporate "death penalty."[3] In all other cases, however, similar to the process followed under the sentencing guidelines for individual defendants (where the sentencing court begins by determining the "base" offense level)[4], under the guidelines for organizational defendants the sentencing court begins by calculating the defendant's "base fine."[5]

§ 8–10

1. See Introductory Commentary to Ch. 8, U.S.S.G.

2. See id.; see also U.S.S.G. § 8B1.1.

3. See introductory commentary to Ch. 8, U.S.S.G.

§ 8–11

1. See id. ("[Chapter 8] is designed so that the sanctions imposed upon organizations . . . taken together, will provide just punishment, adequate deterrence, and incentives for organizations to maintain internal mechanisms for preventing, detecting, and reporting criminal conduct.")

2. See introductory commentary to U.S.S.G. ch. 8.; see also U.S.S.G. § 8C1.1. Such a criminal fine is, of course, subject to the maximum fine permitted by the statute violated.

3. See Pamela H. Bucy, Health Care Fraud: Criminal, Civil and Administrative Law § 3.02[11] at 3–59 (Law Journal Seminar Press 1996); Paul L. Perito, E. Lawrence Barcella, Jr., Compliance Programs, Internal Investigations, and Voluntary Disclosures: Tools for Mitigating Financial Exposure and Avoiding Criminal Liability for Health Care Providers, Health Care Fraud 1996, at J–23.

4. See discussion supra at § 8–4a.

5. See U.S.S.G. § 8C2.1.

§ 8–12. Calculating an Organization's Base Fine

To calculate an organization's base fine, a sentencing court will first find the "base offense level" that the United States Sentencing Commission assigned to the statutory offense in question.[1] The process for finding a base offense level is relatively straightforward. The Statutory Index set forth as Appendix A to the United States Sentencing Guidelines specifies an applicable sentencing guideline section for each federal criminal statute. For example, the Statutory Index specifies that the applicable guideline section for violations of the False Claims Act, 18 U.S.C. § 287, is Sentencing Guideline § 2F1.1, the guideline provision that relates to all "Offenses Involving Fraud or Deceit." In turn, Guideline § 2F1.1 indicates that its applicable base offense level is a level 6. Therefore, if a medical partnership is convicted of submitting a false claim, the partnership's base offense level will be a level 6.

Once a sentencing court has determined the base offense level, it will adjust that number, if appropriate, to account for any applicable "specific offense characteristics." The court will make this adjustment in order to measure the true seriousness of the organization's offense conduct. For example, if the medical partnership's scheme to defraud involved a loss that exceeded $2,000, the partnership's base offense level will be increased in accordance with a table set forth in Guideline § 2F1.1. That table provides as follows:

a. Specific Offense Characteristics

(1) If the loss exceeded $2,000, increase the offense level as follows:

Loss (Apply the Greatest)	Increase in Level
(A) $2,000 or less	no increase
(B) More than $2,000	add 1
(C) More than $5,000	add 2
(D) More than $10,000	add 3
(E) More than $20,000	add 4
(F) More than $40,000	add 5
(G) More than $70,000	add 6
(H) More than $120,000	add 7
(I) More than $200,000	add 8
(J) More than $350,000	add 9
(K) More than $500,000	add 10
(L) More than $800,000	add 11
(M) More than $1,500,000	add 12
(N) More than $2,500,000	add 13
(O) More than $5,000,000	add 14

§ 8–12

1. See U.S.S.G. § 8C2.3.

422

Loss (Apply the Greatest)	Increase in Level
(P) More than $10,000,000	add 15
(Q) More than $20,000,000	add 16
(R) More than $40,000,000	add 17
(S) More than $80,000,000	add 18.[2]

Under this provision, if the convicted medical partnership's false claim involved a loss of more than $120,000, but less than $200,000, the court would increase by 7 levels the partnership's base offense level (a base level of 6) to reflect the seriousness of the partnership's offense. Thus, with this adjustment, the partnership's offense level would be a level 13.

The partnership's base offense level could be increased even further if any of the other specific offense characteristics apply. For example, if the false claim violation involved more than minimal planning, or if it involved more than one victim, the sentencing court would add 2 more levels to the defendant's base offense level.[3] If it involved the conscious or reckless risk of serious bodily injury to a patient, the base offense level would be increased by an additional 2 levels.[4] Or, if the partnership's offense violated a judicial or administrative order, injunction, decree or process not otherwise addressed by the Sentencing Guidelines (such as where the partnership's conduct violates an earlier corporate integrity agreement) the base offense level would be increased by an additional 2 levels. If its level was still below a level 10 after that adjustment, the partnership's offense level would be raised to a level 10.[5]

By way of illustration then, the calculation of the offense level of a medical partnership convicted under the False Claims Act might look something like this:[6]

2. See U.S.S.G. § 2F1.1(b)(1).

3. See U.S.S.G. § 2F1.1(b)(2).

4. See § 2F1.1(b)(4). If this section applies, and after adjusting the base offense level by 2 levels the organization's adjusted offense level is still below level 13, the organization's adjusted offense level will be raised to a level 13. See id. Other specific offense characteristics might also apply. For example, if the partnership made use of a foreign bank account to conceal the nature of its fraudulent activity, and its adjusted offense level was below a level 12, its offense level would be raised to a level 12. See U.S.S.G. § 2F1.1(b)(5). If the partnership's offense jeopardized the safety of a financial institution, or it affected a financial institution and the defendant gained greater than $1,000,000 in unlawful proceeds, the base offense level would be increased by 4 levels, and if it was less than a level 24, the adjusted offense level would be raised to a level 24. See U.S.S.G. § 2F1.1(b)(6).

5. See U.S.S.G. § 2F1.1(b)(3).

6. This illustration is based on a fairly simple, single count, false claims conviction. If, as is the case in many false claims cases, the indictment contains multiple counts, the sentencing court will determine a combined offense level under the provisions in Chapter 3 of the Sentencing Guidelines. See U.S.S.G. § 8C2.3; see also U.S.S.G. §§ 3D1.1–3D1.5.

Base Offense Level (§ 2F1.1(a)):   6
PLUS
Specific Offense Characteristics (§ 2F1.1(b)(3)):
    Loss > $120,000 (§ 2F1.1(b)(1))   7
    More than minimal planning (§ 2F1.1(b)(2))   2
    Violated Corporate Integrity Agt.   2

ADJUSTED OFFENSE LEVEL   17

Once the sentencing court has determined the organizational defendant's offense level, it will be able to determine the defendant's "base fine" under Sentencing Guideline § 8C2.4. That guideline provides that an organization's base fine will be the greatest of:

1) the amount that corresponds to the organization's offense level (specified in a separate table set forth in § 8C2.4);[7]

2) the organization's pecuniary gain from the offense;[8] or

3) the pecuniary loss intentionally, knowingly or recklessly caused by the organization.[9]

The terms "pecuniary gain" and "pecuniary loss" are defined in accordance with 18 U.S.C. § 3671(d). Pecuniary gain encompasses any before-tax profit redounding to the organization as a result of the relevant conduct of the offense, whether derived from actual receipts or cost savings.[10] Pecuniary loss, defined elsewhere in the Guidelines,[11] includes the value of the money, property, or services unlawfully taken by the organization, excluding interest the victim might have earned on such funds but for the offense.[12] If, however, it is determined that organization intended or was attempting to inflict a loss that was greater than the actual loss, that figure will be use.[13]

7. That table provides as follows:

(d) Offense Level Fine Table

Offense Level	Amount	Offense Level	Amount
6 or less	$5,000	23	$1,600,000
7	$7,500	24	$2,100,000
8	$10,000	25	$2,800,000
9	$15,000	26	$3,700,000
10	$20,000	27	$4,800,000
11	$30,000	28	$6,300,000
12	$40,000	29	$8,100,000
13	$60,000	30	$10,500,000
14	$85,000	31	$13,500,000
15	$125,000	32	$17,500,000
16	$175,000	33	$22,000,000
17	$250,000	34	$28,500,000
18	$350,000	35	$36,000,000
19	$500,000	36	$45,500,000
20	$650,000	37	$57,500,000
21	$910,000	38 or more	$72,500,000
22	$1,200,000		

8. See U.S.S.G. § 8C2.4(a)(2).

9. See U.S.S.G. § 8C2.3(a)(3).

10. See U.S.S.G § 8A1.2, Application n.3(h).

11. See Commentary to §§ 2B1.1 (Larceny, Embezzlement, and Other Forms of Theft) and 2F1.1 (Fraud and Deceit).

12. See Commentary to U.S.S.G. § 2F1.1, Application n.7.

13. See id. As discussed in § 8–12, the sentencing court will calculate the loss involved in the offense to determine the organization's offense level. That loss calculation need not be precise if it would unduly complicate or prolong the sentencing process. See id.; see also 18 U.S.C. § 3571(d). Rather, loss need only be a reasonable estimate based on the information available to the court. For example, the loss figure may be based upon the approximate number of victims and average loss to each, or more generally upon the nature and duration of the scheme and the revenues generated by

§ 8–13. Determining the Organizational Defendant's Culpability Score

Once the sentencing court has determined an organization's base fine, it will turn its attention to the organization's "culpability score," a tally designed to measure the organization's relative culpability in the commission of the offense.[1] Every convicted business entity begins with a culpability score of 5 points, to which score points may be added (if, for example, the organization involved itself in, or tolerated, the offense conduct) or subtracted (if, for example, the organization took steps to extract itself from or prevent the offense conduct).

a. Bases for Increasing an Organization's Culpability Score

The United States Sentencing Commission adopted a system of increasing culpability scores premised on the following three beliefs: 1) a business entity is more culpable when persons with significant supervisory or management authority participate in, condone, or are willfully ignorant of criminal conduct within the entity; 2) an even greater breach of trust or abuse of position occurs by virtue of such conduct when the entity is larger and its management is more professional; and 3) as business entities increase in size, the risk of other criminal conduct also increases if pervasive tolerance of the offense in question exists within the management personnel. As a result of these concerns, the Guidelines call for an increase in an organization's culpability score in proportion to the size of organization's workforce, and the extent to which its substantial authority personnel were involved in the offense conduct.[2]

(1) Involvement in or Tolerance of Criminal Activity

In cases where "high-level personnel"[3] either "participated in, condoned," or were "willfully ignorant of the offense," or where

---

similar fraudulent activities. See id. The court will then use that loss figure (calculated for the purpose of determining the organization's offense level) as a starting point for its calculation of the organization's pecuniary loss (for the purpose of determining the organization's base fine). See Commentary to U.S.S.G. § 8C2.3, Application n.2.

§ 8–13

1. See U.S.S.G. § 8C2.5

2. See Commentary to U.S.S.G. § 8C2.5 (background).

3. In organizations or units employing 200 or more, the term "high-level personnel" includes those agents who set policy or otherwise control the organization or unit. See Commentary to U.S.S.G. § 8C2.5, Application n.3. This might include, for example, directors, executive officers, substantial owners, or others in a position of authority over a major unit or business entity. See Stephen S. Cowen, Federal Guidelines for Sentencing Organizations and the Role of Compliance Plans at L–31, L–32, Health Care Fraud 1996 (National Institute on Health Care Fraud).

"tolerance of the offense by substantial authority personnel[4] was pervasive throughout the organization," the organization's culpability score will be increased by 5 points (if the organization or unit employed 5000 or more), by 4 points (if the organization or unit employed 1000 or more) or by 3 points (if the organization or unit employed 200 or more).[5] In cases where "substantial authority personnel participated in, condoned" or were "willfully ignorant of the offense," and the organization employed 50 or more employees, 2 points would be added to the organization's 5–point score.[6] Where the organization employed 10 or more, 1 point would be added to its 5–point score.[7]

(2) Prior Criminal, Civil or Administrative History

An organization's culpability score may be increased by 2 points if the organization (or a separately managed line of its business) committed any part of the offense conduct within five years (or by 1 point if within ten years) of either a criminal adjudication based on similar misconduct, or a civil or administrative adjudication based on two or more separate instances of similar misconduct.[8] The term "separately managed line of business" refers to any subdivision of a for-profit organization that has its own management, enjoys a high degree of autonomy from the organization's managerial authority, and maintains its own books.[9] To determine the prior criminal, civil or administrative history of an organization with a separately managed line of business, a sentencing court will consider only the prior conduct or criminal record of the separately managed line of business involved in the offense conduct for which the organization was convicted.[10]

(3) Violation of an Order

An additional 2 points may be added to an organization's culpability score if the organization committed the offense conduct in violation a judicial order or injunction (other than a violation of a probation order), or if the organization (or separately managed line of business) violated a condition of probation by engaging in misconduct similar to that for which it was placed on probation.[11] If

---

4. "Substantial authority personnel" are those who have been delegated a substantial measure of discretion to act on the organization's behalf, such as all "high-level personnel" as well as others who have substantial supervisory authority (e.g., plant managers, sales managers, and even non-management personnel who have the power to negotiate or set price levels, negotiate or approve contracts, or to exercise other substantial authority on the organization's be-

half). See Commentary to U.S.S.G. § 8A1.2, Application n.3(c).

5. See U.S.S.G. §§ 8C2.5(b)(1)-(3).

6. See U.S.S.G. § 8C2.5(b)(4).

7. See U.S.S.G. § 8C2.5(b)(5).

8. See U.S.S.G. § 8C2.5(c).

9. See Commentary to id., Application n.5.

10. See id.

11. See U.S.S.G. § 8C2.5(d)(1).

the offense conduct violated a condition of probation, 1 point could be added to the organization's culpability score.[12]

(4) Obstruction of Justice

A final basis for increasing an organization's culpability score—obstruction of justice—permits a sentencing court to increase the organization's culpability score by 3 points if it determines that the organization "willfully obstructed or impeded, attempted to obstruct or impede, or aided, abetted, or encouraged obstruction of justice during the investigation, prosecution, or sentencing" of the offense conduct, or the organization "with knowledge thereof, failed to take reasonable steps to prevent such obstruction or impedance or attempted obstruction or impedance."[13]

b.　Bases for Reducing an Organization's Culpability Score

To counterbalance the foregoing set of factors which serve to aggravate an organization's culpability score, the Sentencing Guidelines provide that some factors will reduce that score, the most important of which is the existence of an effective corporate compliance program.

(1) Reduction for Maintaining an Effective Corporate Compliance Program

Three points may be subtracted from an organization's culpability score if the offense occurred despite the organization's maintenance of an effective program to prevent and detect violations of law.[14] No relief is available, however, if either an individual with high-level authority in the organization (or in a unit employing 200 or more) or an individual responsible for administering or enforcing its compliance program, participated in, condoned, or was willfully ignorant of the offense. In addition, participation in the offense by an individual with substantial authority results in a rebuttable presumption that the organization did not have an effective program.[15] The benefits of having an effective corporate compliance program may be lost if, after becoming aware of an offense, the organization unreasonably delays in reporting the offense to appropriate governmental authorities.[16]

A corporate compliance program need not succeed in deterring all criminal conduct to be considered "effective" under the Guidelines.[17] However, to receive credit for its program an organization must exercise due diligence to prevent and detect unlawful conduct by its employees and agents. Thus, at minimum, to be credited with

---

12.　See U.S.S.G. § 8C2.5(d)(2).
13.　See U.S.S.G. § 8C2.5(e).
14.　See U.S.S.G. § 8C2.5(f).
15.　See id.

16.　See id.
17.　See Commentary to U.S.S.G. §§ 8A1.2(3)(k)(1)-(7).

an effective program the organization must satisfy the following seven requisites:

(1) Establish compliance rules and procedures reasonably capable of reducing criminal conduct, to be followed by all of its employees and agents.

(2) Delegate to high-level personnel within the organization responsibility for overseeing compliance.

(3) Exercise due care to prevent assignments of substantial discretionary authority to individuals who (the organization knows, or, with due diligence, should know) have a propensity to engage in criminal conduct.

(4) Endeavor to communicate its compliance rules and procedures to its employees and agents (for example, by mandating their participation in compliance training programs or by distributing understandable materials that describe the procedures).

(5) Undertake reasonable steps to police its workforce's compliance with the standards (for example, by conducting random audits designed to detect criminal conduct or by adopting a confidential reporting system through which employees and agents can report misconduct without fear of retaliation).

(6) Discipline individuals who engage in criminal conduct or who fail to detect such misconduct.

(7) Take all steps reasonably necessary to respond to offenses that are uncovered and to prevent the recurrence of similar offenses.[18]

The precise dimensions of an "effective" corporate compliance program will vary from case to case, depending on the size of the organization, the nature of its business and the organization's prior history.[19] For example, as a general rule, the larger the organization, the more formal its compliance program will be expected to be. Written, standardized rules and procedure will likely be necessary.[20] In addition, the nature of the organization's business may affect the anticipated structure of its compliance program. Where because of the nature of the organization's business certain of-

---

18. See id. HCFA has suggested a number of other compliance features that could be adopted by a corporation, including "conducting their own internal reviews or audits or employer compensation, related party costs, and billing procedures; retaining experts for accounting and medical reviews; centralizing contract review and approval to detect improper remuneration for referrals or provision of free services; and conducting internal quality assurance reviews." HCFA Takes More Active Role in Combatting Fraudulent Claims, 5 BNA Health L. Rptr. 507 (April 4, 1996).

19. See Commentary to U.S.S.G. §§ 8A1.2(k)(7)(i)-(iii).

20. See Commentary to U.S.S.G. § 8A1.2(3)(k)(7)(i).

fenses are more likely to occur, the organization may be expected to take special steps to prevent such offenses.[21] For example, if an organization delegates to its staff substantial discretion to approve contracts or to submit invoices for payment, it may be expected to take special steps to prevent and detect wrongful conduct. Because such discretionary authority carries with it the opportunity for abuse, an effective compliance program will include the adoption of clear standards and procedures designed to thwart and detect such abuse. Finally, if the organization has a prior history of misconduct, it may be expected to take special measures to prevent the recurrence of such misconduct, and repeated improprieties will raise doubts about the effectiveness of organization's response.[22]

(2) Reductions for Self–Reporting, Cooperation, and Acceptance of Responsibility

A health care organization may further reduce its culpability score by varying amounts by reporting offense conduct once discovered, by cooperating with state or federal authorities who are investigating the offense conduct, and/or by accepting responsibility for its criminal conduct. If, for example, the organization reports the offense to the appropriate governmental authorities without an unreasonable delay, fully cooperates with those authorities in their subsequent investigation of the offense, and affirmatively accepts responsibility for its criminal conduct, 5 points may be subtracted from its culpability score.[23] The term "appropriate governmental authorities" includes any federal or state law enforcement, regulatory, or program official having jurisdiction over the offense.[24] To be considered timely, the organization must disclose the offense before it is faced with an imminent involuntary threat of disclosure or government investigation.[25]

A health care organization that fails to disclose its offense in timely fashion may still be entitled to a 2–point reduction in its culpability score if it fully cooperates in the relevant authority's external investigation of the offense and clearly demonstrates its recognition and affirmative acceptance of responsibility for the criminal conduct.[26] Timely and complete cooperation are required. Thus, the organization must begin to cooperate from the time it is first notified of the criminal investigation, and must disclose all

---

21. See Commentary to U.S.S.G. § 8A1.2(3)(k)(7)(ii).

22. See Commentary to U.S.S.G. § 8A1.2(3)(k)(7)(iii).

23. See U.S.S.G. § 8C2.5(g)(1).

24. See Commentary to U.S.S.G. § 8C2.5, Application n.11.

25. An organization is permitted a reasonable period of time to conduct an internal investigation of the offense, and no reporting is required if the organization reasonably concludes that no offense has been committed. See Commentary to U.S.S.G. § 8C2.5, application n.10.

26. See U.S.S.G. § 8C2.5(g)(2).

relevant information of which it is aware, including information regarding the extent and nature of the offense conduct and the individuals involved therein.[27]

A health care organization that chooses not to self-report or cooperate may still be entitled to a 1–point reduction to its culpability score if it affirmatively accepts responsibility for its criminal conduct.[28] A guilty plea by the organization prior to trial accompanied by a candid acknowledgment of its involvement in the offense and any relevant conduct will normally suffice to establish affirmative acceptance of responsibility. Conversely, the reduction will not normally be available to an organization that denies its involvement in the offense conduct throughout trial, and admits its guilt only after it has been adjudicated guilty by the finder of fact. For example, in a case involving the government's appeal of the sentence of an individual defendant, the United States Court of Appeals for the Tenth Circuit held in United States v. Jaramillo[29] that the trial court had erred when it reduced the defendant's sentence for acceptance of responsibility where the defendant had admitted his wrongdoing only after the jury had found him guilty of defrauding the Medicare, Medicaid and CHAMPUS programs.[30]

It is at least conceivable, however, that an organization convicted after trial could still be eligible for the acceptance of responsibility reduction if its claim at trial was not a denial of factual guilt, but rather was designed to assert a legal attack on the prosecution (e.g., where the organization makes a constitutional attack upon the anti-kickback statute).[31]

§ 8–14. Determining a Health Care Organization's Applicable Fine Range

A sentencing court will use a health care organization's culpability score to determine the applicable minimum and maximum multipliers. Minimum and maximum multipliers are specified in a table set forth in Guideline § 8C2.6, which is reproduced below:

Culpability Score	Minimum Multiplier	Maximum Multiplier
10 or more	2.00	4.00
9	1.80	3.60
8	1.60	3.20
7	1.40	2.80
6	1.20	2.40
5	1.00	2.00

27. See Commentary to U.S.S.G. § 8C2.5(g)(1)-(g)(2), Application n.12.

28. See U.S.S.G. § 8C5.2(g)(3).

29. 98 F.3d 521 (10th Cir.1996).

30. See id. at 526.

31. See Commentary to U.S.S.G. § 8C2.5(g)(3), Application n.13.

Culpability Score	Minimum Multiplier	Maximum Multiplier
4	0.80	1.60
3	0.60	1.20
2	0.40	0.80
1	0.20	0.40
0 or less	0.05	0.20

After determining the applicable minimum and maximum multipliers, the court will multiply the organization's base fine[1] by those multipliers to determine the floor and ceiling of the organization's fine range. For example, if the court determined an organization's base fine to be $500,000, and its culpability score to be 5, the organization's fine range would be between $500,000 ($500,000 multiplied by 1.00) and $1,000,000 ($500,000 multiplied by 2.00).

§ 8–15. The Imposition of a Fine Within the Applicable Fine Range

Once the sentencing court has determined the applicable fine range, it is in a position to impose a criminal fine upon the organizational defendant. The fine must fall within the applicable fine range provided by the Guidelines, absent a proper basis for an upward or downward departure.[1] To determine where within the range to affix the fine, the court may consider the policy statement set forth in Guideline § 8C2.8 which suggests a laundry list of factors that might guide the exercise of the court's discretion in this regard. Payment of a fine imposed under the Organizational Guideline chapter is to be made immediately, unless the court finds that the organization is financially unable to do so, in which case payment may be made in accordance with a schedule adopted by the court at sentencing.[2]

§ 8–16. Upward and Downward Departures

A sentencing court may decline to impose a criminal fine within the applicable guideline range if it finds "that there exists an aggravating or mitigating circumstance of a kind, or to a degree, not adequately taken into consideration by the Sentencing Commission in formulating the guidelines that should result in a sentence different from that described."[1] The United States Sentencing Commission expressly provided that certain factors, when consid-

§ 8–14

1. See discussion supra at § 8–12.

§ 8–15

1. See U.S.S.G. § 8C3.1(a). If, however, the maximum guideline fine is greater than the statutory maximum, the statutory maximum shall govern. Similarly, if the guideline minimum fine is less than a minimum fine mandated by the statute, the statutory minimum shall govern. See U.S.S.G. §§ 8C3.1(b) and (c).

2. See U.S.S.G. § 8C3.3. The period for payment shall not extend beyond a period of five years. See 18 U.S.C. § 3572(d).

§ 8–16

1. 18 U.S.C. § 3553(b).

ered in light of the facts of a particular case, may not have been adequately taken into consideration by the guidelines, and may therefore warrant consideration as a basis for an upward or down-ward departure.

a. Substantial Assistance to Authorities—Basis for Upward Departure

The government may move for a downward departure upon the ground that the defendant organization provided substantial assistance in the government's investigation or prosecution of another organization or individual.[2] Such a departure is contingent upon a motion from the government. It is not available upon a motion by the defense or by the sua sponte action of the sentencing court.[3] Once such a motion has been made, the sentencing court may grant or deny it in its discretion after assessing the significance and usefulness of the organization's assistance (taking into consideration the government's view of that assistance), and the nature, extent, and timeliness of the assistance provided. In practice, federal sentencing courts give great weight to the government's evaluation of the assistance provided by an organization. Hence, when a prosecutor indicates that an organization has provided substantial assistance in an investigation or prosecution, a downward departure is likely. Just how far the court will depart from the applicable guideline fine range, however, depends on the facts of the particular case.

b. Threat to a Market—Basis for Upward Departure

The sentencing court may depart upward from the applicable fine range in a case in which the offense committed by a health care organization presented a risk to the integrity or continued existence of a market, whether private (e.g., a financial market, a commodities market, or a market for consumer goods) or public (e.g., government contracting).[4]

c. Members or Beneficiaries of the Organization as Victims—Basis for Downward Departure

When an organization's offense directly victimizes its own members or beneficiaries (other than its shareholders), a downward departure may be warranted if the imposition of a fine upon the organization would simply increase the victims' burden without achieving a counterbalancing deterrent effect.[5] In such cases, the court may forego a fine altogether (e.g., where a labor union is convicted of embezzling pension funds).

2. See U.S.S.G. § 8C4.1.

3. See id.

4. See U.S.S.G. § 8C4.5.

5. See U.S.S.G. § 8C4.8.

d. Remedial Costs Greatly Exceed Organization's Gain—Basis for Downward Departure

Similarly, a substantial fine may not be necessary for either retributive or deterrent purposes in a case in which the organization has paid or has agreed to pay remedial costs arising from its offense greatly exceeding its unlawful gain, and a downward departure may be warranted.[6] Such a departure is not available, however, where high-level personnel was involved in the offense.[7]

e. Compliance Program Mandated by Court or Administrative Order—Basis for Upward Departure

If a health care entity's culpability score was lowered under § 8C2.5(f) for its maintenance of an effective compliance program, but the organization's had implemented that program to comply with a court or administrative order, the sentencing court may depart upward from the applicable fine range to offset the § 8C2.5(f) reduction.[8]

f. Exceptional or Minor Organizational Culpability—Basis for Upward or Downward Departure

The culpability score scale set forth in the Organizational Guidelines caps at a score of "10 or more," which score correlates with minimum and maximum multipliers of 2.00 and 4.00, respectively.[9] In a case in which a health care organization's culpability score would have been above 10 had the scale continued, a sentencing court may decide to upwardly depart from the applicable fine range to account for the actual magnitude of the offense.[10]

Conversely, the court might find in some cases that the organization's culpability for the offense was exceptionally low, warranting a downward departure. However, specific criteria must be met before such a departure will be proper.[11]

§ 8–17. Orders of Probation for Organizational Defendants

In addition to an order of restitution and a criminal fine, the Organizational Guidelines provide that an organizational defendant may (and, in some cases, shall) be sentenced to a term of probation.[1] A term of probation may be imposed when necessary to ensure the organization's compliance with some other aspect of the organization's sentence, such as to ensure payment of restitution to

---

6. See U.S.S.G. § 8C4.9.
7. See id.
8. See U.S.S.G. § 8C4.10.
9. See U.S.S.G. § 8C2.6; see also discussion supra at § 8–13.

10. See U.S.S.G. § 8C4.11.
11. See id.

§ 8–17

1. See U.S.S.G. § 8D1.1.

the victim,[2] or a fine not paid in full at the time of sentencing.[3] A term of probation may also be appropriate to reduce the likelihood of future misconduct by the organization,[4] such as where the organization (with a workforce of 50 or more) does not have an effective corporate compliance program in place at the time of sentencing,[5] or where the organization (or its high-level personnel) engaged in any part of the offense conduct within five years of a prior criminal adjudication for similar misconduct.[6] An order of probation must be imposed upon an organizational defendant if the court declines to impose a criminal fine upon the defendant.[7]

If probation is ordered, a condition of probation must be that the organization not commit any further federal, state or local offense during the probationary term,[8] and a condition that the organization pay a fine, restitution, or perform some community service, unless the court finds that extraordinary circumstances make such condition plainly unreasonable.[9] An order of probation for a felony must last for a period of at least one year, but less than five years.[10] By contrast, probationary orders for misdemeanors have no minimum term, and may span up to five years.[11] While serving out a probationary term, an organizational defendant must tread carefully. A violation of any of the conditions of probation may result in an extension of the organization's probationary term, the imposition of more restrictive conditions of probation, or a revocation of the probationary term accompanied by resentencing.[12] If an organization engages in repeated serious violations of the conditions of its probation, the court may appoint a master or trustee to ensure its future compliance.[13]

§ 8–18. Other Available Sanctions

In addition to the foregoing, a health care organization convicted of health care fraud or abuse can expect its sentence to include a special assessment.[1] Special assessments are mandatory and vary in size with the severity of the offense conduct. If the organization is convicted of a Class B misdemeanor, a $50 special assessment must be imposed (for each count of conviction). If the organization is convicted of a Class A misdemeanor, a $125 special assessment must be imposed (per count). If the organization is convicted of a

2. See U.S.S.G. § 8D1.1(a)(1).

3. See U.S.S.G. § 8D1.1(a)(2).

4. See U.S.S.G. § 8D1.1(a)(6).

5. See U.S.S.G. § 8D1.1(a)(3).

6. See U.S.S.G. §§ 8D1.1(a)(4) and (5).

7. See U.S.S.G. § 8D1.1(a)(7).

8. See U.S.S.G. § 8D1.3(a).

9. See 18 U.S.C. § 3563(a)(2); see also U.S.S.G. § 8D1.3(b).

10. See U.S.S.G. § 8D1.2(a)(1).

11. See U.S.S.G. § 8D1.2(a)(2).

12. See U.S.S.G. § 8D1.5.

13. See commentary to U.S.S.G. § 8D1.5, Application n.1.

§ 8–18

1. See U.S.S.G. § 8E1.1.

felony, a $200 special assessment must be imposed (per count).[2] A convicted organization may also be subject to an order requiring it to forfeit its unlawful gains,[3] to pay the costs of the prosecution,[4] to publicly acknowledge its guilt and to publicize its conviction.[5]

§ 8–19. The Need for an Adequate Corporate Compliance Program in Today's Health Care Marketplace

The full force of the Organizational Guideline provisions can only truly be appreciated when the provisions are considered in tandem. As discussed above, some of the provisions will serve to lower a health care organization's sentencing exposure, while others may substantially increase that exposure. An organization may engage in a preemptive, fine-reducing strike by instituting a corporate compliance program to discourage misdeeds and ferret out wrongdoers.

The mere institution of a program to detect and prevent fraud and abuse, however, will not save an organization if stands idly by while persons with high-level or substantial authority involve themselves in, tolerate or simply ignore criminal conduct. In such a case, even with a compliance program in place, not only would the organization's culpability score be increased by up to 5 points (depending on its size),[1] the organization would also be denied the 3–point reduction that normally is available to organization's with programs to detect such offenses. By contrast, an organization with an effective compliance program in place, whose high level policymaking or managerial staff do not engage in or turn a blind eye to fraudulent or abusive practices, stands to significantly reduce its criminal fine exposure. The following two hypotheticals illustrate.

Hypothetical #1—DME Supply Company.

A president of a DME supply company pays a nursing home and a hospital kickbacks for referrals of program-funded business over the span of 3 years. The kickbacks payments amounted to $100,000 while the program-related profits to the DME supplier amount to just over $1,500,000. The DME supplier is subsequently prosecuted (along with its president) for multiple violations of the anti-kickback statute. The supplier disputes the charges. At trial it is revealed that when the DME supplier first learned of the investigation it shredded documents relevant to the unlawful kickback arrangements. It is also established that the DME supply company had considered, but not yet instituted, a corporate compliance

---

2. See 18 U.S.C. § 3013(a).

3. See U.S.S.G §§ 8E1.2 and 5E1.4.

4. See U.S.S.G. § 8E1.3.

5. See U.S.S.G. § 8D1.4.

§ 8–19

1. See U.S.S.G. § 8C2.5(b)(1)(A).

program; and that, at the time of the offense, the company employed a workforce of 500 persons.

What is the possible criminal fine exposure of the company under the Federal Sentencing Guidelines? The sentencing court is likely to make the following calculations:

Base Offense Level[2]	6
Specific Offense Characteristics:	
Loss > $1,500,000[3]	12
More than minimal planning[4]	2
Adjusted Offense Level	$\overline{20}$
Base Fine[5]	$1,500,000
Base Culpability Score[6]	5
High–Level Involvement[7]	3
Obstruction of Justice[8]	$\underline{3}$
Total Culpability Score	11
Minimum/Maximum Multipliers[9]	2.00/4.00
Fine Range	$3,000,000 to $6,000,000[10]

This hypothetical illustrates the vulnerability of an organization that takes no steps to limit its criminal exposure under the Federal Sentencing Guidelines prior to, or following, the onset of a criminal investigation. The supplier makes matters worse by shredding documents relevant to the investigation, thereby incurring additional culpability points for obstructing justice.

Hypothetical #2—Hospital Overbills Medicare.

During an internal investigation, a large hospital chain discovers that the manager of one of its facilities (employing a workforce of 200) directed his staff to "debundle" the services performed at the facility and thereby overcharge the Medicare program for those services.[11] As a result of this practice, the facility overbilled the Medicare program by just over $1,500,000. The staff of the hospi-

2. See U.S.S.G. § 2F1.1(a).

3. See U.S.S.G. § 2F1.1(b)(1)(M).

4. See U.S.S.G. § 2F1.1(b)(2).

5. See U.S.S.G. § 8C2.4. Because the amount from the table that corresponds to an adjusted offense level of 20 is $650,000, and that amount is less than that gain to the DME supplier, the court will use the defendant's gain as its base fine.

6. See U.S.S.G. § 8C2.5.

7. See U.S.S.G. § 8C2.5(b)(3)(A).

8. See U.S.S.G. § 8C2.5(e).

9. See U.S.S.G. § 8C2.6.

10. The sentencing court could choose to depart upwardly from this range under Guideline § 8C4.11 if it decided the DME company's culpability was exceptional and not sufficiently accounted for by the culpability score. In addition, if the court found that the company operated primarily for a criminal purpose or by criminal means, the court could put it out of business by imposing a fine sufficient to divest the company of all of its net assets. See U.S.S.G. § 8C1.1, subject to the applicable statutory fine limits.

11. Steven S. Cowen deserves credit for much of this hypothetical. See Steven S. Cowen, Federal Guidelines for Sentencing Organizations and the Role of Compliance Plans, Health Care Fraud 1996, L–31, L–36.

tal's compliance unit discovered the wrongful conduct in the course of a routine audit. The hospital had established the compliance program a year earlier to ferret out such criminal conduct. After completing its investigation, the hospital fired the manager after determining that he had wrongfully exercised the substantial authority the hospital had delegated to him to operate the facility. The hospital decided not to share what it had learned about the matter with federal authorities, however. When a subsequent investigation by the OIG revealed the fraud, the hospital was indicted for multiple violations of the False Claims Act. Thereafter, the hospital fully cooperated with the OIG by sharing all it knew about the matter and pleaded guilty to the charges in the indictment prior to trial.

What is the possible criminal fine exposure of the company under the Federal Sentencing Guidelines?

Base Offense Level[12]	6
Specific Offense Characteristics:	
Loss > $1,500,000[13]	12
More than minimal planning[14]	2
Adjusted Offense Level	20
Base Fine[15]	$1,500,000
Base Culpability Score[16]	5
Substantial Authority Involvement[17]	3
Effective Corp. Compliance Program[18]	–3
Cooperating/Acceptance of Responsibility	–2
Total Culpability Score	3
Minimum/Maximum Multipliers[19]	0.60/1.20
Fine Range	$900,000 to $1,800,000[20]

This hypothetical illustrates the substantially improved position of an organization that has taken affirmative steps to limit its criminal exposure under the Federal Sentencing Guidelines prior to, and following, the initiation of a criminal investigation. Both hypotheticals assume the same base fine figure of $1,500,000. However, the

12. See U.S.S.G. § 2F1.1(a).

13. See U.S.S.G. § 2F1.1(b)(1)(M).

14. See U.S.S.G. § 2F1.1(b)(2).

15. See U.S.S.G. § 8C2.4. Because the amount from the table that corresponds to an adjusted offense level of 20 is $650,000, and that amount is less than that gain to the DME supplier, the court will use the defendant's gain as its base fine.

16. See U.S.S.G. § 8C2.5.

17. See U.S.S.G. § 8C2.5(b)(3)(A).

18. See U.S.S.G. § 8C2.5(f).

19. See U.S.S.G. § 8C2.6.

20. The sentencing court could choose to depart downward from this range under Guideline § 8C4.11 if it decided the hospital's culpability was exceptionally low and not sufficiently reflected by its culpability score.

ultimate exposure of the two organizational defendants is dramatically different due to their differing culpability scores (and concomitant multipliers).

Courts and commentators have increasingly signaled that corporate compliance programs are not only beneficial to organizations functioning in today's health care marketplace, they are essential not simply to reduce an organization's potential criminal and civil exposure, but to protect corporate directors from civil liability related to noncompliance.[21] For example, in a recent chapter of the Caremark litigation saga,[22] a chancery court approved a settlement of a shareholder derivative suit brought against the company following Caremark's conviction on mail fraud charges and its related payment of $250 million in criminal and civil fines. Although none of the company's senior officials were implicated in the wrongdoing, some of Caremark's shareholders brought the derivative suit charging that the company failed adequately to supervise employees who had participated in the fraud. While not particularly impressed with the substance of the allegations about the directors' conduct, the chancery court nevertheless approved the settlement. The court held that although Caremark's directors had taken certain steps to ensure compliance by its employees,[23] their failure to provide an adequate corporate information and reporting system was, at least in theory, a basis for rendering them responsible for the losses caused certain lower-level employees' noncompliance with governing laws and regulations.[24]

§ 8–20. The Benefits of Implementing a Corporate Compliance Plan

The benefits of an adequate corporate compliance program are increasingly difficult to ignore. At the very least, as discussed

21. See Adam G. Snyder, The False Claims Act Applied to Health Care Institutions: Gearing Up For Corporate Compliance, 1 DePaul J. Health Care L. 1 (Fall 1996); Gregory J. Naclerio, Hospital Corporate Compliance Programs, Andrews Health Care Fraud Litigation Reporter 3–4 (February 1997); Paul Flanagan and Elizabeth Ryan, "Health Care Providers Caught in the Crossfire: Corporate Compliance Programs Are Now a Necessity," The Health Lawyer, The ABA Health Law Section Newsletter, Vol. 9, No. 3, at 16–20; Memorandum of John T. Boese and Matt T. Morley, Corporate Compliance Programs: Effective Programs May Protect Corporate Directors From Personal Responsibility, at 3; Michael K. McCrory, An Ounce of Prevention: The Case for

Adopting a Healthcare Corporate Compliance Program, Andrews Health Care Fraud Litigation Reporter 3–6 (October 1996).

22. See In re Caremark International Inc. Derivative Litigation, No. 13670, 1996 WL 549894, 907817 (Del.Ch. Sept.25, 1996).

23. Prior to the misconduct, Caremark had set compliance standards, required certain company officers to review certain regulated activities, appointed a compliance officer, instituted an auditing system whereby compliance was to be monitored, and ensured that its employees were trained about the need for compliance and kept appraised of governing laws. Id. at 3–4.

24. See id. at 10.

above, a corporate compliance program operating in good faith will reduce an organizational defendant's criminal fine exposure. It may also stave off costly *qui tam* litigation. Some have even argued that the existence of a corporate compliance program may constitute an absolute bar to corporate criminal prosecution.[1]

A company without a compliance program that becomes an unsuccessful target of a federal investigation will have little choice but to establish a program and operate that program under the watchful eye of federal officials in order to resolve the case. All of the settlement agreements between corporate health care providers and the federal government over the last few years have required that providers develop and maintain a workable plan to show their continuing compliance.[2] For example, the criminal plea and civil settlement agreements signed by National Medical Enterprise (NME) in 1994 to settle charges that it had made unlawful kickback payments required NME to pay a total of $379 million in criminal fines, civil damages and penalties. Under a plea agreement with the government, NME pleaded guilty to six counts of paying unlawful kickbacks and one count of conspiring to defraud the United States, and agreed to establish and maintain an effective "Corporate Integrity Program," the proper functioning of which the HHS would oversee for a period of five years.[3]

The prospect of operating a health care business under the watchful eye of the HHS is bound to be daunting. HHS's oversight over NME's corporate integrity program, for instance, includes the right to examine the hospital chain's books and records to verify its compliance with standards of conduct adopted in connection with the program.[4] If the fear of omnipresent oversight by the HHS fails

§ 8–20

1. See Charles J. Walsh and Alissa Pyrich, Corporate Compliance Programs as a Defense to Criminal Liability: Can a Corporation Save Its Soul? 47 Rutgers L. Rev. 605, 607 (Winter 1995).

2. This will continue. The Fraud and Abuse Control Program mandated by HIPAA and established by the Secretary in January 1997, indicates that HHS will negotiate settlements in the future with an "accompanying compliance agreement or compliance provisions aimed at preventing future wrongdoing ..." See 1 BNA's Health Care Fraud Report 66 (Jan. 29, 1997).

3. Prior to its conviction NME had instituted a compliance program. However, NME's legal staff took insufficient steps to ensure that compliance standards were being met. See 4 BNA Health Law Rptr. 268 (Feb. 23, 1995)

(comments of John Meyers, Associate General Counsel for NME).

4. Not surprisingly, the dimensions of the NME corporate integrity program were strikingly similar to the seven requisites for an effective program described in the Organizational Guidelines. See § 8–13b. NME's Board of Directors was expected to adopt formal standards of conduct that conformed with laws and regulations governing the behavior of participants in federally funded health care programs; each director, officer, employee or other agent was required to acknowledge the standards in writing; the Board was required to certify annually to HHS that the standards had been so acknowledged by its workforce; NME was required to institute a training program to instruct its personnel on how to comply with applicable laws, regulations

to motivate a health care entity to adopt a compliance program, the rewards being reaped by providers with such programs may succeed where fear has failed. Some ably advised health care entities have avoided criminal prosecution altogether by responding quickly to criminal conduct once discovered, instituting corporate compliance measures on their own, and agreeing to cooperate with the government's investigative efforts. In the recent case involving Damon Clinical Laboratories (Damon), for example,[5] Corning Clinical Laboratories, the purchaser of Damon, substantially limited its criminal and civil liability by responding quickly when it discovered that Damon had submitted false claims to the government. Damon had bundled certain medically unnecessary tests with other tests commonly ordered by physicians, and then billed the Medicare program for the bundled tests with knowledge that the bundled tests had not been knowingly ordered by the physicians and were not medically necessary. Following an investigation, Damon pleaded guilty to a one count criminal information which charged Damon with conspiring to defraud the United States. The court imposed upon Damon criminal and civil fines totaling $119 million, which fines were to be paid within one week. As the purchaser of Damon, Corning Clinical Laboratories was vulnerable to prosecution for Damon's misconduct. Corning effectively limited its exposure, however, by immediately terminating the criminal billing practice upon its discovery, and by attempting to prevent its recurrence by the establishing a compliance program at each of the Damon locations.[6] In a settlement agreement negotiated with Corning Clinical thereafter, the government agreed not to prosecute Corning Clinical for Damon's criminal conduct. In turn, Corning Clinical agreed to cooperate with the government in its investigation of Damon, its officers and employees, to institute a corporate integrity agreement with HHS and to guarantee payment of Damon's fines.

§ 8–21. Model Corporate Compliance Plans

Health care entities that decide to adopt a corporate compliance program have not been left entirely at sea. In addition to the

and standards of conduct; each director, officer, employee and agent had to undergo at least one hour of training each year; each NME manager was required to discuss the compliance program with each employee under her supervision; NME was precluded from hiring or retaining any person who had been convicted of a health care offense, or who had been excluded from participation in any federally funded health care program; and NME was required to summarize and evaluate annually in a report to HHS its compliance efforts, and to report any compliance violations within sixty days of discovery. See Plea Agreement and Civil Administrative Settlement Agreement, United States v. NME Psychiatric Hospitals, Inc., No. CR94–0268 (D.D.C. June 29, 1994).

5. See Information and Settlement Agreement, United States v. Damon Clinical Laboratories, Inc., No. 1:96cr10256 (D.Mass. Oct. 9, 1996), reprinted in Andrews Health Care Fraud Litigation Reporter 46–70 (October 1996).

6. See Health Care Fraud Litigation Reporter at 9 (October 1996).

guidance provided by the Sentencing Guideline provisions, the HHS has issued a model compliance plan for clinical laboratories, and it plans to publish more model plans in the future.[1] Clinical laboratories (and other health care entities) can use the model compliance plan to help determine the features that could be incorporated into their own compliance programs. HHS is currently working on a number of other model compliance plans, including a model plan for hospitals and managed care organizations.[2] HHS delayed the issuance of its proposed model compliance plan for hospitals after receiving considerable criticism of the plan from members of the hospital industry.[3] The finalized model plan for hospitals is expected to be distributed by early 1998.

Although similarities between the model compliance plan for clinical laboratories and the proposed compliance plan for hospitals exist,[4] important differences also appear. The terms of the model plan drafted to guide the compliance efforts of hospitals are more general than those included in the model plan for laboratories. The explanation for this difference appears to be that HHS is hoping to create a hospital compliance plan that can be adopted (with appropriate modifications) by hospitals that differ greatly in size, geographic location, financial structure and resources.

The proposed hospital compliance plan is likely to promote HHS's basic philosophy about effective compliance efforts: i.e., adoption of a compliance program will be an empty gesture if it is not "effective," and to be effective a program must be diligent in its efforts to weed out fraud and must be openly embraced by the upper echelons of the hospital's supervisory staff. To this end, clear and well publicized standards of conduct for all employees must be adopted; a compliance officer must be hired; the compliance officer must be given real authority and have access to the hospital's senior staff, board of directors and CEO; hospital employees must be continuously schooled about the hospital's compliance standards, prompted to report suspected acts of fraud, and disciplined for failing to comply with established codes of conduct; and annual audits must be conducted to monitor the hospital's compliance

---

§ 8–21

1. For an excellent summary of the essential elements of the plan, see 1 BNA's Health Care Fraud Reporter 117 (Feb. 26, 1997). The model compliance plan itself can be found in Health Care Fraud 1997 at Appendix A–4 (ABA–CLE National Institute). For other helpful readings on how to structure a compliance plan, see Michael Zeldin, How to Set Up a Money Laundering Compliance Program at P–33, Health Care Fraud 1997 (ABA–CLE National Institute); Ed-

ward J. Hopkins, Compliance Programs in the New World at B–1, Health Care Fraud 1997 (ABA–CLE National Institute).

2. See 1 BNA's Health Care Fraud Reporter 416 (July 2, 1997).

3. See 1 BNA's Health Care Fraud Rptr. 649 (October 8, 1997).

4. For a helpful analysis of the common elements of the plans see 1 BNA's Health Care Fraud Rptr. 117.

efforts.[5] Unlike the model compliance plan for clinical laboratories, the proposed hospital plan may recommend that hospitals conduct a criminal background check on (as opposed to a check of the personal references of) any prospective employee who will exercise compliance oversight authority, and to decline to hire any person who has been convicted of a health care offense or excluded from participation in a federal health care program. This change reflects that HHS's thinking about preventive compliance efforts is still evolving.

§ 8–22. Double Jeopardy Concerns

Some health care providers have looked to the Double Jeopardy Clause of the Fifth Amendment for protection against the debilitating effect of parallel criminal, civil and exclusion proceedings. The Double Jeopardy Clause guarantees that no person shall "be subject for the same offense to be twice put in jeopardy of life or limb."[1] The United States Supreme Court has interpreted the phrase "to be twice put in jeopardy" to prohibit both multiple prosecutions and multiple punishments.[2] As explored more fully below, the constitutional guarantee against multiple prosecutions may be of use to the health care provider who successfully defends against a health care fraud charge and is prosecuted anew by the same jurisdiction. It will be less helpful to the provider who is prosecuted by more than one sovereign, such as where a state government and the federal government seek to prosecute the same provider for the same offense conduct. The double jeopardy prohibition against successive punishment has potential importance for any health care provider who finds herself defending against allegations of programmatic wrongdoing, since the provider may be subject to an assortment of penalties arising out of the same misconduct, including criminal punishment, civil sanctions, an exclusion judgment and an order to forfeit money and property.

a. Multiple Prosecutions

The aspect of the Double Jeopardy Clause familiar to most laypersons is the protection the clause provides to a criminal defendant against successive prosecution by the same sovereign for the same offense. In its simplest form, the clause prevents a prosecutor who is frustrated by an acquittal from prosecuting the accused for the same offense before a second jury in the hope of finally securing a conviction. It provides repose to the already-

---

5. See id.

§ 8–22

1. U.S. CONST. amend. V.

2. See North Carolina v. Pearce, 395 U.S. 711, 89 S.Ct. 2072, 23 L.Ed.2d 656 (1969).

prosecuted defendant from having to defend herself a second time in the same jurisdiction for the same misconduct.

The protection against multiple prosecutions is a shield against successive *criminal* actions. Like a private individual, the government has the right to recover for damages it has suffered as a result of wrongdoing by a health care provider or entity, even if the provider or entity has already been the subject of criminal prosecution.[3] Thus, the double jeopardy prohibition against multiple prosecutions does not protect a previously prosecuted defendant from being the subject of a second trial arising out of the same misconduct if the second trial is civil, rather than criminal, in nature.

Neither does the Double Jeopardy Clause prevent a second criminal trial for the same misdeeds if the trial is brought by a different sovereign.[4] It is not uncommon for criminal conduct to violate simultaneously both a federal and a state statute. When this occurs, the federal and state governments may both have an interest in prosecuting the offender, and as distinct sovereigns, each enjoys the right to prosecute those who would violate its laws without offending the federal double jeopardy guarantee. As put by one court, "the Double Jeopardy Clause does not prohibit the federal government from imposing criminal sanctions following state criminal sanctions since both the state and federal governments have the power, inherent in any sovereign, to independently define and punish an offense."[5] Thus, a state prosecution that follows a federal prosecution,[6] and vice versa,[7] will not violate the federal Double Jeopardy Clause even where the charges of both sovereigns arise out of the same transaction. Although the federal Double Jeopardy Clause will permit such dual sovereign prosecutions, some state courts have interpreted their own state constitutions to mandate a greater measure of protection against multiple prosecutions. In one state, for example, the courts routinely examine the interest an offender has in being free from having to defend herself in consecutive prosecutions for the same acts when determining whether the offender would be placed in double jeopardy by a successive prosecution brought by the state.[8] Other state courts

---

3. See Rex Trailer Co. v. United States, 350 U.S. 148, 76 S.Ct. 219, 100 L.Ed. 149 (1956). If the damage award imposed after such a second civil trial is unduly "excessive," however, the award may violate the "multiple punishment" prohibition of the Double Jeopardy Clause.

4. See United States v. Wheeler, 435 U.S. 313, 316–17 , 98 S.Ct. 1079, 1082, 55 L.Ed.2d 303 (1978). See also Kahn v. The Inspector General, 848 F.Supp. 432 (S.D.N.Y.1994).

5. Chapman v. United States Department of Health and Human Services, 821 F.2d 523 (10th Cir.1987).

6. See Bartkus v. Illinois, 359 U.S. 121, 79 S.Ct. 676, 3 L.Ed.2d 684 (1959).

7. See United States v. Lanza, 260 U.S. 377, 43 S.Ct. 141, 67 L.Ed. 314 (1922).

8. See State v. Hogg, 118 N.H. 262, 385 A.2d 844 (1978).

scrutinize the similarity of state and federal charges brought against a single defendant to determine whether the dual statutory schemes were designed to protect the same or different governmental interests. In Michigan, for example, the state's double jeopardy provision has been read to prohibit a succeeding prosecution in the state unless the interests of the state and the interests of the original prosecuting jurisdiction substantially diverge.[9] Other states have adopted similar approaches under their own state constitutions.[10] In short, even if the federal Double Jeopardy Clause is not violated by a succeeding state prosecution, an existing state double jeopardy provision may offer an embattled health care provider some refuge.[11]

b. Multiple Punishments

Although many regard the Double Jeopardy Clause as simply a bar against a second prosecution of an individual who has already been forced to defend herself for the same offense in an earlier criminal case, the Clause also protects against the imposition of multiple *punishment* for the same offense. Unlike "prosecutions" which may only be criminal, "punishments" may carry a variety of labels, including criminal, civil or administrative. No matter the label attached to the sanction, the Double Jeopardy Clause may be implicated if the sanction is imposed to punish an individual or entity for wrongdoing for which the individual or entity has already received punishment.

As the United States Supreme Court held in *United States v. Halper*,[12] for instance, the Double Jeopardy Clause will be violated where civil damages are imposed on a defendant who has already been criminally convicted and sentenced for the same wrongdoing, if the damage award is so excessive as to constitute a second punishment. The facts of *Halper* help to illustrate how a civil penalty can offend the federal double jeopardy guarantee. Irwin Halper, the manager of a medical supply company, was convicted of submitting 65 false claims to the Medicare program. The submission of the false claims resulted in a total loss to the government in the amount of $585. Upon conviction, Halper was sentenced to a two-year prison term and fined $5,000. After this sentence was imposed, the federal government sued Halper under the civil False

---

9. See People v. Cooper, 398 Mich. 450, 247 N.W.2d 866 (1976).

10. See Commonwealth v. Mills, 447 Pa. 163, 286 A.2d 638 (1971); Northrup v. Relin, 197 App. Div. 2d 228, 613 N.Y.S.2d 506 (4th Dep't 1994); State v. LeCoure, 158 Mont. 340, 491 P.2d 1228 (1971).

11. Not all state courts reject the dual sovereignty approach recognized by the federal courts. See, e.g., Lavon v. State, 586 S.W.2d 112 (Tenn.1979); State v. Franklin, 735 P.2d 34 (Utah 1987); State v. LeCompte, 441 So.2d 249 (La. 1983); Bell v. State, 22 Md.App. 496, 323 A.2d 677 (1974); and Stewart v. State, 652 S.W.2d 496 (1st Dist. 1983).

12. 490 U.S. 435, 109 S.Ct. 1892, 104 L.Ed.2d 487 (1989).

Claims Act,[13] seeking civil penalties for the same conduct for which Halper had been criminally convicted. Based on Halper's conviction, the district court granted summary judgment to the government on the issue of liability.[14] The court then considered the parties' arguments concerning the appropriate remedy for Halper's violations. On its face, the False Claims Act appeared to mandate the imposition of a penalty of $130,000 ($2,000 for each of the 65 false claims submitted by Halper) plus a penalty of $1,170 (twice the government's believed loss) plus the costs of the action.[15] Citing double jeopardy concerns raised by Halper's earlier criminal punishment, however, the district court refused to impose the maximum penalty condoned by the civil statute. Instead the court read the $2,000 per claim provision to be discretionary, and imposed the full sanction for only 8 of the 65 violations. Later on a motion for reconsideration, the district court revised this ruling, and limited the government's recovery to $1,170 (an amount twice its actual loss) plus the costs of the action. On direct appeal from the government, the Supreme Court agreed with the trial court holding that although the government is entitled to "rough remedial justice,"[16] it may not properly seek from a defendant who has previously sustained a criminal sentence a civil penalty that has no "rational relation to the goal of compensating the government for its loss."[17] The Court held further that Halper's was one of those "rare cases" in which the award of the full amount authorized by a civil statute would constitute a second punishment in violation of the Double Jeopardy Clause,[18] and remanded the case to allow the government the opportunity to demonstrate that the district court's approximation of its damages was insufficiently low.

Halper expressly indicates that the question of whether a civil sanction constitutes punishment for double jeopardy purposes "requires a particularized assessment of the penalty imposed and the purposes that the penalty may fairly be said to serve."[19] If a succeeding civil damages award (such as that authorized by the civil False Claims Act) serves "the twin aims of retribution and deterrence" and cannot "fairly be characterized as remedial,"[20] the award will constitute a second punishment violative of the Double Jeopardy Clause.

Counsel for health care providers have relied on *Halper* to challenge a variety of alleged second "punishments" under the Double Jeopardy Clause. Some have used the *Halper* standards to

---

13. See Chapter 2.

14. See United States v. Halper, 660 F.Supp. 531, 532–33 (S.D.N.Y.1987).

15. See 31 U.S.C. § 3729 (1982 ed. Supp. II).

16. Id. at 4529.

17. Id. at 4530.

18. Id. at 449, 109 S.Ct. at 1902.

19. Id. at 448, 109 S.Ct. at 1901.

20. Id. at 448–49, 109 S.Ct. at 1901–02.

challenge civil penalties sought after the imposition of criminal punishment.[21] Others have challenged the government's ability to exclude convicted health care providers from participation in the entitlement programs, arguing that such exclusions constitute impermissible multiple punishment within the meaning of the Clause.[22] Still others have resisted civil forfeiture judgments entered after a criminal conviction.[23]

As might be expected, the courts have not always found it easy to determine when an authorized penalty is so weighty that it ceases to be remedial and becomes punitive. Although the rule of *Halper* clearly establishes that a civil penalty may be so excessive as to create a double jeopardy problem, the decision did not make it clear when an award will cross the line between "rough remedial justice" (to which the government is entitled) and punitive injustice. Moreover, the facts of *Halper* may be of little help to a convicted offender attempting to identify this line. The minor losses apparently suffered by the government in *Halper* ($585) stood in such sharp contrast to the recovery authorized by the statute ($130,000 or more) that it may be difficult to use the case to predict the chances of future double jeopardy claims arising from less troublesome facts.[24] It seems unlikely that cases in the future will present such a yawning gap between the losses attributable to a provider's fraud and the authorized civil penalties.

(1) Civil Penalty Actions Initiated Subsequent to Conviction

As held in *Halper*, a civil damages award may violate the Double Jeopardy Clause as an impermissible second punishment if its lack of a rational relationship to the government's actual losses suggests that the award seeks retributive and punitive, rather than remedial, goals. This rule has been applied to prohibit a sizeable civil damages recovery granted after a criminal conviction,[25] and, by one court, to prohibit the criminal prosecution of certain acts after the award of civil damages.[26]

Early applications of *Halper* suggest that an award of treble the government's demonstrated losses will pose no constitutional problem.[27] The facts of *United States v. Pani* illustrate.[28] In 1983,

---

21. See § 8–21b(1).

22. See § 8–21b(2).

23. See § 8–21b(3).

24. In *Halper*, the False Claims Act authorized a penalty of over 224 times the government's loss from the fraud. Halper's fraud caused the government a $585 loss. The False Claims Act authorized a $2,000 civil penalty for each of the 65 claims, plus $1,170 (twice the government's loss) and the costs of the

civil action. Under this formula, the government's authorized recovery would have been in excess of $130,000.

25. See United States v. Halper, 490 U.S. 435, 109 S.Ct. 1892, 104 L.Ed.2d 487 (1989).

26. See United States v. Mayers, 957 F.2d 858 (11th Cir.1992).

27. See, e.g., United States v. Pani, 717 F.Supp. 1013 (S.D.N.Y.1989). The same conclusion has been reached by

Dr. Kailash Pani, a neurosurgeon, was charged with 9 counts of mail fraud, 63 false claims counts and 49 counts of converting government funds. After trial the next year, Pani was convicted on 4 counts of mail fraud, 3 counts of making false claims and 3 counts of conversion. He was then sentenced to a two-year suspended sentence, fined $40,000, and ordered to make restitution to Blue Cross and Blue Shield of Greater New York and the Medicare program in the amounts of $4,187 and $1,380, respectively. Two years later the government brought an action against the doctor and his corporation under the civil False Claims Act, alleging that the defendants had filed 157 fraudulent claims for payment for surgeries that the doctor had not performed.[29] Sixty-three of the 157 civil claims related to acts that had been the subject of the earlier criminal case, although only three of those sixty-three criminal counts had resulted in counts of conviction. Citing *United States v. Halper*, the defendants challenged the government's civil suit for damages on double jeopardy grounds. The court disagreed. The court found that, unlike Halper, Pani's was "not the 'rare case' of a 'prolific but small gauge offender' subject to a second punishment 'overwhelmingly disproportionate to the damages he has caused.' "[30] In light of the substantial costs incurred by the government in investigating and prosecuting Pani's fraud, the court ruled that a rational relationship existed between the recovery sought by the government[31] and the remedial goal of compensating the government for its losses. Accordingly, no double jeopardy problem was thought to arise from the sovereign's civil suit.

The result in *Pani* confirms that, contrary to early hopes, *Halper* is likely to provide only the most limited help to health care providers struggling to cap their criminal and civil liability. *Halper* itself warns that the decision established a "rule for the rare case,"[32] and the determination of when a penalty is punitive as opposed to remedial "will not be an exact pursuit."[33] "[I]n the ordinary case fixed-penalty-plus-double-damages provisions" will pass constitutional muster,[34] and as shown below, the efforts of providers to extend the decision beyond the context of civil penalties have been largely unsuccessful.

state courts as well. See Kuriansky v. Orvieto, 653 N.Y.S.2d 953, 955 (2d Dep't 1997); Kuriansky v. Professional Care, Inc., 147 Misc.2d 782, 555 N.Y.S.2d 1 (1990); Harvey–Cook v. Miroff, 130 A.D.2d 621, 515 N.Y.S.2d 551 (2d Dep't 1987); Harvey–Cook v. Steel, 124 A.D.2d 709, 508 N.Y.S.2d 220 (2d Dep't 1986).

28. United States v. Pani, 717 F.Supp. 1013 (S.D.N.Y.1989).

29. See id. at 1014.

30. Id. at 1019 (quoting Halper, 490 U.S. at 449).

31. The government sought $32,460 in damages (three times its actual loss, plus $10,000 for each claim, minus the restitution Pani had paid as a result of the criminal judgment).

32. Id.

33. Id. at 449, 109 S.Ct. at 1902.

34. See id. at 449, 109 S.Ct. at 1902, 104 L.Ed.2d at 502.

(2) Exclusion Proceedings Initiated Subsequent to Conviction

Resourceful arguments have been made that other penalties besides civil damage awards might be so burdensome as to place a previously punished health care provider in double jeopardy. Several providers have challenged efforts by the government to exclude convicted health care providers from participation in one of the health care entitlement programs and the courts have acknowledged that the exclusion provisions serve both remedial and punitive purposes.[35] To date, however, the courts have been reluctant to find the co-existing punitive and remedial aspects of exclusionary orders as violative of the Double Jeopardy Clause.[36] In *Manocchio v. Kusserow*,[37] for example, one court considered whether an exclusion penalty violated the double jeopardy rights of a doctor who had been charged with filing a fraudulent claim for payment in the amount of $62.40. To resolve the case, Manocchio pleaded guilty to a misdemeanor. He was then was sentenced to three years probation, fined $1,000 and ordered to pay restitution. After sentencing, the OIG notified Manocchio that HHS would seek his exclusion for the mandatory five-year period. Manocchio resisted exclusion arguing, unsuccessfully, that his exclusion would violate the Double Jeopardy clause as interpreted in *Halper*. On appeal, the Eleventh Circuit expressed the view that although *Halper* may be helpful in framing the double jeopardy analysis, it does not technically apply outside the context of a civil damage award.[38] The court held further that while Manocchio's five-year exclusion might "carry the sting of punishment," the aim of the exclusion provision was nonetheless primarily remedial—it enabled the OIG to shield the Medicare and Medicaid programs from those who would defraud the programs and safeguarded limited taxpayer funds. Consequently, the doctor's exclusion was found not to have violated the Double Jeopardy Clause.

---

35. The legislative history of the exclusion provisions reflects the exclusion provisions' mixed retributive, deterrent and remedial motives. The Senate Finance Committee Report, for example, states clearly that the "mandatory five-year exclusion should provide a clear and strong deterrent against the commission of criminal acts." S. Rep. No. 109, 100th Cong., 1st Sess. 1–2 (1987), reprinted in 1987 U.S.C.C.A.N. at 686. The same Report indicates elsewhere, however, that the basic purpose of the Act within which the provisions are contained is remedial—"to improve the ability of the Secretary and the Inspector General of [HHS] to protect Medicare, Medicaid, [and other social services programs] from fraud and abuse, and to protect the beneficiaries of those programs from incompetent practitioners and from inappropriate or inadequate care." Id., 1987 U.S.C.C.A.N. at 682.

36. See Manocchio v. Kusserow, 961 F.2d 1539, 1541–42 (11th Cir.1992) (because exclusion is a remedial sanction, the constitutional prohibition against double jeopardy is not violated); Kahn v. The Inspector General, 848 F.Supp. 432, 437–38 (S.D.N.Y.1994) (same); Crawford v. Sullivan, 1993 WL 75117 (N.D.Ill. 1993) (same); Greene v. Sullivan, 731 F.Supp. 838, 839 (E.D.Tenn.1990) (same).

37. 961 F.2d 1539 (11th Cir.1992).

38. See id. at 1542, (citing United States v. Reed, 937 F.2d 575, 578 (11th Cir.1991).

(3) Civil Forfeiture Proceedings Initiated Subsequent to Conviction

In addition to the sanctions discussed earlier, health care providers may also be subject to a variety of forfeiture provisions which may lead to the loss of valuable property. Although forfeiture provisions were historically civil in nature, today forfeiture statutes may be either civil, criminal or administrative.[39] Civil forfeitures provisions confer in rem jurisdiction over forfeitable property even in the absence of a criminal conviction or in personam judgment against an individual. Once the government establishes that there is probable cause to believe that property is subject to civil forfeiture, the burden shifts to the property owner to show by a preponderance of the evidence that the property is not forfeitable.[40] By contrast, criminal forfeitures must accompany criminal charges. Thus, upon a conviction, in addition to in personam criminal penalties, a health care offender may be ordered to forfeit property attributable to his crime.[41] Less often used administrative forfeiture provisions authorize executive branch agencies to seek the forfeiture of unclaimed property in an uncontested non-judicial proceeding.[42]

Double jeopardy claims post-*Halper* have primarily concerned the application of civil forfeiture provisions to convicted felons. Federal laws authorize the civil forfeiture of property or proceeds traceable to or involved in money laundering[43] and other health care fraud offenses.[44] These laws enable the government, for example, to seek the forfeiture of fraudulently obtained monies that have been deposited by an offender into a bank account with the intent to promote future fraudulent conduct or to conceal the nature of the proceeds.[45] Also potentially subject to forfeiture are items purchased with the proceeds of fraud, provided the government is able to trace the purchase to the fraudulent profits.[46] These civil

---

39. For an excellent discussion of the forfeiture provisions of concern to today's health care providers and suppliers, see Robert W. Biddle, Michael Schatzow and Allison Lowery, Asset Forfeiture and Freezes in Health Care Fraud Litigation at P–1, Health Care Fraud 1997 (ABA–CLE National Institute, Chicago, Ill.).

40. For a helpful discussion of the way civil forfeiture proceedings work, see Smith, Prosecution and Defense of Forfeiture Cases § 11.03.

41. The forfeiture of property related to drug trafficking violations may be ordered under 21 U.S.C. § 853. The forfeiture of property related to racketeering crimes may be ordered under 18

U.S.C. § 1963. The forfeiture of property related to money laundering, financial frauds, and federal program frauds may be ordered under 18 U.S.C. § 982 and 21 U.S.C. § 853.

42. See 19 U.S.C. § 1608. Although authorized to seek administrative forfeitures, the Department of Justice has adopted a policy of seeking real property forfeitures judicially. See U.S. Dep't of Justice, U.S. Attorney's Manual § 3–2 (1992).

43. See 18 U.S.C. § 981.

44. See 18 U.S.C. §§ 1956 and 1957.

45. See 18 U.S.C. § 1956.

46. See 18 U.S.C. § 981.

asset forfeiture provisions serve a multitude of purposes, many of which are based on principles of deterrence or retribution. The provisions seek, for example, to recover the proceeds of unlawful activity, to eliminate the financial incentives an offender may have to engage in fraudulent conduct, to destroy the structure of a criminal enterprise and to punish criminal activity.[47] Individuals subject to costly civil forfeiture orders after the imposition of a criminal sanction have argued that the Double Jeopardy Clause prohibits such forfeiture judgments as multiple punishment under *Halper*. The Court did not decide in *Halper* whether a costly civil forfeiture might also violate the Double Jeopardy Clause. However, the Supreme Court's recent decision in *United States v. Ursery*[48] suggests that an in rem civil forfeiture judgment imposed on a health care provider is not likely to be considered punishment for double jeopardy purposes. The *Ursery* Court recognized that the government is authorized to bring parallel criminal and civil proceedings based on the same underlying events, and held that the Double Jeopardy Clause does not bar an in rem civil forfeiture simply because prior criminal punishment has already been imposed. Although such proceedings are not automatically exempt from double jeopardy analysis, only "where the 'clearest proof' indicates that an in rem civil forfeiture is so 'punitive either in purpose or effect' as to be the equivalent to a criminal proceeding," will the forfeiture be subject to the Double Jeopardy Clause.[49] If grossly out of proportion to the underlying conduct, however, an in rem civil forfeiture may violate the Excessive Fines Clause of the Eighth Amendment.[50]

§ 8–23. Ex Post Facto Considerations

A final consideration for health care providers subject to punishment for a health care offense is the Ex Post Facto Clause of the United States Constitution which prohibits the enactment of any law "which imposes a punishment for an act which was not punishable at the time it was committed; or imposes additional punishment to that then described."[1] To implicate the Ex Post Facto Clause, a law must be criminal or penal in nature, it must have been applied retroactively to events that occurred prior to the law's enactment, and its application must have redounded to the

---

47. See Anthony G. Hall, The Effect of Double Jeopardy on Asset Forfeiture, 32 Idaho L. Rev. 527, 528 (1996).

48. See ___ U.S. ___, 116 S.Ct. 2135, 135 L.Ed.2d 549 (1996).

49. Id. at 2148 n.3, quoting United States v. One Assortment of 89 Fire-

arms, 465 U.S. 354, 363, 104 S.Ct. 1099, 1105, 79 L.Ed.2d 361 (1984).

50. See Austin v. United States, 509 U.S. 602, 113 S.Ct. 2801, 125 L.Ed.2d 488 (1993).

§ 8–23

1. U.S. CONST. art. 1, § 9, cl. 3.

offender's disadvantage.[2] Where these conditions are met, an offender may not be subject to an enhanced penalty provision not in existence at the time he committed the offense.

As with the Double Jeopardy Clause,[3] if a newly adopted sanction is remedial rather than punitive, the Ex Post Facto Clause will provide its bearer no protection. The courts have used the test enunciated in *United States v. Halper*[4] to determine when a sanction is punitive for ex post facto purposes. Under this test even a sanction expressly labelled as civil may be considered punitive if the provision seeks retributive or deterrent goals and cannot fairly be characterized as remedial.[5] A link between a statutory scheme and a punitive goal may not automatically rouse the Ex Post Facto Clause, however, as the facts of *Manocchio v. Kusserow*[6] demonstrate. Val Manocchio, a medical doctor licensed in Florida, after investigation, pleaded guilty to a misdemeanor charge of filing a single fraudulent Medicare claim for payment in the amount of $62.40. After his conviction on the charge, the HHS sought to exclude Manocchio from further participation in the Medicare program for not less than five years. Manocchio contested his exclusion on the ground that it would violate both the Double Jeopardy Clause[7] and the Ex Post Facto Clause, since Congress had enacted the five-year mandatory exclusion provision after Manocchio had committed the offense. The court rejected Manocchio's argument ruling that although Congress clearly intended to deter similar offenses when it revised the penalty, the primary purpose of the strengthened exclusion provision was remedial, and as such the Ex Post Facto Clause did not apply.[8]

2. See Weaver v. Graham, 450 U.S. 24, 28, 101 S.Ct. 960, 963, 67 L.Ed.2d 17 (1981).

3. See discussion supra at § 8–21.

4. 490 U.S. 435, 109 S.Ct. 1892, 104 L.Ed.2d 487 (1989).

5. See id. at 447–449.

6. 961 F.2d 1539 (11th Cir.1992).

7. See supra at § 8–21b(2).

8. See Manocchio v. Kusserow, 961 F.2d at 1551.

*

TABLE OF STATUTES

TABLE OF STATUTES

TABLE OF STATUTES

TABLE OF STATUTES

TABLE OF STATUTES

TABLE OF STATUTES

TABLE OF STATUTES

TABLE OF STATUTES

TABLE OF STATUTES

TABLE OF STATUTES

TABLE OF STATUTES

TABLE OF STATUTES

467

TABLE OF STATUTES

TABLE OF STATUTES

*

TABLE OF RULES AND REGULATIONS

TABLE OF RULES AND REGULATIONS

TABLE OF RULES AND REGULATIONS

TABLE OF RULES AND REGULATIONS

TABLE OF RULES AND REGULATIONS

TABLE OF CASES

479

TABLE OF CASES

TABLE OF CASES

TABLE OF CASES

INDEX

INDEX

INVESTIGATIONS—Continued
Defenses against—Continued
Fifth Amendment, § 7–14
Fourth Amendment, § 7–15
Joint defense privilege, § 7–16e
Physician-patient privilege, § 7–6a
Psychotherapist privilege, § 7–16b
Sole proprietors, § 7–14
Work product privilege, § 7–16d
Funding and coordination of, § 7–9
Health Care Fraud and Abuse Control Account, § 7–9a
Health Care Fraud and Abuse Data Collection Program, § 7–9b
HIPAA, effect of, § 7–9
National Association of Medicaid Fraud Control Units, § 7–3
Grand Jury
Composition, § 7–12a
Indictment power, § 7–12a
Investigations power, § 7–12b
Prosector, role of, before, § 7–12b
Rules of evidence, § 7–12b
Secrecy, § 7–12a
Subpoenas, §§ 7–11, 7–12b, 7–15
Motions to quash, §§ 7–15,
Overbreadth challenges, § 7–15
Relevance requirement, § 7–15
Investigators, §§ 7–2—7–7
Carriers and intermediaries, § 7–2
Department of Health and Human Services, § 7–4
Health Care Financing Administration, § 7–4b
Office of Inspector General, HHS, § 7–4a
Peer review organizations, § 7–5a
Department of Justice, § 7–5
Federal Bureau of Investigation, § 7–5a
United States Attorney's Offices, § 7–5b
Drug Enforcement Administration (DEA), § 7–6
Inspectors General
For Amtrak (IG/Amtrak), § 7–6
For Department of Labor (IG/Labor), § 7–6
For Office of Personnel Management (IG/OPM), § 7–6
For Railroad Retirement Board (IG/RRB), § 7–6
Medicaid Fraud Control Units (MFCUs), § 7–3
Private Insurers, role of, § 7–7b
State medical and licensing boards, § 7–7a
Whistleblowers, § 7–7c
Of Corporate entities, § 7–14
Of Sole proprietors, § 7–14
OIG authority to investigate, § 7–21a
Operation Restore Trust, § 7–8
Required records exception, § 7–14b
Searches, §§ 7–19, 7–23, 7–24
Subpoena ad testificandum, § 7–12b
Act of production immunity, § 7–14a
Failure to comply with, § 7–12b
Fifth Amendment as limitation, §§ 7–13, 7–14
Grant of immunity, effect of, § 7–14c
Subpoena duces tecum, § 7–12b

INVESTMENT INTERESTS
See Bribe and Kickback Prohibition; Self–Referrals, this index

JOINT VENTURE ARRANGEMENTS
And anti-kickback prohibitions, §§ 3–13b, 3–15a, 3–16a
Exclusion efforts against, § 3–16a(4)

SAFE HARBOR REGULATIONS—Continued
Managed care organizations—Continued
    Increased coverage, § 3–11h(1)
    Medicare SELECT insurers, § 3–11h(4)
    Reduced cost sharing amounts, § 3–11h(2)
    Reduced premiums, § 3–11h(2)
Management contracts, §§ 3–11c, 3–11c(3)
Personal services, §§ 3–11c, 3–11c(3)
Proposed safe harbors, § 3–12
    Cooperative hospital service organizations, § 3–12e
    Investment interests, § 3–12a
    Obstetrical malpractice insurance subsidies, § 3–12c
    Practitioner recruitment, § 3–12b
    Referral agreements, specialty services, § 3–12d
Referral services, § 3–11e
Sale of practice, § 3–11d
Space rentals, §§ 3–11c, 3–11c(1)
Waiver of coinsurance and deductibles, hospital care, § 3–11g
Warranties, § 3–11f

SEARCH WARRANTS
    See also Privileges; Investigations, this index
Increasing use of, § 7–19
Motions for return of seized documents, § 7–10d
Particularity requirement, § 7–19b
Private searches, § 7–19e
Probable cause requirement, § 7–19a
Unauthorized parties in execution of, § 7–19c

SELF–REFERRALS
Advisory opinions, § 4–2
Alternative responses, § 4–2
American Medical Association response, § 4–2
Civil False Claims Act, relationship, § 2–3
Disclosure, §§ 4–2, 4–9
Federal prohibition (42 U.S.C. § 1395nn), § 4–3
    Designated services covered § 4–3
    Exceptions, §§ 4–4, 4–5, 4–6, 4–7
        Ancillary services, §§ 4–5a, 4–5b
        Compensation arrangements, § 4–7
        Employment, § 4–7b
        Fair market value defined for exceptions, § 4–7
        Group practices, §§ 4–5a, 4–5b, 4–5c, 4–7f
        Hospital exceptions, §§ 4–6b, 4–7d, 4–7f
        Isolated transactions, § 4–7e
        Managed care, § 4–5d
        Ownership and compensation exceptions, § 4–5
        Ownership and investment interests, § 4–6
        Personal services contracts, § 4–7c
        Physician practice acquisition, § 4–7e
        Physician recruitment, § 4–7d
        Physicians' services, § 4–5a
        Prepaid health plans, § 4–5d
        Publicly traded securities, § 4–6a
        Purchase of services, § 4–7g
        Rental of space or equipment, § 4–7a
        Rural service providers, § 4–6a
        Supervision requirements, § 4–5b
    Referral, defined, § 4–3
    Reporting requirements, § 4–8
    Sanctions, § 4–3
Hospitals, §§ 1–6c, 4–6b, 4–9
Laboratories, §§ 1–6h, 4–1, 4–3, 4–6b

INDEX

WIRE FRAUD
See False Claims, this index

†